THE MOST DANGEROUS ENEMY

A HISTORY OF THE BATTLE OF BRITAIN

STEPHEN BUNGAY

AURUM PRESS

First published in Great Britain
2000 by Aurum Press Ltd
25 Bedford Avenue, London WC1B 3AT

Reprinted five times

This paperback edition first published 2001

A catalogue record for this book is available from the British Library.

ISBN 1 85410 801 8

12
2007

Typeset in Adobe Minion by M Rules
Design by Don Macpherson
Maps by András Bereznay
Aeroplane diagrams by Roger Hammond
Printed in the UK by CPI Bookmarque, Croydon, CR0 4TD

This book is dedicated to the memory of
Matthew Buncombe
1958–1993
much of whose spirit is reflected in the story it tells

CONTENTS

List of Illustrations

Introduction

The summer was very hot, the school holidays were long, and I was bored.

We lived in Bexley in north Kent, on the edge of south-east London. Bexley was a village then, a few miles south of the River Thames. The railway line up to Charing Cross in London ran along the bottom of the garden, and beyond lay fields and woods. Dad was digging the vegetable patch as usual. I asked him to tell me a story. He had already told me three that day and was getting a bit weary. 'You can read perfectly well yourself,' he said. 'Why don't you find a book?'

Back in the house, I discovered a slim volume on Dad's bookshelf. It was a bit old and tattered, but it was in little writing of the kind grown-ups read, and contained lots of drawings and photographs, so it had to be a clever book.

I took it out into the garden. As I looked through it, I realised that it was about the time when Mum and Dad had been bombed and watched hordes of German planes flying up the Thames. They had grown up in Erith on the south bank of the river, where Nanna and Grandad still lived. Uncle Bill had told me about how he ran into the street one day when the bombers were there and saw a blackened head rolling across the road. He dashed over to have a proper look at it and was disappointed to discover that it was a just a chimney pot. Even so, I wished I could have seen it. It all sounded really exciting. One of our most important fighter stations, Biggin Hill, on the North Downs, was in fact only about ten miles away to the south. The Germans must have flown over my house on their way to London. As I lay in the garden, I was looking up at a battlefield!

The narrative of the action was a bit of a challenge, so I stuck to the photograph captions at first: 'Sheer weight of numbers'; 'The enemy aircraft spun down'; and, best of all, the classic 'Achtung, Schpitfeuer!' I knew about Spitfires already because the boy next door had a model of one I was not allowed to touch, which added greatly to its mystique.

It was time to get to grips with the text.

In it I met for the first time the fat and boastful Göring, who claimed his aircraft were 'definitely superior'. I gazed with satisfaction at a very technical-looking graphic display showing that the Spitfire was the fastest thing in the air.

I nevertheless harboured a guilty admiration for the Boulton-Paul Defiant – not as fast, but it had a wonderful turret with a whole battery of guns that could fire in any direction, which obviously made it very dangerous.

The British were very careful and well organised: 'No squadron was ever thrown into the fight without previous experience of fighting.' The German fighter formations were large and unwieldy. 'Göring still believed in superior numbers. These would win the trick. They had brought him victory in Poland, Norway, the Low Countries, Belgium and France; they might still bring victory in Britain'. Not jolly likely! We shot down 180 planes on 15 August alone and were regularly getting kill-ratios of seven to one. The Germans thought they were superior. Their pilots were brave because they were fanatics, and kept on coming despite the terrible beating they were getting. However, our boys were braver and better still. They were enormously outnumbered, but none of them minded.

The message was clear enough. Göring was a bullying show-off who could beat other foreigners, but soon got his come-uppance when he tried it on with us. We were afraid of no-one, and cut the bad boys down to size if they started pushing the little ones around, no matter how big and ugly they were. The height of moral rectitude was to stand up to bullies. The greatest moral opprobrium was reserved for show-offs.

This little work was a pamphlet published by the Air Ministry in 1941, called *The Battle of Britain*. During the war it sold two million copies, and had a considerable influence on the British public's view of the conflict. It also shaped mine.

The Battle of Britain story as handed down to me is epic myth. People needed myths in 1940. The Nazis were strong on myth, using Germanic legends and heroes and creating a Party mythology with a shabby little pantheon of its own. They deliberately portrayed their own fighter pilots as warrior-heroes. Knowing that the British would not fight for an abstraction, Churchill started a myth for the British in 1940 which still fires the popular imagination.

Britain's lone stand against Nazism in 1940 is as much a national epic as the Trojan war was for the Greeks of Homer's time. The story fulfils the archetypal role of epic literature by defining the identity of a nation through a clash with another – in the contrast with this alien power and also in its relationship to divine powers. The protagonists in the action are heroes.

The British are the ones who saved their army in little ships at Dunkirk, refused to give in, and won against all the odds. Divine providence is at hand. Dunkirk was a 'miracle'. Radar is a magical force in the background, invented by the British. The air battle reaches a point of crisis when another miracle occurs: the enemy makes a fatal error and changes the target of his attacks. As in most epic myths, the hero possesses a magic weapon – in this case not a sword, like Excalibur, but an aeroplane: the Spitfire. Its designer, Reginald Mitchell, was a martyr, sacrificing his health for his vital work. The heroes, as

Churchill intended, are the pilots. Achilles had divine lineage, as many heroes do, but he was pagan. 'The Few' were Christian heroes. Their official sanctification began with the inauguration of the Battle of Britain Memorial at Westminster Abbey by King George VI on 10 July 1947, and has continued ever since.

Myths speak to deep psychological needs and so are extremely resilient.[1] Even the language of the story has repetitive, ritualistic features in common with Homeric epic-myth. Whilst Britain and France had armies, navies and air forces, the Germans had a 'military machine' or 'juggernaut'. Two German aircraft, the Ju 87 Stuka and the Messerschmitt Bf 110 long-range fighter, are always 'much vaunted'.[2] The OED describes the verb 'vaunt', meaning 'to boast or brag', as rhetorical and archaic. I am not aware of having heard or read this word in any other context.

As I left childhood behind, I came to feel that the country of my birth, which had been so heroic, was by most modern measures second-rate. Its economy was failing, the unions were always on strike, and politicians bickered with each other. The past seemed more attractive than the present or the future. As a student, I spent some time in Germany, which was clean, affluent and orderly. Its economy worked and it did not seem to breed football hooligans. All the 'finest hour' stuff began to look rather embarrassing. If 1940 had been a defining moment, what had really happened, and what qualities did people then really display? Were they all gone?

In the 1980s, some books appeared suggesting that admirable qualities had never really been there at all. Clive Ponting has debunked the whole of 1940, Dunkirk and all, 'Dizzy' Allen has debunked the battle, and Corelli Barnett has shown that the British economy was in a parlous state and has even had a go at the Spitfire Herself. By the 1990s, Churchill's time had also come, with some historians questioning whether he was right to continue the war at all, given what it cost. The spirit of Lord Halifax is back.

Some of the debunkers have a crude understanding of myth. The word is used simply to mean 'untrue' and is usually opposed to 'reality'. Debunkers typically oppose it by assembling some facts which they think refute it. As Angus Calder points out, they run up against the Big Fact, which is that the British, even if 'in reality' they were cowardly and incompetent, won the Battle of Britain. Myth is not about correctness or incorrectness: it is about the story that emerges from the totality of facts. The story is about community identity and collective values. Myth can only be challenged by offering alternative explanations of how and why things happened.

In our post-heroic age our scope for reverence is tightly delimited. For my generation, unconditional admiration of anyone or anything has become very difficult. Though the wartime propaganda is obviously a distortion, the debunkers are equally tendentious. We live today in a measured world in which figures and statistics about everything fill the newspapers. The burden of proof we need to accept any proposition is very high. My training, both at university and subsequently in business, has led me to be sceptical about anything until I see the data. By the mid-1980s an enormous amount of research had been done into the facts behind the Battle of Britain, including all the actual losses. I decided to try to sort it out.

I wondered how narrow the odds had really been. I wondered how the two sets of commanders made their decisions. In the mid-1990s, I made numerous excursions to the Public Record Office at Kew, the Imperial War Museum and the RAF Museum at Hendon, as well as spending a week looking through the German military archives in Freiburg to see for myself the documents which bear witness to Germany's actions. The mythology loosened its grip and was replaced by a new and richer tapestry of the interplay of real people. I read the memoirs of some of the pilots and supplemented their accounts by talking to a few of 'the Few' whose stories are less well known. The emerging picture solidified.

Standing back, I reflected on what it all meant from my own perspective at the end of the century in which the events took place. The past is always changing. By the end of the century, 1940 had changed, and it is changing still. It is only just becoming clear that the British have misunderstood themselves. Tony Blair is of my generation. Peter Mandelson was a contemporary of mine at Oxford. Both seem to be searching for a new sense of national identity – or perhaps one should say that they are seeking to re-brand Britain. So now perhaps it is time to reassess the story of the Battle of Britain without the mythology and to reflect on the values it embodies. If the events of 1940 were important for Britain, they were even more so for continental Europe. The Battle of Britain may have been presented to us as a national epic, but it was more to do with the amorphous thing we call 'the West'.

My story is an epic about the deeds of our forefathers. It also contains tragedy and comedy. It shows ugliness and beauty, brutality and compassion, pettiness and greatness. It affirms a set of values. Now that the century whose latter course it determined has come to an end, it is worth re-telling.

Like most epics, it is a song of arms and of men. It is with one of the men that the tale begins.

Prologue

The pilots were waiting nervously at dispersal. They had been at readiness all day, and the afternoon was wearing on. Nobody had any idea what was happening. Nobody told them anything. They had no commanding officer, and the airfield was a shambles.

One of them was particularly quiet. He was a shy young man, just turned twenty. He was the son of a gardener from Reigate in Surrey, an only child. His parents had left him largely to himself. He used to spend hours practising the violin, for which he had some talent, or out in the garden with an air gun shooting the heads off tulips. He had had rickets and been rather sickly. Nobody had ever taken much notice of him. And today, before the sun set, he knew he was going to die.

His name was Robert Doe. Like the other pilots in the squadron, he had never been in action before, but he knew, as they did, that at some point the telephone would ring and order them to scramble, and that this time they would encounter the enemy. He was going to die because he was a useless pilot, the worst on the squadron. But he was going to take off all the same.

He had joined the Air Force because he been fascinated by an early encounter with an aeroplane which had force-landed in a field near his home. The pilot had smiled at him and let him walk round the plane and have a good look. His mother had ticked him off for being late home for tea.

When he joined the new RAF Volunteer Reserve, he was slow to learn to fly, and he did not enjoy aerobatics because he did not like the feeling of being upside-down. But his violin playing had taught him co-ordination and with his delicate hands he was good at handling the controls of an aircraft. He had left school at fourteen to go and work as an office boy at the *News of the World*, so he found the Wings exam a serious challenge. He passed by one per cent. His overall rating was 'average', and in November 1939 he was sent to the newly-formed 234 Squadron at Leconfield near Hull. It appeared to be a bomber squadron, but nobody seemed to know. They were sent all sorts of aircraft: an assortment of biplane trainers, two Blenheims and a Battle. Their squadron leader was involved in a car accident and was replaced by a man called Barnett. He was a lot older than them and rather reserved. He hardly ever flew.

Finally, in March 1940, someone must have decided they should be a fighter squadron because some Spitfires turned up. They practised a lot of formation flying, which made Doe nervous because they had to concentrate on looking at each other rather than looking out for the enemy. On 6 May he was allowed to fire his guns into the sea. That was his gunnery training. On 18 June for some reason they were moved to St Eval in Cornwall. They practised some night flying.

On 7 August one of their Flight Commanders and another pilot were posted. On 13 August, Squadron Leader Barnett was also removed and not replaced. The next day, they were moved to Middle Wallop in Hampshire. They flew in through mist, but managed to land without mishap. Thirty minutes later, however, a raid began, blowing up an ammunition dump and destroying a hangar. Bob Doe escaped injury that time, as he was on a lorry taking some pilots to the mess. He was lucky.

Now it was 15 August. He would not be so lucky again.

At about half past five the telephone went: 'Cressy Squadron scramble'. Bob Doe felt sick, but he ran to his Spitfire and strapped himself in. He was determined to go into action, for he could not bear the thought of being a coward.

The squadron was led by the one remaining Flight Commander, an Australian called Pat Hughes. Bob tucked in behind him and they took off in four 'vics' of three aircraft each, heading towards Portland. They reached their patrol height and flew about for a bit up and down the sun. After one of their turns, they discovered that the rear section was no longer there – there were nine of them instead of twelve. They wondered what on earth could have happened to the others.

All of a sudden, they were surrounded by enemy aircraft. Doe stayed behind Hughes when he turned after a Bf 110, a twin-engined fighter. Hughes fired at the plane and turned away, so Bob followed it and opened fire himself. To his surprise, the German aircraft steepened its dive and plunged into the sea. He followed it down and felt very chuffed. As he pulled up again, a second 110 flew straight in front of him. It had been following him, but had overshot. He fired again, from directly behind. The same thing happened – the aircraft shuddered and ploughed straight on into the sea. He had got two of them.

Just as suddenly as the sky had filled with aircraft, it emptied. He was alone, so he flew back to Middle Wallop and landed. He was alive, and he was not a coward. Three of the squadron's pilots were missing and one had been hit and baled out. Nobody knew what had happened to the missing men.

That night Bob went to bed early and had a think. He wanted to stay alive the following day as well. The main danger, he thought, was from the rear, and he would have to keep a sharp look out behind. He needed to see the enemy before they saw him, so he decided to forget about formations. He was helped in this because from then on the squadron took off in a gaggle, enabling him to take up whatever position he wanted. If he was surprised and saw tracer coming from behind him, he decided, he would push his stick violently forward to get out of the line of fire, even for a few seconds.

What he did not realise then was that all the time he had spent shooting the heads off tulips had made him an excellent shot, and that was very rare. Two months later, he was still alive, and one of his country's leading aces. He had the courage to overcome fear and the determination to develop the skills needed to master his foe. He had little idea at the time what was at stake. He had a job to do, so he got on with it. He knew he was defending his home. Otherwise, he did not think very much about why he was doing what he did.

PART I:
BUILD-UP

1. THE REASON WHY

At half past four on the afternoon of 9 May 1940, the British Prime Minister, Neville Chamberlain, held a meeting with the leaders of the opposition Labour Party, Clement Attlee and Arthur Greenwood, his own Foreign Secretary, Lord Halifax, and his First Lord of the Admiralty, Winston Churchill.

Growing discontent in Parliament over the conduct of the war with Germany had culminated in a Commons debate on the Norway campaign on 7 May. The debate had been a disaster for the Prime Minister. His own speech failed to rouse much support and any military credibility his government may have had was destroyed by Admiral Sir Roger Keyes' bitter attack on the conduct of the naval operations at Narvik. The government whips were finally brought to despair when Chamberlain's old friend, Leo Amery, flung at him the words which Cromwell had levelled at the Long Parliament: 'You have sat too long for any good you have been doing. Depart, I say, and let us have done with you. In the name of God, go!'

The following day the debate had continued. Britain's previous wartime Prime Minister, Lloyd George, had risen to his feet and delivered a violent attack upon the government, singling out Chamberlain. 'The Prime Minister should give an example of sacrifice,' he said, 'because there is nothing which can contribute more to victory in the war than that he should sacrifice the seals of office.' Tension in the House was high when Churchill, who had had direct responsibility for the naval campaign so savaged by Keyes, gave a fifty-minute speech in the government's defence, which some of his listeners found quite incoherent.[1]

The government had won the resulting division by 281 votes to 200. However, thirty-three Conservatives had voted against their government, and sixty had abstained, rendering the vote of confidence, though formally valid, practically indecisive. Chamberlain's only real chance of remaining Prime Minister lay in forming a national government and persuading Labour to serve under him. The purpose of the meeting on 9 May was to see if this were possible.

The Prime Minister formally asked the two Labour leaders if they would join a national government under him or under someone else. He had understood that they favoured Halifax. Having made it clear that they would not serve under Chamberlain, Attlee and Greenwood left to consult with their Party Executive.

After they had gone, Chamberlain informed Halifax and Churchill that it was clear to him he would have to resign, but he had not yet decided who to suggest to the King to replace him. The Labour men had expressed no preference, and under Tory party rules it was the outgoing party leader's responsibility to name a successor.

Churchill said nothing. After a pause, Halifax spoke of the difficulties involved in running a government from the House of Lords. That morning he had told Chamberlain that the idea of being Prime Minister had given him a bad stomach ache, and that Churchill would run the war anyway, whatever his formal office.[2]

The following morning, 10 May, the Germans opened an assault upon Holland and Belgium which was to result in the most rapid and complete victory in modern warfare. The French 2nd and 9th Armies and the British Expeditionary Force (BEF) began to move forward into Belgium, as planned in such an eventuality, thereby generously facilitating the German General Staff's plans for their destruction, whilst the bulk of the French army waited on the Maginot Line. In Britain, the government was a lame duck without a leader.

That evening Chamberlain visited the King to resign. He suggested Churchill as his successor. The King was anxious to appoint the reliable and experienced Halifax, but was swayed by Chamberlain's arguments and the fact that Halifax was reluctant to take office.* The King sent for Churchill at 6 p.m. and asked him to form a government. For his part, Halifax went to the dentist.[3]

Churchill later wrote of his feelings during these extraordinary few days:

During these last crowded days of the political crisis my pulse had not quickened at any moment. I took it all as it came. But ... as I went to bed at about 3 a.m. I was conscious of a profound sense of relief. At last I had the authority to give directions over the whole scene. I felt

---

* John Costello argues that Chamberlain had always wanted Churchill to be his successor. Although he had led Britain's appeasement policy before the war, Chamberlain, who felt personally betrayed, had become convinced that Hitler had to be fought to the bitter end and that Halifax would try to make peace. The only other name ever mentioned in the party was Lloyd George (Martin Gilbert, *Finest Hour*, Minerva 1989, p. 287). See John Costello, *Ten Days That Saved the West*, Bantam Press 1991, pp. 46–464. The King, on the other hand, had always favoured Halifax. See Andrew Roberts, *Eminent Churchillians*, Phoenix 1995, p. 37.

as if I were walking with destiny, and that all my past life had been but a preparation for this hour and this trial.[4]

It was as well that he felt as he did, for the trial was to be severe. His Private Detective, Commander Thompson, reported that as he drove back from the Palace that night, Churchill said to him: 'I hope it is not too late. I am very much afraid that it is.'[5] His appointment itself was a clear enough message to some. 'I didn't realise that things were going to get tough until they sacked Chamberlain and Churchill took over,' wrote one member of the civil defence services after the war. 'We knew he was a tough one.'[6]

It is probably no exaggeration to say that had any other man held that office in the ensuing months, history would have been very different.

Perhaps the most remarkable thing about the Battle of Britain is that it took place at all.

It was a very near-run thing.* That it did take place was due to a single man: Winston Churchill. He gave the Battle its name – before it had begun – and convinced the world that it was inevitable. He claimed he would have been 'torn from his place' had he not led the country into it.[7] This is almost certainly untrue. It was his roar that gave the lion heart. There is no evidence at all that the British nation would not have followed Halifax had he made peace with Hitler.

The government Churchill headed was deeply divided. After Dunkirk, his rival for office, Lord Halifax, made no bones about his belief that Britain had been defeated and had nothing to gain from continuing a hopeless struggle against a continental power with which she had no fundamental conflict of interest and should make peace. Halifax enjoyed support in many quarters, not least in the Conservative party.

Churchill on the other hand remained, in many ways, an outsider. In 1940 he was commonly regarded as a dangerous maverick and war-monger, and had many enemies within the party. Shortly after learning of Churchill's appointment, Halifax's deputy, 'Rab' Butler, spoke to Churchill's Private Secretary, John Colville, in the Foreign Office:

> Rab said he thought that the good clean tradition of English politics, that of Pitt as opposed to Fox, had been sold to the greatest adventurer of modern political history. He had tried earnestly and long to persuade Halifax to accept the premiership, but he had failed. He believed this sudden coup of Winston and his rabble was a serious disaster, but an unnecessary one: the 'pass had been sold' by Mr C., Lord Halifax and Oliver Stanley. They had weakly surrendered to a

---

* In his *Five Days in London*, Yale University Press 1999, John Lukacs argues that the crucial period was in fact the five days from 24–28 May during which Churchill fought Halifax for domination of the Cabinet and just managed to pull it off.

half-breed American whose main support was that of inefficient but talkative people of a similar type . . .[8]

There were, of course, those who had always opposed the war on political grounds. Sympathisers of Oswald Mosley (who himself claimed to support it on the grounds of patriotism) and other members of far-right movements had been identified as potential subversives early on. On 22 May the War Cabinet agreed upon a new 'Defence of the Realm' regulation which was vague enough to let them move against anyone suspected of being a 'fifth columnist', and Mosley was arrested the next day.

The Communist party had, from the first, denounced the war as a capitalist struggle in which workers ought not to participate. Party membership and sales of the *Daily Worker* increased between the outbreak of war and the spring of 1940.[9] The 'Right Club', formed in mid-1939 by the Tory MP Captain Ramsey was an anti-Semitic anti-Bolshevist group which did not see any reason for a war with Germany.[10] It included twelve MPs and a number of lords, and broadly reflected the views of the former King, the errant Duke of Windsor.

Desire for peace was not confined to dukes and politicians. After all, the whole country had sighed with relief after Munich and the cheers which greeted Chamberlain's subsequently vilified 'piece of paper' were genuine enough. No cheering crowds danced in the streets when he announced 'this country is at war with Germany' eleven months later. There were many humanitarians who opposed war in general. The composers Benjamin Britten and Michael Tippett were pacifists, as was the philosopher Bertrand Russell.[11] A negotiated peace had been consistently advocated by John Gielgud, Dame Sybil Thorndike and George Bernard Shaw. Lord Beaverbrook also supported negotiations with Germany until Churchill made him Minister of Aircraft Production.[12]

Once France fell, the case for peace became even stronger. Britain's policy towards Europe had for centuries been that of holding the balance of power, ensuring that no single continental power became dominant. Now, however, the situation had changed. Quite simply, the Germans had won. With the fall of France, no continental allies were available, so the policy had to be abandoned. Britain's reason for going to war had been clear: a guarantee to Poland. There was nothing Britain could do about that any more. She had no army left in Europe, possessed only a weak bomber force, and though the Royal Navy still commanded the oceans, it was useless as an offensive weapon against a continental foe. London, the largest ground target in the world, would be open to destruction from the air. Continuing the war would only bring pointless bloodshed and wreck the country's shaky finances.

Immediately after the Dunkirk evacuation, Britain was defended on the ground by the rump of the BEF – thirteen or fourteen mauled divisions now armed mainly with rifles – fifteen infantry divisions at half their establishment strength and still in training, one partly-equipped armoured division and the Local Defence Volunteers (soon to be re-named the Home Guard),[13] which were a gallant farce. At Dover, there were three anti-tank guns covering 5 miles of coast.[14] The Germans had just defeated a combined Allied army of some 132 divisions. Their own victorious army consisted of about 130 divisions, 10 of them armoured. Further resistance, a rational man would have said, was at best pointless, and at worst risked turning into an appalling tragedy.

Halifax was just that rational man. He had no sympathy for Hitler, but he was a patriot, a humanist, a peace-lover and a professional politician who believed that it was his job to serve the best interests of his country and who knew a lost cause when he saw one.* Before defeating anyone else, Churchill had to defeat him.

Halifax's main aim was to secure the best terms he could before it was too late, in particular before Britain's aircraft factories were bombed to destruction, rendering her completely helpless. As was revealed at the Nuremberg trials in 1946, he met a Swedish businessman called Dahlerus in secret on 20 May, the day that Guderian's leading tanks reached the Channel, cutting off the BEF. He asked Dahlerus to contact Göring with a view to beginning negotiations.

At the meeting of the War Cabinet on 26 May, Churchill announced that he had told the French Premier, Reynaud, that 'we would rather go down fighting than be enslaved to Germany'.[15] Halifax coolly stated that the government's goal must now be that of 'safeguarding the independence of our own empire and if possible that of France,' an unexceptionable statement of how he saw his job as a professional. He explained that the Italian Ambassador had indicated that Mussolini would be prepared to propose a conference and that he had replied that we should 'naturally be prepared to consider any proposals' which could lead to peace in Europe, providing Britain's liberty and independence were assured. Churchill opined that security and independence could not be achieved under German domination of Europe and he was not willing to make any concessions to achieve them. Halifax argued cogently enough and had all the traditions of British diplomacy behind him. The Permanent Under-Secretary at the Foreign Office, Sir Alexander Cadogan, undoubtedly spoke for his minister and probably spoke for his department in describing Churchill as being 'too rambling and romantic and sentimental and temperamental'.[16]

The next day, 27 May, the row between Halifax and Churchill continued at the Cabinet's afternoon session. Though he thought its success unlikely, Halifax

* Although his basic position was clear, Halifax' views, like those of any other sophisticated, intelligent man, were differentiated and complex. He wrote to a correspondent on 19 July of the difficulties involved in overcoming 'the fundamental gulf' between Hitler's desire for a Europe dominated by Germany and his view of Germany simply enjoying 'the position to which her greatness entitles her' without prejudicing the freedom of other nations (Thompson, op. cit., pp. 144–5). Despite the defeat in France, his real desire was to continue Britain's traditional 'balance of power' policy towards Europe.

recommended an approach to Mussolini because it was what the French wanted. Churchill did not care what they wanted: they could give up if they felt like it, though he doubted that they would, but Britain would fight it out to the end. Halifax rejoined that any settlement fulfilling certain fundamental conditions would be better than risking two or three months of air attack. Churchill was only prepared to *listen* to a peace offer, not to make one, and then only if Hitler agreed to give up his conquests. This was too much for the Foreign Secretary, who thought it 'the most frightful rot', and threatened to resign.[17] Churchill took him out into the garden, full of apologies, until Halifax's professionalism overcame his momentary emotional aberration. He could not, he told Cadogan, allow himself to 'do anything silly'.[18]

That evening of 27 May, a Belgian officer crossed the German lines to ask for armistice terms, and shortly before midnight King Leopold ordered a cease-fire as of 4 a.m. the next morning. This left a 20-mile gap between the left flank of the retreating BEF and the sea.[19] It looked increasingly as if the British army was doomed.

With this news fresh in his mind, on the late afternoon of 28 May Churchill convened a broader group, including Lord Lloyd who had opposed the Munich settlement, the belligerent and influential Leo Amery and Hugh Dalton, the Labour Minister for Economic Warfare.[20] Churchill polarised the issue of negotiation with 'that man' by stating that any terms offered would be far too onerous, turning Britain into a 'slave state' and that better terms could be won by fighting on. Having used this speculation to side-step the rational arguments, he got on to his true subject, namely that any parley with the enemy was immoral. He then addressed the group directly:

> I am convinced that every man of you would rise up and tear me down from my place if I were for one moment to contemplate parley and surrender. If this long island history of ours is to end at last, let it end only when each one of us lies choking in his own blood upon the ground.[21]

This may be rhetoric, but it was not idle.* It was clear to those present that he meant it, and his words provoked loud cries of approval all round the table. 'He was quite magnificent', Dalton wrote. 'The man, the only man we have, for this hour.'[22]

At 7 p.m. the War Cabinet met again. This time they all lined up squarely behind their Prime Minister. From then on, Halifax was in retreat.

---

* Churchill's daughter-in-law, Pamela Harriman, relates how, over a family dinner when the possibility of invasion was being discussed, Churchill told his family that they could each take a dead German with them. When she objected that she neither possessed, nor could use a gun, he looked at her gravely and said: 'You can go into the kitchen and get a carving knife.' (*Churchill*, (Part 2) written by Martin Gilbert, BBC-TV Productions 1992.) Particularly in view of the private and personal context, there is every reason to believe that he meant every word.

He conducted a fighting withdrawal. Outside the War Cabinet the Foreign Office continued to pursue its own rational policy despite Churchill's romantic posturing. On 22 June, the day that France fell, 'Rab' Butler, sent for the Swedish Minister in London, Björn Prytz. Butler explained to him that Britain 'would not neglect any opportunity for compromise peace' and that 'no die-hards would be allowed to stand in the way'. During the meeting Halifax called his deputy out and returned him with the message that 'common sense, not bravado, would dictate the British government's policy'. Halifax is unlikely to have dreamt dreams when he was young, and certainly had little inclination to see visions now that he was older. Prytz sent a telegram to Stockholm, ending with the pointed remark that, after some conversations with British MPs, it seemed that 'if and when the prospect for negotiations arises, possibly after 28 June, Halifax may succeed Churchill'.[23] The Germans got hold of this telegram, and it was summarised in a memo from Ernst von Weizsäcker, the Secretary of State at the Foreign Ministry in Berlin on 19 June.[24] It added substance to Hitler's belief that a peace settlement could be reached that summer.

Eventually, time ran out for Halifax. Once the air battle was fully underway the window of opportunity for negotiation began to close. On 20 August, the day on which Churchill spoke to the nation about 'the Few', London received a peace proposal from Göring via the Dutch Foreign Minister, and another via Turkey. Halifax could do little by then. Nevertheless, he encouraged his friend Lord Lothian, Ambassador to Washington and a humane man who wanted to avoid bloodshed, to continue to pursue the opportunities presented by various emissaries in the United States.

In the autumn, Lloyd George himself suggested that the reprieve won by the RAF gave Britain a better negotiating position than it had had immediately after Dunkirk and drafted a memorandum advocating peace negotiations on 28 August. It did not reach Churchill until 1941. He ignored it, though he considered it 'defeatist and treasonable'.[25] There is a fine line between policy disagreements and treason. By then official policy was securely behind him, so he could indeed threaten opponents with that dire accusation.

Halifax's work for peace came to an end only when Churchill sent him to Washington to replace Lord Lothian, who died on 12 December. But by then his cause was lost, for his country was committed to a conflict growing in extent and intensity every month.

Halifax's case was a strong one and he was an honourable man. He lost a battle of wills to a personality whose extraordinary weaknesses had made him an unpopular maverick in Westminster in general and within his own Conservative party in particular. It was the refusal of the two Labour men, Attlee and his deputy Greenwood, to serve under Chamberlain that cleared Churchill's path to the premiership, and his great speeches in the weeks that followed were consistently cheered more loudly on the Labour than on the Tory benches.[26]

The weaknesses which had kept Churchill out of power for so long were precisely the strengths which brought him into power on 10 May. He was not a pragmatist, but a visionary. His vision was intuitive, inspiring and uncannily accurate. For years, he had been using melodramatic rhetoric that seemed hopelessly out of touch with reality. Churchill remained stubbornly true to his convictions and said what he had always said. Slowly at first, then rapidly and suddenly, reality raised itself up to be worthy of him. It finally reached Churchillian heights when Guderian's *Panzerkorps* came to a halt on the cliffs of France and the weary but exhilarated Grenadiers looked out towards Dover. It was to remain at that level all summer.

Churchill's determination to fight Hitler, whatever the cost, was not based on a sober appreciation of British interests, but on deep and long-held moral and historical convictions.

Churchill believed deeply in 'liberal democracy', a form of civil society based on personal liberty, free association and free speech. It was the product of 'the English-speaking peoples', who had developed it out of their internal struggles against tyranny. It was still necessary to fight tyranny wherever it emerged in order to keep liberal, democratic states safe.[27]

It was for the English-speaking peoples as a whole that Churchill always spoke, and the fact that his mother had been American sensitised him all the more to the notion that personal liberty is not the idea of one nation-state, but of the West. The British Empire and the United States were its natural home, but if it were only defended against aggression, it would spread around the world of its own accord.[28] Its principles were embodied in the American Constitution and the British parliamentary system. The principles were few and simple, and relied for their successful realisation on a sense of shared values, common sense and common decency. Unheroic in themselves, these principles sometimes needed heroes in their defence.

The first threat to liberal democracy to arise in the twentieth century was Communism, which Churchill implacably opposed. However, in the 1930s a more sinister evil arose in Europe, in the shape of Fascism. Churchill was one of the earliest to perceive that within the very heart of Europe a dark force had emerged whose virulent malice made it a unique threat to civilisation.

Churchill believed Nazism to be unique in its militant malevolence. It was based on hatred,* but its racial origins made it chillingly arbitrary, as well as pseudo-scientific, and given its proclamation of the master race's need for *Lebensraum*, it was essentially militant.

Somehow, before the death camps and massacres, before the ghettos and pogroms in the east, Churchill sensed that a primitive destructive power had been unleashed which corrupted the mind in its seductive simplicity and corroded the soul through its pseudo-Darwinistic rejection of morality. He realised

---

* Communism is no exception to this, only the basis of the hatred is different – class rather than nationality.

too that it had awesome power, for it linked primitivism with scientism and though nostalgic, was revolutionary. The largest economy in Europe was in its grip, and with it, a people loyal, obedient and capable of being fearsome warriors (as the years 1914–18 had shown), who were also burning with revanchist resentment at the real injustices of the Versailles Treaty. He perceived this instinctively before the evidence so familiar to us today was there, and he was right.

In adopting a moral view of political necessity and the belief that tyrannies were a threat to democracy, wherever they might be, Churchill was working within the American tradition of diplomacy. The British tradition was to see diplomacy as a matter of furthering the national interest by maintaining the balance of power.[29] Churchill's refusal to play by the European rules frustrated Halifax and bemused Hitler. This gives particular point to the theme of the English-speaking peoples, and, for all the differences between them, may well explain why Churchill and Roosevelt were able to understand each other so well.

Churchill's vision of history* and his perception of what had happened in Europe had distasteful but irremediable consequences for his own nation. Nazism had to be opposed until it was extinguished in total defeat, lest the flames should spring again from warm ashes. Britain had to lead this opposition. Churchill had thought she could do so in her traditional way – through alliances – this time, as previously, with France and the smaller states. In June, France left the struggle. It was a terrible blow for him, but he shouldered the burden. He always believed that the British Empire would survive the struggle, even flourish. But in the final analysis he was prepared to have Britain sacrifice herself if need be for the sake of a greater cause. His loyalty was ultimately to a moral rather than a political principle, and he was prepared to accept that one outcome of the war would be the weakening of Britain and the creation of American hegemony. As long as Nazism flourished, none would be safe. He never acted consciously against British interests, but his vision was not in line with that of the Foreign Office. The British had to fight because they were there.

What appeared so irrational and romantic to others had in Churchill's mind its own inexorable logic. His ultimate war aim was the only one which made any sense: victory, 'victory at all costs, no matter how long and hard the road may be'[30]. His short-term war aims followed from this overall goal and were equally clear:

1. To ensure Britain's survival as an independent state, without which there was no chance of taking the war to Germany.

---

* History was always present for Churchill. He understood, perhaps, that the essence of history is the present, for the present is nothing other than what the past has made it, only those most essential elements of the past being retained in the present. That is what makes them essential. One's understanding of the past is therefore a constituent part of one's understanding of current events and a guide as to how to act in it. As Taylor observes, 'History was part of his life' (A.J.P. Taylor, *The War Lords*, Penguin 1978, p. 87).

2. To maintain Britain's belligerence, without which her presence would be a mere shadow on Hitler's flank.
3. To secure the United States' involvement in the war, without which there could be no victory, and with which, ultimate victory was sure.

He had to bide his time with the third aim. The War Cabinet discussed the role of the United States on 28 May. Churchill argued that whilst 'a grovelling appeal, if made now, would have the worst possible effect', a bold stand against Germany would 'command their admiration and respect'.[31] He understood that his aims were linked and sequential. His claim on America could only be a moral one. He understood that America's political traditions made it likely that it would answer an appeal to crusade for democracy and freedom whilst being, at best, indifferent to the fate of the British Empire.

Churchill's struggle to win the hearts and minds of American politicians was more prolonged and even more uncertain in its outcome than his struggle in his own Cabinet.* In May, an opinion poll found that only 7% of Americans were willing to go to war on the side of the Allies. This figure rose somewhat in June, but fell back again thereafter, with the number of Americans expecting a British victory falling from 82% in 1939 to 32% after the fall of France.[32] Churchill guessed, however, that they would admire courage and help a friend in need who was doing his utmost to help himself. In the event, he was not far wrong.

Thus Churchill saw the Battle of Britain as a necessity. It was his battle. He decided to fight it and staked all on its outcome. It was not the only battle of the war on which all seemed to hang, but it was the precondition of all the others. He needed it. So did the civilised world. It was up to him to get it fought.

The primary goal of warfare is to break the enemy's will to fight. Wars are therefore always conducted on two levels, the physical and the moral. A moral victory at the outset by persuading an enemy not to fight at all is clearly the most desirable victory. The purpose of fighting is to inflict physical damage on the enemy until it has an impact on the moral front and he gives up. Fighting only derives significance from its effect on the will to resist.

Churchill fought on the moral front throughout the war. In 1940 he fought at times almost alone. It was on this front that Britain came closest to

---

* His most implacable opponent was the American Ambassador in London, Joseph Kennedy. Being of Irish extraction, he was hostile towards Britain in general and towards Churchill in particular and his sons, including John, brought him back glowing accounts of what they had seen in Germany. He thought that there were plenty of anti-Semites in the United States who sympathised with Germany and whose views should be known to the President, feared American involvement to save the British Empire and thought it was absolutely clear that Germany would win anyway. He also had some personal financial interests in putting an end to the war. He consistently opposed Roosevelt and demanded to be recalled to Washington in October 1940 in order to sabotage the President's chances of re-election. He left London on 28 October, to the relief of the British government. See Costello, op. cit., pp. 130–149 & 392–397.

defeat in May and June, and it was Churchill who saved it. Throughout the war, he also exercised a pervasive influence over the development of strategy and the course of the actual fighting.

Churchill's military ideas were romantic, impractical and often danger-ous. Had Churchill not heeded the advice of his top soldier Sir Alan Brooke, who became Chief of the Imperial General Staff in November 1940, Britain would probably have lost the war before the United States had entered the fray.[33] The main motivation behind many of his ideas was political rather than military, and his overriding concern was to be seen to be aggressive and on the offensive. So it was with the Greek adventure, Dieppe and his obsession with the Balkans and the Mediterranean, and it is in the political realm that justi-fication for his decisions may be found.[34] It was here that Churchill was really at home.

Militarily incompetent, Churchill was a political genius, largely for the same reasons. His goal was to convince the Cabinet, Parliament and the people that his vision should be followed. He had to win over all three, for had any one of them abandoned him, he could not have continued. By June 1940 he had secured the Cabinet, at least for a time. To secure Parliament and the people, his main weapon was rhetoric and he wielded it with mastery. The weapon was one with the man.[35]

Churchill's first speech as Prime Minister was delivered to the Commons on 13 May. It was short and to the point. Having reported on his progress in appointing ministers, he repeated to the House what he had said to those ministers: 'I have nothing to offer but blood, toil, tears and sweat'.[36] Having thus cleared away any illusions from the outset, he elaborated by saying: 'We have before us many, many long months of struggle and of suffering.'[37] This was clearly true, for if Britain were to win the war, it would take many months for her to build up any effective fighting strength. Churchill needed to pre-empt any of the 'the war will be over by Christmas' mentality which was pervasive in 1914. He knew that this war, like the last, would be one of attrition.

Given this black picture the hope he was also to offer would have credi-bility from the outset. He was managing expectations in order to avoid a possible collapse of morale in the future. He then laid out his policy: 'to wage war, by sea, land and air, with all our might and with all the strength that God can give us'. It would be trite to observe that this hardly constitutes a policy. It is a statement of the obvious. But in 1940, the obvious was questionable. The debate that had brought down Chamberlain less than a week before had really been about the vigour with which the war was being prosecuted and the gov-ernment's will to fight. This statement of policy was the one the House needed.

He then slipped in his next major theme of that summer: 'To wage war against a monstrous tyranny, never surpassed in the dark, lamentable catalogue of human crime.' Were the enemy less than monstrous, one might question the sacrifice and ask whether victory, rather than some settlement, was an appropriate goal. Quite logically, therefore, Churchill's next words make the connection with his third theme, the aim of the war: 'You ask, What is our aim? I can answer in one word: victory'. He further justifies this aim with his fourth major theme: the awesome historical nature of what was at stake:

> victory at all costs, victory in spite of all terror, victory, however long and hard the road may be; for without victory, there is no survival. Let that be realised; no survival for the British Empire; no survival for all that the British Empire has stood for, no survival for the urge and impulse of the ages, that mankind will move forward towards its goal.'[38]

Using the well-tried device of triple statement, elaborated each time, he laid out his goal as a necessary consequence of what all would have wished for: survival.[39] Churchill was not going to try to persuade the British, of all people, to suffer and die for an idea or for mankind as a whole. Neither, of course, does he say what mankind's goal is. He could not do so, for he did not know, any more than anyone else does. It was enough to suggest that it has one. The overall message would be repeated in different forms time and again: in saving themselves, the British would save civilisation, and thereby the whole of mankind.

Having lifted his audience's eyes towards a great cause, Churchill ends by offering reassurance based on the solidarity of comradeship and the strength within the audience itself:

> But I take up my task with buoyancy and hope. I feel sure that our cause will not be suffered to fail among men. At this time I feel entitled to claim the aid of all, and I say, 'come, then, let us go forward together with our united strength.'[40]

'It was quite a good little warlike speech' opined the then editor of *The Times*, Geoffrey Dawson, generously.[41]

His leitmotivs spell out Churchill's vision. They form a simple, coherent whole that could be expressed as five propositions.

1. we face a monstrous evil which is a threat to the whole of the civilised world;
2. if we can stand up to it, we will save not only ourselves, but the whole of mankind;
3. our ultimate goal must be victory, for this is an evil so virulent that it must be utterly extinguished;
4. the road to victory will be long and hard, and involve much pain and sorrow;
5. but if we all support each other and stick together, we can do it.

This was the message he delivered again and again that summer, to Parliament, to the British people, to the occupied countries, and to America.

Churchill's first address to the nation came in a BBC broadcast on 19 May. Broadcast at 9 p.m., he began work on it at 6 p.m.[42], an indication of the extent to which he simply said what was flowing through him at the time.

The bulk of the speech was a warning that things were going badly in France. However, he singled out the performance of the RAF, saying: 'My confidence in our ability to fight it out to the finish with the German air force has been strengthened by the fierce encounters which have taken place and are taking place.'[43] This, the most encouraging message about the fighting in the speech, is at once the most sinister. Churchill lost no opportunity to make it clear what he expected was to come, and repeats his message a few lines later: 'After this battle in France abates its force, there will come the battle for our island – for all that Britain is and all that Britain means.' The phrase 'Battle of Britain' is not quite there, but it is forming.

Four of his main leitmotivs are sounded in this speech: the aim of the war ('Our task is not only to win the battle – but to win the war'); the nature of the enemy ('the foulest and most soul-destroying tyranny which has ever darkened and stained the pages of history'); the cause ('rescue not only Europe but mankind'); and strength through solidarity, which, as usual, formed his peroration:

> Arm yourselves, and be ye men of valour, and be ye in readiness for
> the conflict; for it is better for us to perish in battle than to look
> upon the outrage of our nation and our altar. As the will of God is in
> heaven, even so let it be.[44]

This is more or less what he was to say to the colleagues he sought to rally on the 28 May. Here the form is biblical, there it was cinematically blood-curdling.

The battle in France took its course and the evacuation from Dunkirk began on 26 May. The BBC did not tell the country what was going on until 31 May.[45] Vice-Admiral Bertram Ramsey, who was in charge of the evacuation, finally closed down Operation Dynamo at 1423 on 4 June.[46] 364,628 troops, of which about two thirds were British, had been taken off the beaches and landed safely.* That day, Churchill addressed the Commons.

The speech lasted about half an hour. Churchill reported the facts about the closing stages of the battle, and then used reversed expectation management, saying that he had expected to have to announce 'the greatest military disaster in our long history'.[47] He continued to conjure up the spectre that had haunted his mind a week previously, of a British army completely destroyed,

---

* A good number of the French ones were at all events to return to France to fight its last battle, and perished or entered captivity there.

the core of future armies gone. Instead of saying what had happened, Churchill kept up the tension by turning to the smoke and noise of battle, describing the strength of the enemy, the gallantry of the army, then of the navy and the evacuating forces, and then of the air force.

In paying tribute to all those involved in the 'miracle of deliverance' he cast a note of caution, implying that the struggle was just beginning:

> We must be very careful not to assign to this deliverance the attrib-
> utes of a victory. Wars are not won by evacuations. But there was a
> victory inside this deliverance, which should be noted. It was
> achieved by the air force.[48]

He singled out the RAF, partly because of many bitter complaints from the returning troops, who could see little of what was going on, that the 'Brylcreem boys' had left them in the lurch, and partly because he knew he would be turn-ing them into particular heroes in the coming weeks.

He stressed the importance of the target for the Luftwaffe, stressed how hard they had tried and he even stressed their courage. Despite the worst they could do, then, the army got away, and, he said, the enemy had 'paid fourfold for any losses which they have inflicted'.[49] We know now that this was nonsense, but the figures were derived from combat reports, and nobody knew any better.[50]

Churchill's purpose in presenting such figures was to reassure the public:

> When we consider how much greater would be our advantage in
> defending the air above this island against an overseas attack, I must
> say that I find in these facts a sure basis upon which practical and
> reassuring thoughts may rest.[51]

He laced the account with what today read like *Boy's Own* style yarns, which were again from the best sources – 'Very large formations of German aero-planes . . . have turned on occasion from the attack of one quarter of their number . . . Twelve aeroplanes have been hunted by two. One plane was driven into the water and cast away by the mere charge of a British aeroplane, which had no more ammunition'[52] – and claimed that the RAF's machines were superior to those of their foes.

There then follows a passage which shows him first groping towards the image of 'the Few', though it is as yet – the full phrase was not to come until 20 August – without its Shakespearean ring:

> The great French army was very largely, for the time being, cast back
> and disturbed by the onrush of a few thousands of armoured vehi-
> cles. May it not also be that the cause of civilisation itself will be
> defended by the skill and devotion of a few thousand airmen.[53]

This shows to what extent the notion of 'the Few' has been misunderstood. Whilst the phrase usually conjures up a handful of Spitfires pitting themselves against hordes of bombers, what Churchill meant was that the number of protagonists in any air battle would be very small, which is perfectly true. Britain was delegating the decision over its fate not to a vast mass of soldiers struggling in the mud, but to a select group of young men whose business was so technical that nobody else could be involved. It was to be a meeting in battle of the two countries' elected champions, and it is in this vein that he continues, drawing comparisons with the Knights of the Round Table and the Crusaders. He was preparing the ground for his battle and beginning his deliberate myth-making.[54]

He summarised the result of the French campaign, whilst stressing once more that relief should not blind people to the fact that the country had suffered 'a colossal military disaster'.[55] Nevertheless, the country would be able to 'ride out the storm of war, and to outlive the menace of tyranny, if necessary for years, if necessary alone.'[56]

Storms are natural. They happen from time to time, they are unpleasant and frightening, but in the end one survives and the sun reappears.

He continued: 'At any rate, that is what we are going to try to do. That is the resolve of His Majesty's Government – every man of them. That is the will of Parliament and the nation.' This was a plain lie. Nobody knew this better than Churchill. But it was a necessary one, both for the public and his colleagues. It made it very difficult for Halifax to continue to pursue his policy of negotiation with anything approaching openness. Whether or not it was the will of Parliament (it probably was) or the nation (it may have been) few could say. Churchill was at any rate going to make it so.*

He carried on by stating that France and Britain would continue to fight to the death and would not 'flag or fail'. His final words, a single extraordinary sentence, begin with his most defiant expression yet of the theme of sacrifice and end with a coda developing the leitmotiv of solidarity further than before to encompass his vision of the English-speaking peoples:

> We shall go on to the end, we shall fight in France, we shall fight on the seas and oceans, we shall fight with growing confidence and growing strength in the air, we shall defend our island, whatever the cost may be, we shall fight on the beaches, we shall fight on the landing grounds, we shall fight on the fields and in the streets, we shall fight on the hills; we shall never surrender, and even if, which I do not for a moment believe, this island or a large part of it were subjugated and starving, then our Empire beyond the seas, armed and guarded

---

* It is symptomatic of the naivety of de-bunkers such as Ponting that they present the disunity of the country as a revelation. Had all 50 million inhabitants of Britain been of one mind, an absurd notion in itself, Churchill's main task of creating unity would have been superfluous.

by the British Fleet, would carry on the struggle, until in God's good time, the new world, with all its power and might, steps forth to the rescue and the liberation of the old.'[57]

Beginning with the fighting still going on in France, Churchill moves through the elements of land, sea and air as if opposing a cosmic force and then moves back to the concrete realities of invasion. The famous asseverations follow the natural course of a retreat from the beaches, ending in the hills – which neither the Romans nor the Normans had been able fully to subdue. His gaze then moves out again to remind people that they are part of a great empire, that even the Nazis cannot seriously challenge the Royal Navy, and that beyond that the English-speaking peoples will eventually unite in their common cause. But he asks, as he had asked the Cabinet on 28 May, for patience.

Britain was not really alone; it formed part of an international brother-hood. It had its task to do, but deliverance was just a matter of time. It had to endure.

Churchill did not fail in his intended effect. 'This afternoon,' wrote Harold Nicolson, Labour MP and Parliamentary Secretary to the Minister of Information Duff Cooper, 'Winston made the finest speech I have ever heard. The House was deeply moved.' Several Labour members cried, as did Churchill.[58] Labour MP Josiah Wedgwood thought it 'worth a thousand guns, and the speeches of a thousand years'.[59] Labour MP and Minister of Economic Warfare Hugh Dalton found it 'very grim and determined,' designed, he thought, 'to pull ostrich heads out of the sand both here and in the USA.'[60]

Dalton saw its wider significance, for it was indeed aimed at America as much as at Britain. Here, for the first time, all three immediate war aims played their part.

Parts of the speech were read out by an announcer on the BBC that evening.[61] The Tory MP Major General Sir Edward Spears, who was acting as Churchill's personal representative and had brought de Gaulle to England, was listening in France. He wrote afterwards that it established Churchill firmly as 'the supreme leader' and continues in an almost mystic vein that it was as though the British people had been given 'a password, the significance of which only we could grasp, it bound us in a great secret understanding.' It was as if the British people were passing through 'an intense fire and light that burnt out everything mean and selfish in us, leaving only a common purpose and a common unity, fusing into the single soul of the British people.'[62] These are heady sentiments for an old soldier.

Listening at Sissinghurst Castle in Kent, directly on the invasion route from the coast to London, Vita Sackville-West wrote to her husband Harold Nicolson that the words, 'even repeated by the announcer' sent 'shivers (not of fear) down my spine.' She felt above all the 'whole massive backing of power and resolve behind them, like a great fortress.'[63]

The impact on thousands of simpler souls must have been comparable. The moral front was firming up.

It was not yet solid. The Cabinet was growing unruly again, with the leading Tories Leo Amery and George Lloyd this time lobbying for 'practical changes' in 'our system of government'.* On the same day, 17 June, the new French government formed by Marshal Pétain on the previous day sued for peace. Lloyd George had still not responded to the offer of a post and when Chamberlain suggested to Churchill that he might be waiting to be Britain's Pétain, Churchill growled back: 'Yes, he might, but there won't be any opportunity.'[64]

On 18 June 1940, the 125th anniversary of the Battle of Waterloo, at 3.49 p.m., Churchill addressed the Commons again. He spoke for thirty-six minutes.[65]

The Prime Minister reviewed the history of the lamentable collapse on the Continent, dismissed the search for scapegoats there and, with characteristic magnanimity, the hounding of former appeasers at home. He outlined the forces available for home defence, making the point that the existence of the Royal Navy made a sea-crossing a perilous undertaking, and then considered the threat from the air.

He asserted that the RAF, though less numerous than the Luftwaffe, was still very powerful and had so far proved itself to be superior. In support, he quoted more statistics on relative loss-ratios and suggested that they might be improved upon in a conflict over England, as many pilots would be recovered. He addressed the possible impact of bombing, and used the example of Barcelona to show that resolute people could stand up to it. He expressed once again his conviction that the French government should continue to resist, and as he warmed to his theme, he screwed up the emotional tension in talking of Britain's sense of comradeship with the French people:

If we are now called upon to endure what they have been suffering, we shall emulate their courage, and if final victory rewards our toils, they shall share the gains, aye, and freedom shall be restored to all. We abate nothing of our just demands; not one jot or tittle do we recede. Czechs, Poles, Norwegians, Dutch, Belgians have joined their causes to our own. All these shall be restored.[66]

Here his main themes have been sounded: the cause, the aim of the war and an offering of solidarity to the conquered nations of Europe.

He then ended by drawing all his themes together in a coda of 180 words.

---

* It may be significant that both were passionate Imperialists, Amery then being Secretary of State for India and Lloyd, Secretary of State for the Colonies. Despite their support for Churchill and for the war they may have harboured justified misgivings about its impact on Britain's long-term ability to sustain its empire.

These words have given the Battle of Britain its name. They make it clear that it was not about a few aeroplanes having some dogfights. They define an integral part of what it has meant to be British for the two generations after the one which heard it broadcast on the radio that summer evening, and maybe for some generations to come. At the time, it secured Churchill a victory on the moral front and announced the imminent commencement of his battle. It was the Supreme Commander's final manoeuvre to bring his forces into contact with the enemy.

> What General Weygand called the Battle of France is over. I expect that the battle of Britain is about to begin. Upon this battle depends the survival of Christian civilisation. Upon it depends our own British life, and the long continuity of our institutions and our empire. The whole fury and might of the enemy must very soon be turned on us. Hitler knows that he will have to break us in this island or lose the war. If we can stand up to him, all Europe may be free and the life of the world move forward into broad, sunlit uplands. But if we fail, then the whole world, including the United States, including all that we have known and cared for, will sink into the abyss of a new Dark Age made more sinister, and perhaps more protracted, by the lights of perverted science. Let us, therefore, brace ourselves to our duties and so bear ourselves that, if the British Empire and its Commonwealth last for a thousand years, men will still say, 'this was their finest hour.'[67]

This passage has a pedigree going back to Pericles. It takes the form of a Greek funeral oration, called an *epitaphios*, from which 'epitaph' derives. In an *epitaphios*, the dead are praised and the living comforted by the thought that the fallen had been worthy of their ancestors. Churchill's words are an inverted *epitaphios*. The living are called upon to be heroes so that their descendants will regard them as worthy ancestors, and say (in some future epitaph) that 'this was their finest hour'.

The opening sets out three facts in one simple sentence each. We move from France and the past, to Britain and the present, and then broaden the geography to 'Christian civilisation' and the future. It is a shock. The forthcoming battle is not just for territory but for the moral values represented by the West.

Most of his listeners could have had little idea what that all meant so Churchill makes it very simple. Everything they know around them is threatened, as is history itself and all that generations have striven for. The battle is not only for space, but for time, the threat not only to an island home in the present but – extraordinarily – to the past. The achievements of two thousand years of history could all be annulled. With this annulment the future could be lost as well. We have to survive, for everything depends on our survival.

Survive, and victory will be ours, for then, as according to Churchill, Hitler knows, he will lose the war.

Then follow the two possible outcomes of success or failure, presented as a set of contrasts: light versus dark; upward, forwards movement versus downward, backwards movement.[68] The conclusion, presented as inexorable ('therefore'), is that the storm must be weathered.[69] But there is no call to heroism, no suggestion that what is required is supererogatory. It is enough to do what Nelson asked of his men in his famous signal at Trafalgar: 'our duty'.[70] The result, even if the empire lasts for a millennium – an ironic echo of the 'thousand year *Reich*' – will be a supreme historical achievement: 'their finest hour'.

In the Commons, the speech did not have the impact of its predecessor. Perhaps it was too odd, too visionary. His speaking performance is reported to have been less accomplished.[71] Nevertheless, given indications from the Ministry of Information on 17 June that there was the danger of a serious rift between Parliament and people unless the Prime Minister gave a strong lead, Duff Cooper prevailed on Churchill to talk on the radio that night, despite his tiredness and his dislike of the medium.[72]

Nicolson thought he sounded 'ghastly' on the wireless.[73] The newspaper owner Cecil King thought he was either ill or drunk and wrote in his diary that it was 'the poorest possible effort'.[74] Colville's lady dinner companion that night remarked that it was like listening to a bishop. Churchill did the whole broadcast whilst smoking a cigar, which, together with his lifelong difficulty in pronouncing the letter 's', may account for King's impression that he was the worse for drink.[75]

Whatever civil servants or newspaper proprietors thought, Churchill had the attention of the nation. The albeit rather rudimentary audience research carried out by the BBC at the time showed that 51% of the population listened to his first broadcast as Prime Minister on 19 May. The size of his audience increased with every broadcast, reaching almost 60% on 18 June, and it increased further after that.[76] A Home Office report on public opinion conducted the following day records some comments about the delivery but found that the anxiously awaited speech was considered 'courageous and hopeful'.[77] Some of his sophisticated listeners, like 'Rab' Butler's Private Secretary, Chips Channon, who was of the mould of the mainstream Conservative party and the Foreign Office, admitted that although Churchill left him unmoved, the nation would no doubt be impressed.[78] It was impressed enough by his performance throughout the summer that a Gallup Poll conducted in July gave Churchill an extraordinary 88% approval rating and in October, as the bombing of London was intensifying, 89%.[79]

Whatever the shades of opinion at the time, the end of this address surely ranks as one of the greatest political statements of modern times. It is worthy to stand alongside Lincoln's Gettysburg address as one of the seminal visionary texts of Western civilisation, made at one of the most significant climacterics of twentieth-century history. A 'half-breed' American who had a peculiar lisping speech defect, stood in the House of Commons and transformed his government's policy of refusing to recognise the latest shift in the local balance of power into a struggle for the fate of the world. In so doing, he reaffirmed and reset the identity of his nation.

After he had done so, the Battle of Britain began.

2. THE THREAT

By June 1940 it was not at all obvious why Germany should continue to fight Britain. After all, Germany had attacked Poland. Britain and France were the nations which declared war, as a result of which Germany found itself in a conflict which it had risked, but not sought. Nevertheless, after the fall of France, the Germans created a plan for attacking Britain.

Germany's overall policy was determined by one man. He had obligingly laid out the whole purpose of his career and his vision of Germany's future whilst in prison in 1924–5 in an autobiography to which his publisher gave the catchy title *Mein Kampf*.[1]

Perhaps the best one-line description of Adolf Hitler is the one Churchill gave after the war: 'a maniac of ferocious genius, the repository and expression of the most virulent hatreds that have ever corroded the human breast'.[2] *Mein Kampf* is a precise reflection of that genius, and its author never swerved from the path it lays out. Hitler himself says that his ideas were all formed when a youth in Vienna, and that he subsequently had to learn little and to alter nothing.[3]

It is indeed a repository of hatreds, and they are expressed with ferocious virulence. German politicians of right and left, Austria and the Habsburg Empire, democracy and capitalism, Socialism and Communism, and above all the Jews, who are somehow linked with all of these, are savaged with fervour. For only two things does Hitler consistently express admiration: the ordinary German soldier of World War I, and Great Britain – her soldiers and her statesmen, her institutions and her empire.

Britain is first mentioned as the home of Parliament, an institution Hitler claims to admire as an 'exalted form of self-government', whilst regarding it as quite inappropriate for Germany.[4] He derides Wilhelminian Germany's stupidity in making an enemy out of England by building a fleet, and expresses resentment at the anti-English propaganda of the war, for it led to an underestimation of their enemy which was to exact 'the bitterest retribution'.[5]

Her position as a colonial power made England unique in Europe and the only nation which was clearly of no interest to Germany in terms of territory. She was a natural ally, and making an enemy of her was wilful, arbitrary and reckless, for she was a most dangerous foe:

> England . . . always fought with whatever weapons were required for success . . . the resolve to do battle and to carry on the fight with ruthless tenacity never altered.[6]

Hitler returns to his theme at some length towards the end of the second volume of his book, where he considers Germany's alliance policy. He castigates German pre-war politicians for indulging in an irrelevant pursuit of colonies which turned Germany's most valuable potential ally into an enemy.

He continues by analysing the history of British foreign policy. For three hundred years, he says, Britain had sought to protect its interests by maintaining the balance of power in Europe, whilst itself having no interest in territorial acquisition there. Britain, therefore, unlike France, had no interest in eliminating German power, in fact it wanted a strong Germany to act as a brake on France. Britain simply sought to restrain Germany from becoming *too* strong. Her leaders were entirely pragmatic, forming alliances and fighting wars purely on the basis of self-interest, supporting the weaker against whichever power happened to be the strongest. The total collapse of German power in 1918 was against British interests, for it created a vacuum which could allow France to become over-dominant once more. England, he says, whilst not wanting Germany to be a world power, has no essential conflict with Germany in Europe. He concludes that Germany has two potential European allies:

> Taking a cool, dispassionate look at the world today, it is above all these two states, England and Italy, whose most natural selfish interests are at least not in fundamental conflict with the basic existential needs of the German nation and indeed might, to some extent, be identified with them.[7]

The problem, as he saw it, was that Germany (in 1925) was too weak and vacillating to be a worthy partner.[8]

Whilst exaggerating Britain's anxiety of a resurgent France, these passages define fairly accurately the classical foreign policy position represented by Halifax in 1940. Hitler did not imagine that winning England over would be easy, as he expected the Jews to do their best to prevent this happy alliance from being formed. But he ends the chapter by recommending that every attempt be made to do so. Germany should at least try to deal with France without British interference. Then if all went well, she would invite Britain and Italy to join her in destroying Communism and acquiring the territory she needed in the east.[9]

The real goal of German policy and the mission of the Nazi movement was to rid the world of Judaism and to conquer living-space in Russia. France had to be eliminated because of its implacable opposition to Germany's very existence, but Russia was the ultimate goal. Russia offered the only territorial option for Germanic expansion. Hitler also believed that it represented a real threat in itself because it had been taken over by a corrupt Jewish-Bolshevik movement which saw Germany as its next great target. Waging war against Russia therefore recommended itself on grounds of security alone, but had the added advantages of eliminating Bolshevism, dealing world Jewry a shattering blow and enabling the German race to fulfil its need for space to grow at the expense of the inferior Slavs.[10]

In Europe in 1925 it was not fanciful to see the Soviet Union as a threat. Winston Churchill would have agreed. Communism was militant and the new Soviet state was engaged in a strong ideological export drive. There were plenty of Communists in Germany and indeed, in the chaos after World War I, a Soviet Republic had been briefly declared in Bavaria. It is nevertheless ironic that Hitler should regard the anti-Semitic regime run by Stalin as some sort of Jewish plot.[11] It may have been because Marx was a Jew, but Hitler did not generally need any facts in order to denounce anything he disliked as Jewish. His view of them was metaphysical, akin to the view of the Devil in medieval theology.

Hitler's subsequent actions were entirely consistent with this programme. Those of his generals who later professed themselves to be bemused by the reluctance Hitler showed in 1940 to wage an all-out war against Britain had not troubled to inform themselves about their leader's clearly stated intentions. One can have some sympathy with this omission, as *Mein Kampf* is not a gratifying read. Most of the 8–9 million copies sold or distributed in Germany during its author's lifetime remained largely on the bookshelf.[12]

Hitler unequivocally wanted peace with Britain, and after the fall of France appeared to have every prospect of getting it. If he could not get it, he wanted Britain to be neutralised so that it could not interfere with his plans for the east.

But he understood his foe, and always recognised the possibility that Britain could act irrationally against its self-interest. One passage from the first volume of *Mein Kampf* is prescient.

> ... people will not die for business, only for ideals. There is no better proof of the superior psychological insight the English have into the workings of a people's soul than the way they managed to motivate their fight. Whilst we battled for bread, England fought for 'freedom', and not even for her own, no, but for that of the small nations. We laughed at the impudence of this or were annoyed by it, which just showed how thoughtless and stupid the so-called statesmanship of Germany had become even before the war. No-one seemed to have the faintest idea any more about the nature of the power which can make men resolve to give up their lives of their own free will.[13]

That was the fly in the ointment. Paradoxically, the nation of shopkeepers was also a nation of idealists. When the issue arose again, Churchill led the British down this very same path.

The Nazis were tireless in their attempts to gain Britain as an ally, or at least to secure her neutrality.

The leading role in this was played by Göring. In an interview with the British Air Attaché in 1935, he announced that Germany already had 1500 bombers (which was a hopeless exaggeration) and on being told that this meant Britain would rearm, welcomed the news, remarking that in the next war the two countries would be fighting side-by-side to save Europe from Communism. In 1937, he promised Lord Londonderry (who had been Secretary of State for Air from 1931–1935) that if the British Empire were menaced, Germany would come to its aid, and told the British journalist G. Ward Price and the Canadian Prime Minister that all Germany wanted was a free hand in the east. The same message was repeated to the British Ambassador, Sir Neville Henderson, on one of Göring's hunting parties, and again to Lord Halifax, who visited Göring's hunting exhibition in November 1937. He saw Ward Price once more at his fantastic villa, Karinhall, in March 1938, just after the Austrian Anschluss and a few months before the Czech crisis. He explained, whilst they played with the enormous train set Göring had had set up there, that Germany wanted to keep the British Empire strong and regretted the sense of belligerence creeping over Britain. Ward Price passed this on to the British government. Göring continued to communicate with Halifax during the last months of peace, sometimes directly and sometimes through the Swede Dahlerus, and sustained his diplomatic offensive directly with Chamberlain right into the winter of 1939–40.[14]

Churchill was not left out of the loop, as he recorded after the war. The German Ambassador to Britain, von Ribbentrop, visited him in 1937 to repeat the basic themes: Germany wanted the friendship of Britain, would 'stand guard' for the British Empire, would at most ask for a few of its old colonies back, but must have a free hand in the east, where she needed White Russia and the Ukraine as *Lebensraum*. All that was asked was that Britain should not interfere. Churchill replied, in front of a map, that Britain most certainly would interfere if Germany sought to dominate Europe. 'In that case,' von Ribbentrop replied, 'war is inevitable.' Churchill took due note of this, but added that England would bring the whole world against them. Von Ribbentrop left in a huff.[15]

During the last days of August 1939, Hitler used all the diplomatic means at his disposal to avoid war with Britain and was furious when the British government honoured its guarantee to Poland on 3 September.[16] It was the first time things had not gone his way. However, his victorious campaign in France offered new hope, and as it neared its completion, Hitler talked repeatedly to his generals about making peace with Britain. On 23 May, OKW issued an order halting his Panzers short of Dunkirk, thus allowing the BEF some vital time to escape. Hitler confirmed the order the following day. The 'halt order', which outraged his generals, has been said to be because of a loss of nerve, because of the exposed flanks of the armoured columns, because the tanks needed time to re-fit and repair, because Hitler thought the ground in Belgium was bad tank country, because of the need to conserve strength for the coming show-down with the French, and because Göring promised Hitler that the Luftwaffe could wipe out the BEF on the beaches without help from the army. In 1970, Basil Liddell Hart sparked off controversy by putting forward the view, based on his conversations with generals such as Blumentritt, that Hitler in fact wanted to avoid inflicting a humiliating defeat on the British, as they would then be unwilling to negotiate.[17] People rarely make decisions for a single reason. All of these considerations probably played a role.

Attempts to reach a settlement with Britain continued, and Hitler had every reason to suppose they had a good chance of success. After all, he was aware that Halifax was actively using Göring's Swedish channels and that Churchill's position as Prime Minister was far from secure.[18] A diplomatic solution was infinitely preferable to him than wearing out his forces in the west or conducting an extremely risky invasion.

The possibility of invading Britain is first mentioned in German records on 21 May, when Hitler broached the subject with Admiral Raeder.[19] General Jodl prepared a paper on the continuation of the war against England which Hitler read on 30 June after France had capitulated and he had enjoyed himself sight-seeing.

The general feeling in the German High Command was that the war was over, and just a little more force had to be applied to England in order to make her realise it. Jodl envisaged three measures: an intensification of the air war against shipping, the British economy and the RAF; terror attacks on the civil population; and the landing of troops. He gave the top priority to the elimination of the RAF, but seems to have believed that if the British were subjected to air attack and a siege which would reduce their food supply, their will to resist could be broken and the government would capitulate. A landing was a final resort to be undertaken only after England had been weakened economically and control of the air secured. However, he thought that all this would be unnecessary, for reason would surely prevail. Britain could not threaten Germany herself, so a continuation of hostilities was pointless.[20]

Whilst their expectations were quite reasonable, Churchill's failure to fulfil them placed the German High Command in a very difficult position, as is made clear by Jodl's muddled thinking. Whilst it was true that Britain could not immediately threaten Germany, neither was it easy for Germany to threaten Britain. Britain is a very hard country to defeat. With their control of the seas, the British can land troops where they like and get them home again if they get into trouble, as had just happened. They also have a dangerous talent for making friends and influencing people, so that even if the British do not have troops of their own fighting you somewhere, they are likely to have an ally somewhere else who is.

Perhaps it could be different in 1940. England had no more allies on the Continent, and, crucially, it could now be attacked from the air. A strategy for neutralising or possibly even defeating Britain therefore might be feasible. The one chosen was crucially dependent on the time available.

Hitler had two basic options: a long siege or a quick decision.

A siege meant using U-boats and air power to cut Britain's sea-lanes and wreck her economy. It would take many months, but it might work. However, he would then have to either postpone his plans for Russia or face a war on two fronts. He was impatient to get on with things, and he was worried about the Russian threat. He really wanted a rapid decision.

That meant establishing air superiority and backing it up with the threat of invasion. It was possible at any time that if they began to lose the air war, the peace lobby in the British government would gain the upper hand and negotiate. Air power was still an unknown factor. After Warsaw was bombed, the Poles capitulated. After Rotterdam was bombed the Dutch capitulated. The threat of bombing helped the French to make up their minds to evacuate Paris. Might not the bombing of London create such unrest that the government would be forced to come round?

Thus it was that Jodl saw this as a possible quick solution. Economic warfare meant a long siege. Invasion would be quick. Terror bombing might be either – nobody knew, but there was a lot of theory and some evidence suggesting that it could be quick, albeit the evidence from the bombing of Guernica during the Spanish Civil War pointed the other way. However that might be, it was crucial for the Germans to decide on the time-span and the basic strategy, for each meant deploying different forces and attacking different targets.

They did not find it easy to make up their minds. The longer they spent doing so, the more they were forced into a siege – and for this they were poorly equipped. In May 1939, Luftflotte 2 had carried out a war-game to ascertain how Britain's war economy and sea-lanes could be attacked from the air. They concluded that apart from mining, they lacked the means to do this effectively.[21] With U-boat production peaking at only six a month in 1940, in July the Kriegsmarine had a grand total of twenty-seven operational submarines.[22] The Luftwaffe had abandoned the long-range heavy bomber. The German economy was ill prepared for siege.

Some bold men had advocated seizing the chance offered by Dunkirk before France surrendered. Milch went to see Göring on 18 June and proposed landing paratroops in a *coup-de-main* to take the exposed airfields in southern England and supply them by air, supported by Stukas and Bf 109s. Göring told him it was far too risky, and in any case he only had one parachute division available.[23] Milch's daring was shared by Kesselring, who advocated a similar strike whilst the British were in disarray.[24] He was dumbfounded to learn that instead of this, a partial demobilisation of the Wehrmacht had been ordered before France had even been fully defeated.[25] June and July slipped away without decisive action whilst diplomacy was tried and Hitler waited for the British to negotiate.

Throughout July, diplomatic activity and military preparations ran in parallel. Feelers were put out through Sweden, Italy, Switzerland and Spain, where there was also an attempt to involve the Duke of Windsor in a peace move. It was only after this had failed, on 1 August, that Hitler issued Directive 17 for the prosecution of the air offensive against Britain.[26]

The German people were impatient. A Gestapo survey carried out in June showed that most Germans were resentful at Britain's apparent determination to continue the war and eager to teach them a lesson.[27] On 6 July, the song 'Denn wir fahren gegen Engelland' was broadcast over the radio for the first time.[28]

After the war, some German generals claimed that Hitler was never serious about invading Britain and it was all a bluff. It would be more accurate to say that it was an example of Hitler's usual technique of backing up his attempts to gain political ends with the threat of force. Much lay between nuisance raiding and an invasion and those were the possibilities most interesting to him.

So it was that the Luftwaffe was tasked with making the threat to Britain real, always with the hope that an air campaign alone would bring the British to the negotiating table. The air campaign had three aims:

1. To fulfil a basic pre-condition of invasion by establishing air-superiority over the invasion area of south-east England and thus both make the threat of invasion very real and give Hitler the option of carrying it out.
2. In so doing to weaken the RAF to such an extent that Britain would feel herself to be very vulnerable to attack from the air, and therefore become more willing to negotiate.
3. By these same measures, to begin the process of isolating Britain and weakening her war-making capacity, so that a siege could simultaneously begin.

The Germans were keeping their options open. The Luftwaffe felt supremely confident. They had superiority in front-line numbers and had prevailed with ease against every foe. Their young service was the most combat-experienced air force in the world. They did not know a great deal about their enemy across the Channel, but that did not worry them unduly. Having arisen from the ashes of 1918 the Luftwaffe had become a force before which Europe quailed.

In fact, that enemy had been preparing a defence against the very sort of attack they were about to launch for about as long as the Luftwaffe had been in existence. These efforts had been originally galvanised by the painful experience that enemy had suffered at the hands of the Luftwaffe's own predecessor, the '*Luftstreitkräfte*' of the German army, some twenty-five years before.

3. THE ASSAILANT

The war-time Commander-in-Chief of the US Air Force, General Carl Spaatz, once observed that 'it was the German air force which dominated world diplomacy and won for Hitler the bloodless political victories of the late thirties.'[1]

For the Nazis the Luftwaffe was as much a political weapon as a military one. Its potency came from the world's fear of air power. They broadcast every new technical development they made, even resorting to trickery. For example, the specially constructed aircraft with which Willy Messerschmitt set a new world speed record in 1939 was claimed to be an ordinary Bf 109 fighter.[2] The biggest piece of stage-management took place during the occupation of the Rhineland in March 1936, when the Luftwaffe only had ten fully-armed fighters in operation. Aircraft were photographed on airfields, flown to others, had their cowlings re-painted overnight and were photographed the next day as if they were different aircraft. Mechanics were dressed in flying overalls to pose as pilots. It worked.[3]

Before war broke out, most of the world believed the propaganda. Once it had broken out, the strength of the Luftwaffe and the fear of air attack played a major role in Halifax's arguments for peace.[4] The perceived strength of the Luftwaffe also had a strong impact on American assessments of British chances of survival. Charles Lindbergh and the US Ambassador in London, Joseph Kennedy, were both particularly impressed by it, the latter telling the State Department on 31 July 1940 that the Luftwaffe had the power to put the RAF 'out of commission'.[5] Roosevelt himself believed in May that the Germans had a five-to-one superiority in the air and that the British would be unlikely to 'withstand the assault for many weeks'.[6] He differed from his Ambassador only in finding the prospect unwelcome.

That the Luftwaffe existed at all is due to that fateful document, the Versailles Treaty. Inspired by hatred and formulated in haste, it was signed in June 1919, and with that the German Air Service was dissolved. Germany's fleet of aircraft was handed over to the Allies, and the country was forbidden to support an air force or manufacture military aircraft.[7]

So Germany did not. Instead, it built commercial aircraft which could easily be converted into bombers, sports aircraft which could serve as fighters, formed a state airline to build up a transport fleet and encouraged gliding clubs in order to train future pilots.

The man who first guided this ingenious development was General Hans von Seeckt, who worked in the so-called Ministry of Defence in Berlin. The ministry was in effect a General Staff. From the beginning it included 180 officers from the former German Air Service and its senior figures included Kesselring, Sperrle, Stumpff and Wolfram von Richthofen, a cousin of the 'Red Baron', Manfred von Richthofen, who would lead the air campaign against England.

Germany had been forbidden to build large commercial airliners by the 1922 Paris Air Agreement, but this lapsed in 1926. In order to help create a strong industry and provide it with a good customer, the Civil Aviation Minister, Ernst Brandenburg, ordered the formation of a single national airline, the Deutsche Lufthansa, out of Junkers Airways and Aero-Lloyd, both subsidiaries of the Deutsche Luftreederei, a transport company formed in 1919.

The new company had three directors, two from Aero-Lloyd and one, an ex-pilot called Erhard Milch, from Junkers. Professor Hugo Junkers did not take kindly to the enforced merger of his company and began a campaign against it and Milch, whom he regarded as a traitor. By September 1929, however, Milch had survived Junkers' sabotage attempts and also ousted his fellow directors to become Lufthansa's first Chairman. Milch was not above politics. Amongst the candidates at the 1928 Reichstag elections one of the more attractive to him was an old flyer called Hermann Göring who managed to win a seat with some financial support quietly provided by Lufthansa.[8]

Erhard Milch was born in 1892 into a fiercely patriotic north German family. He served in the artillery on the Eastern Front in 1914–15 before joining a reconnaissance unit of the air service, and in 1918 served once again in the army. In these posts and in helping to suppress insurrectionists in post-war Germany, Milch showed the vision, independence of mind, courage, energy, organisational ability and ruthlessness which enabled him to become the real designer and builder of the Luftwaffe. He was impressed by Göring on their first meeting and even more impressed by Hitler when they first met in 1930. The feeling was mutual, and Lufthansa worked closely with the Nazis even before they came to power.[9]

Von Seeckt encouraged gliding so strongly that by 1929 some 50,000 Germans were members of the *Deutscher Luftsportverband*, which was in effect a civilian reserve. He needed to create the cadre around which these civilians could be formed into an air force, so from 1923 he sent selected Lufthansa personnel to a secret and illicit training establishment at Lipetsk in Russia. It was run by Hugo Sperrle.

By the time the Nazis gained power in 1933, the core of the Luftwaffe already existed. In 1934 the Reichswehr Ministerium (Defence Ministry) became the Reichskriegsministerium (Ministry of War), which showed commendable honesty. Hitler thought that Göring would have the right political appeal to be Air Minister, and Milch agreed to become his deputy.

Hermann Göring was born in Bavaria in 1893 and, inspired by his friend Bruno Loerzer, joined the air service in 1915. He served as a fighter pilot throughout World War I, finishing it as Commander of the legendary Geschwader 1, having taken over from Baron Manfred von Richthofen. With twenty-two official victories he ranked forty-sixth on the list of German aces.

His career since then had been bound up with the history of the Nazi party. He was in many ways a remarkable man. He was highly intelligent, forceful, self-confident and energetic, as he was to demonstrate to his captors during his trial at Nuremberg, where he dominated proceedings. However, in the abortive Munich Putsch of November 1923, he was shot in the groin and evacuated to Austria, where doctors treated him with morphine. This began a life-long addiction to the drug. Its general effects have been described as follows:

> Morphine is capable of rendering a person of honest character completely untrustworthy, of producing delusions that in turn result in criminal actions, of increasing glandular activities and of generating side-effects like outpourings of immense vital energy and what the pharmaceutical textbooks describe as 'grotesque vanity'. The morphine addict may find his imagination stimulated, his oratory more fluid, but then a state of languor supervenes, followed on occasions by deep sleep.[10]

Göring was to demonstrate these characteristics throughout the rest of his career.

Milch wanted the air force to be independent of the army, and as his boss was Hitler's right-hand man, he got what he wanted. He set about building up the Luftwaffe, estimating that he would need eight to ten years. Göring was a politician who had happened to be a pilot, so all matters of technology and organisation were dealt with by Milch. He planned a massive expansion in aircraft production – 800% in two years – and matched it with growth in training facilities.

On 1 March 1935, Hitler officially announced the existence of the Luftwaffe as a separate branch of the Wehrmacht (the armed forces), with Göring as its Commander-in-Chief, General Walther Wever as Chief of Air Staff and Milch as Secretary of State for Air. Like Athena, the Greek goddess of war, who sprang fully armed from the head of Zeus, the Luftwaffe at its birth already had 1,888 aircraft and about 20,000 men. And just as Athena was Zeus' favourite, so the Luftwaffe, which unlike the army and navy was actually created by the Nazis, was, for a time at least, Hitler's favourite amongst the armed forces.

Hitler made Milch a general of the Luftwaffe in 1936, a move which did not go down well with Göring. Hitler had expressed dissatisfaction with Milch's expansion plans, as they were too slow for his ambitions, and Göring openly insulted Milch when he raised objections to moving any faster. Milch was fully aware that the increased pace meant that the Luftwaffe would lack depth in infrastructure and numbers. He wanted a real air force, not just one which only existed in propaganda.[11]

During the course of 1936, Göring undermined his deputy, whom he increasingly saw as a threat, and introduced his old flying chum, the Great War ace Ernst Udet, into a position of increasing power. Udet was popular amongst the flying fraternity, but completely lacked Milch's considerable administrative and technical skills. Thus it was that Udet was given two appointments ideally suited to displaying these lacunae in his talents, becoming Inspector of Fighters and Dive-Bombers and Director of the Technical Department. Nazi that he was, Göring did not like too many competent people too close to him and believed that the future belonged to the warrior-hero. He was one himself, and Udet was another. Together, they introduced romantic amateurism into the very top of the new service.

This was symptomatic of a leadership problem the Luftwaffe never solved. When the first Chief of Staff, the extremely able General Walther Wever, was killed in a crash in 1936, he was replaced by Albert Kesselring. Kesselring did not get on with Milch, so was replaced within a year by Hans-Jürgen Stumpff. This did not work out either, so in 1939 Göring replaced Stumpff with Hans Jeschonneck. Jeschonneck had passed out brilliantly from the Kriegsakademie, worshipped Hitler and feuded with Milch.[12] To some extent, personnel problems were inevitable given the new service's rate of expansion. In 1935, the Luftwaffe had 1,100 officers and 17,000 men. By 1939, it had grown to 15,000 officers and 370,000 men, an overall expansion rate of over 200% per annum.[13] Most were simply pilots, army officers or pure technicians.

But added to this factor came the nature of the Nazi regime. Apart from its emphasis on ideology, it placed a premium on intrigue and personal loyalties, in this case mainly to Göring. His relations with Milch had deteriorated to open conflict by the end of 1936. Responsibilities were left deliberately unclear and those in power adopted a divide-and-rule policy towards their subordinates.[14] As Milch icily observed to Göring shortly after the war began, *divide et imperat* was a motto the Romans had applied to their enemies, not to their friends. Göring made no reply.[15] In Nazism the relationship between the individual and the tribe of the *Herrenvolk* was mediated by little except pack loyalty to whoever was the local alpha male at the time. Rational debate and decision-making were therefore rendered very difficult.[16] Despite the jealousies within the RAF, rational debate was allowed, so major decisions were strongly influenced by reality. Avoidance of reality was of the very essence of Nazism and this was to reach its ultimate realisation in the febrile fantasy world of Hitler's bunker in the spring of 1945.

The first major decision the Luftwaffe had to make was about equipment, in which the first issue was the strategic bomber. Wever championed the concept in Germany, drawing on a study carried out by Dr Robert Knauss in 1933. Knauss argued for a force of 400 heavy bombers to act as a deterrent. The army was jealously opposed to this (as it was in Britain), but more importantly, German industry lacked the capability to produce such a force. The military aircraft industry was a shadow in 1933, and by 1934, after a period of hectic expansion, employed barely 17,000 people, just half as many as the British aircraft industry at that time, which was before Britain's rearmament had begun.[17]

Wever did not argue for an autonomous bomber force. A war-game held in 1933–4 had convinced the Wehrmacht that a bomber force alone could not destroy an enemy's air fleet. But Wever did believe that long-range bombers were an important weapon, and in 1935 he ordered two four-engined types. On Wever's death, Kesselring cancelled the orders whilst Milch was on holiday, and on his return Milch reluctantly agreed, in view of the resource constraints faced by the industry.[18]

In the rush to create a new air force, an unexpected opportunity presented itself when a civil war broke out in Spain in 1936. In November of that year, Germany secretly sent a 'volunteer corps', known as the 'Legion Cóndor' to support Franco. Good pay attracted a lot of volunteers, who were rotated for six-month periods to give as many pilots as possible operational experience. The force was commanded by Hugo Sperrle, with Wolfram Freiherr von Richthofen as Chief of Staff. It had about 200 fighters, bombers and reconnaissance aircraft, and in May 1937 the Heinkel He 51 biplanes equipping the fighter force were replaced with the new Bf 109Bs. The other major equipment change was the relegation of the three-engined Ju 52 to a transport role, and the introduction of the Do 17 and He 111 as bombers. The military aims of the Cóndor Legion were to achieve air superiority, which the 109s soon did, and to support ground forces. They all learned extremely valuable lessons, especially about fighter tactics. Werner Mölders was the prime mover behind this and Wolfram von Richthofen worked out the technique and tactics of air-to-ground co-operation. These lessons were integrated and systematised by the Lehr Division (technical development unit), formed in 1937.

The world also learned lessons from Spain. In 1937, a force of forty-three Cóndor Legion bombers and fighters got through to the small town of Guernica, the seat of the Basque government. They were attacking an important military target, a road bridge. The bombers discovered what every other bomber force discovered when it tried to attack specific targets: they could not bomb it accurately, and so had to attack the general area of the target. The civilian death toll was claimed to be 1600, even as many as 2500, though modern research suggests about 300 to be closer to the truth. The poor souls were 'collateral damage', but the international press portrayed the raid as a deliberate act of terror. The world received the news in muted horror. Its emotional impact was captured in Picasso's famous painting, which still gives the most vivid available impression of the impact of the new air weapon on the civilised European mind. Guernica became a symbol of the terrors a new war would bring and of the power and the ruthlessness of the Luftwaffe, which was very useful for Hitler.

Inside the Luftwaffe, events like Guernica were subjected to a more dispassionate analysis than in the world at large. Whilst it was recognised that bombing did affect civilian morale, a report by Naval Staff Officer Hauptmann Heye, who interviewed pilots in 1938, concluded that attacking non-military targets was not 'a suitable means of breaking an opponent's resistance', and emphasised the alienation of the population it caused.[19] It also became clear how hard it was for bombers to hit targets, especially at night. This had three consequences: firstly, it convinced Udet even more of the need for dive-bombers; secondly, it resulted in a change of production priorities from a ratio of three bombers to every fighter to two bombers to every fighter; and thirdly, it led to heavy investment in developing radio direction systems as a navigational aid. The result of this was the '*Knickebein*' system that made the raid on Coventry in November 1940 possible.[20]

The Spanish Civil War put the Luftwaffe on the world stage and the Nazis exploited its impact for propaganda purposes. However, behind the formidable façade, the Luftwaffe from the outset had a number of concealed weaknesses which its leaders were unwilling to face and were largely incapable of solving. These were in the areas of aircraft production, crew training and command and control.

Milch's early achievements in aircraft production were prodigious. He set up his first annual production plan in 1934, placing an order for 4,021 bombers, fighters and reconnaissance aircraft, the bulk of which were to be used for training. The industry produced 1,968 machines in 1934 and 3,183 in 1935, prompting Milch to increase the targets, resulting in a production figure of 5,112 in 1936. Hitler was not interested in training, however – he was too impatient for war. He wanted a striking force fast, and in 1937 re-tooling began for production of the new types being rushed into service, and production was put under Udet's control. In 1937, Germany produced a total of 5,606 machines, of which 2,651 were front-line combat aircraft. This was not nearly enough, and Udet lacked the skills and personality to get the industry to do better.[21] That it could was revealed in 1944 when Speer took over, and production, despite round-the-clock bombing by the RAF and USAF, reached nearly 40,000. But in the 1930s there was no centralised control and manufacturers did largely as they pleased. Many valuable technicians and engineers were called up for national service. The industry was also short of raw materials, but there was no attempt to plan priorities. The emphasis was on short-term numbers.[22] The Luftwaffe was designed to fight a short war, and entered what was to become a war of attrition with no reserve.[23]

Pilot training paralleled aircraft production. The original four flying train-ing schools were not added to, albeit one naval air training school was created. The standards were very high, but again the numbers were lacking. In 1939 the General Staff refused a proposal for expansion on the grounds that resources were needed for new units at the front. Not only that, the main training aircraft, the Ju 52, was needed for transportation and the training units were raided by the operational commanders as soon as the war began. Final training was made the responsibility of front-line units, each of which had a training squadron. Operational development was made the responsibility of two *Lehrgeschwader*, groups of fighters and bombers formed around a cadre of instructors. Once again, there was no strategic reserve. Once the war began the relatively light casualties in Poland led to a further underestimation of needs, and it was only after the start of the Russian campaign that the need, which by then was obvious, was acted upon.[24] By then it was too late.

At first, this did not matter. It started to matter during the Battle of Britain, and the first crisis came in early 1941, when the lack of bomber pilots, in particular those capable of flying the very effective but tricky Ju 88, first became manifest. Bomber pilots needed two years of training as against the one needed for fighters.[25] With this failure to think long-term, the Luftwaffe sowed the seeds of its own future destruction. It meant that the losses incurred during 1940 had a far-reaching effect.

The other major area left to improvisation was that of technology. At the national level, the Nazi party spread its nefarious influence here as everywhere else. Large numbers of scientists left Germany in the 1930s. Those that were left were made to concentrate their efforts on gadgetry of minor short-term value or on wonder-weapons. The Nazis were as unwilling to co-operate with civil-ian scientists as they were with businessmen, and responsibility for research was split up between various competing political bodies in accordance with the divide-and-rule principle.[26]

The warrior-hero mentality of the Luftwaffe itself also led to the neglect of available technology. On 15 August 1940, a Spitfire flown by Pilot Officer Ralph Roberts of 64 Squadron became disorientated after a dogfight and landed at Caffiers, a German fighter airfield in France. The aircraft was examined by technical experts who concluded that it was carrying 'the most modern com-munications equipment, better than ours; a discovery of great tactical and technical value to us'.[27] This can only have been a VHF radio. The Germans had neglected basics like communication in the air. This was not through lack of capability, but through choice.

Ulrich Steinhilper was, by chance, made Communications Officer of his fighter wing in January 1939. He describes in detail how from that point his attempts to install radios in the 109s, let alone to develop proper procedures in the air, were frustrated and ridiculed at every turn by the Cóndor Legion veter-ans, led by his Commanding Officer, Adolf Galland.[28] Galland argued that radios were unnecessary as pilots could communicate well enough in the air by waggling their wings as they had in World War I and in Spain, and that the radios just added weight. This romantic amateurism, based on the Richthofen-inspired cult of the heroic individual, dogged the Luftwaffe until 1940, and seriously affected their operations over England. When Johannes Steinhoff developed night-fighting techniques, which demanded good radio communication, he was ridiculed, and Steinhilper's own radio direction finding experiments met with derision.[29]

Technical developments were prompted by operational experience. It was Kesselring's appraisal of the Spanish experience that led to the development of navigational systems like 'Knickebein'. But this was an isolated example. There was no systematic planning. From 1941, when the British went over to the offensive in the air, the Luftwaffe simply responded to new developments, and was therefore always one step behind. The exceptions were the wonder-weapons so appealing to Hitler. Because of poor planning and prioritisation neither of the two major ones, jet propulsion and rocketry, had a significant impact on the outcome of the war.

The Luftwaffe was originally organised into four regions, called 'Luftämter', each responsible for the defence of their own part of Germany. In 1939, the Luftämter were re-designated 'Luftflotten', or 'Airfleets', which soon lost their regional role as they were to be used offensively outside their territories. They were themselves divided into corps and divisions, like an army. The Airfleets could be made up of any combination of fighter or bomber units depending on their task.

Fighters and bombers were organised into Geschwader, or Groups. Each Geschwader normally had three Gruppen (wings) and each Gruppe three Staffeln (squadrons). In addition, most Geschwader had a Staffel or even a fourth Gruppe for training. During the Battle of Britain these units were based in southern France or Germany and did not form part of the Order of Battle.

The basic operational unit was the Gruppe, which was usually based at the same airfield and tended to fight as a whole. There was thus a structure between the Airfleet and the squadron, which helped in the sharing of information and in giving greater leverage to the experienced air leaders.

Bomber units were called 'Kampfgeschwader', shortened to 'KG', fighter units 'Jagdgeschwader' ('JG'), dive-bomber units 'Stukageschwader' ('StG') and heavy fighter units 'Zerstörergeschwader' ('ZG'). Each was commanded by a 'Geschwaderkommodore' who led a staff flight ('Stabschwarm') of about four aircraft in the air. Each of the three 'Gruppen' was led by a 'Gruppenkommandeur' with another staff flight of his own. Although a Geschwaderkommodore was usually a colonel or even a general and a Gruppenkommandeur a major, the role was independent of rank and far more junior officers were promoted into leadership positions during the Battle. The three Staffeln which made up a Gruppe were each led by a captain or a major, the equivalent of a squadron leader in the RAF.

Gruppen were usually equipped with the same model of aircraft and often flew together. They were the largest units which could be controlled whilst in the air, at least until action began, when the Staffel or its component parts fought independently. Both Gruppen and Staffeln were numbered consecutively through the Geschwader, the Gruppen designated by Roman numerals and the Staffeln by Arabic. Thus 1., 2. and 3./KG1 were the first three Staffeln of KG1 and together made up I./KG1, the first Gruppe of KG1, which flew He 111s. II./KG1 consisted of 4.,5. and 6./KG1 and also flew He 111s. III./KG1 consisted of 7., 8. and 9./KG1, which flew the Do 17.

On 1 May 1939, the Geschwader were re-numbered. Airfleet 1 was given numbers 1 – 25, Airfleet 2 numbers 26 – 50, Airfleet 3 numbers 51 – 75 and Airfleet 4 numbers 76 – 100, giving plenty of scope for future expansion which never took place. The different Geschwader types used the series of numbers independently of each other.[30] The primary logic for the numbering of the main Luftwaffe units of 1940 (despite some anomalies) was as follows:

	Airfleet 1	Airfleet 2	Airfleet 3	Airfleet4
Single-seater fighters	JG1, 2 & 3	JG26 & 27	JG51, 52, 53 & 54	JG77
Heavy fighters	ZG1 & 2	ZG26	–	ZG76
Bombers	KG1, 2, 3 & 4	KG26 & 27	KG51	KG76
Dive-bombers	StG1, 2 & 3	–	–	StG77

In practice these units did not necessarily operate under their 'parent' Airfleets. There were also constant transfers and re-designations of the units themselves. For example, the original I./StG26 became II./StG2 almost immediately, and the original StG51 became StG77. After the occupation of Norway, Airfleet 5 was set up there and assigned KG26, the newly formed KG30, JG77 and part of ZG26. As forces were reorganised for the Battle of Britain, the remaining units were divided between Airfleets 2 and 3.

The two Lehrgeschwader formed exceptions to this general rule. LG1 had three Gruppen of Ju 88s attached to Airfleet 3, a fourth of Stukas attached to Airfleet 2 and a fifth of Bf 110s attached to Airfleet 3. LG2 had two Gruppen of Bf 109s with Airfleet 2 and some Bf 110s and Do 17s with a reconnaissance role, split between the Airfleets (see Appendix I).

In addition to these units there were various specialised reconnaissance, coastal and air-sea rescue units attached to various levels of the organisational hierarchy, as well as a few independent specialist Gruppen.

The Luftwaffe attracted a broad cross-section of the German population, offering those with the talent an escape from foot-slogging. Like the 'Brylcreem boys' of the RAF, they were admired and envied by others, being rather resentfully known as 'Schlipssoldaten' (literally: 'neck-tie soldiers') by the army.[31] The speed of the Luftwaffe's expansion in the late 1930s meant drawing on every possible source. After March 1935, men were transferred wholesale from the army, Lufthansa and the gliding clubs, but the army was expanding too, and after managing to scrounge 6000 men from them in 1936, Göring got no more from the generals.[32] He had then to rely on conscripts and volunteers, most of whom entered at seventeen to serve between two and twelve years. The Luftwaffe, unlike the army, was made to represent the Nazi ideal of dissolving class barriers, with easier relationships between officers and men and largely meritocratic promotion amongst flying personnel. This attracted a lot of good people, especially those of an individualist, anti-authoritarian bent, and there are stories about many of the famous aces like Wick and Marseille which show they were temperamentally as intolerant of authority as Tuck or Bader were on the other side.

Training was thorough despite a teacher-pupil ratio of 1:6, rather than the 1:4 which was considered ideal, and pilots joined their units with some 250 hours in their log-books, with bomber crews taking extra courses equipping each crew member to do the work of every other.[33] However, the Luftwaffe shared the army's lack of technically trained personnel. Only 5% of Luftwaffe generals and General Staff officers had technical qualifications, and this was not helped by Jeschonnek's denigration of technology and engineers. Tactics and operations were stressed at the expense of intelligence and supply.[34]

Training was a dangerous business. Nobody had very much experience with fast monoplanes with retractable undercarriages, and the new fighter, the Bf 109, did its bit to make gory inroads into the ranks of young recruits. Testosterone also played its part. Many young pilots were reckless, and stunts over the homes of parents and girlfriends often ended in combustion. Spectacular accidents were as much part of life as 'wizard prangs' were in the RAF and were known as 'Californian' crashes.[35] In 1937, for example, 147 men were killed and 2422 injured, with 108 aircraft written off and a further 1290 damaged.[36] Göring rightly became very concerned, but the pattern was to continue throughout the war.

Although the new service was revolutionary in cutting through class barriers in German society, it soon introduced new class distinctions of its own. After the Spanish Civil War, veterans of the Cóndor Legion became a group apart. They had earned good money, so most had cars and tended to think they had a licence to misbehave.[37] Their combat experience led them to think they knew it all, and they showed a romantic disdain for new technology and rejected anything which was not practised in Spain, including night flying. They also formed a clique favouring promotion from within.[38] This clique literally died out as the war progressed, but had a strong influence over the Luftwaffe of 1940.

The expansion process was still in full swing when war broke out on 3 September 1939. There were only 2,577 aircrews available, which was 69% of establishment and of those only 1,432 (38% of establishment) were fully qualified. The situation was most serious for the bombers, who were only able to operate at 32.5% of full strength, and least serious amongst fighters, which had 83.5% of their establishment strength operational.[39] The force that attacked England in 1940 was at its peak in terms of quality and relative numbers. From then on, more and more corners were cut in training as attrition took its toll. Those that were left had to bear a heavy burden.

In the 1930s, the Luftwaffe harboured no illusions that air power alone could win wars. With most of its staff recruited from the army, this was only to be expected, and it took its part next to the army and navy as part of the Wehrmacht, the German armed forces. As such its High Command, the 'Oberkommando der Luftwaffe' (OKL) was in theory subject to the supreme command of the armed forces, 'Oberkommando der Wehrmacht' (OKW). Its operating principles stated that 'decision in war can only be achieved by the co-operation of the three services'. As the destruction of the enemy's armed forces were to be achieved primarily by the army, the main aim of the air force was to support this. This implied building medium bombers, dive-bombers and fighters.[40]

There was another reason to concentrate on smaller aircraft: the obsession with numbers. Three twin-engined machines could be produced for every two four-engined ones and Göring took the simple view that 'the Führer will not ask how big the bombers are, but how many there are.'[41] Numbers impressed not only the Führer but the outside world as well. The result of this thinking was to rush into service types that were to remain the mainstay of the bomber force throughout the war before they had been properly evaluated.[42]

The aircraft industry had been told what to expect in 1933 during the first diplomatic crisis Hitler created by withdrawing from the League of Nations. Braced for foreign intervention, Milch called the top industry executives together for a meeting at which Göring dramatically announced to them that Germany had to become an air power within a year.

The Nazis used their usual methods to deal with opposition. The ageing and stubborn Hugo Junkers owned what was still the largest aircraft production facility in Germany, so with a combination of threats, blackmail and intimidation Milch settled his own score with him and appointed a new General Manager who turned Junkers into a mass-producer of the vital Ju 52 transport machine.[43] Junkers was exiled from his home town and died in Bavaria shortly afterwards. His fate encouraged the others to be co-operative.

The process of aircraft specification and production was in Udet's hands. He had little idea how long it took to get new designs into production and was at the mercy of the managers of the rival firms who put more store on having a wide range of new designs on offer than on producing existing types in large numbers. The Luftwaffe developed eighty-six new designs during the war, of which only a handful went into large-scale production. When Milch himself took over the job after Udet committed suicide in 1941 he found such chaos that he cancelled most new types and insisted on modifying established ones to make up the production shortfalls. The industry only reached its productive potential under Speer's radical measures in 1944. The Luftwaffe of 1940 was a lot smaller than it might have been.[44]

The first new bomber to arrive was the Dornier Do 17. It was conceived in 1934 as a fast passenger carrier, but its slim fuselage, which was to give it the nickname 'the Flying Pencil', made it cramped and unsuitable as an airliner. A test-pilot suggested that it would make a good fast bomber, and it went into production in 1936 as the Do 17E, capable of carrying 2,200 lbs (1,000 kg) of bombs at a maximum speed of 230 mph. At a Swiss air-show in 1937, a stripped-down version flew at a speed of 284 mph, making it faster than any fighter then in service, which made good propaganda.[45]

The most prolific production version was the Do 17Z, which entered service in 1939. It cruised at 246 mph, and carried between four and eight machine guns grouped in various positions around the cockpit.[46] In accordance with Luftwaffe philosophy, the crew was grouped together in the glazed nose area, which aided communication and was thought to improve morale.

The first aircraft designed from the outset to carry bombs was the Heinkel He 111, which first flew in 1935. A commercial version was displayed in January 1936, but by then the first military production batch had already been built. Early versions flew with the Cóndor Legion, and this experience led to the belief that an armament of three machine guns was sufficient. In 1939 the He 111H appeared with a redesigned glazed nose, a ventral gondola to accommodate another gun and Junkers Jumo engines rather then the DB 601s previously used, as these were needed for the Bf 109, and production was constrained. Experience in France indicated that two further gun positions were needed in the fuselage to protect against beam attacks. Of the five crew positions, the gondola was the most unpopular, becoming known in some units as the 'Sterbebett' or 'deathbed'. However, the He 111 was very stable and easy to fly, with the same bomb-load and almost the same performance as the Do

17Z.[47] Both these aircraft were comparable in performance to their British counterparts with one significant exception: they only carried about half the bomb-load. They were not designed for razing cities to the ground.

The weapon most beloved of the Luftwaffe High Command was, however, the Stuka. The reason for the interest in it was that up to 1939, the Luftwaffe had no effective bomb-sight. Consequently, the results achievable through dive-bombing had a special attraction.[48] This was particularly so as accuracy was the key to ground support. Most targets were small, in the proximity of friendly troops and could only be taken out by a direct hit.

The driving force behind the dive-bomber was Udet. He had brought two Curtiss Hawk dive-bombers back from the US in 1933, became convinced by the concept and began lobbying. Once the Luftwaffe had been formed he became Inspector General of Stukas and set up a tender between Heinkel, Arado, Blohm und Voss and Junkers, who presented their aircraft in June 1936. The Heinkel and Junkers designs came out on top[49] and when Udet crashed the Heinkel, the choice fell on Junkers. The result was the Ju 87, which came to arrogate to itself the generic German term for dive-bomber – 'Sturzkampfflugzeug' or 'Stuka' for short.

Deliveries of the first model, the Ju 87A-1, began in 1937. It was a crude-looking but very rugged machine, designed with its unique purpose in mind, no attempt being made to maximise performance through streamlining. It also had the advantage of being simple to produce and so helped to swell pre-war numbers. Uniquely amongst bombers of the time, it had a fixed undercarriage. As a result, its maximum speed was under 200 mph, which mattered little, as it was deliberately slowed in the dive by the use of dive-brakes. Its defensive armament was also perfunctory: one rearwards firing machine gun. It was never intended to fight its way through to a distant target alone by massing defensive cross-fire. It was designed for an environment in which local air superiority had already been achieved.

A few were sent to Spain, and vindicated expectations in actions against bridges, roads and shipping. In 1938 the more powerful B model appeared, with a new canopy, enlarged tail surfaces, spats instead of trousers around the undercarriage legs and a single forward-firing machine gun in the port wing. The main production variant, the B-2, cruised at 175 mph at 15,000 feet and had a maximum speed of 232 mph, with the ability to carry a 1100 lb bomb 370 miles. It was thus some 25 mph slower than the obsolete Fairy Battle and carried a similar bomb-load over a shorter range. The RAF withdrew the Battle from front-line service in June 1940, one month after its disastrous début.

Such was Udet's enthusiasm for dive-bombing, however, that he made dive-bombing capability a requirement for *all* future German bombers. The first victim of this obsession was the Junkers Ju 88. This excellent fast medium bomber first flew on 21 December 1936, a response to a specification laid down by Milch in 1935.[50] Unlike the Stuka, it was a sleek design and in March 1939 a cleaned-up prototype set up a new speed record of 321 mph.

However, despite the general desire for rapid production of large numbers of aircraft, in 1938 the dive-bombing requirement was imposed on the new design. As a result of the need for a strengthened fuselage, dive-brakes and sundry extras, the Ju 88's weight doubled to 12 or 13 tons, and production was delayed. Diving the 4.2 ton Ju 87 at 90° was a task which average crews could master. Despite the assurances of the test-pilot that the Ju 88 could be dived at 80°, in practice most of its crews came down in far shallower dives, greatly reducing their bombing effectiveness, so that the dive-bombing requirement bore little fruit.[51]

The other penalty was that only sixty Ju 88s had been delivered by the end of 1939.[52] Göring's solution was to increase the production targets. Milch tried to solve the problem, and during the Battle of Britain he toured Ju 88 units collecting complaints about this fine but bastardised design, and sent a report to Göring listing thirty-two of them. Göring visited Junkers and was told that the new version, the A-4, would solve all the problems, so left it at that. It did solve a lot of them, but in 1940 there were far fewer Ju 88s in operation than had been envisaged.[53]

This was fortunate for the RAF, for, though complex, the Ju 88 was a superb aircraft going on to serve in many roles, including that of night-fighter. The main variant to fly during the Battle of Britain was the A-4. It had a crew of four, a defensive armament of four machine guns and could carry 4000–5500 lbs of bombs over 1900 miles. With a maximum speed of 293 mph, it was 50 mph faster than its two stable-mates whilst carrying twice the bomb-load. The RAF quickly recognised it to be the toughest bomber target, as its strong construction enabled it to absorb a lot of damage. It required more skill to fly than the other two bomber types, and it was tricky to handle on take-off and landing.[54] This was a small price for the crews to pay for increased chances of survival.

The Luftwaffe also needed a new fighter. In the mid-1930s, just as in Britain and everywhere else, Germany's front-line fighter was a biplane, the He 51. Just as in Britain, there was some controversy in Germany over the virtues of biplanes and monoplanes, but it was resolved more easily because Heinkel had produced a fast mail carrying monoplane, the He 70, for Lufthansa in 1932. Its success gave the monoplane lobby in Germany a decisive boost and also attracted the attention of the Chief Designer of Supermarine, Reginald Mitchell, who was intrigued by its flush riveting and elliptical wing.*

As a result, the fighter specification drawn up by the German Air Ministry in early 1934 was for a monoplane with a retractable undercarriage and a top

---

* It has often been claimed that the Spitfire's wing was developed from the He 70. This is denied by Mitchell's aerodyamicist, Beverley Shenstone, who points out the great differences between the two wing sections, but adds that on inspecting an He 70 at the Paris Airshow he was impressed by its smooth riveting and wrote to Ernst Heinkel to ask how he did it. He used the He 70 as a benchmark for aerodynamic smoothness during working discussions on the Spitfire, and this was the main influence the German aircraft had on Mitchell's team. See Price, *The Spitfire Story*, p. 18.

speed of 280 mph, almost exactly the same as specifications F.36/34 and F.37/34 issued to Hawker and Supermarine in the same year, resulting in the Hurricane and Spitfire. Focke-Wulf, Arado and Heinkel were asked to bid, but, at Milch's insistence, Messerschmitt's team at the Bayerische Flugzeugwerke was excluded from the tender.

Willy Messerschmitt had begun designing gliders in 1921 when he was only twenty-two. Most of them crashed for a variety of reasons, including structural instability. Undeterred, he went on to set up the Bayerische Flugzeugwerke (BFW) at the old Rumpler site in Augsburg, Bavaria, in 1926 and turned to powered aircraft.

His first airliner for Lufthansa, the M20, crashed on its first flight in 1928, but nevertheless went into production. In 1930, BFW's first military aircraft, the M22 twin-engined bomber, crashed on a test flight, killing the pilot. In October, an M20 crashed on landing at Dresden, killing all seven occupants, including the wife of a Lufthansa official. Another went down in April 1931. Lufthansa cancelled further orders for the M20 and BFW faced bankruptcy.[55] Milch was not disposed to order anything else from this dangerous source.

However, in 1933 Göring asked one of his old fighter pilot friends, Theo Croneiss, to join BFW to re-build it and, in a secret note, asked him to get to work on a fast mail-carrier (i.e. a fighter). After a series of arguments with Milch, BFW was finally put onto the tender list for the new specification, under the understanding that no production orders would result, and the design team set to work in March 1934. They were already working on a four-seater set to become the Bf 108, and this experience strongly influenced the fighter.

The work was carried out in the main by the Head of the Project Office, Robert Lusser, the Chief Design Engineer, Richard Bauer, and Messerschmitt himself. They did not get on, as witnessed by the tense and accusatory correspondence which flowed between Lusser and Messerschmitt. Nevertheless, only fifteen months later, in May 1935, the prototype Bf 109 had its maiden flight, just six months before the Hurricane. Given the shortage of good aero-engines in Germany, it was powered by a Rolls-Royce Kestrel, and the test-pilot, Hans Knoetzsch, landed in an exuberant mood, saying that the new machine handled perfectly.[56]

The prototype was flown to the Rechlin Experimental Establishment, and when it came in to land its undercarriage collapsed. The repaired machine went on to trials at Travemünde in October, and to the surprise of all, Udet awarded BFW a contract for ten aircraft. The Heinkel entry, the He 112, won a similar order. The He 112 was strong and fast, but of a complex construction and it lacked the superb handling characteristics of the Messerschmitt design. Heinkel modified the design many times until it matched the Bf 109, but by then its rival was in full production and the He 112 was cancelled. This did not prevent many RAF pilots from claiming to have seen and shot down He 112s in 1940.

So, amidst acrimony and jealousy the Bf 109 was born. Milch disliked Messerschmitt and resented Udet for awarding him the contract. Their differences were not settled, but led to intrigue, with personal spite taking precedence over the interests of the Luftwaffe.

The controversy around Messerschmitt's designs was not entirely undeserved. When none other than Rudolf Hess put on a dazzling aerobatic show in a Bf 109B near Berlin, he landed having bent the metal at the junction of the wings and the fuselage. The join was strengthened.[57] The first Bf 109 sent to Spain crashed on take-off. The second was damaged on landing. The first production Bf 109B crashed at Augsburg after side-slipping too steeply, killing its pilot. So things continued. The problem was the strong torque, making it swerve to the left on take-off, coupled with the narrow undercarriage, which, like the Spitfire's, folded outwards, but unlike the Spitfire's was fixed to the fuselage rather than the wings, making it even narrower. The problem got worse throughout the aircraft's career, as more powerful engines were fitted. The Bf 109G, introduced in 1942 and produced in greater numbers than any other, gained the reputation of a killer.

However, 33,000 Bf 109s were built, a record for any military aircraft. The reason was that once in the air it was very fast and very manoeuvrable. In the hands of an expert pilot such as Johannes Trautloft, who tested out the first Bf 109s sent to the Cóndor Legion, it was a formidable fighting machine. Trautloft's enthusiasm showed that for all the problems, Messerschmitt had got the essentials right. 'The new Bf 109 simply looks fabulous,' Trautloft wrote in his diary. 'The take-off certainly is unusual, but as soon as I am in the air I feel at home in the new bird. Its flight characteristics are fantastic ... To fly the 109 is really a joy.'[58] It experienced a number of trivial teething problems, but by April 1937 it was ready to go into action in Spain and the Bf 109 was triumphant.

Messerschmitt's design was based on the simple principle of building the smallest possible airframe capable of housing a powerful engine. The result was a high wing-loading, but also great responsiveness. One innovation was to install leading edge slats to delay the stall at low speeds. The design chosen for the slats was British. It came from Handley-Page.[59]

The news that the British were installing eight machine guns into their fighters caused some consternation, for the 109's wings were not large or strong enough to take more than two. The alternative was to use cannons, and these arguably resulted in a more effective armament, despite the recoil problems they created, which in the test-bed were so severe that they threatened to destroy the wing.[60] The early two-bladed propellers were replaced, as in the case of the British fighters, with three-bladed automatic variable-pitch propellers, which resulted in similar improvements in performance.[61]

Word soon got round. In the summer of 1938 an American friend of Udet's, Major Al Williams of the USMC, flew a Bf 109D at Kassel. He was extremely enthusiastic, realising it was far superior to any fighter the United

MESSERSCHMITT Bf 109E-3 & E-4

DISTINCTIVE FEATURES

MG-FF 20mm Oerlikon cannon carried in each wing, each firing 8-9 rounds per second, and each with 60 rounds of ammunition – enough for about 7 seconds. Whilst one strike from one of these explosive shells could be lethal, their low muzzle velocity limited their penetration power and the low rate of fire made them more use to average marksmen than average shots. The MG-FF-M fitted to the E-4 improved matters. This was the only difference between the E-3 and the E-4.

Fuel-injected Daimler Benz DB601Aa 12 cylinder in-line engine developing 1,175 hp on take off, an improvement on the 1,050 hp of the DB 601A which powered the E-1. By July 1940 the Jagdgeschwader flew a mixture of E-1s and E-3s, both gradually being replaced by E-4s. The slightly more powerful DB601N, using 96 octane fuel, was fitted to the E-4N and the E-7.

Hollow airscrew hub, designed to take a further cannon. In practice, it was not fitted to the 109E. It became standard equipment on the 109F which did not begin to appear on the Channel front until March 1941.

250kg (551lb) high explosive or armour piercing bombs which could be fitted to the pylon of the E-7 as an alternative to the fuel tank as well as to the E-4/B flown throughout the Battle by 3rd Staffel of Erprobungsgruppe 210. The standard E-4 could be retrofitted in the field with a bomb-rack, which is what was done in late September. However, only the E-7 could take a fuel tank.

Two MG 17 7.9mm (rifle calibre) machine guns synchronised to fire through the propeller arc, which worked best when the engine was doing 1,800 rpm. They each fired at about 17 rounds per second (990 rpm) and 1,000 rounds were carried for each gun.

Two types of hood armour were fitted to the E-3 and E-4, the later squared-off one giving slightly improved vision. Both were heavily barred and hinged on the right. They were interchangeable in service.

Supercharger air intake. The supercharger gave the DB601 a better high-altitude performance than the Merlin III.

Early wooden and later 300 litre (79 gallon) jettisonable steel fuel tanks which could be fitted to the fuselage pylon on the Bf 109E-7. Only 414 had been produced by the end of October 1940, as opposed to 1,246 E-3s and 496 E-4's, and only LG2 flew it regularly. There is no recorded instance of extra fuel being carried. LG2 usually fitted bombs instead.

Narrow undercarriage folding outwards from the fuselage, making ground loops a constant hazard.

Pilot's back and head armour. All RAF reports on wrecked 109s also mention an armour plate fitted in the fuselage. The Luftwaffe began fitting this in the field from July.

Leading edge slats which came out near the stall to smooth the air flow and facilitate low-speed manoeuvering. They moved smoothly on the ground, but at high speed they would come out with a bang and make the wings snatch.

FuG 10 HF radio, a different model from that carried by Bf 110s and bombers, with which they could not therefore communicate. Frequencies could not be modified in the air.

L-shaped self-sealing petrol tank carrying 400 litres (88 gallons) of 87 octane fuel. The Luftwaffe realised during the Battle of France that it was very vulnerable from behind and added armour plating to protect it.

Rudder trim tab which was adjusted on the ground and was then fixed. The rudder itself was cambered to counteract the strong torque of the engine. Even so, flying was hard work for an inexperienced pilot and landing was always tricky.

Struts to strengthen the tail unit, a last throw-back to the days of biplanes.

States then possessed, and in October 1938, no less a person than Charles Lindbergh took to the controls, with similar results.[62] Lindbergh later campaigned for American neutrality in the war and was marked out as a German sympathiser.

Development followed and in 1939 the first Bf 109E-1s, known as the 'Emil', were delivered. They were the first to have the new fuel-injected 1050 hp DB 601A engine, which gave the Emil a top speed of 357 mph at 12,300 feet and the unrivalled service ceiling of 36,000 feet. In late 1939 the E-1 variant was replaced in production by the E-3 with the slightly more powerful DB601Aa engine which produced 1175 hp for take-off. Like the E-1, the E-3 had two machine guns on top of the engine cowling, but the E-1's pair of wing-mounted machine guns were replaced by two far more deadly MG-FF cannon. It had the facility to mount one further cannon in the nose, firing through the propeller spinner, but in practice this was never fitted because of the vibration it caused. The E-4 version, which began reaching units in the early summer, differed only in mounting the improved MG-FF/M cannons in the wings. During the Battle of Britain, some E-1s were still in service, but the most numerous varants were the E-3 and E-4.[63]

The other specification issued in 1934 was for a long-range fighter. The idea was that a powerful offensive fighter would carve out a path for bombers in enemy airspace, eliminating fighter opposition. The concept was christened the 'Zerstörer' ('Destroyer'), and this contract was placed exclusively with BFW. The result was the Bf 110, which went into service in 1938. The term 'Zerstörer' does not apply specifically to the Bf 110, but is a generic term for a heavy fighter, a twin or multi-seater usually designed for long-range operations. Thus the Germans referred to Defiants and Blenheim fighters as 'Zerstörer'.[64] The name comes from the naval designation of a destroyer as a small, fast vessel which protects the fleet. The fighter-bomber version of the Bf 110 was given a propaganda name of its own, though it never caught on: the 'Jaguar'. Milch had little time for the Zerstörer concept, which was backed by Göring, and thought that the unique award of the task to Messerschmitt could serve to blacken his reputation.

In November 1938, about a third of the existing fighter units, seven Gruppen in all, were re-designated 'schwere Jagdgruppen' ('heavy fighter wings') and began re-equipping with the Bf 110. These units in fact retained Bf 109s for some time, as problems with the early Bf 110s still had to be ironed out.[65] By the outbreak of war, 195 Bf 110s were in service.

The Bf 110 was blooded in the Polish campaign of 1939, where it formed the bulk of the Luftwaffe's fighter force, the Bf 109s being held back for home defence. It experienced no serious opposition, and its first contact with the RAF was with the unfortunate Wellingtons that attacked Wilhelmshaven on 18 December, which it shot out of the sky with ease. With four machine guns and two cannons in the nose, it was a formidable bomber-killer and its top speed of 349 mph at 22,965 feet meant that it could easily catch them.

The experience in Poland seemed to confirm that the Bf 110 could operate very effectively as an offensive fighter. However, its acceleration was sluggish and it was not remotely as manoeuvrable as single-seater fighters, with the result that when confronted with them it needed its speed to get away, relying on its single rearward-firing machine gun to protect itself. At sea-level its maximum speed dropped to 294 mph, which was not enough to get away from a Spitfire, though it could still out-run a Hurricane. The problem was not with the machine but, as Milch had surmised, with the concept. The Bf 110 was not an escort fighter, but a fighter-bomber, and both its failure as the former and its potential as the latter were to be demonstrated in the summer of 1940.

By the mid-1930s, people in Britain had started to get worried about the Luftwaffe. By late 1936, Hitler had begun to worry that about the fact that the British were getting worried. He feared that the propaganda was working too well, and would lead Britain to re-arm. He therefore instigated an open exchange of information between the RAF and the Luftwaffe.

Milch was also anxious to set right the enormous exaggerations of German air strength appearing in the British press and invited Air Commodore Douglas Evill (who in 1940 was to become Senior Air Staff Officer (SASO) at Fighter Command) and Air Vice-Marshal Christopher Courtney to Berlin. He gave them a lot of accurate information, with the rider that it could go to the Air Ministry but not the Foreign Office. A return visit to Britain followed in 1937, during which Milch met Churchill, and in July the founder of the RAF, Lord Trenchard, visited Berlin. Kesselring denounced Milch for high treason, to no effect.[66] The only recrimination made against him was that Hitler complained some years later that Milch betrayed the secret of radar to the British.[67]

After his visit to Berlin, Evill wrote a report ending with a balanced and accurate assessment:

> The final conclusion is that within twelve months the Germans will have strong and highly organised air defences, and a large and well-equipped air force which would be very difficult to destroy if that were to prove necessary. An impression is given that, if only for professional reasons, they would even then prefer to have further time to consolidate this force before putting it into operation. Whether they have the resources to do so and the political stability to proceed for several years at the present pace is beyond comment in this paper; but, if the answer is yes, it is impossible to avoid the conclusion that Germany in 1940 will possess a thoroughly well-organised air force of high efficiency and morale.[68]

The French view was less balanced, but no less accurate. After a visit to Luftwaffe installations in August 1938, the C.-in-C. of the French air force, General Vuillemin, concluded that his forces would not last a week against them.[69] In the event they managed about ten days.

However, the perceived strength of the Luftwaffe had two serious negative consequences for them. It did indeed stimulate British rearmament and led them to take their potential enemy very seriously, and it fooled Hitler himself. Seeking to gain more resources, Göring and Milch put on a show for the Führer at the experimental establishment at Rechlin in April 1939. Hitler left with the impression that a lot of experimental weapons were about to go into service and got a wholly misleading impression of the strength of the Luftwaffe.[70] This influenced his decision-making until well into the war.

As Evill observed, the men who ran the Luftwaffe wanted more time. Hitler threw them into a major European war, which he soon turned into a world war, without any strategic reserve of aircraft and without the production capacity to create one. The Luftwaffe was powerful enough to do a lot of damage and once the fighting began, its reputation went before it. It soon became clear that in the air the Germans were formidable adversaries. But behind the scenes, the professionals were sitting in Whitehall, not in Berlin. The instrument Milch had created was an iron glove covering a spongy hand. Despite appearances, the Germans were taking a terrible gamble, staking all on a first round knock-out. If this could be thwarted, their longer-term prospects were grim.

Yet for all that, the gamble started to pay off. The Germans did indeed achieve first round knock-outs, not just one, but a whole series of them, against Poland, against Denmark and Norway, against Holland and Belgium and then, almost incredibly, against France. By June 1940, in an extraordinary ten-month run, the Wehrmacht had just about broken the house. There was just one player left. Hitler was on a winning streak and it looked as if one more knock-out blow could and would be achieved. In fact, he wanted to leave the table, count his winnings and turn to a different game. The trouble was that the other player would not let him.

4. AIR DEFENCE

On the night of 19/20 January 1915 the first bombs ever to be dropped on Britain fell on King's Lynn in Norfolk. The British civilian population had thereby had the honour of being the first ever to be attacked from the air by a foreign country.

On 8 September of the same year the first ever bombs were dropped on London. The raiders in each case were Zeppelin airships. It was not until one year later, on the night of 2/3 September 1916 that the Royal Flying Corps managed to destroy one of these ungainly intruders. So momentous an event was this that the pilot involved, Lieutenant Leefe-Robinson, was awarded the VC.

In time, these large, slow machines began to be intercepted with some success. However, on 28 November 1916, a lone German bomber dropped six small bombs on London and made off unharmed. Its successors proved far harder to stop than the Zeppelins. On 25 May 1917, twenty-one giant Gotha bombers flew over the Essex coast, turned south, crossing London, and proceeded east over Kent, finally dropping their bombs on Folkestone, where they killed 92 people and injured another 260. A total of no less than seventy-four British fighters took off in attempts to intercept them, but none made contact. The guns around Dover opened fire, but misjudged the bombers' height and did no damage. One Gotha came down in the sea because of engine trouble and another crashed on landing.[1]

The material damage inflicted by Germany's air raids on the UK during World War I was not very great, but the lessons were disturbing. The campaign had cost the Germans about sixty bombers in all, only some twenty of which were lost as a result of action by the defences, the remaining forty falling victim to some kind of accident. At the end of the war the British were employing 200 fighters and 450 guns in home defence.[2] The guns were ineffective and the fighters rarely even found their potential targets. The loads carried by bombers, only fifteen years after the Wright brothers' first flight, included bombs weighing a ton.

The conclusion was spelled out by the Prime Minister, Stanley Baldwin, in an address to the House of Commons in 1932:

> I think it well . . . for the man in the street to realise there is no power on earth that can protect him from bombing, whatever people may tell him. The bomber will always get through.[3]

The bulk of the British civilian population had not experienced the direct effects of warfare since they fought each other between 1642 and 1651. Now they were in the front line. Not only that: they were, in Lord Northcliffe's words 'no longer an island'[4]. Only an Englishman can fully understand the dread implications of that doom-laden phrase.

We live in a world today in which we know not only that London can take it, but that Berlin and Tokyo and Leningrad and Hanoi and every other city subjected to bombardment from the air can take it. In the 1930s there was a widespread belief that civilians subject to air attack would panic. In 1917, the C.-in-C. Home Forces, Field Marshal Lord French, banned his anti-aircraft guns from firing at enemy raiders because of the effect he feared the noise would have on jumpy civilians. They were subject to real danger from falling shell fragments, and given the anti-aircraft guns' record against the enemy, he reasonably concluded that they were more dangerous to his own side.[5] Protecting civilians against air attack looked like an impossible task.

This was, at all events, based on interpretation of selected evidence. Also in 1917 the Minister of Munitions, none other than Winston Churchill, produced a paper in which he argued:

> It is improbable that any terrorisation of the civil population which could be achieved by air attack would compel the government of a great nation to surrender . . . In our own case, we have seen the combative spirit of the people roused, and not quelled, by the German air raids. Nothing we have learned of the capacity of the German population to endure suffering justifies us in assuming that they could be cowed into submission by such methods, or indeed, that they would not be rendered more desperately resolved by them.[6]

This view was indeed to be borne out by events. It would explain Churchill's phlegmatic acceptance of the bombing of London in 1940 and thereafter. It equally fails to explain his support of the area bombing of Germany later in the war.*

---

* He repeated his views about the inability of bombing to break civilian morale in a reply to Sir Charles Portal, the Chief of the Air Staff, in September 1941. His support of strategic bombing was largely pragmatic: he saw it as the only way in which Britain could strike at Germany and was desperate to pursue the war actively with all and any means at the country's disposal. He did not think it would win the war. See Hastings, *Bomber Command*, pp. 120–1.

If experience was not encouraging, the imagination offered unbridled terror. The technology involved in aeronautics was entirely new. Nobody had any idea what the potential of aircraft was. The Wright brothers had made the first-ever powered flight in a heavier-than-air machine on 17 December 1903. It lasted twelve seconds. Ten years later, aeroplanes could stay in the air for over an hour, travelling at speeds in excess of 100 mph. Twenty years later, aircraft could fly at 200 mph, cover hundreds of miles and carry several thousand pounds of bombs.

The general public's view of conventional bombing in the 1930s was in many ways similar to its view of nuclear warfare today. Writers added to the consternation. H.G. Wells wrote his novel *The War in the Air* in 1907, and it was serialised in the *Pall Mall Magazine* the following year. His vision is one of mass panic and mass destruction as the world is engulfed by Armageddon, ending in 'The Great Collapse'. It was to be another year before Blériot crossed the Channel. What would happen as reality began to catch up with the vision?

A number of airmen were bent on making it do so. The Italian General, Giulio Douhet, first articulated the idea that future wars would be won by air power alone. The major role of air forces, he argued, was an offensive one and their prime instrument the bomber. In the US, General Billy Mitchell developed similar ideas and in Britain they were strongly advocated by the First Marshal of the Royal Air Force, Lord Trenchard. It was also assumed, based on the experience of the trenches, that bombers would drop not only high explosive bombs, but gas. Cities and populations would be wiped out.

The events of the 1930s tended to add credence to this. The Italians' use of gas bombs in Abyssinia and the air attacks on Shanghai and Nanking by the Japanese received wide newspaper coverage. The bombing of Guernica, interpreted as a deliberate attack on civilians, caused outrage and horror.

With its Commander-in-Chief being one of the main exponents of the theory of strategic bombing, the RAF put its emphasis on developing a force of bombers, albeit without much success.* However, despite the rapid shrinking in the size and funding of the RAF from 1919 onwards, defence was not entirely ignored. In 1923 a committee formed for the purpose set up the first plan for defending the country's airspace from attack across the Channel. It was assumed at the time that the most likely enemy was France and the most likely target was London.** The committee set up an air-fighting zone of AA guns

---

* Despite all the talk, Britain still lacked a strategic bombing force at the outbreak of the war. Most of the types in service during the 1930s were light or medium bombers. Despite their enormous differences in doctrine, the bomber forces of Britain and Germany were comparably equipped in 1940, apart from the lack of a British dive-bomber.
** London was the world's largest target, being at the time the largest city in the world in terms of area. In his pre-war speeches Churchill called it 'a tremendous fat cow tied up to attract the beasts of prey' (Hough & Richards, p.308).

around London, with sound locators and observers stationed near the coast.[7] However, the service had major commitments overseas, and at home the bomber still had priority.

It was not until 1934 that a government assailed by warnings about German air strength issuing from the isolated but stubborn MP for Epping, Mr Churchill,[8] began to look more closely at defence, and voted for a five-year general expansion plan for the RAF. The breakthrough came in 1936, when, because of the complexity of its administration at home, the RAF reorganised into Commands: Bomber, Fighter, Coastal and Training.[9]

On 6 July 1936, Fighter Command was born, and a new Commander-in-Chief appointed, who bore the imposing name of Hugh Caswall Tremenheere Dowding.[10]

Dowding was appointed on 14 July 1936 and on that day paid his first visit to his headquarters, a 166-year-old mansion called Bentley Priory, near Stanmore in Middlesex. Dowding turned up at Bentley Priory at 9 a.m., showed his security pass and was greeted not by the customary pomp and ceremony, but by one Sergeant Cornthwaite, with whom he looked around the new premises.[11]

Born in 1882, Dowding was the oldest of the RAF's senior commanders.[12] He began his military career in the artillery, but had joined the RFC at the beginning of World War I, and saw action in the air on the Western Front before being transferred home to improve standards of training. After the war he became Director of Training, had an operational position in Transjordan and Palestine and finally became a member of the Air Council for Supply and Research in 1930 before taking over the new command. He therefore knew what it was like to be a pilot, had senior operational experience, understood how to build and run an effective air fighting force and had spent five years studying the latest technologies available to the air force.

An abstemious non-drinker, Dowding hated show and fuss. His RAF nickname was 'Stuffy'. His biographer, Basil Collier, describes his appearance to the young men of 16 Squadron under his command in 1915:

> his soft voice and quiet manner, his air of abstracted concern with things outside their ken, his curiously withdrawn, almost abashed gaze and his disconcerting habit of mixing praise with blame, seemed an apparition of almost incredible aloofness.[13]

His asceticism had a tragic background, for his wife had died after only two years of marriage, and he lived with his sister. His only son, Derek, whom he had brought up alone, joined 74 Squadron as a Pilot Officer on 1 July 1940, which could hardly have added to his father's peace of mind. Whilst his pre-war achievements as a skiing champion fitted the RAF mould, his interests in spiritualism did not, and he mystified his colleagues. Intensely private, he formalised most of his contacts with other people and had no close friends. One of those closest to him was the head of AA Command, General Sir Frederick Pile. Pile spent about an hour with him every day, and called him 'the outstanding airman' he met during the war. Pile also said that he was 'a difficult man, a self-opinionated man'.[14] He was an odd fish.

In July 1936, therefore, Britain finally had a single man, albeit a strange one, in control of its air defence, with not only the fighter force, but Anti-Aircraft Command, Balloon Command and the Observer Corps under his direct control, and with responsibility for supply, control, reporting and the air-raid warning network. Fighter Command was fortunate in having as its head a man who knew all the issues involved, understood technology, had thought about how to apply it, and was able to draw on practical experience gained at all levels of air operations. The unified command also meant that the strategic bomber lobby had someone within the RAF to compete with its claims on resources.

Dowding found the political ally he needed in 1937, when Neville Chamberlain became Prime Minister. Hitherto, most of the scepticism within Britain about strategic bombing had come from the army and navy, because they wanted money for themselves. Chamberlain was sceptical for moral reasons. He was horrified by Baldwin's view that: 'The only defence is offence, which means that you have to kill more women and children more quickly than the enemy if you want to save yourself.'[15] He therefore insisted that air rearmament change its priorities and put more emphasis on fighter defence.

In this, his Minister for Co-ordination of Defence, Sir Thomas Inskip, played a significant role. Inskip was originally supposed to cut defence expenditure. Guided by the fact that fighters are cheaper than bombers, he was also sceptical of the Douhet-Trenchard emphasis on bombers. However, instead of cutting fighter production as well, he built up fighter numbers and became an important ally of Dowding.[16]

Dowding was an articulate proponent of an alternative to the Douhet doctrine. He also believed in deterrence, but it was based on the fear of the fighter:

> The best defence of the country is the fear of the fighter. If we were strong in fighters we should probably never be attacked in force. If we are moderately strong we shall probably be attacked and the attacks will gradually be brought to a standstill . . . If we are weak in fighter strength, the attacks will not be brought to a standstill and the productive capacity of the country will be virtually destroyed.[17]

He calculated that he needed forty-five squadrons to defend Britain from a threat across the North Sea. But will alone did not make the equipment materialise. Britain needed time. Chamberlain knew this and it may have contributed to his desire to do a deal with Hitler over Czechoslovakia at Munich in 1938. Be that as it may, he did his country and the free world an immense service by pushing for the build up of Fighter Command in 1937.

However, all the fighters in the world were of little use if they could not find their enemy. The experience of 1915–18 suggested that this was not a trivial matter. Nor was it apparent how the fighters could be controlled. Clearly, they could not just be sent into the air in the hope that they would find something worth shooting at.

Nobody else in the world had spent as much time thinking about these critical command and control issues as Hugh Dowding, and he set to work to create a system which is still known as the Dowding System and is essentially unchanged today.* If genius really is an infinite capacity for taking pains, Dowding, stuffy as he was, was a genius.

The first key steps he took date from his time on the Air Council between 1930 and 1936.

The RAF's air exercises in 1934 had shown the ineffectiveness of the sound location technology which had been developed to detect aircraft. As a result of a report about this by the scientist A.P. Rowe, the Secretary of State for Air, Lord Londonderry, set up a committee under the scientist Henry Tizard to examine in general the question of how scientific advances could help to strengthen air defence. One of the ideas generated was for a 'death ray'. No-one took this very seriously, but Tizard asked Robert Watson-Watt of the National Physical Laboratory to demonstrate scientifically that it would not work.

In the course of doing so, one of Watson-Watt's staff pointed out that although radio beams did not harm human beings, they were affected by the presence of aircraft, and might therefore be used to detect and locate them.

It was generally known that radio waves reflected off solid objects. This had been demonstrated by Heinrich Hertz towards the end of the previous century. Shortly thereafter, a German engineer suggested that they could be used to help ships detect each other at sea. This idea lived on in Germany and in 1934, the head of Germany's naval signals research, Dr Rudolf Kühnold, was able to get a 'picture' of a warship in Kiel harbour. Soon, his apparatus had a range of seven miles, and was also able to pick up aircraft. The German navy was not very interested in this application, but did install radar in its warships to aid gun-laying, as the British discovered when they examined the wreck of the scuttled *Graf Spee* off the River Plate in 1939. However, the Luftwaffe was

---

* As attested to by the air defence specialist Air Commodore Joan Hopkins speaking fifty years later (in *Battle For Britain*, TVS productions for ITV, written by Suzanne Campbell-Jones, 1990), who regards the way in which Dowding pulled the whole thing together as 'in some ways a stroke of genius'. She makes the point that not only are the principles unchanged but the warning time is also similar. Aircraft travel much faster than in 1940, but the equipment also has a far greater range. The net result is the same.

interested and by 1938 had a detection system called 'Freya' and the 'Würzburg' gun-laying radar in use.*

In Britain, Watson-Watt's team set about getting the theory to work, and on 26 February 1935, a Heyford bomber was seen to displace a radio signal transmitted by the BBC. The Director of Scientific Research, H.E. Wimperis, reported this to Dowding who declared it to be 'a discovery of the highest importance'.[18] The pace quickened and by September 50-mile detection ranges were being achieved. This convinced the Air Defence Sub-Committee that a chain of twenty transmitter-receiver stations should be set up around the coastline. Promising results in the 1937 air exercises convinced the Air Ministry to expand the chain, known as Chain Home (CH). In 1940 it was complemented by the low-looking Chain Home Low (CHL) network.[19]

Watson-Watt and Rowe decided to call their system 'Radio Direction-Finding' (RDF) because in the early days they were pessimistic about being able to use it for this purpose and hoped the name would mislead unfriendly agents. Later in the war, the American term 'radar' (radio detecting and ranging) became universal. The stations were built in great secrecy and darkly referred to as AMES, standing for 'Air Ministry Experimental Stations'. The large numbers of people recruited to work in them were told their jobs were secret and not to be discussed with anyone. They were not told a great deal themselves. They were simply asked to volunteer to become such things as 'Clerk Special Duties' on the understanding that the job would not consist of clerical duties as they knew them.[20]

The new technology enabled skilled operators to estimate four things: the elapsed time between the emission of a signal and its reception revealed the *range* of the target; by using a device called a goniometer the *bearing* (i.e. direction of flight) could be assessed; the shape and behaviour of the 'blip' (i.e. the amount of interference with the transmitted radio signal) indicated the *strength* of the raid; and by switching in and out of different receiver aerials, *height* could be estimated.[21] The quality of the information depended crucially on the skill and experience of the operators, as judgement as well as calculation played a role. They had to work very fast, or their information was useless. They were also under pressure, as lives depended on the accuracy of their reports. The pressure was the greater if they suspected, as was soon to be the case, that the hostile forces were heading for them.

Of the four pieces of data, the hardest to assess was height.[22] Unfortunately, this was the piece of information of the greatest tactical importance to the pilots. Its unreliability was endemic, as different atmospheric conditions could affect the readings, and as they were unknown and constantly changing, no adjustments could be made. Pilots soon became aware of this and throughout

---

* This was one reason why early RAF raids on north Germany were so badly mauled. (See Deighton, *Fighter*, Grafton Books 1987, pp. 109–112). The Germans invented radar a year before Watson-Watt's team got on to it. When Germany began to be attacked in strength by British Bombers in 1941, the Luftwaffe quickly set up a radar-based night defence system under the control of General Kammhuber. Unfortunately for Bomber Command, it worked very well.

the war they treated altitude information (given in thousands of feet or 'angels') with suspicion. Once the air battle began in earnest, experienced fighter leaders in the air started to add a few thousand feet to the instructions they got from controllers, causing some tensions with senior commanders.

RDF was the first detection line, but it pointed out away from Britain's shores. Once inland, aircraft were tracked visually by the Royal Observer Corps, an organisation which Dowding inherited from the man who set up London's original air defence system in 1917, Major General E.B. Ashmore.[23] They were also the prime intelligence source for low-flying aircraft which got below the radar net in what is today the standard method for evading detection, a method not systematically used at the time.[24] By 1940 there were about 30,000 observers covering the UK, organised into 50 observer posts in each of 31 groups. Every post had a phone link to its group which in turn was linked to the Observer Corps Centre at Horsham and thence to Fighter Command HQ at Bentley Priory.

Fighter Command HQ was the central processor of all information from the air-raid warning system. It passed its information out along the nerve fibres of the Fighter Command organisation, which was simple and resilient. Dowding created three groups, each with responsibility for the airspace in a particular area. 11 Group covered the South-East, 12 Group the Midlands and 13 Group the North and Scotland. On 8 July 1940, given the new threat to the south coast, 10 Group was set up to cover the South-West. The Groups were split into Sectors which were given letters but were usually known by the name of their Sector Station, which was the airfield controlling them. 11 Group, with headquarters at Uxbridge, consisted of seven Sectors lettered A, B, C, D, E, F and Z, controlled from Tangmere, Kenley, Biggin Hill, Hornchurch, North Weald, Debden and Northolt respectively. The sectors had smaller 'satellite' airfields under them where squadrons were stationed (e.g. on 10 July Kenley was home to 64 and 615 Squadrons and also controlled 111 and 501 Squadrons at its satellite, Croydon). Airfields belonging to other commands such as West Malling or Detling could also be used during operations as temporary bases or re-fuelling depots.* Sectors were able to control up to six squadrons, but most usually controlled two or three.

---

* Visitors to such airfields were not always welcome, though, especially if they came from another Command. Deighton relates the frosty reception accorded to 609 Squadron when it was temporarily transferred to Warmwell, a Coastal Command station. They were given no proper facilities and were told off for being late for meals. Understandably, this did not go down well with their C/O, Squadron Leader Darley. (See *Fighter*, pp. 227–8.) This indeed runs counter to the 'nation united' theme of Churchill's mythology, but is not all that surprising. The RAF was still the RAF, and as in any organisation there were rules and responsibilities. Coastal Command was not responsible for looking after Fighter Command pilots, Fighter Command was. The Warmwell Station Commander no doubt thought it was good of him to find some space for a fighter squadron to sleep in, but had better things to do than run around looking for beds and blankets for them. He had noted that there was some fighter activity overhead, but that was to be expected and he had the Battle of the Atlantic to fight. He did not want his station disrupted or diverted from that purpose by the presence of a few of Dowding's glamour boys. It was an ungenerous and narrow attitude, but will be familiar to anyone who has worked in a large organisation, whether military, public or private.

It was at the filter room at Bentley Priory that all the information on raids was collected, assessed and compared with known friendly flights. A filter officer gave each raid a number, and then transferred the track to the Operations Room and simultaneously to the group controllers, who passed them on to the sector stations. The sectors passed them on to the Observer Corps. In essence, then, data flowed from the periphery to the centre which processed it into information and then passed out the information to the organisation. The unified command structure allowed Dowding to sit with his AA Commander Frederick Pile, and make decisions about gunnery defence which could immediately be relayed to his fighters.

Fighter Command itself did not take any tactical decisions about the air fighting. Operational command rested with the groups, and it was they who decided when the direction of a raid was clear and when to send up which aircraft.[25] They passed the orders to the sectors specifying which units to send up and which raids to intercept. The sectors were then responsible for bringing their units into contact with the enemy, specifying which direction and height to fly at. Thus the group made tactical decisions: it determined the targets of its attacks, when to attack them and what forces to use. The sector had the tactical responsibility of bringing those forces to bear by guiding them onto the enemy and giving them a tactical advantage. They were also responsible for getting their pilots back, helping them to navigate and telling them where to land, which was not necessarily at their home airfield. They identified them thanks to IFF (Identification Friend or Foe) which changed the radar signature of British fighters, and tracked them by means of a radio device called 'pip-squeak'.

Plotting was done in a similar way at Fighter Command, the Groups and the Sectors. In the centre of each room was a large table with a grid-lined map drawn on it showing the group and sector boundaries and the airfields. Hostile raids were plotted by WAAFs who worked in three shifts of about ten each, and were known as the 'beauty chorus'. It was widely believed that the more attractive they were, the higher up the chain of command they were allowed to work, the loveliest being reserved for Fighter Command HQ. At the sector stations, each of them was assigned to a radar station and Observer Corps centre within the sector. The WAAFs were equipped with telephone headsets and croupier's rakes with which they moved wooden blocks representing each raid. A floor supervisor told the plotters who to plug their telephones in to. The blocks representing the raids had numbers slotted into them to show the raid designation, e.g. H06 for 'hostile 6', with an estimate of the strength underneath it, e.g. '30+', to show the minimum size positively indicated by the radar blip. Arrows were placed behind the blocks to show the direction of the raid. There was a clock on the wall with each five-minute segment colour-coded red, blue or yellow, and the arrows were coloured to show during which segment they had been updated. One could therefore see how up-to-date the information on the table was and the course of each raid. Friendly aircraft were plotted in a separate room and other WAAFs put their blocks on the board, showing the units concerned, their strength and their height.

The plotting system was a masterpiece of graphic design. Using the simplest of methods, it showed at a glance the deployment of forces in three-dimensional space and used colour to convey the dimension of time. This was critical, for in air fighting, information aged extremely rapidly.

Above the beauty chorus, arranged around a balcony like a theatre, on what Churchill called the 'dress circle', were the men who used the information they supplied. At a sector station there were typically eight, each with a specific role. At the centre sat the Senior Controller who controlled the squadrons based at the sector station. On his left sat an Assistant Controller who dealt with other squadrons, and flanking them sat two Deputy Controllers, one listening in to other sectors and the other dealing with air-sea rescue. On either side of the Deputy Controllers were 'Ops A', who was in permanent contact with group, and 'Ops B' who got through to dispersal and actually scrambled the pilots. On the wings of the balcony sat liaison officers who were in direct contact with Observer Corps Headquarters and AA Command respectively.[26]

Work on the system began in 1937 and it was still being refined and strengthened in 1940. No less than nine CH and twenty-two CHL stations were built during the Battle of Britain itself. It was a remarkable creation. It brilliantly solved the problems of dealing with massive amounts of data from a wide range of sources in a very short time and using it to exercise control over the fighting. It was a system for managing chaos. Its intelligence-gathering capability extended to the period after an engagement, enabling Dowding and his generals to blow away the fog of war very quickly. It possessed a Defence Teleprinter Network (DTN) connecting all RAF stations and Headquarters. After raids, the DTN was full of information gathered from returning pilots in de-briefs as well as from those who stayed on the ground. As a result 'loss details, combat reports, ground damage reports, casualties, aircraft and equipment requirements were easily disseminated throughout the whole system.'[27] Its fundamental excellence and its ultimate success in practice can be attributed to a number of features.

Firstly, its organisational structure was simple and roles were very clear. Everyone knew what they had to do. It was not parsimonious with information: plot data was shared widely and passed simultaneously to several levels at once.[28] Bentley Priory gave out information simultaneously to groups and sectors and sectors could plug into local Observer Groups once they knew something was up in their area[29]. It was in effect an analogue intranet. Whilst it was used to transmit orders down the chain of command, it was also designed to allow anybody in the system find out what they wanted when they wanted from anybody else. It was a network organisation based on telephone lines rather than e-mail.

This sounds as if it would create confusion, with everybody talking to everybody else and everyone copying everyone on everything. However, all of those involved knew what they could and could not do with the information, and the decision-making rules were very logical. Only Fighter Command itself was in a position to sort out the data on raids, because it alone had a complete overview. However, it could not possibly control all its squadrons directly. Dowding saw his role as akin to a Chairman of the Board, who needed Operating Chief Executives at group level to deploy his forces.[30] The groups were large enough to form effective operating units without being overstretched. Sectors had too narrow a view of things to be able to make effective force-deployment decisions, but were needed to guide the squadrons onto their targets, a task that would have been impossible at group level.

Secondly, it was robust. Communications went mainly through the country's existing telephone system and if they went down, GPO engineers were there within minutes to carry out repairs. They twisted broken wires together and the lines were up again. The first war-time commander of 11 Group, Air Vice-Marshal Ernest Gossage, had a series of 'stand-by' Operations Rooms constructed a few miles from the sector headquarters[31] which came into use during the Battle.[32] The radar towers themselves looked vulnerable, but in fact they proved to be very hard to bomb. They were small, off-putting targets – pilots tend almost instinctively to veer off as they see a mass of wires approaching – and, most importantly, being open steel constructions, (a bit like the Eiffel Tower) they did not contain a blast but allowed it to disperse and were therefore hard to damage.[33] Only vulnerable dive-bombers or low-flying aircraft had the accuracy to hit them, but even then luck was needed to damage them substantially. The most vulnerable parts of the stations were the wires attached to the masts and the equipment and telephone lines around them, but these were easier to repair than the masts themselves.

In May 1940, work began on duplicate transmitters to build further redundancy into the system, and two pools of twelve MB 2 mobile stations were created, one for the north and one for the south. Jamming was anticipated by the introduction in 1939 of anti-jamming equipment fitted to all the stations. In fact, the Germans did not attempt jamming of any sort until September 1940, and it was ineffective.

Thirdly, it was flexible. The spans of control of both sectors and groups were very elastic, so Dowding could move squadrons around easily. They just flew off, taking their ground crews with them in transports, and the next day another unit would be there. There was also flexibility in command during a battle, as both groups and sectors could take over temporary control of others' squadrons. Each group could call on the support of any other at any time. In general this worked very well, especially between 10 and 11 Groups, which presented a seamless front to the enemy, but it failed to work between 11 and 12 Groups. This was not a fault of the system as such but was at root a clash of personalities and of doctrines.[34]

Fourthly, it was run against a rigorous system of performance measures, most of which were time-based, so that it was subject to constant improvement. The skill of the operators was paramount to the system's effectiveness. Estimating numbers from the size and nature of the blip was a matter of experience and was carefully practiced.[35] One key metric was the time needed to establish tracks. The filter room at Bentley Priory was discovered early-on to be a bottleneck – small wonder – so the standards for filter officers were raised and three technical assistants with science degrees were drafted in and trained. The time lags went down.[36] The rate at which sectors had to be informed was specified: they needed one plot per minute per raid.[37]

The pilots had to practice in order to ensure that they could keep within allotted times according to their 'state', which was recorded in the 'tote', a large blackboard on the wall of the operations rooms with a column for each squadron. A system of light bulbs showed each squadron's 'state'. A squadron was categorised as 'released' (not available for action), 'available' (airborne in twenty minutes), at 'readiness' (airborne in five minutes) or at 'standby' (airborne in two minutes).[38] When at standby, pilots sometimes sat in their cockpits with the engine running, but they could not do so for long.* So getting off the ground fast was generally a matter of climbing in whilst the engine was started by ground crew. The speed with which pilots could respond to a 'scramble' translated into extra height and that could be a matter of life and death, especially in 11 Group, so they ran like hell. At the height of the Battle, squadrons had reduced the time from the 'scramble' order to the last plane leaving the ground to ninety seconds.

For it to work, everybody in the system had to practice.[39] The early months of the war, during which activity was of low intensity, proved to be invaluable. Everybody had something to learn. Sector controllers, for example, who were themselves experienced pilots, had to put their squadrons in a tactically favourable position, preferably up-sun and above the enemy. They also had to be decisive and reassuring. The Tangmere Sector Controller, Squadron Leader David Lloyd, has commented:

> The important thing was to make a right-enough decision, soon enough. If you then found it was not the right decision, it should be left as long as possible without doing any damage before one gave the correct order. But one should never, never give contradictory orders one after another.[40]

The correctness of this judgement is borne out by Alan Deere's account of what it was like to be a poorly controlled pilot. He writes of his involvement in

---

* In hot weather a Spitfire could only idle for seven minutes before overheating. Its radiator was behind the right undercarriage leg, which restricted the airflow into it when on the ground. Hurricanes cooled off better, but could still not wait for much more than ten minutes. See the commentary of the Battle of Britain Memorial Flight pilot, Air Commodore Cliff Spink, in the video *Pilot's Eye – The Spitfire*, The Creation Company Films Ltd, 1993.

the notorious early 'cock-up' known as the 'Battle of Barking Creek' that his squadron was receiving so many vectors (instructions to fly in a certain direction) that it was impossible to follow them.[41] This incident, hushed up at the time, took place on 6 September 1939, when people were nervous as well as inexperienced. A radar plot was identified as hostile and several squadrons scrambled by different sectors. There were no hostiles, but two Hurricanes were shot down by Spitfires, with AA batteries joining in for good measure.[42] This also showed that the Observer Corps, gunners and pilots needed to work at aircraft recognition.

The system had one critical effect beyond warning of attacks which was equally far-reaching. It enabled Dowding to utilise and manage his assets: the fighters and the pilots. Had it not existed, Fighter Command would have had to keep planes in the air the whole time, flying standing patrols as they had in France. The number of aircraft necessary to provide a firm defence line under such conditions would have been several times the fifty-two squadrons Dowding regarded as was the minimum safety level in 1940. The country did not have them, and the RAF could not have managed them if it had. The system was a pre-condition of being able to defend British airspace with a reasonable number of fighters.

It also enabled Dowding to utilise the aircraft he had fully and to manage his pilots properly. A pilot in the sky was himself a wasted asset, wasting further resources in terms of fuel and engine hours.* Only a pilot engaging the enemy was a utilised one. As it was, standing patrols still had to be flown and small targets searched for, and the drain on resources was bad enough. Alfred Price has calculated that on 18 August, one of the busiest days in the whole Battle, only 45% of the 886 sorties were flown to counter the three major Luftwaffe attacks. 56 sorties (6%) were standing patrols to protect shipping (necessitated by the shorter warning times over the Channel) and the remaining 49% were flown to intercept lone reconnaissance aircraft.[43]

The system had two weaknesses, however: a lot of vital operations were conducted above ground in unarmoured accommodation; and, paradoxically for a maritime nation, there was no adequate air-sea rescue service.[44]

The filter and operations rooms at Bentley Priory were underground and well protected, as was 11 Group HQ at Uxbridge. However, the sectors had their operations rooms in ordinary buildings above ground on their sector airfields, with the exception of Tangmere, which had a concrete bunker. In principle, the operations rooms were vulnerable, but they were small and hard to hit. The real penalty for the lack of protection was lost lives.

---

* A Merlin engine needed to be stripped and reconditioned after 240 hours. Under normal operating conditions this was equivalent to about 9 months in service, though few aircraft actually survived over 100 hours of operational flying. At the height of the Battle, pilots were flying up to five hours a day For example, on 18 August, the hardest-worked squadron, No. 43, put up 63 combat sorties from its 13 Hurricanes, an average sortie rate of 4.8 per machine. It is reasonable to assume an average flying time of an hour per sortie.

The loss of life caused by pilots drowning was even more serious, for theirs were lives that ultimately defined the boundary between success and failure for Fighter Command.

British pilots wore a lifejacket known as a 'Mae West', which is a tribute to the role that remarkable woman played in young men's fantasy lives. Unlike many of their German counterparts they had no dinghy and no fluorescence to mark their position. The summer temperature of the Channel rarely rose above 14°C which gave a downed pilot a survival time of about four hours.[45] If he happened to be wearing regulation dress, his survival time was far shorter, though, as the collar of the standard officer's Van Heusen shirt shrank in contact with sea water and throttled the wearer.[46] The wearing of silk scarves as an alternative, which many outside Fighter Command thought a mere affectation, was a life-saving measure, and also prevented chafing when turning the neck to look behind.

There was no search and rescue organisation, just the hope that any passing boat would do the good turn of picking the pilot up. The life-boat service would be alerted if he were seen going down. Before the war, Bomber and Coastal Commands had had priority for equipment and a conference in 1939 placed air-sea rescue under Coastal Command. Some launches were ordered, but were not in operation by the time the Battle started. Not until pilots were drowning in sufficient numbers to call attention to the oversight was anything done. On 22 August, RAF launches were passed to the operational control of the local naval authorities, and Fighter Command got twelve Lysanders to help look for downed pilots.[47] No proper air-sea rescue service was formed until 1941.

This blot of amateurism on an otherwise totally professional approach contrasts with the astonishingly thoroughgoing amateurism of the German intelligence services to which most of the features of Dowding's system remained a closed book. This is in spite of the fact that many of the details had been shared with the French, whom the Germans could have interrogated in June or July had they wished to do so. The Germans knew all about radar and used it themselves to great effect. They had in fact invented it first. It was in the application of radar technology to create a command and control system that the British were pioneers.

The Dowding system had an early impact on the minds of Germany's young flyers. The first small doubts about their ability to break their opponent came to many of them over Dunkirk, when they first encountered Spitfires. The second came to them when the assault began and they noticed that the Spitfires always seemed to turn up at the right place and the right time.[48] The Luftwaffe's pre-eminent fighter pilot Adolf Galland summed it up after the war:

> From the first the British had an extraordinary advantage, never to be balanced out at any time during the whole war, which was their radar and fighter control network and organisation. It was for us a very

bitter surprise. We had nothing like it. We could do no other than knock frontally against the outstandingly well-organised and resolute direct defence of the British Isles.[49]

This overstates the case. The German front-line flyers may not have been aware of their own raid detection system, but it worked, and later in the war it got very sophisticated.[50] What none of them understood was the nature of the radio-based fighter control system linked in to the British detection network.[51] Galland's words bear witness to the psychological impact of realising that the air defence of Great Britain had been the object of much attention and was not being run by amateurs. It was a shock.

However, detecting enemy bombers was only part of Dowding's problem. Once they had been located, he needed fighters which could intercept them and shoot them down.

5. THE FIGHTERS

In 1929, the RAF's main front-line fighter was a biplane, the Bristol Bulldog, which had a maximum speed of 174 mph. At the end of that year the RAF introduced into service the Hawker Hart light bomber. It was capable of 184 mph in level flight. Clearly, if fighters were to shoot down bombers, there was a problem. They could not even catch them. If they did, there was another problem. The Bulldog, like most other contemporary fighters and almost all its predecessors from the previous war, was armed with two machine guns. It was becoming apparent that this did not offer sufficient firepower to knock down the increasingly sturdy bombers.

The difference in performance between fighters and light bombers had already been eliminated in 1926 with the introduction of the Fairey Fox light bomber which, with a top speed of 156 mph, was as fast as the Siskin and Gamecock fighters then in front-line service.[1] The Bulldog re-established a gap for a year until the Hart for the first time put bombers ahead of fighters.

The Hart could only carry 520 lbs of bombs, so it was not the threat to civilians that the Gothas had been. If there was a threat to them it came from heavy bombers, but the fastest of these in 1929, the Boulton-Paul Sidestrand, could manage only 140 mph. Biplane fighters were always able to catch the heavier bombers, and the docile and lumbering Sidestrand was unlikely to have terrorised anyone. The fighter version of the Hart, the elegant Hawker Fury, appeared a year after it, and, with a top speed of 207 mph, gave fighters a narrow edge again.

Nevertheless, the performance of the Hart was chastening, and in 1930 the Air Ministry decided to issue a challenge to the aircraft industry by formulating a new fighter specification called F.7/30. It called for a machine capable of 250 mph and armed with four machine guns, and it was widely regarded as impossible to fulfil.[2] Although almost every British aircraft company studied the proposal, nothing resulted in an order. The Air Ministry pondered further.

In 1933, Squadron Leader Ralph Sorley was posted to the Operational Requirements Branch at the Air Ministry. He was convinced, even then, that war with Germany was inevitable, and admits to having been a 'fanatic' about the need to develop a fighter which could defeat German bombers.[3] The problem he focused on was how to kill a bomber once it had been caught. His starting point was his own experience:

> Like so many others, I had spent many years trying to hit targets with one, two, or even four machine guns, and I confess, with singularly poor results. Others were so much better, but I guessed that if one could hold the sight on for longer than two seconds, that was better than average. We were now going to have to hold it on at appreciably higher speeds so the average sight might be even less than two seconds.'[4]

RAF fighters still used the vast stocks of Vickers guns left over from 1914–18. In 1934, a new Browning gun with the much higher rate of fire of some 1,000 rounds a minute was being tested. Sorley sat down to think and add some theory to his experience:

> By dint of much blotting paper, arithmetic and burning of midnight oil, I reached the answer of eight guns as being the number required to give a lethal dose in two seconds of fire. I reckoned that the bomber's speed would probably be such as to allow the pursuing fighter only one chance of attack so it must be destroyed in that vital two-second burst.[5]

The next problem was where to put all these guns. The old Vickers guns were usually mounted in front of the cockpit, firing through the propeller by means of an interrupter gear. The wings were too flimsy to take more than a single Lewis gun fixed above the centre of the top wing. All the guns had to be near the pilot so that he could clear the frequent jams. However, the interrupter gear limited the rate of fire. Sorley's calculations showed that in order to build up the density of bullets needed to be lethal over any part of the target, the rate of fire of the Brownings could not be restricted. This meant putting the guns in the wings, outboard of the propeller-arc. This in turn meant that the wings had to be very rigid, the guns had to be very reliable, because the pilot could no longer clear jams, and the firing mechanism had to be pneumatic rather than mechanical. All of this was revolutionary. It implied the need for a flying gun-platform quite unlike the design of any aeroplane then in service.

Aware of the radical implications of his theory, Sorley kept it quiet until he had tested it in practice. In the course of many discussions with friends aided by large quantities of sherry, he became convinced that the concept was correct.

In 1934, with the help of a friend of his, Major Thompson, he got hold of an old aircraft and set it up on a firing range. They fired at it with eight guns from a range of 400 yards and cut through the structure in so many vulnerable places that it was clear that two seconds were indeed lethal.

Sorley approached Dowding to confess that he had destroyed one of his old aircraft, and tell him of the implications. He discovered to his surprise that he was flying this particular kite with a tail-wind, for Dowding told him that he had already placed an order for two experimental monoplanes in order to try out the new features designers were talking about, such as retractable undercarriages, enclosed cockpits and flaps, and to exploit the exciting developments in aero engines at Rolls-Royce in the hope of not only fulfilling, but going beyond the existing F.7/30 specification.

These specifications were F.36/34 and F.37/34 ('Experimental High Speed Single Seat Fighter') and had been issued to Hawker and Supermarine respectively as a result of their efforts on F.7/30. Sorley went off to see the two Chief Designers, Sydney Camm at Hawker and Reginald Mitchell at Supermarine. Both had been intending to fit four machine guns on the top of the fuselage of their designs, but when Sorley explained his reasoning, they enthusiastically turned to their thoughts to putting eight guns in the wings, which gave them the added bonus of being able to slim down the fuselage.[6]

Speeds continued to rise. In April 1935 the Bristol company demonstrated a new bomber known as 'Britain First' which it had developed with funding from Lord Rothermere, the owner of the *Daily Mail*, who was impatient at the lack of results from official specifications. This prototype reached 307 mph, about 70 mph faster than the fastest fighter, the Gauntlet. The aircraft, which was to become the Blenheim, was a low-wing metal monoplane.

In the same month the Ministry produced a new specification, F.10/35. It required 'as many guns as possible' but suggested eight (the decision already having been taken to use the American Browning, produced by Colt). Speed was specified as a minimum of 310 mph at 15,000 feet, but at least 40 mph more than 'the contemporary bomber', which in practice now meant 350 mph.* The rate of climb which had been specified in F.7/30 was eight and a half minutes to 15,000 feet,** and still applied, but the required

---

* Speeds always vary with altitude, some aircraft being faster at lower levels than higher, others the other way round. It is misleading to give an aircraft's 'top speed' with a single number. It normally means 'in level flight' at a given altitude and is airspeed, not speed over the ground i.e. it is what the machine is capable of under its own power, unaided by the forces of nature. Gravity makes aircraft speed up in a dive, making maximum diving speed a lot higher than its level flight performance, and a tailwind can make its speed over the ground a lot higher than its speed relative to the air around it.
** Rate of climb was very important in an interceptor as this determined how quickly it could get up to meet the enemy. It was also important in combat because height always conferred an advantage.

service ceiling (maximum altitude) was increased slightly to at least 30,000 feet. Endurance (maximum flying time) was to be ninety minutes.* F.10/35 also revealed the influence of young Turks like Sorley by specifying some design features, including an enclosed cockpit and a retractable undercarriage (which was an aerodynamically determined 'must' at the speeds envisaged).[7]

Sorley did not make himself popular with many of his superiors. The RAF did not like monoplanes. In 1912 two monoplanes had broken up in the air, so the Secretary of State for War, Colonel Seeley, banned them.[8] Some of his aviators facing the Fokker monoplane three years later no doubt wished that the German Air Ministry had shown a similar concern for the well-being of its pilots. The ban only lasted for five months, but the mud had been thrown and some of it had stuck. Air Chief Marshal Sir Robert Brooke-Popham, a man whose views had some weight given that he was then C.-in-C. Air Defence of Great Britain, liked open cockpits and thought eight guns was 'going a bit too far'. Indeed it was, for there was nowhere to put them on a biplane. Eight guns meant monoplanes.[9] Sorley persevered, however, and got F.10/35 approved.[10]

The biplane school had a lot of arguments and almost all of past experience on their side. The majority of pilots favoured biplanes. The key to fighter combat was widely believed to be manoeuvrability. That implied low wing-loading, which in turn implied two sets of wings. Many pilots thought that the innovations being discussed by designers were fine in theory but introduced too much complexity for the rigours of war service. Retractable undercarriages, flaps and variable pitch propellers were all devices which added weight and could go wrong, adding to servicing needs in the field and adding to the pilot's work-load. Enclosed cockpits created a feeling of claustrophobia, made baling out more difficult and added a barrier of perspex between the pilot's eyeballs and his enemy. Goggles were already a necessary evil. If the perspex were curved, it introduced distortion, and any perspex could get scratched or mist up. It may, as Sydney Camm wrote after the war, have been obvious to the industry that the biplane had had its day,[11] but it was not obvious to pilots.

Getting more speed meant using more powerful engines. With a team led by their Experimental Manager Ernest Hives, Rolls-Royce had built many of the power plants for the British entries to the Schneider Trophy seaplane races in the 1920s. These racing engines were called the 'R' series, and were developing almost 2,000 bhp by the end of the 1920s, though only for short periods. This was fine for racing, but durability was needed from an engine for commercial or military use. These big engines developed such heat that they could

---

* A few minutes of combat at full throttle could reduce endurance, and hence range, considerably. The Spitfire Mk I had a maximum range of 575 miles, but if it spent fifteen minutes in combat at maximum power this reduced to just under 400.

not be sufficiently cooled by air flowing round them but needed a liquid cooling system of their own. The goal was to get more and more sustained power out of as compact a unit as possible, and the experience with the 'R' series resulted in the PV XII engine, based on the Kestrel V 12, which by early 1934 was producing 1,000 bhp on a sustained basis. Rolls-Royce had taken to naming its engines after birds of prey, though with British understatement, they tended to choose the smaller ones. They had had the Falcon, the Buzzard and the Kestrel, so the new engine was named the Merlin.

The pursuit of speed led inexorably in the direction of monoplanes. Biplanes have a greater wing area, and therefore develop more lift. As a result, they are more manoeuvrable, but they are also slower because of the drag inherent in the extra wings and the struts and rigging they necessitated. The monoplane was a cleaner conception, and so potentially faster. The core issue was how to catch bombers. Whatever pilots wanted, the Air Ministry had to have more speed.

Sydney Camm at Hawker had set the pace of military aircraft development in the early 1930s with his family of excellent fighters and bombers, which had included the Hart and Fury. Camm believed that this gene pool was not yet exhausted. In October 1933, he began working on converting the Fury into a monoplane, based around the Rolls-Royce Goshawk engine. In early 1934, the Merlin inspired him to have a real go at F.7/30. He submitted his design for the 'Fury Monoplane' to the Air Ministry in September 1934 and there was a conference on the mock-up in January 1935. On 21 February 1935 Camm received a contract for one experimental high-speed fighter, which was Dowding's specification F.36/34. When Sorley turned up, his eight gun requirement fitted Camm's conception perfectly. The prototype which flew on 6 November 1935 was christened the Hurricane.*

The machine was fast, docile and manoeuvrable. With its proven lineage, it was vice-free and easy to fly. It had a strong frame of tubular steel and duralumin, making the whole aircraft very strong. This frame was built out with wooden runners and covered in fabric, making it easy to build and repair with the technology in common use. Eight guns fitted easily into its thick, sturdy wings and could be grouped together to give it a good concentrated bullet pattern; together with its flying properties which made it a very steady gun platform, this made it a fine bomber-killer. As easy to handle on the ground as in the air, it had a wide undercarriage which made it stable and capable of operating from rough forward airstrips. The guns and engine were readily accessible, making the Hurricane relatively easy to re-arm and maintain.

Approval was not universal, however. Whilst the prototype was undergoing trials at Martlesham Heath in early 1936, Ralph Sorley paid a visit to watch

---

* Just as Rolls-Royce liked birds, so Hawker liked high winds. The Hurricane was followed during the war by the Typhoon and the Tempest.

it on the firing butts. In a hand-written note at the end of his 1945 article about the eight-gun fighter he added:

> The armament officer was evidently in difficulty and when I asked how things were going he replied: "Whoever the b . . . f . . . was who put so many guns in this thing, and new type guns at that, I'd like to know." I didn't inform him.[12]

Hawker were nevertheless so sure they had a winner that they tooled up for production of 1,000 machines. In June 1936 the Air Ministry obliged by ordering 600, and in November 1938 ordered 400 more, so Hawker's entrepreneurialism paid off.[13]

The first unit to convert to Hurricanes was 111 Squadron at Northolt, which took its first delivery of Hurricane L 1547 in November 1937. Their C/O, Squadron Leader John Gillan, who had a keen sense of publicity promptly covered himself and the new fighter in glory in February 1938 by flying from Edinburgh to Northolt at an average speed of 408 mph. It was all over the papers and made the Hurricane every little boy's heart-throb – for a while. What the papers did not say is that nature had lent a hand with a benign hurricane of its own. Gillan's professional colleagues were less impressed, and christened him 'Downwind Gillan'.

111 Sqadron had the job of working up the new machine for operations, recommending modifications and ironing out the faults which are bound to exist in any piece of new technology. It was, for example, the first RAF fighter to have a retractable undercarriage, a change many pilots were still getting used to in 1940. Following his squadron leader and flight commander, James 'Sandy' Sanders, who had joined 111 in 1936, was the third pilot to fly L1547, and he took every opportunity to do so. One of the squadron's tasks was to display the machine to other units and in February 1938, Sandy was the first to take one to Tangmere, home to 1 and 43 Squadrons. Everybody on the station turned out to watch him come in to land, including 'Prosser' Hanks, Peter Townsend, Caesar Hull and Freddie Rosier. At the end of Sandy's landing run, the right undercarriage leg folded as he was turning. His audience were delighted, throwing their hats in the air. The Hurricane was not damaged and Sandy calmly set about rectifying the situation. Still in the cockpit, he beckoned to some airmen who lifted up the wing, while he pumped furiously at the undercarriage handle. Slowly the wheel came down, and, honour restored, Sandy was able to take off back to Northolt. The hydraulic system was not perfect and had got a small air-lock, a potential problem revealed for the first time by this incident. From then on a notice was fitted inside the cockpit reminding the pilot to continue pumping the handle after the green light came on showing the undercarriage was down until the undercarriage locked solid.

Even when it was not sitting on a tail-wind, the Hurricane could still achieve a creditable 320 mph at an optimum of 18,500 feet, and could reach

20,000 feet in 9.8 minutes. It had made the biplanes it replaced obsolete and comfortably outperformed the fastest new bombers then entering service.*

The Hurricane's moment of glory was to be tragically short, however. She was very good, but a somewhat plain and homely country girl, well-behaved and reliable. Her time in the limelight was to be cut brutally short by the appearance on stage of a real glamour-puss, a lady of such refined but curvaceous beauty and class that she instantly seduced every young man who climbed into her cockpit, and with such charisma that the public as a whole just stopped and stared every time she passed. They still do.

In 1919, at the age of only twenty-four, a former engineering apprentice from Stoke-on-Trent called Reginald Joseph Mitchell had become Chief Designer of the Supermarine Aviation Works. The company was based on the coast at Eastleigh near Southampton and specialised in seaplanes. Fortuitously, this got it involved in producing racing monoplanes for the Schneider Trophy seaplane races that in the 1920s were one of the driving forces behind the quest for speed in aviation. Mitchell's designs enjoyed great success. His S.5 won the trophy in 1927, and his S.6 won in 1929 and then set up a new air speed record of 357 mph. In 1931 the S.6B won the trophy for the third time in a row, allowing Britain to keep it for good. For good measure, it then broke its parent's speed record and set up a new one of 407 mph.[14]

Mitchell was already ill, and in 1933 he took a holiday in Europe to convalesce from a serious operation for cancer of the rectum. He had been told that the risk of the disease recurring within the next four years was considerable, but far lower thereafter. After talking to some German aviators, he returned convinced that there would be war. Convinced too that he could influence the outcome of the conflict he saw coming, he devoted himself to work.[15]

Given his intimate involvement with Hives' team from Rolls-Royce in the Schneider Trophy work, Mitchell was well placed to exploit the Merlin and wanted to take up the challenge of F. 7/30. Unlike Camm who thought forward, extrapolating from what he knew, Mitchell thought backwards, retrapolating from what he could envision. He believed in monoplanes from the outset, backed up by his Schneider experience, and in 1934 produced his response to this specification, the Type 224, a low-wing monoplane. His main problem was cooling the engine, a Goshawk. He put the liquid coolant in large fixed undercarriage spats, making it look a bit like a streamlined Stuka, but it still overheated. In any case, it could only do 228 mph. Mitchell modified it, producing the improved Type 300, but the Air Ministry was unimpressed.

In November 1934, the Chairman of Vickers[16], Sir Robert McLean, authorised Mitchell to go ahead with further work on the Type 300 based this

---

* The Blenheim Mk I only began to be delivered to the squadrons in March 1937, and with a top speed of 265 mph it was over 50 mph slower than the Hurricane. The aircraft that only two years before had seemed revolutionary, had already become vulnerable to modern fighters by the time it entered service.

HAWKER HURRICANE MK I

DISTINCTIVE FEATURES

Glycol header tank. The use of ethylene-glycol meant that the cooling system could be one third to one half of the weight of a pure water-based one, but the tank was vulnerable to fire from the front. Hurricanes attacking bombers often suffered hits in this tank which was followed by a stream of white vapour and an overheating engine.

The powerplant was the Rolls-Royce Merlin III, driving a three-bladed Rotol or De Havilland constant speed variable pitch propeller and developing 1,050 hp on take-off. Unlike the DB 601, the Merlin had a float carburettor and cut out when under negative g. To follow a 109 into a dive a Hurricane had to corkscrew, or lose a few seconds' power. Either way, the 109 gained valuable seconds.

The oil tank was housed in the port inner wing. It was also vulnerable to bombers' defensive fire.

Four 0.303 inch (7.7mm) rifle calibre Browning machine guns in each wing, outboard of the propeller arc, with a rate of fire of 20 rounds per second (1,200 rpm). Each had 300 rounds of ammunition, enough for about 15 seconds firing, delivering 160 bullets per second. They were initially harmonised at 400 yards, but this was soon reduced in practice to 200-250 yards. Grouped in a single bay, the Hurricane's guns could be swabbed out and re-loaded more quickly than those of the Spitfire. Ducts carried warm air from the engine into the bays to prevent the guns from freezing at altitude. One Hurricane was experimentally fitted with two Oerlikon cannon and was flown by F/L Roddick Smith of 151 Squadron from 6th July, who claimed a Dornier on 13 August. It was replaced by a machine armed with four Hispanos on 3 September, and F/L Rabagliati of 46 Squadron claimed a Bf 109 in it two days later when he 'borrowed' the machine in Smith's absence.

The Hurricane's thick wings were strong enough to support the weight of the aircraft, so the undercarriage legs were fitted to them and retracted inwards, creating a broad, sturdy base, enabling the aircraft to operate from rough grass strips and making landing and take-off accidents less of a problem on any runway.

Reserve gravity petrol tank containing 28 gallons (127 litres) of 100 octane fuel. Because it was sandwiched between bulkheads and also because it was hard to remove, it was at first not covered by Linatex sealing material. It was as vulnerable as the glycol tank when making attacks on bombers, and the resulting fires, sending flames of blow-torch intensity through the instrument panel at the pilot, prompted Dowding to order the retrofitting of Linatex and the addition of an armoured panel between the tank and the pilot.

Armoured windscreen.

Pilot's back armour.

The fuselage aft of the cockpit was a mixed wood and metal frame covered with fabric.

Main fuel tanks, one in each wing root, carrying 34.5 gallons (157 litres) of 100 octane fuel, giving a total of 97 gallons capacity. They were covered with Linatex, but were vulnerable from the rear, and some pilots believed that they, not the fuselage tanks, were the main cause of Hurricane fires.

TR 9D HF radio transmitter/receiver. Squadrons were upgrading to VHF radio, which gave greater range and clarity, during the course of the summer. By September, the sets were being delivered at the rate of 680 per month. In order to communicate, squadrons had to have the same equipment.

The thick wings were very sturdy and easily accommodated eight guns, but they produced much higher drag than those of the Bf 109 or Spitfire. The National Physical Laboratory advised Hawker on the basis of wind tunnel tests that reducing the thickness-to-chord ratio below 20% would not improve drag, so having obtained 19%, Camm's team left it alone. The NPL later discovered that they had been wrong. The wings were originally fabric-covered, but this was changed to stressed metal on the production lines in 1939 and most earlier examples had been retro-fitted by May 1940. All control surfaces remained fabric-covered.

time around the new Merlin. A month later, the Air Ministry issued a contract worth £10,000 and formalised it on 3 January 1935 with Dowding's F. 37/34 specification.* So Mitchell went back to his drawing board and started again, going for speed above all. He wanted as thin a wing and as narrow a fuselage as possible, and a retractable undercarriage to reduce drag. He was uncompromising at every turn, resisting anything which might impair performance, insisting, for example, on a retractable radiator to cut down drag in flight.

The wing was his masterpiece. His aerodynamicist, Beverley Shenstone, has commented:

The elliptical wing was decided upon quite early on. Aerodynamically it was the best for our purpose because the induced drag, that causing lift, was lowest when this shape was used: the ellipse was an ideal shape, theoretically a perfection. There were other advantages as far as we were concerned. To reduce drag we wanted the lowest possible wing thickness-to-chord ratio, consistent with the necessary strength. But near the root the wing had to be thick enough to accommodate the retracted undercarriage and the guns . . . A straight-tapered wing starts to reduce in chord from the moment it leaves the root; an elliptical wing, on the other hand, tapers only very slowly at first then progressively more rapidly towards the tip.[17]

The wing also featured 'wash-out'. It had a slight twist along it which meant that during tight turns the wing root would stall before the tip, giving the pilot a safe warning. Many blessed Mitchell for that.[18] The thinness of the wing did mean having the undercarriage fold outwards, making it far narrower than the Hurricane's inward-retracting undercarriage, with resulting loss of stability on the ground. It also meant that it was not so easy to install the guns. They could not be grouped together and it therefore took longer to re-arm them than those on a Hurricane, which were in a single bay.[19] During further work the familiar problem of over-heating arose. The design team moved over from water to ethylene glycol, which has a very high boiling point and greatly

---

* Some, including Sir Robert McLean, have propagated the idea that the Spitfire was produced against the opposition of the Air Ministry. All of Mitchell's work on fighter design was in fact carried out against the background of official specifications, and he worked very closely with Air Ministry men, such as Sorley. The Spitfire was a private venture for precisely one month. See McLean's letter to *The Times* of 18 August 1957 and the corrective correspondence from Marshal of the Royal Air Force Sir Edward Ellington (then CAS) and Air Marshal Sir Ralph Sorley (14 September 1957). The image of the lone visionary hero struggling against the stupidity of officialdom makes for a popular story, but it is the stuff of legend. Sir Sydney Camm commented on it himself in a letter to Air Marshal Robert Saundby of 14 May 1965: 'It was certainly wrong to say that there would have been no Hurricane or Spitfire had certain pre-war Ministers had their way but I think it is true to say that it started off as a private venture, with of course the friendly co-operation of the Air Ministry; in fact you will recall that I worked very closely in those days with them.' (Saundby Papers, RAF Museum, Hendon, Box 8).

improved efficiency, allowing the amount of coolant and therefore the weight of the cooling system to be reduced by two thirds.

The design team was a real team: they thought for themselves, developed different views, and debated them, improving the outcome. Mitchell's Chief Assistant, Harold Payn, thought manoeuvrability could be improved by increasing the size of the ailerons and thought the length of nose imposed by the in-line Merlin unacceptable.[20] Mitchell replied that 'the general manoeuvrability of the machine is not affected by the size of the ailerons, but rather by the ease with which aileron can be applied' and was willing to accept the poor view over the nose as it could only be improved 'with the sacrifice of performance by increasing the size of the body.'[21] He added that the pilot's seat could be raised at a later date if it proved necessary. It never did. The view was poor, but it was a compromise pilots were willing to live with.* The ailerons were a problem, for they became very heavy at high speed, but Mitchell was right again. The answer was not to increase their size, but to cover them in metal instead of fabric, and from late 1940 onwards this was done at the instigation of the Spitfire Test-Pilot Jeffrey Quill.[22]

The fighter first flew on 5 March 1936.[23] The small audience was elated by the first trouble-free twenty minutes. Over the next days and weeks, the hard work of refinement and development began. It was not to end until some ten years later. The last Spitfires to be operated as front-line fighters by the RAF were flown by 809 Squadron from Hong Kong in 1952. The basic design was so brilliant and so advanced that it was capable of further development until its power, weight and firepower doubled. It was the only Allied aircraft to be in the front line when the war began and on the day it ended.

On 3 June 1936 the Air Ministry placed an order for 310 of the new fighters. They were a snip at £4,500 each, one of the best investments British governments have ever made.

The Air Ministry also accepted the suggestion that the fighter be called the Spitfire. Vickers appeared to think of aeroplanes as bad-tempered women. They had previously come up with 'Shrew'. Mitchell did not approve of his graceful and serene Lady being denigrated in this way and was overheard to caustically remark that it was 'just the sort of silly name they would give it'.[24] The suggestion came from the Vickers' Chairman, Sir Robert McLean, who called his daughter Ann 'a little spitfire'.[25]

Its designer died on 11 June 1937 just three years and ten months after the original operation when he had been told the cancer had a good chance of

---

* The long nose meant taxiing in a snake-like movement in order to see ahead, but, more seriously, it remained hard to judge a deflection shot in the air because the target was covered by the nose. However, few pilots ever mastered deflection shooting and the majority of kills were made within 15° of dead astern, so the weakness probably had few real consequences. When the Merlin 62 was installed on the Mk IX, the nose was lengthened further to accommodate it, and the later Griffon-engined Spitfires had veritable snouts. Pilots facing Focke Wulfs did not complain. Mitchell's philosophy of sacrificing everything to performance was vindicated by experience.

recurring within four years. No Spitfires had yet been produced. He had been very ill during the last days, but he had earned his place amongst the few who determined the outcome of the air battle to come.[26] If he is the first of 'the Few', his Chief Draughtsman, Joseph Smith is surely the second. For over a decade, Smith led the team Mitchell had formed, preparing the hand-built prototype for production and continuing its extraordinary development, an achievement as unique in its way as Mitchell's own.

The first unit to be equipped with Spitfires was 19 Squadron, which got the first one on 4 August 1938. They loved them, but found a few problems with leaks and the engines were difficult to start. The pilots also had to get used to controlling a swing at take-off and then changing hands to operate the manual pump which brought up the undercarriage, a common complaint. But their graceful new machines took them up to 20,000 feet in seven and a half minutes and then allowed them to whip along at over 350 mph. They were responsive, reliable and turned very tightly. If the Hurricane was a bomber-killer, Spitfire pilots felt confident about taking on any other fighter in the sky.

The Spitfire was rather less well built than a Messerschmitt, with generally inferior skinning, and the Merlin, fine engine that it was, was less advanced than the fuel-injected Daimler-Benz DB601 that powered the 109.[27] Even in the 1940s the German engineering industry, which was to conquer world markets after the war, turned out better designs of military equipment than the UK or US.[28] However, the Spitfire, which as a design was quite Teutonic in its uncompromising commitment to quality and performance, did not betray in service the failings of the economy which produced it. This placed its pilots in a privileged position compared with most Allied fighting men throughout the war. Even after America's entry, Allied soldiers were consistently far worse-equipped than their German counterparts, especially in tanks, but also in small arms.[29] The Spitfire's design proved to be more robust than that of the Bf 109, for the later versions of the Messerschmitt fighter, the 109G and the 109K, were no match for its Spitfire contemporaries, the Mark IX and Mark XIV.[30] Mitchell had taken piston-engined fighter design almost as far as it could go, which is remarkable given its early provenance. The photoreconnaissance Mk XIX of 1944 could cruise beyond the reach of the first jet fighter, the Me 262. Not until the advent of the first swept-wing jets in 1949 was there anything else in the sky which could catch it.[31]

Anyone watching a period film or going to an air-show today can see that Mitchell's little creation has charisma. The man who nursed it through its development, and loved it more than anyone, Jeffrey Quill, once remarked in 1942 that the Spitfire is a piece of mechanical engineering, differing little other than in size and shape from the Forth Bridge. Likewise, the Mona Lisa is paint on canvas.[32] Some sobriety is needed in assessing the role played by the Spitfire and the Hurricane and in comparing both with the Bf 109, for it is an emotional subject.[33] However, it is clear that in 1940 the Spitfire fascinated the Luftwaffe and the British public alike. The former admired it and were always

VICKERS SUPERMARINE SPITFIRE MK I

DISTINCTIVE FEATURES

Four 0.303 inch (7.7mm) rifle calibre Browning machine guns in each wing, outboard of the propeller arc, with a rate of fire of 20 rounds per second (1,200 rpm). As in the case of the Hurricane, each had 300 rounds of ammunition, enough for about 15 seconds firing, delivering 160 bullets per second. However, the thinness of the wing meant that those of the Spitfire were fitted in three separate bays, which meant that even a practiced crew needed ten minutes to re-arm the aircraft. In the quest for better bomber-killing capability, 19 Squadron flew Spitfires armed with the 20mm Hispano cannon. They were called Mk1Bs to distinguish them from the standard Mk1As with eight machine guns. The cannon constantly jammed because the spring-operated feed mechanism failed under high g-forces. On 4 September the Mk1Bs were withdrawn, and replaced with some old Mk1As. The jamming problem was solved by a new belt-feed mechanism and from the introduction of the Spitfire MkV in February 1941, the most common Spitfire armament was two 20 mm Hispanos and four machine guns.

Glycol header tank, vulnerable to defensive fire from bombers.

Upper fuel tank containing 48 gallons (218 litres) and lower fuel tank containing 37 gallons (168 litres) of 100 octane fuel, giving a total capacity of 85 gallons. Positioned between bulkheads, it was the least vulnerable petrol tank of the three main fighters.

The power plant of the Mk I was the Rolls-Royce Merlin III, as in the Hurricane. The Mk II had the slightly more powerful 1,140 hp Merlin XII, giving a better performance at high altitude. Deliveries were made to 611 Squadron in August 1940, followed by 19, 74 and 266 Squadrons in September. However, the overwhelming number of Spitfires which flew in the Battle of Britain were Mk Is.

The Spitfire's wing roots were strong enough to take the undercarriage legs, but they folded outwards and gave a less stable platform than the Hurricane's. The risk of taxiing accidents was increased by the poor forward vision, which necessitated a snaking movement on the ground, but there was far less tendency to ground-loop than with the 109.

Armoured windscreen.

Pilot's head and back armour.

TR 9D HF radio.

Tapering all-metal elliptical wing with a thickness-to-chord ratio of 13% at the root and only 6% at the tip. This was the most aerodynamically efficient wing shape known in the 1930s, so it was adopted despite the difficulty of forming the curved metal parts needed to make it. Like Hawker, Supermarine were advised by the National Physical Laboratory that a thickness-to-chord ratio of below 20% gave little improvement in aerodynamic efficiency. Mitchell did not believe them, and was proved to be right some years later. The only sub-sonic wing section to have superior properties was the laminar flow airfoil adopted in 1940 by the German émigré Edgar Schmued when he set about designing the P51 Mustang for North American. The Spitfire's control surfaces were still covered with fabric, and the aircraft became difficult to roll in a dive. This was corrected, at Jeffrey Quill's instigation, by fitting metal ailerons, which only began to happen after successful operational tests on 19th November 1940, too late for the Battle of Britain.

shot down by Spitfires, never Hurricanes. The standard warning cry of 'Achtung, Indianer!' ('look out, bandits!') often became 'Achtung, Spitfire!' as approaching Hurricanes were spotted. The British public set up Spitfire funds to buy more of them for their fighter boys and they were sure that all the aluminium pots and pans they donated to the war effort went into Spitfires.[34] It became a symbol of 1940 and is now *the* icon of the Battle of Britain. It plays the mythological role of a magical weapon, the equivalent of Achilles' armour, of the swords Excalibur or Nothung. Its power is unique: the power of eros.

Oddly perhaps for such a phallic machine, the Spitfire has always been female and always clearly upper-class. Her main Test-Pilot, Jeffrey Quill, describes how on landing after his first flight in the prototype, K 5054, it was only after touch-down that he felt the mild buffeting associated with the wing stalling, and adds: '"Here", I thought to myself, "is a real lady."'[35] In recalling his first flight, Bob Stanford-Tuck commented 'If it comes to war, this is the girl for me,'[36] and has observed quite explicitly: 'Some men just fall in love with yachts or some with women, strangely enough, or motor cars, but I think every Spitfire pilot fell in love with it as soon as he sat in that nice tight cosy office with everything to hand.'[37] Sailor Malan has recorded his first experience in similar terms: 'The Spitfire had style and was obviously a killer . . . Moreover, she was a perfect lady. She had no vices. She was beautifully positive. You could dive till your eyes were popping out of your head . . . She would still answer to a touch.'[38] First encounters with her often had erotic overtones. 'We continued flying our mixed bag of aircraft until about 20 March when a solitary Spitfire landed and taxied over to our hangar. We were told it was ours. Our hearts leapt! We walked around it, sat in it, and stroked it. It was so beautiful I think we all fell a little bit in love with it.'[39] Her charms knew no borders: 'Americans raved about her and wanted to have her; Poles were seduced by her; men from the old Dominions crossed the world and the oceans to be with her; the free French undoubtedly wrote love songs about her. And the Germans were envious of her.'[40]

Bob Doe flew both the Spitfire and the Hurricane during the Battle of Britain. When I asked him about them he compared the Hurricane to 'a brick-built shit-house', sturdy and reliable, which did not shake about when the guns were fired. The Spitfire was so sensitive it was quite hard to keep the guns on. In order to be able to control it properly, he abandoned his flying boots and wore light shoes, controlling the rudder with the tips of his toes. He controlled the joystick with his fingertips. An average pilot, he thought, was better off in a Hurricane. However, if you were good, you could get more out of a Spitfire. It became part of you. It was an absolute joy.[41]

I am not a pilot, so I took this in good faith. In the meantime, I have been privileged to find out for myself, courtesy of Carolyn Grace, who owns the two-seater Mk IX, ML 407, based at Duxford. Piloted by aerobatic pilot Peter Kynsey, well strapped-in after a three-minute lesson on how to use the parachute, we snaked along the grass to the end of the runway, peering either side of the nose to see where we were going. Peter did the final checks and run-up and then, as the Merlin roared, we bumped off down the runway. The bumping lasted for a few seconds, then everything became smooth. That was the sign we were airborne. Once we had turned north at a few thousand feet, we tried her out. Peter put her into a right-hand bank of about 40 degrees and then said: 'Now I'll show you how we get out of trouble'. With that the whole aircraft rolled into a similar left-hand bank. There was no noise, no juddering, hardly a sense of movement, just instant response. We levelled off, and I had control. Peter trimmed her for straight and level flight and then suggested I hold the stick between my right thumb and forefinger. 'Now', he said, 'just apply a little pressure through your finger. Don't move your finger or your hand. Just apply a little pressure.' I did. We began to climb. I released the pressure and we levelled off. I applied the pressure through my thumb and we went into a shallow dive.

Now I wanted to test That Wing and see the effect of wash-out. Peter put her into a left hand bank again and began to turn, tightening all the time. The ground was just beyond the tip of the wing, and I could feel the g. As the turn tightened there was suddenly, distinct through the growl of the engine, a low drumming sound from the left outside the cockpit. I could sense a slight vibration from outside. I knew it was the inner wing stalling, but it felt like the machine was alive, talking to us: 'Now boys, be gentle.' She was not complaining, just looking after us. I had flown Cessnas before, but it was nothing like this. We pulled out and finished the flight with an exhilarating low run over Duxford and a victory roll. The Spitfire may not have supernatural powers, but the power she does exert can only be compared to that of a beautiful and sophisticated woman. In that non-mythological sense, she is indeed magical.

Improvements to both the new fighter types followed their introduction into service. New three bladed, constant-speed, variable pitch propellers were fitted[42] and 100 octane aviation fuel was imported from the US to replace the 87 octane fuel then in use.[43] Armour plating was added below and behind the pilot's seat and armoured windscreens fitted. The Spitfire's petrol tank was lined with a substance called 'Linatex' to prevent fuel leakage through bullet holes and prevent fire. The same was done to the two main tanks in the wings of the Hurricane, but it was not done to the Hurricane's reserve tank just in front of the pilot. This tank was hard to get at and it was thought that the armour there would be sufficient protection. This proved to be wrong and had terrible consequences for a good number of Hurricane pilots. When it became apparent what was happening, getting the reserve tanks covered in Linatex became one of Dowding's highest priorities.

The state of aeronautical technology in the middle of the twentieth century can be compared with computer technology at the end of it. The rate of change was so high that aircraft had a very short life at the forefront of technology.[44] The Blenheim, the world's fastest bomber in 1935, was obsolete in 1939. Going to war in an obsolete machine meant swift death for most. This was to be sadly demonstrated by a third fighter which entered service in March 1940, well after the Hurricane and Spitfire: the Boulton-Paul Defiant.

One of the most successful British fighters of World War I, the Bristol Fighter, had been a two-seater. In 1935, the Air Ministry issued Specification F. 9/35, calling for a two-seater with a power-operated gun turret. An air staff memorandum from June 1938 shows some of the thinking behind it:

> The speed of modern bombers is so great that it is only worthwhile to attack them under conditions which allow no relative motion between the fighter and its target. The fixed-gun fighter with guns firing ahead can only realise these conditions by attacking the bomber from dead astern. The duties of a fighter engaged in 'air superiority' fighting will be the destruction of opposing fighters . . . For these purposes, it requires an armament that can be used defensively as well as offensively in order to enable it to penetrate into enemy territory and withdraw at will. The fixed-gun fighter cannot do this.[45]

Whilst some of the stated premises were correct, the conclusion was not. It was thought that it was an advantage to divide up the work of flying and shooting between two people and that the armament could be used both offensively and defensively, whatever that means. The Bristol Fighter had in fact been armed with a fixed forward-firing gun operated by the pilot, who flew it like a single-seater with an added sting in its tail.

The response to F. 9/35 came from Boulton-Paul, which created a two-seater fighter around their own new four-gun turret. It first flew on 11 August 1937.[46] The turret was heavy and, as might be expected with such an innovation, unreliable at first. But it seemed to many to be a good idea, especially against bombers.

Churchill, no less, seems to have flirted with the idea that turret-armed fighters were best, and in 1938 the Deputy Chief of the Air Staff, Air Vice-Marshal William Sholto Douglas, ordered Dowding to form nine squadrons of Defiants, informing him that 450 had been ordered. 'For work over enemy territory,' he stated, 'a two-seater is best'.[47] It was a British heavy fighter, a Zerstörer. Dowding vigorously opposed this and prevailed to the extent that when the Battle of Britain opened, the Defiant equipped only two squadrons, 141 and 264.[48] They were very proud of them. Their tragic tale was only an incident in what followed, but it was to show how critical fighter performance had become and how easily, but for Dowding, Spitfire and Hurricane production could have been curtailed in favour of a machine which would have lost the Battle of Britain within a few weeks.

Having got his fighters, Dowding needed young men to fly them. Personnel expansion began to get under way in 1936. From then on there were three ways in which a young man could join the RAF and get his lascivious hands on one of its wonderful new flying machines.

The first was to join the RAF proper to train as a pilot at Cranwell, which established a standardised training programme in 1933. Technical colleges at

Halton, Cranwell and Flowerdown trained groundcrew from whose ranks some later became pilots. The introduction of short-service commissions ensured that a reserve was created between the wars.

The second was to join the Auxiliary Air Force, which Trenchard had created in 1925. Like the Territorial Army, it consisted of groups of men from a particular area who trained at weekends. However, they were not just any young men. The first to be formed, 601 (County of London) Squadron, was raised by Lord Edward Grosvenor from amongst his old wartime friends and fellow members of White's Club. The Right Hon. Edward Guest formed 600 (City of London) Squadron largely from solid, wealthy frequenters of the City. So the tone was set. The auxiliaries quickly gained a reputation for their wealth, high living, flouting of regulations of all kinds and for looking down on the RAF (whom they called 'coloured troops') who in turn looked down on them as 'pampered pimpernels' and amateurs.[49] But by 1940 the weekend flyers were as effective in the air as any regular squadron. Fourteen auxiliary squadrons flew in the Battle, about a quarter of the total.

The third entry route was opened up in 1936 when the government created the Volunteer Reserve to train 800 young men a year. The principles were similar to the auxiliaries, but money was not a requirement, and it was in this way that a far broader range of the population entered the ranks. About a third of Fighter Command's pilots in 1940 entered the service through the RAFVR. However, as the bulk of them were not gentlemen they could not be officers, and most of them joined their squadrons as Sergeant Pilots.[50]

This policy did not go down well in Commonwealth countries, and it was also opposed by Sir Arthur Harris when he took over Bomber Command.[51] It did not have a good effect on morale. Sergeants and officers had separate messes and officers were expected to lead formations even if some of the sergeants were more experienced. The two groups were expected not to fraternise too much, and sometimes got told off for doing so. But in general it was up to the individuals themselves to be snobbish or friendly, and as the war went on the distinctions eroded.[52]

Opening itself up to all-comers was something of a revolution for the RAF. The reason for keeping officers and sergeants apart had deep roots. It was officially believed not only that the best background for a pilot was hunting, shooting and fishing (which has some truth to it) but that only public schools could be expected to produce men with the right 'moral fibre', lack of which was the technical term for cowardice, the dread 'lack of moral fibre' or 'LMF'.* One contemporary medical officer expressed the view that 'breeding very definitely is of great importance. It is unlikely that the son of a coward would

* The RAF was particularly ruthless in dealing with it, more so than the USAF. One of the most humane and courageous of all airmen, Leonard Cheshire, has admitted that there was simply not enough time to be compassionate. Psychological breakdown was regarded as contagious, so as a commander under the extreme pressures of war, Cheshire himself was uncompromising. See Wells, op. cit., pp. 200–201.

himself become a hero, for it is remarkable how heroism often runs in families.'[53] If pedigree of family or school were in doubt, a candidate's qualifications were tested to see if he had 'the right stuff'. Sandy Johnstone recalls that before he was allowed to join 602 (City of Glasgow) Squadron, who were auxiliaries, he had to go through a 'dining in' night to test his social acceptability and his behaviour when drunk.[54]

The selection of candidates for flying training was as yet untainted by any objective considerations of aptitude. A Flying Personnel Research Committee had been formed on 11 January 1939, and one of its tasks was to design flying aptitude tests, but the work was still at an experimental stage in 1940.[55]

Training was dangerous. In 1937, the RAF suffered 156 training fatalities and in 1939, 218, an average of 1 per 5,000 hours flown.[56] Bomber Command lost 8,000 aircrew in accidents throughout the war, about 15% of its total casualties.[57] The causes were the same as in the Luftwaffe.[58]

In an attempt to clamp down on some of the testosterone-driven behaviour, pilots were forbidden to fly below 2,000 feet. This rule was one of the most commonly broken, but efforts to enforce it were not always as rigorous as they might have been. At the end of 1937, Flight Lieutenant 'Sailor' Malan of 74 Squadron, then based at Hornchurch, and soon to become one of the most celebrated pilots in Fighter Command, was court-martialled for beating-up his girlfriend (i.e. flying low over her house) in a Gladiator. Unfortunately for him, his girlfriend's neighbour was a 'femme seule', a young single mother with a toddler. The little boy was scared out of his wits by the aircraft roaring over his head. His mother managed to write down the code lettering of the aircraft of a piece of card with her lipstick and sent it to the Undersecretary of State for Air. There was a court-martial, and Sandy Sanders, who was senior to Malan, was the escorting officer. At the hearing, Malan's defending officer, 'Baldy' Donaldson, who was known for his wit, explained that the woman claimed her little boy had been terrified by the defendant, a particularly gallant officer who had come all the way from South Africa to defend the country in its time of need. He then asked the woman whether she would ever allow her son to join the RAF in a future time of need. 'Never!' she said. 'Gentlemen,' concluded the defence, 'this woman is biased against the RAF.' Malan got away with a severe reprimand.

Given the propensity of even the most gifted young men towards breaking the wonderful new flying machines, and the tendency for them to develop faults even without the depredations of the 'Brylcreem boys', the RAF needed a new army of groundcrew to put right the damage and keep them in the air. During its period of expansion the RAF supplemented its skilled fitters, trained in an apprentice scheme set up by Trenchard, with less skilled flight riggers, responsible for the airframe, and flight mechanics, responsible for the engine. They were at the bottom of the RAF hierarchy, and knew it, but most pilots, whose lives depended on them, formed close relationships with them, and veterans are frequently lyrical in their praise for the work they performed under often arduous conditions. In the summer of 1940, their jobs were to become dangerous too.

6. THE BOMBERS

The dominant image most of us have of the Battle of Britain is of British fighters taking on the whole of the Luftwaffe in daylight over England. There is another view, one which had received scant attention, of British bombers taking on German defences at night over France and Germany.

> There was no fighter Battle of Britain. I was at Lympne in light bombers in 1940. There was some fighter activity overhead but no more than you would expect. We went out every night, destroying the German invasion barges in the Channel Ports. That was why the Germans never came. We fought the real Battle of Britain.

The obvious overstatement represented by this view of one RAF veteran of 1940 bears witness to the pain lying behind it. Ignoring the role British bombers played in the Battle gives a false impression of the cost to both sides, and fails to take into account the impact of British offensive activity in weakening the invasion forces and in tying down German fighters. Whilst most of these attacks were carried out by Bomber Command crews, Coastal Command was also involved in reconnaissance and some of the actual attacks. Defending Britain against invasion was a task carried out by the whole of the Royal Air Force.

The men who fought with Bomber Command did not, on the whole, have a good war and they have had a rather miserable peace as well. Their war was long and very dangerous, and in peacetime the reputation of their principal leader, Sir Arthur Harris, has been sullied because of his unwavering pursuit of area bombing. When a statue to him was finally unveiled in 1992, it was defaced a few months later. Dowding's has never been damaged.

Bomber Command's wartime losses of 55,573 aircrew were the heaviest in the RAF, and half those of the whole of the British army.[1] The young men who died were amongst their country's educational élite, for flying a bomber was a technical business needing skilled navigators, flight engineers and bomb aimers as well as pilots.

At the beginning of the war, Bomber Command was highly confident. It had 280 aircraft of four main types, the Whitley, the Hampden, the Wellington and the Blenheim. The first three all cruised at about 160 mph and could take a 4,000 lb bomb-load about 1,200 miles. The Blenheim Mk IV was lighter and faster, being capable of taking a 1,000 lb load 1,460 miles, cruising at 198 mph. They had all been designed for specific tactics. They would operate by day in order to be able to find their targets, and by flying in massed 'box' formations would put up a screen of defensive fire no fighter could penetrate. Their targets were German warships and ports, well away from civilians.[2] At night, they would scatter leaflets in order to explain to the Germans that the war was not a good idea and to suggest that it be called off and that everyone should go home.

In addition there were ten squadrons of Fairey Battles sent to France to operate in support of the army. The Battle dated from 1933, when it elicited little enthusiasm but was ordered anyway because it was better than nothing.* It was very slow and clearly obsolete in 1939. It was probably in fact a good deal worse than nothing. The men who flew it were a gallant but tragic band.

Bomber Command's first operation was launched one hour after war was declared. It did not find the target, and nor did the second. Early the next day a reconnaissance flight identified naval vessels in the harbours of Brunsbüttel and Wilhelmshaven. Fifteen Blenheims left for Wilhelmshaven and fourteen Wellingtons set out for Brunsbüttel. Five Blenheims and two Wellingtons were brought down by flak and fighters. The shipping was barely molested.[3]

In October and November activity was desultory. On 14 December, however, twelve Wellingtons of 99 Squadron attacked a German convoy north of Wilhelmshaven. They were shot at by flak and then attacked by fighters. A thirty-minute air battle followed. Six Wellingtons were lost, including two which collided. On 18 December, twenty-four Wellingtons set out for more shipping targets in the same area, two turning back early with technical problems. The Freya radar operators did not scramble their fighters at first because they could not believe the British would attack them with such a force in broad daylight with visibility of 50 miles. When they finally did intercept them, the mixed force of Bf 109s and 110s found that the formation had been broken up by flak, and shot down twelve of the twenty-two which had reached the target area.[4]

---

* At that time, Britain and Germany were playing a political numbers game called 'air parity'. Politicians wanted to say that they were keeping up with German aircraft production numbers and trusted that if the numbers looked good no-one would ask questions about the quality of the machines involved (see Crossland, op. cit., p. 41). Whatever amusement this game may have afforded the politicians playing it, it was to cost the lives of several hundred extremely brave and skilful men who were sent to their deaths in these things seven years later.

The German pilots involved claimed thirty-four victories, three times the actual losses inflicted. The German Air Ministry checked all the combat reports carefully for consistency, eliminated double counting and confirmed twenty-six of the claims, narrowing the gap between illusion and reality to a factor of only two. The gunners on the Wellingtons thought that *they* had won on points, claiming a total of thirteen definite kills and twelve 'probables'. In fact, the Germans lost two Bf 109s in the air and a further one was written off after crash-landing. A large number of the surviving machines on both sides, including all the Wellingtons and all the Bf 110s involved had damage which kept the repair workshops busy.

The loss rates showed that unescorted bombers could not survive in daylight. This conclusion was very threatening to Bomber Command for it jeopardised the doctrine on which its very existence was based. An alternative explanation had to be found.

The leader of the Wellington formation, Wing Commander Richard Kellett of 149 Squadron, provided Bomber Command with what it needed by maintaining a very strict and tight formation amongst the flight of four aircraft he led directly throughout the engagement. Only one of these machines had been lost, and from the list of claims submitted by this flight, it seemed that they had inflicted a small but significant defeat upon the intercepting fighters.

So it was that, having experienced loss rates of between 30% and 50% on three out of four major operations conducted since the war began, 3 Group of Bomber Command concluded:

> There is every reason to believe that a very close formation of six Wellington aircraft will emerge from a long and heavy attack by enemy fighters with very few, if any, casualties to its own aircraft.

Accordingly, on 21 December it issued Operational Instruction 21, which stated:

> With the intention of combining useful training and operations, sweeps will continue to be carried out . . . If enemy aircraft are encountered, gunners will be able to practise shooting at real targets instead of drogues . . .[5]

Thus Wing Commander Kellett, through his skill, courage and dedication to duty, condemned many of his colleagues to death over the coming months. The Germans continued to believe that the British had been bent on suicide. Despite some chivalrous and humanitarian misgivings on the part of some of its fighter pilots, the Luftwaffe continued to co-operate with Bomber Command's training programme and sent up targets for its air-gunners, though they inconsiderately attacked the bombers from their blind spots rather than flying directly at their guns, as had been planned. Over at Fighter

Command, senior officers muttered that they had told them so, and the fighter pilots waited longingly for the Luftwaffe to try the same thing in reverse. They did not do so because they did not espouse the theory of strategic bombing by an independent bomber force.

Post-war literature has drawn its own conclusions about these events. They showed that bombers had difficulty finding their targets, even by day, in poor weather. If they found the target and wanted to hit it, they had to go in low, where they would be shot down by flak. To escape the flak they had to fly higher, where they would be shot down by fighters. Unescorted bombers were dead meat. In order to get through to somewhere and come back, they had to fly at night. Night operations were started and soon revealed that targets had to be very big and near water which reflected moonlight so that they could be found. Until more sophisticated navigation aids came into operation, most targets were accordingly on the coast or by a river.

In May 1940, the Battles sent to France were annihilated. The courage of their crews was recognised with two VCs, which might have gone to any of them. Bomber Command was left to face further months of sacrifice in warding off the danger of invasion as the Wehrmacht assembled in the Channel ports.

It had been decided by the War Cabinet on 15 May 1940 to attack the oil industry, communications and also forests and crops in Germany, concentrating on the Ruhr. This began the night-time strategic bombing campaign which was to last until 1945. Once the threat from the Luftwaffe emerged, the Chiefs of Staff reconsidered. They considered Bomber Command's forces to be central to the air defence of the country:

> we cannot resist invasion by fighter aircraft alone. An air striking force is necessary not only to meet the sea-borne expedition, but also to bring direct pressure to bear upon Germany by attacking objectives in that country[6]

The influence of the strategic bombing doctrine can be seen here, but it also shows that a force conceived of as purely offensive was to be used in a strategically defensive role. This was to some extent a face-saver for Bomber Command, as it was at this time totally incapable of carrying out the role for which it had been intended.

The Whitleys, Hampdens and Wellingtons were accordingly directed at aircraft factories in Germany in addition to their industrial targets, and the Blenheims attacked airfields during the day. The RAF intended to attack the Luftwaffe in much the same way as the Luftwaffe was going to attack the RAF. On 3 July, harbours and shipping were made the overall priority target. A lot of mine-laying operations were carried out and attempts made to disrupt inland waterways in Germany to prevent the passage of invasion barges. The then head of Bomber Command, Air Marshal Charles Portal, objected to having his command diverted from its offensive role 'for the purpose of bolstering Fighter Command, the AA defences and the ARP before these have really been tried and found wanting', but changed his mind in August as the threat became more evident.[7] From August, the Blenheims attacked the assembling invasion fleet as well.

The invasion fleet presented the bombers with targets that they could both find and hit. The targets were large and on the coast and therefore detectable at night. Air defences had had to be improvised, so there were only a few Freya radars to help the German fighters. There is a sense in which, by coming to the Channel, Hitler gave Bomber Command the only sort of targets they could usefully attack until a proper strategic bomber force could be built up. It may even have saved the lives of crews who would otherwise have been sent over the North Sea alone and achieved nothing. The airfields were a different matter, as the bomber crews were to learn to their cost. Attacking them was also of doubtful value. The Luftwaffe had several hundred in operation, so achieving significant disruption would be almost impossible.

The political use of bombing for retaliation was also considered early on. The Minister of State for Air, Sir Archibald Sinclair, wrote on 23 July that all Britain's bombers had the range to reach Berlin and could drop 65–70 tons of bombs on the German capital every night for a week. Given sufficient preparation, this could be increased to as much as 200 tons for a single heavy blow.[8] A month later, Berlin would indeed become a target.

Bomber Command's effort against the invasion forces peaked during September, when some 60% of its strength was directed at the Channel ports. For several nights the whole of the available force attacked the barges. Between the beginning of July and the end of October, 36% of Bomber Command's sorties were flown against invasion shipping, and destroyed about 12% of the assembling craft. A further 17% were against airfields and 14% against the German aircraft industry.[9] One could therefore say that two-thirds of Bomber Command's effort during the Battle of Britain was in direct support of its fighter colleagues.

Coastal Command's main role throughout the war was to protect convoys and attack enemy shipping, but it began conducting anti-invasion patrols from the day war was declared. In May 1940, Coastal Command was made primarily responsible for reconnaissance over enemy-held coastline to detect any build-up for an invasion. It flew an average of forty visual reconnaissance sorties a day. The Photographic Reconnaissance Unit (PRU) was also attached to Coastal Command throughout the Battle of Britain, and flew 681 sorties, of which 492 were successful.

After Dunkirk, Coastal Command was given responsibility for anti-shipping patrols from Norway to the Channel ports and its bomber squadrons also joined Bomber Command in mine-laying operations ('gardening') and carrying out strikes against dockyards, oil terminals, shipping and airfields. From July to September, Coastal Command aircraft dropped 26 tons of bombs on airfields and 205 tons on the other targets. This was little in comparison with Bomber Command, but they braved the same dangers.[10]

The total of 9,180 sorties flown by Bomber Command between July and the end of October was itself dwarfed by the 80,000 or more flown by Fighter Command. But some of 'the Few' flew bombers.

7. STRENGTH FOR BATTLE

A dolf Galland has characterised the state of the Luftwaffe in 1940 with the phrase 'too little too late'. British pilots facing mass bomber formations and swarms of Bf 109s might well have laughed with incredulity, but Galland was right.

Mass production started too late, for Hitler thought he could fight a lazy war. The German economy was not placed on a war footing, for the Nazis wanted their people to conduct their struggle for national existence whilst continuing to enjoy all the comforts of peace-time. Whilst the British prepared for blood, toil, tears and sweat and went onto rationing, the Germans were to have holidays and all the consumer goods they desired. Although German output of consumer luxuries dropped after 1938, it still continued, and the war ouput of Nazi-run industries was far lower than Britain's in 1940 despite spending almost twice as much. They were less efficient.

The numbers tell the story.

AIRCRAFT PRODUCTION 1932–45

Source: Overy, op. cit., pp 21 & 150

The German figures show the rapid pre-war rise to a peak in 1937, slowed by a slight decline in 1938 as the bulk of production shifted to the new types. Production rose almost 60% between 1938 and 1939 and by another 23% in 1940. Despite a significant effort in 1943, the full potential of the aircraft economy was not exploited until Speer rationalised production in 1944, at the height of the Allied bombing offensive. Some of the increase is due to a shift in mix, as Speer concentrated on fighters, which were cheaper to produce. This was the only year of the war in which German production exceeded that of Britain.

British production was lower than Germany's in the pre-war years, but this was less important as the types being produced were mainly outdated. British rearmament got into swing in 1939, with the bulk of the fighters manufactured being Hurricanes and Spitfires, which did matter. In 1939, Britain produced only 350 aircraft less than Germany produced. The British effort continued steadily and Germany was out-produced by 47% in 1940, by 70% in 1941 and 54% in 1942. Not until 1943 did the gap narrow.

Galland's view is substantially borne out: Germany was losing the economic air war against Britain from the beginning. From 1941 it was taking on the Soviet Union and from 1942 the United States. By 1944, the economic war mattered less as the Luftwaffe had already lost the military war. It had by far its best chance of winning in 1940.

This graph understates the numbers problem faced by the Luftwaffe even in 1940, for France manufactured 2,113 aircraft in the first five months of 1940, and the countries of the British Commonwealth another 1,100.[1] Even though French production was not of comparable quality, the Luftwaffe still had to defeat them, and suffered attrition in the process.

The picture which emerges is of one country which took the war seriously from the beginning and put the whole of its economic resources behind the war effort, and another that did just enough to produce a formidable façade, but was then caught on the run when its enemies survived the first shocks.

As Evill had noticed on his visit to Germany in 1937, Luftwaffe Chiefs such as Kesselring were nervously aware of this.[2] Milch had planned to be ready for war in 1942. When Hitler provoked the Czech crisis in 1938, raising the real prospect of war with Britain, Göring was shocked to receive a report from General Felmy that an exercise had shown that the Luftwaffe was in no condition to take on the RAF. After the invasion of Poland, Hitler's eagerness to attack France provoked similar anxiety within the Luftwaffe High Command. They were not ready, but by that time Göring's boasting had made it impossible for him to tell Hitler the truth without losing face or worse.[3].

The Nazis did not understand the economics of war, and, like the Japanese, relied on the superior skill and the warrior ethos of their fighting men to win. Their propaganda efforts back-fired, for the British expected German production to be far higher than it was and so planned for high numbers themselves.[4]

The British aircraft industry in 1940 was in fact more productive and more efficient than the German one, outproducing it with smaller numbers of workers until 1944. However, attaining that efficiency took a great deal of effort. The Air Ministry placed its first order for 400 Hurricanes in June 1936, but the first production Hurricane did not roll out of the assembly sheds at Brooklands in Surrey until 12 October 1937, which was almost two years after the prototype had flown. The ministry had expected to have its first fifty by September.[5] The production capacity of the British aircraft industry had been allowed to decline so far over the previous twenty years that it could barely cope. Similarly, it was only due to the energies of Ernest Hives, who became General Works Manager in 1938, that Rolls-Royce could manage to meet an order for 3,350 Merlins.

The production of the Spitfire was even more problematic. Mitchell's radicalism ensured that, unlike the Hurricane, the Spitfire was difficult to produce, especially the wing, and his modernity ensured that existing production techniques could not be employed. It was all metal, hard to make and hard to repair.* There were endless delays. Supermarine only had 500 employees and it was also committed to producing the Walrus and Stranraer seaplanes. The British aerospace industry of the 1930s was not only small, but was technologically little more than a set of cottage workshops, and the Spitfire was something it had not reckoned with.[6] A new set of production facilities was required to mass-produce it properly.

In 1936, the government had conceived the idea of building dedicated factories to 'shadow' aircraft production at existing works. On 15 July 1938 work began on building an entirely new works at Castle Bromwich near Birmingham under the supervision of Lord Nuffield's Morris Motor Works. Lord Nuffield and his men knew how to mass-produce cars, but knew nothing about aeroplanes. The project was plagued by changes to the production specification from the Air Ministry, the management's ignorance of aerospace technology and squabbles between the car unions and management over money.** Delays

---

* Corelli Barnett ruefully compares the 13,000 man-hours needed to make a Mk V airframe with the 4,000 for an Me 109G (*Audit of War*, p.148). The Spitfire also took two-and-a-half times as long to make as a Hurricane, though Barnett does not mention this. He is nevertheless correct that Willy Messerschmitt took production needs into account in his design. Mitchell took nothing except performance into account. This was one of the consequences. Maybe Mitchell would have done better to do so, but the advantages of his design over the 109 have also to be considered. Even German engineers would have had trouble with the wing, which allowed every Spitfire pilot to outturn any 109, and despite all the incompetence it could muster even British industry finally managed to make 22,000 Spitfires. Heinkel had rejected the elliptical wing after his experience with the He 70 because it was so difficult to manufacture in quantity. For a less tendentious account of the aircraft economies of all the war-time belligerents see Overy, op. cit., pp. 149–184, and for that of Britain Sebastian Ritchie, *Industry and Air Power*, Frank Cass 1997.

** Workers at Castle Bromwich ended up being paid far more than those at Southampton. This was not an isolated case of unions putting their interests before the war effort. In the period of Dunkirk there was a strike at a colliery and another at the A.V. Roe aircraft factory. In August 1940, the De Havilland aircraft factory at Edgware lost 4,426 days over 'the transfer of four capstan fitters from the firm to other work of national importance'. See Andrew Roberts, *Eminent Churchillians*, pp. 256–7.

continued into 1940, until, bullied by Lord Beaverbrook, Nuffield resigned. Beaverbrook put Vickers men in charge. To meet the June target of ten Spitfires, machines were surreptitiously transferred from Eastleigh. In July, Castle Bromwich finally succeeded in producing some itself, a modest twenty-three. In August it produced thirty-seven and in September fifty-six.[7]

From the introduction of the slightly more powerful Mk II in August, Spitfire production shifted steadily to Castle Bromwich. The vast majority that fought in the Battle of Britain, however, were Mk Is made at various works belonging to Supermarine and its sub-contractors which were arrayed around Southampton, on the vulnerable south coast.

Lord Beaverbrook's involvement was Churchill's idea. On 11 May 1940 he invited Beaverbrook to head up a Ministry of Aircraft Production, whereupon his Lordship forgot his misgivings about continuing the war and accepted. The new ministry reported directly to the War Cabinet and set priorities depending on the needs of the moment, which in 1940 was for fighters. Beaverbrook's main method seems to have been to bully people and then to claim the credit for what they achieved. His action with Lord Nuffield is one instance where these methods were successful. Others were less so. He sent teams of 'investigators' around the country to interview managers in the aircraft industry to see if they were up to their jobs. One of their victims was the General Manager of Supermarine, who had been dealing with, and overcoming, the problems of early Spitfire production. He was dismissed and shortly afterwards he shot himself.[8] It is at best unclear how this helped the war effort.

Beaverbrook was appointed in May. In June, fighter production rose and it continued to do so. It looked like magic. The two events succeeded each other, so a causal link suggested itself to many, at least to those who did not know what it takes to mass-produce entirely new products. Few people did know, and Beaverbrook had a marvellous marketing machine. It made him a hero. The many people who had actually solved the problems in the years and months before he appeared could not afford marketing men and did not own newspapers.[9]

By contrast, the German Air Ministry did not contain just one bully, but was full of them. It was also bureaucratic and run by party men who had no understanding of business economics. Constant minor modifications disrupted production runs, and on the basis of divide-and-rule, potential scale effects were left unexploited. Professional industrialists were kept at arm's length by the ideologues of the party and simply ordered about. Neither Volkswagen nor Opel were integrated into aircraft production until late in the war. Negotiations were drawn-out and when Opel finally agreed to co-operate, production orders were changed just after it had tooled up, and re-tooling had to begin.[10] The British innovation of shadow factories, whilst difficult to get started, gave it a major advantage as the war continued and was copied in the United States.[11]

In 1940 the Luftwaffe was stronger in relative terms to its enemies than it was ever to be again. The failure to exploit the industrial strength it possessed was due to dilatory amateurism on the part of its leaders. Fighter production plans were actually reduced between July and September, and thanks to the army's obstructing the transfer of resources, even they were not met. In the crucial field of single-engined fighter production, the British consistently out-produced Germany by well over two-to-one throughout the months of the Battle.

So it was that the Luftwaffe had to deliver its knock-out blow fast. With every passing month, its enemy was growing appreciably stronger. The British were desperate for time. When the Germans attacked France they faced the problem of keeping their existing forces intact whilst continuing to fight, and they also faced the uncertainty about how many fighters they needed to defend the country against an enemy who was getting far closer than anyone had expected.

In 1923, the then Secretary of State for Air, Sir Samuel Hoare, set out a programme to create a Metropolitan Air Force of fifty-two squadrons of all types.[12] It was never implemented. In the 1930s a whole succession of schemes came and went, based on the notion of 'air parity', whereby, in the words of Stanley Baldwin, 'air strength would not be allowed to fall below that of any continental power.'[13]

By 1938, in view of Germany's rising strength, a new scheme provided for forty-two home defence squadrons. Dowding said he would be satisfied with forty-one squadrons on whose presence he could rely. By the time the war broke out, the Air Ministry predicted the need for fifty-two. In May 1940, when discussing the question of whether to send more fighters to France, Sir Archibald Sinclair told the War Cabinet in May that home defence needed sixty squadrons, a figure confirmed by the CAS, Sir Cyril Newall. In June he said it needed fifty-seven. Dowding stuck to fifty-two.[14]

He had started sticking to it thirteen days after war broke out, when the Air Ministry decided to send four of the thirty-four squadrons then in existence to France, and talked about sending four more. They had thereby turned on what Dowding dubbed 'the Hurricane tap' and turning it off again was to consume much energy.[15] Dowding saw this as his mission, and pursued it with his usual single-mindedness, something which has obscured the role played by others in this difficult political and military issue.

The aircraft flowing from the tap were mainly Hurricanes, but initially included a few old Gladiator biplanes. This almost had fateful consequences, which were narrowly averted by the presence of mind of one of Dowding's pilots who came, by a curious set of circumstances, to be taking a Gladiator to France.

In early 1939, the celebrated Harry Broadhurst had taken over 111 Squadron from John Gillan. In common with most of the squadron, 'Sandy' Sanders took a dislike to his new C/O, whom he regarded as a prima donna, and having spent his childhood fighting for his rights against four beautiful sisters and his mother, all of whom he considered to be prima donnas, fighting prima donnas had become a bit of a habit. Broadhurst was an extremely good pilot, but his men disliked the way he would talk about his aerobatic skills, especially by doing a roll off the top of the loop on take-off, as he had done at the 1938 Hendon air display, in a machine with the guns removed to make it lighter. So one grey Sunday morning in September, Sandy took off in a Gauntlet with the guns still in it to do the same thing, just to show that anyone could do it. Unfortunately, the war had just started and a number of senior officers were arriving at Northolt for an important conference just as Sandy was carrying out his stunt. Himself a very experienced pilot, he completed an immaculate roll off the top of his loop in the unmodified aeroplane. When he landed, in recognition of his skill and sense of timing, Broadhurst put him under arrest.

He took him to the then AOC 11 Group, Air Vice-Marshal Gossage, to decide what to do with him. Gossage knew Sandy's mother, so he just asked the young pilot what he would like to do. Sandy replied that he would like to go to France. 'Off you go then,' the AOC replied. So, on 4 October 1939, Sanders was posted to 615 Squadron, which was earmarked for duty in France.

His punishment was what he had asked for, but it was in fact a double insult. Though an RAF regular, he had been posted to fly with auxiliaries. Also, despite being one of the most experienced Hurricane pilots in the RAF, this meant he had to fly Gladiators. However, he did go to France, for on 15 November 1939, 615 lined up at Croydon along with 607 Squadron to head for Merville. There was an official inspection before they left, and, appropriately enough, 615's Honorary Air Commodore, the First Lord of the Admiralty, Winston Churchill, turned up with his wife to see his boys safely off.

Gladiators were armed with two machine guns at the sides of the cockpit and one under each wing, at about waist height. These guns could only be cocked for action on the ground. The pneumatic system that operated them was unreliable and even rocking the wings could set them off. As 615 were escorting their ground crews in two Ensign aircraft, and were expecting to fly into action, they had their guns cocked.

Sandy was leading the flight, so Churchill and Clementine naturally chose his machine for a close inspection. Churchill being Churchill, he showed a particular interest in the guns. His wife being a woman[16] she sat in the cockpit asking 'what is this?' and 'what is that?'and as Churchill was bending over in front of the machine gun under the wing, she started fiddling with the firing mechanism. Fighter pilots need to have fast reactions, and Sandy was a very good fighter pilot. So it was that he may have saved the future Prime Minister from a premature demise at the hands of his spouse, and thereby changed the course of world history. The squadron took off and landed at Merville without further incident.[17]

At a meeting of the War Cabinet on 13 May 1940, Sinclair and Newall warned against sending any more squadrons to France in addition to the six which by then were already there. Churchill agreed. The Cabinet discussed whether or not to bomb Germany but Chamberlain and Sinclair feared reprisals against the British mainland, which they felt was weakly defended, so no raids were ordered.

That night, a telegram arrived from the BEF's Commander in France, Lord Gort, asking for more fighters. It was followed the next morning by a telegram from the French Prime Minister, Reynaud, asking for ten squadrons. Churchill was reluctant to respond, Newall warned that once they had left Britain the squadrons would never return, and so Churchill put Reynaud off with a vague message of support. Reynaud was not put off, and called Churchill at 7 a.m. on the morning of the 15 May, excitedly begging for assistance. Churchill reported this to the Chiefs of Staff meeting at 10.30 a.m. and summoned Dowding to hear his views. Dowding stressed the dangers if things were to go badly and urged that no more fighters be sent. At the War Cabinet meeting at 11 a.m., Churchill suggested bombing the Ruhr precisely in the hope of reprisals, as this might take the pressure off France and would enable Fighter Command to take on its enemy on its own terms.

At the Chiefs of Staff meeting the next day, 16 May, Newall read out a message from Gamelin pleading for the ten squadrons again and saying that without them, all was lost. This time, in view of the 'new and critical situation', he agreed to sending some and the other Chiefs of Staff agreed. Churchill thought it 'a very grave risk', but necessary in order to bolster the French. Newall thought four squadrons would do, Churchill suggested six, but Sinclair, referring to Dowding's comments the previous day, held that four was the maximum, and so it was decided, with two further squadrons held in readiness. That afternoon, Churchill left for France.

In France, Churchill was subjected to even more intense pleas. Churchill said he did not see that more fighters would make a difference but the French disagreed. In the end, Churchill wrote in his evening telegram to the War Cabinet that six extra squadrons should be sent to France in addition to the four agreed that morning, as it 'would not look good historically' if France should fall for lack of them. Colville found the telegram 'terrifying'. Newall decided to fulfil the request by having three squadrons fly out to French air-fields in the morning, return to England, and be relieved by another three in the afternoon. When he returned, Churchill made it clear that he expected a 'supreme effort' from the French in exchange for the air support offered.

In the meantime, Dowding had been at his desk hard at work. Deeply disturbed, he decided to put his thoughts down on paper. He composed a ten point memorandum for the Air Ministry, and sent it to the Air Council on 16 May. It has become one of the most celebrated documents in RAF history.

Addressed to the Under Secretary of State for Air, Harold Balfour, Dowding's two-page memorandum expressed the hope that victory might yet be gained in France, but assumed that if it were not, Britain would fight on. He reminded the Air Ministry that they had agreed that fifty-two squadrons would be needed for home defence, rather than the thirty-six then available. He pointedly demanded a statement 'as to the limit on which the Air Council and the Cabinet are prepared to stake the existence of the country' and that this limit then be rigorously adhered to, pointing out that the estimate of fifty-two assumed that attacks could only be launched at the east from across the North Sea, not on the whole south coast from just over the Channel. He repeated that ten squadrons had already gone to France and that the home defences were already depleted. He concluded:

> I believe that if an adequate fighter force is kept in this country, and if the Fleet remains in being, and if the home forces are suitably organised to resist invasion, we should be able to carry on the war single-handed for some time, if not indefinitely. But if the home defence force is drained away in desperate attempts to remedy the situation in France, defeat in France will involve the final, complete and irremediable defeat of this country.[18]

Newall wrote a note about the subject, appended Dowding's document to it and circulated it to his fellow Chiefs of Staff. They discussed it and converted it into a report of their own. It thereby had the official backing of Britain's most senior military leaders. The Air Council replied to Dowding a week later. They did not answer his questions, but asked him to prepare to cover an evacuation and to dispose his home forces so as to protect the aircraft industry in particular.[19]

On 19 May, Dowding's opposite number at Bomber Command, Air Chief Marshal Sir Edgar Ludlow-Hewitt, had a late-night conference with Churchill. Following that meeting Churchill issued a minute in which he stated that no more squadrons would leave Britain whatever the need in France. It had become clear that the BEF might well have to be evacuated and that if this were to happen, strong air cover would be needed. This cover could best be provided from Britain. In addition, Churchill pushed for the formation of an additional ten fighter squadrons from the training schools.

This note provoked an angry response from Churchill's own scientific adviser, Professor Lindemann. He felt that the war would be decided in France and that every risk should be taken to strengthen the French cause. But Churchill stuck by his decision, saying so to the War Cabinet the next morning.[20]

This decision was undoubtedly correct. The fighters would have made no difference in France, but did make a big difference in Britain. The French did not need them anyway, because they had plenty of their own. After the war, the French government looked into the question and found that large numbers of French fighters had been held in storage units. The French Air Force Commander, General Vuillemin, testified that at the end of hostilities he had more aircraft available than at the beginning.[21] Colville records that in the summer of 1941, Churchill and Sinclair agreed that the French had acted shamefully in calling for more fighters when they knew all was lost.[22]

Dowding's anxiety was partly due to his lack of faith in the French air defences, something he had made clear in correspondence with Newall in 1939.[23] He had inspected them in 1939 and formed a dim view of their capabilities.[24] He knew that no Hurricane sent out there would come back.

The drama nevertheless continued during and after the Dunkirk evacuation. Dowding was reluctant to use his full strength over Dunkirk, and backed Churchill in resisting further French demands thereafter. In the emotionally charged meetings in France in which he tried to persuade the French to stay in the war, Churchill had to argue his case alone, and he was not helped by the changing estimates of actual and required strength which emanated from the Air Ministry. The War Cabinet discussed the issue again on 3 June, with the Chiefs of Staff recommending that no more than six bomber and three fighter squadrons be allowed to operate from French airfields. Dowding was called in and produced a graph showing fighter wastage in France. He stressed how difficult it would be to build up the home defence force as it was. Were Hurricanes to continue to be expended at the rate they had been from 8–18 May, he claimed, there would be none left at all by the end of the month. His case was unanswerable.

Churchill nevertheless raised the matter again the next day, pointing out that there were now forty-five squadrons in Britain as against twenty-nine a few weeks before. Beaverbrook's Ministry of Aircraft Production had managed to greatly increase output. Sinclair argued that Fighter Command had become disorganised and that there was now a pilot shortage, which was a bolt from the blue. Faced with another demand from Reynaud, whom he was desperately trying to keep in the fight, Churchill called together his senior airmen, including Dowding, on the morning of 5 June, saying that they had to do something. Dowding stuck to his guns.

They had barely finished their meeting when another message arrived, this time from Vuillemin, demanding another ten squadrons immediately and a further ten as soon as possible. Churchill sent out a delaying message in return.

On the evening of 6 June, Reynaud's personal representative in London, Jean Monnet, came to appeal to Churchill in person. By this time, the British had had enough. They began to suspect that it was a ploy to blame them for the French defeat. Churchill argued that the equivalent of twelve squadrons had been operating over France the previous day. The final decision was taken at a Defence Committee meeting on 8 June. The question now, Churchill opined, was one of survival. He wrote to Reynaud that any additional British fighters sent to France could only be a make-weight. 'We believe,' he wrote, 'that if we do not, by an act of strategic folly, leave ourselves utterly defenceless, Hitler will break his air weapon in trying to invade us.' Henceforth, they would keep their fighters in Britain, for if properly used there they would 'enable us to break his air attack, and thus break him.' 'That,' he added, 'is what we are going to try.'

The final French plea came on Churchill's final visit to France on 11 June. It was a pathetic and anguished meeting, continuing the following day. Despite enormous political, moral and emotional pressure, Churchill did not cede a single fighter. Four days later, on 16 June, General Pétain asked Germany for an armistice.[25]

Halifax visited Dowding at Bentley Priory a few days later, and told him what had just happened. Dowding got up and looked out of the window, then turned round and said: 'Thank God we're now alone.'[26]

Dowding had acted out of deep conviction and was totally obdurate in his pursuit of a principle. He also felt that he was fighting a lone battle. He was worried that his boss, Newall, would give way, and assumed that the Air Ministry were against him. He was quite wrong about both. The War Cabinet and the Chiefs of Staff had to weigh up the balance in which the stakes were very high – they could not afford to have their main ally make a separate peace because they lacked a few fighters. Churchill's agony of mind can be imagined. Dowding did not have his responsibilities and never had to face Paul Reynaud. However, Dowding's stubborn defence of his principle was important in strengthening the resolve of the decision-makers. Had he wavered, the 'final, complete and irremediable defeat of this country' could have followed.

In the meantime, Churchill was pursuing Sinclair over his remark about being short of pilots. Writing to him on the evening of the cabinet meeting, Churchill said it was 'the first time this particular admission of failure had been made by the Air Ministry'. Until then, he said, they had heard only that there were thousands of pilots for whom there were no machines. Following Beaverbrook's success in 'clearing up the muddle and scandal of the aircraft production branch', Churchill hoped that his old friend Sinclair could do the same on the personnel side.[27]

This brief missive set off a flurry of activity at the Air Ministry which was to go on for weeks as anxious civil servants tried to explain to Sinclair the meaning of the numbers they had given him, and Churchill tried to get some action. Fighter Command was expanding, and new squadrons were being formed for which pilots had to be found. The training organisation was pushed to keep up. However, the main reason for the shortage was that it had been decided to create one. Once the fighting began in earnest in May, Dowding decided to raise the establishment number of pilots on a squadron from twenty-one to twenty-six in order to give them all more of a chance to rest. At a stroke of his pen, Fighter Command became under-strength.

When Sinclair explained all this to the Prime Minister in his reply on 5 June, Churchill homed in on the resources devoted to training and the output being delivered. As production got into gear over the summer, the lag in pilot output grew worse, as freshly painted Hurricanes and Spitfires stood idle. Whereas Fighter Command's expansion had previously been constrained by lack of machines, pilots had now become the bottleneck. Sinclair busied himself trying to increase the throughput of the training organisation by shortening certain parts of the courses.

After he had got back to Churchill on this, Churchill replied on 18 July saying that the training methods were good and should not be interfered with too much, but he was then on to something else. 'According to figures that have recently been furnished by your department, only three out of every ten pilots with Wings are operational,' he observed. 'Of the remaining seven, two are pilots with Wings still under instruction, two are instructors and the rest are air staff, administrative, technical or those with other non-operational duties.' In other words, 30% of the RAF's trained pilots were flying desks. Churchill said he would be grateful if Sinclair were to give the matter his 'earnest consideration'.[28]

This unleashed a frenzy of data-gathering and analysis. The analysis produced paralysis, prompting Churchill to write again on 9 August, just as the Battle was about to begin in earnest, asking what was going on and demanding a reply the following day. There followed some strained correspondence.

Dowding had, for his part, been badgering to get pilots from Bomber Command and the Fleet Air Arm, with some success, and foreign pilots were being taught English as fast as possible. Churchill was still convinced that more could be found, and he vented his frustration in a note to Sinclair on 25 August when he said that he had with his own eyes seen 'enormous numbers' of pilots in staff roles walking around at Hendon, and that Sinclair's 'dominant idea' should be 'strength for battle'. He thought Hendon could provide two squadrons for a start. He urged Sinclair to comb and comb and to question every non-military activity in the RAF: 'The tendency of every station commander is naturally to keep as much in his hands as possible. The admirals do the same. Even when you have had a thorough search if you look around a few weeks later you will see more fat has gathered.'[29]

The results of such vigilance are reflected in the figures.

Force strength, the number of aircraft available to each side, can be given in terms of first-line strength or serviceable strength. The former is the number of aircraft available in front-line units. Because at any given time some aircraft will be being overhauled, serviced or repaired in those front-line units, the actual number of aircraft available to fly on combat duty at any given time is smaller than this. They may develop small engine faults, mechanical problems or instrument problems and so be out of action for a day or a few hours. The number of serviceable aircraft varies literally by the hour, even when the unit is not in action. When the unit is involved in intense action, the number varies even more. After a major day of action, a large number of aircraft are rendered unserviceable, but come back into the line over the next few days. That is why large reserves had to be available to make sustained action possible. The German Fighter Commander Theo Osterkamp used the rule of thumb that in peace-time, 90% of aircraft at the front were serviceable, in war-time, 75%.[30] Reports were filed every day.

At the outbreak of war, the comparative strengths of the German and British air forces were as follows:[31]

	First-Line Strength	Serviceable Aircraft	Serviceability Rate (%)	Reserves	Total First-Line and Reserves
Germany	3,609	2,893	80%	900	4,509
Britain	1,911	1,600	84%	2,200	4,111
British strength as % of German	53%	55%		244%	91%

These figures are for all types of aircraft, including transports. 'Reserves' are aircraft held at depots or aircraft storage units ready for delivery to squadrons, but not actually in service. They show how the Luftwaffe put as much as it could into the front-line, which, with a comparable serviceability rate, gave it almost double the immediate battlefield strength of the RAF. It needed it, for it had first to deal with the 400 aircraft of the Polish Air Force and then the 1,800 of the French. However, if the war were to be long, the RAF's strength in reserves would allow it to almost make up the balance.

Once the war began, these numbers quickly changed. Given the spectacular nature of Germany's rapid victories over Poland and France, it tends to be assumed that it suffered few losses. However, in Poland the Luftwaffe had 285 aircraft destroyed and 279 damaged, a total of 564, or 20% of its serviceable machines. Although this was a small price to pay for such a decisive victory, it was still a weakening which had to be made good if the far more powerful enemies in the West were to be subdued. The Polish Air Force lost 333 aircraft, which effectively wiped it out, but in terms of aircraft destroyed alone, it is only

48 more than the Luftwaffe.[32] Many of the Luftwaffe's machines were lost to ground fire and accidents, for it was used to support the army as well as to defeat the Poles in the air. Intensive operations of any kind, even if highly successful, cause considerable attrition, at a rate everyone had underestimated at the time.

Before embarking on the main attack on France and the Low Countries, the Luftwaffe supported the Norwegian operation in April 1940, a completely successful campaign which nevertheless cost them 260 aircraft, as against 169 for the British.[33] Once again, many losses were suffered because the Luftwaffe, unlike the RAF, had such a wide variety of support tasks, and seventy-nine of the total were accidents. The overall impact of steady low-level attrition may be judged by the fact that between the outbreak of war and the beginning of the French campaign, the Luftwaffe lost a total of 1,460 aircraft and suffered damage to another 1,074. In other words, they had had to replace or substantially repair 88% of the machines operational at the outbreak of war before the 'real' war even began. Over 40% of these losses were suffered in training.[34] Making them good was hampered by material shortages, particularly of steel, but front-line strength had been increased by over 20% (822 aircraft) by March 1940. However, as usual reserves were not built up, and serviceability fell to 70%.[35]

The brief but fierce campaign in France brought a sudden dramatic increase in attrition for both sides. The Luftwaffe assigned some 2,750 aircraft to the campaign and were opposed by about 1,200 French and 416 British machines, giving them a numerical superiority of about 3:2 in force strength.[36] However, they enjoyed a significant technical lead and as they had the initiative and could choose the point of combat, they usually had a far greater numerical superiority in the air.

Overall, the campaign in the West which began on 10 May cost the Luftwaffe 1,428 aircraft destroyed – about half its operational strength – and another 488 damaged. The RAF lost 959 aircraft, half of which were fighters.[37] The RAF withdrew, licking its wounds, with Dowding issuing grim warnings and all expecting a massive blow to fall almost immediately. That it did not is partly because the Luftwaffe was barely capable of delivering it. The losses had been incurred in a short space of time, and whereas the British were able to rebuild their critical defensive strength by concentrating all their efforts on fighter production, the Germans had to re-stock their bomber units as well as the fighters to create the balanced offensive capability required.

This was just as well, for the RAF's withdrawal had not been orderly. A lot of aircraft and equipment were abandoned as airfields were hurriedly evacuated and many pilots only just made it. 615 Squadron operated from four aerodromes in eleven days, and Sandy Sanders only just made it. On a patrol near the Franco-Belgian border he shot down a Do 17 but was hit by return fire and crash-landed near Valenciennes, suffering a severe blow to the head which almost knocked him out. Despite being half-concussed, he made for the station and got a train, but it was attacked near Béthune, so he got out and walked into the town with his parachute on his back. He met a German tank coming the other way, so he left his parachute in a doorway and hitched a lift to Abbeville in an RAF lorry. There at about 2 a.m. he found a long-nosed Blenheim bomber parked on the edge of the aerodrome. He had never flown a Blenheim or any other twin-engined aircraft before, but he nevertheless decided to use it to try and get back to England. The night was pitch black. There were no lights in the aircraft, there was no flare-path, he could not see the instrument panel and he did not know where the starter buttons were. While Sandy was fumbling around in the dark, a number of other people had hopped on board the three-man Blenheim before he managed to find what he was after and take off. He was in fine pitch, the undercarriage was locked down, and he could not do more than 110 mph or get above 700 feet.

He did not know how much petrol he had, but he made for his old station at Northolt, came in over the Western Avenue and landed safely in semi-darkness just short of the mess at about 3.15 a.m. As his grateful passengers got out, he went to find the duty officer. There was nobody there. The whole airfield was deserted. So he got on the phone and a WAAF answered. He asked for the Station Commander, only to be told that he was not to be woken before 8 a.m. After all he had just experienced, and with his head still throbbing, Sandy became quite vociferous and told her to put him through. When the Station Commander answered, Sandy went for him. 'How dare you!' he said. 'Do you realise that I've just landed and there's not a soul around and we could have been the Germans?' 'Do you realise who you are talking to?' asked the Station Commander. 'I don't care,' came the reply. 'What do you mean by saying you are not to be disturbed until 8 a.m.? Do you think the Germans are going to wait until you're out of bed?' So Sandy was put under arrest again for showing lack of respect and insubordination.

As before, he was sent to see the AOC the same morning, 20 May. He ordered a car and sent Sandy down to join up with a few Gladiators based at Manston. After rejoining his squadron, he flew continuously during what remained the Battle of France and the Dunkirk evacuation. He had a close call on 22 June when, after an eventful sweep over northern France, he landed on a farmer's field on the clifftops near Ventnor on the Isle of Wight after a wave-top flight across the Channel in thick fog. He took off again with the assistance of some locals who helped him to refuel with car petrol and then held the tail of his Hurricane down while he opened the throttle. When they let go he went up like a lift and flew to Kenley. This second escape from France called for all the experience he had gained on Hurricanes from his days at 111. A novice would never have managed it. It was a sign of what was to become brutally clear over the weeks to come: that flying and fighting experience meant the difference between life and death.

By the beginning of July, the opposing air forces had the following numbers of aircraft at front-line units:[38]

	Luftwaffe	RAF
Single-seater fighters	1,107	754
Two-seater fighters	357	149
Bombers	1,380	560
Dive-bombers	428	0
Reconnaissance	569	–[39]
Coastal	233	500
Total	4,074[40]	1,963

Of the British single-seater fighters, 546, or 72%, were serviceable. The Luftwaffe's serviceability rate for the end of June is unknown, but on 11 May, when the French campaign opened, it was 73%.[41] This tallies with Osterkamp's rule of thumb for a wartime air force, so it was probably about 75% when the Battle opened. British rates were low in the aftermath of Dunkirk, with a lot of replacement aircraft having faults ironed out. Overall, the Luftwaffe was over twice as strong.

With some 1,000 aircraft in Bomber and Coastal Commands, the RAF had the capacity to hit back at its assailant in kind, but the structure of the RAF shows how, despite the strategic bombing doctrine, it had in fact become relatively stronger in fighters than in bombers.

The defensive battle during the day would effectively pit the 48 squadrons of 754 Hurricanes and Spitfires against 1,464 fighters and 1,808 bombers. The British fighter pilots, from that point of view, were outnumbered by almost four and a half to one. In comparing like with like, however, the Hurricanes and Spitfires would be taking on 1,107 Bf 109s, a ratio of one and a half to one. Most of the other aircraft in the sky (including the Bf 110s) were potential victims. From the Luftwaffe's point of view, its fighters had to cripple their opponents with a numerical superiority of 3:2, which is a narrow margin on which to stake a bid for air superiority. There was little room for mistakes.

All of this deals with relative force strength. It has nothing to do with strength in the air. The Luftwaffe could choose to use any number of their aircraft on any one raid, and the British long believed they were holding back up to half their bombers.[42] The British could also choose what numbers to send up to engage any raid. Subject to the constraint of one side having to commit all its forces at any time, relative strength in the air was a matter of choice.

From the point of view of a British fighter pilot, the odds were daunting. When he was scrambled to meet a large formation, the only friendly aircraft he saw were his dozen or so companions. Squadrons like this might often wade into formations of 100 or 150 bombers and fighters, and the Germans always seemed to have more of them. He did not see what happened before or after the ten minutes or so of frantic fighting in which he was usually engaged, and did not know whether in the course of the hour it spent over England, the hostile formation might itself be attacked by a total of 100 or 150 British fighters. He just knew that he was up against it, and this, the feeling that things depended on him and his few pals, acted as a spur to his efforts. Like most soldiers, he had no idea of the overall shape of the battle he was engaged in. He had to keep going up, because there seemed to be nobody else.

8. SEALION

W hen the last British ships carrying soldiers back to England pulled away
from Dunkirk on the afternoon of 4 June, they left the Germans masters of the Channel coast. Whilst the Germans found this very agreeable, it also
left them with the problem of having to decide what to do about what the
Luftwaffe's Chief of Intelligence had called their most dangerous enemy.

The parlous state of the British army recommended swift action. It was at
its weakest in June immediately after the Dunkirk evacuation, and grew steadily
stronger from then on.[1] Despite this, such an undertaking, using airborne
forces, would have been extremely risky.[2] If the paratroops had been got across
the Channel, they would have to have been re-supplied, either by sea or by air,
and it is doubtful whether this was at all feasible. Nevertheless, one historian has
reconstructed a possible course of action which could have given the Germans
victory in July. It depended on the Luftwaffe being able to saturate the invasion
area in order to gain local air superiority for a critical period, and on the British
Admiralty being unwilling to fully commit the Royal Navy because of the need
to keep the fleet in being as a bargaining counter in the case of negotiations.[3] If
achieved, it would have been a victory against the odds, and so the German
General Staff judged it at the time. It was never seriously considered.

Whatever its military chances of success, the preparations actually made
for an invasion were politically serious and involved considerable cost to the
German economy. They were always planned as a contingency, dependent on
the outcome of the Luftwaffe's efforts. The chances of an invasion being successful critically depended on the achievement of air superiority over the
invasion area. Preparing for invasion was in many ways an inviting course to
take, for it was the line of least resistance.

Overall German strategy was directed by the Supreme Command of the
Armed Forces (Oberkommando der Wehrmacht or OKW), of which Hitler,
backed up by Generals Keitel and Jodl, was the C-in-C. To them reported the
three services. The Army High Command (Oberkommando des Heeres or

OKH) was headed by Field Marshal von Brauchitsch, whose Chief of Staff, General Fritz Halder, kept a valuable diary detailing much of what went on. The Navy High Command (Oberkommando der Marine, OKM) was headed by Admiral Raeder and the Luftwaffe High Command (Oberkommando der Luftwaffe or OKL) was, nominally at least, run by Göring. As his deputy, Milch attended all the important meetings, but Göring saw the attack on England as his battle, and he generally worked directly with Kesselring and Sperrle.

The overall direction for the Battle of Britain and the invasion planning was determined by two directives, one from OKW and one from Hitler (No. 17), issued on 1 August. The timetable of meetings and decisions leading up to them ran in parallel with a steady intensification of the fighting in the air.

22 June: France surrendered and Hitler issued a ban on the Luftwaffe flying over British airspace in order not to provoke her.[4] Göring ordered the Luftwaffe to engage the RAF wherever they were met, including over the Channel, but not to cross it.

30 June: Jodl issued his paper on the continuation of the war against Britain. Halder had a meeting with the Secretary of State at the Foreign Office, von Weizsäcker, in which von Weizsäcker told him that Hitler's attention was directed firmly towards the east. As she had as yet made no concrete peace proposals, England would probably need a further demonstration of military power before coming round. This was the first indication that Hitler was thinking about Russia. The difficulties, Halder noted, lay less in the present situation than in the future, for the maintenance of hostilities would inevitably lead to an overstretching of Germany's resources.[5]

1 July: General Halder met the Chief of the Naval Staff, Admiral Schniewind. They both thought that air superiority was needed and speculated hopefully that that might suffice in itself. Schniewind stressed the importance of the weather, and they agreed the threat from British surface ships could be limited by using minefields and U-boats. Both men appear to have departed satisfied that they had understood one another. They had not.[6]

2 July: OKW issued a request (signed by Keitel), to submit planning documents for an invasion, stating that the Führer had decided that a landing in England could be a viable option under certain circumstances, the most important of which was establishing air superiority. The Luftwaffe's submission was to specify whether and by when 'decisive air superiority' could be achieved.[7]

4 July: Made aware by von Weizsäcker that Russia could be on the agenda and anxious not to be caught napping by a sudden demand for plans, Halder gave General Marcks, the Chief of the General Staff of the 18th Army, the job of putting some first ideas together about how the Soviet Union could be attacked. He then heard a report about the Luftwaffe's preparations for the attack on England. The goals were to destroy the RAF, its supply system and aircraft production and, as a secondary goal, to damage the Royal Navy. The British were said to have a good early-warning system, but to be outnumbered by about two to one.[8]

11 July: Admiral Raeder visited Hitler at the Berghof, his chalet in the Bavarian Alps near Berchtesgaden. Raeder's main aim was to win Hitler over to a siege, arguing that a concentrated air attack on the British mainland and combined air and U-boat attacks on Britain's sea-lanes would be the best way to make her sue for peace. He argued that invasion should be a last resort. Hitler agreed.

OKH met again to discuss England and hear a further report from the Luftwaffe. It was estimated that air superiority would take fourteen to twenty-eight days to achieve. For the first time, it was mentioned that England was thought to be approaching Russia over an agreement about Iran. This was the first indication of the line of thought Hitler was to develop that England only continued to resist because she expected help from the Russians. The Germans may have got wind of a letter Churchill wrote to Stalin on 25 June, which did not mention Iran and went unanswered.[9]

12 July: Jodl issued a memorandum for what he called Operation Löwe (Lion), which, to the annoyance of the navy, he described as 'a river-crossing on a broad front'.[10] This was a notion that was seductive to the army, but rivers are not tidal, not subject to violent storms and are generally not patrolled by the enemy's High Seas Fleet.

13 July: Hitler met von Brauchitsch and Halder, who had prepared detailed plans for an assault by 39 divisions, about 500,000 men. Unsurprisingly, the army were confident of success if the navy could give them the sea transport they required. Hitler authorised further preparations on this basis, and then held forth about grand strategy, explaining that he did not want to inflict a military defeat on Britain, as this would mean the end of her empire and that would bring no benefit to Germany but only to Japan and the United States. He was puzzled by the continued lack of peace proposals from the British, and thought this must be because they were putting their hope in Russia. Recalling his earlier decision to reduce the strength of the army by thirty-five divisions in order to make manpower available for the economy, Hitler scaled down the reduction to fifteen divisions.[11]

16 July: Hitler issued Directive No. 16. It opened thus:

> As England, despite the hopelessness of her military situation, has so far shown herself unwilling to come to any compromise, I have there-fore decided to begin preparations for, and if necessary to carry out, an invasion of England.
>
> The aim of this operation is to eliminate Great Britain as a base from which the war against Germany can be fought, and, if necessary, the island will be completely occupied.

The invasion was to be planned on a broad front. Preparations were to be ready by mid-August, and were to include the moral and physical weakening of the RAF to the point that it could offer no serious opposition to the landing. The army plan formed the basis of the Directive, albeit with the front shortened to Ramsgate-Isle of Wight. The navy was to furnish an invasion fleet and protect it. The Luftwaffe was to prevent the RAF from intervening, attack coastal strong-points, break initial resistance on the ground and destroy reserves. In addition, it was to disrupt communications and attack British surface vessels before they reached the invasion area. Hitler demanded plans to be submitted at the earliest opportunity showing how this was to be achieved.

Hitler gave this operation the new name of 'Seelöwe'(Sealion).[12]

One might be forgiven for thinking that the Luftwaffe was to defeat Britain by itself, leaving the navy to run a ferry service and the army to walk ashore and mop up anything left. Göring and his commanders ignored the Directive, as they were more interested in their own plans which were being made in parallel, and thought an invasion unlikely anyway. The navy thought Hitler and OKW were out of their minds. On 19 July, Raeder sent a long memorandum to OKW, moaning that the Directive placed an unfair burden on the navy relative to the other two services – which was nonsense – and pointing out that the task allotted to it was way beyond its capabilities – which was quite true.[13]

21 July: Two days after his Reichstag speech, Hitler held his first proper joint services conference in Berlin, attended by Raeder, von Brauchitsch and the Luftwaffe Chief of Staff, Jeschonnek.

Hitler seems to have done most of the talking. He said that the English were stupid not to negotiate. They were probably trying to use Russia to create trouble in the Balkans and cut off Germany's oil supplies. The news via Washington was that the British considered their own position to be hopeless, and the British Ambassador in Washington regarded the war as lost. The group discussed the possibility of a Cabinet consisting of Lloyd George, Chamberlain and Halifax.[14]

Hitler then stated that he needed to clear up the question of whether a direct operation could bring England to her knees and how long it would take. An invasion, he said, was very hazardous. What about air assaults and submarine warfare? They would have to take effect by mid-September. Jeschonnek suggested that they should launch a large-scale attack on the RAF, lure their fighters into the sky and shoot them down. Raeder gave no clear answer. What did become clear was that the 'river-crossing' idea was nonsense and that it would be impossible to achieve surprise. It was also clear that the navy could not meet the mid-August deadline for completing preparations. Hitler asked Raeder to go away and tell him how long the navy would need to get ready. He wanted the air assault to begin in early August and to launch the invasion on about 25 August if the Luftwaffe were successful. By the autumn the weather would in any case be a prohibitive factor.

Hitler then turned to his main topic, which he had convinced himself was a related one: Russia. The Russian problem had to be dealt with. Halder had already prepared some preliminary thoughts on the strength of forces needed to eliminate the Red Army. Detailed plans were to be prepared.[15]

25 July: the ban on flying over England was lifted.[16] The navy had been at work on what they saw as their main task, namely torpedoing the army's plans. Raeder accordingly saw Hitler again to assure him that every effort was being made to complete preparations by the end of August, but that the results were highly uncertain. Hitler set up a conference for when Raeder could produce a plan, 31 July.

28 July: Raeder launched his torpedo. Its explosion at OKH caused much consternation. The navy announced that ferrying the first wave of troops across would take ten days, even if the landing were conducted on a far narrower front than planned. 'If that is true,' recorded Halder, 'all previous navy statements are a lot of nonsense and a landing is not possible at all.'[17] The planning started again, on the basis of different assumptions.

29 July: an angry General Halder prepared a counter-attack on the navy, claiming that their statements about the transport problem were rubbish and demanding a new plan.

More gratifyingly, the Luftwaffe reported that it would be ready for a major assault by the end of the week. They were expecting an attrition rate of about 10% per month, which they could cope with. There followed a resumé of Oberst Beppo Schmid's intelligence report on the RAF, which gave cause for confidence that a 'decisive result' could be achieved. About 50% of the Luftwaffe's bomber strength was to be used in the air campaign, the rest held in reserve to support the invasion.[18]

30 July: Halder listened to a report about a meeting held with the navy in Berlin the previous day. It was the usual tale of woe. The recommendation was to wait until the following May when the new battleships *Bismarck* and *Tirpitz* would be ready.

In view of all this, OKH considered their options. They could either postpone the invasion into the period of poor weather or wait until the following spring, but they would thereby lose the initiative. Alternatively, they could attack British colonies in the Mediterranean and North Africa, or just wait and lay siege to the island. They concluded that the best option would be to stay friendly with Russia and prepare for a long war against England.[19]

31 July: Raeder, von Brauchitsch and Halder arrived at the Berghof. The Luftwaffe was conspicuous by its absence. Raeder reported that the conversion of the Rhine barges needed as transport would take until 15 September, and that the only days on which a landing could be contemplated in 1940 were 22–26 September, when unfortunately the weather was usually bad. Only a narrow front landing could be contemplated. All in all, it would be best to wait until the spring of 1941.

Hitler considered that in view of the growing strength of the British army, the September date should be adhered to. If the Luftwaffe were successful the invasion should take place. A naval memorandum of 30 July stated quite clearly that the invasion could not be protected against the Royal Navy and that, critically, resupply could not be guaranteed during the autumn weather. The Kriegsmarine wanted to kill Sealion completely.

Raeder left, and Hitler agreed with his army commanders that the air offensive would begin around 5 August and he would decide whether or not to launch the invasion in the current year some eight to fourteen days thereafter. 'Something', he said, 'must have happened in London. The English were right "down" *(the text uses the English word)* but now they seemed to have got up again.' Smashing Russia would deprive England of her last hope. Russia must be knocked out in the spring of 1941.[20]

1 August: Hitler issued Directive No. 17 and OKW issued a further directive going into more detail.

Directive 17 announced that Hitler had decided to intensify the air and sea war against England in order to create the pre-conditions for her final defeat. He ordered the Luftwaffe to 'overcome the British air force with all means at its disposal and in the shortest possible time'. The targets were the flying units, their ground organisation and observation apparatus, and the aircraft and radio industry. They were then to concentrate on attacking ports through which food was imported and internal food stocks. As the opportunity arose, shipping was also to be attacked. The Luftwaffe was at all events to ensure that it remained sufficiently strong itself to subsequently support the invasion. Hitler reserved to himself the right to order terror attacks on civilians in retaliation for any launched against Germany. The air assault was to be launched on 5 August or as soon thereafter as weather permitted.[21]

As Directive 17 shows, the issue of decision versus siege had not been resolved. All were agreed that establishing air superiority was the pre-requisite of everything else, and the Luftwaffe was left to get on with it. The navy hoped it would fail and the army awaited events. Everybody hoped that air action alone would be decisive, as Göring expected it to be, which was why Sealion did not interest him very much. The Luftwaffe's plans were designed to bring Britain to the negotiating table with or without an invasion.

Perhaps the Kriegsmarine assessed Sealion's prospects most realistically. They were in awe of the Royal Navy. Liddell Hart reports that many German naval officers thought the war was lost on 3 September 1939, when Britain declared war on them.[22] Admiral Raeder fatalistically opined in a memorandum issued on the outbreak of war that the German navy was 'so inferior in numbers and strength to the British fleet that, even at full strength, they can do no more than show they know how to die gallantly . . .'[23] His predictions proved to be correct.

By July 1940, the German navy had already lost one pocket battleship, three cruisers and ten destroyers (all during the 'phoney war'). Its two battleships were still being fitted out, its two battlecruisers had been torpedoed and were being repaired and its remaining two pocket battleships were also in dock under repair. There were one heavy cruiser, three light cruisers and nine destroyers left. The Royal Navy had five battleships, one aircraft carrier, ten cruisers and fifty-seven destroyers in home waters alone, with more on escort duty, and a powerful Mediterranean fleet which could be used as reinforcement.[24] Small wonder Raeder quailed at the prospect of protecting a fleet of fragile river barges.

It is tempting but idle to speculate about whether Sealion could have succeeded. Historians have argued both sides of the case.* However, it can be assessed as a plan.

The best that can be said for Sealion is that it was a terrible gamble. Everything had to go right: the three services had to co-operate very closely; the RAF had to be neutralised, the Royal Navy had to be deterred by mines, U-boats and air attack (bearing in mind that the Luftwaffe had only a handful of obsolete He 115 torpedo-bombers and did not have a bomb heavy enough to penetrate the deck armour of the British battleships); and the weather had to be benign. The river barges taking the troops across were to be towed in pairs by tugs and could make about three knots. They would be swamped by anything more than a light swell, which was up to force 2.[25] When one compares these preparations with the effort the Allies put into conducting the operation in reverse four years later, it is hard to see Sealion as anything other than a plan of desperation. By the time they landed in Normandy in June 1944, the Allies had carried out five combined-operations sea landings, spent a year planning, and had complete air and sea supremacy. Admittedly, they faced far more formidable defences, but they had secured for themselves every advantage an attacker could have. Still they thought it risky. Only a decisive victory in the air could have given Sealion any prospect of success. All depended on the other part of the plan – the Luftwaffe's Eagle assault.

* In his *Britain Invaded*, Century 1990, Adrian Gilbert reconstructs a scenario ending in a German victory. Fighter Command is exhausted in July and is forced to abandon forward airfields. The Germans get ashore, despite heavy naval losses, and use the captured airfields for re-supply. The Luftwaffe successfully counters RAF opposition and prevents the Royal Navy from seriously disrupting the supply lines. The Wehrmacht gains a ground victory so quickly that the British government is forced to capitulate. In *Operation Sealion*, Thornton Cox 1975, Richard Cox gives an account of a war game in which re-supply fails, the Royal Navy does intervene and a German bridgehead is contained, forcing its surrender.

9. EAGLE

Fighting a battle is without doubt the messiest of all human activities. That is why military professionals put so much emphasis on order and planning. Plans always get disordered, in part because that is what the other side is there for, and to some extent they will always succeed.

Many old soldiers subscribe to the 'cock-up' theory of war, which maintains that the side which wins just does as little as possible, so that not much can go wrong, and waits for the other lot to cock it up. If anything is organised it will produce a cock-up and is therefore counter-productive.

There is a touch of hyperbole about this, but the cock-up theory has a lot going for it. History suggests that winning plans are very simple and that battles are lost rather than won. The winners make fewer mistakes than the losers.

Let it not be thought that this belittles generals. Given every army's inherent disposition towards them, preventing cock-ups requires enormous skill, energy and determination. Great generals avoid becoming exposed to them in the first place. Good plans minimise cock-up potential, which comes in various forms.

The first kind is ignorance. Ignorance is inherent and tends to increase as a battle progresses. Nobody can have a look around the other side of the hill, but a general can try to find out as much as possible about the enemy's strength, dispositions and intentions. What he does not find out before hostilities commence will be even harder to find out afterwards. In battle, units will get mixed up, rendezvous will be missed, and friendly troops will fire on each other. A plan which relies on this not happening will go wrong.

The second is the uncertainty produced by factors beyond control, which is also inherent. The greatest uncertainty is the weather. Rain can change firm cavalry or tank ground into impassable mud. Cold can freeze weapons and soldiers. High seas can swamp landing craft, storms can wreck harbours, wind can blow bombers off course, clouds can obscure targets. Good plans are robust enough to work under any conditions.

The third is complexity. The more complex a plan is, the more likely it is to break down under pressure, the critical element being communications. A chain of interdependent timed events will usually break. If the air force is to bomb enemy positions, then the artillery put down smoke, then the tanks clear the minefields, then the engineers blow up the bunkers, then the infantry go in, something will go wrong, e.g. the air force will take off late and bomb the tanks. Not only does complexity need to be minimised, but communications should be so robust that everyone can find out if there is a change of plan. Even so, someone will forget to tell somebody.

The fourth is equipment. It will either be at the wrong place at the right time or the right place at the wrong time or will not work. Radios will break down, engines will not start, guns will get the wrong sort of ammunition, spares will be delivered for the wrong type of tank, petrol will be sent to the cook, beans will be sent to the front line and condoms will be sent to the padre. In action, maps will be of the wrong place and guns will jam. The wise will not make brand new, untested equipment the corner-piece of their plans, because it will not work, and they will keep a supply, recovery and maintenance and repair organisation near the front.

The fifth is the opposition. It is remarkable how many military plans assume that the enemy will co-operate fully, and equally remarkable how seldom they do so. When, in May 1940, on one of those rare occasions, the Allied High Command did indeed do exactly what the German General Staff hoped it would, many Germans thought it was too good to be true, and must be a trick. By and large, though your own side have huge potential for cocking-up your strategy, you should expect your opponent to actively help them in this, and you should therefore not have any critical point in your plan dependent on his doing one particular thing. He probably will not be able to even if he wants to, because his side will cock things up as well.

Not making mistakes is not easy, but it is easier than coming up with a brilliant masterstroke. However, the German General Staff had just managed to execute one of the most extraordinary masterstrokes in military history, totally defeating within days the combined armies of the two most powerful nations in Western Europe and their allies against whom they had previously struggled in vain for four years. They were on a roll. Maybe the Luftwaffe, which had performed quite brilliantly, could do it again.

Kesselring gives some insight into the state of planning at OKL. There were no combined services meetings. 'Central purpose was lacking', he wrote in his memoirs:

No definitive instructions were given about what my Air Fleet had to expect in the way of tactical assignments or what provision had been made for co-operation with the army and navy. I found this the more disheartening because, in the light of verbal instructions given me on 6 August [*at Göring's conference at Karinhall*], I could presume that the air offensive which started two days later was intended to be the prelude to Sealion. But in the very first days of the offensive it was conducted on lines quite at variance with those instructions and never harmonised with the requirements of an invasion.[1]

At its simplest, the requirement of the Luftwaffe was to achieve local air superiority over the invasion area, south-east England, and in so doing to remain sufficiently intact to support an invasion or threaten British cities from the air.

In essence, air superiority involves so reducing the enemy's strength in the air at the place and time of critical military developments, that he is unable to effectively impede any of your own air or ground operations.

The Germans knew about air superiority: they had established total air superiority in Poland by wiping out the obsolete Polish Air Force in the first days of the campaign; and they had established local air superiority in France. Without destroying the Allied air forces in their entirety, the Luftwaffe so dominated the airspace above the crucial break-through points in the Ardennes that those Allied aircraft which bravely attempted to interfere with their Panzer columns were slaughtered without achieving anything.

The Allies achieved it before invading France in 1944. They dominated the skies to such an extent that German aircraft hardly appeared at all, and Allied bombers and fighter-bombers were able to operate at will over the invasion beachhead. There was no great air battle above Normandy.[2] Yet the Allies had not destroyed the Luftwaffe by June 1944. They had so reduced it and so disrupted its ground infrastructure and command and control systems that it was unable to concentrate sufficient strength sufficiently rapidly to have an effect on the Battle.

The examples of the Polish and French *Blitzkriegs* on the one hand, and Normandy on the other, exemplify the two models which the history of air warfare offers as to how air superiority can be achieved. The first is through a rapid and overwhelming strike delivered in a very short space of time. The second is through long-term attrition.

In Poland and France the Luftwaffe had delivered surprise blows in the opening moments of hostilities which destroyed as many or more aircraft on the ground as in the air, dislocated the opponent's command and control systems, and co-ordinated their effort with attacks by ground forces on the enemy's ground forces.

Such blows are designed to create air superiority for a limited but crucial period of time. The ultimate expression of it is a tank on the runway.

Permanent air superiority can only be established through the second method: prolonged attrition and the destruction of the enemy's aircraft industry so that he cannot replace his losses. This is what the Allies did to the Luftwaffe from 1943–4. They engaged it in continuous combat until its loss rate exceeded its replacement rate and its strength was sapped away. It took several years.

Kesselring understood the dilemma. It was clear, he writes, that:

> although we might gain a temporary ascendancy in the air, perma-
> nent air supremacy was impossible without the occupation of the
> island, for the simple reason that a considerable number of British air
> bases, aircraft and engine factories were out of range of our
> bombers.[3]

The Luftwaffe had been given five weeks, from 8 August to 15 September, to
achieve its aim. It had therefore to achieve a quick decision, but the only way to
achieve it was through attrition. In order to put tanks on the runways, it had to
combine the two basic strategies. Moreover, it was not easy to know when
local air superiority had been achieved. The best indication would be the
amount of opposition met.

To gain temporary local air superiority in the short-term, the fighter
opposition would have to be either surprised on the ground or shot down in
the air. This meant achieving a favourable kill ratio high enough to reduce
Fighter Command to ineffectiveness within five weeks and leave the Luftwaffe
fighter force sufficiently intact to protect the invasion against British bombing
attacks.

The only alternative was to attack the population in the hope that that
would force capitulation. This was a wild card. Hitler had expressly forbidden
any attacks on civilian targets and in particular on London. It was a fall-back
option.

Against the background of Hitler's desire to reach a diplomatic settlement but nevertheless to plan for an invasion, the Luftwaffe High Command
set about creating plans of its own. They had at their disposal three Airfleets:
Airfleet 2, under the command of Albert Kesselring, Airfleet 3 under Hugo
Sperrle and Airfleet 5 under Hans-Jürgen Stumpff. Ultimate direction rested
with Göring as Commander-in-Chief of the Luftwaffe. These four men and
their staffs were responsible for planning and running the forthcoming
battle.

The Luftwaffe had been built up by Milch. Göring understood and cared
little about the issues that should have concerned him: logistics and supply,
equipment and training, the use of technology, strategy and tactics. He did not
make much effort to analyse what was going on, and sometimes appeared not
to care. As Hitler's chosen successor, he had his fingers in too many pies to ded-
icate himself fully to the job of leading the Luftwaffe.[4] He nevertheless
possessed some of the intellectual qualities of a commander. After the war,
German survivors have tended to blame him for all that went wrong, but his
interventions in the Battle were not all misguided – though some indeed were.
The real problem was the manner in which he exercised command, which
tended to demoralise his direct reports and his men, leading to the resentment
evident in the likes of Galland.

Göring was quite prepared to pursue petty feuds to the detriment of morale. He disapproved of the Kommodore of JG53, Hans-Jürgen von Cramon-Taubadel, because he had married into a family whose Aryan credentials were less than perfect. So in July, he ordered the unit to paint out its 'Ace of Spades' insignia, of which it was very proud. They painted red bands around their cowlings instead. In retaliation, when Wolf-Dietrich Wilcke took over III./JG53 in August, he had the Swastikas on the tails of his Bf 109s painted out, which was both an expression of solidarity with his Kommodore and a signal to Göring.[5] His standing was very low within JG53.[6] They got their Ace of Spades insignia back on 20 November.

Göring was first and foremost a Nazi politician, skilled at scheming and using people. He ran the Air Ministry on a divide-and-rule basis and did nothing to improve the ruinously bad relationships Milch, Jeschonnek, and Udet had with each other and with him. He possessed considerable charm and was a good communicator when he chose to be, as witnessed by Mölders and Galland, to whom it nevertheless rang hollow. The Luftwaffe was not run by a team but by a set of isolated individuals who had to look out for themselves and tried, if anything, not to co-operate.

Those individuals were of a very different mould.

The largest of the German Airfleets, Airfleet 2, was commanded by Albert Kesselring. He was born in 1885, the son of an academic and scion of one of Bavaria's oldest families. Given a classical education, he joined the army in 1904, in part to assert his independence from his father, and was commissioned in the artillery. During World War I he served in France, distinguishing himself through his coolness and professionalism during the period of the Allied offensive in Artois in 1917. In 1918 he was given a General Staff appointment, and noted the value of control of the air.

In the chaos of post-war Germany, he helped to suppress the Communist revolution in Bavaria, and was amongst those officers selected to remain in Germany's 100,000-man army. In 1933, he was singled out, despite his protests, to head the administrative office of the clandestine Luftwaffe, and quickly decided to make the best of the inevitable by learning to fly at the age of forty-eight. His energy and organisational talents were invaluable. He became Chief of Air Staff, and finally, on the outbreak of war, was given an operational command as Head of Luftflotte 1 for the invasion of Poland. In 1940, whilst he was engaged in organising Poland's air defences, the Commander of Luftflotte 2 in France, Hellmuth Felmy, was sacked after one of his planes force-landed in Belgium on 10 January, carrying full details of the Wehrmacht's invasion plans. Kesselring was appointed to succeed him.

Kesselring was one of Germany's ablest field commanders, as he was to prove when he took over command of the Wehrmacht in Italy, and tied down superior Allied forces in that tough and scaly underbelly of Europe until the war's end. His commanding General in 1917 had written a glowing report of him, commenting on his intellectual power, his sound grasp of tactics, communication skills, tireless industry, his loyalty to his superiors and his ability to inspire those below. He was in many ways the model of a German soldier.

As an air force leader, Kesselring's intellect alone secured for him a reputation for competence. Theo Osterkamp met him on Nordeney in 1933, just after he had taken up his new post. Kesselring came over as a 'chevalier of the old-school', modest, eager to learn and with a charming smile. Despite his modesty, Osterkamp wrote, Kesselring had deep knowledge and a clear vision of the Luftwaffe's future. 'What a delight it must be,' he added, 'to be privileged to work with a man of such calibre.'[7]

Yet despite the enormous amount of effort he put into the Luftwaffe from 1933 onwards, he remained a soldier rather than an airman. In Poland and France the Luftwaffe operated in support of the army, a role in which Kesselring felt quite at home. The Battle of Britain was something which had never been tried, and he was facing men who had spent the best part of their careers working out how to defeat an attack by an enemy air force.

As a man, however, he was a leader of high distinction. He was courageous, independent-minded and unusually amiable. He earned the sobriquet of '*der lächelnde Albert*' ('smiling Albert') and his organisational skills were matched by an understanding of human nature and a sure touch with his men. In the crisis he faced in 1917 he had restored his troops' shattered confidence when they faced defeat. Easy-going on the outside, he was tough as nails on the inside and incisive in his decision-making. It is doubtful whether, given the experience pool they had available, the Germans could have found a better man anywhere in their armed forces to carry out the role allotted to Kesselring in 1940.[8]

The Commander of Airfleet 3, Hugo Sperrle, was from the western part of south Germany, Swabia, and was just one year older than Kesselring, but a lot less of a smiler. When Hitler confronted the Austrian Chancellor Schuschnigg at the time of the Anschluss, he chose Sperrle and General Reichenau to accompany him. They were, he told Milch, his two most brutal-looking generals.[9]

Lacking Kesselring's charm, he was, however, the only long-term professional airman. A World War I flyer, he commanded the training school in Russia in the 1920s and became the first Operational Commander of the Cóndor Legion, bolstering morale in the difficult days before the new Bf 109s arrived in Spain. Regarded as difficult and wilful, he was nevertheless highly competent, and enjoyed Hitler's confidence. His personality ensured, however, that he remained a commander rather than a leader, for he was not only pompous, but, according to Speer, demonstrated sybaritic leanings second only to Göring, whose girth he also challenged.[10] After the Battle he was not displeased to be able to stay in France to enjoy the tranquillity of the occupation and turn to high living, art and wine.[11]

The other Airfleet involved in the Battle, Airfleet 5, was based in Norway and was effectively in action on only one day, serving thereafter to provide its sister fleets with reinforcements. Its commander, Hans-Jürgen Stumpff, had a distinguished career with the Luftwaffe, dating from 1933, and during his earlier career as an infantryman, had been considered as a potential Commander-in-Chief of the army. Having started as Head of Personnel at the Luftwaffe, Stumpff indeed succeeded Kesselring as Chief of the Luftwaffe General Staff. However, despite his efficiency, his retiring personality combined with the usual wrangles with Milch left him as nothing more than a quiet administrator, and he left the post in early 1939. In May 1940, after the occupation of Norway, Stumpff was given Command of Luftflotte V and stayed in Norway until 1944.

In his first Directive of 30 June, Göring set out the mixed purpose of destroying the RAF and cutting off Britain's overseas supplies, with the emphasis on the former. This reflects the general indecision over siege versus decision, and effectively just gave the go-ahead for a re-deployment, the intensification of air fighting, and the launching of harassing attacks on the RAF, ports and transportation. It stipulated that only weakly-defended targets should be selected and that attacks should be carried out under suitable weather conditions and allow for surprise. These attacks were to be small scale, being designed to probe the defences and ascertain their strength, and civilian targets were to be avoided. The purpose was to prepare for the main offensive, and to secure the defence of the newly conquered territories. The Directive calls for close co-ordination between the Airfleets, but ends by stating that until the RAF had been defeated, it should be attacked without regard for any other tasks. The possibility of an invasion is not mentioned.[12]

This document mundanely states what the operational commanders already knew about the basics of their job. No wonder Kesselring felt abandoned. By then, at the latest, he and Sperrle realised that they were going to have to plan and conduct the campaign for themselves, so they hesitantly set about doing so.

On 11 July, Jeschonnek issued a further order, this time mentioning the armament industry as well as the RAF as a target, allowing two to four weeks for the defeat of the RAF, and giving official sanction to preliminary attacks on shipping in the Channel, which Göring's Directive did not mention. Kesselring and Sperrle had already begun attacking Channel convoys. They were not sure what else to do. This gained official sanction in a conference Göring held at Karinhall a week later. The stated rationale for it was to give the aircrews some training.

The plans were prepared in the last week of July and were discussed at a meeting convened by Göring at the Hague on 1 August, an occasion which he graced by appearing in a new white Gala uniform. All the Fliegerkorps as well as the Luftflotten had prepared something. The process had been abruptly ended by a note from Hitler on 29 July that the Luftwaffe should be ready to attack within twelve hours of the order to do so being issued.

The state of the operational units' deliberations is revealed by what is known about the content of the plans. Fliegerkorps VIII under von Richthofen in Luftflotte 3 recommended the use of its Stukas to attack RAF ground installations. Within Luftflotte 2, Loerzer's Fliegerkorps II stressed attacks on London in order to flush up the British fighters, enabling them to be destroyed in the air. This suggestion was thought to be a good one, but had to be abandoned for the time being because Hitler had forbidden attacks on London; Grauert's Fliegerkorps I recommended first attacking the RAF and the motor and aircraft industries, then attacking the Royal Navy and ground targets when the invasion started, and also blockading Britain by rendering its harbours unusable. It also considered some terror attacks against major cities for good measure. The British should be lured into the air with a mixed first wave followed by a second wave of massed fighters to shoot them down. Attacks on ground installations and airfields were rejected.[13]

This confusion of banalities cannot be ascribed to incompetence. Oberstleutnant Deichmann, who worked on the plan for Fliegerkorps II, had himself laid out very clearly in a lecture held in Berlin in 1936 the futility of trying to attack all and every target in a country and the need to select the key targets after a thorough and careful intelligence appraisal.[14] The planners knew full well what they ought to be doing. The confusion came from the requirements stipulated by OKW, and from Göring's failure to create a unified planning process. The meeting on 1 August brought the chaos into the open.

Sperrle thought that the RAF could be defeated *en passant*, and wanted the main effort directed against ports and supplies. However, Göring had excluded Britain's southern ports from the target list on 21 August because they would be needed by the invasion forces. Kesselring in any case thought that attacking ports would result in heavy losses and, influenced by recent reports from Osterkamp that the RAF were refusing to intercept fighter sweeps, wanted to draw British fighters into battle by attacking the one target they would have to defend, namely London.

However, Kesselring was fundamentally sceptical about attacking the British Isles at all. He advocated persuading the British to negotiate by attacking Gibraltar and only then turning on London. Deichmann, Kesselring's own Chief of Staff, disagreed with the emphasis placed on London, as this would mean that the crucial Bf 109s would be operating at the limit of their range, and the British could simply withdraw their forces to airfields north of London and engage the Luftwaffe from there with impunity.[15]

Göring rejected Kesselring's views. He stated that according to intelligence reports, the British had at most 4–500 fighters,[16] and outlined a three-phase plan for destroying them, which consisted of attacking targets in three concentric circles around London over a period of two weeks. For the first five days the attacks would take place on a line outside a 100–150 kilometre radius of the city, for the next three days it would move up to within 50–100 kilometres and for the final five days inside 50 kilometres. It was quite simple.

Theo Osterkamp ventured to comment on this. Osterkamp was the doyen of the veteran fighter pilots in the Luftwaffe and its favourite old star. Known as 'Onkel' ('Uncle') Theo, he had been credited with thirty-two victories in World War I and had won the *Pour le Mérite*, the 'Blue Max'. He had commanded a fighter training school and when war broke out was made Kommodore of JG51, the first fighter unit to arrive on the Channel coast. On 13 July he claimed his sixth and final victory of World War II. He was at that time the only fighter leader to have actual experience of fighting the RAF over the Channel.

He said that radio intercepts had identified the British units active in the area around London, and estimated their strength at 5–700 fighters and growing, with the dangerous Spitfires being increasingly evident.

Göring angrily interrupted Osterkamp to tell him that this was nonsense. The Luftwaffe's intelligence was excellent and anyway the Spitfire was inferior to the Bf 109, and Osterkamp himself had reported that the British were too cowardly to come up and fight.

Osterkamp corrected him. The listening service had reported that the RAF had orders to avoid pure fighter-fighter combats. They were not stupid enough to engage in wasteful attrition against fighters which by themselves could do no harm. Göring retorted that that amounted to the same thing, and turned to the question of numbers.

Sperrle and Kesselring recommended conserving the bomber force until Fighter Command had been decisively weakened by fighter action. They wanted first of all to attack the ground organisation and aircraft industry by night. Göring declared that that was ridiculous, for JG51 alone had shot down 150 planes, which was enough of a weakening. (Osterkamp swallowed at this, for the figure of 150 was the number of claims submitted during the whole of the French campaign for all Allied aircraft destroyed in the air and on the ground.) With the number of bombers available, the few fighters the British still had would be of little consequence. Sperrle and Kesselring pointed out that they had about 700 operational bombers between them. Göring had spoken publicly about 4,500. Osterkamp too was taken aback and was to be even more sobered when he discovered that the 1,200–1,500 fighters he thought the Luftwaffe had turned out to be more like half that. Göring is reported to have sat down in shock and murmured: 'Is this my Luftwaffe?'[17]

This shows how far Göring was from actual operations. He remembered the pre-war figures used for propaganda purposes, and had no grasp of the impact of attrition once fighting began. The Luftwaffe had lost 285 machines in Poland, 260 in Norway and 1,428 in the Battle of France. Similar numbers were damaged in each campaign, and of the rest many were temporarily unserviceable. Front-line strength was being rebuilt, but it took time.

Having allowed reality to make this unpleasant intrusion into the proceedings, the conference members did get as far as discussing tactics. The first day of the main attack was to open with small raids of mixed fighters and bombers, followed by massed fighters ten to fifteen minutes later to carry out the main business of shooting down the British fighters flushed up by the initial sally, and then a massed bomber raid escorted by Bf 110s, just in case the British had anything left. This would be done three times in succession. These plans were elaborated the next day in telephoned instructions from OKL to the Airfleets. Göring's summary of the conclusion of the conference was also issued the following day.[18]

Sealion was a bad plan. Eagle barely merits the name of 'plan' at all. It amounted to little more than flying over England, dropping some bombs on various things to annoy people, and shooting down any fighters which came up as a result. Given that the German General Staff had just planned and executed one of the most innovative, brilliant and decisive conceptions in military history, Eagle was astonishingly amateur.

The first thing wrong with it was the process by which it was developed. It was not only done without the army and navy, it was not even done by the Luftwaffe as a whole, but by separate operational units guided by nothing more than platitudes and a wish-list. Kesselring, Sperrle and Stumpff should have locked themselves away with Milch, their Corps Commanders and the Intelligence Staff for a week to agree on targets and tactics.

The second failing is the unclear aim. It was clear that the RAF – or was it just Fighter Command? – was to be destroyed, but in addition, ports, merchant shipping, the Royal Navy, the aircraft industry, transport infrastructure and industry had all appeared, disappeared from and returned onto target lists for the pre-invasion offensive, let alone what was contemplated for the invasion itself.

The third problem was the complete failure to think through how the RAF was to be defeated. The naïve assumption was that if British fighters came up to fight they would be shot down. The OKL Staff, from Göring down, took this as read, and the illusion persisted in Kesselring's mind even after the war. In his memoirs he wrote:

> Our difficulty was not to bring down enemy fighters – in Galland, Mölders, Oesau, Balthasar etc., we had real aces, while the huge figures of aircraft shot down are further proof – but to get the enemy to fight.[19]

The British, of course, had Malan, Tuck, Frantisek, Lock, Lacey and so on. In broad terms the number of aces or potential aces in every air force is about the same. In assuming his fighters would win all the air battles, Kesselring was placing his bets on two key advantages: the greater experience of his fighter pilots and their superior tactics. The question was how quickly the British would learn, a process which had already begun.

However, even if the British pilots did not learn at all, the Luftwaffe had a problem. Given that the Luftwaffe's own fighter arm had to remain sufficiently intact to protect an invasion fleet against British bombers, and assuming, as the Head of Luftwaffe Intelligence Beppo Schmid did, that the British had 675 serviceable fighters, the Luftwaffe, with about 725, would have to consistently achieve kill ratios in the air of better than 2:1 in order to eliminate Fighter Command and have a reasonable number of fighters left itself. A kill ratio of 1:1 would be no good, because the Germans would eliminate themselves, and they had to remain intact.

Osterkamp calculated that in order to protect the invasion beaches he would need two whole Geschwader (i.e. about 150 aircraft) over the beachhead all the time. Even if each Geschwader were to fly three sorties a day, this implied a strength of twelve Geschwader, i.e. 900 fighters, somewhat more than the Luftwaffe had to begin with.[20] This suggested that they could not really afford any net losses at all. Given that they could accept a gross attrition rate of about 10% per month, they could really only afford to lose about 75 aircraft, which meant that they had to get a kill ratio of the order of 5:1 in order to reduce Fighter Command's initial strength by 50% – leaving aside the question of the British replacement rate. The goal of a 5:1 kill ratio is indeed the one which Osterkamp set JG51 when they took up their positions on the Channel coast in early July.[21] Accordingly, he instructed his pilots only to attack when the tactical situation gave them a sure kill for almost no risk.

That would not do, however. The Luftwaffe had five weeks, which meant shooting down a hundred British fighters a week in order to eliminate them, assuming they too had a replacement rate of about 10% per month. This implied intense air activity, and it meant taking chances. If they just waited for the best hunting opportunities, the German fighters would not inflict enough damage in the time available. It was no good getting a kill ratio of 5:1 if the total British losses were too small in absolute terms. If the British lost a hundred fighters in five weeks and the Germans only twenty, the British would still be able to fight over the beaches, and the Luftwaffe would not have achieved its goal. The Luftwaffe needed big air battles every day. The weather alone would probably prevent this.

A few simple considerations of the orders-of-magnitudes involved, calculations which no-one except Osterkamp seems even to have considered, show that Eagle was a pipe-dream. It would have been hard enough to realise even if favourable kill-ratios could be achieved, but getting as much as 3:1 in the air usually requires significant technical superiority. All these considerations leave out the question of the British command and control system. Radar installations are given a perfunctory mention in the final target list, but as long as they were there, surprise was impossible and the British had the initiative in terms of which raids to engage with which forces.

When Stumpff returned to Airfleet 5, he told his staff that the plan would not work. It would cost them lives and machines, but they had to get on with it.[22]

Under the best possible assumptions Eagle would have been hard put to achieve very much of military significance, though it would look impressive and trying to carry it out would certainly cause a lot of damage. What if something were to go wrong?

It is not difficult to assess the plan's cock-up potential. Almost nothing at all was known about how the defence system worked, the nature of the targets or the British aircraft industry's output; the weather could effectively wreck the whole timetable if it were to turn bad; if it were to turn very bad and ground everybody for long enough, the British would thereby win by default; two Airfleets with fighter, bomber, dive-bomber and Zerstörer arms were spread between Denmark and Brittany, with another one in Norway. They were responsible for setting their own targets and all had different ideas about what was important. Fighter and bomber units could not talk to each other in the air, as their radios could not carry multiple frequencies; serviceability rates had been declining since the war had ceased to be phoney, and the Luftwaffe was now operating from improvised bases. Serviceability was running at 70–80% and declining. In addition, the newest piece of equipment, the Ju 88, was causing complaints amongst crews.

Finally, there was the opposition: the British were supposed to come up in large numbers and allow themselves to be bounced by formations of Bf 109s. They did not do so. It was a first indication of more unsporting behaviour to come.

10. THE DEFENDERS

The summer of 1940 was a watershed in the history of the Third Reich. During its course, the German High Command made the most important strategic decisions of the war, and broadly determined its future course. Without fully realising they had done so, and starting from a position of triumphant dominance, they effectively ceded the initiative to the British. By simply staying in the war, at the level of grand strategy the British imposed on the Germans a constrained and uncongenial set of options.

Within the context of their air offensive, the Luftwaffe were able to choose the time and place of attack. However, the Dowding system gave the British the choice of which raids to intercept, when and in what strength. Thus in the realm of campaign strategy, the outcomes also largely depended on British actions.

The defences were controlled by Dowding and his four Group Commanders: 11 Group in the south-east under Air Vice-Marshal Keith Park, 10 Group in the south-west under Air Vice-Marshal Sir Quintin Brand, 12 Group, covering the Midlands, under Air Vice-Marshal Trafford Leigh-Mallory and 13 Group covering the north of England and Scotland, under Air Vice-Marshal Richard Saul. Dowding's role was to manage their resources. He had been successful so far, but it was not in fact clear how long he would remain their leader.

Dowding was, at fifty-eight, the oldest C.-in-C. of a Command in the RAF, and had held that position for two years, after which it was normal to move on. He justifiably expected to be a candidate for Chief of Air Staff, the most senior position in the RAF, but in February 1937 the job had gone to Cyril Newall, who was junior to him, and he was told that he could expect to be retired in 1942 at the age of sixty, which was normal. The main reason for passing him over then and for his subsequent treatment, was his personality. He was regarded as obstinate and uncooperative, and to be too narrow in outlook for the top job. In August 1938 he had been told that he would retire in

June 1939. After some confusion caused by a newspaper report in February 1939 about his impending retirement, Newall wrote to him on 20 March asking him to stay on until March 1940. One day before this latest expiry date, Newall extended it to 14 July. His patience at an end after all this messing about, Dowding began an irritated exchange of correspondence on the subject with Newall and his political boss, the Secretary of State for Air, Archibald Sinclair. Sinclair finally wrote to him on 10 July 1940, the day on which the Battle of Britain 'officially' began, and a new date of 31 October was agreed.[1]

This is not exactly a model example of personnel management. However, there were reasons for all the shilly-shallying. Dowding's professional competence was never in question, and it was apparent to all that his knowledge of the defence system was unrivalled. There was no-one to replace him with anything like the same set of qualifications. Political and military circumstances were changing rapidly, and each new crisis made the need for Dowding seem more urgent. The Munich crisis, the subsequent acceleration in Fighter Command's expansion, and the imminence of an all-out attack by the Wehrmacht in the spring and by the Luftwaffe in the summer of 1940 each time made it seem inopportune to let him go. The successor who was named for him in August 1938, Air Vice-Marshal Courtney, was injured in an accident three days before he was due to take over in June 1939, so he stayed on then as well.

The other reason for retaining him was that Dowding enjoyed the support of Lord Beaverbrook, who remained an admirer and lifelong friend, and of Churchill, who recognised the vital contribution he had made to Britain's defences. Churchill, at all events, saw the need to postpone Dowding's retirement for only as long as the direct threat to Britain was there. As a student of *Mein Kampf*, Churchill expected Hitler to turn east once his attack on Britain had been broken. The only way to get at Germany then was by bombing, and he therefore expected to shift resources towards Bomber Command in the future.[2] Once the defence battle had been won, Dowding could be released from Fighter Command.

The manner of Dowding's actual going on 25 November 1940, planned though the event was, caused much personal rancour to those concerned. The issues have been clouded because of the involvement in them of two of his immediate subordinates. In appointing these men, Dowding had unwittingly and simultaneously made one of the most important decisions of his life and lit the fuse of a bomb that was to explode underneath him. Fighter Command was to embark on the most crucial battle it ever fought with a leader on the brink of dismissal and as a house divided.

On a spring day in 1918, Manfred Freiherr von Richthofen, the 'Red Baron', had been buried behind Allied lines, his coffin borne by six officers of the newly created Royal Air Force and a guard of honour drawn from the Australian troops who shared with Captain Roy Brown the claim to have shot him down on 21 April. Amongst the fifty or so British airmen who had gathered to pay their respects was the Commander of 48 Fighter Squadron, Major Keith Park.[3]

Born in 1892 of a Scottish father and English mother who had emigrated to New Zealand, Keith Park joined a steamship company at nineteen and spent three years as a purser before joining up in 1914. Like his future adversary Kesselring, he joined the artillery, serving in Gallipoli and then on the Western Front. Wounded in October 1916, he recuperated in England and applied to join the RFC. After some time as an artillery spotter, he joined 48 Squadron, the first to be equipped with Bristol Fighters, and by the end of the war was accredited with fourteen victories. To this first-hand experience of air-fighting he added the salutary one of being bombed on an airfield, and showed an early ability to reflect on the broader implications of what he had experienced. In 1922, while at staff college, he wrote an insightful piece on the lessons of the war, making four points: the need for aircraft dispersal on the ground; the need for fast ground-strafing aircraft keeping up continuous attacks in order to neutralise enemy airfields; the need for fighter-sweeps rather than close escorts to establish control over airspace; and the need to appraise tactics thoroughly on the ground rather than leaving it to improvisation in the air.[4] He was fortunate indeed that the Germans did not read these notes.

Park spent his time between the wars in a variety of administrative and operational flying roles in fighters, and then, in July 1938, stepped in to replace the original choice, Arthur Harris, as Senior Air Staff Officer at Bentley Priory, Dowding's Chief of Staff.

For the next two years, Park was engaged in determining tactics and in working up the defence system.[5] His contribution to this was substantial. He was responsible for introducing the practice of filtering radar plots at Bentley Priory before passing them on to the Groups. Dowding initially opposed this idea, but when Park did it anyway and showed him the results, he agreed.[6] Park worked harmoniously with Dowding, who developed the deepest respect for him. On 20 April 1940, Park took over 11 Group.

He was uniquely qualified for the job. He had almost twenty-five years of experience with fighters covering almost all aspects of operations and command, culminating in the unrivalled opportunity to refine the actual weapon he was now required to wield. He was also a superb leader.

His competence was clear and he showed it. Like Dowding, he was very task-oriented, and he was ruthless with any he found wanting. He came across as a tough, no-nonsense character with a head for detail as well as the big picture. He was rational, questioning and independent-minded, and had repeatedly demonstrated both physical and moral courage. Somewhat austere and stern, and regarded as ambitious, he was judged unreservedly by all who worked with him to embody the highest standards of integrity. Brought up as a practising Christian, he retained his faith till the end of his life.

Some who met him found him vain and humourless, and thought him more respected than liked by his men. None of those who served under him whose comments have been recorded shared that view. He repeatedly showed how he could put quite junior people at their ease with his informality and humour and cared nothing for rank, which certainly put some people's backs up. He lacked the education and urbanity to be a popular colleague within the higher reaches of the RAF, and this was to become a problem for him. Several of his pilots, however, have said that they all worshipped him. When he was at Malta in 1942, he once stopped his car to give a lift to a humble fitter. 'From my position, he was almost God!' his passenger has recalled, but a God 'without a tribe of staff officers following, seeing for himself what was going on.'[7]

Park's skills as a team builder stemmed from his ability to communicate, and his demonstrated concern for the welfare of his men and women. He was a good listener, who showed he was listening and could express himself clearly and concisely, the sort of 'no-nonsense' talker pilots like. When faced with near-rebellion at a training depot in 1919, he quelled the discontent with a short, relaxed address given in a hangar.[8] When his battered pilots returned from France in 1940, he went round to their airfields in his own Hurricane and told them they had done very well.[9] Throughout the Battle of Britain he would leave his HQ every evening in his Hurricane which he named 'OK 1' and tour the airfields, especially those which had been hit. He came to listen, to discuss and to encourage. His men identified with him completely.

He knew that nature had not been generous enough to endow him with charisma, so he set about creating a charismatic image. Well before Montgomery tried similar things, he created some 'signatures' for himself to make him a recognisable character to his men. In 1940 it was 'OK 1' and the white overalls he always wore when flying her.[10]

He demanded, and got, better facilities for his pilots, including better accommodation and some entertainment. He took the business of decorations for his men very seriously at times when one might have imagined he had other things on his mind, and his care extended down to the lowliest aircraftmen and mechanics. Typical of his attitude is an incident which took place when he was on a liner on his way to the Middle East in early 1942. Some young pilots on board appeared on the boat-deck, which was reserved for senior officers, and were ordered off by a Major. Park heard of this and informed the other senior officers on board that 'these young gentlemen have faced and will face dangers that none of you will ever meet. They will share any facilities on board this ship equally with you.' This practice abruptly stopped on Park's disembarkation.[11]

Such examples may also serve to demonstrate how Park could rub colleagues up the wrong way. He did not have a great deal of charm, and had no small-talk. The vanity often commented upon showed itself in undue sensitivity to criticism, his one identifiable weakness. He had one other problem, which he could do nothing about – his health. In 1925, he was passed unfit for flying duties in any capacity due to 'a history of neurasthenia and general debility'. Somewhat amusingly in the light of his later performance, this led to the judgement that 'he would not stand stress'. His physical condition was not good. In 1930 he was laid low by flu, and despite his courageous attempts to cover it up, he suffered from repeated bouts of ill-health throughout his career.[12] This did not prevent him from living to the age of eighty-two and in 1940, at the age of forty-eight, from taking on the most awesome responsibility of any military commander anywhere in the world at that time.

It had already become clear in late 1939 that the task of running 11 Group as originally conceived was too great, so Park (at that time SASO at Fighter Command) and Dowding decided to create 10 Group, taking over the three western-most sectors of 11 Group.[13] It became operational on 8 July 1940. The man chosen to command it was a South African, Air Vice-Marshal Sir Quintin Brand. Born in 1893 in Johannesburg, Brand won the MC, DSO and DFC as a fighter pilot in World War I, shooting down a Gotha on the last night raid on England. He achieved a measure of fame in 1920 when he made the first flight from England to Cape Town in a Vickers Vimy, for which he was awarded a knighthood. He subsequently held positions as Director General of Aviation in Egypt, and Director of Repair and Maintenance before taking up his new operational job. He was well respected, competent and courageous, and above all he got on very well with his more dynamic and dominating colleague at 11 Group. This was not true of the man commanding Park's northern neighbour, 12 Group.

Trafford Leigh-Mallory was born only one month after Keith Park in July 1892 in Cheshire, the youngest child of the local rector. After taking a degree in history at Cambridge, he joined a territorial battalion of the Liverpool Regiment in 1914, was wounded in June 1915, and applied to join the RFC. He returned to France as a member of No. 5 Squadron in July 1916 and flew over the Somme battlefield in a B.E.2 whilst Park was in action below with his artillery battery. After a period in England, he was made Commander of 8 Squadron which flew two-seater reconnaissance machines.

After the war he had a brief spell as Inspector of Recruiting and then moved to the School of Army Co-operation at Old Sarum. In 1927 he became the Commander of the School, where he remained until 1931, when he was moved to the Air Ministry. In 1934 he was given command of one of the first flying training schools at Digby, and his performance there convinced his superiors that he was fit for higher things and needed a posting abroad. He was sent to Iraq and saw through the troubles there until he was recalled to England as AOC 12 Group at the end of 1937.[14]

He proved to be a good organiser, and built up 12 Group from scratch. However, this was his first appointment in fighters, and when it came to finding a man for 11 Group, Park, though junior to him, was chosen instead. Leigh-Mallory regarded this as the plumb job in Fighter Command, and felt rather resentful. At the time, it was by no means clear that 11 Group would assume such importance, as no-one imagined that an enemy would be able to array itself all along the French coast. However, it was already clear that Leigh-Mallory did not get on with Dowding.

In October 1938, he had requested that twenty-nine of the forty-one fighter squadrons in the Command be allocated to 12 Group, a request Dowding refused, observing to Park that his request showed 'a misconception of the basic ideas of fighter defence'.[15] Leigh-Mallory clashed with Dowding again in September 1939 over the disposition of his squadrons.[16] Bad feeling between them had reached such a point by February 1940 that Park recalls Leigh-Mallory storming out of Dowding's office and telling him that 'he would move heaven and earth to get Dowding removed from Fighter Command.'[17]

Dowding did not learn of the incident until Park made it public in 1968. What he did notice at the time was that Leigh-Mallory showed great zeal for independent action which went as far as going against his orders.

Leigh-Mallory did not have the depth of competence in handling fighters shown by Park and Dowding. From his career development alone, one could hardly expect him to. Nevertheless, he was respected by his men, (though he did not seek contact with them in the way that Park did), and he was far better than either Park or Dowding at getting along with colleagues and superiors. He was outward-going, affable and easy to get on with. He clearly identified more than either Dowding or Park did with people at his own level, but he could be harsh towards those of lower rank.[18] He knew he knew less than Park and relied on advice,[19] a good thing in itself if the advice was balanced. On the other hand, he was more likely to go his own way than seek advice from colleagues or superiors.

Air Vice-Marshal Richard Saul, who commanded 13 Group, which covered northern England and Scotland, had flown as an observer in World War I and won the DFC. He was an excellent sportsman and highly thought of, becoming SASO at 11 Group in 1938 before taking over 13 Group in 1939. He was hard-working, efficient and friendly, and handled his squadrons well. In the main his force effectively constituted a strategic reserve.

In planning how to meet their enemy, the British had to choose between two basic strategic views, each one of which had advocates.

The first view was founded on the belief that the Luftwaffe would give up if their attacks proved to be very costly, regardless of what damage they inflicted.

This view was held by several officers at the Air Ministry, notably the Deputy Chief of Air Staff, Air Vice-Marshal William Sholto Douglas and Air Commodore Stevenson, and also, with provisos, by Leigh-Mallory. Sholto Douglas gave a very clear statement of his case in the discussions of defence strategy that took place before the war, writing in 1938:

> It is immaterial in the long view whether the enemy bomber is shot down before or after he has dropped his bombs on his objective. Our

object is *not* to prevent bombers reaching their objectives, though it would be nice if we could, but to cause a high casualty rate among enemy bombers, with the result that the scale of attack will dwindle rapidly to bearable proportions.[20]

His opinions did not change during the course of the Battle. In a minute written on 17 December 1940, after it was over, he states:

The best, if not the only way of achieving air superiority is to shoot down a large proportion of enemy bombers every time they come over. It would be better to do this before they reach their objective if possible, but I would rather shoot down fifty of the enemy bombers after they have reached their objective than shoot down only ten before they do so.[21]

The other view was that the Germans would give up if they were convinced that they were not achieving their aim. The prime goal of the defence was therefore to remain in being and offer undiminished and constant opposition, thus denying the Luftwaffe air superiority. As long as a cost was imposed for entering British airspace, how high it was mattered less than keeping one's own force in being, and being able to impose the cost again the next day. The objective would be to both minimise one's own losses in the air and damage to the defence system on the ground. It followed that it was better to break up a raid and prevent it from damaging its target by shooting down ten raiders in the process than allowing it to bomb an airfield or radar installation, which would impair the defence's ability to meet the next raid, and shoot down fifty.

The assumption behind this is that an enemy will give up if he becomes convinced that he is getting nowhere, for even if his losses are moderate, it is senseless to accept even moderate losses for no return.

This view was espoused by Dowding and Park, and was the strategic principle which guided the tactics they employed in the air throughout the Battle. It was clear to them that the Luftwaffe's aim was to eliminate Fighter Command, so they had to ensure that the defences were not seen to weaken.

Prima facie, Sholto Douglas had a reasonable case. However, neither he nor anybody else was able to specify *how* high the German losses had to be in order to be unacceptable to them. Neither side of the argument had any evidence to go on at the time because no-one had ever tried to defend a country against large-scale air attacks.

There can in fact be little doubt that the principle adopted by Dowding and Park was correct. The British bomber crews in France went into action knowing they had little chance of survival, but did so because they were ordered to and because they believed there was a chance, albeit a small one, of success. Bomber Command tolerated losses of 80% on raids in the first months of the war until they realised that they were doing no damage. It is the realisation that the aim is not being achieved that makes an opponent, however determined, give up. Had the Luftwaffe commanders had good evidence that their attacks were weakening the defences and that their bombing was rendering airfields inoperable, they would have been willing to sacrifice a lot of crews and aircraft to finish the job. If they had good evidence to the contrary then *any* further losses incurred in trying to do so would have been a useless sacrifice.

The tactics flowed from this principle. Park had to ascertain which raids were serious and guard against being caught by surprise by possible further raids designed to catch fighters re-fuelling on the ground. He had to engage the most dangerous raids early-on in order to protect the ground targets. It was vital not to be caught on the ground and important to engage when in as advantageous a tactical position as possible. Speed of reaction was critical. Achieving all this would be demanding, but it was what the system was designed to do. As bombers were the only aircraft which could cause damage on the ground, they were the main target. If the Germans sent over fighter sweeps, they should be left alone.

The basic tactical unit was the squadron.[22] Park decided how many to deploy against each threat and when to send them into action. In attacking any one raid, he could either use his squadrons together at the same time or individually over a period of time. Until he faced very large single raids he chose deliberately to do the latter, for several reasons.

Firstly, it was fast and simple. Each squadron detailed to attack just carried out its orders without waiting for any others. The pilots could scramble, head straight for the enemy, attack and get down again.

Secondly, it reduced the risk of suffering a major defeat. If the intercepting force were to be caught on the climb by a gaggle of 109s, only one squadron would be lost.

Thirdly, each small formation would be harder for the escorts to detect than one large one, and would tend to confuse them, as British units would often be coming from different directions. If the escorts made the mistake of diving as a body on the first British fighters to appear, the coast would be clear for the next ones.

Fourthly, Park's fighters would be able to enter a target-rich environment, shoot at anything and get out fast, rather than exposing themselves as they queued up to attack or spending half their time avoiding collisions and shooting at each other.

Finally, raids could be subjected to almost continuous attack. German crews would learn that they could expect no let up, that the whole of the sky over southern England was a potential death-trap. This continuous pressure increased their stress and made it harder for bomber commanders to restore order if formations got disrupted.

It may seem intuitively wrong to commit forces piecemeal. To many at the time, the image of a bomber fleet as a column of Redcoats and a fighter squadron as a band of Indians would have appeared aberrant.* However, Park's principles had nothing to do with the number of aircraft used to intercept raids, but simply the operating unit employed. If the raid were very large, two squadrons could engage it at one time. Park wanted complete flexibility, and that was very important, for he had to react to any number, sequence or size of raids. Park could say to his squadron leaders, as Nelson had said to his captains at Trafalgar, that he wanted a 'pell-mell' battle and that no-one could go very far wrong if they simply closed with the enemy. Like Nelson, Park minimised cock-up potential.

As the fighting in France came to an end, Dowding had to reorganise his force and deploy it to meet an enemy now coming from the south, a few minutes flying time away.

On 20 May, Fighter Command had 30 Spitfire and Hurricane squadrons on its Order of Battle, plus six of Blenheims and one of Defiants. In terms of actual numbers, this meant 247 Spitfires and 99 Hurricanes. The energies devoted to re-building the command during June may be gauged by the fact that after heavy fighting over Dunkirk and continuous skirmishing thereafter, at 9 a.m. on 1 July the number of squadrons available to Fighter Command had increased from 37 to 58. There were 29 squadrons of Hurricanes with 347 operational aircraft, 19 of Spitfires with 199 aircraft, as well as 69 Blenheims and 25 Defiants.[23] Spitfire losses over Dunkirk had not been made up, but Hurricane production was such that strength had been substantially re-built. With 546 operational Spitfires and Hurricanes in all and 912 pilots for them, aircraft production was seen to be the factor limiting strength in the air.

Fighter Command as a whole needed a reserve with which to make good losses and keep up the strength at the front. Dowding provided for one through his force dispositions. On 1 July they were as follows:

| | Number of Squadrons | | | | |
	Spitfires	Hurricanes	Blenheims	Defiants	TOTAL
11 Group	8	17	5	0	30
12 Group	5	3	2	1	11
13 Group	6	9	1	1	17
Total	19	29	8	2	58

* Except in the Luftwaffe. Their jargon for 'enemy aircraft', the equivalent of the RAF's 'bandit', was 'Indianer'. Whether the choice is to be ascribed to a deep understanding of air fighting or a predilection for the cowboy stories of Karl May, still a favourite with German children today, is a mystery shrouded in the mists of time.

| Proportion of aircraft strength (%) | | | | |
Spitfires	Hurricanes	Blenheims	Defiants	TOTAL
11 Group	14	34	6	0	54
12 Group	7	6	3	2	18
13 Group	10	14	2	2	28
Total	31	54	11	4	100

Whilst placing over half of his operational strength in the critical south-east under 11 Group, Dowding sent no less than seventeen squadrons to the far north to rest and re-fit, including several which had been badly mauled in France. Others amongst these seventeen had only recently been formed. For the rest he put all of his Blenheim nightfighters in the south but otherwise mixed Spitfires and Hurricanes.[24]

Dowding did not put seventeen squadrons in 13 Group primarily to defend the north, though it also achieved that, making the Luftwaffe's reconnaissance efforts perilous, and giving them a nasty shock when they attacked the north in strength on 15 August. His main purpose was to form a reserve, the very thing Churchill was appalled to find lacking in France.* Dowding had to mix Spitfires and Hurricanes, for if all the fighting and all the losses had fallen on one type, they would have quickly run out of replacements. The Blenheims were in the process of converting to night-fighting and were needed in the south to protect vital targets, including London. Dowding was unhappy with the Defiant, but both squadrons had done well over Dunkirk (though not as well as they thought) and he gave them another chance.

Dowding held a conference with his four Group Commanders at Bentley Priory on 3 July to discuss the likely moves of the enemy and what they would do in response. Leigh-Mallory thought that prior to invasion, the Germans would spend a week or so attacking airfields with heavily escorted bomber formations. Dowding hoped they would. If they did, Fighter Command would exhaust them and start cracking their morale before the invasion had even begun. He said he hoped they would spend a month that way, but he feared that if they tried it at all, it would only be for twenty-four hours.[25] The Germans were about to play right into his hands.

---

* On 16 May, Churchill flew to France to meet the French generals face to face. On hearing from Gamelin that the front had been broken, he asked 'Où est la masse de manoeuvre?' and received the shocking reply 'Aucune.' Churchill was dumbfounded. 'It had never occurred to me,' he wrote, 'that any commanders having to defend 500 miles of engaged front would have left themselves unprovided with a mass of manoeuvre.' (*Their Finest Hour*, p. 38).

Meanwhile, the peoples of occupied Europe sought to recover from the shock of the past few weeks' events and come to terms with their new situation. Some welcomed the 'new order'. They admired the energy and military skill of the Germans, and many in France did not regret the overthrow of their worn out and corrupt government. A new and vital force was sweeping Europe into a new era, casting all the uncertainties of democracy, with its endless squabbles and divisions, into the dustbin of history. In the occupied countries some people discovered that the 'wicked Huns' were polite and law-abiding, so perhaps things were not all that bad.

Outside Europe, opponents of the British Empire rejoiced. Gandhi wrote in an Indian newspaper that Germans of future generations would 'honour Hitler as a genius, as a brave man, a matchless organiser and much more.' Teilhard de Chardin wrote from Peking that 'we are watching the birth, more than the death of a world . . . the world is bound to belong to its most active elements. Just now, the Germans deserve to win because, however bad or mixed is their spirit, they have more spirit than the rest of the world.' Churchill and Roosevelt, he thought, seemed 'grotesquely antiquated'. How could anyone believe that an anachronistic and almost bankrupt Empire led by a garrulous, ageing reactionary with a tendency to hit the bottle could prevail against this young and vibrant new force which embodied the spirit of the modern age?[26]

Thus as the smoke cleared over the ruins of Dunkirk, the Luftwaffe, fresh from supporting the army in the final defeat of France, moved unit by unit to new airfields along or near the Channel coast.

They had destroyed the Polish air force on the ground, swept the French air force from the skies, massacred the British bombers sent against them and brushed aside the few Hurricanes they found in their path. Whilst they had failed to prevent the evacuation from Dunkirk, it hardly mattered, as the fleeing army was effectively disarmed. They had learned to respect the Spitfires they had met there, but there were not many of them, and the RAF had comparatively little experience of air combat. The British, as they knew from World War I, were a stubborn lot, and defeating them would not be quite the pushover that Göring seemed to think. But none of them had any real doubt that within a few weeks the air over southern England would be patrolled by Messerschmitts.

Their mood was probably not unlike that of the French noblemen who gathered in their splendour outside Agincourt and looked across the field to where a tired and bedraggled array of English archers sheltered behind a line of pointed sticks which they had stuck into the ground in front of them as a forlorn and final hope that it would protect them from destruction.

Göring's young eagles little suspected that they were about to impale themselves on the most fearsome air defence system in the world.

PART II:
BATTLE

11. THE ENEMY AT THE GATE

On the afternoon of Sunday, 14 July 1940, Charles Gardner, a young BBC radio reporter, arrived with a recording van on the cliffs above Dover. A few miles out, a small convoy was steaming through the Straits. His engineer had just set up his microphone when Gardner spotted the shapes of aircraft above the ships.

Over the next few minutes he gave the nation its first eye-witness account of the Battle of Britain. He was full of admiration for the fighter pilots he had met in France, and full of excitement at what he saw.

> Well now [he began], the Germans are dive-bombing a convoy out at sea. There are one, two, three, four, five, six, seven German dive-bombers, Junkers 87s. There's one going down on its target now. A bomb! No! – There, he's missed the ship! He hasn't hit a single ship. There are about ten ships in the convoy but he hasn't hit a single one and . . .

Gardner's voice rose in pitch.

> But the British fighters are coming up. Here they come! The Germans are coming in an absolutely steep dive, and you can see their bombs actually leave the machines and come into the water. You can hear our anti-aircraft guns going like anything. I am looking round now. I can hear machine gun fire, but I can't see our Spitfires. They must be somewhere there. Oh. Here's a plane coming down.

The voice paused for a moment as Gardner scanned the sky trying to make out what was going on. Then he continued, his excitement even greater.

> Somebody's hit a German and he's coming down with a long streak – coming down completely out of control – and now a man's baled out

by parachute. It's a Junkers 87 and he's going slap into the sea. There he goes – *smash!* – A terrific column of water!

Now, then – oh, there's a terrific mix-up over the Channel! It's impossible to tell which are our machines and which are German. There's a fight going on, and you can hear the little rattle of machine gun bullets. *[There is a dull* crump *in the background.]* That was a bomb, as you may imagine. Here comes one Spitfire. There's a little burst. There's another bomb dropping – it has missed the convoy again. You know, they haven't hit the convoy in all this.

The fight seemed to be over. It had been remarkably brief. Gardner thought he could see two more parachutes, but then corrected himself – they were seagulls. Just as well he was not responsible for confirming claims. He reassuringly affirmed that no damage had been done, except to the one Stuka, and he watched the parachute float down into the sea. There were no boats to pick the man up. 'He'll probably have a long swim ashore,' Gardner remarked.

There was silence. In the meantime, a small group of observers had gathered near the BBC van. Suddenly, Gardner's voice broke the silence:

Oh, there's another fight going on, away up, about twenty five or even thirty thousand feet above our heads. Oh, we have just hit a Messerschmitt! Oh, that was beautiful! He's coming right down . . . You hear those crowds? He's finished. Oh, he's coming down like a rocket now. An absolutely steep dive. Let us move round so we can watch him a bit more . . . No, no, the pilot's not getting out of that one.

Gardner tried to get a view of the crash, but could not do so, for it was behind a hill. He had been watching somebody die. All he could actually see was smoke. 'We cannot count that as a definite victory because I did not see him crash,' he added, as if explaining the rules by which umpires kept score.

He further explained to his listeners how hard it was to make sense of anything up there because of the speed of the events. Fights seemed to last for a matter of seconds. The sky filled and emptied within a minute. Despite saying that it was impossible to tell friend from foe, he identified every crashing fighter as a Messerschmitt. He was probably watching an engagement taking place at 10–15,000 feet. Had it been at 25–30,000 feet, as he more dramatically said it was, he would have seen only vapour trails. But even at a lower height, the aircraft would have been nothing but silhouettes against the sky.

Then Gardner spotted something else. Completely absorbed by what he could see, he reacted as if his listeners were standing next to him on the cliffs:

Hello? Look, there's a dogfight going on up there. There are four, five, six machines whirling and turning around. Now – hark at those

machine guns going – there's something coming right down on the
tail of another. Here they come. Yes, they are being chased home!
There are three Spitfires chasing three Messerschmitts now. Oh, boy!
Look at them going! There is a Spitfire behind the first two. He will
get them. Oh, yes. I've never seen anything so good as this. The RAF
fighters have really got these boys taped. Our machine is catching up
the Messerschmitt now. He's got the legs of it, you know.

Like a spectator cheering on a runner in a race, Gardner suddenly transplanted
himself into the cockpit: 'Now right in the sights. Go on, George! You've got
him! Bomb! Bomb!'

He came back to earth: 'No, no, the distance is a bit deceptive from here.
You can't tell, but I think something definitely is going to happen to that first
Messerschmitt. I wouldn't like to be him.'

The crowd gathered together and peered towards France, just twenty miles
away.

I think he's got him. Yes? Oh, look. Where? Where? I can't see them at
all. Just on the left of those black spots. See it? Oh, yes, oh, yes – I see
it. Yes, they've got him down. Yes, the Spitfire has pulled away from
him. Yes, I think that first Messerschmitt has crashed on the coast of
France all right.[1]

The recording was broadcast, unedited, about four hours later. Today, we are
used to getting very recent or even live broadcasts from war zones. This was a
first. The general public had never before heard an unexpurgated eye-witness
account of a military engagement recorded as it actually happened only hours
after the event itself. They had been able to read newspaper reports by eye-witnesses since William Howard Russell had written articles for *The Times* from the
Crimea in 1854, but they had never heard a recording made on the spot, complete with the sound of bombs and machines guns. It created a sensation.[2]

The letter columns of *The Times* were soon filled with reactions, one of the
first, published on 17 July, coming from a former pilot of World War I who had
become a clergyman, the Reverend R.H. Hawkins from Carlisle:

As a pilot in the last war, will you allow me to record my protest
against the eye-witness account of the air fight over the Straits of
Dover given by the BBC News on Sunday evening? Some of the
details were bad enough; but far more revolting was the spirit in
which the details were given to the public. Where men's lives are concerned, must we be treated to a running commentary on a level with
an account of the Grand National or a Cup Final tie? Does the BBC
imagine that the spirit of the nation is to be fortified by gloating
over the grimmer details of fighting?[3]

Another former serviceman, Major-General Guy Dawnay, who was probably equally aware of what lay behind phrases like, 'Oh, he's coming down like a rocket now', added his voice two days later:

Thank you for printing Mr Hawkins' protest against the latest deplorable manifestation by the BBC in their eye-witness account of the air fight in the straits. The BBC standard of taste, feeling, understanding and imagination is surely revolting to all decent citizens.[4]

However, the letters page on that day contained other reactions which were quite different. A C. Fisher from north London disagreed with the Revd Hawkins:

It was something quite different from 'an account of the Grand National or a Cup Final'; to me it was inspiring, for I felt that I was sharing in it, and I rejoiced unfeignedly that so many of the enemy were shot down, and that the rest were put to ignominious flight. My uplift of heart was due to a better understanding, which the BBC enabled me to get, of the courage and daring of our pilots, and of the reality and nature of the victory they are achieving for us. We are proud of their feats, and such a description as Mr Gardner gave made it possible for us to rejoice with them. I fancy that his commentary caught something of the spirit of the pilots themselves. If our cause is a just and worthy one, then to rejoice in its success is the obvious thing.[5]

The two ex-servicemen, who had experienced war first-hand, appealed to universal moral principles of sensitivity and decency. The civilian, who had not, but who did feel threatened by the sudden unaccustomed proximity of enemy bombers, felt reassured by being told what was going on, and by the evident prowess of his defenders.

The BBC felt itself to have been called to account, and on 22 July, the man responsible for the broadcast, F.W. Ogilvie, replied to the critics. 'British fighting men do not wage war with long faces,' he opined.

The high gravity of German troops is alien to them. Theirs is a spirit of cheerful realism, and, in a total war, is it not also the spirit of the British people as a whole? That young men, on a fine July Sunday afternoon, fight to the death over the Channel instead of bathing in it is horrible. But it is, alas, through no fault of our country, a fact. The young men face this fact without loss of their native high spirits. Do civilians want it presented to them in any other way?[6]

Thus the nation debated how it wanted the war to be reported and the impact of reporting on moral sensibilities. It was a highly civilised debate. On the

23rd, General Dawnay replied, thanking Mr Ogilvie for his 'courteous' rebuke, saying that he merely wanted to say that 'the football match technique' was 'inappropriate' and hoped that the expression of his views would 'induce in the BBC a finer sensitiveness in dealing with these superb transactions'.[7]

As Gardner was an eye-witness, many felt what he said was incontrovertible. In fact, as he more or less says himself, he had little idea what he was seeing.

Gardner had witnessed the only sizeable raid of the day, which was carried out by the thirty or so Stukas of IV./LG 1 escorted by a similar number of Bf 109s from III./JG 3. They were intercepted at about 15:15 by 'A' Flight from 615 Squadron, which was on patrol, and seven more Hurricanes from 151 Squadron at Rochford. They were joined by twelve Spitfires of 610 Squadron, and the remaining Hurricanes from 615's 'B' Flight, led by 'Sandy' Sanders, operating from the forward airfield of Hawkinge behind Folkestone. Some of the Spitfires Gardner saw were almost certainly Hurricanes. 615 got through to the Stukas and Pilot Officers Collard, Gayner and Hugo all hit the machine piloted by Oberleutnant Sonneberg of IV./LG 1, which is the one Gardner saw go into the sea. Neither Sonneberg nor his wireless operator survived, the wireless operator being reported missing. Each of the three pilots filed a claim for a Ju 87. Collard was awarded one confirmed and Gayner and Hugo shared another. The man on the parachute was almost certainly Pilot Officer Mudie of 615 Squadron who was shot down by the escorts. He was picked up by a naval vessel very badly burned and he died the next day.

When the Stukas made off the fighters were still engaged, and some Spitfires of 610 pursued the Messerschmitts over the Channel until they had to break for home, short of fuel. The one Gardner saw pursuing two of them was probably that of Pilot Officer Litchfield, who was credited with one Bf 109, his only confirmed victory before he was killed himself four days later. One Bf 109 of III./JG3 was written off on crash-landing at Boulogne, its pilot wounded, and another landed with damage at Wissant, though the pilot was unhurt. The crash behind the hill is a mystery, unless Gardner was in fact looking out at France, which was only 20 miles away, and it was one of the Messerschmitts of JG3. It was probably Mudie's Hurricane, which crashed in St Margaret's Bay. A Hurricane of 111 Squadron crashed taking off from Hawkinge that day, which would indeed have been behind a hill from where Gardner was standing. The time of this event is, however, unrecorded.

One can see from this how confusing air fighting was, even if you were standing on the ground with nothing to do but watch. Gardner connected a crashing Stuka with a parachute, though they were unrelated. He did not realise that one of the losses was a Hurricane. However, he was witnessing a small British victory. The convoy was undamaged, and the Germans lost two aircraft destroyed and one damaged for the loss of one British pilot and his machine. Churchill sent a message of congratulation to his boys at 615 Squadron. Their only regret, according to the Squadron's Operations Record Book, was that 'Green section missed the fun'.[8]

Gardner's broadcast was followed at 9 p.m. by one from the Prime Minister. Gardner had no doubt served to get everyone in the mood, for Churchill conjured up the picture of an island fortress 'girt about by the seas and oceans where the Navy reigns; shielded from above by the prowess and devotion of our airmen', calmly awaiting the assault. All had just heard how true that was, a clever piece of programming by the BBC. Here, too, they heard for the first time of the two attributes of the airmen – 'prowess and devotion' – which Churchill was to single out most memorably a month later. The RAF had inflicted losses of five to one, he said, though these were only preliminary encounters. Then, in direct contrast with the words to come, he spoke of the many people ready to defend Britain's shores; of the Home Guard; of a million and a half soldiers under arms; and went on to speak of vast numbers of unknown souls who would render faithful service in the war. 'This,' he declared, 'is a War of the Unknown Warriors'. All were determined to carry on so that 'the dark curse of Hitler will be lifted from our age.'[9]

The following day, Dowding wrote to Churchill to tell him 'how profoundly moved I was by your Sunday broadcast. You said what we all think but are too inarticulate to express.'[10]

Gardner brought home to the British public the fact that the enemy was at the gate, and starting to knock on it hard. Churchill told them that they were not going to get in. Dowding had to keep the gate shut.

12. THE CHANNEL: JULY

In his Directive of 30 June, Göring had ordered his commanders to attack targets of opportunity with small forces, in order to familiarise themselves with their future areas of operation and to gain insight into the strengths and weaknesses of the defences. He stressed the need for the Luftwaffe to preserve its own strength and for units to co-ordinate their actions. He added the specific goal of closing the Channel to British shipping as soon as possible, assigning the task to von Richthofen's VIII Fliegerkorps.[1] To this was added Loerzer's II Fliegerkorps in the Pas-de-Calais.[2]

Being of an easy disposition, and taking the view that the job was not too difficult, Loerzer delegated it to Oberst Johannes Fink, the Kommodore of KG2, who was to liaise with Richthofen. Fink was given the title of 'Kanalkampfführer' – Channel Battle Leader. This was a bit of a mouthful, so it was usually shortened to 'Kanakafü', which was marginally preferable to his other sobriquet of 'Kanalarbeiter' – 'sewer-rat'.[3]

Not one to stand on his dignity, Fink set up his command post in an old bus on the cliffs at Cap Blanc Nez, just beyond a statue commemorating Hubert Latham, a French citizen of English extraction who had narrowly missed becoming the first man to fly the Channel when his rival Blériot beat him to it. He had tried to make it two days after Blériot's triumph, but his engine failed and he landed in the sea.[4] From his bus, Fink could see radio tower masts on the English coast, which he realised were to do with fighter control. The scale of the system and its effects were nevertheless to take him completely by surprise.[5]

One of the first things the Germans did was to set up a mobile Freya radar station of their own on Cap Blanc Nez to track their main target: shipping.[6] It was operational from the end of July, complementing the reconnaissance flights sent out every morning to locate convoys.

Theo Osterkamp, the Kommodore of JG51, was based at Wissant, just down the road from Fink. 'Onkel' Theo knew the British of old, and was quietly concerned that the 'Lords', as he always called them, would not be a push-over.[7]

Osterkamp was a little confused by the role given to his new neighbour. His own job was clearly spelled out in a passage of Göring's order of 30 June which was underlined for emphasis: 'Until the enemy air force has been broken, the over-riding principle behind air operations is to attack the enemy's flying units at every favourable opportunity, by day and by night, on the ground and in the air, without regard to any other tasks.'[8]

Osterkamp had set about this by taking his Geschwader out over England on 'freie Jagd' operations ('free-hunting' fighter sweeps) to pounce on any RAF fighters he found there. Targets were few for, as Osterkamp began to realise, Park had expressly forbidden the interception of pure fighter sorties, so JG51 turned to attacking the patrols Fighter Command was forced to put above the Channel convoys.

Now, however, Osterkamp's fighters would have to give up their sweeps and act as escorts for Fink's bombers. This would keep Kent free of Messerschmitts and keep the Messerschmitts tied to the role of protecting rather than hunting, which was quite a different kettle of fish. Fink assured Osterkamp that the Stukas would attract a lot of British fighters, which would give him the opportunities he was looking for, but Osterkamp disagreed. Escorting Stukas meant staying close to them and chasing off fighters which approached. Hunting meant operating freely and seeking out the enemy.

So Fink and Osterkamp reached a 'gentleman's agreement' that Fink would use Bf 110s as close escorts and give the Bf 109s the freedom they needed. Osterkamp had his doubts about the Bf 110, but was willing to give it a try.[9] The subject of their gentlemanly discussion was to become a dilemma and finally the source of a rift within the Luftwaffe High Command that grew in seriousness as the weeks went on.

In the meantime, the Luftwaffe's operations took on a pattern which lasted until the launching of Eagle.

Every morning, single aircraft from the meteorological units ('Wettererkundungsstaffeln') attached to each of the three Airfleets would fly sorties to report back on current and developing weather conditions, particularly cloud cover, in their operational areas. General reconnaissance flights were sent out throughout the day to photograph ports and airfields inland, report on damage from night raids and to look for shipping. If attractive targets were found, attacks would be launched. Then, usually at dusk, single or small groups of bombers would be sent out on nuisance raids. If the weather were bad, raids might be carried out in daytime, using cloud cover. Typical targets were docks, factories, oil installations, railway stations, airfields and ships, and the raiders reported back on the state of balloon, searchlight and AA defences. They ranged all over Britain, including Wales, Scotland and Ulster, in order to build up a complete picture of the defences and to show the British that they were vulnerable everywhere.[10] Dusk was also the prime time at which

mine-laying was carried out, both by bomber units and the specialist seaplanes of the Coastal Detachments ('Küstenfliegergruppen').[11]

The strategic role of these operations was to gain target information for
Eagle and to seal off the Channel to shipping. The purpose of the latter was in
part to disrupt internal transportation, but more importantly to prevent the
Royal Navy from interfering with Sealion between the Straits of Dover and the
Navy's main Channel base of Portland, which was a particular target. Mines
caused continuous losses to shipping. Churchill had been particularly concerned about the threat from magnetic mines at the beginning of the war, but
by now counter-measures were in place.[12]

Night raiders were able to operate with impunity, as Fighter Command
still had no effective airborne radar, nor any effective night fighter. However,
daytime reconnaissance, particularly over land, was perilous. All four Fighter
Command Groups were active, shooting down raiders as far north as the
Pentland Firth, between the Scottish mainland and the Orkneys.[13] Between 10
July and the beginning of the assault on the mainland on 12 August, RAF
fighters are known to have shot down thirteen reconnaissance aircraft and
damaged another four. Five more were lost to unknown causes, which probably included further losses to fighters. The unusually high proportion of
aircraft destroyed was due to the fact that the defending fighters had no escorts
to worry about and so had time to finish the job. Also, some of their victims
whose machines were crippled failed to make the long journey home over the
sea. Of the thirteen, four crashed into the Channel and four into the North Sea.
Only one, a Do 17P attacked by 74 Squadron on 10 July, made it back over the
Channel, but it crashed at Boulogne, a write-off. With this one exception, the
crews of the reconnaissance machines were all killed or captured.

Before it crashed, however, this Dornier was to send out the message
which 'officially' began the Battle of Britain.

The weather was bad. Eight convoys were at sea, some within range of
Luftwaffe fighters. Unusually, therefore, this particular Dornier could be given
an escort, which consisted of the whole of I./JG51. As it approached North
Foreland the crew of the Dornier spotted a large convoy, codenamed 'Bread',
heading into the Straits of Dover. Six Spitfires of 74 Squadron, based at
Hornchurch, were scrambled to intercept and engaged the Dornier and its
escorts at 1100. The Dornier was crippled, two Spitfires were damaged by the
escorts, and everybody went home. Hoping to find some stray British fighters
near the convoy, another Staffel of Bf 109s went prowling over Dover as I./JG51
returned, and were met by Spitfires of 610 Squadron from Biggin Hill. The
Spitfire flown by Flight Lieutenant A.T. Smith, who was leading the squadron,
was damaged in the skirmish and force-landed at the forward base of
Hawkinge.

'Bread' was a tempting target, and Fink decided to go for it. He put
together a force of Dorniers from his own KG2, escorted, in accordance with

his arrangement with Osterkamp, by the Bf 110s of III./ZG26, with free-ranging Bf 109s from JG51 flying above. Fighter Command's initial response to the early action had been in line with its habitual parsimony: to send a flight from 32 Squadron to guard the ships. They were scrambled from Biggin Hill at 1315. However, sixteen minutes later, at 1331, British radar detected Fink's planes forming up over Calais. As the Germans clearly meant business, 56, 111 and 74 Squadrons were scrambled, and were on their way when the pilots from 32 Squadron spotted their foes at 1335, announced a raid of sixty-plus and suggested they be reinforced.

The result of this was the largest dogfight yet seen over the Channel, which is what prompted official historians to see 10 July as the opening day of the Battle.

111 Squadron went into line abreast and charged the formation head-on. They tore through them and one of their number, F/O Higgs, hit a Dornier with his wing. Higgs bailed out and his Hurricane plunged into the sea. His body was washed ashore at Noordwijk on the Dutch coast in August after over four weeks in the water. The collision was also the end for the Dornier, which was commanded by the Staffelkapitän of 3./KG2, Hauptmann Krieger, and went in near Dungeness Buoy. He and another crew member were picked up and captured by the British, but the two other crewmen perished.[14]

The squadron diary records that Higgs rammed the Dornier.[15] Other accounts suggest that Higgs was attacked on his approach by Hauptmann Walter Oesau of III./JG 51.[16] He may have been hit and lost control. Definite cases of ramming are rare, and a collision seems more likely.

The rest of 111 got through the bombers, turned and attacked the rear aircraft. The formation had broken up and the other British fighters joined in. There ensued a huge mêlée involving the British fighters, the bombers and their escorts.

As the raid ended, 64 Squadron arrived to harass the Bf 110s back to France. The Bf 110s had begun to confirm Osterkamp's scepticism. Three were lost, together with their crews, one possibly to AA fire, and another two returned damaged. KG2 also lost three Dorniers, with two more damaged, and JG51 lost one Bf 109 with its pilot and two more damaged. For this, they had only been able to damage four RAF fighters, Higgs being the only pilot casualty.[17]

The head-on attack had split up the formation, which resulted not just in turning the bombers into easier targets, but in messing up their bombing attempts. Only one bomb out of some 150 dropped by KG2 scored a direct hit, sinking a 700-ton sloop. No cargo was lost, as the convoy was in ballast. The RAF's kill-ratio in the air was six to one, which was very high, and not often to be equalled. The German fighters had failed both to protect the bombers and to shoot down British fighters. Fighter Command had responded to the threat with speed and flexibility, and 11 Group's scrambles had fed five squadrons into the fight which had successively distracted the escorts, broken up the bombers, inflicted losses in the subsequent dogfight and harried the retreating Bf 110s.

Meanwhile, Luftflotte 3 had been active. In the late morning they dispatched some solitary raiders against Bristol and Southampton, and sent the Ju 88s of III./LG1 to attack Falmouth and Swansea. They approached from the west, confusing the radar operators on the Lizard about their intentions, and when 92 Squadron were scrambled from Pembrey they were too late to intercept the raiders. However, the Observer Corps accurately reported the presence of a single Ju 88 (probably doing post-raid assessment) to the training airfield at Stormy Down. Stormy Down was under the command of Wing Commander Ira 'Taffy' Jones, an RFC veteran who had claimed forty kills when flying with 74 Squadron during World War I. Jones relates that he could see 'the blighter' through his binoculars and finally got fed up with the Observer Corps constantly ringing the telephone. So he took off in an unarmed Hawker Henley which was used for target-towing, positioned himself up-sun and dived on the Junkers from 15,000 feet. Feeling 'the old joy of action' coursing through him, Jones grabbed a Very pistol and fired it at the German bomber, watching the lights floating down in front of it. The Junkers dived and headed for the sea. Jones followed it until the rear gunner opened up on him, upon which common sense finally prevailed over bravado and Jones returned to base.[18]

If Fighter Command's 'first day' gave cause for confidence in the future, Bomber Command's 'first day' was a dreadful continuation of the gallant folly of the past. In support of their colleagues' fight against the Luftwaffe, 2 Group of Bomber Command ordered off six Blenheims of 107 Squadron to attack the airfield at Amiens which was the base of II./KG1. They had no fighter escort, and though the weather was not good it was not bad enough to protect them. As they approached low over the airfield, the flak opened up before the Bf 109s arrived and five of the six aircraft were shot down. Three crews were killed, two taken prisoner.[19] Perhaps the greatest effect of this sort of raid was to add to the body of evidence which convinced the Luftwaffe commanders that low-level attacks in daylight were suicidal, and hence to be sparing in using them themselves.

These losses did not redress the balance, however. The day's air fighting cost the Luftwaffe ten aircraft destroyed and six more damaged. Another three were written off and six damaged in accidents. Only one RAF fighter was destroyed and eight damaged through Luftwaffe action. One more, a Hurricane of 111 Squadron, was damaged by RAF action when it was attacked by a Spitfire over Hawkinge in the early evening. That day, the weather was as deadly as the enemy. At 6 o'clock in the morning, before a shot had been fired, Sgt Clenshaw of 253 Squadron died when his Hurricane crashed in murky conditions off the Humber. When the disaster overtaking 107 Squadron is added in, the total British aircraft losses for the day from all causes stood at seven against the Luftwaffe's thirteen. The Luftwaffe claimed thirty-five. Assuming they knew about the Blenheims, as they had wrecks to count, they imagined that the RAF had lost thirty fighters. They had actually hit nine, only one of which was lost. The RAF had also lost another which the Germans knew nothing about.

So thick was fog of war that the Wehrmacht's liaison officer at OKL, General Otto Stapf, reported to Halder the following day that the RAF would be neutralised in some two to four weeks.[20]

That day, 11 July, the Luftwaffe was to have more success. A Do 17 reconnaissance machine of Fliegerkorps VIII reported five steamers and a warship 15 km south-west of Portland. Three Hurricanes of 501 Squadron were on patrol over it. Von Richthofen sent off forty-four Stukas of I. and III./StG2 to attack it, escorted by eight Bf 109s of III./JG27. Before the Hurricanes could interfere with the Stukas, JG27 pounced on them, shooting one down. By the time six Spitfires of 609 Squadron arrived, the Messerschmitts had gained height again and bounced them in turn, shooting down two. No Stukas were hit, and they sank the old armed yacht HMS Warrior.

Hoping to reinforce this success, von Richthofen launched more Stukas, but this time entrusted their protection to the Bf 110s of III./ZG76 in their first operation over the Channel. As they gained height, the Zerstörer crews found it rather unnerving to be flying over water, and the silence was uncanny. They had the strong feeling that the British were watching them.

So they were. But the menacing absence of response was just a mistake. The raid was reported as a single aircraft, so only six Hurricanes from 601 Squadron were scrambled from Tangmere. When they got there the Stukas had launched their attack and were at sea-level, way below their escorts. The Hurricanes destroyed one Stuka, and when the Bf 110s came down to protect them, engaged them as well. Once advised of their error by 601, the controllers scrambled 87 and 238 Squadrons, which appeared out of the blue as the raiders were withdrawing.

III./ZG76 were under strict instructions to protect the Stukas whatever the cost, and this they did, paying a heavy price. Between them, the British pilots shot down four of them. One of them was flown by Oberleutnant Hans-Joachim Göring, the Reichsmarschall's nephew, described by one of his colleagues as 'a boisterous young man' who 'stupidly tried to take on the whole RAF'. His aircraft plunged out of the sky in a screaming dive and hit the ground on the Verne heights overlooking Portland Harbour. Leutnant Friedrich-Wolfgang Graf von und zu Castell, who nobly tried to help him, suffered a similar fate. Uncle Hermann was not amused and 'stirred up quite a fuss', having been assuming that the Gruppenkommandeur, Hauptmann Dickoré, would be taking special care of his nephew. The men of III./ZG76 were shocked to suffer four losses on a single mission, for France had been a walk-over and they just assumed it would continue. They had little appetite at dinner, consuming a lot of liquor instead.[21]

Further German assumptions were to be challenged that day. Luftflotte 3 assumed the RAF were fully occupied over Portland, so in the early evening they launched twelve Heinkels of I./KG55 and more Bf 110s on a final attack on Portsmouth. These were met again by 601 Squadron and 145 Squadron, which shot down three of the Heinkels.

These actions had lessons for both sides.

Standing patrols over convoys were vulnerable. It was hard for the pilots to sustain the concentration necessary to keep a good look-out, and relatively easy for enemy fighters to see them, manoeuvre into a good position and dive on them from out of the sun in a single slashing attack known as a 'bounce'. This is what Osterkamp wanted to do.

Equally, when scrambling defenders, it was critical to get a good estimate of the strength of the opposition. The readings of the experienced radar operators around Dover on the 10th had been accurate, but when the girls got it wrong, the intercepting fighters could be sent into a trap, as happened to 609 on the 11th. In the afternoon, only the direct observation of 601 Squadron's pilots got enough machines off the ground to prevent losses and have an impact. However, even when mistakes had been made, Fighter Command's reflexes were fast, and the use of forward airfields allowed reinforcements to reach the scene of fighting quickly. Fresh fighters, arriving when attacking formations had been split up and were low on fuel and ammunition, could inflict serious damage.

It was equally becoming clear that only Bf 109s could protect bombers and inflict losses on Hurricanes or Spitfires. Bf 110s could only protect bombers by offering themselves as more attractive targets, which in many ways they were. They were only dangerous from in front (unlike the bombers which had few blind spots) and were scarcely more manoeuvrable. Indeed, the Ju 88, despite its teething problems, was an altogether more formidable opponent.

In the course of this second day, 11 July, the Luftwaffe had destroyed six RAF fighters, killing three of the pilots, and damaged four more. In doing so they lost sixteen aircraft, with five more damaged, a loss-ratio of over two to one in favour of Fighter Command. Bomber Command lost four aircraft that day and during the following night. The Luftwaffe's claims, at fourteen, were far more accurate than on the previous day. Indeed, though they did not destroy them all, they actually hit the number they claimed. The reason for the difference in the accuracy of claims is probably that the dogfight above 'Bread' was large and confused, inviting multiple claims, whereas each action on the 11th was smaller. There were also fewer Bf 109s involved. This meant that any single-engined fighter going down was British and anything else was German. It might also just be that the absence of large numbers of fighter pilots anxious to earn their Knight's Cross led to greater realism.

One of the German losses on the 11th was a Heinkel He 59 seaplane, shot down into the Channel by an Anson of 217 Squadron Coastal Command. Four crewmen were later discovered near the Channel Islands and captured.[22]

The RAF's first encounter with these seaplanes, which were painted with red crosses and had civilian markings, had been on 1 July, when 72 Squadron had intercepted one in murky weather near a convoy off the Sunderland coast and shot it down. The British authorities' interest in them had been further stimulated on the 9th, when pilots of 54 Squadron had encountered one. It was from Seenotflugkommando 1 and had been sent out from Boulogne under fighter escort to rescue survivors of an attack on a convoy. They found it and forced it down. The He 59 became stranded on Goodwin Sands at low tide. The Walmer lifeboat towed it off to Deal, and the crew were made prisoners of war and interrogated to find out what they were up to.

While the Air Ministry considered the matter, Fighter Command issued an order to all pilots on 14 July to ignore the red crosses and attack them. On the 29th, the Air Ministry pronounced that the aircraft were 'being employed for purposes which HM Government cannot regard as being consistent with the privileges generally accorded to the Red Cross', and that any of them flying in operational areas would do so 'at their own risk and peril'. By the time the Air Ministry order had been issued, British fighters had shot down four more and damaged another. The vulnerable seaplanes continued to be in peril all summer.

Goebbels predictably made much of this at the time. Kesselring, whom the Allies put on trial for war crimes in 1946, condemns the policy in his memoirs, stating:

> There may be two opinions on the justice and admissibility of this order; but anyone who has seen, as I have, the constant attacks made in defiance of international law on a German air ambulance and a crew in the water by Hurricane flights can have only one.[23]

Indignation, and more, was genuinely felt by ordinary German pilots, who also point out that the Heinkels rescued British as well as German airmen.* The claim that the aircraft were radioing back the position of convoys is dismissed as an excuse. Ulrich Steinhilper witnessed one of these incidents on his first combat mission. He found it 'utterly sickening', ascribing the orders for this 'criminal behaviour' to Churchill:

> To me and the other German pilots these attacks were viewed as nothing short of murder. Eight-gun fighters and fighter-bombers tore into these rescue aircraft which were armed with nothing more lethal than a flare-pistol. Even more sickening was when we saw these attacks driven home by multiple passes over a downed or damaged aircraft ensuring there were no survivors.[24]

---

* British policy was pointed out to foreign journalists such as William L. Shirer as a violation of the Geneva convention. Shirer was aware that the Wehrmacht used the Red Cross to try to protect gasoline trucks and other pieces of military hardware. He did not believe their reports until he read Churchill's own justification of the policy after the war. See Shirer, *The Nightmare Years*, Bantam 1985, pp. 572–4.

Dowding makes no apologies and states the fundamental reason for the policy:

> We had to make it known to the Germans that we could not countenance the use of the Red Cross in this manner. They were engaged in rescuing combatants and taking them back to fight again, and they were also in a position, if granted immunity, to make valuable reconnaissance reports. In spite of this, surviving crews of these aircraft appeared to be surprised and aggrieved at being shot down.[25]

Dowding takes a ruthlessly military view of the issue, in which he is as consistent as he is dispassionate. With more German than British airmen coming down in the Channel, the Luftwaffe stood to gain more from an effective rescue service than the RAF in any case. British policy remained consistent. The RAF never did use the red cross on air-sea rescue planes when they finally set up their own service in 1941.

One of the 54 Squadron pilots who forced the He 59 ashore on the 9th was Alan (known as 'Al') Deere. A New Zealander who was among the first contingent of his countrymen to join the RAF in 1937, he grew up in the countryside of South Island, where he had experienced a major flood and an earthquake by the time he was twelve. He was attracted by the excitement of flying and, when the war came, thought it would all be a great adventure. He had a narrow escape in 1938, when he was replaced at the last minute as a passenger on a plane which subsequently crashed, killing all on board. In May 1939 he passed out through lack of oxygen while flying at height and came to only just in time to pull out, suffering from a burst ear-drum. He flew with 54 Squadron over Dunkirk, where he was knocked out force-landing on a beach half-way between Dunkirk and Ostend, came to, got to Dunkirk itself, and was bombed on the destroyer taking him to England. He claimed seven victories and got the DFC. On the 9th, he and two of his comrades held off the escorts of II./JG51 while P/O Johnny Allen forced the seaplane down. Deere shot down one Bf 109, only to find another heading straight at him. Both pilots opened fire, but within seconds they collided, with the 109 passing just over Deere's cockpit, smashing his propeller and rudder. He managed to land at Manston and return to the squadron. So it was that by the beginning of the Battle of Britain, Deere had already used up six of his nine lives. His Intelligence Officer put in his report that Deere had run out of ammunition and rammed the 109. Deere observed that he might be mad, but not as mad as that. He just did not have time to get out of the way.[26]

Dowding dined with Churchill at Chequers on the 13th. He told the Prime Minister that the only thing that worried him were his dreams. He had dreamt the previous night that there was only one man in England who could use a Bofors gun and his name was William Shakespeare. He found it deeply disturbing. This may have been a way of conveying that, whilst he was confident, concern about resources was on his mind even when he was asleep. Churchill seemed to have few doubts, declaring that the previous four days had been the most glorious in the history of the RAF. It had met the test and shot down the enemy at the rate of five to one.[27] They went on to discuss various technical matters, including the Germans' use of radio beams for target location, and the Defiant. One of the two squadrons equipped with it had been brought down from Scotland to West Malling in Kent the previous day. What they said about this aircraft is not recorded, but it was a subject on which they differed. No doubt Churchill talked of its success over Dunkirk. No doubt Dowding expressed his reservations. However that may be, they came to talk about Dowding's retirement. Churchill expressed his confidence in him, and said he wanted him to remain on the active list without any retirement date being set. Dowding conveyed this to his superiors in his correspondence with them the following day.[28]

The Channel fighting continued at a low level. On the 16th Hitler issued Directive 16, ordering preparations for Sealion as a contingency. On the evening of the 19th in the Reichstag he celebrated the creation of new Field Marshals and created the unique title of 'Reichsmarschall' for Göring. He then delivered his 'last appeal to reason' speech, in which he said he saw no point in continuing the war, and tried to separate the interests of the British people from the belligerence of Churchill's government. He actually quoted Halifax's own words to Dahlerus, appealing to Britain to be governed by 'reason and common sense.' At the same time he made it clear that if the war were to go on, he would deal 'the final blow' to a structure already set tottering by unscrupulous politicians. Most of his audience were convinced that his offer would be accepted. It was a bit of a shock when, within an hour, the offer was rejected in a BBC broadcast. Halifax broadcast an official rejection from the Government on the 22nd. Churchill later declared that the BBC made the immediate response entirely off its own bat.[29] When asked about an official reply, Churchill responded that he had no intention of replying to Hitler himself, as he was not on speaking terms with him.[30]

If the Germans' diplomatic efforts came to nought on 19 July, their military efforts had enjoyed more success. Nine convoys had been at sea, so in the expectation of action, 11 Group had ordered 141 Squadron, the one equipped with Defiants, from West Malling to Hawkinge. They had not yet been in action. Despite their misgivings, Park and Dowding decided to use them on the strength of the successes enjoyed by 141's sister squadron, 264, over Dunkirk.

At 1223, 141 were ordered off to patrol twenty miles south of Folkestone. Nine machines took to the air. At about the same time, Theo Osterkamp decided to make use of the break in the weather to lead III./JG51 on a 'free hunt' sweep. The Gruppenkommandeur of III./JG51, Hannes Trautloft, suddenly saw the Defiant formation below him, heading south. With the sun behind them, Trautloft's men dived down to attack. It was 1245. Four Defiants fell in Trautloft's first pass. The Messerschmitts stayed, and shot down another as it sought cover in the clouds. Their hunt was interrupted by the arrival of 111 Squadron, which shot down one of the Messerschmitts and allowed the four remaining Defiants to get back to Hawkinge. They touched down at 1300. Two of them had been hit. One of them crashed on landing, the other was a write-off. Within half an hour, the fresh squadron had lost seven aircraft and twelve pilots and gunners. The shocked survivors were withdrawn back north over the next few days. Osterkamp too, who saw what happened, was moved. Spirits were high that night at III./JG51's base at St Omer, but, he observes, despite the laughter, the faces of his young flyers were beginning to be marked by a growing awareness of their own mortality.[31]

When the news came through to Dowding, Churchill was with him. On hearing it, Churchill looked grave. Dowding had been right. He was, Dowding said, very conscious of the fact that a lot of his men had died. Churchill glanced at him, nodded and turned away.[32]

This disaster made 19 July Fighter Command's worst day so far. It lost ten aircraft to the Luftwaffe's four. Three British bombers were also lost that night. On very few other days during the Battle of Britain would Fighter Command lose more aircraft in combat than the Luftwaffe. It was as well for Dowding that the absolute numbers involved were so small.

When Hurricanes and Spitfires were involved, however, the balance of losses was largely a result of the tactical situation. The following day, tactical advantage allowed Fighter Command to score a success over the unfortunately-code-named convoy 'Bosom'. This convoy was sailing east from Dorset and Park was confident that it had been seen. Accordingly, in the late afternoon he anticipated German intentions by stationing elements of two Hurricane squadrons, 32 and 615, above it, and two Spitfire squadrons, 65 and 610, above them. Earlier attempts to station 601 Squadron above it failed because their leader, Sir Archibald Hope, could never remember the code-names of convoys, and understood the controller, an old chum of his, to be asking him to patrol Bosham, a village outside Chichester. This made perfect sense, especially as Bosham was the home of a nice pub called The Ship, a regular squadron haunt, and worthy of vigorous defence. When 601 arrived over Bosham, and the controller asked whether they could see where the ships were, Hope corrected: 'Where The Ship is', and then realised there had been some misunderstanding. Such was the quality of HF radio.[33] When they got to where they should have been, all they found on the water was an He 59, so they tried to force it to the shore. They failed, and its crew abandoned it. It subsequently sank and the crew were never seen again.

At about 1800, when 'Bosom' was about ten miles off Dover, it was approached from the east by Stukas of II./StG1 with a strong escort from JG51. The patrolling British fighters pounced on the Stukas, damaging four, and shot down two Bf 109s in the ensuing dogfight. They lost two Hurricanes of 32 Squadron with a third damaged, and one Spitfire from 610.

The dispositions of the British fighters were in line with an instruction Park issued on the same day, to place Spitfires at height to engage fighters and Hurricanes below them to stop bombers from slipping through.[34] In practice, things did not always work out so cleanly.

The 21st saw Göring call his commanders to Karinhall for a conference. The operational goals remained unchanged but for the addition of British warships as explicit targets. He warned that Eagle could be launched soon.

Göring broached for the first time the question of how fighters should be employed. He stressed that combined Bf 109 and Bf 110 forces should be used to press forward to deal with defending fighters before the bombers were sent in. Only weak bomber forces were to be used at this stage to lure the enemy up. He also stressed that fighters were to be used offensively and given maximum operational freedom. If they were tied to the bombers they could not act decisively, could not exploit their potential and would suffer heavy losses. The bombers should, if the worst came to the worst, rely on tight formation flying and their own defensive armament for protection. To ensure the effective co-ordination of fighters, he decided to create a unified leadership for them.[35]

This was enacted on the 27th, with the appointment of 'Onkel' Theo Osterkamp as 'Jagdfliegerführer 2', in charge of the fighter forces of Airfleet 2, most of which arrived at the Pas-de-Calais in the last week of July, and Werner Junck as his opposite number at Airfleet 3. Acronyms being *de rigueur* in the Luftwaffe, Osterkamp was actually known as 'Jafü 2'. Whilst the new Jafü felt honoured and thoroughly approved of the fighter forces being directed by someone who understood how they worked, he was also rather confused. He was responsible for the tactical operations of the fighter forces of the Airfleet, which meant taking such vital decisions as the strength of escorts, when to carry out sweeps, which units should take-off and when – i.e. a rather similar role to the Group Controller in Uxbridge. However, he was also to report to Fliegerkorps II, which effectively meant he had to take orders from Loerzer as well as Kesselring. In practice, indeed, Göring added orders of his own. Osterkamp's job was only made workable by the laziness of Bruno Loerzer, who left for his Headquarters in Ghent and only once turned up in Wissant. His main concern, Osterkamp observed, seemed to be what to have for break-fast.[36]

'Onkel' Theo's place as Kommodore of JG51 was taken by the man who was then Germany's leading ace ('Experte' in Luftwaffe parlance), the illustrious Werner 'Vati' Mölders. Credited with fourteen victories in Spain, Mölders was the main inventor of the Luftwaffe's fighter tactics. This replacement of a wise uncle by a skilful father was the first of a series of moves to place the leading young aces at the head of the Bf 109 Geschwader. The Germans knew that most of the kills were scored by a few expert pilots and that the inexperienced were vulnerable. Of the ten pilots lost by JG51 in July, half had failed to score at all, and the remainder had on average only two kills apiece.[37] The Experten on the other hand were amassing claims at a dizzying rate. On 24 July, the man being talked about as the main challenger to Mölders, Adolf Galland, had arrived at the Channel at the head of III./JG26 determined to beat his friend into second place.

The very day after Mölders' elevation, 28 July, Galland very nearly had pre-eminence guaranteed for him. Early that afternoon, on his first mission as Kommodore, Mölders led a force drawn from I. and II./JG51 towards Dover as escorts for a convoy raid, and Galland was there as high cover with III./JG 26. 74 and 257 Squadrons were scrambled at 1350, followed by 41 Squadron. There are various accounts of what then transpired.

The most common is that Mölders tangled with 74 Squadron and was raked by their leader, 'Sailor' Malan, when trying to get a bead on one of his men; others have Malan bounce him. An alternative version of events is that 74 Squadron were engaged with JG26, and that Mölders was in fact hit by F/Lt John Webster of 41 Squadron as he pursued his colleague F/O Lovell.[38] This version may lack the romantic appeal of a duel between two famous aces, but is almost certainly the truth. Whoever is right, 74 Squadron lost two pilots with their machines, with two more Spitfires damaged, and Lovell's Spitfire was hit. JG51 lost one Messerschmitt and two were damaged, one of which belonged to Mölders, who was also wounded in the leg. He was lucky. The aces made most of the kills, but most of them were also hit themselves, often when they were concentrating on a kill, as Mölders was. As the dogfights grew larger, the likelihood of this increased.

Malan was one of the names beginning to be mentioned on the British side. Because tactics were the official preserve of the Air Fighting Development Unit, individual air leaders in the RAF had less influence on them than their counterparts in the Luftwaffe. Within these limits, Malan became the most influential pilot within 11 Group.

Thanks to his early career in the Merchant Navy, Adolf Gysbert Malan was known, fortunately perhaps, as 'Sailor' rather than as Adolf. Like his other namesake Adolf Galland, Malan traced his ancestry to French Huguenots. Given the uncertainties of maritime life, he decided to join the RAF in 1935. Passing out as 'above average', he was posted to 74 Squadron in November 1936. His qualities were recognised early on, so it is not surprising that the RAF did not allow the wrath of a young mother to blight his career. Following his Squadron Leader's posting to Fighter Command HQ, Malan took over 74 on 8 August 1940, having effectively led it in the air for some time.

With sixteen claims and two DFCs to his credit, all gained over the previous ten weeks, Malan was by then already a leading ace. Just coming up to thirty, he was older than most pilots and this, together with his solid physique and Sean Connery-style good looks, added to his natural authority. He was quiet and serious, but had powerful charisma. One of the squadron's fitters has recalled: 'I think Malan was the most wonderful man I ever met. Certainly, in all my long service in the RAF, I never met another like him.'[39]

There was, by all accounts, something deeply impressive about this man. He was modest and unfussy, an expert and a professional, but above all a team-builder. He was not interested in scores, although when the battle ended he was the RAF's top-scorer. One of his Flight Commanders, Harbourn Mackay Stephen, has commented:

> I don't really know how many I shot down. Much has been written about the competition between individuals in their quest to be top scorer. Such competition in my experience did not exist. We all did our job, which was to destroy as many of the enemy as we could. If the opportunity presented itself then we took it as an individual, a section or a squadron ... We were not in there for personal glory but as part of a team, and in 74's case a very well disciplined team.[40]

Malan's pilots held him in awe and he drove them hard with constant practice. Under his leadership his Flight Commanders, John Mungo-Park and Stephen, became a formidable fighting pair and excellent leaders in their own right. Malan was extremely aggressive in the air and unusual in being driven to some extent by a hatred of the Germans.

He learned very fast and gave clear and insistent voice to his opinions. After action over Dunkirk he had 74's guns re-harmonised at 250 yards instead of 400. Based at Hornchurch, he discussed tactics with the C/Os of the other two squadrons there, abandoned official RAF tactics and had 74 fly in loose fours instead of vics of three. After the Battle of Britain he formulated his famous 'Ten Rules of Air Fighting' which were widely circulated within Fighter Command. Unfortunately, during the Battle itself his views were unofficial.

13. THE MEN

On 17 August, a few days after the assault on the British mainland had begun, Leutnant Hans-Otto Lessing, a fighter pilot with II./JG51, wrote home to his parents. The previous day, he had scored his fifth kill. This was, he wrote, the hundredth victory of his wing:

> And of these Hauptmann Tietzen, my Staffel commander alone has nineteen! I witnessed most of his kills. It is fantastic, the way he shoots. He is the boss, he moves us into position and selects the victims, and we have to do little more than cover him. There is a wonderful sense of teamwork in the Staffel. With his twentieth victory, the Ritterkreuz will be due. For me, the award of the Iron Cross, First Class, has been imminent since my fourth kill.
>
> Our own losses are only moderate. Seven in the entire Gruppe, and of these three certainly survive in captivity. We are in the Geschwader of Major Mölders, the most successful Geschwader. Ours is the most successful Gruppe and our 5th Staffel, with thirty-seven victories, the most successful Staffel.
>
> During the last few days the British have been getting weaker, though individuals continue to fight well. Often the Spitfires give beautiful displays of aerobatics. Recently I had to watch in admiration as one of them played a game with thirty Messerschmitts, without itself ever getting into danger; but such individuals are few. The Hurricanes are tired old 'puffers'.
>
> This is only a short letter. One would have to write a book to give even a brief picture of events. I am having the time of my life. I would not swap places with a king. Peacetime is going to be very boring after this!
>
> Your
> Hans-Otto[1]

Hans-Otto need not have worried about becoming bored in peacetime. The following afternoon, at 1735, together with his admired boss, Horst Tietzen, Hans-Otto Lessing was killed by a 'tired old "puffer"'. They went down into the sea off Whitstable, the victims of two Polish pilots of 501 Squadron, which flew Hurricanes. Tietzen's body was washed up on the coast some time later. He had a single bullet wound to the head and his pistol was missing. Hans-Otto was never found.

This letter, poignant as it is in its context, gives some insight into the warrior-hero ethos of the Luftwaffe's fighter arm. Morale is clearly very high, and it is also clear that the writer regards war as tremendous fun – or at least that he wanted his parents to think he did. The main theme of his letter is how successful he and his unit have been. Though he uses no sporting analogies, he is passionately interested in his performance in terms of the score, not with a view to defeating the enemy, but with a view to beating rival units on his own side. The war itself is merely the occasion for him to develop his technical skills. A true professional, he admires a skilled and daring foe as much as anyone on his own side, whilst remaining confident of his own side's overall superiority. He seems to have fought without hatred.

The Luftwaffe was out to create warrior-heroes. Its clinging to a pseudo-knightly ethos was just as archaic as the class distinctions in the RAF, but given a modern twist. It encouraged score-chasing by individual pilots and Goebbels used them as propaganda material. During the Battle, the rivalry between the leading contenders for the number-one spot, Mölders, Galland and Wick, became intense, and the Wehrmacht newspaper *Signal* published voluminous photos and articles about their exploits. When he died, Horst Tietzen was in fourth place. The drive to build up his score affected how he flew. Tietzen's wingman would indeed have been expected to do 'little more than cover him', and he would have gone for the best opportunities himself. 'Vati' Mölders stressed that the most important thing for a young pilot was to get his first victory without too much trauma, but in practice the pressure on the leaders to score led to this wise advice being ignored.[2] The RAF, in contrast, refused to officially recognise aces and only reluctantly co-operated with press interest in the likes of Tuck, Malan or Bader.

The philosophy behind decorations was also different. The Luftwaffe had an output-driven incentive system, with a certain number of victories needed for each decoration. With twenty kills, Tietzen got a Ritterkreuz (Knight's Cross), albeit posthumously.[3] In the RAF, DFCs tended to be awarded for 'distinguished service', but the criteria were less explicit. The highest decorations, including the VC, were input-driven. The VC was 'for valour', in other words, extraordinary courage, whether or not it was militarily effective.

The Luftwaffe, the only arm of the German armed services to grow up entirely afresh under the collectivist Nazi régime, and the only one led by a Nazi politician, was highly individualistic. In the fighter units, it fostered a form of personality cult around the leading aces. Having to reinvent itself anew in

1935, it looked back to the famous individuals of World War I as its source of inspiration. Every unit had its own insignia, even down to the level of the Staffel, and whilst some Geschwader were given emblematic names like 'Edelweiss' (KG51) or Löwe ('Lion' – KG26), others were named after the great men of the past such as 'Immelmann' (StG2) and, of course, 'Richthofen' (JG2). Being new, the Luftwaffe was also easier to politicise and other units were named after Nazi heroes like 'Schlageter' (JG26) or 'Horst Wessel' (ZG26).

The traditions of World War I were kept literally alive by the presence of veterans like Osterkamp in leadership positions. Its most prestigious fighter unit, JG2 'Richthofen', was led by Major Harry von Bülow-Bothkamp, who had led the Jagdstaffel 'Boelcke' during the First World War and scored six victories. In 1940 he was forty-two. The most unusual of the veterans was the nearest Germany got to Douglas Bader, Oberstleutnant Joachim-Friedrich Huth, who had lost a leg in World War I and had been given the very demanding job of leading ZG26. He was forty-four.

Air fighting is a young man's business, and in the course of the summer Göring replaced most of these veterans. In the RAF, Dowding had already instituted a policy that no man over twenty-six was to lead a squadron in the air. Göring was less concerned about age than about selecting the leading aces. He left Huth where he was. When Galland took over JG26, he was only three years younger than the man he replaced, the former Olympic medallist Gotthard Handrick. However, he was a far more successful pilot.

This was part of the Luftwaffe's emphasis on individual stardom and it had some negative aspects. At the margin, some of the most successful gave the impression that they were after their own glory rather than the success of the unit, and the view became widespread that some of them were building their scores at the expense of their protecting wingmen, the poor old 'Katschmareks'. Ulrich Steinhilper reports on such discussions in JG52 which increased in frequency as the battle continued:

The debates nearly always came back to the subject of battle honours and decorations, mostly prompted by the NCOs who felt more aggrieved than the officers. Why was it, they would ask so often, that the decorations are, in the main, only handed out to those with the highest scores? Wasn't it clear that it was those who were flying ahead and insisting on strong formation discipline around them who were also running up the highest personal scores – almost exactly matched by the losses from their own formations – losing one Katschmarek after another for another white stripe on the tail of their aircraft? And who was it who was suffering the most, they would ask. Of course, it was the NCOs who generally flew at the rear or on the flanks.[4]

Those known to be plagued by a chronic desire to have a Knight's Cross and its various accoutrements (Oak Leaves, Swords and Diamonds) dangling around

their necks were said to be suffering from 'Halsweh' (a sore throat).⁵ Adolf
Galland was one well-known sufferer, and he used his position first as
Gruppenkommandeur of III./JG26 and then as Kommodore of the whole
Geschwader to hand-pick his wingmen.

At the beginning of the battle, Galland's Katschmarek was the superb
young pilot Joachim Müncheberg. During this period he got four victories,
which was considered outstanding for a wingman. On 22 August, when
Galland took over the whole Geschwader, he gave in to pressure from
Müncheberg and made him the leader of the 7th Staffel.⁶ Thereupon
Müncheberg's score rose to twenty by mid-September, which got him his
Ritterkreuz, and by the time of his death in March 1943, stood at 135.
Müncheberg's place was taken by Oblt. Horten. He flew forty-five missions
with Galland until the end of September, witnessing twenty-five of his victories, but only getting into a firing position himself eight times and making
seven claims (an unlikely total). On the last day of September, Walter Kienzle,
a potential Gruppenkommandeur, flew as Galland's wingman and was shot
down over Kent. He was captured, badly wounded.⁷ Using the best pilots like
this was not a good way to employ resources.

The pressure to score also produced some transparent cases of dishonesty.
One story has it that a famous German ace returned from a combat to claim
three Spitfires. His ground crew discovered that his guns had not been fired.
His score went up, but his standing fell and the tale soon did the rounds.⁸ It was
not good for morale.

Nevertheless, there can be no doubt that Galland himself was a superb
fighter pilot and a hard but highly effective leader. Under him, JG26 became by
general consent the most successful fighter Geschwader of the Luftwaffe, claiming 285 victories for the loss of 56 pilots, a ratio of over 5:1.⁹ On 26 August,
Milch inspected a number of units at the front, including JG26. He describes
III./JG26, which had hitherto been commanded by Galland, as first class,
whereas I. and II./JG26 were 'not on the same level'.¹⁰ Galland's promotion to
Kommodore undoubtedly improved the effectiveness of the whole
Geschwader.

He did not make life easy for his men. He gave his Gruppe some tough
feed-back after their first mission over England, when two pilots were lost for
only two claims. Nor did he have much time for weak novices. Once, when
flying together with JG26, Steinhilper overheard some of their radio transmissions. The silence was broken by a frightened voice calling out 'Spitfire hinter
mir!' ('Spitfire on my tail!'). A few seconds later, the trembling voice repeated
with greater urgency, 'Spitfire immer noch hinter mir. Was soll ich tun? Immer
noch hinter mir!' ('Spitfire still behind me! What should I do? He's still behind
me!') He should probably have bunted into a dive. Galland's voice came over
the R/T with an alternative suggestion: 'Aussteigen, Sie Bettnässer!' ('Bale out,
you bedwetter!').¹¹

The word for 'fighter' in German is 'Jäger' ('hunter'), and the Luftwaffe's tradition was that of a hunting club. The war was a wonderful opportunity for the gifted few to engage in a dangerous but exhilarating sport. At the beginning of the war trophies were collected. Mölders and Galland actually went hunting in their spare time, and after Galland had visited to Berlin at the end of September to collect Oak Leaves to add to his Knight's Cross for forty victories, he joined Göring and Mölders for a deer hunt at the Reichsjägerhof in East Prussia. It was seen as an entirely appropriate way for the three of them to be spending their time.

The image of the hunter sits uneasily alongside the image of the 'Knights of the Air'. A hunter stalks prey that is often defenceless, and kills it unde-tected. A knight is supposed to joust in one-to-one combat against an opponent equally well-armed. This did not stop the Germans from thinking of themselves as both. It is striking how many German pilots interviewed after the war agree that air fighting was chivalrous.[12] All deny that they would have obeyed an order to shoot at parachutes. Galland explicitly mentions a conver-sation he had with Göring in which the question was posed. Galland replied that he would neither obey nor pass on such an order and reports that Göring clapped him on the back and said that he would have reacted in the same way in 1918. The suggestion, he said, came from 'Party circles'.[13]

Numbers of their opponents nevertheless claim to have seen friends shot up on parachutes. Some men who baled out were found on the ground riddled with bullets. One witness was Pilot Officer Dennis David, who flew with 87 and 213 Squadrons:

> Johnnie Cock was shot up and had baled out at 20,000 feet. On his way down, one of those 109s came round and started shooting at him. His parachute cords went ping! ping! ping! – beginning to sep-arate him from his chute canopy as the bullets flew around him. I managed to get behind that murderous Hun and shot him down. I circled Johnnie till he hit the water, because I wasn't going to let another Hun shoot him down.
>
> I came to know and like some Germans later on. But I hated the enemy then for what they tried to do to Johnnie Cock and what they did to Johnnie Dewar, our squadron leader, later in the battle. He parachuted out, but when we found his body, it was riddled with bullets. Some of our people say what wonderful men the German pilots were personally. But I still feel that men who could shoot boys in parachutes are not people I want to know.[14]

One should bear in mind that parachuting through an air battle involved the risk of being hit by mistake, and it is always possible that aircraft which appeared intent on murder were aiming at another plane. One should also bear in mind that the writer could not possibly have heard a 'ping! ping! ping!' sound over the roar of his own engine, but no doubt saw the cords snapping.

The intent to kill men on parachutes has never been unambiguously established, though there are some cases – on both sides – in which the
circumstantial evidence is strong. They remain isolated examples.

However that may be, Dowding later wrote that the Germans would have
been fully justified in ordering their pilots to shoot at parachutes, as British
pilots, landing on their own territory, would be fighting them again the next
day. He did not expect his pilots to do it to the Germans, however, as they were
potential prisoners of war. He added that he was glad to say that in most cases
the German pilots refrained from exercising their rights.[15]

The young men on the other side of the Channel were by and large just as
happy to be doing what they were doing as their opposite numbers were. What
that meant has been summed up most succinctly of all by one of their number,
Paddy Barthropp: 'It was just beer, women and Spitfires, a bunch of little John
Waynes running about the place. When you were nineteen, you couldn't give a
monkey's.'[16]

Indeed the degree of psychic and somatic fulfilment offered by a life filled
with 'beer, women and Spitfires' seemed to most who enjoyed it then, and to
many who contemplate it now, to leave little wanting. The RAF was not a
hunting fraternity, but a flying club, the best flying club in the world.

Although the RAF had admitted all social classes to its ranks, a public
school ethos permeated the service. The men were 'chaps' and the squadron
was treated like a sports team: 'Understatement, restraint and humility were
virtues of leadership. Bragging or showing emotion was eschewed. It was especially important not to admit weakness and "showing a stiff upper lip" was
more than a wartime cliché. In this pattern, courage and leadership were insep-
arable from the character of a man.'[17]

The behaviour expected in Fighter Command goes back to the indiffer-
ence to danger evinced by Wellington's officers, but by 1940 it had been largely
seen through as an act and grafted onto schoolboy behavioural norms. It was
recognised that courage is not fearlessness but the overcoming of fear. There
was no disgrace in openly showing its symptoms. Many pilots got jumpy about
the phone ringing. One of the most successful and respected pilots of the
battle, 'Ginger' Lacey, was sick beside his aircraft every time the Tannoy went.[18]
There was a lot of laughter about macabre events, and cheerfulness became an
important virtue:

> The thing that sticks out in my mind was the laughter. Some of the
> things we laughed at might be regarded as a bit macabre. 'Old so-and-
> so ended up on his back and they had to get a crane to lift his aircraft
> to get him out.' The fact that old so-and-so was in hospital was nei-
> ther here nor there. It was still a hell of a laugh.
>
> We didn't take ourselves too seriously. If anybody was heard
> waxing a bit heavy, and asking if any of us would survive another

week, he'd be laughed out of the room. It was taboo to admit that you were in any sort of personal difficulties. We were kids, but at the same time at the top of our profession. We were demonstrating that we were better than the enemy and were saving our country.[19]

Professional pride and technical skill, about which Wellington's officers cared little, were important, but if you tried to out-do your colleagues they would usually find a way of taking you down a peg or two. Non-fatal accidents were a source of amusement, but you did not want to prang too many kites, or you might become the butt of too many jokes. Showing off or seeking publicity was looked down upon. Word quickly got round if anyone was felt to be pulling strings or to have too great a regard for their own interests. The worst thing anyone could do was be caught acting heroically.

Courage was whatever it took to do the job well, and that meant primarily endurance and continued aggression in the air. Most of them kept going because they had a job to do, and they were the only ones who could do it. The closest thing to heroism was displaying humour:

While we were closing in, the first Stukas were peeling off and going into their dives, one after the other. I thought, 'What's the CO going to do? Is he going in behind this lot?' But I realised there was no going behind them. They were stretching out right across the Channel. He just eased off towards the second echelon of Stukas and said: 'Come on chaps. Let's surround them.' And there were just eight of us! That was Lovell-Gregg. He didn't come back.[20]

The fear of fear was very strong. Here is a revealing account from a pilot who had twice returned to base with a faulty undercarriage which the maintenance crews found to be in order:

I started getting some strange looks . . . When we went off on the third trip of the day, I prayed to God harder than I had ever prayed in my life that the undercarriage would come up so that I could prove that I wasn't trying to stay out of action. To my intense relief, the undercarriage finally came up.

I was desperately frightened of being thought a coward. Every mission during the Battle of Britain was potentially a life or death situation, but I was much more concerned about that than about risking my life fighting the Germans.[21]

The ethos of Fighter Command resulted in a force which thought so highly of itself, it never imagined it could be beaten. On 27 May, at the time of the Dunkirk evacuation, Flight Lieutenant Ronald Wight, a Flight Commander with 213 Squadron who had already seen action in France, wrote to his mother:

Well, another day is gone, and with it a lot of grand blokes. Got another brace of 109s today, but the whole of the Luftwaffe seems to leap on us – we are hopelessly outnumbered. I was caught napping by a 109 in the middle of a dogfight and got a couple of holes in the aircraft, one of them filled the office with smoke, but the Jerry overshot and he's dead.

If anyone says anything to you in the future about the inefficiency of the RAF – I believe the BEF troops were booing the RAF in Dover the other day – tell them from me we only wish we could do more. But without more aircraft we can do no more than we have done – that is, our best, and that's fifty times better than the German best, though they are fighting under the most advantageous conditions.

I know of no RAF pilot who has refused combat yet – and that sometimes means combat with odds of more than fifty-to-one. Three of us the other day had been having a fight and were practically out of ammunition and juice when we saw more than eighty 109s with twelve Ju 87s. All the same, we gave them combat, so much so that they left us alone in the end – on their side of the Channel too. This is just the work that we all do. One of my Sergeants shot down three fighters and a bomber before they got him – and then he got back in a paddle steamer.

So don't worry. We are going to win this war even if we have only one aeroplane and one pilot left. The Boche could produce the whole Luftwaffe and you would see the one pilot and the one aeroplane go into combat . . . The spirit of the average pilot has to be seen to be believed.[22]

Unlike Hans-Otto Lessing, Ronald Wight was up against it and engaged in serious war. He stresses the skill and determination of everyone in the face of great odds, and he feels superior to his enemy, who only seems to have numbers on his side. He is part of a great team of 'grand blokes' who are taking losses but will prevail in the end or go down fighting. He shows no knowledge of, or interest in, the relative performance of individuals or his unit. He makes no bones about being caught napping himself, but he uses it as a case of turning the tables on an advantaged enemy. Still, it could hardly have comforted his mother.

The impression he gives is that every pilot in Fighter Command is undaunted by odds and willing to take on anything. There may be an element of bravado in this for Mum's consumption. There were of course cases of pilots refusing combat. Both Deere and Tuck, for example, have related stories about cases of LMF (i.e. cowardice) on their squadrons.[23] But these cases were few and far between, and dealt with rapidly so that they remained isolated. So many pilots actually did pile in at daunting odds, that the sentiments expressed in this letter must have reflected how most of the pilots felt.

Ronald Wight continued to fight in the spirit he depicts. He was one of those who attacked the 165 raiders Sperrle sent against Portland on 11 August, and in the biggest dogfight seen up to then, in which the British were outnumbered by 2:1, he was shot down and killed.

Weaknesses in squadron leadership were usually discovered quite quickly. People were replaced or, as was the case in 234 Squadron for a time, the senior Flight Commander took over.[24] At the other extreme, some outstanding leaders began to emerge from the fighting. Some, like Townsend of 85 Squadron, Thompson of 111, or Johnny Kent of 303, simply possessed the competence, personal integrity and social skills necessary to turn their men into followers, and hence themselves into leaders. Others, like Tuck, Bader or Malan, were also tactical innovators and their influence spread more widely, but very slowly.

The problem in Fighter Command was caused by the ones in the middle: brave, honest and sometimes inspiring men who lacked both knowledge of air fighting and the instinct to question official doctrine. Dowding realised during the battle that heavy losses were incurred in units led by 'gallant and experienced' officers who, because of their lack of combat experience, led their pilots into a trap or were 'caught while climbing by an enemy formation "out of the sun"'.[25] This problem tended to solve itself through the brutal effects of natural selection. The men tended to follow the one who most seemed to know what he was doing, regardless of rank. Fighter squadrons were staffed entirely by officers and NCOs. There were no 'squaddies' ready to blindly obey orders, and it was in any case often hard to tell in the air whether a pilot was being insubordinate. By and large, and usually with pain, natural selection worked.

The main attraction to the RAF's recruits was the glamour and social status of flying. Most training was about flying not fighting, and many were there because they loved aeroplanes and thought it was all great fun. They were not military men in the traditional sense, and the idea of having to kill people came as a shock to some of them, as it did to Peter Townsend.

The son of a civil servant of the Empire, Townsend was born in Burma and grew up in Devon. He went to Haileybury and fell in love with aeroplanes when his father took him to a local air display. He passed through Cranwell and was posted to No. 1 Squadron in 1935. After some time in Asia, he returned to 43 Squadron in Tangmere in 1937 and was depressed to find that his flying club had been invaded by a lot of new people 'with a different style'. He was even more depressed to find that they were training for war. He rebelled, he has written, 'against the thought of flying being used as a means to kill', for it went against all it had meant to him, and he seriously thought about leaving the RAF. By the time of Munich, however, he had become rather bellicose towards the 'swaggering, bullying Germans', and discovered that the new boys were actually quite good chaps. He first saw action with 43 Squadron, helping to shoot down some lone raiders, and in May took over command of 85 Squadron in Debden.[26]

In many ways, Townsend embodied an old English ethical ideal. He was indeed a 'verray, parfit gentil knyght'. Modest and completely charming, he never uttered a profane word, which was rather unusual, even in 1940. He was motivated not by any ideology but by a straightforward set of values, which the Germans had started to violate.

Few of 'the Few' felt any ideological motivation. People who thought too much suffered. A combination of the ordinary patriotism taken for granted at the time and black crosses in the air was enough to make the issues clear. The Nazis were an unpleasant lot, always marching and shouting, and the pilots were not going to have any of that sort of nonsense over in England. RAF drill corporals were bad enough.

There were some, though, given to deeper reflection. Richard Hillary was a member of Oxford University Air Squadron when the war started, and he joined up in part to find something meaningful to do and in part to prove that, undisciplined aesthete though he might be, he was a match for 'Hitler's dogma-fed youth'. His ideals were embodied by Goethe: individualism, free thought, enlightenment, self-realisation. He made close friends with a Cambridge contemporary, Peter Pease, the son of Sir Richard and Lady Pease of Richmond. This handsome, reserved Etonian had very different motives for fighting. He was a committed Catholic, and explained to his bemused friend that Hitler had to be defeated, because if he won:

> All courage will die out of the world – the courage to love, to create, to take risks, whether physical, intellectual or moral. Men will hesitate to carry out the promptings of the heart or the brain because, having acted, they will live in fear that their action may be discovered and themselves cruelly punished. Thus all love, all spontaneity will die out of the world. Emotion will have atrophied. Thought will have petrified. The oxygen breathed by the soul, so to speak, will vanish, and mankind will wither.

Hillary was still struggling with that when they both joined 603 Squadron at Turnhouse in Scotland in the summer of 1940.[27]

On the outset of war the attitude to the enemy was neutral. Once the Battle of Britain began, attitudes hardened. The British knew that they were facing heavy odds and the threat to their homeland was very real. Far fewer British pilots than German ones talk about chivalry, and hatred of the enemy was far more common. It was often prompted by a sense of outrage that the Luftwaffe was invading British air space without an invitation:

> I'd say there was no chivalry at all. You mean between the German Air Force and the British? I'd say absolutely none. Not as far as I was concerned. I hated them. They were trying to do something to us. They were trying to enslave us.[28]

During the Battle of Britain was the only time I really felt . . . a territorial possession. One used to look down and see one's own country, one's own people, and see these hideous great hordes of aircraft flying over. One thought, 'Bloody hell', you know – one can't possibly allow this to happen.'[29]

Later in the war, I flew in the Middle East over desert. You'd look down and there was a lot of sand. It meant nothing to me. But flying over Kent and Surrey and the green fields of southern England and the Thames Estuary – that was home. The fact that someone was trying to take it away or break it up made you angry.[30]

Who the Hell do these Huns think they are flying like this over OUR country in their bloody bombers covered with Iron Crosses and Swastikas?[31]

This is all a long way from the Edwardian ethos of the World War I pilot Cecil Lewis, who apologises for referring to his enemies as 'Huns', adding in a footnote:

It has been suggested that this word has an ugly connotation, and that I should not use it. But we always referred to our friends the enemy as 'Huns', just as the infantry knew them as 'Fritz' or 'Jerry', and nothing derogatory was, or is, intended.[32]

By 1940 the world had lost its innocence, grown up, and got a lot nastier.

Although the territorial instinct could not have loomed as large, the Commonwealth members of the RAF were similarly motivated to their British counterparts. In 1940, Fighter Command was an international force. Some 80% of the pilots were British, but nearly 10% were from Commonwealth countries, and most of the remainder from occupied Europe. They and the other foreign pilots flew alongside their British comrades in regular squadrons. Almost every one had a few non-British pilots in its ranks.

The men from Commonwealth countries were to make up a disproportionate number of the RAF's aces. This is probably because they tended to be more questioning of official doctrine, and also because more of them grew up on farms, where they learned how to shoot.

Of the men from the Commonwealth, the largest national contingent was from New Zealand, which had 129 officially accredited pilots in the battle, 4.4% of the total. The RAF began serious recruiting in New Zealand in 1936 when expansion was getting into swing and, given that the New Zealand Air Force consisted of 20 officers and 107 NCOs, any New Zealander who wanted to fly had little choice but to join the RAF. The first arrived in July 1937, including Al Deere and his mate, Colin Gray. Another of the New Zealand contingent was Brian Carbury, a shoe salesman who joined up because he had got bored with his job. The Oxbridge pair Richard Hillary and Peter Pease found him in the bar when they arrived at 603 Squadron and he greeted them warmly.

Australians also joined the RAF before the war and in 1940 there were thirty in Fighter Command. Australia wanted to send complete RAAF squadrons to Britain, and six were offered to the RAF on 20 September 1939. However, the first Australian fighter squadron in Europe did not arrive until April 1941.[33] One of the thirty pilots already there was Pat Hughes. He had joined the Royal Australian Air Force in 1935, and transferred to the RAF on a short service commission. He was a Flight Commander at 234 Squadron when Bob Doe arrived. More experienced and more mature than the others, he effectively led the Squadron. He took Bob Doe under his wing and Bob listened hard to what he had to say.

The second largest Commonwealth contingent after New Zealand was provided by Canada, with 100 pilots or 3.4% of the total. Most of these had come to Britain under their own initiative before the war for a variety of reasons, but predominantly because they wanted to fly. The RCAF had few vacancies and particularly stringent educational requirements for entry, so the RAF was the obvious alternative.[34] After 1933 the Canadian and British governments co-operated officially, with selected short service commission officers being sent from Canada after receiving flying training. After the outbreak of war, the formation of Canadian units was seen as a political necessity, and so, under the British Commonwealth Air Training Plan, 242 Squadron was formed from Canadians in the RAF. The disaster in France in 1940 galvanised the Canadian government into sending its only properly-equipped fighter squadron to Britain, and in June No. 1 Squadron RCAF arrived, complete with their own fourteen Hurricanes. They were moved to 11 Group in July and were in the thick of it from mid-August.[35]

The remaining twenty-seven Commonwealth pilots in Fighter Command came from South Africa and what was then Rhodesia. All of these were volunteers who joined on their own initiative, for their governments were too concerned with events on their own continent to officially send forces to Britain. By 1941, the SAAF was fully committed in North Africa. Some of those who joined up were of British parents who had emigrated to Africa, but were themselves educated in Britain, so joining the RAF was natural. Others, like Malan, went to greater lengths. One can be grateful that he, in particular, did.

The RAF was in a real sense beginning to deploy the resources of an Empire. However, it did not end there, for the German occupation of Europe brought Fighter Command a windfall of 276 pilots from the Continent, the largest group of whom were the 146 Poles, fully 5% of the Command's strength and the largest single non-British contingent. Their contribution to what was to come was to be quite extraordinary.

The Polish Air Force was founded in 1918 and saw action in Poland's successful war against its new Soviet neighbour between 1919 and 1921. Its personnel were drawn largely from the cavalry and they continued its traditions of gallant and undisciplined knight-errantry. Spared the slaughter of the trenches, Poles could still be romantic about warfare, especially as they saw in it their only salvation from centuries of oppression. The Air Force attracted entrants from all levels of society, chosen on far more rational grounds than in other countries: good eyesight, speed of reaction and physical fitness. Given its small size, the new service could afford to be choosy, so its recruits were very good and its training programmes at least as thorough as those of Britain or Germany.[36]

However, when the Germans attacked Poland, the Air Force was in the process of re-equipping with modern machines. Most of their 392 combat aircraft were obsolete, so they did not last long against the 1,941 modern aircraft the Luftwaffe launched against them. They learned to fight during the battle for their homeland, but on 17 September, the Russians attacked their defensive positions in Eastern Poland from the rear, and collapse was rapid. No less than 8,500 Polish airmen got away to the West. Some made their way to France, and within nine months found themselves in the same position. Via many circuitous routes, they followed their government into exile and trickled over to England.

The British thought the Poles were a bit unruly and assumed they needed a rest after what they had been through. They set about civilising them and teaching them English. For their part the Poles discovered that English cooking was even worse than its reputation, being particularly affronted at what the island race did to the noble cabbage, and that English girls were not only far prettier than their reputation but remarkably Polonophile to boot. This latter discovery greatly accelerated their linguistic progress, and few had not mastered the phrase, 'You very beautiful', within a few days and, 'You me go pictures', within a week.[37]

Dowding was cool towards them, but as their English improved enough to enable them to understand commands in the air, they were sent to squadrons. Even so, on 29 July he told the Secretary of State for Air, Archibald Sinclair, that he was 'extremely apprehensive about the infiltration of foreign pilots into British fighter squadrons', partly because of the language issue and partly because he thought it might undermine morale. He therefore pressed for the formation of all-Polish squadrons. So it was that in August, all Polish airmen became members of the Polish Air Force, and two fighter squadrons, 302 and 303, based on the remnants of Air Regiments from Poznan and Warsaw respectively, were set up, with British squadron leaders and flight commanders.[38] Two bomber squadrons, 300 and 301, were also formed and took part in raids on the Channel ports. Sixty-six Poles flew with 302 and 303 squadrons during the Battle of Britain.

The remainder opted to remain in their British units, where they felt more than at home. They coped with the ways of the English. When Flight Lieutenant Brzezina and Flying Officer Szczesny arrived at 74 Squadron in

August, they were quickly and perhaps inevitably dubbed Breezy and Sneezy. They were treated like squadron mascots, and loved it. Ludwik Martel, who flew with 54 and 603 Squadrons, writes that he twice refused to transfer to a Polish unit. 'I felt so happy amongst these comrades, I can honestly say that I never had such relationships again in my life . . . It is impossible to describe how charming they were, how kind . . . My most cherished memories date from 1940 to 1941, when I was in an English squadron.' Boleslaw Drobinski felt the same.[39]

Dowding was one of the first to realise that, far from undermining morale, the Poles had improved it. As soon as they got involved in the fighting, it was not only the girls who loved them. After the battle, Dowding wrote that, 'had it not been for the magnificent material contributed by the Polish squadrons and their unsurpassed gallantry I hesitate to say that the outcome of the battle would have been the same.'[40] Johnny Kent was despondent when he learned that his first operational posting was to 303. 'All I knew about the Polish Air force was that it had only lasted about three days against the Luftwaffe and I had no reason to suppose that they would shine any more brightly operating from England,' he wrote.[41] When he left them to take over 92 Squadron, he had a 'quite fantastic' party and was very sorry to leave.[42]

The record of 303 in particular was indeed unsurpassed. Although only entering battle on 31 August, they were, with 126 accredited kills, the highest claiming squadron in Fighter Command. Such were the suspicions raised by their claims that their station commander at Northolt, Group Captain Vincent, flew with them on one occasion and reported back, rather shaken, that 'what they claimed, they did indeed get!'[43] Moreover, despite their reputation as reckless daredevils, 303's claims-to-loss ratio, at 14:1, was the fourth best in Fighter Command. The highest-claiming pilot in the battle, Josef Frantisek, flew with 303, though he was, ironically, a Czech who had escaped to Poland when his country was occupied in 1938. When he died in an unexplained accident on 8 October he had added seventeen confirmed kills to those he had gained in Poland and France.[44]

There were good reasons for the Poles' outstanding performance. They were all very well-trained, battle-experienced pilots. Many had been flight or squadron commanders in Poland, and they often ignored their less combat-experienced British officers.[45] They always got in very close, so it seems likely that their claims were indeed more genuine than average. And they were driven by hatred. They had seen brutality in the air and on the ground in Poland, and were animated by patriotism of a seriousness and vibrancy unknown in Britain. They felt a passionate desire to avenge their defeat.[46] Boleslaw Drobinski put it like this:

> When you seen [sic] the Swastika or black cross on the aircraft your heart beating gets much quicker, and you decided that you must get him or you get shot yourself. It's a feeling of absolute . . . vengeance.[47]

This is more than the territorial feeling or indignation felt by many of the British. Poland was occupied. It made a difference.

Czechoslovakia had been occupied longer than Poland, and it made a difference to the 88 Czechs in Fighter Command as well. Their Air Force, formed in 1929, had never had the chance to go into action. Some flyers moved to Poland, some directly to France. Once there, they, like the Poles, had to move on again, and some reached England, where they stayed. In July, 310 Squadron was formed, followed by 312 in September. Two bomber squadrons were also set up, and remained in the RAF for the duration of the war. As in the case of the Poles, they were very good pilots, but their British commanders were a little taken aback by some of their ways. Flight Lieutenant Gordon Sinclair was made a flight commander in 310:

> The Czechs were totally disciplined. They did what was expected of them, though not necessarily what they were told to do, because they knew sort of instinctively what they were supposed to do. The young ones were very frightened of their commanding officer. One day, early on, one of these lads crashed a Hurricane in landing. The undercarriage buckled up. They quickly had a court martial among themselves and they were going to shoot him behind the hangar. Douglas Blackwood and I discovered what was going on and said: 'You can't do that sort of thing. We run the show, not you.'[48]

There were two other smaller groups of exiles: twenty-eight Belgians and fourteen Free French. Some of the Belgians had already flown Hurricanes, so when they arrived they were posted directly to various RAF squadrons equipped with them. No Belgian units were created in 1940, though in 1941 Belgian flights were created in 609 and 131 Squadrons, and in November an all-Belgian unit was formed, followed by another some months later.

The French were also sent to serve with British squadrons, and two in particular, René Mouchotte and Jean Demozay, were to achieve distinction after the battle. Mouchotte became the commander of 341 'Alsace' Squadron and shared, with the Canadian Ray Charles, Biggin Hill's 1,000th claim on 15 May 1943. He was killed on bomber escort duty late that August.[49] Demozay, who had acted as an interpreter for No. 1 Squadron in France, joined them himself in October. He later commanded 91 Squadron and the French bomber wing Groupe Patrie. He ended the war as Air Schools Inspector for the French Air Force, only to die in an accident in December 1945.[50]

The exact number of Americans in Fighter Command is uncertain because some pretended to be Canadian in order to get round their government's enforcement of its neutrality. There were probably about eleven. Three of them got past FBI agents at the Canadian border and tried to join the Finnish Air Force to fight the Russians, but by the time they got to Europe that war was over so they ended up in 609 Squadron and fought Germans instead.

They were volunteers of the purest sort, for it was not yet their war. They fought for fun or for freedom. It was hard to tell.[51]

Among the Americans was the film producer, stockbroker and Olympic bobsleigh champion Billy Fiske, who joined English society when he married the former wife of the Earl of Warwick in 1938. He joined 601, the 'Millionaire's' squadron in order to be able to fly with the friends he had in it. On 17 August he became the first American to die in the war.[52] These early volunteers were the forerunners of the 240 Americans who joined the three 'Eagle' squadrons of the RAF created in 1941 and forming an experienced nucleus around which the formidable fighter force of the US 8th Air Force was then built.

Thus it was that Fighter Command, though predominantly British, was a diverse, international force, with men of different backgrounds and different motivation. This heterogeneity was overlaid with the unifying ethos developed by the service. To all appearances, they had much in common with their enemy. They were the same age, had the same high spirits and spent their time doing much the same things. Many pilots talk about the 'universal fellowship of the air', the bond that unites all those who love flying. Underneath this there were significant if subtle differences between the RAF and the Luftwaffe, as well as crass differences between the societies and systems they represented which were to have a telling effect on their performance.

One thing both sides had in common was the nature of the dangers they ran. Apart from the odd collision, the RAF and the Luftwaffe wrought destruction upon each other with bullets. Fired at more than 200 yards, they could be stopped by plate armour. Inside 200 yards, they could kill even a protected pilot. In addition, the British had the de Wilde incendiaries, and the Bf 109 fired explosive cannon shells. Both caused worse wounds than ordinary bullets.

Some bullets killed pilots, or incapacitated them so that they went down with their machines. Sometimes bullets hit oxygen bottles, which exploded, as petrol tanks could. These were probably the cause of the mid-air explosions reported by witnesses, in which aircraft just disintegrated. They also provided pilots with the quickest death. Bullets were also comparatively merciful and pilots did not discuss them much. Their first fear was fire.

A British pilot sat behind eighty-five gallons of high octane fuel. A Bf 109 pilot sat on top of eighty-seven. If the stuff caught fire, it developed temperatures of several thousands of degrees within seconds. Pilots talked of 'blow-torch' intensity. Skin flaked off instantly and hung in shreds, and flesh cooked. The smell was repulsive. Pain set in later, but it could, in one form or another, last a lifetime. The horrific nature of these injuries, often inflicted in just a few seconds before baling out, stimulated innovative surgery. The most celebrated example in Britain was Archibald McIndoe's burns unit at East Grinstead. It was experimental, so his patients from the time have christened themselves 'The Guinea-Pigs' and formed a club which holds reunions.[53]

Neither air force provided its pilots with flame-proof suits, so they wrapped themselves from head to foot, despite the hot days in the summer. RAF pilots had to hope a scramble did not catch them too inappropriately dressed. There were cases of pilots throwing a jacket on over pyjamas while running for their cockpits.[54] Goggles were worn largely to protect the eyes, but the rubber of the oxygen mask would melt in a fire, making it a dubious benefit. The main protection against fire was to get out fast. One pilot reckoned that the most time you had to leave the cockpit was eight seconds. That meant you would never fly again, but would get away with about twelve operations. If you took nine, it would mean being a patient of McIndoe's for the rest of the war. Ten meant you would never reach East Grinstead.[55]

Pilots usually tipped their parachute packers 10/- (50p) when they re-packed their parachutes after use, a handsome sum for a young man paid 11/6d a day.[56] If not used, the parachute was re-packed once a month anyway, but it rarely got to that. The money was well spent, and only a few parachutes failed to open. Few pilots who fought for more than a couple of weeks did not bail out once, and many did so several times. When fighters were hit the survival rate amongst pilots was 60–70%, and most of these baled out, though the temptation with a machine that was damaged but still flying was to remain with it. Standard procedure for British pilots was to turn their Hurricanes and Spitfires on their backs, undo their straps, push and be sucked out by the air pressure. When in more of a hurry, they simply slid back the Perspex canopy and stood up in the open cockpit. The concern was to be in a position to fall clear. The main danger was to avoid hitting the tailplane or getting the chute caught up in it.

Getting out was not always that easy, however. At speeds over 180 mph, the canopies of the British machines would not slide open,[57] and the pilot had to pull hard at a toggle catch above his head, fighting the air pressure which wanted to move the canopy forward. The toggle was connected by a wire to pins holding the base of the canopy in its grooves, and with a bit of luck a good tug of the toggle pulled them out and the canopy flew off. If the pressure was too great, as it could become during a dive, or if the grooves for the canopy had been bent by bullets, locking the canopy in place, there was a crowbar on the side of the cockpit. Being trapped in a blazing machine was probably every pilot's greatest fear. Some ended this way, and if they had their radios on 'transmit' their comrades and the controllers at the sector stations heard their friends' dying screams.

German pilots had an even tougher challenge. The hood of a 109 was heavy and swung open on a hinge to the right of the cockpit. When fully open, the left side of the canopy was only just clear of the cockpit, which meant that the pilot was always in danger of banging it with his head.[58] An unconscious pilot could not open his parachute. It also meant that the pilot had to bail out to the left – though the air pressure usually decided the direction of exit on the pilot's behalf – which was unfortunate if the left wing was on fire. Accordingly, the hood was fitted with a fast-release mechanism so that it could be jettisoned. If it failed to work, the pilot had to try to open the canopy in the normal way and hope that the slipstream rid him of the encumbrance it then represented.[59]

Unhappiest of all were the gunners of the Defiants. It was not chance that their casualties were worse than those of Defiant pilots. The turret escape-hatch was electrically operated and if this mechanism failed, as it usually would if the aircraft were damaged, there was no way out.

Force-landing was frequent and usually successful providing the under-carriage was up. None of the single-seaters ditched well, however. The engine was heavy and the radiator on the underside of all three types scooped up water, adding to the weight. They all started to nose-dive towards the bottom of the Channel in a matter of seconds.

Most meetings with the inhospitable waters of the Channel or North Sea began on the end of a parachute. The shock of the cold was bad for an unin-jured man, worse for a wounded one, and the salt water added pain to shock. Injuries could make it hard to escape from the parachute. If that were accom-plished, trembling hands then had to find the tube to blow up the life jacket, a demanding task if the sea were at all rough. There is always a swell in the Channel at the best of times. Those with the strength then swam towards the shore if they knew where it was, the others floated and waited. They had about four hours to be found before hypothermia took them. If they were found by British seamen, British pilots had to make sure they were identified as such, as merchantmen had not appreciated the attentions to which the Luftwaffe had subjected them since Dunkirk. The best method was to call them 'fucking bas-tards' as this provided incontrovertible proof of nationality.[60]

In addition to their He 59 seaplane air-sea rescue service, the Germans anchored rescue buoys for downed airmen off the French coast. They called them 'Rettungsbojen Generalluftzeugmeister' and the RAF called them 'lobster pots'. They each contained four bunks and were a thoughtful gesture, but most of them broke loose.

So great was their fear of the Channel that many German pilots took pis-tols with them so that they could make a quick end of things. This became so widespread that the Luftwaffe authorities banned side-arms in early September.

So it was that, if they thought about it, pilots on both sides hoped for a bullet or an explosion. Either was preferable to death by fire or death by water. Neither side liked fighting over the Channel, but the contest for it was growing in intensity.

1. A sombre Churchill leaving 10 Downing Street for the Commons on 18 June 1940, followed by his personal private secretary, Brendan Bracken. In his hand are notes for the speech he delivered at 3.49 in which he announced that the Battle of Britain was about to begin.

2. A photograph believed to have been taken on 1 July 1940 of the Luftwaffe High Command, including Göring (sixth from right), standing on Cap Blanc Nez to peer at their 'most dangerous enemy'.

3. Major General E.B. Ashmore, who founded the Observer Corps in 1924 and was the architect of London's air defences in 1917 which, though ineffective at the time, formed the basis of what became the 'Dowding system'.

4. The man who, with the help of large quantities of sherry, came up with the idea of the eight-gun fighter - Squadron Leader Ralph Sorley, pictured in 1943 as an Air Marshal.

5. Robert Watson-Watt, who in 1935 made proposals to his boss Henry Tizard called 'The Detection of Aircraft by Radio Methods' which resulted in the development of Radio Direction Finding (RDF), later universally known as radar.

6. The lattice tower of the CHL station at Hopton in East Anglia.

7 & 8. The engineers who made an effective defence possible: (left) Supermarine's Reginald Mitchell, designer of the Spitfire, photographed in 1929 with Henry Royce, who led the development of the Merlin prototypes and (right) Hawker's Sydney Camm, who designed the Hurricane.

9. British industrial innovation: the Spitfire 'shadow factory' at Castle Bromwich in the West Midlands. In 1940 it was plagued with problems and the vast majority of Spitfires were assembled at Supermarine's works in Southampton.

10. Hermann Göring in a romantic and heroic pose, in one of a series of photographs taken to commemorate his promotion to the unique rank of Reichsmarschall on 19 July 1940. He holds his new baton and is wearing his Grand Cross, Knight's Cross and the Pour le Mérite he won during World War I.

11. The brilliant and energetic Erhard Milch, the man from Lufthansa who by 1939 had built the Luftwaffe into a formidable front-line force in only five years, but did not have time to create the back-up in reserves, production and training he wanted.

12 & 13. The operational commanders of Airfleets 2 and 3: the jolly Bavarian Albert Kesselring, who joined the Luftwaffe from the Army in 1933, and the rather less genial Swabian Hugo Sperrle, one of Germany's most experienced senior airmen, sometime Commander of the clandestine training operation in Russia and the Condor Legion.

14 & 15. The Jafü and the Kanakafü. Oberst Theo Osterkamp, First World War flying ace and Kommodore of JG51 until his promotion to command the fighter forces of Airfleet 2; and Oberst Johannes Fink, Kommodore of KG2, who was put in charge of the battle for the Channel and led the first bombing raid of Eagle.

16. RAF reconnaissance photograph of invasion barges at Dunkirk taken on 19 September 1940.

17. *Above left:* Air Chief Marshal Hugh Dowding, C-in-C Fighter Command, and builder of the defence system.

18. *Above centre:* Dowding's SASO, Douglas Evill, pictured as Air Marshal in 1945.

19. *Above right:* Air Vice-Marshal Trafford Leigh-Mallory, pictured in 1944, who in 1940 was Commander of 12 Group and succeeded Park at 11 Group in December.

20. *Left:* Air Vice-Marshal William Sholto Douglas, Deputy Chief of the Air Staff in 1940, who clashed continually with Dowding and replaced him at Fighter Command in November.

21. *Below:* The Secretary of State for Air and Leader of the Liberal Party, Sir Archibald Sinclair, talking to Douglas Bader on a visit to 310 (Czech) Squadron at Duxford on 26 October in the aftermath of the meeting at the Air Ministry on the 17th.

22. Much polished wood and silver on display at the Air Council in July 1940. Left to right: Sir Harold Howitt, Air Marshal Sir Christopher Courtney, Park's predecessor at 11 Group Air Marshal Gossage, Under-Secretary of State Captain Balfour, Sinclair, the Chief of the Air Staff, Air Chief Marshal Sir Cyril Newall and the Permanent Under Secretary of State, Sir Arthur Street.

23. Pilots of 615 Squadron in France in early 1940 clustering around Flight Lieutenant 'Sandy' Sanders as he shows them their flight plan on a map. 615 kept their Gladiator biplanes until early May, changing to Hurricanes just in time for the German attack on France. The machine gun under the wing of Sandy's Gladiator may well have been the one Churchill was standing in front of the previous November while his wife fiddled with the firing mechanism.

24. Air Vice-Marshal Keith Park, who, having worked closely with Dowding as his SASO for two years, took over 11 Group, the largest and most important, on 20 April 1940. From then until his unceremonious dismissal on 18 December he conducted the day-to-day air defence of south-east England in such a way that his opponents dubbed him 'defender of London', and Lord Tedder could observe after the war that 'if ever any one man won the Battle of Britain, he did'.

14. THE CHANNEL: AUGUST

Convoys were a problem for Dowding. There were lots of them, and all needed protection. Because the warning times over the Channel were so short, the only way he could protect them was to mount standing patrols, which were exhausting for the pilots, gave the attackers the tactical initiative and wasted resources. Furthermore, he did not want to fight over the sea, where downed pilots would be lost. Churchill, on the other hand, liked the idea of using convoys as 'bait' and told Admiral Pound over dinner on 9 August that he hoped the practice would continue, though he did admit that 'the surviving bait are getting a bit fed up.'[1] The Admiralty had already drawn their own conclusions and Churchill did not interfere.

By the end of July, the Straits of Dover had become known as 'Hellfire Corner'. On the 25th, convoy CW8 lost all but two of its ships making the passage west, and two destroyers, *Boreas* and *Brilliant*, which sallied out from the Royal Navy's base at Dover to escort them, were damaged and forced back. The Admiralty decided that the losses to the convoys were becoming prohibitive, and on the 26th cancelled all daylight merchant movements through the Straits. When RAF reconnaissance flights showed large guns being installed near Calais to bombard Dover, it was enough to convince the Navy to abandon Dover as a base, and move to Harwich and Sheerness.[2] The following day, the 29th, daytime naval movements also ceased. The Kanakafü had almost achieved his goal. By day at least, the English Channel was German.

The Air Ministry could see what was happening and did not like it. That day, secret cipher signal X853 from Sholto Douglas landed on Dowding's desk. It suggested that strong offensive action should be taken against E-boats (German motor torpedo boats) in Boulogne, the airfields at St Inglevert and Calais-Marck, and the new gun emplacements. It also suggested that Dowding co-operate with Bomber Command so as to attack just after the Germans had landed after a major sortie.

Dowding's feelings on receiving this message need little imagining. His Senior Air Staff Officer, Douglas Evill, prepared a careful briefing note the following day which tried to take the suggestion seriously, but, given all the difficulties, mooted that it would be unwise to undertake such attacks in great strength. Next to the passage dealing with fighter cover, the margin has the comment 'NO' in large blue letters, with the double line Dowding habitually used to mark things he did not like. The plan more or less died in a meeting he had at the Ministry the same day. Instead, two squadrons of Fairey Battles belonging to Coastal Command were held at readiness at Eastchurch for operations against E-boats. They were never used. On 5 September, signal X853 was officially cancelled.[3]

This was an example of the sort of intervention from above which Dowding found maddening. Having rescued his boys from France, he was now to send them back again. The air over Calais was constantly full of German aircraft, making it impossible to detect anything but very large raids until they left for England. Given the time needed to alert Bomber Command, there was no hope of catching the raiders just after their return. He could only too well imagine what would happen to any of his planes which got to the Calais area. The Luftwaffe had managed to stuff nearly 500 Bf 109s into the area between Calais and Boulogne, and the effectiveness of their light flak had been experienced often enough by Bomber Command. All the Luftwaffe's plans for its own offensive devoted considerable attention to the needs of its own air defence.[4] Trying to attack them in their bases would throw away every advantage Dowding had carefully built up for his pilots. The answer to trouble with E-boats was not to send through any targets for them. He was relieved that the Admiralty, if not the Air Ministry, had begun to see sense.

On the other side of the Channel, whilst the Kanakafü might allow himself some feelings of satisfaction over the absence of British shipping off Dover, his friend the Jafü was hardly helped by it. The further beyond the Channel he had to go to fight Fighter Command, the harder his task became. Everybody wondered what to do next. So there was a lull.

Hitler issued Directive 17 on 1 August, requiring the Luftwaffe to begin to destroy the RAF at any time from the 5th onwards, depending on the weather. OKL met the same day in The Hague to review their plans. In his notes from the meeting, Göring emphasised the need for fighters to conserve fuel, and, in a significant change, ordered escorts not to move too far away from their charges or to fly off in pursuit of single enemy aircraft. In a telegraphic message to the Airfleets, the concern over 109s not running out of fuel was repeated, with the order to mark out the areas of French coastline closest to England with lights and smoke to help them get in. The message also ordered specific attacks on the identified 'radio transmission devices' in the first wave of the attack in order to knock them out. In a war game on the 4th, the commanders went through everything again, and the resulting review on the 6th added nothing – the concern about fighters not running out of fuel is there yet again – except to permit attacks on any naval vessels which might try to disrupt sea rescue operations.[5] All seemed to be ready. Eagle was fixed for 10 August.

The preoccupation with fuel is telling. The Bf 109 was something of a gas-guzzler, but this had been of little concern either to Willy Messerschmitt or the Luftwaffe High Command. It carried 87 gallons of fuel and its range at cruising speed was about 412 miles, a little less than a Spitfire. Both had been intended as short-range interceptors.

Suddenly, it mattered. It is about 100 miles as the crow flies from Calais to London. The Bf 109s rarely had the privilege of flying like crows. They had to form up, zig-zag when escorting, and usually got into fights. The Luftwaffe crammed as many 109s as it could into Calais-Marck, Coquelles, St Inglevert, Audembert and other even less salubrious airstrips in the Pas-de-Calais, but they still had only ten minutes' fighting time over London. Beyond London, the bombers would be on their own, or have Bf 110s to engage some of Fighter Command's attention.

The Germans had a few drop-tanks. Some were made of wood and leaked, so were not very popular. There were others of light aluminium, but the racks needed to fit them were in short supply, with the fighter-bomber units having priority. The issue of range was to constrain the options of the Luftwaffe commanders and sap the nerves of their fighter pilots, as they constantly worried whether they would get home or have to ditch in that terrible stretch of water that acted as a moat for the island fortress they were to assault. Having control of the Straits meant little to the pilots.

Meanwhile, the lack of activity had encouraged the Admiralty to allow a number of convoys to sail, though they passed through the Straits at night. On the evening of 7 August convoy CW9, consisting of twenty merchantmen and nine naval escorts, left the Medway to slip through 'Hellfire Corner' undetected in the darkness, bound for Swanage. The British did not know that the Germans were using radar, and the Freya unit at Cap Blanc Nez picked them up. E-boats attacked in the morning twilight, sinking three ships.

The day dawned cloudless, with visibility of 50km. As the ships headed west out of the Straits of Dover, Sperrle took up the challenge and ordered von Richthofen to destroy the convoy, which the RAF had code-named 'Peewit'.

At 0930, fifty-seven Stukas took off to attack, accompanied by twenty Bf 110s and thirty Bf 109s. They sank four ships and damaged seven others. At 1600, eighty-seven Stukas with sixty-eight mixed escorts launched a second assault over Weymouth Bay. To all intents and purposes, they finished the job. Out of 'Peewit''s twenty merchantmen, four reached Swanage unscathed, six were so badly damaged they had to make for other ports, seven were on the bottom of the Channel and the rest were damaged. However, achieving this had cost von Richthofen dear.

Luftflotte 3 lost eight Bf 109s, four Bf 110s and ten Stukas destroyed and two Bf 109s, two Bf 110s and eight Stukas damaged. They claimed twenty Hurricanes and Spitfires. The RAF actually lost thirteen destroyed and five damaged. It had been the heaviest day's fighting so far.

The squadrons which had probably done most damage to the raiders had been 145 and 43. 145 squadron were in action three times and claimed ten confirmed and thirteen 'probables', warranting congratulatory messages that evening from Sinclair, Newall and Park. However, five of their pilots were posted missing. Park expressed the 'sincere hope' that some of them would turn up, as had often happened in the past. None of them ever did.[6]

43 Squadron claimed six confirmed and nine 'probables' for the loss of two pilots. Pilot Officer Tony Woods-Scawen claimed a couple of Stukas and got back with a shot-up Hurricane and 'multiple foreign bodies in both legs'. Tony was one of a pair of brothers in Fighter Command. They were perhaps unusual in that they joined the RAF for reasons of love.

Patrick Woods-Scawen, the elder son of a widowed accountant, grew up in Farnborough in Hampshire, and had become fascinated by the planes he saw at the airfield there. He joined on a short-service commission in 1937, and a year later Tony, his younger brother, did the same. This was not a simple case of following in his brother's footsteps. Both had fallen in love with a local girl they had grown up with called Una Lawrence, whom the boys called 'Bunny'. She had promised to marry Patrick when he became a squadron leader. Tony wanted to beat him to it. Patrick joined 85 Squadron, where he was very popular and known as 'Weasel'. His squadron leader, Peter Townsend, called him 'little Patrick who smiled with his eyes'. He saw action in France, winning the DFC.

This was a bit of a blow for Tony – he did not want Patrick to become too much of a hero before he had had a chance. He was posted to 43 Squadron at Tangmere, where he was nicknamed 'Wombat' because he looked a bit like a rabbit and was as blind as a bat. He was in action over Dunkirk, where he made a couple of claims, but got shot down and took a week to get back to England. The 8th of August had been his first day of combat since then.

That evening he went home to Farnborough to repair his legs and see Bunny. He persuaded his brother's fiancée to help him pick the foreign bodies out, and pressed her to marry him instead. She said she would in a fortnight. She was joking, of course, or thought she was. She was not quite sure. Tony took it as seriously as he took anything, and booked a friend's cottage near Tangmere for the honeymoon.[7]

Eagle was postponed again. The 10th was squally and thundery. It was put off for a day and then till the 13th. However, the 11th dawned fine and both Airfleet commanders decided to exploit the weather.

Kesselring opened by trying to draw up British fighters. He sent the Bf 109s and Bf 110s of the special trials unit Erprobungsgruppe 210 on a strafing run of Dover, where they shot down some barrage balloons and dropped some small bombs. Park interpreted this as the prelude to a serious attack, and ordered squadrons forward from the Sector stations. Several of them ran into

Bf 109s on sweeps. Once it was clear what Kesselring was up to, Park kept his forces back, and only a few small clashes resulted.

Meanwhile, a worthwhile target had been found: convoy 'Booty' off the Essex coast. This was a bit far for Bf 109s, so Erprobungsgruppe 210 were chosen to attack with their Bf 110s, followed by some Dorniers of KG2 escorted by more Bf 110s of ZG26. They found 'Booty' at 11.50, just before 17, 74 and 85 Squadrons found them. The British fighters destroyed four Bf 110s, (two from Erp.Gr. 210 and two from ZG26) and three Dorniers as well as damaging six more of the attackers. Somewhat unusually, the Bf 110s also inflicted casualties, shooting down three fighters and damaging another three.

As this action was fizzling out, Kesselring sent in another raid against a convoy in the Thames estuary, this time with an escort of Bf 109s. 74 and 111 Squadrons intercepted over the coast of north Kent in the gathering cloud. 74 suffered no losses, but the engagement was a disaster for 111. They lost four Hurricanes and their pilots, and another pilot ran out of fuel and wrote off his aircraft on crash-landing. On the other side, two Bf 109s crashed into the sea off Margate, probably as a result of this action.

The main action of 11 August was, however, initiated by Sperrle, well to the west. The target was not a convoy, but the important naval base of Portland, which pokes provocatively into the Channel from the coast of Dorset, about halfway between Exeter and Bournemouth.

At 0935, fifty four Ju 88s from I. and II./KG54 and some twenty Heinkels from KG27 took off from France, preceded by sixty-one Bf 110s from ZG2 and thirty Bf 109s from JG2. They were not part of von Richthofen's forces, but drawn from Fliegerkorps IV and V, Luftflotte 3's main bomber strength, signalling that this was not part of the battle for the Channel. With about 165 aircraft, it was the largest single force yet to attack Britain.

It was picked up just after 10 o'clock and identified as '100-plus'. Brand scrambled forty-two fighters from five squadrons to meet them. 11 Group sent in thirty-two Hurricanes from the three squadrons of the neighbouring Tangmere sector (601, 145 and 1) to support them. These seventy-four aircraft were therefore attacking a force twice their size, but containing a similar number of fighters, only half of which were Bf 109s.

The German escorts arrived ahead of the bombers at 1009 and formed holding circles at 20–25,000 feet five miles south-east of Portland. The intercepting fighters attacked the Bf 110s, and a massive dogfight began. The bombers tried to slip in underneath – as Park feared – but were met by some of the late arriving squadrons, and became embroiled in the fighting as it sank, as dogfights often did. JG27 arrived on the scene to cover the German withdrawal, and as the main action petered out, He 59s, under further Bf 109 escort, came to pick up survivors.

The aircraft losses on both sides were almost exactly the same. The returning German pilots claimed fifty-seven kills, including two Curtiss Hawks, which the RAF had never possessed.[8] The RAF lost sixteen fighters, most of them to Bf 109s, and a further seven damaged, some by return fire from the bombers. The Luftwaffe lost eighteen of the attacking force – five bombers, eight Bf 109s and six Bf 110s – as well as two He 59s. Another five Bf 110s and a bomber were damaged. In Portland, the oil storage tanks burned.

At Chequers, where Churchill was having lunch with Air Marshal Bowhill, Dowding's opposite number at Coastal Command, there was high excitement. Colville was made to get on the phone to Bentley Priory to get the lunchtime score. German air superiority was clearly less than had been feared, opined Churchill. 'The swine had needed three days in which to lick their wounds' before coming again. That afternoon he went out to a rifle range and practised with a revolver, a cigar still gripped between his teeth, and talked constantly about the best way of killing Huns.[9]

Given the high proportion of Bf 110s among the escorts, Fighter Command might have expected a better score. It would have been better if Park's instruction of 20 July to attack in two layers had been followed, and more interceptors had headed straight for the bombers once the high escorts had been engaged. But this action was under the control of 10 Group, and since becoming operational on 8 July it had only really been tested in the battle over 'Peewit'. The Portland raid was its biggest battle by far, and would have tested even the most experienced controllers at 11 Group. Given the size of the group of escorts, the plot of which would for a time have merged with that of the bombers, the radar operators would have had difficulty in identifying them as fighters, and realising that the bombers were following them lower down. Fighter Command could afford to lose sixteen aircraft, but not the fourteen pilots who died in them. It could not allow things to continue in this fashion. Everybody had to learn. Fast.

Luftflotte 3 was also in some disarray at its losses. Sperrle knew that Eagle had been postponed till the 13th, but he also needed to get ready for the softening-up attacks planned for the morrow. For him as for the British, it was the personnel rather than the aircraft losses that were the greatest concern. He had also lost fourteen pilots over Portland, as well as thirteen other crew. Amongst the missing were two Gruppenkommandeure and one Staffelkapitän. Kesselring's Luftflotte 2 also lost one Staffelkapitän. He could not afford to lose senior officers at that rate. And the real show was only just about to begin.

The Luftwaffe planners worked feverishly through the night of Sunday 11 August 1940 to prepare for the offensive on the 13th. The attacks intended for the following day, just to clear the way, would be unprecedented. The Luftwaffe would no longer mess about with ships and secondary targets, but go for the heart of their enemy.

In Bentley Priory, Dowding expected them. The day's hectic action had been a clear sign that something was brewing. He was grateful convoy sailing had reduced, for it relieved him of the need to mount wasteful patrols. He hoped the fighting would move over the mainland, for then he would lose fewer pilots in the neutral waters of the Channel. He hoped the Luftwaffe would launch their attacks in large formations, for they were easy to track and would give his controllers plenty of warning. He was grateful that the wastage of his squadrons in France was over. He wanted to fight the enemy on prepared ground, to take them on in the way he had always planned for. He wanted them to attack Britain. Then he could break them.

15. THE NUMBERS GAME

In the Battle of Britain, the role of intelligence was crucial, for it not only determined plans but also shaped perceptions and expectations. It was the understanding each side had of what was happening to their opponent which determined the decision to carry on or give up.

Both sides gathered competitive intelligence from a variety of sources. Prior to the outbreak of hostilities, their Embassies collected general economic, geographical and technical data,[1] and some information had been openly exchanged during the visits of 1937 and 1938. Once the war had begun, some nuggets filtered in from foreigners, and some use was made of spies, most of it ineffective or downright misleading.* More reliable was the monitoring of low-grade radio-traffic by the British 'Y' service and the German 'Horchabteilung' run by Martini, which enabled both to construct a picture of the other side's order of battle. Both sides also flew reconnaissance flights. Whilst the British were mainly concerned with counting invasion barges in the Channel ports, a fairly straightforward matter, the Germans had to assess the damage their bombing was causing, a far more difficult task.

The Germans certainly did not lack services devoted to gathering foreign intelligence. The State had six, including Göring's own Research Office, which was politically very useful to him throughout his career, the Nazi Party had another three, including the Sicherheitsdienst (SD) which was run in conjunction with the Gestapo, and the Wehrmacht (the Armed Forces) had one for

---

* In May 1940, for example, a mysterious stranger approached Michael Golovine of Rolls-Royce in a Budapest café, and handed him a parcel containing the fuel pump from a DB601 engine, the device which allowed the Bf 109 to bunt without its engine cutting out. When Golovine tried to give the injection unit to the British Air Attaché, he said he did not want it, and it never got to England (Wood & Dempster, op. cit., pp. 73–4). OKW ran a spy called 'Ostro' to report on the British aircraft industry, particularly on production figures. Unfortunately for them, he was a double-agent, and his contribution to the RAF's ultimate victory was considerable (see Horst Boog, 'German Air Intelligence in the Second World War' in Michael I. Handel (ed.), *Intelligence and Military Operations*, Frank Cass 1990, pp. 370–3).

each of the Army, Navy and Luftwaffe, plus the Abwehr (the equivalent of MI 5 and MI 6) under Admiral Canaris, which together with the War Economy Staff and the Foreign Economy Branch reported to Keitel at OKW.

The intelligence-gathering operations within the Luftwaffe consisted of the 5th Abteilung (Department) attached to the OKL General Staff, which was set up on 1 January 1938 and run by Oberst Beppo Schmid; a Cipher Office run by General Wolfgang Martini, and the usual Reconnaissance and Aerial Photography branches. Below OKL, each operating unit down to the level of Geschwader had Intelligence Officers (designated Ic) who reported to the operations branch (not to the 5th Abteilung). These officers were responsible for troop welfare, propaganda and censorship as well as intelligence.[2]

The result of all this was more *embarras* than *richesse*. As usual in Nazi Germany, most of these organs were rivals, hated each other and fought for influence. There was no co-operation and little co-ordination, despite calls for it after the Polish campaign.[3]

This might not have been disastrous had the content of the information gathered been good. Before the war, it was fairly realistic, but once hostilities commenced, it became increasingly optimistic, because that was what the leadership wanted to hear. Schmid in particular had a reputation for embellishing his reports to please Göring.

The first report made about Britain was completed by the 5th Abteilung of OKL in July 1939 and code-named 'Studie Blau' (Blue Study). It served as the main source of information about Britain, and appears to have been largely descriptive with few judgements.[4] However, judgements were forthcoming from Schmid in his assessment of the air situation in Europe issued in May 1939, in which he opined that Britain was one to two years behind Germany in the air, with obsolescent aircraft and a weak air defence, making her 'very vulnerable from the air.'[5] This was not the conclusion of the war-game carried out by Luftflotte 2 that month.

On 22 November 1939, Schmid issued a far less sanguine strategic paper called 'Proposal for the Conduct of Air Warfare against Britain'. Here he describes Britain as 'the most dangerous' of all Germany's possible enemies, for, unlike France, she was capable of prosecuting the war alone. 'As long as Britain is undefeated,' he wrote, 'the war cannot be brought to a favourable conclusion.' He recommended the immediate adoption of a siege strategy. The report was noted with interest and laid aside.[6]

Schmid claimed after the war to have warned the Luftwaffe leadership against engaging in an air war with Britain without sufficient preparation. He claims to have realised that the Luftwaffe, not the Kriegsmarine, would have to take care of the Royal Navy, and that the British could well pull out all the stops and increase their production considerably. He went so far as to claim that in the light of Studie Blau, a prudent Luftwaffe leadership would never have started the Battle of Britain.[7] However, a series of reports he issued in 1940 led OKL to believe that the Battle of Britain could not only be won, but would be a push-over.

These reports were summarised in an overall survey of the RAF produced in response to the OKW planning request of 2 July. It was dated 16 July, and pithily lays out all the Luftwaffe's illusions:

- both the Hurricane and the Spitfire were inferior to the Bf 109F (which was not yet in production) and only a skilfully handled Spitfire was better than the Bf 110;
- the number of operational airfields in southern England was severely limited;
- the British aircraft industry was producing 180–300 front-line fighters a month (the true figure for July was 496) and would decrease;
- command at all levels was inflexible, with fighters being rigidly tied to their home bases, and Station Commanders were non-flyers (most flew regularly).

The report concluded that the Luftwaffe was 'clearly superior to the RAF as regards strength, equipment, training, command and location of bases.' All these errors amount to a chronic underestimation of the enemy. But in addition, Schmid made an important overestimation and two crucial omissions. He overestimated the number of light flak guns available to the RAF for low-level defence by a factor of two, which, when added to the knowledge that their own light flak was extremely effective, helps to explain the Luftwaffe's reluctance to launch low-level attacks.[8] He also omitted to mention the repair and mainte-nance organisation which put damaged aircraft back into service with great rapidity and, most astonishingly of all, did not even mention radar. He did cir-culate a letter to the Airfleets about radar on 7 August, concluding that it tied units to their home bases and made assembly at critical points difficult. So much for 'the most dangerous of all possible enemies'.[9] The only thing Schmid got about right was the current operational strength, which he put at 675 serv-iceable fighters.

This report was reinforced by a far more comprehensive one issued on 10 August, just before Eagle began. Schmid claimed that, being based on the latest captured material, this report was by far the most accurate ever produced. It includes detailed tables on monthly aircraft production, which gave great weight to imports from America and included figures for repaired aircraft. He gauged British fighter production to be running at about 250 a month from all sources in July, August and September, well below German output of just under 450 a month (300 a month new plus 150 a month from repairs). In fact, British primary production alone ran at just under 500 a month throughout the summer.

However, Schmid's documentation is impressive, and his argument that the British aircraft industry should be knocked out swiftly is backed up by an accurate table of all the key production sites, including the Spitfire works at

Southampton and the Hurricane factories at Kingston-upon-Thames and Brooklands.

His detailed qualitative comparisons of the aircraft of both sides put great stress on the poor offensive armament of British fighters, from which he concluded that whilst British bombers could only operate over Germany at night, Luftwaffe bombers would be able to survive in daylight over England. The overall impression of the report is of overwhelming German superiority in both numbers and quality.[10]

The very comprehensiveness of this report is part of the problem. In many of the comparisons he makes, Schmid is quite right. For example, the Bf 110 was generally markedly superior to British types in its class such as the Blenheim fighter. However, it would never meet the Blenheim in combat. In what was to come, only the features of the Bf 109 and the Hurricane and Spitfire mattered, and Schmid simply concluded that the Bf 109's superior armament was decisive.[11]

Schmid's work was based in part on the interceptions of radio traffic from Martini's 3rd Abteilung. The 3rd Abteilung knew about radar. On 3 August 1939, they sent a Zeppelin airship fitted out as a radio laboratory to fly up the north-east coast of Britain to pick up signals. The airship was swamped by the powerful transmissions, and its crew concluded that it was all interference from the National Grid. The flight left the Luftwaffe none the wiser.[12] By 1940, the 3rd Abteilung had nevertheless worked out that squadrons were being directed from the ground – they had learned most of the call-signs used – but they were not going to betray their secrets to a rival department.[13] Jeschonnek also knew about radar, and had identified its key weakness. In a staff report issued under his name on 1 May, he confirmed the existence of an 'electrical reporting device' on the English coast. He was unable to say whether similar devices were in use in France, nor whether it could distinguish friendly from enemy aircraft. However, he did say that it was unable to detect low-flying aircraft at long distances.[14] The concern at the time was the Battle of France, and no consequences seem to have been drawn from the report in the Battle of Britain. The Germans appear to have remained uncertain about the capabilities of the radar system, and in particular its inability to detect low-flying aircraft, for some time, for they were still probing it in early 1941.[15]

As time went on, Schmid's estimates of British strength moved ever further away from their reasonably accurate starting point. Thus the Luftwaffe High Command became increasingly deluded about what was happening. The reason for this was the combined effect of the underestimation of production and the reliance on pilots' claims in order to estimate losses inflicted.

Claims are usually used to show who got what. This may be of interest to the participants, but it is knowing the total losses inflicted on the enemy in the air, whoever caused them, that matters. Because of its importance, both sides insisted on rigorous criteria for confirming claims, which had to be independently witnessed by another pilot or verified through the location of the crash-site. Despite this, it is an endemic feature of all air-fighting that claims are too high, by a factor of at least two. There are good reasons for this.

The first is simply mistakes, usually made by inexperienced pilots. If he was firing at an enemy machine and it dived steeply away, belching black smoke, a callow pilot might well think he had a kill. In fact, engines usually emit smoke when an aircraft bunts. They can also get into spins, fall out of control and then recover low down out of sight.

The second is that verification is very difficult and also dangerous. To be accurate, the observing pilot, who is usually fighting for his life himself rather than playing umpire, would have to follow the victim from the first bullet strikes on it through to its eventual demise on the ground. All he would usually be able to see would be several planes firing at each other, catch a glimpse of one spinning down a few seconds later, and then perhaps an explosion on the ground some time after that. All three impressions might be connected. On the other hand the spinning plane may have recovered in cloud and gone home, and the crash be of an entirely different machine actually shot down in a dog-fight some miles away. When moving at 200–300 mph in three dimensions, large distances are covered very quickly. Young pilots often tried to follow down aircraft they had hit. This usually turned them into victims themselves. The experienced forgot about confirming claims and kept their precious height for better purposes.

The third is that many aircraft did not crash within view on land anyway, but in the Channel or on the other side. Some were shot-up, crash-landed on their home base and were written-off. Others looked as if they were stricken, but got home and were repaired in a day.

The net result of all this is the main cause of over-claiming: multiple claims. Sometimes the same aircraft would be seen by different pilots at different altitudes and in different stages of disintegration and be identified as different machines. Often the same machine would be attacked by several pilots in separate incidents. The crash would be confirmed and they would all claim it. The multiples involved could be quite significant. For example, on 18 August, one Ju 88 which crashed at Ide Hill in Kent was claimed by five pilots, each of whom had attacked and hit it, and each of whom correctly identified the crash site, whilst identifying the victim variously as a Do 215 and He 111 as well as a Ju 88.* On 15 September, one of the most celebrated of German losses, the Dornier which crashed on Victoria Station and was also reported as having bombed Buckingham Palace, was claimed by nine pilots. Another less dramatic example on the same day is a Heinkel which force-landed at West Malling and was claimed seven times as a definite, twice as a probable and once as damaged.[16]

---

* Price, *The Hardest Day*, pp. 81–2. The last pilot to hit it was Sandy Sanders, who saw it go in. He aimed at the cockpit to kill the pilot, which was what he believed was the only way to be sure of a bomber. 'Of course, you could claim whatever you liked,' he has said. 'You could always say it went into the sea.'

From this it can be seen that in the speed and confusion of a battle, honest pilots can make genuine claims that nevertheless lead to a completely erroneous view of the damage inflicted on the enemy. The claims for the Victoria Station Dornier were made by pilots from four different squadrons which did not cross-check their claims. In the RAF, claims were assessed by unit intelligence officers, but all they could do was to eliminate gross errors and duplication between pilots of their own unit. It is hard enough for peace-time researchers spending weeks comparing log-books, timings, verbal accounts and comparing all with registered losses and crash-sites to establish what went on. So what was anyone to do in wartime?

Because of its nature, over-claiming rises with the number of aircraft engaged on each side. If two lone opponents meet in an empty sky, both will have a fairly clear idea of the outcome. If four dive on forty, knock two down in flames and dive away, they will probably get their claim about right. If fifty meet fifty and a huge mêlée begins, most pilots will take short bursts at several targets which fly briefly into view, whilst all concentrate on avoiding collisions. Five plumes of smoke from stricken machines would be seen by most of the ninety-five who are left, most of whom fired and many of whom think they hit something. When claims come to be assessed, the five could easily become several times that number. Big air battles are not only less lethal than small ones, but inherently increase confusion and as a consequence the difficulty of accurate loss-reporting.

During the battle, the equivalent of the 'fog of war' was the ratio of claims to actual losses inflicted, which could be called the 'delusion factor'. A delusion factor of two is about average. Below two is quite good; three is dangerously misleading. Throughout, the British had the advantage of being able to count wrecks and having to estimate only what went into the Channel. The Germans had the added disadvantage that their warrior-hero ethos greatly increased the temptation to make fraudulent claims, of which some examples have been noted. The Luftwaffe's delusion factor did not only lead to faulty command decisions, but also lowered morale. Göring began to suspect that dishonesty was rife – ignorant as he was, he could think of no other reason for the discrepancies – and it was one factor which led to the breakdown in trust between the Luftwaffe and its leadership during the course of September.[17]

Intelligence was less important to the defenders. Before the battle began it was as bad as the Germans', but in contrast with theirs, it grew in accuracy. Importantly, fuelled by the Luftwaffe's very effective pre-war propaganda, it erred on the right side, that of over-estimation. This did not affect dispositions or tactics.

In June the RAF's Air Intelligence section estimated German front-line strength at 2,500 bombers (there were 1,808), a similar number of fighters (there were half that) and a reserve of 7,000. These estimates were queried by Professor Lindemann and the Air Staff and, with some help from Ultra, the view reached in July was of a total strength of 4,800 – only a little too high.[18]

However, there was a strong belief that the Germans had substantial reserves and could sustain a long campaign. Fighter Command accordingly prepared itself for one, aiming to maintain its ability to inflict damage on any raid with undiminished strength, no matter how long the Germans kept coming.

The most important thing for the RAF was to get a reasonably good idea of the Luftwaffe order of battle from radio intercepts operated by the 'Y' Service. By August this was in place and remarkably accurate. During the course of the fighting additional information was gleaned from a new source – captured German aircrew. They were bundled away to an interrogation centre at Cockfosters, and even those captured early in the summer were shocked to discover how much the British already knew about them. When the Staffelkapitän of 9./ZG76, Oberleutnant Kadow, was interrogated on 11 July, he was startled when, on learning his name, his questioners already knew his unit, his position as its commander (which was not obvious from his rank) and the fact that another pilot picked up at Weymouth during the same action was one of his men. By mid-August, new prisoners were confronted by RAF intelligence officers who seemed to know more about their units than they did. They found the experience very disturbing.[19]

The British had scored a major intelligence coup early in the war by breaking the German's Enigma code, used for the transmission of high level secret information, by using a device called 'Ultra'. It gave information about overall moves of forces, but was of limited day-to-day value and Dowding was only put onto the list of those circulated with the Ultra decrypts on 16 October, when most of the serious fighting was over. However, some information gleaned from Ultra, such as the plan for Luftflotte V to attack northern England on 15 August, was probably passed on to him.[20]

Nevertheless, Dowding was faced by some problems because of the claims made by his pilots which the press published and made much of. Sinclair cross-examined him about the matter in August because the Americans were growing sceptical about the differences between the British claims and those made in the German press. His immediate response was to tell Sinclair that the Americans would soon find out the truth because if the Germans were right they would be in London in a week.[21] The RAF was genuinely interested in the truth, so Intelligence officers began counting wrecks. During the second week of August, they found 51, whereas claims had been made for 279. They suggested that another 80% had come down in the sea, but nobody really knew. Just how much in the dark the best-informed were can be seen from the fact that Dowding, in a letter to the Air Staff, estimated that claims were about 25% too high. In fact they were as a rule 200–300% too high. During the war, the only real way of knowing was to do as Dowding suggested to Sinclair: wait and see the results.[22]

What mattered for decision-making was that the Luftwaffe remained in total ignorance of the figures it most needed to know: Fighter Command's aircraft and pilot losses relative to their replacement rate. As a result, it was flailing about in the dark. German losses were less important. They were a limiting factor – if they got too severe, the Luftwaffe would be unable to cover the invasion – but assuming the sort of ruthlessness usually displayed by German generals, one would expect OKL to be ready to sacrifice a lot of crews in order to realise its aim.

The Battle of Britain took the course it did because the major decision-makers in the Luftwaffe did not know or understand what was actually going on. In the time since the Battle of Britain took place, by dint of painstaking research on the part of historians, many of them amateurs, we have slowly moved into the privileged position of having access to accurate information not available to the participants, as well a lot of the information they did have. The data about aircraft and pilot losses is difficult to assimilate and interpret, but it is very rich, and when the detail is put together, it is possible to understand what the protagonists thought was happening, what was actually happening and why. Repeated analysis would be tedious, but an audit of the first month's fighting over the Channel will reveal patterns that determined the events to follow.[23]

During the battle of the Channel between Wednesday, 10 July and Sunday, 11 August 1940, German airmen filed claims for the destruction of 381 British aircraft. They actually destroyed 114 fighters and 64 bombers, a total of 178. Many of the bomber losses were due to flak, so would not be included in the 381. So, making allowance for a few justified claims for bombers, it seems reasonable to suppose that the Luftwaffe believed it was destroying Fighter Command at three times the rate it actually was.

The Germans went to great lengths to verify claims. There were separate forms for the claimant and witnesses, all of whom had to state what damage was done and how the victim crashed. Extant Luftwaffe combat reports are rare, but copies of those filed by Leutnant Marx of Erprobungsgruppe 210 for 27 July have been published.[24] They were painstaking, and the evaluation procedure was strict. It appears almost certain from a comparison of this particular claim with RAF combat reports that Marx shot down F/O P.A.N. Cox of 501 Squadron off Dover at 1850. His Hurricane was also claimed by Fw. Fernsebner of III./JG52 a short while earlier. 'Pan' Cox died twice for the Luftwaffe, thereby posthumously doing his bit for his cause by adding a little to the illusions of its commanders.

Some of them knew full well that the reported numbers were illusory. Jafü 2, wise old bird that he was, had seen for himself when flying on operations how over-claiming arose. He mentally adjusted claims downwards, but he had no rule of thumb to go by, so even he was not really able to build up an accurate picture of the reality of the fighting.[25]

Appearance and reality come closer if the figures for damaged aircraft are included. The total of these two is the number of aircraft actually hit in combat, and a lot of the claims can be explained by a pilot's false estimation of the lethality of the hits. There is nevertheless no doubt that the Luftwaffe's rigorous system was designed to identify kills; the claimant and his witnesses had to stipulate whether the victim caught fire, blew up or hit the ground. This corresponds to the RAF's 'Category 3' damage classification, meaning either an aircraft failing to return or a write-off – in other words a total loss (defined in the table on p. 195 as 'destroyed'). The term 'damaged' covers a broad range. The RAF's 'Category 1' meant that the necessary repairs could be effected on the station, which meant the machine could be in action again within a few days. 'Category 2' meant repairable at a maintenance depot or by a contractor. This took the machine off-strength for far longer. For the sake of simplicity, this distinction has been ignored here. The Luftwaffe had a more precise damage classification system, giving the level as a percentage. In practice, up to 40% corresponded to the British 'Category 1', 40–60% to 'Category 2' and 60% and above meant an airframe write-off with parts available for cannibalisation.

The fighting was in fact only part of the picture (see p. 195). During the month of the 'Kanalkampf', Fighter Command lost 162 aircraft destroyed and 174 damaged. Of these, forty-seven and sixty-eight respectively, were caused by accidents. Adding in the one destroyed and three damaged by their own side, it emerges that fully one-third of the destruction to RAF fighter aircraft was wrought by RAF pilots. In one month, they had put nearly 18% of the Command's front-line aircraft strength temporarily or permanently out of action. At this rate, were it not for replacements, Fighter Command would cease to exist by the end of 1940 through its own efforts, without any help from the Luftwaffe.

The destruction was not only meted out to aircraft. Of the 107 fighter pilots killed in the period, eighteen died in accidents. Another five were injured. The situation was so serious that the Secretary of State for Air had convened a meeting of the RAF top brass in Whitehall in early April to discuss the matter. In opening the meeting, he noted that since the start of the war, accident rates had soared, particularly of avoidable mishaps arising out of low flying and low aerobatics.[26]

Dowding believed this was down to station commanders being too preoccupied with military duties to supervise flying as closely as they had in peacetime. Taxiing accidents had increased, in part because operations in marginal conditions – which in peace-time would have been cancelled – were now tolerated. Pilot error was often also a case of faulty cockpit drill, which Dowding thought could be helped by better design of a horn warning that the undercarriage was not down, and more rapid production of handbooks for new aircraft. In general, most of the measures to control accidents were to increase levels of airfield supervision, increase awareness and institute a reward for safe stations.[27]

Clearly, three months later, after the war had ceased to be 'phoney', the problem had not been solved. The accidents seem to have been the consequence of Fighter Command pushing itself to the edge and taking risks because

Fighter Command aircraft losses, 10 July–11 August			
Cause	Destroyed	Damaged	Total
Bf 109	87	52	139
Bf 110	6	10	16
Bomber	13	38	51
Collision	4	1	5
Flak	1	1	2
Friendly	1	3	4
Unknown	3	1	4
Total Combat	115	106	221
Accidents	47	68	115
Grand total	162	174	336

it was at war. Some of the accidents (about 12%) were clearly due to mechanical failures, most commonly engine failure. Some 8% were down to operating in marginal weather conditions. In the bulk of cases, the causes were not really known, but pilot error accounted for most. A lot were due to inexperience. Landing was the most common hazard. Five machines were damaged because the pilots forgot to lower the undercarriage. One of those guilty of this was the man who was to become the RAF's top scorer in the Battle, Josef Frantisek, who damaged his Hurricane by landing wheels-up on 8 August. Like his fellow Czechs and the Poles, he was used to planes with a fixed undercarriage. Exactly two months later he crashed on a routine patrol and was killed in circumstances never explained. Taxiing accidents accounted for another 7%, but were probably also largely due to lack of control or misjudgements.

However, the largest single factor aggravating the accident rate was Fighter Command's desperate effort to develop a night-fighting capability. Twenty-eight accidents, fully one quarter of the total, took place on night flying practice. Six of them were fatal. Dazzled by the glare of their exhaust stubs, good pilots undershot or overshot runways or just disappeared in the night, sometimes hitting the ground because they misread their altimeter, sometimes becoming disorientated in the blackness, sometimes simply getting lost. This high price was paid for scarcely any reward in terms of night interceptions. The answer, as Dowding was well aware, was to fit airborne radar into a fast, well-armed two-seater with a skilled, dedicated operator. There was such a solution: Bristol Beaufighters fitted with airborne interception (AI) radar. However, it was only on 27 July that the first Beaufighter was handed over to the RAF. It was mid-September before a squadron was operational and not until mid-November that it got its first night kill.[28] In the meantime, the slow, lightly armed Blenheims had to do. The attempt to use Hurricanes and Spitfires in this role is a measure of the pressure Dowding was under to meet the night threat. It did little good.[29]

A quarter of Bomber Command's eighty-seven losses were due to accidents, mostly on training flights. The causes of fifty-two of the rest are unknown, but took place on operations. Of these the thirty which came down at night were probably mostly the victims of AA fire, though a few may have been shot down by night fighters. The Germans had no more success with single-seaters in this role than the British did, and it was not until October that General Kammhuber began organising proper lines of searchlights and sound locators for night defence. They did not begin using ground radar until 1941, and airborne radar not for another year.[30]

Of Fighter Command's combat losses of 115, no less than 87, three quarters of the total, were caused by Bf 109s. They also accounted for half of those damaged – fifty-two. This shows the Luftwaffe's belief that they could only defeat the RAF by engaging it in a fighter battle to have been basically correct. It also shows the vital importance of the Bf 109. As far as can be ascertained, Bf 110s only shot down six Hurricanes or Spitfires and damaged ten others. Bombers accounted for all but a few of the rest, their air gunners shooting down thirteen of their assailants, and damaging thirty-eight. They were more formidable opponents than is often presumed, and many British pilots have testified to the accuracy and determination of their return fire, which could make even the lone reconnaissance machines far from easy prey.

However, they were far less deadly than the Bf 109. Of the 139 British fighters hit by Bf 109s, 63% were shot down and destroyed. Of the 51 hit by return fire from bombers, only 25% were shot down. More tellingly, of the eighty-nine British pilots killed in combat, sixty-nine were in aircraft hit by Bf 109s and only five in aircraft hit by bombers. To put it another way, Bf 109s killed 50% of the pilots in the machines they hit, whereas bombers killed the pilot only 10% of the times they hit the plane. There are two main reasons for this.

The first is that the Bf 109s were aggressively trying to kill, usually from behind. Having passed through the thin structure of a fuselage, the first thing their bullets would meet would be the back of the pilot's seat. If he were lucky, they would be stopped by its armour plating, but a lot of them got through. A bomber, on the other hand, was simply trying to defend itself and carry out its bombing mission. An attacking fighter would typically be flying straight towards it, and the first thing its bullets would hit would be a large engine or a toughened windscreen. A lot of the damaged fighters had hits on the glycol cooling system at the front of the engine. When hit, it streamed white smoke, giving the inexperienced eye the look of catastrophe and providing further material for false claims, but most of the pilots damaged in this way broke off and got home with a hot engine. The pilot himself was only really vulnerable at the end of his attack when he flew past the bomber, exposing other parts of his machine, but even then he was a fast-moving target.

The second reason was the cannon fitted to the Bf 109. The rifle-calibre machine guns of the bombers, even if accurate, did far less lethal damage. The Bf 109 was the real killer. A single exploding cannon shell could wreck a fighter, and they could penetrate seat armour if fired from a close range. However, the cannons had a low muzzle velocity and the shells often exploded on impact with metal. They therefore tended to blow holes in fuselages rather than pilots if the pilot was flying the all-metal Spitfire. Hurricane pilots were not so lucky.[31] The Hispanos the British were experimenting with had greater penetrative power, but given 19 Squadron's difficulties in getting the shells to leave their barrels, they were irrelevant in the Battle.

The Bf 109's victims were Spitfires and Hurricanes in exactly equal number – sixty-three of each – as well as six Defiants and seven Blenheims. Bombers also scored hits on equal numbers of each type: twenty-five of each. This suggests that, given that two-thirds of Fighter Command squadrons flew Hurricanes, the Spitfires were being worked harder by the controllers. However, there was a significant difference in the result, for the Spitfires had a far better rate of survival. Of those sixty-three hit by Bf 109s, only thirty-one were destroyed as opposed to damaged, whereas of the same number of Hurricanes, forty-five were destroyed. The contrast in the casualties caused by bombers was even more stark. Of the twenty-five Spitfires hit, only two were destroyed; of the twenty-five Hurricanes, eleven were destroyed. This is reflected in the pilot casualties. Of the total number of pilots killed, fifty-one flew Hurricanes and only twenty-five flew Spitfires.

One reason may be that the Spitfire's superior speed made it a harder target and meant it was better able to get away from a Messerschmitt on its tail. The more important reason is that Hurricanes were not just more vulnerable to cannon fire, but also burned well.

The wing tanks of Hurricanes had been fitted with a covering of sealant called 'Linatex', but the gravity tank in the fuselage in front of the pilot had not been, partly because it was hard to get at and partly because it was assumed to be protected by the engine and a bulkhead. As a result, a Hurricane had a tendency to catch fire. When it did, a sheet of flame would leap into the cockpit and the wood and fabric fuselage ensured the fire spread rapidly. It was fire as much as anything which led to the total destruction of an aircraft and put the pilot's life in greatest danger. Pilots talked of 'Hurricane burns'. That the Hurricane was so much more likely to be destroyed when hit by air gunners in bombers suggests that fire, rather than the difference in performance between the two aircraft, was indeed the main reason why Spitfire pilots should have felt particularly grateful for their mounts.

This issue was of such concern to Dowding that he had Hawker retrofit the fuselage tanks of Hurricanes with Linatex as a matter of priority, which they did at the rate of 75 a month.[32] Pilot Officer Tom Neil and his colleagues on 249 Squadron were well aware of the problem but concluded it was the two wing tanks that were the main problem.[33] They were particularly vulnerable from behind, whereas the fuselage tank was between the cockpit and the engine with a bulkhead behind it. This was a feature of the design and could not be cured. Despite its ruggedness, the Hurricane was less able to bring its pilot home. Flying a Hurricane was twice as dangerous as flying a Spitfire.

Dowding was doing his best to protect his Hurricane pilots, but the greatest thing he could do to protect them all was to secure a cessation of Channel convoys. *Where* they fought had an enormous impact on their chances of survival. Of the eighty-nine pilots killed in combat, ten died in or over the North Sea and no less than fifty-eight in or over the Channel: in all, almost 80% of the pilots lost. Of course, that was where most of the fighting took place, and some pilots were dead when they hit the water. But the recovery rates suggest that the sea was itself responsible for a lot of the deaths. Only four wounded and three unhurt pilots who baled out over the Channel were fished out. Seven are known to have drowned. There may have been others. Peter Townsend was the only pilot shot down in combat over the North Sea over this period to be rescued. In contrast, eighteen pilots baled out over land or crash-landed and survived, half of them unhurt. The cold, murky waters surrounding Britain were lethal. The men in the convoys forming the 'bait' were not the only ones getting a bit fed up.

The two victims of flak are not strictly Fighter Command casualties at all. They were Blenheims of 236 Squadron, Coastal Command. They have been included because they were hit when on a raid on Querqueville aerodrome on 1 August, which was part of the RAF's fight against the Luftwaffe.

The price the Luftwaffe paid for inflicting all this damage was heavy. General Stapf reported to Halder on 29 July that the Luftwaffe would be ready for its main offensive by the end of the week and was expecting losses of 120–150 machines a month, about 10% of its operational strength, which it was well able to replace.[34] That month, *before* beginning its main offensive, the Luftwaffe lost 301 machines from all causes – double the upper estimate – and another 196 were damaged, a grand total of 497. It did not augur well (see table on p. 199).

The cost to the Luftwaffe of simply staying in being was 85 aircraft a month written-off and 96 damaged in accidents, a total of 181. As in the case of the RAF this is just over one third of the total losses. They are spread across all aircraft types in rough proportion to their numbers, though the rates are a little higher for the bomber units. This was probably due to the difficulties crews were having with the new and complex Ju 88, for although it made up only about 30% of the Luftwaffe's bomber strength at this time, it accounted for 43% of the accidents. The exact causes of most accidents is unclear, but

Luftwaffe aircraft losses, 10 July – 11 August

Type	Destroyed	Damaged	Total
Bombers	72	33	105
Stukas	22	20	42
Bf 109s	61	23	84
Bf 110s	27	17	44
Reconnaissance	18	5	23
Seaplanes	16	2	18
Total Combat	216	100	316
Accidents	85	96	181
Grand Total	301	196	497

from what is known, they seem to be similar to those afflicting the RAF, with a few curious differences.

Mechanically, engine failure is the most common cause, cited in forty cases. This is 22% of the total, more than twice the rate in Fighter Command. It is possible that this reflects the remarkable reliability of the Rolls-Royce Merlin, but there is a more sinister reason for the high rate in the Luftwaffe. Maintenance engineers at Erprobungsgruppe 210 had trouble with engines and suspected sabotage on the part of foreign workers in the Messerschmitt plant at Augsburg. When an engineer from Daimler-Benz accompanied a pilot on a flight test, the Bf 110 crashed.[35] The most likely explanation for this type of accident is indeed the work of the forced labourers, many of them Poles, who were beginning to fill German factories.

Take-off and landing were just as perilous for most German pilots as for British. In the case of the Bf 109, though, leaving and regaining the ground was a particular challenge. Of the forty-eight accidents involving them, twenty-three happened on take-off or landing. In five of these cases, the aircraft were write-offs.

For all this, the accident rate relative to the numbers of aircraft involved was significantly lower than in Fighter Command. Not forcing Bf 109 pilots to fly at night made a big difference. It is also noticeable that there is no report of anyone trying to land wheels-up. As the Luftwaffe effectively came into being in the monoplane era, fewer pilots had years of old fixed-undercarriage habits to break, and there may have been greater general familiarity with the aircraft. However, unless one believes that the Luftwaffe showed a higher level of Teutonic discipline than the RAF – which is possible – the remaining difference probably reflects the fact that in July Fighter Command was being worked harder. It was flying more sorties, including standing patrols, never less than 500 a day and in one case 1,000. Many pilots in 11 Group were in action several times a day, whereas for most of the German flyers such intensity was yet to come. At the beginning of August, many units had yet to see action over Britain.

The pilot casualty rate, however, was somewhat higher: 33 killed in 181 incidents, a rate of 18%. The rate of injury was also higher. There is no good explanation for this, except that some of them were doing things in which a mistake is fatal: two pilots of Erprobungsgruppe 210 were killed on dive-bombing practice. The Messerschmitts they flew were not designed for the task, and had neither dive-brakes nor the automatic pull-up mechanism of the Stuka.

The fighting itself exacted a toll of 216 aircraft destroyed and 100 damaged. Of these, 80% can be definitely attributed to British fighters, and it is likely that fighters also played some role in the fate of the 32 cases in which the cause is unknown. To these could be added four collisions with British machines. Of the rest, ten were destroyed and three damaged by AA guns, a small return for the ammunition they expended, and the remaining seven destroyed and nine damaged were the results of Bomber Command's almost forgotten and highly dangerous activities over their airfields. Of these losses, almost half were inflicted in a raid on the airfield of Haamstede on one of the Dutch islands of Zeeland on 7 August. It was home to a Staffel of II./JG54 and they were just taking off to intercept when the bombs fell amongst them. Haamstede is near the coast, and they had very little warning. Manston was to experience something very similar within the week.

The pattern of the losses is revealing. British fighters hit 100 bombers (including 17 from reconnaissance units). If we assume that they were also primarily responsible for the unexplained operational losses, the total rises to 114. Of these, no less than 80 were destroyed, 70% of the total. This is a slightly higher ratio of destroyed to damaged machines than that achieved by the Bf 109s against British fighters (63%). Even if we just take bombers known to be the victims of fighter attack, the ratio is the same. It is a telling testament to the power of Sorley's eight machine guns, and probably also reflects the behaviour typical in fighter pilots of concentrating on damaged aircraft – easier to hit and offering the chance of a definite 'kill'. Twenty-two Stukas fell to the fighters' guns, with another nineteen damaged, a surprisingly more balanced ratio, given the Stuka's vulnerability. Half of these losses were suffered in the battle over Convoy 'Peewit' on 8 August.

The losses amongst Bf 110s were twenty-seven lost and seventeen damaged, with twenty-five of their pilots killed or captured and another four wounded. Twenty-two of those lost and all of those damaged fell to fighters, which meant Spitfires and Hurricanes were inflicting on them a humiliating loss ratio of 4:1. There are reports from some of their earliest actions of their forming circles immediately on being attacked. Circles of Bf 110s could neither shoot down British fighters nor protect their own bombers.

But the aircraft most vulnerable of all to the guns of British fighters was the Bf 109. RAF pilots managed to get a bead on 70 of them, and of those they destroyed 54, some 77%, a markedly higher destruction ratio than the 63% which the Bf 109s achieved in return. This may be because damaged machines had further to fly to make it home and force-landed in England or ditched and so were lost. But it also looks as if Spitfires and Hurricanes were even more deadly than the Bf 109 itself, and that in fighter combat their eight Brownings were at least as destructive as the two cannon and two machine guns of the Bf 109E.

These figures may reflect the fact that the British were using a unique type of incendiary ammunition. Two inventors, a Belgian called de Wilde and a Swiss called Kaufman, demonstrated an incendiary round in December 1938, and the Air Ministry bought the design. Captain Dixon of the Royal Arsenal was not very impressed with it, however, and designed from scratch one of his own, which was in production by May 1940. The original name was kept to make the Germans think it was the old de Wilde bullet.[36] It impressed Dowding who observed that 'it was extremely popular with pilots, who attributed to it almost magical properties'.[37]

Considering both air forces as a whole, they were wreaking destruction on each other at roughly similar rates. From 10 July to 11 August, the RAF lost 115 fighters and 64 bombers in combat, a total of 179. This is not far short of the Luftwaffe's total combat losses of 216. But for the Luftwaffe to achieve its ends, its forces had to shoot down more than 115 fighters a month, which British factories could easily replace. They also had to remain intact to cover the invasion, which meant that they could not afford to lose three aircraft themselves for every two they shot down. Nor could they tolerate the losses in personnel. They had managed to kill eighty-nine fighter pilots and wound another twenty-eight. But doing so had cost them the lives of 153 pilots, with 45 wounded, and another 20 in British prison camps. Pilot losses were running at almost 2:1 in Fighter Command's favour. The loss of aircrew added to the disproportion. In addition to pilots the Germans lost 251 airmen killed in combat, another 55 wounded and 53 captured.

The German fighter pilots themselves, of course, had no idea of any of this. During the Channel fighting they themselves had been shooting down more British fighters than they lost in combat with them. They destroyed eighty-seven and damaged fifty-two for the loss of fifty-four destroyed and sixteen damaged in return. This means that the German fighter pilots were achieving a favourable kill ratio of 1.6:1 and an overall hit ratio of almost 2:1. Given that they over-claimed by a factor of three, they believed things were going well and they were actually achieving the 5:1 ratio Osterkamp thought they needed. The overall picture is different, for the British fighters were under explicit instructions to target bombers rather than fighters. Taking all types together, Fighter Command shot down at least 172 German aircraft and damaged another 79, a total of 251, which rises to 283 if the unknown cases are added. They themselves lost 115 shot down and another 106 damaged, a total of 221. They were thus achieving a favourable kill ratio of at least 1.5:1 and an overall hit ratio of 1.3:1.

So it was that both sides thought they were winning, and morale on both sides remained high. Some of their ignorance was merciful. Statistically, a green pilot on either side going into action for the first time had three rolls of the die. First roll: four, five or six and you get back with your aircraft undamaged; one, two or three and your aircraft is hit. Second roll: four, five or six, and you bale out or force-land unhurt; one, two or three and you are injured. Third roll: five or six and you recover from your injuries; one, two, three or four and you are dead.

16. EAGLE DAY

A t 6.30 in the morning on Monday 12 August, the roar of Daimler-Benz engines disturbed the peace of a fine, clear dawn in the small French town of Denain. The ground crews had been up for a long time fitting bombs to the aircraft, which was strange, because the machines which took off and then headed north-west for Calais were fighters, a mixture of Bf 109s and Bf 110s. They landed at Calais-Marck, re-fuelled, and at 8.40 took off again in four groups on the same north-westerly heading, taking them towards Dover.

The unusual unit to which these aircraft belonged was called Erprobungsgruppe 210. It was, as its name says, a test group, perhaps best translated as 'Operational Trials Wing 210'. It was set up on 1 July to develop techniques for delivering small weights of bombs with high precision onto small targets from low altitudes, in a shallow dive. The unit consisted of two Staffeln of Bf 110s and one of Bf 109s, and they were expected to perform as fighters after delivering their payloads. They were the first fighter-bombers. Willy Messerschmitt was designing an aircraft expressly for this role, designated the Me 210. Hence the unit's name. They were attached to Loerzer's II Fliegerkorps in Airfleet 2.

The men were not hand-picked. The crews of three existing Staffeln, 1./ZG1, 3./StG77 and 4./JG186[1], which combined the skills of men trained on Zerstörer, Stukas and Bf 109s, were simply put together under the leadership of a Swiss-born German national, Hauptmann Walter Rubensdörffer. They were helped by a special training officer, Hauptmann Karl Valesi, the leading Luftwaffe expert on the use of the Bf 109 as a dive-bomber. Part of the idea was to see what average pilots could achieve. Rubensdörffer, a veteran of the Spanish Civil War, had previously been based at the Experimental Trials Centre at Rechlin, and was a daring and utterly dedicated man. He said that when he died, he wanted his ashes to be scattered in the air from an aeroplane.

Erprobungsgruppe 210 was the only unit formed by the Luftwaffe specifi-cally for the air campaign against England. Its insignia was a yellow gunsight graticule superimposed over the red shape of the island that was its target. They first went into action on 13 July, and had already lost ten airmen in combat and another five, including Hauptmann Valesi, in accidents. But 12 August was to be their busiest day by far.

As the twenty or so aircraft headed out over the Channel, they were picked up by the radar station at Rye. From their speed they were clearly fighters. The filter room at Bentley Priory hesitated, giving them an 'X' designation, meaning 'unidentified'. Just before they reached the coast, they confusingly turned west and then split into four groups. One Staffel carried on to the radar station at Dover and watched the masts sway as their bombs landed in the compound. One scored eight hits on the radar station at Pevensey, severing the electricity cables, one put Rye itself off the air and the fourth group, led by Rubensdörffer, sped inland and dropped the whole of their payload into the radar compound at Dunkirk just west of Canterbury. They all landed back in Calais without having seen a British fighter.[2]

The CH stations at Dover, Pevensey and Rye were down. The part of the map protected by the CHL equipment at Dover was well covered by its neighbours at Fairlight and Foreness. But Dunkirk was the only CH station left to give long-range high cover over Kent. In a few minutes, a gap had been torn in the CH cover between East Kent and West Sussex. The first intact CH stations west of Dunkirk were at Truleigh and Poling near Arundel and at Ventnor on the Isle of Wight. The latter, on the southern coast of the island, had particularly good coverage.

It was the CHL station located next to the CH station at Poling that was the first to pick up something big heading towards Brighton at 1145. The plots became confused, but within twenty minutes the Observer Corps confirmed that a huge force was moving towards Portsmouth and the Isle of Wight. It was Sperrle's main contribution to the day: sixty-three Ju 88s of KG51 led by their Kommodore, Oberst Dr Fisser, with up to 150 Bf 110s and Bf 109s from two Zerstörer and three Jagdgeschwader which formed up in a huge circle far above them. Over Spithead, the bulk of the Junkers turned north through the balloon barrage, and, braving intense AA fire, delivered a devastating attack on the dockyards and town. The other fifteen aircraft split off to the south. Once over the middle of the Isle of Wight, they entered a shallow dive and, disturbed only by the fire of three Bofors guns, dropped seventy-four bombs in and around the Ventnor station. Fifteen of them were direct hits. Ventnor was down.

As the raiders tried to leave the area, British fighters arrived in succession, fifty-eight in all, and, together with Portsmouth's AA guns, had accounted for eleven of KG51's machines before the bulk of the German escorts engaged. Knowing that their best chance of getting kills was in the first dive, the German fighters spent fifteen minutes waiting for a tempting target. In the meantime, the bombers were savaged, one of the victims being Dr Fisser himself. Fighter losses on both sides ran at about ten each, with the Bf 110s predictably losing heavily.

Kesselring was keen to exploit Rubensdörffer's opening success. By midday, Erprobungsgruppe 210 was ready to take off again. Reinforced by eighteen Dorniers of KG2, they appeared over Manston airfield at 1250.

Manston was permanent home to only one unit, 600 Squadron, a night-fighter Squadron equipped with Blenheims. However, it did put up a number of occasional guests. The main guests on 12 August were 65 Squadron, who, whilst based at Rochford, were using Manston as a forward base.

During the morning 65 had been scrambled to intercept a raid on two small convoys off North Foreland, had an inconclusive tussle with the escorting Messerschmitts, and landed again at about 1115. When the raiders arrived they were formed up on the grass with engines running, waiting to take off in response to a warning received ten to fifteen minutes before. Remarkably, only one Spitfire was damaged. The rest of 65 Squadron got off the ground and joined 54 Squadron in a confused mêlée with their assailants.

65 Squadron had one illustrious supernumerary. On 5 August, the Spitfire test pilot Jeffrey Quill had got himself posted to 65 Squadron in order to see for himself how the Spitfire performed in combat. He was sitting in his cockpit watching his leader on the left when he became aware of a reverberation to his right. Looking across, he saw a hangar roof and a lot of earth in the air, and a Bf 110 pulling out of a dive. He slammed the throttle open and took off with the image of smoke and bomb-bursts in his rear-view mirror. In the air, he was vulnerable until he picked up more speed and altitude, but suddenly a Bf 109, travelling very fast, swept up in front of him. He fired at it and pushed the throttle through the gate to get maximum power, but the 109 sped on and disappeared into clouds. That was it for Quill, but Manston was blanketed in smoke and reduced to confusion by the 150 or so bombs which fell on it while he was taking off.[3]

Lympne on the Kent coast, used as an emergency landing ground, was attacked both in the morning and the afternoon, and then, shortly after this second raid, it was the turn of nearby Hawkinge, a satellite airfield lying just behind Folkestone. It was the target of Erprobungsgruppe 210's third mission of the day. They wrecked one hangar, damaged another, destroyed several stores and two houses in the Airmen's Married Quarters and left twenty-eight craters on the aerodrome. Six airmen were wounded and two Spitfires damaged. The raiders were reported to be Ju 88s.[4]

The evening saw three small raids on coastal towns in Kent which Kesselring conducted to test the damage done to the detection system. As the light faded, so did the Luftwaffe's sense of satisfaction. Radio traffic clearly indicated that the defenders had located all three raids precisely. For all that, the Luftwaffe felt it had some real successes. It had totally destroyed Manston and rendered Hawkinge and Lympne unserviceable. In addition, it had shot down forty-six Spitfires, twenty-three Hurricanes and one Morane 406 for the loss of half that number.[5]

Fighter Command had in fact lost twenty aircraft in the air and two Blenheims of 600 Squadron written off on the ground during the attack on

Manston. All three airfields were operational the following morning after the debris had been cleared and the bomb-craters filled in.

Rye RDF station had come back on the air at noon. The other two in Kent were working within six hours. The most serious damage had been at Ventnor. It was out of action for three days because the power supply had been cut and a mobile generator had to be brought in. The damage to the towers themselves had been as superficial there as at the other stations. The RAF was also relieved to discover that despite some worries about them, the WAAFs did not panic when they were under attack. In fact, Dowding praised the women at the radar stations in particular for their courage under bombardment.[6] In order to further mislead the Luftwaffe about its success at Ventnor, dummy radio signals were sent out as repairs were going on.

This attempt to blind Fighter Command had been half-hearted, in part perhaps because some, like Kesselring's Chief of Staff, Oberst Paul Deichmann, wanted the British to know when they were coming so that the 109s could engage them in a big dogfight. Deichmann's view was not shared by many of his airmen, who realised that they were being observed by the evil eye of these invisible signals from the time they left France. It meant that almost every sortie was intercepted. There could be no easy missions over England.

The desire for a decisive aerial engagement had affected the fighters escorting KG51, and given Park the opportunity to hit the bombers with individual Squadrons one after another whilst the 109s circled. KG51 lost 17% of its strength, and feelings ran high. By pursuing his tactics, Park was driving a wedge between the fighter and bomber commanders. He presented them with a stark choice: either carry on with loose escorts and sweeps and risk continued heavy losses to the bombers; or shackle more of the fighters to the bombers in a close escort role, which would make them far less threatening to Park's men. Tactically, Park had the initiative. The only solution for the Luftwaffe was to do both – but that would take an awful lot of fighters.

If the resources dedicated to the attacks on the radar chain had been inadequate, their execution had been brilliant. Erprobungsgruppe 210's first operation against the British mainland fully vindicated their methods. They were as accurate as Stukas at their best, but far less vulnerable, and flying fast aircraft at low level had achieved surprise against these coastal targets. For all that, they had not achieved their goal. They needed to go back again and again to do that.

That night, Bomber Command was out as usual. The target for that night was an aqueduct on the Dortmund-Ems canal, which was a choke point in Germany's inland waterways, important for the movement of barges to the invasion ports. Five Hampdens from 49 and 83 Squadrons made the difficult low-level attack. After the first two had been shot down and the next two damaged, the last aircraft, piloted by Flight Lieutenant Roderick Learoyd, flew through the flak and searchlights to score a near miss. His behaviour in conducting the attack and in nursing his crippled aircraft home won Learoyd the

Victoria Cross. The canal was blocked for ten days, which significantly hampered the projected timetable for the invasion.[7]

The 13th of August was Eagle Day. Göring had wanted three days of good weather, and on the evening of the 12th, it looked as if he would get it. Across northern France, staff and ground crews worked away to get their units ready for the morning. In fact, the 11th and 12th had been fine, despite the forecasts, so he could in fact have gone ahead before. The weather was about to be contrary again. Before dawn, weather reconnaissance machines reported thick cloud forming over the Channel. In the early hours, Göring, who did not want Eagle Day to go off half-cock, postponed the planned operations again, this time till the afternoon.

The result was a classic cock-up, the product of two classic causes: the weather and communications. The honour of leading the first mission on this historic day had been given to Oberst Johannes Fink, who, his task as Kanakafü complete, had reverted to his role as Geschwaderkommodore of KG2. His Dorniers had taken to the air between 0450 and 0510 to meet up with their escorts over the Channel. These were Bf 110s of ZG26, led by Germany's famous one-legged pilot, the WWI veteran Oberstleutnant Joachim Huth. The staff at Luftflotte 2 HQ were frantically signalling the cancellation order to every unit, but for some reason it did not get through to Fink's II. and III. Gruppen.[8] It did get through to Huth, however. ZG26's radios were tuned to a different frequency from the bombers, so he could not communicate with Fink. Somewhat at a loss as he watched the bombers flying on, Huth performed a series of aerobatics in front of Fink's Dornier to try to get him to turn back. Fink thought he was showing off. Then the escorts disappeared.

Fink flew on round the north Kent coast towards his targets, Sheerness and the airfield of Eastchurch on the Isle of Sheppey, knowing that his return flight path would take him across the heart of 11 Group's territory. It was a brave thing to do, but counter to a set of orders issued by Kesselring on 4 August which stipulated that bombers were to abort their missions if their escorts failed to turn up or broke off.[9] Fink probably continued because he did have some escorts in the shape of the Bf 109s of the 3rd Staffel of Erprobungsgruppe 210 led by Oberleutnant Otto Hinze. The 109s had yet another set of crystals and did not get the recall order either.[10]

This had the makings of a massacre, but Fighter Command managed some cock-ups of its own. For some reason, the radar operators missed the Dorniers. Glimpsing them indistinctly in the low cloud, the Observer Corps thought the raid was quite small and mistook its bearing. Five squadrons were scrambled, but only 74 Squadron intercepted, to be joined later by 111 and 151, which put in attacks on the bombers as they appeared between the clouds. Five Dorniers were lost, but both targets were bombed.

When he got back, Fink was furious, delivering such a tirade over the telephone to Kesselring that 'Smiling Albert' had to go to his airfield in person to placate him.[11] Fink nevertheless reported success, even if more dearly bought than need have been: they had destroyed ten Spitfires on the ground and wrecked Eastchurch airfield.

They had in fact destroyed one, and had been lucky to do that. It belonged to 266 Squadron, which had moved down to Tangmere from 12 Group on the 9th and were using Eastchurch temporarily for convoy protection patrols. The report of Spitfires on the ground added credence to the Luftwaffe's belief that Eastchurch was a fighter station. In fact it was used by Coastal Command. KG2's sacrifice made no contribution at all to the battle against Fighter Command, and the Luftwaffe would conduct seven more futile raids on Eastchurch between Eagle Day and the first week of September. They would also be well spaced out, giving the station plenty of time to repair the damage each time and get ready for the next.

Göring's postponement order appears not to have reached Airfleet 3 at all. At about the same time that Fink and his men were getting on their way – between 0500 and 0520 – twenty Ju 88s of I./KG54 took off to raid the airfield belonging to the Royal Aircraft Establishment at Farnborough, and between 0505 and 0535, eighteen more from II./KG54 formed up to attack the army co-operation airfield at nearby Odiham. At 0550, eighty-eight Ju 87s of StG./77 also set off for Portland. The raids were escorted by about 60 Bf 110s of ZG2 and V./LG1, and 173 Bf 109s from JG27, JG53 and JG2, who flew ahead on a sweep.

The Stukas' targets were obscured by cloud, so they turned back. However, the two sets of raiders from KG54 flew on, experiencing what Airfleet 3's operational records describe as 'strong and stubborn' fighter defences from the coast to the targets and half-way back across the Channel. The intercepting fighters were from Middle Wallop, Tangmere and Northolt, and they shot down four Ju 88s and one Bf 109 from JG2. No less than eleven Ju 88s suffered varying degrees of damage. In return the escorts claimed six RAF fighters and the bombers claimed fourteen. In reality, the Bf 109s shot down one and damaged another and the bombers damaged five, of which two had to be written off, the other three being repairable. Out of the twenty claimed, the actual British losses were three aircraft, with just three pilots wounded.

Having returned unscathed from this escort mission, V./LG1 took off again at 1110 on a mission described as a 'freie Jagd' over Portland, led by their Gruppenkommandeur, Horst Liensberger. It may be that this was intended to lure up fighters before a second raid by KG54 went in and that by this time the cancellation order had arrived. After the aborted Stuka mission of the early morning, Airfleet 3 did not attempt to bomb Portland until the late afternoon. Whatever happened, the twenty-three Bf 110s found themselves alone and ran into trouble, losing six machines (including two written off on crash-landing), with three more damaged. They hopefully claimed nine Spitfires. They had tangled with the Hurricanes of 601 Squadron, of which they shot down one and damaged two. Liensberger found time to scribble a couple of postcards in which he put a brave face on things, saying it was a hard day

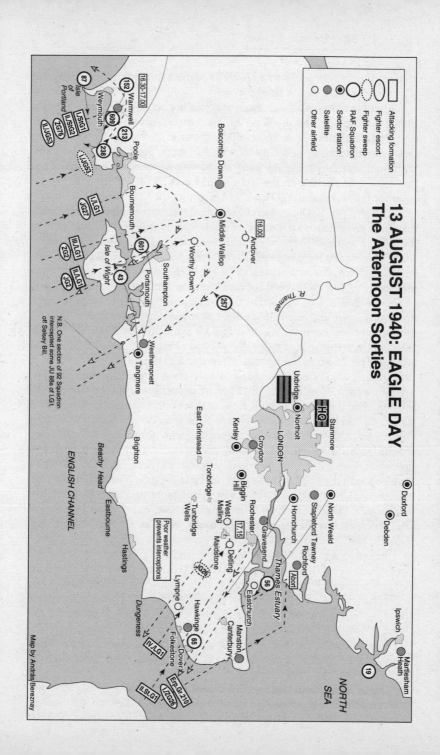

13 AUGUST 1940: EAGLE DAY
The Afternoon Sorties

Map by András Bereznay

against a plucky enemy which had some impressive stunt pilots in its ranks, but that things would turn out alright.[12]

After the morning's fiasco, Eagle was finally given the official go-ahead at 1400. It was Sperrle who provided the main thrust, sending fifty-eight Ju 88s from I., II. and III./LG1 to bomb the airfields at Boscombe Down, Worthy Down, and Andover, and fifty-two Ju 87s from StG1 and StG2 against Warmwell and Yeovil. I./JG53 went ahead on a sweep curving round from Poole to Lyme Regis, with the rest of JG53 and III./ZG76 providing escort cover for the Stukas and JG27 and ZG2 escorting the Ju 88s of LG1.

The whole of 10 Group took to the air. It was impossible for the German fighters to protect such a large and unwieldy formation and in the confusion of the fighting one Staffel of Stukas from II./StG2 was massacred by 609 Squadron while their escorts were embroiled with other fighters above. Six out of nine were shot down. The weather was still so poor that it was impossible to bomb most of the targets. StG1 could not find Warmwell and StG2 gave up on Yeovil, so they both had a go at Portland. I./LG1 abandoned its attempt to reach Boscombe Down and bombed Southampton instead. One aircraft of III./LG1 dropped its bombs near the important Sector Station of Middle Wallop by mistake, but the rest managed to hit the old grass airstrip at Andover which had been used for bombers but nobody cared about any more.[13]

To the east, Kesselring decided to have another go. Erprobungsgruppe 210 took off at 1515 escorted by ZG26 to attack Southend, but they aborted the mission when they found unbroken cloud cover over Essex, and returned after the escorts had had a little tussle with 56 Squadron, dropping their loads over Canterbury on the way. Meanwhile, Kesselring sent the only two Stukagruppen attached to Airfleet 2 across Kent to attack two airfields. II./StG1 tried to find Rochester, but failed and returned without incident, and IV./LG1, also equipped with the Ju 87, tried to find the Fleet Air Arm base at Detling, with JG26 out on a sweep ahead. Detling was free of cloud, and the Stukas bombed it, killing the Station Commander amongst sixty-seven others. All the Stukas returned safely, for the weather made interception as difficult as bombing. JG26 lost one Bf 109 over Folkestone.

So ended the day designed to be the beginning of the end of Fighter Command. Even if the attacks had succeeded brilliantly, they would have done Fighter Command little damage: only Middle Wallop was a fighter station and its assailants missed it altogether. But the obvious failings of execution spread anger and recrimination throughout the Luftwaffe. There were stories too about a Staffel of Stukas being wiped out, stories which spread fast. The Luftwaffe knew the day had not gone well. But at least they had destroyed eighty-four RAF fighters, a lot of them on the ground, many more than the forty-seven they lost themselves.[14]

One of their claims was Tony Woods-Scawen. He had got shot up as was usual for him, and crash-landed his Hurricane, which blew up after he had scrambled out. Still, he put in a claim for two He 111s as 'probables'. The rest of 43 Squadron claimed Ju 88s, which made more sense, as they had in fact attacked KG54. Tony's problem was not just a matter of aircraft recognition. He had had TB as a child and ever since his eyesight had been impaired. He had got into the RAF by memorising the eye-test card. It was no wonder his planes were always getting damaged, but he was particularly loved in the Squadron for always coming back for more and being an especially gutsy little chap.

Eagle Day was one of Fighter Command's best days. It lost only thirteen aircraft in combat and one on the ground. All but three pilots survived. The RAF lost another forty-seven aircraft of various kinds on the airfields bombed, a loss possibly worth the confusion it caused on the other side of the Channel. The first report to reach Downing Street that evening was of seventy-eight German planes destroyed for the loss of three pilots. Colville describes it as an 'astonishing result', which indeed it would have been. As it was, the truth still justified his comment that it was 'indeed a victory and will do much for public morale'.[15]

However, it was one of Bomber Command's worst days. As long ago as April, Portal had sent a note to the Air Ministry about the dangers and the pointlessness of attacking airfields in Scandinavia. Nevertheless, in the morning, twelve Blenheims of 82 Squadron took off to attack KG30's base at Aalborg in Denmark. The weather played a role here too. The Blenheims had been ordered to turn back if the weather was good, and out to the east the skies were clear. For some reason, they continued. One pilot did turn back, claiming fuel problems. He was court-martialled. He was also the only one to return, the rest of the Squadron falling to flak and fighters, as so often in the past.[16] Twenty airmen died, and the lucky thirteen who survived were taken prisoner. The Luftwaffe did not have a monopoly on folly.

The morning of the 14th was quiet. In the early afternoon there was a big dogfight over the Goodwin Sands between JG26, who were escorting some Stukas, and about forty British fighters. I./JG26 stayed close to the Stukas, and this time managed to protect them, while the other two Gruppen flew more loosely. For once they enjoyed the sort of success the Luftwaffe had always expected, shooting down three British fighters and damaging two more for the loss of only one Bf 109. The Stukas were numerous enough to be an effective bait, but the 109s were not tied down by them, and JG26 had a goodly number of aces. Amongst those claiming were the 'Experten', Ebbighausen, Schöpfel, Galland and his wingman Müncheberg. The Stukas managed to sink the Goodwin lightship. Just why they wanted to do so is unclear.

With the defences thus preoccupied, Erprobungsgruppe 210 struck again at Manston. It was a repeat of the 12th, except that Manston's AA defences destroyed two Bf 110s. A hangar with three aircraft was destroyed, and the Commanding Officer of 600 Squadron got a black eye from a stone which ricocheted off the adjutant's steel helmet.[17] There were also fifty craters to be filled in.

Sperrle restricted himself to a number of small raids on an assortment of airfields that did little damage. Both Airfleets were preparing for the morrow.

Sperrle had been summoned to Karinhall with Kesselring, Loerzer, Grauert and Osterkamp to explain how it was that Eagle Day had turned out such a mess. That evening plans were authorised to be put into operation, if the weather permitted, by the staff officers of the two Airfleets, who would be joined for the first time by Airfleet 5 in Norway. The RAF was to feel the power of the entire Luftwaffe and be subjected to pressure at all points.

Dowding needed to do little. His system had passed its most severe test so far. On the morning of the 14th his old friend Pile found him more animated than he had ever known him, as close to jubilation as 'Stuffy' had ever got. He was nevertheless clear that it was going to be a long haul, so he moved squadrons between the Groups, without greatly changing the strength of the Groups themselves. Just as Park was the prime mover in deciding which squadrons should be withdrawn from 11 Group, so the AOCs of the other Groups selected which ones to send south.

The hardest hit squadron was 145, which had lost eleven pilots with another two wounded since 10 July, all but one in the five days from 8–12 August. This is the sort of sustained but concentrated punishment which can break morale. Dowding took them right out of it, posting them to 13 Group at Drem to rebuild the unit, and Saul sent the Scots auxiliaries of 602 (City of Glasgow) Squadron down from Drem to the Sussex coast at Tangmere's satellite, Westhampnett, in their place. 74, which had lost five pilots, was moved to 12 Group at Wittering in Cambridgeshire, and 238, which had lost seven, stayed in 10 Group but was moved out of the way to St Eval. 266 Squadron, recently arrived in Tangmere from 12 Group, was moved to Hornchurch, and 249 Squadron, also from 12 Group, was moved south for the first time.

Dowding was careful about introducing too many inexperienced units at once. Two other Squadrons which had lost five pilots, 111 and 601, were kept in 11 Group. In both cases, four out of the five had been killed on 11 August. This would have been a shock to both of them, but was an isolated instance. Both units were to vindicate Dowding's decision the next day.[18]

17. THE GREATEST DAY

The Luftwaffe's early reconnaissance flights on the morning of the 15th showed that the cloud was clearing from the north. As Kesselring's Chief of Staff, it fell to Oberst Paul Deichmann to decide whether or not to carry out the planned attacks. As the skies over the south began to get clearer, he decided that the carefully co-ordinated operation, designed to stretch the defences to their limits, was on.

The first targets were Hawkinge and Lympne once more, which were hit by two groups of Stukas with a heavy Bf 109 escort just before midday. The interception was a race between 54 and 501 Squadrons trying to get at the Stukas and the high escorts trying to get at them. In the event the 109s got there first, diving from above and shooting down four of them.

More buildings collapsed on the airfields, but the most serious effect of the bombing was never intended. Four of the bombs meant for Hawkinge missed the target and fell on the roads outside. They severed the cables carrying power to the CH station at Rye and the CHL stations at Foreness and Dover. The Kent radar screen was down again, and it took all day to get power back to the three stations and put them on the air again. This damage, inflicted by chance by only four bombs aimed at something else, was in fact more disruptive than that inflicted by the multiple precision-aimed bomb-loads three days before. The Germans never had any idea what they had achieved.

These two attacks were followed by a snap raid on Manston which destroyed two Spitfires on the ground and rattled some new recruits who had arrived just in time to be bombed on the 12th. It was becoming clear that Manston was a prime target; only three miles from the sea, it could not be effectively protected from fast, low-level raiders.[1]

These airfield raids were in part designed to keep the defenders' attention focussed on the south. They were expected to be weaker and less alert in the north, where Luftflotte 5 could bring its forces into play. In fact, 13 Group's radar operators had been put on full alert because of a convoy sailing from Hull at midday. So it was that at 1205 they reported a raid heading for Edinburgh. As the plot gained in strength and shifted south, the controller scrambled 72 Squadron from Acklington, 605 from Drem and put 79 on 'standby'.

The Germans had wanted them to pick up the first northerly plot. Anxious to leave nothing to chance, Stumpff had sent two Staffeln of He 115 seaplanes towards Dundee as a feint to draw off fighters. He knew fighters were there because they regularly shot down his reconnaissance planes. The seaplanes were to turn back before they reached the coast. This they did.

The main raid consisted of 72 He 111s of KG26, led by Oberstleutnant Fuchs, which took off from Stavanger at 1000. They were supposed to head for the airfields of Usworth in Durham and Dishforth in Yorkshire. Unfortunately, Fuchs' navigator took them 3° north of their planned heading, carrying them almost to where the seaplanes were and creating a very large plot on the radar screens. The plot moved south as the navigator realised his error, and KG26 moved towards their escort, twenty-one long-range Bf 110Ds of I./ZG76, led by their commander, Werner Restemeyer. When 72 Squadron discovered them, they reported a raid of 100 plus, and 41, 607 and 79 Squadrons were scrambled as well.

72 Squadron were about 4,000 feet above the German force and heading straight for them, closing at over 400 mph. Both formations stood out in the clear skies and one of the British pilots asked his leader, Ted Graham, if he had seen them. Graham had a bad stutter and there was a pause before he stammered: 'Of course I've seen the b-b-b-bastards – I'm t-t-t-trying to work out w-w-w-what to do!' Unlike most of his colleagues further south, he had the luxury of being able to manoeuvre without the presence of Bf 109s, and he took his Squadron out to sea and up-sun before leading them in a diving attack on the escorts which carried them through to the bombers below. Restemeyer's Messerschmitt blew up, and another came down on the Durham coast. The formation disintegrated, some of the Heinkels jettisoning their bombs and making for the cover of clouds. Within five minutes, the other fighters arrived and began the work of execution. Eight more Heinkels and six more Bf 110s fell, the latter losing a third of their number. The disproportion of their losses relative to the bombers shows just how vulnerable these long-range Bf 110s were when loaded with fuel. The dramatic explosion of Restemeyer's machine is thought to have been caused by the ignition of petrol gas in his ventral tank.[2] Two Hurricanes of 605 Squadron were damaged by return fire, and force-landed near Newcastle. One machine was a write-off and one of the pilots was wounded. The Hurricane of 605's leading ace, F/Lt Archie McKellar, who had been leading them, also landed with minor battle damage.

These events had brought 12 Group to a high state of readiness. At 1305, a forty-plus raid was located apparently heading for the fighter aerodromes of Church Fenton and Leconfield, and 616 and 73 Squadrons based there were scrambled at 1307. Hugh Dundas was among the twelve pilots of 616 who took off, surprised to be scrambled and indignant about having to leave in the middle of lunch. He had not been in action since Dunkirk, where he had had a narrow escape, but now he was lucky again. The raiders turned out to be sixty Ju 88s of KG30 which had crossed from Aalborg. They appeared to be without escorts, but were in fact escorting themselves. About half of them were Ju 88Cs, a 'Zerstörer' version of the bomber which exchanged its bomb load for machine guns and cannon fitted into a solid nose. They proved to be no more effective in this role than the Bf 110. As the force crossed the coast they swung south-west to bomb the Bomber Command airfield at Driffield, destroying ten Whitleys on the ground and damaging six others, but they lost two bombers, and, reflecting the same pattern as in the action further north, six of the Ju 88C fighters, which went down without damaging any of their assailants. A further Ju88 bomber and a Ju88C were damaged.

As the survivors of KG30 were heading back to Aalborg, a new plot developed over the Pas-de-Calais. The main cause of the build up were the eighty-eight Do 17s of KG3 getting into formation. Disguised by this, Erprobungsgruppe 210 took off at the same time and headed round the north coast of Kent at high speed. Still off the air because of the earlier power failure, North Foreland CHL station did not see them, and it was not until they were approaching Harwich that they were identified and 17 Squadron ordered off from Martlesham Heath. The second flight of 17 Squadron was just taking off as Rubensdörffer's men arrived over the airfield at 1510. The 109s of the 3rd Staffel led the attack with a dive-bombing run (leading to their being mis-identified as Ju 87s) and zoomed off to play the role of pure fighters. They put Martlesham out of action for forty-eight hours, and when 17 were joined by 1 Squadron in pursuit of the Bf 110s, the Bf 109s of Erprobungsgruppe 210's 3rd Staffel above bounced them, shot down three of their number and damaged two more. The fighter-bombers had proved to be devastatingly effective in both roles, and Erprobungsgruppe 210 landed back at Calais-Marck with no losses. They debriefed, re-fuelled and bombed up again, and got ready for their final mission of the day.

Meanwhile KG3, with 130 Bf 109s from JG51, JG52 and JG54 above them were approaching Deal, as JG26 sped in front of them on a sweep. Three Squadrons were sent against them, followed by four more, but they could not get through to the bombers. The bombers did get through to their targets, however: Eastchurch once more, and the Short Bros factory at Rochester, which was damaged so badly that production of the Stirling, the first of Britain's heavy bombers, was disrupted for three months. Though the air fighting was confused, the German pilots got the best of it, with height and numbers on their side. The aces of JG26 again claimed heavily, and some of the claims were undoubtedly correct. Certainly they themselves did not lose a plane that day.

There followed a series of small raids on airfields, towns and radar stations in Kent, and though little damage was done, few interceptions were successful.

11 Group was getting swamped, but Luftflotte 2's effort was not sustained. It could not be. With four whole Geschwader in the air as well as I./LG2, Luftflotte 2 only had one Geschwader of Bf 109s left. They needed extra cover for returning aircraft and were too wary to totally denude their own defences. What if something were to go wrong in Osterkamp's absence? Göring always fell into a rage when RAF intruders were not shot down. The risk was too high. Yet the returns could have been great.

Instead, as the activity in the east died down, Airfleet 3 went into battle, the last of the three to do so. Between 1500 and 1900 KG27 sent out a number of Heinkels on harassing raids, several of which were broken off because of poor visibility and fighter opposition. The first main thrust, however, was undertaken by 12 Ju 88s of I./LG1 against Andover and 15 from II./LG1 against Worthy Down, escorted by II./ZG2 and II./ZG76. The raiders took off between 1515 and 1545 and were intercepted at 1715. There was no particular reason why this should not have been co-ordinated with Airfleet 2, but the command structures were separate and Kesselring and Sperrle themselves, whilst they did not row, often differed. So they fought their own campaigns.

The raiders got through, but they did little damage, and 601 Squadron in particular dealt savagely with them, shooting down five out of the seven Ju 88s of one Staffel.

At 1600, 47 Stukas of I./StG1 and II./StG2 took off to attack Warmwell, escorted by about 60 Bf 109s from JG27 and JG53 and the 40 or so Bf110s of V./LG1 and II./ZG76. Meeting strong fighter opposition, they decided to attack their secondary target instead and so they appeared over the long-suffering naval base of Portland at 1730.

Just to the north of Portland, at Middle Wallop, Bob Doe was waiting to die. He took off with the rest of 234 Squadron and intercepted this raid, along with 213 and 87 Squadrons. He was not alone in claiming Bf 110s, for Luftflotte 3 lost thirteen of them, including the Gruppenkommandeur of III./ZG76. Even the Stukas, with four losses, had a better survival rate.

The final act of this dramatic day seemed from its weight to be almost an afterthought, but involved targets dwarfing in importance all the others attacked so far: the Sector Stations at the centre of 11 Group's network, Biggin Hill and Kenley.

As JG26 crossed the Kent coast on its final sweep of the day, it was followed at high altitude by a small group of Dorniers heading for Biggin Hill. JG26 bounced 151 Squadron over Dover on their way back at about 1900 and handled them very roughly, shooting down three and damaging two. Making landfall at 1815, the Dorniers headed into Kent, unloaded their bombs and flew back unopposed. They had bombed West Malling, a satellite airfield still under construction, several miles south-east of Biggin Hill.

Kenley was entrusted to Erprobungsgruppe 210. They took off on their last sortie of the day at 1815. Given that they were penetrating far further inland than they had at Manston, and that, unlike Martlesham Heath, Kenley was within range of Bf 109s, they were given an escort from I./JG52. They met up, but somehow lost contact in the early evening haze and the escorts, frustrated and anxious, returned to base. As one might expect, Rubensdörffer pressed on.

Coming in over Sevenoaks, he had of course been observed all the way, and 111 Squadron were scrambled from Croydon, together with 32 Squadron from Biggin Hill. Rubensdörffer spotted fighters above him as he saw the airfield below, and went in to attack his target as the Hurricanes dived on him. The 110s carried out their run in a 45° dive with the eight Bf 109s of 3rd Staffel bringing up the rear. Bombs fell on the airfield buildings and also among the factories outside the perimeter. But Erprobungsgruppe 210 was now fighting for its life. As 32 Squadron arrived and engaged the 109s, John Thompson's 111 Squadron hounded the Bf 110s into their usual defensive circle. The Bf 109s themselves tried to form a defensive circle between the British fighters and the Bf 110s, but lost them in the mist.

Suddenly, on an order from their leader, the Bf 110s broke for home, several of them having already been hit. A frantic chase began, with 111 and 32 pursuing their quarry across Kent, Surrey and Sussex. Between 1850 and 1915, one after another of the Bf 110s went down, leaving wrecks at Redhill, Crawley and Ightham, with a fourth force-landing at Hawkhurst. One almost managed to reach the coast, but was attacked by two more fighters. Its engines died and it was forced to make a belly-landing at Hooe near Bexhill.

Leutnant Horst Marx, flying a Bf 109, stuck by his leader. Rubensdörffer spoke to him over the R/T saying that his wireless operator was dead and he himself wounded, but then Marx was hit and baled out south of Tunbridge Wells, his aircraft crashing at Frant. Moments later, Rubensdörffer's machine hit the ground near Rotherfield with one of its engines on fire. Marx stopped a police car heading to the scene of Rubensdörffer's crash, surrendered to the policemen, and went with them. Rubensdörffer was dead. In his pocket was a letter from Kesselring congratulating him on the award of the Iron Cross First Class.[3]

Two more of the Bf 110s which landed back at Calais-Marck were damaged, one of the pilots being hospitalised for two months. As the shaken pilots compared notes, the suspicions several of them had had during the attack itself hardened into certainty. They had attacked the wrong airfield. Seven aircraft had been lost and thirteen men, including their brilliant leader, had been killed or captured in attacking Kenley's satellite airfield of Croydon.

They themselves had killed six airmen and sixty-two civilians. The craters were quickly filled in, though the smell from the Bourjois soap and perfume factory next door to the airfield, which had taken a direct hit, hung around Croydon for days. Erprobungsgruppe 210 had not just failed to attack Kenley, but had contravened Hitler's direct orders by hitting part of London. Despite that, Rubensdörffer was posthumously awarded the Knight's Cross four days later.

On 15 August, in the absence of its senior Commanders, the Luftwaffe flew more sorties than on any other day of the Battle of Britain – over two thousand. It had caused a lot of destruction, in particular to the resources of Bomber Command, and not a few deaths. But the most serious effect the day's activities had on Fighter Command was the chance cutting-off of the power supply to three radar stations, and by evening that was restored. The Luftwaffe had destroyed thirty-four RAF fighters, two of them on the ground, but the price was grievous. They did not lose the 182 machines claimed by the RAF, but seventy-five was enough to do their country loss. 15 August became known in the Luftwaffe as 'Black Thursday'.

That evening, as the Commanders returned to their Airfleets from their conference at Karinhall, it took some time to put things in perspective. They had not had a good day themselves.

Göring had started with a few rebukes about weather reconnaissance and radio communications, specifically on Eagle Day itself, which seems to have been an attempt to blame somebody else for the chaos he caused then.

However, his main concern had been losses. The fate of the Stukas over Portland on the 13th had disturbed him, and he stipulated that each Stuka wing was to be protected by three fighter wings: one to stay with them, one out ahead over the target and one flying top cover. Fresh fighters were needed to cover their return. When he allowed his mind rather than his emotions to work, Göring often made sense, and the prescription he gave was precisely the one enacted so successfully by JG26 on the 14th. However, the recipe was profligate in its use of Bf 109s, for it would take more than one whole Geschwader to protect each wing of Stukas. Luftflotte 2 might manage this, but Sperrle only had three Jagdgeschwader to protect a force of seven Stuka Gruppen. He would either have to restrict the use of Stukas or compromise Göring's demands.

Sperrle had come in for some stick on his use of Bf 110s, whose losses were clearly causing Göring major concern. 'We do not have that many Zerstörer,' he noted, 'and have to work economically with them.' He singled out V./LG1's disastrous '*freie Jagd*' as a breach of orders, and said again, as he claimed to have done many times before, that Bf 110s were only to be used when the ranges involved made it necessary, or to allow Bf 109s to break off combat.

Park's policy of causing bomber losses was working. Both of Göring's orders were a reaction to this, and would put increasing strain on the German single-seaters, which were already flying several missions a day. They would increasingly be the constraint governing the weight of attacks the Luftwaffe could deliver.

Göring had more to say about targets. He wanted to focus entirely on the RAF and the aircraft industry. Ships, including the Royal Navy, were just targets of opportunity, and he mentioned the previous day's attack on the Goodwin Lightship as a waste of effort (though in fact the escorts had been successful in this action). Again he stressed economy of effort. He wanted night and bad weather raids restricted to small groups of volunteer crews who knew the targets well. These were nuisance raids designed to wear down the population, and should also be directed at the RAF. In passing, he questioned the need for the current frequency of air raid warnings over Germany itself, as the economic disruption they caused was out of proportion to the damage Bomber Command was inflicting.

His most important remarks were lapidary and appear almost as afterthoughts. He questioned the wisdom of continuing to attack radar stations, as none had as yet been put out of action, and the British had 'a lot of radio stations'. His comments are couched more as a suggestion than an order, as if he did not think the matter terribly important. However, he was quite explicit in ordering that airfields which had been 'successfully attacked' one day should not be attacked the following day, presumably because he regarded it as a waste of effort.[4]

With these two comments, Göring more or less guaranteed the survival of 11 Group's infrastructure on the ground.

Back at their Headquarters, Kesselring, Sperrle and Stumpff reviewed the results of the 15th. The conclusion for Luftflotte 5 was clear. It never went into action again on a large scale. The loss of Rubensdörffer was a blow to Kesselring, and he was very concerned about the mistake in identifying the target. But for all that, a lot of damage had been done to airfields and 110 British fighters had been destroyed in the air. In the past week's heavy fighting, even allowing for some exaggeration, the RAF must have lost half its front-line fighter strength. The answer was to carry on.

Over at Middle Wallop that evening, Bob Doe was also having a think. He was working out how best to stay alive. He decided that if he saw tracer bullets coming from behind, he would push the control column straight forward and dive, and he repeated this to himself every night so that it would become an automatic reaction. He also agreed with another pilot, Sergeant Harker, that they would form a pair and look after each other's tails.

Somewhere near East Grinstead, Al Deere was in the back of an RAF ambulance whose driver was lost. Deere had chased a 109 over the Channel to Calais-Marck in the early evening, only to realise that he had thereby foolishly put his seventh life in peril. He was himself chased back to Dover by several 109s whose attacks damaged his Spitfire, and he baled out, landing near Ashford. The ambulance driver was trying to get to Kenley. The detour via East Grinstead was fortuitous, as it enabled Deere to get his wounded wrist put in plaster. He spent the night there and sneaked out the following morning while the celebrated burns surgeon Archibald McIndoe was trying to negotiate a longer stay in hospital for him because he looked as if he needed it. Deere caught a train and was back at Hornchurch by midday.[5]

The results of the 15th had caused great excitement in Downing Street. During the day, the Prime Minister had been given a hard time in the Commons. He was drawn into a petty brawl with an Independent MP about his motives for urging rearmament in 1936. When he then announced that he had agreed to give the Americans ninety-nine-year leases on some bases in the Caribbean and Newfoundland in exchange for fifty destroyers desperately needed for convoy protection, the news was very badly received by members of the Tory right, and another squabble started.[6]

However, as the reports of mounting German losses came in through the day, Churchill got more and more animated, until he ordered a car and drove off to Stanmore to see for himself. He returned with the news that German losses were over a hundred, had Colville ring up Chamberlain to tell him, and declared the day to be 'one of the greatest in history'.[7] In his later account, Churchill calls Dowding's foresight in keeping fighters in the north 'an example of genius in the art of war'. The result was politically important to him, for he knew his hold over the Commons was tenuous: 'Henceforth, everything north of the Wash was safe by day'.[8]

18. THE HARDEST DAY

Needing to regroup after the action of the 15th, the Luftwaffe launched no attacks until the end of the following morning. When they came, they were more threatening than those of the day before.

West Malling was the first airfield to be hit, a raid on Hornchurch being thwarted by a combination of poor visibility and 54 Squadron. More bombers got through to the Royal Aircraft Establishment at Farnborough and scattered bombs over Surrey and Wimbledon. In practice, it was impossible to attack military targets without dropping bombs on London. In the course of these late-morning actions, 266 Squadron encountered II./JG26, led by their Gruppenkommandeur Karl Ebbighausen, who had seven victories to his credit and was scoring fast. The fight was a disaster for 266, who lost four Spitfires. Two of the pilots, including Squadron Leader Wilkinson, were killed and the other two injured. II./JG26 suffered only one loss, but it was Ebbighausen, who according to some reports collided with Wilkinson. Other reports claim that Wilkinson, who was a friend of R.A.B. Butler's Parliamentary Private Secretary 'Chips' Channon and had turned down the job of Equerry to the Duke of Kent in order to get on operations, was shot up after taking to his parachute. 266 had only been in the south for a week. They had been in action on the 12th and 13th and had already lost three pilots. They seem to have bounced JG26, but did not notice other Bf 109s above them and were bounced in their turn. Such was the price paid by newcomers to battle.[1]

There was a grim, but significant postscript to this dogfight. One of 266's pilots, twenty-two-year-old Sub-Lieutenant Henry La Fone Greenshields, who had been posted to them from the Fleet Air Arm, survived the initial combat and bravely, perhaps foolishly, pursued the Germans over the Channel. He was shot down and killed, the squadron's fifth casualty, his Spitfire crashing into a canal bank in Calais. The Germans recovered his body and found an unposted letter in his tunic describing how his unit had been bombed at Eastchurch on the 13th. This confirmed their erroneous belief that Eastchurch was a fighter station, and does something to explain their interest in this Coastal Command base.[2]

The most important attacks of the day were carried out by Stukas from Airfleet 3. At 1300, the fifty-four Ju 87s of I. and III./StG2 appeared over Tangmere. After his light forays against Middle Wallop, this was only the second time that Sperrle had chosen a valuable airfield target, a Fighter Command Sector Station. At the same time, twenty-eight aircraft from III./StG1 made for Lee-on-Solent, and twenty-two from I./StG3 for Portsmouth. No doubt mindful of the previous day's admonitions, Jafü 3, Werner Junck, committed his entire fighter force. The 84 Stukas were thus protected by 214 Bf 109s from three Geschwader, as well as 43 Bf 110s from ZG2 and the 11 machines which V./LG1 could still manage to put into the air. This was close to the ratio Göring had demanded. It was certainly a maximum effort as far as Luftflotte 3 was concerned.

But no plan can guarantee success every time. Eight British squadrons intercepted. In the raids on Portsmouth and Lee-on-Solent, the Germans' tactics worked: the escorts kept the interceptors busy and the Stukas bombed and got home. Over Tangmere, they did not. As the Stukas came out of their dives, it was above all Tangmere's own 43 Squadron which got amongst them and did terrible execution. Nine Stukas from StG2 failed to return, and six more were damaged.

Though the fighter protection had not worked, the bombing had. Most of the buildings were hit, power and water supplies were cut off and fourteen Spitfires and Hurricanes undergoing repair had to be written off. Despite this, all of Tangmere's resident fighters were able to land there.

A more damaging event was taking place a little to the south-west. Despite Göring's opinion on the matter, which he had not in any case expressed very forcefully, Sperrle thought the radar stations were still worth a try. So he detailed a small force, just eight Stukas, to have another go at Ventnor while this huge activity was going on just to the north of them. 152 Squadron tried to intervene but became embroiled with Bf 109s. The Stukas hit Ventnor with twenty-two bombs, and this time it was off the air for seven days. A Mobile Reserve Station was set up at Bembridge on the east of the Island on the 23rd, but its performance remained very poor.

The German escorts had not inflicted a great deal of damage in the air fighting, but they did succeed in bringing down 601 Squadron's celebrated American volunteer, P/O Billy Fiske. He crashed on Tangmere badly burned and died of shock the next day. He was the first 'official' American to die in World War II, and much was made of the event on both sides of the Atlantic.[3] The Germans also brought down P/O James Nicolson of 249 Squadron, but not before he stayed in his burning Hurricane long enough to earn himself Fighter Command's only Victoria Cross of the war.[4]

They also got Tony Woods-Scawen again. He had been with 43 Squadron in its blistering attack on the Stukas over Tangmere, in which they claimed 17, two of which were due to him. But he was hit in the radiator and while making his way back home he was set upon by four Bf 109s. He crash-landed on the Isle of Wight and knocked out three of his front teeth. He took the ferry to Southampton and decided to spend the night in a hotel. He called his adjutant the next morning and told him to send someone over to pay his bill if the squadron still wanted him.[5]

Throughout all the sound and fury, it was the smallest raid, that on Ventnor, which had had the biggest impact on the defence. That afternoon, two Ju 88s appeared out of the blue over RAF Brize Norton in Oxfordshire, and put their wheels down as if to land, hoping to be mistaken for Blenheims. They then opened up their throttles, dropped thirty-two bombs on the hangars, and made off unscathed. The bombs destroyed 46 aircraft. They were mostly trainers but, relative to the resources involved, the raid was a major success. A little later, a handful of Bf 109s from I./JG52 strafed Manston, destroying a Spitfire and a Blenheim and damaging two more, as well as disrupting repairs. Speed and surprise, stealth and cunning, and precision rather than weight of bombs were what achieved success for the Luftwaffe throughout the campaign. Yet the pattern was not clear to them.

Late in the afternoon, still exhilarated by the reports from the previous day, Churchill called in on Park's HQ at Uxbridge, which was conveniently on the way from London to Chequers and was to become a favourite stop-over for the Prime Minister. He was accompanied by his Chief-of Staff, General Ismay, who recalled feeling 'sick with fear' when he saw 11 Group had nothing in reserve whilst new hostile plots developed. As they left for Chequers in the evening Churchill said to him: 'Don't speak to me; I have never been so moved.' He had seen Park commit all his forces. He well remembered the dreadful answer to his question when, a few weeks before, he had asked General Gamelin where his reserves were: 'Aucune'. He did not see the forces of 10 and 12 Groups on the plotting table at Uxbridge. He did not know what calculations about raid sizes, turnaround times and so on Park was making. He did not fully realise that an aircraft not intercepting was an aircraft wasted. He simply saw that the margins within which Park operated seemed to be very narrow. After about five minutes in the car, he leaned over towards Ismay and said: 'Never in the field of human conflict has so much been owed by so many to so few.' These words so struck Ismay that he repeated them to his wife when he got home.[6]

During the fight over Tangmere, in his second day of action, Bob Doe had shot down a 109, and later had a go at an air-sea-rescue flying boat. However, on landing he was disconcerted to be told by Pat Hughes that he had shot another 109 off Doe's tail. Doe had never seen it.[7] He sat down in the evening and had another think.

His neck sore from looking around, Doe abandoned his collar and tie for a silk scarf, and decided to search the sky more systematically. He realised that simply looking out was no good. Instead he resolved to quarter the sky and search it, paying attention to movement in the area of his peripheral vision, and regularly looking behind. He resolved to increase the distance between himself and the other aircraft.

The following day, the 17th, the Luftwaffe launched no attacks at all, despite the fine weather. This gave Fighter Command time to carry out repairs and time for the pilots to rest. The previous night, Bomber Command had flown 150 sorties over Germany, ranging from the Ruhr to the distant towns of Leuna, which contained a major chemical complex, and Augsburg, where Messerschmitts were built. Seven aircraft failed to return. On the night of the 17th it flew another 102 sorties, again to Germany and also against airfields in Holland, Belgium and France. This time, all the aircraft returned.[8]

Beppo Schmid issued an intelligence appraisal in which he estimated, on the basis of reported claims and his estimates of production, that the British had only 300 serviceable fighters left. In fact there were 855 serviceable machines with the squadrons, 289 at storage units and another 84 at training units, a total of 1,438, twice as many as at the beginning of July.[9] Expecting weakening opposition, the Luftwaffe Commanders spent the day preparing for major action on the 18th.

Following Göring's idea of moving the fight steadily inwards, Luftflotte 2 planned to attack four major stations further inland: Hornchurch, North Weald, Biggin Hill and Kenley. They were all Sector Stations. Despite the losses suffered by StG2 on the 16th, Sperrle planned to use his Stukas again in even greater numbers, sending a relatively fresh Geschwader, StG77, into action against the airfields at Gosport, Ford and Thorney Island near the Hampshire coast (none of which had anything to do with Fighter Command) and the radar station at Poling in Sussex. All the fighter forces of both Airfleets would be committed, with the absence of Mölders and Galland, whom Göring called to Karinhall. The stage was set for what would become known as 'the Hardest Day'.[10]

Sunday 18 August dawned fine but hazy. By midday the haze had cleared, and radar reported a build-up over Calais which grew into the biggest plot they had yet seen. There were 60 He 111s of KG1 who were to deliver a high level attack on Biggin Hill, 48 Do 17s and Ju 88s of KG76 which were to attack Kenley, and all but three Gruppen of Osterkamp's fighters, 410 Bf 109s and 73 Bf 110s, which were to protect them.

KG1's plan of attack was straightforward, but KG76 were planning a three-stage assault on Kenley. First, twelve Ju 88s from II. Gruppe were to dive-bomb the buildings; then the Do 17s of I. and III. Gruppen were to crater the runway from high altitude; and, finally, the specially-trained 9th Staffel from III./KG76, flying Do 17s, were to go in at low level, without fighter cover, to finish the place off. They were the only bomber force in the Luftwaffe to be employed as a unit on low-level attacks. Otherwise this form of attack was left to sneak raiders such as those who hit Brize Norton, or the fighter-bombers of Erprobungsgruppe 210.

This plan showed enterprise and its results would be of special significance. A major success could lead to a more general change in tactics. However, it was also complex. Complex plans usually go wrong. So did this one.

As the main force joined up over Calais to rendezvous with their escorts, they headed into cloud and their formation lost cohesion. By the time they had formed up again they were six minutes late, with the Ju 88s well to the rear. So when, after a taxing piece of navigation, the low-flying 9th Staffel thundered over the southern perimeter of Kenley airfield at 1322, they were the first to arrive instead of the last, and were greeted by the defender's full fury, from the ground and the air. Though they passed under the radar screen, they had been tracked accurately by the Observer Corps, and in the Ops Room, the plotters watched as the raid marker moved steadily in their direction. They felt a sense of detachment as the final observation placed the 'hostile' marker on top of them, and then they heard the Bofors guns start up just outside. While gunfire shot up at the Dorniers from the ground, together with special rockets firing parachute cables – an experimental weapon designed to deal with low-level attacks – 111 Squadron from Croydon laid into them from above.

615 Squadron was now based back at Kenley. Since getting back from France, Sandy Sanders had been engaged in further intensive conflict with the Luftwaffe and his superiors. During early August the Squadron operated from Hawkinge in separate Flights. On 5 August, when Sandy was flying back, he suspected he had a mechanical problem, so when he got to Kenley he did a slow roll at the edge of the airfield to test his aircraft. From the airfield it looked as if he was below tree-top height, but in fact he was at a safe altitude above the Caterham Valley. His Station Commander called him in to rebuke him for 'endangering His Majesty's aeroplane', whereupon Sandy told him that it was perfectly safe, and in any case he ought to get into an aeroplane himself and do some fighting. He was sent to his room under arrest and told to fly to Hawkinge again at 7 o'clock the next morning.

He damaged some Heinkels off Brighton on the 16th, but the 17th was quiet, so being fully aware of what had happened just three miles up the road at Croydon, he called up 11 Group operations and told them that the Germans would be hitting Kenley next, so would they request that 12 Group send some fighters to patrol their airfield when they were scrambled? He was therefore not very surprised when, just before 1300 on the 18th, he was scrambled and ordered to climb to the right, towards Biggin Hill, which was just six miles away.

He was at about 6,000 feet, followed by P/O Douglas Hone, when a string of bombs came down between them, just feet away from his Hurricane. Alerted in this way to an enemy presence, he looked up and saw some Dorniers above him. He pushed the throttle through the gate, climbed up more steeply and opened fire. His aircraft stalled on its back and spun down. A parachute floated down next to him whilst he was still inverted, and he pulled out. As he did so, he saw a Do 17, and gave chase towards Biggin Hill. As the Dornier turned, a Ju

88 banked steeply in front of him, giving him an excellent full-deflection opportunity. He let rip, aiming for the cockpit to kill the pilot – in his view the only way to get a bomber down – and the Junkers went straight in and blew up in some woods at Ide Hill, a few miles south of Biggin Hill and close to Churchill's private residence at Chartwell.

Over Kenley, the leading Dornier of the left-hand section of three came in higher than the others and was an easier target for the gunners. It caught fire and flew into one of the parachute cables that had shot up from the northern perimeter, dragging it down onto a bungalow just beyond the edge of the airfield. The wing of another Dornier hit a second cable, but the pilot banked right and the cable slid off. The pilot leading the right-hand section was hit in the chest by a round from a Lewis gun, and slumped forward, moaning 'Nach Hause!' ('Get me home!'). His navigator, Wilhelm Illg, grabbed the controls and eased the plane up. The aircraft leading the formation lost an engine but staggered on, pursued by Hurricanes from 111 Squadron, to crash at Leaves Green, just north of Biggin Hill. The Commander of 9./KG76, Hauptmann Joachim Roth, who had performed the expert piece of navigation which had led him and his men to their nemesis, was killed in the crash, though his pilot, Rudolf Lamberty, struggled out of the wreckage badly burned.

Within three minutes of their appearance over Kenley's southern boundary, two Dorniers were down and all the others were damaged. The survivors had to battle home under constant attack. Two of them did not make it.

Three of the Dorniers got back into some sort of formation for the flight back, but one of them lost its left engine, began to fall behind, and finally had to ditch off the French coast. One of the others tried to fly back alone, but also lost an engine and ditched off Le Touquet. The surviving crew members of both machines were picked up by the German Navy after about three hours in the water. Of the five remaining in the air, two landed at airfields, one crashlanded on sand-dunes near Calais, another crash-landed in a field near Abbeville, and the last to get down was the one now piloted by its navigator, who managed a wheels-down landing at St Omer airfield. His pilot died on the way to hospital. Oberfeldwebel Wilhelm Illg was awarded the Knight's Cross for his initiative, determination and bravery in bringing his plane home.

Kenley had been fiercely defended, both on the ground and in the air. Whether or not 11 Group had followed Sandy's advice, they had sent along his old comrades of 111 in the nick of time while he was trying to get at the Biggin Hill raiders. However, the defence was not conducted without cost.

111 were led in by Sandy's old friend, Flight Lieutenant Stanley Connors, whom of course they called 'Conny' rather than Stanley. Conny was a 'very, very nice, gentle sort of person', and also a first-class fighter pilot with twelve confirmed kills to his credit. He came in extremely close to his quarry to get a kill, but by so doing flew into the same ground fire savaging the Dorniers. Whether he was hit by friendly fire or a machine-gunner on a Dornier we will never know, but his Hurricane caught fire. An eye-witness from Keston Home Guard

watching from the valley just west of Biggin Hill has reported that he saw a burning Hurricane firing repeatedly at a Dornier flying up the valley from the south, with another behind. The first crashed at Leaves Green, the second flew on. The Hurricane crash-landed in an orchard, throwing the pilot clear. Staying clear for fifteen minutes to let the ammunition explode, the Home Guardsman then approached the wreck but the pilot was dead. His name tag read 'P/O Connors S.D.P.' By staying in his burning plane to continue the attack on the enemy he acted much as Nicolson had done over the Solent two days before. Nicolson survived and got Fighter Command's only VC of the war. Connors died, so there was no combat report for the authorities to consider.[11]

The AA gunners brought down a second Hurricane, already damaged by return fire from the Dorniers, as it was returning over Kenley trying to make it back to Croydon. It crashed near Godstone. Its pilot, Harry Deacon, baled out and landed with a bullet in the leg, only to have a shotgun thrust in his face by a youth asking if he spoke English. He uttered some Anglo-Saxon monosyllables to prove that he did. Two further Hurricanes were brought down by the bombers. The pilot of one crash-landed on a golf course at Epsom. He was then faced not with a shotgun but with golf clubs, and established his identity by pulling out a pack of Players cigarettes. The other plane was hit by a machine-gunner on one of the Dorniers which subsequently ditched, and the pilot, Harry Newton, who had had to crash-land just one week before, baled out with severe burns. He walked to a road and passed a young couple on a tandem bicycle. Such was his appearance that the girl fainted.

When the Do 17s of the high-level attack arrived over Kenley they were already fighting off savage fighter attacks and, whilst some of their bombs fell on the airfield, others scattered over Caterham, Whyteleafe and Purley and around the railway line to East Grinstead. When the Ju 88s arrived last of all, they found Kenley so swathed in smoke that dive-bombing was impossible, so they left and attacked West Malling instead. One of their number was unlucky, however, being attacked and knocked out of the formation by P/O Wlasnowolski of 32 Squadron. It was hit by four more British fighters as it lost height, and it was to this machine that Sandy Sanders, along with Peter Brothers of 32 Squadron, fighting with particular determination in the knowledge that his pregnant wife was down below in Westerham, delivered the *coup de grace*.

The nine tons of bombs dropped by 9./KG76 did a lot of damage, destroying all but one of the hangars, damaging most buildings and cutting the power supply, which put the airfield out of action for two hours. Four Hurricanes and several other training aircraft were destroyed on the ground, and nine RAF personnel were killed. The eighty or so tons of bombs dropped by KG1 on Biggin Hill in a fairly undisturbed bomb-run landed mainly on the landing ground and the woods to the east, and the station carried on as normal. However, four Dorniers of 9./KG76 were destroyed and all the other five damaged, two seriously. Apart from them, the Kenley raiders of KG76 lost another four

Dorniers and four damaged. KG1's ineffective attack on Biggin Hill, by contrast, cost them only one He 111 destroyed and one damaged. Cock-ups apart, the lesson for the Luftwaffe seemed clear.

As the raiders streamed back to France, Ulrich Steinhilper's unit, I./JG52, were sent out to cover their return. However, once they had taken off, they were diverted to strafe Manston again. Their signals officer had been listening in to the British radio frequencies and realised that a lot of fighters were using Manston for re-fuelling. Crossing the coast over Margate, they headed south and came in low without warning over the long-suffering airfield. They destroyed two Spitfires of 266 Squadron and a Hurricane of 17 Squadron, whose pilots had just landed and only narrowly escaped. Steinhilper hit a petrol bowser and flew off satisfied he had done his job, but nagged by the knowledge that he had also killed someone who had been standing near it. It had been a man, not an aeroplane. He found it hard to take.

Ulrich Steinhilper had been in action for the first time only a week before and he had found that hard to take, too. He had joined the Luftwaffe in 1936 when a recruiting officer visited his school near Stuttgart. His mother was a schoolteacher in a small Swabian town nearby and had been coming under pressure from local Nazi officials for continuing to give Jewish children piano lessons. Her husband was in the Party, but that did not help, so Ulrich hoped that if her son were in the Luftwaffe, they would leave her alone. Besides, he was technically-minded and he liked aeroplanes. He joined I./JG52, where his first Staffelkapitän was Adolf Galland, with whom he soon clashed. Galland moved on, but Steinhilper stayed where he was, seeing no action in France or over the Channel until on 11 August he and his colleagues encountered a Blenheim attacking an He 59 rescue seaplane and shot it down. He found the whole thing sickening.[12]

Oberleutnant Gerhard Schoepfel was leading III./JG 26 that day whilst Galland was in Berlin.[13] They had been detailed for a '*freie Jagd*' in front of bomber formations raiding Kenley and Biggin Hill. They flew high over Dover and then Schoepfel spotted a squadron of Hurricanes climbing below them, with a weaver behind the rear section. It was 501 Squadron heading for Canterbury. Schoepfel told his pilots to stay high to cover him, moved into the sun and then dived on the weaver. He opened fire at 100 yards, sending the Hurricane down in flames, and zoom-climbed. He repeated this action three times, each time picking off the rearmost man. With his fourth attack he got too close and pieces from the exploding Hurricane hit his own machine, spreading oil over the cockpit canopy. Unable to see, Schoepfel disengaged, and some of his men dived on the remains of 501. An inconclusive dogfight ensued.

In two minutes, one Messerschmitt had destroyed four enemy aircraft, an unprecedented feat. One pilot was killed and the other three wounded. One of Schoepfel's surviving victims, P/O Kenneth Lee, has commented: 'He did it so neatly, I never knew what hit me.'[14] It was indeed a textbook attack, using surprise, height and speed and getting in close.[15] This was the sort of thing the

Luftwaffe had to do all the time in order to win the air battle. The vulnerable formation used by 501 was also out of the textbook, and might have been designed to facilitate the sort of attack Schoepfel executed. Once surprise was gone, the Hurricanes avoided further losses in the dogfight. Schoepfel maintained surprise for as long as he did by deliberately attacking alone – when his colleagues joined in and evened up the odds against him, they failed to get a single kill. There were lessons here too, this time for the RAF.

Luftflotte 3 was about to undergo an experience from which the Luftwaffe drew a further lesson it deemed unambiguous, regarding not low-level attacks, but the use of Stukas.

At about 1330, 109 Ju 87s, the entire operational strength of Stukageschwader 77 and I./StG 3, took off to attack the airfields of Gosport, Ford and Thorney Island and the radar station at Poling. Gosport housed a torpedo development unit, Ford was a naval air station and Thorney Island was a Coastal Command base. Fifty-five Bf 109's from JG2 flew ahead on a sweep, and the delights of providing close escort were the privilege of thirty-two 109s from JG53 and no less than seventy from JG27, who drew the short straw.

The attacks on Poling and Ford went in unopposed, but over Gosport the top cover were attacked by 234 Squadron, and lost three 109s. Then Hurricanes from the 'Stuka party' specialists 43 and 601 Squadrons tore into I./StG77 just as it was moving into line astern prior to its dive. The close escorts were themselves by now embroiled with 234 Squadron and could do nothing except hope that the dogfight moved lower. 602 Squadron then arrived from nearby Westhampnett, Tangmere's satellite airfield, and caught II./StG77 just after it had bombed Ford and was pulling out over the rooftops of Bognor. III./StG77, which had attacked Poling, joined the II. Gruppe in fleeing for home, only to make the less welcome acquaintance of 152 Squadron and the Blenheims of 235 Squadron Coastal Command, whose home base of Thorney Island the Stukas had just bombed. The last to arrive were the Hurricanes of 213 Squadron from Exeter, in time to pursue some of the escorts now at sea-level and heading for France, low on fuel.

This shambles was a disaster for StG77. The II. Gruppe lost three of its aircraft in the air and one written off on landing; the III. Gruppe lost two with two more damaged; but the I. Gruppe, which had been caught forming up, lost ten out of the twenty-eight participating in the attack, had to write off another and had four more damaged. If that were not bad enough, the escorts lost eight 109s, with only two pilots recovered by German air-sea rescue to fight another day. In exchange for this total of seventeen Stukas and eight Messerschmitts, Fighter Command lost five aircraft and suffered damage to seven more, but only two pilots were killed. The aircraft loss ratio was 5:1 in favour of the defenders. StG77 lost a total of twenty-six aircrew killed, including I./StG2's Gruppenkommandeur, Hauptmann Meisel, six taken prisoner and six wounded.

Most unusually, Luftflotte 3's post-action report the next day (always called an '*Erfolgsmeldung*' – literally a 'Success Report') commented on the losses of the Stukas. It attributed them to 'British fighters gaining local superiority due to particularly favourable weather conditions' and carrying out a pursuit up to 30km over the Channel.[16] StG77's Aircorps Commander, von Richthofen, confided to his diary that 'a Stuka Gruppe has had its feathers well and truly plucked'.

What really struck von Richthofen were not the overall losses of the Stukas, which at 15% were high but bearable in the short run if they were achieving results, but the near destruction of one Gruppe, whose losses ran at 50%. This was on top of losses of nearly 30% to another single unit, I./StG2, in the Tangmere raid on the 16th, and the loss of 70% of one Staffel of II./StG2 on the 13th. Earlier losses, such as those over convoy Peewit, had been heavy but acceptable. It was becoming clear, however, that any unlucky Stuka unit caught without its escort would be almost wiped out. It was also becoming clear that there was at least one such unlucky unit on every major sortie. Some re-thinking was called for.

The hardest day was not over. By 1700, 58 Do 17s of KG2 were on their way to Hornchurch and 51 He 111s of KG53 were making for North Weald, with 120 Bf 109s and 20 Bf 110s around them. 11 and 12 Groups detailed 143 Hurricanes and Spitfires to intercept, giving the British parity in fighters, and a small numerical superiority over the Bf 109s, though in the event only 103, almost all from 11 Group, made contact. They clashed over north Kent and Essex and the defenders felt a sense of jubilation when both raiding forces turned back, dropping their bombs on the army barracks at Shoeburyness and the Royal Marine barracks at Deal. The reason for this was not the fighter opposition, but that both the primary targets were obscured by cloud. After the events over Croydon, Kesselring was particularly sensitive about throwing bombs about near London. Only four of the bombers failed to return. Most of the fighting had been between the fighters, with Fighter Command losing nine and the Luftwaffe ten. Amongst the latter were two of JG26's budding *Experten*, one of whom was killed and the other taken prisoner. This was also the day on which JG51 lost one of its leading aces, Horst Tietzen, who with seventeen victories was at the time only just behind Adolf Galland and Walter Oesau in the Luftwaffe league tables.

On the day that Germany lost a leading ace, Britain took another step towards gaining one. 234 Squadron had claimed five Bf 109s and suffered no losses during the fight above Gosport. One of the Bf 109s was claimed by Doe. It had been his fourth victim. He had begun to feel more confident, and when he sat down that night, he thought about his offensive flying. He decided to exchange his flying boots for shoes, so that he could control his Spitfire more precisely. He had also noticed that opening fire at 400 yards was ineffective, and had his guns re-harmonised at 250 yards. Unlike many of his comrades, he had had a period training as an air gunner on Ansons, so he understood something about deflection shooting. One more kill and he would be an ace. He was to get it, a Ju 88, three days later.

While Bob Doe and his colleagues had been holding off the escorts, Tony Woods-Scawen had been with 43 Squadron hammering the Stukas. Tony's plane had been damaged again, but that evening the news came through that he had been awarded the DFC. Now he was quits with his big brother. Two days later, he proposed to Bunny again, and this time she really did say yes. She had to break the news to Patrick two days later, and she was in floods of tears. 'That's all right, Bunny', he said, 'it can't be helped', and he offered to help pay for the cottage near Tangmere.[17]

In the air fighting, the Luftwaffe lost sixty-nine aircraft destroyed and thirty-one damaged, to Fighter Command's thirty-four destroyed and thirty-nine damaged. The RAF lost another twenty-nine destroyed and twenty-three damaged on the ground. The total aircraft losses were about equal, but Fighter Command achieved a kill ratio of 2:1 in the air. Adding together all the material losses, both sides suffered more damage than on any other day. Thus 18 August was, in that sense, the Hardest Day of the Battle of Britain.[18]

19. THINKING AGAIN

Göring had spent the Hardest Day at Karinhall with Mölders and Galland. Apart from awarding them *'das goldene Flugzeugführerabzeichen mit Brillianten'* (Pilots' Badges in Gold with Diamonds), Göring took the opportunity to berate them about the bomber losses, missed rendezvous with the escorts and general lack of aggression on the part of the fighter arm. This did not go down very well, but he quickly became reconciliatory and suggested that the solution lay in promoting high-performing youngsters like themselves and putting the old hands out to grass. He had decided amongst other things to make them both Kommodore of their respective Geschwader as of the 22nd. They were dismissed. So they left.[1]

At midday on the 19th, after reading the reports from the front, Göring summoned his commanders once more for a review of events. It was not a pleasant affair, but it was critically important.[2]

He called for a critical examination of the errors made so far, above all to avoid losses. He was clearly becoming anxious about the cost of the past week's work. Hitler's Directive 17 had explicitly stated that the Luftwaffe was to remain strong enough to support Sealion. Moreover, the Luftwaffe was Göring's power base. Its failure would be bad enough, but a severe weakening would be worse. The past week's fighting had cost him nearly 300 aircraft compared with 200 for the previous month. So it was that he emphasised the need to preserve the strength of the Luftwaffe, to ensure that the men were well cared for and to issue clear orders so they were not kept in a constant state of readiness, which he knew would wear them down.

That theme gave him the opportunity to definitively pass the buck for the cock-up on Eagle Day. Cutting short preparation time increases losses, he claimed: 'It is better not to embark on a mission than to rush it or to change even small details of orders at the last minute.' (On one copy of the memo, the recipient has underlined this sentence and, as well he might, put a large exclamation mark against it in the margin.)

The core theme of the conference was fighter protection. The fighter leaders had differing views, some advocating nothing but sweeps, others combinations of sweeps and close escorts. Göring wanted each fighter leader to make up his own mind and do whatever he saw fit, the only proviso being that he keep enough fighters back to protect his own base when the others returned to refuel. Perhaps the Luftwaffe's concern for the safety of its own fighter airfields was some small gain for the sacrifices of the Blenheim crews who tried to raid them. Göring also recommended using information from the listening services to find out when British squadrons were landing, and attack them then, perhaps in the knowledge of JG52's success in this.

Göring listed a number of forms fighter sweeps might take, but stressed again that they should be kept constantly changing and that the leaders of the flying units were to be given free reign: 'Fighting methods are largely a question of leadership. Unit commanders are therefore to be given as much freedom of action as possible.' Göring's faith in his Wing and Group commanders stemmed from his intention to follow the appointment of Galland and Mölders with a wholesale purge. In his follow-up note to the Airfleet Commanders, he specified that the leaders of flying units should be drawn from their own ranks and be appointed on the basis of skill and experience rather than rank.

The first issue for escorts was meeting up with the bombers in the first place, so to avoid repeats of the missed rendezvous of the past, bombers were instructed to pick up their escorts from the fighter airfield. It was recognised that no bomber formation larger than a Gruppe could be properly protected, and that the escort had to consist of several Gruppen of Bf 109s. Göring stressed that as many fighters as possible were to be left free for sweeps, albeit that these should be co-ordinated with bomber raids. Overall, fighter usage was to be strengthened. The burden was clearly on the 109s. The Bf 110 was only to be used when the 109's range was insufficient. Bombers were to be used only in sufficient numbers to draw up British fighters.

Göring's earlier prescriptions about escorting Stukas were repeated, and were realistic except for the idea that one group of escorts would dive with them, which, lacking dive brakes, they could not do. The dive itself was in fact about the only time the Stukas were safe.

More significant was the final sentence: 'Until the enemy fighter force has been broken, Stuka units are only to be used when circumstances are particularly favourable.' With this withdrawal of the Stukas from general operations, the only precision bombing instrument the Luftwaffe had left was Erprobungsgruppe 210.

Göring also turned to targets. Fighter Command was the absolute priority. Bomber Command airfields were only to be attacked if there was little risk of losses. The aircraft industry was to be attacked only by small groups of aircraft in bad weather, which the coming week promised. It was to be the main target of night attacks. In attacking any target, only crews familiar with the area were to be used, and escorts used as far as possible with the same bomber unit.

The thrust of all this was to minimise losses, prevent mistakes over target identification and avoid the mix-ups of the past week. There was nothing about its effect on the RAF. Not a great deal was known about that, after all, but it was a matter of some importance and might have been worthy of some consideration.

In addition to the personnel changes, the Airfleets were to be reorganised. Sperrle was to transfer the mass of his fighters to Kesselring to give him the numbers he needed and place them as close to England as possible. Airfleet 3 was to concentrate on night attacks and Airfleet 5 was also restricted to night sorties and nuisance raids.

The Luftwaffe spent most of the following week reorganising itself. From the 22nd onwards, the Jagdgeschwader got new Kommodoren. Galland and Mölders took up their new posts, Hauptmann Günther Lützow took over JG3, Major Trübenbach JG52 and Hauptmann Johannes Trautloft moved from III./JG51 to be Kommodore of JG54. Shortly thereafter, Major Schellmann took over JG2 and Major Günther von Maltzahn JG53. It was a truly revolutionary move. These men had the rank of Flight Lieutenant or Squadron Leader and were given control of Fighter Groups, each consisting of the equivalent of nine squadrons. Their promotion led to a string of others lower down as they themselves were replaced. These moves did not enjoy universal acclaim. There were those who resented the preferential treatment given to the golden boys, and would have preferred to be led by men less concerned with their own scores.[3]

Whilst the young aces given these positions were expected to continue to lead their Groups in the air, another measure was taken to preserve the alarming losses among experienced senior commanders. Since the beginning of August, the Luftwaffe had lost one Geschwaderkommodore, seven Gruppenkommandeure and thirteen Staffelkapitäne as well as two Fliegerkorps Chiefs of Staff. Leading from the front was threatening to deprive the organisation of its core cadre. In contrast, the most senior RAF casualty of the Battle was a Wing Commander.[4] Henceforth, only one commissioned officer was allowed to fly with any Luftwaffe crew.

All the Bf 109 units in Luftflotte 3 except JG2 were moved to the Pas-de-Calais, as was I./JG77, which had been based in Northern Germany. The Stukas of von Richthofen's VIII Fliegerkorps were also moved there ready to support the invasion. If 'favourable circumstances' were to arise, they could also be given the protection they clearly needed. In the event, such circumstances did not arise until 1 November when one Staffel of StG1 attacked shipping off the Nore. By then, it was all over bar the shouting.

This dislocation and the predicted poor weather led to a lull in the fighting. The Luftwaffe's redeployment clearly meant that when it began again in earnest the brunt of the daylight fighting was going to fall even more on 11 Group.

Dowding did some redeployment of his own. On the 19th, he decided to move the two remaining squadrons which had suffered most before Eagle Day, 111 and 601, to Debden – still in 11 Group, but north of London. Peter Townsend's 85 Squadron swapped places with 111. Patrick Woods-Scawen would now join his brother in the thick of it. Dowding also moved 64 from Kenley to Leconfield in 12 Group, swapping them with 616, which had been in action against Luftflotte 5 on the 15th. Finally, Dowding posted the shattered remains of 266 back to Wittering on the 21st after two weeks in the front line. To add to their trauma in the air on the 16th, they had, in a rare piece of bad luck, been the ones caught on the ground refuelling at Manston on the 18th when Steinhilper's squadron launched their opportunistic attack. Two of their Spitfires had been destroyed and the rest damaged by the strafing Messerschmitts.

Dowding also had four additions to his Order of Battle. 302 (Polish) and 310 (Czech) Squadrons had become operational on the 18th. They were based at Leconfield in Yorkshire and Duxford in Cambridgeshire respectively. Number 1 Squadron of the Royal Canadian Air Force also became operational on the 19th, and, most importantly of all, the wild men of 303 (Polish) Squadron, formed on 2 August, were allowed to patrol inland aerodromes. It was felt that their English was not yet quite good enough for them to be declared fully operational. They had to wait until the last day of the month for that.

Park was not idle, and on the 19th issued an instruction to controllers containing his reflections on the previous week. Given that the targets being attacked were now over land, he wanted all interceptions to take place over land as well to avoid losing pilots in the Channel. He wanted interceptions to engage escorting fighters with minimal forces and to concentrate on the bombers. And finally, he wanted a squadron up over any threatened airfield once a raid had crossed the coast. In the case of the three Sector Stations north of London, Debden, North Weald and Hornchurch, he wanted his controllers to ask 12 Group or the Fighter Command Controller to provide the squadrons needed to patrol them.

The next day, Park sent a message to the Commanders of his Sector Stations for distribution to the squadrons, congratulating them on the Group's performance on the 18th and encouraging them to attack bombers at every opportunity, before they reached the target, when bombing and when returning. He stressed that fighters were only attacked in order to uncover the bombers, and once more recommended head-on attacks when there was a large escort.

In a week which saw the Luftwaffe fly upwards of 1,500 sorties a day designed to knock out Fighter Command, every blow had been parried. The Luftwaffe had rarely achieved surprise, and rarely caught fighters on the ground. In the air, it had only occasionally managed to cripple a squadron by bouncing it. When serious losses were inflicted in a single action this was generally because the unit concerned was inexperienced and still using the RAF's prescribed tactics. Most of the veterans in 11 Group had already abandoned them. On every day, Fighter Command inflicted far more serious losses in return, and by doing so had secured the tactical initiative. The losses had forced the withdrawal of the Stuka and restricted the use of the Bf 110 which, together with the need to protect bombers, forced the Luftwaffe to use its limited force of Bf 109s ever more intensively.

By carefully choosing which raids to intercept and avoiding the potentially dangerous fighter sweeps, Park and his controllers had greatly reduced, though not nullified, their effectiveness. The greatest threat to their ability to do this was the damage to the radar system, which had lost some of its reliability. This was Park's single most difficult challenge.[5] Whilst the radar installations were indeed difficult to destroy, they could be disrupted. What was needed was luck and persistence. The Luftwaffe had had some of the former, but lacked the planning discipline to show the latter. With the withdrawal of the Stuka, the greatest threat to these small targets were the twenty to thirty hard-working aircraft of Erprobungsgruppe 210, but they needed to hit each radar station once or twice a day, and there were ten such stations between the Isle of Wight and the Thames Estuary alone. Nevertheless, even their disruption could seriously degrade Park's defensive capability. Not to attempt this systematically was a strategic error of the first order.

The airfields were a similar story. The only one to really suffer was the most exposed, Manston, and it suffered because it was attacked so often. Even so, it had not ceased to operate. Even if it had this would have been little more than an inconvenience, for it was just a useful re-fuelling site. Only attacks on Sector Stations could inflict real damage to the command and control system. The three 11 Group Sector Stations south of London, Tangmere, Biggin Hill and Kenley, had each been attacked only once. Biggin Hill was almost unscathed, Tangmere was damaged but only lost power for a short time and never ceased to function, and Kenley, the most severely hit, was out of action for a total of two hours. The serious damage at Tangmere had been inflicted by Stukas and at Kenley by 9./KG76's low-level attack. Losses to both sets of attackers influenced the Luftwaffe Command in its decision not to use these successful methods on a large scale.

The core problem for Kesselring and Sperrle was that they literally did not know what they were doing. Any grass landing strip with a few buildings around it seemed to warrant a raid, but concentration of effort was absolutely vital to their success. They did not have long, for Sealion was due in mid-September. Some of the most serious damage they did was by accident, and by and large the most threatening attacks were the smallest. Eagle had indeed revealed what Churchill, no less, was to characterise as the essence of war: 'a catalogue of mistakes and misfortunes'[6].

The 20th saw little action in the air. Manston was strafed again by 109s, Erprobungsgruppe 210 lost a Bf 110 on an anti-shipping raid, and another raid detected over the Thames Estuary was roughly handled. The Luftwaffe lost seven aircraft in combat, the RAF only two.

However, it being almost a year since war had been declared, Churchill addressed the Commons that afternoon to review the general war situation. He had spent the previous day working on the speech at Chequers.

He compared the situation favourably with one year into the previous Great War, saying the country was stronger than it had ever been. He then came to consider the 'great air battle' which had 'attained a high intensity'. He expected it to continue for some time, for if, after Hitler's 'boasting and blood-curdling threats ... his whole air onslaught were forced after a while to tamely peter out, the Führer's reputation for veracity of statement might be seriously impugned.'

Churchill went on to claim that the course of the fighting had so far been favourable. He praised the Ministry of Aircraft Production, rightly observing that Britain's production was outstripping Germany's, and saying that the longer the struggle continued, the more rapidly Britain would achieve parity and then superiority in the air.

He then paid tribute to the pilots, finally using in public the phrase that had come to him four days before:

> The gratitude of every home in our island, in our Empire, and indeed throughout the world, except in the abodes of the guilty, goes out to the British airmen who, undaunted by odds, unwearied in their constant challenge and mortal danger, are turning the tide of world war by their prowess and their devotion. Never in the field of human conflict was so much owed by so many to so few.

On 14 July, Churchill had said that this was a war of vast numbers of 'Unknown Warriors'. For a brief span, these vast numbers of people had to stand by and watch as the war was fought by a few thousand airmen, though many Unknown Warriors toiled on the ground repairing airfields and making sure 'the Few' could get back into the air. His phrase echoes the words Shakespeare gave Henry V before the Battle of Agincourt, when the King addresses his men as 'we few, we happy few, we band of brothers'. Churchill was wont to compare the fighter pilots with knights. Here it was again.

He continued immediately, in less-celebrated words, to ask that his listeners not forget the bomber pilots who went out over Germany every night and the daylight bombers, who bore a heavy burden and 'whose unflinching zeal' it had been necessary 'on numerous occasions to restrain.'

He ended the speech by challenging his opponents in the Commons, saying that co-operation with the United States would, 'like the Mississippi', just keep rolling along. 'Let it roll,' he proclaimed, 'let it roll on full flood, inexorable, irresistible, benignant, to broader lands and better days.'[7] Britain desperately needed American arms and American money.

Returning to Downing Street with Colville, Churchill sang 'Ole man river' in the car all the way. The speech had seemed to drag, Colville noted, and the House, not used to sitting in August, was languid. Still, the bit about Hitler's reputation for veracity of statement being seriously impugned had been rather good.[8]

History has not recorded what the surviving bomber crews of 82 or 107 Squadrons thought about the alleged attempts to restrain their zeal. The fighter pilots' reactions to being immortalised as 'the Few' were varied. One based in Scotland with 13 Group after taking a pounding at Dunkirk thought that the chaps down south must be pretty brave and thanked God he wasn't one of them. Alan Deere, who was one of them, said to his colleague George Gribble: 'By Christ he can say that again. There aren't many of us left.' 'It's nice to know someone appreciates us, Al,' Gribble replied. 'I couldn't agree more about that bit about mortal danger, but I dispute the "unwearied".'[9] Some of those in 12 Group wondered why they were doing 'bugger-all' and why they couldn't 'have a bash'. Another pilot warned his colleagues: 'Careful, chaps, the PM has seen our mess bill'.[10]

Others felt less need for irony. Asquith's daughter, Lady Violet Bonham-Carter, wrote to Churchill that his sentence would 'live as long as words are spoken and remembered. Nothing so simple, so majestic and true has been said in so great a moment of human history.'[11]

Such phrases came less readily to the minds of the increasingly exhausted pilots. However, it was clear to a lot of them that people's hearts were indeed going out them. 'There was tremendous kindness,' one of them has recalled. 'It was a lovely feeling. I've never felt that Britain was like that again.'[12] Indeed, some of them felt quite proud. 'It was the first time I realised we might have done something unusual,' recalled Bob Doe. 'I hadn't realised it until then.'

20. HUNTERS AND HUNTED

The history of combat in the air is short but very well documented. A pilot has to detail every flight in his log-book and, after an operational sortie, pilots are de-briefed. In 1966, an American, Herbert K. Weiss, collated and analysed some historical data and published it in an article called 'Systems Analysis Problems of Limited War'. He concluded that over 90% of pilots had only a 50:50 chance of getting through their first decisive combat without being shot down. After five decisive encounters their survival chances increased by a factor of twenty. Further data suggests that only about 5% of pilots score five or more victories (thus becoming 'aces') but that these 5% score about 40% of all victories claimed in the air. This data remains consistent across all the campaigns he analysed in the two World Wars and Korea.[1]

The Battle of Britain is no exception. Between 1 July and 31 October 1940, RAF pilots made 2,698 claims, an average of just under one each for the 2,927 pilots who officially flew in the campaign. Examination of the claims made by the aces, defined as all those making five or more claims over the period reveals that these 104 pilots made 806 claims between them.[2] This top 3.5% of pilots therefore made about 30% of claims, broadly in line with Weiss' findings.

The sky contains two very different groups of pilots: a small group of hunter-killers and the majority who are the hunted. Amongst the hunted are the experienced who know how to get away from the hunter-killers, and who also hunt themselves without often killing. And there are the novices who either learn survival fast or simply provide the hunter-killers with targets.

Today, air combat is usually broken down into five elements: detection, closing, attack, manoeuvre and disengagement.

Detection is the first and most important. In World War I this depended on seeing the enemy. In World War II it still depended largely on sight, but it helped to have a controller telling you over the radio roughly where your enemy was. The sky had to be systematically quartered and searched. In perfect conditions, a single aircraft can be picked up at a range of about two miles; in haze it is less. A large formation can be seen from far further away, perhaps four miles. An aircraft approaching head-on is harder to acquire visually because it is smaller and offers no relative movement. In the air above the clouds, the sun is bright and effectively blocks out about 15% of the field of vision. Flying up-sun makes an aircraft virtually invisible.

Once seen, an aircraft had to be identified as friendly or hostile. This was no simple matter, as you normally had only the distant outline to go on, and this changed with the angle at which the aircraft was seen. Recognition book-lets accordingly contained silhouettes from a variety of angles. Small Battles of Barking Creek took place frequently throughout the war, usually without sub-sequent enquiries.[3]

Once an aircraft had been identified as hostile, the one who detected first chose whether or not to close or await a better opportunity. He had an advan-tage if he was flying higher than his potential adversary because by diving he could gain speed and so put in a shot and zoom away before his opponent could react. He would enjoy a huge advantage if he had not himself been seen, for then he could surprise his enemy and have a chance of shooting him down without himself getting shot at. The decision had to be almost instantaneous.[4]

Closing lasts as long as a decision to break off is possible and then merges into the attack phase. In 1940 the time was not long, even at the maximum range at which visual detection is possible. A fighter spotting a bomber for-mation on the same course four miles away flying 50 mph more slowly than he was, had a minimum of three minutes twenty seconds before he was on them. Being faster, he could extend this as he wished. Two fighters flying towards each other at 300 mph who saw each other two miles away had twenty seconds before they met. One of them had to do something to avoid an encounter. Closing times would be less than this in poor visibility and clouds could pro-duce immediate surprise encounters. The usual unit of measurement was seconds.

In closing, the attacker would try to make himself hard to see by moving between his victim and the sun, and try if he could to approach from above. If his enemy was a single-seater, he would try to get behind him, where he would be hard to see and his intended victim was vulnerable. If the target was a bomber, attacking from behind might be more dangerous than from in front or the side (a so-called 'beam attack'), depending on the nature of the oppo-nent.[5]

By the time of the attack itself, the dice would normally be heavily loaded. Surprise was the norm. Four out of five fighter victims never saw their attacker. The bombers usually did, of course, especially if flying in formation, but mostly they could do little other than wait.

The attacker now had to get in a shot. In 1940, most fighters had enough ammunition for twelve to fifteen seconds' worth of firing, so the pilot could not keep the gun button depressed waiting to hit something. The relative closing speed of the aircraft determined how much time he might have to aim.

If the target were flying in any relative direction other than head-on or on the same course, the attacker had to take a deflection shot. This meant allowing for the speed, direction and distance of the target, and then shooting in front of it so it flew into the stream of bullets.[6] A fighter travelling at 300 mph across an attacker's line of flight travelled 36 feet in the quarter-second that bullets moving at twice the speed of sound would take to reach it. So, for a full-deflection shot at 400 yards, the pilot had to aim one-and-a-half plane lengths in front of the target. At many angles this meant the target would, at the point of firing, be under the nose of a Spitfire, Hurricane or Bf 109, and therefore could not be seen. This had to be done in the few seconds available whilst manoeuvring at over 300 mph, avoiding being buffeted in the opponent's slipstream, countering any evasive action on their part and keeping a watch on one's tail.

It will come as no surprise to learn that not many pilots ever mastered this, and that the vast majority of kills were made from within 15° of dead astern. The manuals issued to Luftwaffe fighter pilots discouraged deflection shooting as a waste of ammunition and recommended von Richthofen's method, which was indeed to get in directly behind and open fire from close range.[7] It soon became apparent that kills were made by people who got up close, meaning 100–200 yards. Then there was not only a better chance of hitting, but the hits were more likely to be lethal. Eight Brownings fired 480 rounds in three seconds. Because of vibration, each gun produced a cone of fire. At 400 yards, the cone gave a density of 7–8 rounds per square foot, meaning that luck was needed to hit anything vital. Accordingly, the guns of Spitfires and Hurricanes were re-aligned or 'harmonised' to produce a single converging cone of fire.[8] This was initially set at 400 yards. Experienced pilots had theirs re-set, as Bob Doe had done, for 250 yards or less.[9] The maximum effective range of a rifle-calibre machine gun was about 300 yards. Even so, pilots tended to underestimate ranges and open fire too early, often thereby giving away their presence.

Most decisive fighter encounters ended within a few seconds of the attack. One aircraft dived on another from behind or out of the sun, opened fire for two to three seconds at close range and then either dived away or zoom-climbed, using the extra speed gained in the diving attack either to escape or gain height for another attack. This was the aerial ambush called a 'bounce'.

However, if neither side had an initial advantage, or the attacker was spotted, or missed, the fourth phase of manoeuvre could take place, the classic 'dogfight'. If a bounce was detected in time, the defender would turn to face the attacker, presenting a small target, and offering return fire. Running away was the most dangerous thing to do, as the attacker, being in a dive, would always be faster. He would inevitably catch up and have a non-deflection shot from behind. The more planes there were on either side, the more likely a dogfight was, as there were more eyes to prevent a bounce from occurring. The main object of the dogfight was to get on the opponent's tail – hence the name. The German word for 'dogfight' is '*Kurvenkampf*' i.e. turning fight.

It was in dogfighting that the manoeuvrability as well as the speed of an aircraft was important, the key factor being the turning radius. The tighter the turn, the greater the ability to get behind an opponent. Dogfights ended either in a victory, a voluntary disengagement, or an enforced disengagement.

Enforced disengagement was perilous. Realising that your opponent was out-turning you in a dogfight and then trying to break away could give him the chance he had been waiting for, especially if he could tell you were close to stalling and anticipated a disengagement. The usual method of breaking off was to dive away. That was fine at 10,000 feet, but apt to end in an unwelcome confrontation with nature if attempted at 500 feet. An advantaged attacker intent on his kill also ran the risk of disengaging too late. Long-lived pilots knew how long to stay.

The essence of air-fighting in the pre-electronic age was not the duel but the ambush. Sustained dogfighting was exhausting and rare. The large aerial mêlées which took place during the Battle of Britain consisted of numerous short individual engagements during which pilots would shoot at numerous different opponents. The 'Knights of the Air' often fought more like medieval foot soldiers peering through a visor and slashing with an axe at anyone they thought might be on the other side.

About 5% of pilots mastered the skills needed for consistent success in air combat. They possessed a set of qualities that set them apart from the rest.

Better flying ability was the first and most obvious factor. 'Good flying never killed anyone' is an old air force adage. Yet good flying did kill some people. It depended on how they used their ability. Some superb aerobatic and formation flyers, particularly in the RAF, flew into battle as if they were at the Hendon air display and never came back. 'It helped to fly crudely, as I did, and not be bound by the rules,' Brian Kingcombe of 92 Squadron has commented: 'The good pilots – often the squadron commanders – were often killed quickly because they flew too well . . . If you went skidding around the sky you were a more difficult target.'[10] Stanford Tuck, a brilliant aerobatic pilot, used to fly in a rough, undisciplined way. The importance of flying ability was to become so intimate with the aircraft that it could be flown by instinct. The pilot would concentrate on fighting, during which he would exploit his aircraft's performance to its absolute limits. Tuck was able to make his plane almost a part of him.[11]

The second factor was good eyesight. Most successful fighter pilots were long-sighted and the best of them practised distance vision. 'Sailor' Malan used to fix a dot on the wall, look away and then turn his head and see how quickly he could focus on it. Looking was a skill and improved with experience. One pilot has said that it took him about four trips to get 'tuned in'.[12] Bob Doe stresses the need for systematic searching, the importance of peripheral vision ('You normally saw them first about ten to twenty degrees off the point at which you were looking') and the increased difficulty caused by high altitude ('Above twenty thousand feet . . . aircraft at the same level seemed to be lower').*

The third was a mental capability not analysed until the 1980s. It is now called 'situational awareness' – the ability to be aware of a multiplicity of different, rapidly changing events and maintain a mental picture of their overall shape. At its most simple, it was a matter of knowing what was going on and what one was doing and therefore maintaining a measure of control.[13] It required experience, and improved with it, but some experienced pilots never developed it. It could also be lost during combat, for it required a reserve of mental capacity that could simply be used up, a phenomenon known as 'task saturation'. There are cases reported when opponents who had been flying well at some point appeared to give up and just fly straight and level. It had all become too much.[14]

The combination of these three qualities would ensure survival in the air, and with a little time turn a potential victim into a hunter. However, it would not produce an ace. Those with the high scores were not just hunters but hunter-killers, and for that they needed the rarest quality of all, the ability to hit the target.

The closest one can get today to experiencing what pilots had to do to shoot something down is to go clay-pigeon shooting, or better still, on a mixed shoot involving birds with different flight characteristics. Imagine then that rather than swinging a shotgun you have to control an aeroplane in order to hit the target. Imagine too that the birds can shoot back.

Early experience with shotguns characterises the lives of the famous aces. They seem to have got their eye in early. Malan grew up on a farm in South Africa and got his first gun from his father when he was a boy.[15] Tuck was the son of an army captain, loved shooting,[16] and was 'a singularly precise judge of height and distance'.[17] Galland was the son of the manager of the Westerholt estate in Westphalia and taken on his first hunting trip when he was five.[18]

One quality that all fighting men need is courage. It is often assumed that the more a soldier has, the better he will be. In air fighting at least, this is not necessarily so. The courage needed in a military airman is the courage of resolution. Pilots had to be brave enough to overcome their fear and carry on doing their job, to fly aggressively and close with the enemy or to push on through flak and fighter attacks and to hit the target. They had to find the strength to do this every day. Most of them did. The most successful were

---

* The RAF's flying goggles, designed by one Group Captain Livingstone, were intended to reduce glare as well as to protect the eyes in case of fire, and could be fitted with a dark visor. The Flying Personnel Research Committee reported in 1940 that they had been 'highly spoken of in most units to which they have been issued' (AIR 6/59). Their interviewees may have just been being polite. All of those pilots to whom the author has spoken claimed ignorance of any such visor and said that they would not have used one in any case as they wanted as little as possible between the sky and their eyeball. The distortions of a Perspex canopy were bad enough. See BobDoe, *Fighter Pilot*, pp. 29–30.

particularly determined to win. But they also wanted to survive, and their determination was subject to calculation and judgement. If the situation was not in their favour and they had the choice, they went home. Heroes did not live long.

In this, there was a difference between the two sides in the Battle of Britain. The Germans sought to preserve their strength by discouraging heroics. Steinhilper reports how his Staffelkapitän, a veteran of Spain, drummed into them that they should not attack unless there was little risk to themselves and they were certain of success.[19] Theo Osterkamp, Kommodore of JG 51 in July, gave his men exactly the same instructions in his pre-battle briefing.[20] The British pilots, on the other hand, were under orders to intercept whatever they happened to find. They were usually outnumbered, and rarely had the choice of position. They usually just piled straight in from wherever they happened to be.[21]

Courage beyond this, though admirable as a human quality, was usually militarily ineffective. An excess of courage could result in foolhardiness or imprudence.[22] Those who made valour the better part of discretion usually paid with their lives.

During the war, the RAF won 21 VCs, but only one fighter pilot was rewarded with Britain's highest decoration. On 16 August Flight Lieutenant Nicolson of 249 Squadron took off at about 1305 at the head of a flight of three Hurricanes. Whilst climbing with the sun behind them they were bounced and all three aircraft hit. Nicolson's Hurricane caught fire and he was about to bale out when a Bf 110 shot past him. He stayed in the cockpit and opened fire at about 200 yards until he could bear the heat no more and took to his parachute. His ordeal was not over, however, for just as he was landing, as he laconically notes in his combat report, he was shot in the buttocks by an over-zealous member of the Home Guard whose pilot-recognition was not as good as it might have been. Badly burned, he was taken to hospital, where he learned on 15 November that he had been awarded the VC.[23] 'Now I will have to go and earn it', he is reported to have remarked, and telegrammed his wife: 'Darling. Just got VC. Don't know why. Letter follows. All my love. Nick.'

Acts of bravery had to be witnessed to qualify for an award, but fighter pilots fight alone, which is why Nicolson's award remained unique. Nicolson's act was not witnessed either, as his two comrades had troubles of their own to contend with.[24] But his wounds were unambiguous enough and his superiors were looking for an example it was thought valuable to honour.[25]

However, it must be said that, in the cold light of military logic, he might have done better to have saved himself sooner. His wounds kept him out of the rest of the battle. As long as he was able to fly, he himself was of greater value to his side than one downed Bf 110, even if he did get it, for had he remained in action he could well have shot down several. Unlike the infantryman, who can be easily replaced, a fighter pilot can rarely sacrifice himself with profit. It is part of the hunter's task to stay alive and killing.

This was a long way from knights-at-arms. That romantic idea stemmed from the genuine feelings of World War I pilots who clung to notions of honour and individual combat based on skill in contrast to the arbitrary mass murder of the trenches. In his classic autobiography *Sagittarius Rising*, published in 1936, RFC veteran Cecil Lewis was able to write of his admiration for a skilled opponent:

> And if at last he went down, a falling rocket of smoke and flame, what a glorious and heroic death! What a brave man! It might just as well have been me. For what have I been spared? To die, diseased in a bed! Sometimes it seems a pity.
>
> So, if the world must fight to settle its differences, back to Hector and Achilles! Back to the lists! Let the enemy match a squadron of fighters against ours. And let the world look on! It is not as fanciful as you suppose. We may yet live to see it over London.[26]

These were prophetic words, but they are also a delusion, complete with Hector and Achilles, shared willingly by many, including, for a time at least, some of the more impressionable young pilots who read Lewis's book. The Luftwaffe fighter arm fed itself on the Knights of the Air mythology, inspired by their role model, Baron von Richthofen. Richthofen was in fact a classic hunter-killer, who did not joust with an equal opponent if he could help it. Of his eighty claims, twenty-eight were other fighters. The remaining two-thirds were slow, less manoeuvrable two-seaters. Air fighting was not about jousting. It was about gaining and exploiting advantage whilst putting oneself at as little risk as possible. It classically involved creeping up on someone who had not seen you and shooting him in the back. The skill lay in gaining that initial advantage. Those who did not attack with an advantage rarely scored victories. Those who did not minimise the risk to themselves rarely survived. Richthofen, amongst others, showed the way, but not because he was a Baron.

Whilst they did not follow a medieval code of chivalry, the combatants did largely adhere to some rules of play. They espoused them because it was in their mutual best interests to do so. The main one amongst airmen was that they did not shoot at opponents who baled out and were parachuting to safety. Analogously, soldiers do not usually kill prisoners.[27] In every other way, air fighting was utterly ruthless. As long as he was still in his aircraft, an airman was a legitimate target, whether wounded or not. This may be because his potential killer saw only a machine, a fact often commented upon by pilots of both sides. They were shielded from the grisly effects their machine gun bullets had on the human body, and this significantly raised the threshold at which emotions like pity and moral impulses like mercy begin to operate. Once on a parachute, an enemy became a helpless human being, so killing him required hatred rather than a desire to add to one's score. Every pilot was also aware that the next time it could be him. Between machines, it was no holds barred. An aeroplane cannot put up a white flag and surrender, an option almost always open to a soldier, perilous and uncertain though the act of surrender may be.

In fact, for fighter pilots, the ideal victim was a cripple, and cripples were sought out. The French knights at Agincourt found no honour in killing an opponent who had lost his horse and arms and was struggling, wounded, to reach safety. Few soldiers at any time stalked the battlefield looking for unarmed, wounded men to kill. On the contrary, they would often leave them alone, for they had lost their threat value. However, neither the RAF nor the Luftwaffe had any compunction about attacking a bomber limping home at low level with one engine down and a dead rear gunner. They would often continue their attacks until they set the victim on fire so that they could get a 'confirmed' kill rather than a 'probable'. Bomber crews were very aware that losing an engine and dropping out of formation was highly dangerous, and there are many examples of damaged machines being attacked by a disproportionate number of fighters, even when there were plenty of other targets in the sky, the damaging of which would have had greater military value.[28]

Very few pilots exhibited all the skills needed on their first combat. They needed time to learn, and to gain time they needed luck. Air fighting of the intensity of the Battle of Britain provided precious little time at all. It would have been like passing your driving test and entering a Grand Prix the next day, knowing that somewhere among the competitors are the best drivers in the world. The difference is that if you meet them, and they are on the wrong side, they will kill you.

The most unfortunate new pilots were those who flew into their first engagement as the rear aircraft in a small flight, a perfect target for the hunters. Lacking their flight commanders' skill, they were less able to get the best out of their machines on the climb and therefore tended to lag behind their leader. Thus they advertised their inexperience and attracted proportionately more attacks. As, say, one of three, they had well over a 30% chance of being chosen as the victim.

Hugh Dundas, whose father, though of modest means, had been 'born in the purple', became fascinated by stories of World War I aces during his childhood and left Stowe in May 1939 to join the Auxiliaries of 616 'South Yorkshire' Squadron. It was an offshoot of 609 'West Riding' Squadron, founded by his godfather, in which his admired elder brother John was already serving. He was rather taken aback when war broke out, but it did not affect him much until 616 flew to Rochford to relieve 74 Squadron in late May 1940. His encounter with the recently-blooded pilots of 74, including the hard, business-like Malan, somewhat dampened his schoolboy spirits, but still did not fully prepare him for his first action, which was over Dunkirk. He had no idea what was going on, except that there were others out there trying to kill him:

> With sudden, sickening, stupid fear I realised that I was being fired on
> and I pulled my Spitfire round hard, so that the blood was forced

down from my head. The thick curtain of blackout blinded me for a moment and I felt the aircraft juddering on the brink of a stall. Straightening out, the curtain lifted and I saw a confusion of planes, diving and twisting . . .

At some stage in the next few seconds the silhouette of a Messerschmitt passed by my windscreen and I fired my guns in battle for the first time – a full deflection shot which, I believe, was quite ineffectual.

I was close to panic in the bewilderment and hot fear of that first dogfight. Fortunately instinct drove me to keep on turning and turning, twisting my neck all the time to look for the enemy behind. Certainly the consideration which was uppermost in my mind was the desire to stay alive.

. . . When, at last, I felt it safe to straighten out I was amazed to find that the sky . . . was now quite empty . . . At one moment it was all you could do to avoid collision . . . The next moment you were on your own. The mêlée had broken up as if by magic. The sky was empty except perhaps for a few distant specks.

It was then that panic took hold of me for the second time that day. Finding myself alone over the sea, a few miles north of Dunkirk, my training as well as my nerve deserted me. Instead of calmly thinking out the course which I should fly to reach the Thames Estuary, I blindly set out in what I conceived to be roughly the right direction. After several minutes I could see nothing at all but the empty wastes of the North Sea . . . At last I saw two destroyers . . . The sight of the two ships restored to me some measure of sanity and self-control. I forced myself to work out the simple problem of navigation which sheer panic had prevented me from facing. After a couple of orbits I set course to the west and soon the cliffs of the North Foreland came up to meet me.

Soaked in sweat, I flew low across the estuary towards Southend pier. By the time I came in to land . . . a sense of jubilation had replaced the cravenness of a few minutes earlier . . . now a debonair young fighter pilot . . . sat in the cockpit which had so recently been occupied by a frightened child . . .[29]

The first thing to make the nineteen-year-old Dundas aware that he was in an air battle was the sight of tracer bullets around him. Totally confused, he reacted defensively, pulling round hard, which was the right thing to do: keep on turning. Mitchell had seen to it that his Spitfire would not only keep him alive as long as he did so – for the 109s could not stay with him – but also benignly warn him of an impending stall with an inner-wing judder if he overdid it. So she did. It may have been difficult to build, but that wing saved many a frightened young man's life.

Dundas reached his physical limits before the machine did. Most people start to black out at a force of 4–5 g. The Spitfire could withstand double that. Flying it to its limits was necessary for survival, but felt dangerous and imposed considerable physical strain. Not all the novices did so.

When Dundas straightened out, he saw his attackers for the first time, and was presented with a target, passively. He saw only a silhouette and perhaps it triggered a memory of his aircraft recognition manuals. Firing at full deflection, he was no doubt right in supposing that he missed. The confusion produced disorientation and the disorientation produced panic. His only instinct was to turn, which again was the right thing to do to increase the odds of survival.

Suddenly, he was alone. At 300 mph, an aircraft could move a mile away from the scene of action in twelve seconds. A bit of cloud could mean that a furious dogfight could be taking place unseen only a few hundred yards away. He was still in the battle area, and it was then, after his involuntary disengagement, that he was exposed to the greatest danger. He panicked because he was lost, but he had reason to be afraid, for being alone he could easily have been bounced. His blind flight to the north probably saved him, for had he stayed a few miles away from Dunkirk in order to work out his proper course, a pair of roaming Messerschmitts could well have got him whilst he was looking at his compass.

As familiar sights arose, he recovered his sense of orientation and the panic left him. His recovery, which he treats with irony, is also significant. In part, his exultation was due to his survival and was quite justified by the statistics, which he mercifully did not know. But it also demonstrates the resilience of youth. The self-delusion was an important part of his development. His experience did not break him, but gave him confidence. Pilots had to believe they were the greatest or they could not carry on. Such delusions were dangerous only if they continued at the moment of battle. They explain how it was that Dundas could get into his cockpit for his next mission.

Dundas was lucky to be caught up in a large dogfight, terrifying though this experience was. He was less likely to be singled out and the overall casualty rates in large fights were lower than in small ones. The most fortunate novices gained their first experience against inferior fighters or lone reconnaissance aircraft. The nature of combat depended enormously on the kinds of aircraft engaged. They posed very different challenges.

21. TACTICS

I t has become a truism that every generation of military leaders enters a new war prepared to fight the last one. That rebuke cannot be levelled at the RAF in World War II. Its development of tactics in the 1930s was revolutionary. It believed that any future conflict would be totally unlike the conflagration of 1914–18 and that the extraordinary pace of technological change in aeronautics rendered the experiences of the great aces redundant. It tried to work out what would happen instead.

Fighter Command's mission was to stop the bomber. Given the range of fighters and the fact that France was an ally, it was assumed that no hostile fighter could reach UK airspace, which meant that bombers would be unescorted. Dogfighting would in any case be impossible at 300 mph, as pilots would black out, so the issue was purely one of fighters versus bombers.

Bombers would fly in tight, massed formations, concentrating their defensive firepower. Given what Sorley had ascertained about the weight of fire needed to bring down a bomber, the answer was clearly to mass fighters in formation to bring a large number of guns to bear. Exploiting the RAF's undoubted skill at disciplined formation flying, squadrons would attack together according to six basic patterns, the Fighting Area Attacks, all of which were laid out in the Training Manual of 1938 and formed part of standard air drill.

There was another reason why these tactics were laid out in such detail and so rigidly rehearsed. The rate of expansion of the RAF in the late 1930s led some senior officers to believe most of their new pilots would not be good enough to be let loose on their own, and would need to go into action under the tight control of their more experienced leaders.[1] Like Kitchener's New Army preparing for the Battle of the Somme in 1916, the new Fighter Command had to be mothered. The results when tested were to be similar in effect, though not, fortunately in extent.

The standard RAF fighter formation was the V-shaped 'vic' of three. A squadron consisted of two flights, A and B, each made up of two sections of three, the smallest tactical unit, with Red and Yellow sections in A flight, and Blue and Green in B flight.

In Fighter Attack Number 1, designed for lone bombers, a section would move into line astern (Indian file) and each successively attack from the rear. In Number 2, they would approach from below and then each climb up from behind, fire until their ammunition was exhausted and break away to allow the next to take his turn. Number 3 involved the whole section staying in a vic and firing together at a formation from behind. Number 4 was a variation of Number 2 suitable for a formation of bombers, Number 5 had the section move to line abreast to shoot at a string of bombers, and Number 6 was for a whole squadron dealing with nine bombers and is so complex that it would be tedious and futile to describe it.[2]

The Fighting Area Attacks were very complex, with endless variations attempting to cover every eventuality and actually covering only a few, so that simply selecting which attack to make took some mental agility. When manoeuvring for them, the attackers were perfect targets for escorting fighters. The Fighting Area Attacks were neither old-fashioned nor conservative – on the contrary. They were simply unrealistic. As most of those who attempted to put them into practice were rapidly shot down, they gradually fell out of use, but they continued to be learned in some units until early 1941.[3] Their persistence was all the more remarkable in that Park had criticised them as early as 1938 when he was Senior Air Staff Officer at Fighter Command, urging that air leaders be left to use their initiative.[4] When he was at Northolt with 111 Squadron, Sandy Sanders worked with both the Air Fighting Development Establishment and the Air Fighting Development Unit, which were responsible for devising tactics, and added his own protest that they should be left to fly loosely and not use tight formations just because they were good at them. However, he was just a Flying Officer and it was the Air Commodores who called the shots.

So it was that initiative was not just discouraged but forbidden. The 1938 directive for Fighter Command Attacks contains this sentence: 'Squadron Commanders are not to practice forms of attack other than those laid down, unless they have been specially authorised by Headquarters, Fighter Command.'[5] This effectively meant that some degree of insubordination would be a requirement of survival.

In practice, the tactics fighters used against bombers depended on whether they were confronted with single aircraft or formations, and what the escorting fighters were doing.

Bombers flew in formation for two reasons: one was defensive, to protect themselves from fighters by bringing their guns together in mutual support to create overlapping arcs of cross-fire; and the other was offensive, to get a concentrated bombing pattern.

The smallest Luftwaffe bomber unit was a group of three called a 'Kette' which flew in a 'V' like the RAF vic. It says much about RAF fighter tactics that they thought about their fighters in the way the Luftwaffe thought about their bombers. The most common tactical unit was the Gruppe and when a Gruppe flew together the Ketten were grouped together in one of four basic formations.[6]

The first was to have each of the Gruppe's three Staffeln in line abreast, each Staffel having its Ketten in line astern, with the Staffelkapitän in the lead aircraft. The central Staffel was slightly ahead of the two flanking ones and led by the Gruppenkommandeur, who was generally the observer, not the pilot as in Bomber Command. The leader not only navigated, which was the most important task, but also gave orders to change direction, change formation and to bomb. The bombers could cover each other defensively and sometimes 'stepped up' the formation by having each successive Kette fly about 500 feet higher than the one in front, allowing gunners more opportunity to engage targets simultaneously without the danger of hitting each other. The more cohesively they flew, the more likely they were to survive and the better their bombing concentration was likely to be.

The second formation had each Staffel form an arrow-head, the third involved each Staffel forming a V, and the fourth was Ketten in line astern, in which the whole Gruppe split into Ketten and followed each other.

The bomb-aimer used a Lofte bombsight into which were entered the details of the bombs to be dropped and the altitude from which the attack was to be carried out. It then fed course corrections to the pilot, and released the bombs automatically. Optimal altitude for bombing on a clear day was between 13,000 and 17,000 feet, but bombers operated at anything between 10,000 and 20,000 feet depending on weather conditions. The most dangerous time for the crew was the bomb-run, during which the aircraft was committed to an attack and had to fly straight and level. It lasted about forty seconds.

The bomber crews' task was, if the navigator got it right, simple but dangerous. They had to keep going, stay in formation and drop their bombs when their leader told them to, enduring whatever the enemy threw at them, which in the main were flak and fighters. They knew they were prey from the outset and the role would never change. Performing that job in daylight took an increasing amount of courage. Unlike fighter pilots, bombers crews could not have too much of it.

The most effective way to break up a bomber formation was to attack it head-on and fly on through it, a tactic frequently urged by Park himself.[7] At a closing speed of 500 mph, there was only time for a two- to three-second burst. The odds on breaking up the formation were above average because of the bomber pilots' instinctive temptation to swerve in order to avoid colliding with the oncoming fighter, a very real danger. If they did swerve, the bombers then risked collision with each other, which sometimes happened. If the formation broke up, the fighters could turn and pick them off piecemeal.

The attacks also made it possible to target the leader who was controlling the bombing.

It had a particularly intimidating effect on the Germans because in all three main bomber types the crew were sitting together in the nose with only Perspex between them and their attacker. The fighter pilot had a bullet-proof windscreen and an engine in front of him, and presented a small target. Notwithstanding that, it required unusual nerve.

111 Squadron, which was taken over in February 1940 by the formidable and austere Squadron Leader John Thompson, were known as strong proponents of these tactics, and opened the 'official' Battle of Britain with a head-on attack over convoy 'Bread'. It was very effective, but Higgs' fate shows the risks involved, and head-on attacks called for skill as well as guts. 111 lost Flying Officer Ferris in a head-on attack over Marden on 16 August, when he hit a Dornier belonging to III./KG 76.[8] As the number of old hands in 111 diminished, so did the number of head-on attacks. Views on them differed. Some thought that if you learned how to time the break, they were no problem. Others thought they were strictly the preserve of 'a few brave buggers' and 'bloody dangerous', although there were 'one or two lunatics who revelled in it'.[9]

An alternative was to try from the first to attack from behind, fighter escort permitting, either diving through the formation from above or attacking the rear and flanks, though some squadrons tried to go for the leaders. Diving meant only a short time for a shot, but a fighter flying at diving speed through a formation would be difficult to hit and could zoom-climb for another go.* An attack on the rear or flank of a formation at similar level gave more time for shooting, and was the most common method, given that German bombers were poorly protected from behind.

In as much as a pilot was capable of aiming at anything, he went for the engines. If he could knock an engine out, the bomber would lose height and speed and have to leave the formation, becoming far easier prey. Some pilots, however, espoused Malan's bloodthirsty view that it was best to hit the fuselage in order to kill or wound the crew. He argued that if the bomber then did in fact return home the results would have a demoralising effect on the rest of the unit. Few pilots had the shooting skill to make the choice.

Another method, preferred by Tuck, was to try a shallow dive out of the sun, wherever it happened to be, and go through the formation at a good speed without firing. The attacker would then pull out underneath them, climb fast, and fire at the unprotected bellies from close range. This avoided any armour plating they might have. According to Tuck, this 'always produced instant results'.[10]

---

* A Spitfire's maximum diving speed was 470 mph, about the same as a Bf 109's and over 100 mph higher than its 'maximum' speed in level flight. The Hurricane's was 380–390 mph. See Rod Smith, 'In Defence of the Spitfire' in *Aeroplane Monthly*, August 1995, p.30.

The bombers could still fight back, of course. It is often said that they were poorly armed, but their highly-trained gunners were very good shots, and did a lot of damage. Because they were faced with a small frontal target during the fighter's attack, they usually hit the engine if anything, and most damage from the defensive fire of bombers was done to aircraft rather than pilots. Fighters often crash-landed with damaged engines or holed glycol tanks.

The dangerous stage for the fighter was breaking away. If it delivered an attack at the same level and overtook its target, the gunners had a non-deflection shot from behind. This time there was no engine to protect the pilot, only his armoured seat-back. If the attacker climbed away too steeply too soon, he gave the gunners a target it was hard to miss. The best method was to break out and down at full throttle, banking away from the bombers' flight path to reduce the amount of time the gunners had for a shot.[11]

To shoot down a bomber required getting in close. Destroying them was not as easy as had been suspected. Many still flew back to base with upwards of 100 bullet holes in them and the British themselves found wrecks which showed that they could take a lot of hits before being knocked down. This was despite the use of DeWilde incendiary ammunition as well as the standard ball and tracer. Dorniers were the easiest to shoot down. Heinkels, which were fitted with some 600lb of armour plating, were tougher nuts to crack and the very robust Ju 88 was toughest of all. All the bombers had self-sealing petrol tanks.

The suspicion was raised that even Sorley's eight machine guns were not destructive enough.[12] The experience from France had indicated as much, and it was well known that the Bf 109 was armed with cannon. Accordingly, the first squadron to have received Spitfires, No. 19, took delivery of three new ones fitted with two Hispano 20 mm cannon in June. These aircraft were known as Mk 1Bs to distinguish them from the normal eight-gun Mk 1As.

After many frustrations with stoppages, due in the main to an unreliable cartridge-case ejection system and the fact that the guns tended to freeze above 20,000 feet, the squadron tried out some aircraft armed with four machine guns in addition to the two cannon.* This armament worked well without

* Those sharing Corelli Barnett's iconoclastic bent will delight in the fact that Germany had a series of reliable and formidable cannon already fitted to the Bf 109. Further pleasure can be derived from the fact that when it did turn to cannon, the RAF had to adopt a French design, just as it used American-designed machine guns. Enjoyment of this need only be tempered by the fact that the German guns were simply an adapted version of the anti-aircraft gun designed and manufactured by the Swiss firm Oerlikon, and that even they had not mastered the recoil problems imposed by the MG FF/M. Although provision was made for the Bf 109 E series to have a cannon firing through the propeller spinner, it was never fitted because of the vibration it caused. The virtues of cannon versus machine guns were as much a matter of controversy in the Luftwaffe as in the RAF (cf. Spick, *Luftwaffe Fighter Aces*, pp. 54 & 82). Sadly, it must further be noted that the British extensively redesigned the Browning so that it could be used in the air, and that it took the RAF and a British design team, with all the legendary incompetence of British engineers, to actually turn the Hispano into a reliable working weapon whose weight and velocity of fire made it so deadly and efficient a weapon that the Americans adopted it after the war.

adding too much weight, and in November, 92 Squadron took delivery of Mk 1Bs fitted out in this way. Throughout the Battle of Britain, however, 19 Squadron was the only unit armed with cannon. On 4 September, in despair over the constant jams, the squadron took over Mk 1As from a training unit, and began to get more kills.*

Once a bomber was isolated, it was in trouble. It could only head for cloud or protect its underside by getting down to the deck and jinking – flying as erratically as possible to make itself a difficult target. The lone reconnaissance aircraft the Luftwaffe sent over England were inherently vulnerable. The men who flew in these were very courageous and usually fought back hard.

The usual approach when attacking a single bomber was from astern, and the best way to deal with return fire was to ignore it. The results of such interceptions were inevitable unless the bomber escaped into cloud, or over-eager British pilots in section strength all attacked at once and got in each other's way. In one disastrous incident in the early morning of 10 October, a flight from 92 Squadron intercepted a lone Dornier over Tangmere. Possibly showing the effects of fatigue at this late stage in the battle, two of the British aircraft collided, killing both pilots. The next man to attack, Sergeant Ellis, took a hit in the glycol tank – a typical bomber-inflicted aircraft injury – and had to crash-land, writing off his Spitfire. The three remaining colleagues then attacked – with what feelings one can imagine – and damaged the Dornier, but it escaped into cloud and eventually crash-landed in France with its photographs intact.[13] Lord Haw-Haw enjoyed himself that evening, which was a quiet one at Biggin Hill.

Underestimating these lone scouts was a mistake. On 11 July, in filthy weather, Squadron Leader Peter Townsend found a lone Dornier from KG2, which he had been scrambled to intercept. Meeting it coming towards him, he got behind it in a hurry, afraid that it would disappear in the cloud. The German rear gunner opened up at long range as Townsend closed in from behind. Townsend opened fire when the range shortened, but the return fire continued as he got closer. As he overtook the bomber at the end of his attack, Townsend's Hurricane was an easy target and it took hits in the engine. The Dornier crash-landed in Arras St Léger with 50% damage and three wounded crewmen. Townsend took to his parachute and landed in the North Sea. He was picked up by a trawler within a few minutes and arrived at Harwich much the

---

* See Robinson, op. cit., pp. 36–50. It was not until the Spitfire VB made its appearance in the summer of 1941 that the reliability problem had been solved. Bader was still against cannon, claiming that they encouraged pilots to open fire from too far away, and remaining sceptical about the assurances that the problems had been solved. He was very familiar with them, as 19 Squadron flew from Duxford as part of his wing. He continued to fly an aircraft with eight Brownings for as long as he could get one (see Burns, pp. 174–5). Malan, on the other hand, greeted the new armament with enthusiasm. He may have been influenced by an experience he had on 5 February 1941, when he and A Flight of 74 Squadron expended the enormous total of 6,541 rounds in bringing down a Dornier Do 215, which Malan suspected was trying out new armour plating (Franks, *Sky Tiger*, pp. 93–4).

worse for rum. Greeted by one of his Flight Commanders on the jetty, Townsend was rather pleased with himself. His Flight Commander, on the contrary, thought it the height of ignominy to get shot down by a Dornier of all things, and his loyal men saw to it that Townsend's status as a warrior-hero suffered accordingly.[14] He was luckier than he thought. He was the only pilot to be rescued from the North Sea throughout the battles over the convoys.

During the battle, the men of Fighter Command rarely had many options, and usually just went straight for the bombers from wherever they happened to be, which was often climbing from below. If the escorts were too high or not alert, the attackers had a brief opening, which they usually exploited to the full.

By the summer of 1940, the Junkers Ju 87 Stuka had come to symbolise the Blitzkrieg, and with it, German military success. It had had an enormous psychological effect on ground troops, partly because Stukas seemed to be everywhere, partly because they gave anyone on the ground the impression that they were diving straight for them and partly because, at the instigation of Udet, they had been fitted with sirens to give them a terrifying wail. None of this affected someone sitting in another aeroplane.

Some explanation for German success was needed in the aftermath of their shock victories, and the Stuka was seized upon in the public mind. In Battle of Britain mythology it is always 'much-vaunted', to point the fact that the British gave it its come-uppance.[15] Although the Germans were not slow to exploit its propaganda value, most of the stories about the Stuka's powers came from its victims. The trail of fire and broken armies the Wehrmacht had laid across Europe seemed to suggest there could be something to it.

As part of the complete Blitzkrieg package, operating in effect as flying artillery to keep the Panzers moving, Stukas were extremely valuable. They could get anywhere within 200 miles of their base and could thus attack positions the artillery could not reach, especially as heavy artillery would quickly be left behind by the tanks. They were robust enough to operate from forward airstrips and could be radioed for support and join the action at short notice. They were the only bombers consistently capable of hitting pin-point targets.

One condition of their success was local air superiority. The Luftwaffe wanted to use them against England because it had them and they ought to have something to do. They were indeed ideal for attacking shipping. However, in attacking England, the very issue was establishing air superiority in the first place.

Several things contributed to their inability to survive in hostile air space.

The first was that they were very slow. With a top speed of some 230 mph, the Ju 87B was the slowest aircraft operating in any numbers on either side, slower even than the 257-mph Fairey Battle. Both types were technically obsolete in 1940, but the Ju 87's dive-bombing capability and more adaptable design offered it a far longer useful life than the mediocre Battle.[16]

The second was its bombing technique.[17] For accuracy, Stukas had to bomb into the wind, which meant that, having reached the target, their attack position was determined by the weather rather than the presence of the enemy. They had to break formation, move into line astern, and manoeuvre into position, ready to start their dive from 13,000 feet. During all this, they were very vulnerable. They were harder to attack in their half-minute dive, though with their dive-brakes out to slow them down and ensure bombing accuracy, they dived at only 300 mph. Four seconds before bomb-release, a horn sounded in the cockpit, and ceased at 2,275 feet. That was the signal for the pilot to release the bomb and an automatic pull-out system then hauled the nose up out of the dive for him. The Stuka would then zoom-climb, giving the rear gunner the chance to spray the ground with his machine-gun to help cover the next attacker, before levelling off at low altitude and heading for home. At this point the Stuka was also very vulnerable.

The third was that if it was attacked, it could not defend itself, for it was as ungainly as a heavy bomber, but less well-armed. It only had two forward-firing machine guns, which it had no hope of bringing to bear on a competently-handled fighter, and one rear-facing machine gun which did not frighten even the most nervous novice pilot with eight Brownings and an engine in front of him.

The fourth was that it could not be defended by anybody else either.[18] The Stukas were so slow – they climbed at only 120 mph – that on the way out Bf 109 escorts used to wait until they were half-way across the Channel before even taking off. Once they had caught up with their ugly charges, they had to fly on a zig-zag path to stay with them, which both used up precious fuel and made the 109 pilots themselves vulnerable to being bounced, something of which they passionately disapproved. Given the height from which the Stuka's dive started, the escorts also had to fly lower than they were wont, adding to their danger. Once the Stuka dived, it was on its own. Every young blood in the Luftwaffe fighter arm wanted to bounce Spitfires from 30,000 feet, not circle round a Stuka at 2,000 feet, where even a Hurricane could both bounce him and then outperform him in a dogfight if it happened to miss on the first pass.

The fifth was that when it was hit it had an alarming tendency to disintegrate, catch fire or blow up. Sorley's guns were more than enough to hack through a Stuka. As one rear gunner/radio operator has since commented: 'We radio operators felt as though we were human armour plate – armour plate to protect the pilot sitting behind us!'[19] Their main hope was that their mounts were so slow the British fighters would misjudge their aim and overshoot.

The final reason was that, in attacking prepared positions on the British mainland rather than troops in the field, the Stukas would run into low-level AA guns and possibly have to face targets protected by barrage balloons, which made life between 1,000 and 5,000 feet more exciting than even the hottest pilot would wish.

Small wonder then that Dowding's young men soon christened a Stuka attack a 'Stuka party'. They were all eager for invitations and tended to crash them if they chanced upon one.

The Messerschmitt Bf 110 is the other aircraft in the Luftwaffe's inventory to have attracted to itself the fixed epithet 'much-vaunted'.[20] Göring did have a weakness for vaunting, and he called the Bf 110 units his '*Eisenseiten*' ('Ironsides') in a reference to Cromwell's troopers. Given the delight the British take in giving boastful Toads a humbling lesson, this aircraft has come in for a lot of self-satisfied criticism.

The Bf 110 was probably the best machine in its class, and popular with its pilots.[21] Reaching 340 mph at 32,000 feet, it was a good 80 mph faster than the comparable Blenheim 1F twin-engined fighter, had a higher ceiling and was far better armed. With four forward-firing machine guns and two 20mm cannon, it was a very effective bomber-killer, as Bomber Command discovered almost as soon as war broke out.[22] It was less vulnerable than the Defiant, with a longer range and significant bomb-carrying capability. Some versions had a strengthened undercarriage which allowed them to carry 2,200 lbs of bombs, as much as the He 111 or Do 17. It was even faster than the Hurricane and could give a Spitfire a run for its money. The Allies pursued similar design concepts themselves with marked success later in the war.

The Luftwaffe's mistake was to imagine that the Bf 110 could operate as a long-range daylight air superiority fighter, like a beefier, longer-legged 109. Though fast, it had poor acceleration and poor manoeuvrability. Osterkamp realised this, commenting that it would take a prize wrestler to move the joystick at the speeds flown in combat.[23] Werner Mölders had come to the same conclusion before the war when he tried it out against a 109 in a mock dogfight against his brother Viktor, who flew with ZG1. Piloting the 110, even Werner could not stay on his brother's tail.[24] It could no more dogfight than could the Blenheim, and the British sensibly turned their nine squadrons of Blenheim fighters over to night-fighting before embarrassing massacres occurred. It took embarrassing massacres to convince Göring to do the same.

The first real embarrassment came in June, not at the hands of the British, but of the Swiss. Since the outbreak of war, they had vigorously defended their neutrality, and the Swiss Air Force had attacked several German bombers that had violated their air-space. On 4 June some Heinkels appeared, escorted by ZG1 and, though heavily outnumbered, Bf 109s from a Swiss border surveillance patrol attacked them and shot down a Bf 110. Incensed, Göring sent thirty-two Bf 110s of II./ZG1 on a mission to deliberately violate Swiss airspace and provoke a combat. They orbited the Jura mountains and succeeded in getting attacked by fourteen Swiss Bf 109s, which shot down four of them and chased off the rest at a cost of one damaged 109. After that Göring left the Swiss alone.[25]

Despite being aggressively flown by some very good pilots, the Bf 110s soon found that any Spitfire or Hurricane could easily get on their tails and was not deterred by the single machine-gun they had to ward it off. The problem of manoeuvrability was fundamental to a twin-engined design. The large wings with the engines on them created huge resistance to rolling. In attacking, the Bf 110s' successes came in the main through a bounce – it was after being bounced and hit by 110s that James Nicolson won his VC.

If attacked themselves or forced into a dogfight, the Zerstörers' standard tactic was to fly round in a circle, which their crews christened the 'circle of death', in order to protect each other's tail. Sometimes the whole circle moved on a single course, though it was difficult to keep this up for long.[26] As long as it was intact and at sufficient height, the circle had some offensive as well as defensive purpose, as it could dominate a large area of sky, and an aircraft could dive out of it at any stage on a target appearing below. However, when practised over hostile territory, the circle tactic created a problem for its members, for at some stage they had to break and run for it, and then they were vulnerable.[27]

As this tactic was refined, procedures were thought out in some units for breaking in different directions, but this called for a level of discipline not always present in the heat of battle.[28] The circle was itself not very effective, as the British fighters could either dive on it or break into it and use their tighter turning radius to pick off 110s from inside it. The circle also had to be complete for it to work at all, and when it was formed too slowly it could easily be attacked.

Though ineffective as a fighter, when used as a fighter-bomber the Bf 110 represented a real threat to Fighter Command. The only unit consistently to use it like this was Erprobungsgruppe 210, which first saw action against convoys on 13 July. The Bf 110s effectively became fast Stukas, carrying a similar or larger bomb-load which they could deliver over greater ranges with equal accuracy. What might have happened had more of these aircraft been used in the same way will thankfully remain one of history's counterfactuals.

By 1940, the fighters of most air forces could successfully challenge most bombers. The key issue in deciding air superiority was fighter-fighter combat. The Bf 109 was a formidable weapon and its pilots knew how to use it.

The fighter force which assembled on the coast of France during July 1940 was by far the most experienced and tactically advanced in the world. The experience individual pilots gained during the Spanish Civil War, useful though it was, was of far less significance than the opportunity it gave the Luftwaffe to develop fighter tactics. Less than a third of the Luftwaffe's 1940 personnel had served there, but the lessons learned were embodied in their organisation, tactics and training, so that all benefited. These tactics were so good that their principles have been adopted by every air force in the world and are still in use today.

The prime movers in these developments were the Luftwaffe's leading pilots, and in particular Werner Mölders. Successful combat experience was deemed all-important. Mölders was highly successful and what he learned in combat was offically institutionalised in training, which was often carried out by the Spanish veterans themselves. With its origins in combat, it emphasised fighting rather than flying.[29] Thus, for example, the young Helmut Wick who joined up in 1936 and did not go to Spain, describes how in his first action on 22 November 1939, when attacked by French Curtisses, he remembered the lessons given to him by Werner Mölders and acted accordingly.[30] The challenge Mölders and his colleagues faced in Spain was not how to stop large bomber formations from attacking cities, but how to support ground forces by gaining air superiority against the agile Russian fighters introduced by the Republicans. His tactics are based on fighter-fighter combat.

When they went to Spain, Luftwaffe fighter units flew in tight vics of three just as RAF fighters did. When they returned, they flew in widely spaced units of four called a 'Schwarm'.[31] Each Schwarm consisted of two 'Rotten', or pairs, which formed the basic fighting unit. Within the pair, the leader, the 'Rottenführer', had the job of making kills and his wingman, the 'Rottenflieger' (or in Luftwaffe slang 'Rottenhund' or 'Katschmarek') had the job of protecting the leader's tail, particularly when the leader was making a kill. The wingman was not to think about where he was flying or what to do next, but was to follow his leader, usually flying about 200 yards behind, to one side and slightly above him, and keep his head turning. Thus whilst the Rotte flew aggressively, one of its members concentrated on its defence. A lone pilot, even if he was very good, was far more vulnerable than a pair, and wingman and leader tried never to be separated.

The spirit behind the Luftwaffe's flying can be seen in its language. A 'Schwarm' is a swarm of bees, a flock of birds or a shoal of fish, creatures which move freely together, but with a guiding pattern and logic to their movement. 'Rotte' is the word for a pack of dogs (hence the term 'Rottenhund'), and also means 'gang' or 'band' of men. It well conveys the principles the Luftwaffe wanted to get into the heads of its pilots: the flexible but purposeful aggressiveness of a band of hunting animals. The RAF terms 'flight' and 'section' equally reflect a prime concern with rigid, geometrical patterns of flying. There was another side to it, however, reflected in the term the pilots themselves usually used for a wingman. 'Katschmarek' is a Polish word for an old family retainer. A lot of wingmen felt themselves to be no more than humble servants whose duty it was to protect a great ace while he was adding to his score. Often the way they did so was by offering an attacker an easier target.

Two pairs made a Schwarm. The pairs flew some 300 yards apart, as this was about the turning radius of the 109 at combat speed, the second pair being staggered in height and position. The Rottenführer of the leading pair was the Schwarmführer. The whole Staffel consisted of three Schwärme and would once again stagger the formation so that it covered about a mile and a half of sky.

A Staffel flying like this was inconspicuous itself (and looked very undisciplined to an RAF regular officer in 1939) but could search large areas of sky in all directions. Each pilot had only one flying job to do: follow his respective leader. Given the simplicity of the flying task, everybody could be on the lookout and concentrate on fighting. The Schwarm could turn in a cross-over, with each Rotte reversing position, without any throttling back to stay in formation. If the leader were to be attacked, his wingman could pursue the attacker. If a Schwarm were attacked, the two pairs could split and likewise sandwich an assailant.[32]

When out hunting, the leader had only one job: to find victims for himself and his hunting pack. When victims were found, the leader was the one to go for them, which in part explains the high scores built up by Germany's leading aces, the 'Experten'. The Messerschmitts would fly high and look for bounce opportunities. In the RAF's terminology a 'fighter sweep', this was the 'freie Jagd' – a 'free hunt'.

Fighter Command flying practices might have been designed to make its fighters vulnerable to being bounced. The vic of three forced two of the three pilots to concentrate on keeping formation rather than watch their tails or the sky. In a turn the inner two had to throttle back, whereas a fighter pilot wanted to leave his controls alone as much as possible and always keep up full speed in the combat zone. The Germans dubbed the vics 'Idiotenreihen' ('rows of idiots'), which says it all. Squadrons arranged themselves in section echelons, either to opposite sides or both to the same side, which meant that three out of four section leaders had to keep an eye on the whole section in front. As they realised that squadrons flying in this way were blind to the rear, the RAF introduced 'weavers', one or two aircraft of the rear section flying on a zig-zag weaving course (using up more fuel than the others) above and to the rear of the squadron to 'guard' it from behind. The job of weaver tended to go to the most junior pilot. Most were never seen again.

The British were at a severe disadvantage in the process of adopting good tactics. They had fewer pilots who had worked out the principles of air combat, and these were needed for fighting, not training. Standard RAF training practically ignored fighting. Nothing was systematised and things spread by word of mouth. In this the lack of structure between squadron and Group level was a disadvantage, for the best leaders did not have the leverage of their German counterparts. Galland influenced the performance of a Gruppe and then of a whole Geschwader.

In August 1940, James Edward ('Johnnie') Johnson, who was to become the top-claiming ace on the Allied side during the war, was still in training at an Operational Training Unit (OTU) at Hawarden in Cheshire. There he was taught how to fly Spitfires, but not how to fight in them, despite the fact that the instructors were battle-experienced. The fledgling pilots were longing for information about the Bf 109, turning circles, deflection shooting, how to keep a look-out and so on, but all they got were a few vague chats in the bar.

No lectures on combat tactics had yet been written. The instructors' priority was to 'keep the sausage machine turning'. As a result most of the sausages were dead meat when they arrived at their squadrons.[33]

The knowledge was available. Major Oliver Stuart, an RFC veteran, wrote a book called *The Strategy and Tactics of Air Fighting*, based on the experiences of the top aces of World War I, in order to let future generations benefit from what they learned.[34] It was published in 1925, and some of it was dated by 1940, but the basics are all there: the value of surprise, gained by height and a position up-sun; how to quarter the sky; the use of the bounce (called the 'dive and zoom' attack); the need to turn into the enemy if attacked; and how a single machine with a superior position can attack a group without this being 'too hazardous a proceeding'.[35] To official argument that the human body could not withstand the g-forces involved in high speed manoeuvring, rendering dogfighting obsolete, Stuart rightly replied: 'a method will be found – if it requires finding – by which the fastest fighters will be enabled to manoeuvre freely at their maximum speeds.'[36] This prediction still holds good, for as speeds increased well beyond their 1940 limits, 'g-suits' were invented to allow pilots to cope. The demand for such books existed, and rose during 1940. Johnnie Johnson relates how they sent someone to London to buy a novel about World War I they had heard contained some useful information. The booksellers knew about it, but all the copies had already gone at six times the cover price.

In retrospect, the neglect of available knowledge seems almost criminal. However, at the time the RAF itself was not clear about tactics. Park favoured sections of four and encouraged debate amongst his squadron leaders about the best formation to use. However, they all disagreed with each other, as can been seen from the comments from four squadrons on a suggestion circulated by the Intelligence Officer of 504 Squadron in September 1940.[37] Malan experimented with looser formations based on two pairs. Some thought he was mad:

> Somebody said Sailor Malan's squadron is spreading out in formation on patrol. It seemed like a mistake. It seemed highly dangerous. Somebody said, 'They'll all get shot down.' The Germans were flying their loose formations, but we thought it was very untidy. It took us a while to learn.[38]

Dowding later wrote that he came to doubt whether the organisation of a squadron into four sections of three was best for dogfighting, and thought it should be replaced by three sections of four, allowing the four to split into two pairs. However, he states, it was 'undesirable to make any sweeping changes during the Battle' and observes that it would in any case 'upset standard arrangements for accommodation.'[39]

In war, more is usually better. There are nevertheless many examples of few beating many. In air fighting numbers count in the long run, especially if the game is one of attrition, but in an actual aerial engagement, they count for less than they do on the ground or at sea. A single pilot with the initiative could carry out an ambush and escape before anybody knew he was there. Hard to detect during closing, a small number of attackers engaging a large number of defenders could also shoot at almost any target and be confident that it was an enemy. In modern jargon, they were operating in a target-rich environment, and tended to mete out more damage than they suffered. They were only disadvantaged if the enemy was alert and had such numerical ascendancy as to be on the tail of almost every attacker. In general, a single squadron on a single pass could cause more destruction than several squadrons together in a huge mêlée.

A large, unalert formation in vics was like a battalion of Fenimore-Cooper's Redcoats marching through the forest as though on parade. A high-flying Schwarm of Bf 109s was like a party of Indians waiting in the undergrowth to ambush the end of the line. They could get three or four aircraft in one pass. If that happened once or twice, squadrons could be wrecked.

Roland Beamont flew Hurricanes with 87 Squadron in France. At 1730 on 16 May, the seventh day of the German offensive, 87 Squadron was ordered up from Lille to patrol the battle area in a wing together with 85 and 504 Squadrons. It was Beamont's third action.

> We made a fine sight as thirty-six Hurricanes formed up in the late afternoon sun in three squadron boxes, line-astern, four sections of vic-threes to a squadron. I was flying No. 2 in the right-hand section of 87 Squadron, leading the wing, and it made one feel brave looking back at so many friendly fighters. And then without fuss or drama about ten Messerschmitt 109s appeared above the left rear flank of our formation out of some high cloud. The Wing leader turned in towards them as fast as a big formation could be wheeled, but the 109s abandoned close drill and, pulling their turn tight, dived one after the other onto the tail sections of the Wing. Their guns streamed smoke and one by one four Hurricanes fell away. None of us fired a shot – some never even saw it happen – and the enemy disengaged, while we continued to give a massive impression of combat strength over the battle area with four less Hurricanes than when we started.[40]

Beamont recounts this through RAF eyes: the 109s did not 'abandon close drill', they never practised it at all. They were flying as a regular Staffel in three Schwärme. Beamont felt safe and strong in the formation. He was only safe because he was at the front – the formation was very exposed, and its size made it an attractive target that was easy to see. It was also unable to manoeuvre. The weak looked strong and the strong looked weak.

Smaller engagements produced higher casualty rates. The percentage of aircraft losses was roughly inversely proportional to the number of participants.

If two lone fighters met, the result would either be joint disengagement or victory for one, a casualty rate of 50%. In a fight involving three or four, one might be shot down, a casualty rate of 25–30%. In a mêlée of 100 aircraft, the most anyone could do was to avoid collisions, watch their tail and take pot-shots at any target which appeared in front of them.[41] Casualty rates were unlikely to reach double figures. At the same time, the number of multiple claims went up because of the confusion, so big dogfights seemed more lethal than they actually were. In 1940, few people had the experience or the insight to understand what was really going on.

In dogfighting small differences in the characteristics of the three main fighters became critical, as pilots tried to get everything they could out of their machines. Whilst 19 Squadron was carrying out flying trials on the Spitfire at Duxford in 1938, Dowding paid them a visit and opined that, although the Hurricane could take on any German bomber, including the Ju 88, the 109 was more than a match for it. He then asked 19 Squadron's C/O, Squadron Leader Cozens, whether the Spitfire could take on the 109. If it could, Fighter Command was prepared for war. The pilots were confident, but only real fighting would tell.[42]

The Bf 109 was not for the claustrophobic.[43] It was so small that movement was restricted, and moving the joystick fully left and right for aileron control especially difficult. At high speeds the controls became very heavy, with a tendency for the ailerons in particular to freeze up because of the pressure of the air flowing over them.* The canopy was hinged and had to be lifted open, and its heavy bars, adding to the space constrictions and the pilot's low, reclining position, made rearward vision very difficult, although this seating position did in fact allow a pilot to withstand about 2 g more before blacking out than a more upright configuration.** Forward and downward view was also very restricted. Its best feature was the well-designed flying panel and controls,[44] with simple, smooth throttle operation, and it was clearly well-engineered, a view confirmed from the outside. An added refinement was the instalment of leading-edge slats on the wings, which extended automatically at low speeds to prevent stalling.

As an airframe design, the Bf 109 had two strengths relative to the Spitfire. It had a superior rate of climb to the Mk I and also climbed at a steeper angle,

* On these two points compare the results of the trials carried out by the R.A.E. at Farnborough on a captured Bf 109E in May 1940: 'Owing to the cramped Me 109 cockpit, a pilot can only apply about 40lb sideways force on the stick, as against 60lb or more possible if he had more room ... The time to 45° bank of 4 seconds at 400 mph, which is excessive for a fighter, classes the aeroplane immediately as very unmanoeuvrable in roll at high speeds' (*Hurricane and Messerschmitt* by Bowyer and Ishoven, p.301).
** Adolf Galland reports how, when first getting into a Bf 109, he made some critical remarks about visibility, only to be informed by the chief test pilot that rearwards visibility would not be needed as no aircraft was fast enough to catch up with the 109 (Galland, Introduction to Martin Caidin, *Me 109*, Purnell's History of World War II Weapons Book no. 4, 1968). This proved to be a little over-optimistic. On the effects of position on blacking out see the deliberations of the RAF's Flying Personnel Research Committee in AIR 6/59.

particularly at low airspeeds.[45] However, it was harder to fly. For some reason, it had no adjustable rudder trimmer. The 109 had strong engine torque, and tended to want to move right. Its rudder was asymmetric, with a camber on one side to counteract this.[46] Nevertheless, to fly it straight at any speed and especially at take-off, the pilot had to keep his foot on the left rudder bar. At high speed, the controls got very heavy and the pressure he had to exert was considerable. This tired him and also made it harder to actually bank left.[47]

However, the most significant technical advantage the 109 enjoyed over both British fighters was due not to the airframe but the engine. The DB 601 was fuel-injected, whilst the Merlin had a float-carburettor. When the Merlin was subject to negative g (creating excessive upward force rather than downward force), which would occur in moving into a dive (a manoeuvre called 'bunting'), the fuel supply to the engine stopped and the engine would cut. The 109 had no such problems. Its pilots quickly discovered that if they bunted suddenly, a pursuing fighter's engine would cut out if it followed. This was only for a few seconds, but it was enough to let the 109 escape. If the Spitfire were to corkscrew to avoid the negative g, it would still take longer to get into the dive than the 109. Thus German pilots had an escape manoeuvre.*

The negative g was unpleasant for the pilot, though, and the 109's classic method of disengagement was a half-roll and dive. As it did so, the engine gave off a belch of black smoke, leading to false claims by inexperienced RAF pilots.** By the same token, the standard escape for a Spitfire or Hurricane was a corkscrew dive, which exploited the aircraft's higher rate of roll. The 109 could go straight down faster, but had trouble following a twisting dive.[48] One variant on this a British pilot could use was to half-roll into a steep dive and pull out suddenly. If his pursuer followed the dive he could not pull out as fast because of the heaviness of his elevator, and the Spitfire would be climbing away above him. When the Royal Aircraft Establishment discovered this during their evaluation of the 109, they recommended that British pilots try diving and pulling out at low level, and watch their opponent fly into the ground.[49]

---

* It was only once fighting began that the importance of this feature became apparent to Rolls-Royce. The carburettor had the advantage of introducing fuel to the engine before the supercharger, increasing the supercharger's performance as well. The DB601 sacrificed a loss of supercharger power (affecting high altitude performance) for the advantages of fuel injection. The first solution to the float carburettor problem was devised by one Miss Shilling of the RAE, who invented a restricter orifice which stopped all the fuel from being flung upwards in a negative-g dive. This inevitably became known to the pilots as 'Miss Shilling's orifice'. Later, the Bendix Strömberg carburettor was put into production and eliminated the problem completely. See *Forty Years of the Spitfire*, ed. East & Cheeseman, Proceedings of the Mitchell Memorial Symposium, Southampton, Royal Aeronautical Society 1976, pp. 86 and 100–101.

** Novices could make bigger mistakes than that. Colin Gray, a New Zealander who ended the war a Wing Commander with twenty-seven claims, reports that in his first combat he was shocked to see black smoke coming from his wings and thought he had been hit. He pulled round to find his attacker, but then realised that it was cordite smoke from his own guns. (Price, *Spitfire*, p.174). That gives some indication of how much combat training the RAF gave its pilots before sending them to meet the Luftwaffe.

On the other hand, the 109 could also use its low-speed climb advantage to get away, with the steep angle making it even harder for a Spitfire to keep it in its sights.

With its narrow undercarriage and strong torque, the Bf 109 was no lady. She was a potential man-eater, said to have killed 1,500 learners in the first two years of the war, most of them during take-off or landing.[50] But once in the air in the hands of an experienced pilot, she was perfectly suited to the tactics the Luftwaffe adopted. With its high rate of climb and high diving speed, the Bf 109 was ideally suited to hunting trips at 30,000 feet, bouncing a victim in one pass and then away. It could not be caught on a dive. Small wonder that this relatively safe manner of deployment was the one the fighter units lobbied for.

The Spitfire was almost as small as the Bf 109 and had similarly restricted forward vision, though this was only a practical problem on the ground, requiring taxiing to be done in a snaking movement. Rearward vision was poor, but better than the Bf 109's, and the view through the sliding canopy was also better, despite the distortion produced by its curvature.* Canopies were polished all the time, for in the air a scratch or speck of dirt could be mistaken for an aircraft. Small rear-view mirrors, like a car's, were fixed above the front windscreen in an attempt to improve the view behind. They were about the size of make-up mirrors, and if a pilot did see an attacker in it, it generally meant he was about to be shot down.

Stick movement was freer than in the 109, though as with the Messerschmitt the ailerons tended to freeze at high speed until the Spitfire test pilot Jeffrey Quill had their fabric covering replaced with metal. The lay-out of the instruments was inferior to the 109,[51] and on the Mk I the pilot had to cope with a hand-change after take-off to pump up the undercarriage.

The Spitfire was slightly faster than the 109 at low level, the knowledge of which made Bf 109 pilots particularly anxious as they wave-hopped to France after their mission. Its deficits at high altitude were made up for in the Mk II by the improved supercharging and extra 100 or so hp of the Merlin XII, but production of the Mk II only began in August 1940.

Despite this slight under-performance at high altitude, the Spitfire was quite as capable of delivering a lethal bounce as a Bf 109. In its case, however, it was not one pass and away, but one pass and stay, for the Spitfire was a superb dogfighter.

In the dogfight, both the Spitfire and Hurricane could turn inside the Bf 109 because of their lower wing loadings. 109 pilots trying to hold them in

* Day judges the 109 to be 'a good 100% worse' in this respect (ibid.). Later in the war, Spitfires were fitted with 'tear-drop' bubble canopies and the rear fuselage cut down to improve vision. The Air Fighting Development Unit flew a Mk VIII modified in this way in August 1943 and reported on the results with enthusiasm (see Price, *The Spitfire Story*, pp. 178–9). From 1944, an increasing number of Spitfires, mainly the Griffon-engined Marks, were given tear-drop hoods. In 1940 the manufacturing methods for these canopies had not yet been mastered.

similar turns bore the risk of losing their wings as the pressure built up. This was suggested by experience and confirmed in a comparative test on a captured Bf 109E conducted by the Royal Aircraft Establishment at Farnborough in May 1940. Pilots' standard reaction when a dogfight began was to turn.[52]

Leutnant Erwin Leykauf, who flew with JG 54 during the battle, maintains that the Bf 109 had a smaller turning radius than the Spitfire, and claims to have shot down six Spitfires by out-turning them. He comments that many Bf 109 pilots would not go far enough, losing their nerve when the leading-edge slats came out with a bang, thinking they had been hit. For the old hands, he says, manoeuvring only began when the slats were out.[53] Len Deighton has even produced a diagram, based on calculations, claiming to show that the Bf 109 could turn tighter than the Spitfire or even the Hurricane. Leykauf's experiences were probably against inexperienced British pilots who did not fly their machines to their limits.[54] Under realistic combat conditions, if a 109 behind a Spitfire stayed with it in a turn, the Spitfire could be on its tail within a good shooting distance (250 yards) after seven and a half turns, which would take about two minutes. A Hurricane could do so in less.

The Hurricane was by far the largest of the three fighters and the pilot sat higher up. He had a better forward view and plenty of room to swing his joystick around. However, the Hurricane was between 10 and 30 mph slower than the Bf 109E, depending on altitude. One pilot has commented: 'a lead of 10 mph was a great advantage, one of 20 was usually commanding, and one of 30 or more indicated obsolescence in the slower aircraft'.[55]

During the Battle, Park tried whenever possible to send Spitfires against the 109s whilst Hurricanes attacked the bombers. Excellent gun platform that it was, the Hurricane, which equipped two-thirds of Fighter Command squadrons in 1940, accounted for the majority of the bombers lost by the Luftwaffe. It was at its best at about 15,000 feet, which is where the Heinkels and Dorniers were mostly to be found, but at high altitude the performance gap with the 109 became very dangerous.[56]

However, encounters between Hurricanes and 109s were numerous and the Hurricanes were not always worsted. This was because most of the fighting took place below 20,000 feet and a lot of it was dogfighting, where the Hurricane's tighter turn made a difference. Clearly, Messerschmitt pilots always tried to bounce. If they succeeded, their chances of success were no different whether they were attacking Spitfires or Hurricanes. Opportunities to bounce Hurricanes were proportionately more frequent because of the Hurricane's lower rate of climb.[57]

If the bounce failed, however, and the fighting descended, as it tended to, the odds were more even. The 109 could generally get away if it wanted to, but its job was to protect the bombers as well as shoot down fighters. In order to do that it had to mix it with Hurricanes and then its opponent was not so very different from the Spitfire, and the tactics on each side were similar. Hurricanes which were attacked usually turned or corkscrew-dived.

A low-flying 109 disengaging from a dogfight or running for home with low fuel could just as easily be surprised by Hurricanes as by Spitfires, though Hurricanes could not chase and catch them. Perhaps the greatest factor working in Hurricane pilots' favour was the widespread belief of their opponents that the Hurricane was easy meat. It made them overconfident and opened up room for mistakes.

22. SUMMER'S LEASE

The battle, which re-opened in earnest on 24 August, was now to all intents and purposes fought out between Park and Kesselring. It was essentially a battle of attrition, which in itself bears witness to the fact that Eagle had failed. Kesselring went all out to destroy Fighter Command in the air and on the ground, and for the first time the selection of targets showed some sense of purpose. Almost every significant raid was directed against an airfield and, as the Germans slowly grew wiser, they tended to be Fighter Command airfields.

Kesselring's main constraint was his fighter force. It was about the same size as Fighter Command, and used just as intensively – the German pilots flying up to three or four sorties a day – as that of their British opponents.[1] It also had range limitations. When Kesselring targeted the airfields north of the Thames – Hornchurch, North Weald and Debden – he had to make a difficult trade-off between using Bf 109s at the limit of their range and exposing his bombers. If Bf 109s were used and got involved in dogfights anywhere much beyond the Thames Estuary, they would either have to break off the action after no more than about ten minutes or risk having to ditch in the Channel. The idea of losing a whole Gruppe because it ran out of fuel and had to ditch was as much of a nightmare for Göring as it was for his pilots. From the earliest discussions, he had always stressed the need for the fighter pilots to take no risks with their fuel. They needed little encouragement to keep their eyes on the red light that went on in the cockpit when they had only 15–20 minutes flying time left, meaning it was time to go home.[2]

On the other hand, Kesselring knew what would happen if he left the task of bomber protection to the Bf 110s, and Göring had explicitly demanded that they be used sparingly. Kesselring faced a brutal choice. He could either lose bombers and Zerstörer or lose fighters. He had been ordered not to do the former. If he did the latter, he would blunt and possibly even break the only instrument he had which could destroy Fighter Command. The risk of that was high – every stricken plane was a lost pilot. Unlike the British, he did not even have a large reserve of aircraft. He could not afford to lose men or machines.

The crucial elements of 11 Group's ground organisation were the Operations Rooms at the Sector Stations. Without them, Park could not control his fighters because none of the information from the radar system could be translated into orders to scramble and got out to the squadrons. Taking out an Operations Room meant either a direct hit on what was one of the smallest and least conspicuous buildings on the airfield, or cutting off the power supply, which, with a bit of luck, extensive cratering around it might achieve. Kesselring was effectively aiming blind at six single-storey brick buildings of some 2,000 – 2,800 sq. ft surrounded by blast walls, located at Kenley, Biggin Hill, Hornchurch, North Weald, Debden and Northolt – and a concrete bunker at Tangmere. He might, had he known about them, also have aimed at Fighter Command and 11 Group Headquarters themselves, but both were well underground and nothing in the Luftwaffe's arsenal had any prospect of destroying them.

In planning his attacks Kesselring followed the principles agreed with his Chief on the 19th, and tried everything: large and small bomber forces, sneak attacks, strafing runs, feints, large forces which then split, saturation, multiple attacks, follow-ups – everything. He may not have been a career airman but, as he was later to show the Allies in Italy, he was a very good general indeed. He was clever, wily and imaginative. It is doubtful whether anyone else in the Luftwaffe could have run the battle better than he did. But in Park he met his match.

Kesselring's forces were gathered by the evening of the 23rd, and when the 24th dawned clear, he began with raids on Dover and Manston.

Manston was being used as a forward base by 264 Squadron, which had moved from 12 Group to Hornchurch on the 22nd. Erprobungsgruppe 210 had hit Manston again the same day. 600 squadron had moved to Hornchurch, 65 Squadron were in action on the other side of the Channel, and 54 Squadron, who also used Manston more than they would have liked, were absent as well. Although there were no casualties, some buildings were damaged and a temporary armoury set on fire. The firemen who extinguished the blaze were all commended for bravery.

After the demise of 141 Squadron in July, 264 were the only remaining squadron operating the Defiant, led by Squadron Leader Philip Hunter. 'He was a brilliant pilot,' one of his men has said of him. 'Everyone thought the sun shone on him. He seemed to be invulnerable.'[3] They were scrambled at about midday to meet the raiders, Ju 88s from KG76. Hunter was last seen trying to pursue a Ju 88 out towards France. Two others failed to return.

The raiders, however, did return. They attacked Manston again in the afternoon, and communications were cut. This was the sixth time it had been attacked. Appropriately, perhaps, it was Erprobungsgruppe 210, the unit which had put the first nail into Manston's coffin, that also hammered home the last.[4] There were no living quarters left and unexploded bombs littered the place. Communications were restored two hours later, and two firemen who kept water supplied with a hand-pump next to an unexploded bomb were awarded the George Medal.[5] But Fighter Command decided to evacuate the remaining personnel and only use Manston as an emergency landing-ground. Al Deere, along with the rest of 54 Squadron, was heartily relieved, and could not understand why it had not been abandoned sooner. The remaining Defiants returned to Hornchurch badly shaken by Hunter's death, and soon after they arrived discovered that Hornchurch was Kesselring's second target of the day. They managed to get up just as the bombs started falling. Two of them collided in the rush, and another was shot down. A short while later, 54 Squadron landed. It looked as if the Luftwaffe knew they had left Manston for Hornchurch, and were following them.[6]

As this was going on, another raid approached North Weald. About twenty bombers got through 11 Group's defences and hit messes, married quarters and stores. At about 1600, with all his units engaged, Park called on Leigh-Mallory to cover his airfields north of the Thames. Only 19 Squadron arrived, but they were flying the Spitfires armed with 20mm cannon, and most of them jammed. They did little good.

Park was not amused. He heard a story that Leigh-Mallory had ordered his squadrons to form a wing over Duxford before going in to action, but somehow nobody quite understood, and by the time they got over Essex the raiders had gone. 310 Squadron were Czechs and had only just become operational. Their English was adequate, but only just. It had been a cock-up.

There was another cock-up over at 10 Group. The Mobile Reserve Station at Bembridge detected something, but the plot was unclear. Expecting Stukas again, the controllers sent 609 Squadron in at 5,000 feet to slaughter them as they came out of their dives. There were no Stukas now, and 609 found themselves stuck between an AA barrage and the escorts which were up-sun at 10,000 feet, ready to slaughter them. They got away by the skin of their teeth. Portsmouth was bombed.

Night raiders were still operating more or less with impunity. They could not do any damage of military significance because they could not aim accurately, but they were able to cause destruction and kill civilians. All Fighter Command had were a few Blenheims and the odd Hurricane and, without airborne radar, successes were rare. Night flying was not for novices. Sailor Malan had made the headlines when he shot down two Heinkels on the night of 18/19 June. Just after midnight on 24 August, Sandy Sanders took off from Kenley and shot down a Heinkel of KG55 over Hastings. Park sent him a congratulatory telegram. He was earmarked to help to develop effective night-fighting techniques.

The next morning, Kesselring sent some Staffeln of Bf 109s to fly up and down the Sussex coast, but Park ignored them. In the afternoon, Sperrle attacked Warmwell and, although the defenders went in higher this time, some bombers got through, damaging some hangars and the sick bay. Kesselring launched a final sally in the evening, met by an exhausted 32 Squadron, which lost another pilot in exchange for two bombers. They landed with eight men left. They were sent north two days later.

Early on the morning of the 26th, Luftwaffe reconnaissance aircraft saw a lot of fighters on the ground at Kenley and Biggin Hill, so Kesselring decided to go for them. A big fight started over north Kent during which the recently-arrived 616 Squadron were bounced and lost seven aircraft, with two pilots dead and four wounded. Hugh Dundas had been lucky again, though it did not feel like it. He was not there because he had himself been bounced and shot down on the 22nd, three days after arriving at Kenley from Leconfield. He had been the 'weaver'. He was sitting in hospital in Canterbury when he heard that two of his close friends were dead and several others badly burned. One of the dead, George Moberley, had visited Hugh in hospital the night before to tell him he would be killed, and that he wanted him to have his belongings.[7]

264 entered the same fray as 616 and lost three more Defiants, though they took some Dorniers with them. Nevertheless, the defenders stopped the raids, which turned back because the escorting Bf 109s had used up too much fuel during the fighting.

In the afternoon a new raid developed, heading for Debden and Hornchurch, but Park sent everything he had against it, and all but half a dozen heroic Dorniers also turned away as the Bf 109s' red warning lights came on, and they had to go back. 85 Squadron made a notable début in the south, as Peter Townsend led them in a head-on attack with his Flight Commander Patrick Woods-Scawen just behind. They claimed eight and one 'probable' for the loss of one Hurricane. The new Canadian squadron, declared operational on the 19th, also charged in on their first action, but lost three aircraft and a pilot.

This last raid on the two northern airfields caused recriminations on both sides. Park had called for support from 12 Group again, and again they were late. It turned out that 310 Squadron had the wrong radio crystals in some aircraft. They had nevertheless engaged, losing two Hurricanes and two more damaged whilst claiming three bombers. 19 Squadron never found the raiders. On the other side of the Channel, Kesselring faced anger from his bomber leaders. They claimed he had used too many Bf 109s on sweeps over Kent and not enough on protecting them. They also claimed that the Bf 109s they did get avoided combat in order to preserve fuel and seemed more concerned about protecting the Bf 110 escorts than the bombers. There were calls for increased use of Bf 109s as close escorts.

At 1600, Sperrle launched what was to be his last major daylight raid for three weeks. He sent 55 Heinkels of KG55 and all his fighters against Portsmouth. It was repulsed by five 11 Group and three 10 Group squadrons. Henceforth, Luftflotte 3 concentrated on night bombing against factories and ports as far north as Liverpool. Fighter Command still had little opposition to offer in darkness.

One of the Squadrons sent to meet Sperrle's raid was 234. Bob Doe had got ahead of the rest of the Squadron and found himself alone, when he spotted a gaggle of about fifty Bf 109s, probably JG53. Knowing that numbers were trumped by surprise and that he would be difficult to see, he climbed above them and dived on the rear of the formation in a perfect bounce. Opening fire at 300 yards, he hit his target, but his target's slipstream hit him and his engine cut. Aware that the other fifty Messerschmitts were beginning to take an interest in him, he continued his dive until his engine restarted, keeping an eye on his damaged victim, who had turned away towards France. His diving speed enabled him to avoid the others and with his Merlin restarted he pursued the lone 109, keeping a careful eye on his fuel gauge. At low level the Spitfire was faster, and he slowly caught up with his prey. Getting very close, he opened up. His target spewed out coolant, the undercarriage dropped and several pieces flew off it. He returned to base feeling rather pleased with himself, as well he might. He had just enough fuel left to taxi to dispersal.[8] Eleven days after his first combat, the worst pilot in the squadron had taken on odds of fifty-to-one and triumphed. The spring chicken had become a hawk.

Park had been concerned about getting all the squadrons his controllers scrambled to engage. Poor visibility on the previous days had frustrated some units and left those that had met the raiders outnumbered. Accordingly, he issued Instruction No. 6, in which he asked engaging squadrons to call out their position and the size of the raid before attacking, so that others could be summoned. It was to take effect from the following day.[9]

There was in fact little activity on the 27th. However, Park gave expression to his frustration over the events of the 26th by issuing a terse instruction to his controllers to go through Fighter Command Headquarters whenever they needed support from 12 Group. His Instruction is pointedly and provocatively worded, starkly contrasting the co-operative behaviour of 10 Group with that of Leigh-Mallory, whom he blamed by implication for the bombing of North Weald, Debden and Hornchurch. He was willing to put up with the slight delay inevitably involved in going through Bentley Priory, he stated, in order to ensure the supporting squadrons were where they were needed, when they were needed.

Park copied the instruction to Evill. He averred that not receiving assistance that had been promised shook the confidence of station commanders, and asked for Fighter Command's co-operation. Evill diplomatically sent a note to his controllers asking them to do as 11 Group asked, as 'AOC 11 Group has represented that it may on occasions be more satisfactory to him to ask for this support to be definitely arranged by the Command Controller.'[10] Trouble was brewing.

The 28th finally saw the end of the Defiant as a daylight interceptor.

Shortly after 0800 the familiar build-up was detected over Calais. As the raid crossed the coast, it split, the Dorniers of I./KG3 making for Eastchurch and the Heinkels of III./KG53 for Rochford. The 33 bombers were accompanied by 120 Bf 109s. Four squadrons of fighters were scrambled, including the Defiants of 264, who spotted the Heinkels. They did not spot Adolf Galland, now Geschwaderkommodore of JG26, leading his old III. Gruppe up in the sun. He bounced them. Three of them fell, including their new leader, S/L Garvin, one force-landed at Petham, south of Canterbury, and two limped home.

III./KG53 got through to Rochford, but did little damage, and I./KG3 managed to drop a hundred bombs on Eastchurch without putting it out of action.

At 1235, thirty Dorniers appeared over Rochford again, and left about thirty craters. The three Defiant crews who had got back took off again with murder in their hearts, believing one of their colleagues had been machine-gunned whilst on his parachute, but they were too late, which may have been as well for them.[11] When they got back, the five serviceable Defiants remaining on strength were transferred to the 12 Group airfield of Kirton-in-Lindsey in Lincolnshire.

The third raid of the day was a trick. Five Gruppen of Bf 110s and six Gruppen of Bf 109s imitated bombers and flew up the Thames Estuary. Six squadrons intercepted, losing five aircraft, but German fighter losses that day were also heavy. Fourteen Bf 109s failed to return, both Galland and Mölders losing the adjutants of their Geschwader. 85 Squadron had been the first to attack, and managed to get in a bounce on JG51. They claimed six for no loss. They probably did indeed get four, with Townsend and Patrick Woods-Scawen responsible for one each and the Squadron's star pilot, Sergeant Sam Allard, getting two.

Park lost fifteen fighters, including the three Defiants and two more shot down by their own side. One of the unhappy pair of pilots attacked by their friends was Alan Deere, who used the eighth of his nine lives that day. He baled out near Detling, from where he was flown straight back to Hornchurch, along with the Defiants' new leader, Squadron Leader Garvin. He has written of his mood at the time:

> The strain had almost reached breaking point. The usually good-natured George was quiet and irritable; Colin, by nature thin-faced, was noticeably more hollow-cheeked; Desmond, inclined to be weighty, was reduced to manageable proportions; and I, though I had no way of knowing how I appeared to the others, was all on edge and practically jumped out of my skin when someone shouted unexpectedly over the R/T. But still we continued to operate – there was no alternative.'[12]

As George Gribble had said, they were in fact all desperately wearied by 'their constant challenge and mortal danger'. So was every pilot in 11 Group. What

Deere describes are the symptoms of combat exhaustion, which is not tiredness. At some point men in this condition will break. Deere thought that, with no leader and only four experienced pilots, 54 Squadron should have been withdrawn then. In fact they carried on until 3 September. Deciding when to pull squadrons out was a fine judgement.

54 Squadron were getting new neighbours, for, as the Defiants left Hornchurch, 603 Squadron were flying in. When Richard Hillary and Peter Pease arrived they found that the rest of the squadron had already been in action, unfortunately against this fighter feint. Three Spitfires and their pilots were missing already, and a fourth was damaged with its pilot in hospital. It is possible that some of these newcomers were responsible for the attack on Al Deere. At all events, 603 Squadron filed three claims.

Ironically, it was at this time that the Luftwaffe's Jagdgeschwader were being issued with bright yellow paint and instructions to paint their cowlings, rudders and wingtips. The pilots were not told why, and speculated that they were special markings for the invasion.[13] In fact it was an aid to aircraft recognition, to make sure that mistakes such as those which had just cost Fighter Command two aircraft did not happen to them. Given the numbers of aircraft now in the sky, avoiding friendly fire took precedence over camouflage. British pilots who saw the new colour-schemes quickly decided that they marked out élite units, which flattered not only their opponents but them too, as it was surely more honourable to be shot down by an élite pilot than by an ordinary one. It was convenient that all the enemy fighters belonged to élite units. Henceforth 'yellow-nosed bastards' began to rival the more traditional 'snappers' as a sobriquet for Bf 109s.

The 28th was also the day Churchill chose for a visit to the defences of the south coast, including Manston. He did not like what he saw there, and minuted Sinclair, Newall and Ismay that night.

'I was much concerned,' he wrote, 'to find that, although more than four clear days have passed since it was last raided, the greater part of the craters on the landing ground remain unfilled, and the aerodrome was barely serviceable.' He berated the 'feeble method of repairing damage' and demanded that the '150 people available to work' be given the equipment needed. He expected craters to be filled in within twenty-four hours and recommended the use of well-equipped mobile units to do so.[14] There he left the matter. Churchill was having no truck with the degrading of aerodromes to emergency status only. The man who had made the call to 'fight on the beaches' was not going to abandon any airfields, no matter how prudent it might be.

Kesselring did nothing till mid-afternoon on the 29th. In fact, as he well knew, he needed to keep up constant pressure, and this pause might have been a sign that the strain was telling on his fighter pilots. He had nothing in reserve.

As if to prove the point, when he did make his move at 1500, it turned out to be a small group of bombers acting as bait for almost the whole of his fighter force, over 500 Bf 109s. This was taking the principle of high fighter-to-bomber ratios *ad absurdum*, and Park was not fooled. Despite having thirteen squadrons in the air, he ordered them not to engage and, though he was too late to avoid some dogfighting, Kesselring did not get the big mêlée he was seeking. 85 Squadron was badly hit this time, losing three Hurricanes, and 603, having no luck at all, being scrambled against fighters for the second time in a row, suffered damage to two Spitfires and lost two more that evening to free-hunting 109s. Richard Hillary was one of the lucky ones, though. He was flying number two to Brian Carbury, who opened up on the leader of a Staffel of Bf 109s. When the Messerschmitt turned to avoid Carbury, Hillary got it, and landed feeling satisfied 'with the essential rightness of it all'. It had seemed a fair fight.[15] On the German side, JG3 had a particularly bad day, losing seven Bf 109s in all and another damaged.

The next day, 30 August, Kesselring began with some probes, and then sent over a series of multiple attacks of fighters, followed by escorted bombers crossing the coast every 20–30 minutes. Fighter Command had come to expect three attacks a day separated by intervals of a few hours. Now the effect was to saturate the defences and make the target unclear. By midday the whole of 11 Group was airborne and 48 Observer Posts reported combat overhead. Kesselring hoped that by creating confusion raiders could slip through to bomb and the Bf 109s could get in some bounces.

Despite losing five Heinkels from KG1 in a raid on Farnborough airfield, the Luftwaffe had some success of both kinds in the morning. A Staffel of Ju 88s eluded 19 Squadron, sent from 12 Group to patrol Biggin Hill, to drop their payloads without loss, but the bombs fell mainly on the village rather than the airfield. Some forty to fifty bombs put Detling out of action until the following morning. In the air, some 109s managed to bounce 222 Squadron, which had arrived in Hornchurch from Kirton-in-Lindsey the previous day, and were flying about in vics with a weaver above. The weaver disappeared at about 1210 and force-landed in Rainham. He had been very lucky. Others were not.

253 Squadron had arrived at Kenley the day before from Prestwick, changing places with 615 Squadron. 253 were not very experienced, so a few old hands of 615 were left behind to 'look after them', as 615's Operations Record Book puts it. One of the old hands was Sandy Sanders, who had met a girl at Kenley and so lobbied to stay in the dangerous south. 253 were ordered off at 1050 when it looked as if Kenley was under threat. Twenty minutes later they tangled with a mixture of fighters and bombers over Redhill and lost three Hurricanes and two pilots.

253 had transferred south with one supernumerary. Tom Gleave had commanded them at Dunkirk, but on 20 July he was promoted to Wing Commander and handed the unit over to his former pupil Harold Starr. Dowding had by then fixed the maximum age of a squadron commander at twenty-six, but Gleave remonstrated with his AOC, Saul, and got permission to

stay with the squadron as a pilot despite his advanced age of thirty-two. Shortly after Starr had led the bulk of the Squadron off on their first combat mission, Gleave was ordered to lead a flight off to patrol Maidstone. Just before midday, he ran into a massive gaggle of Bf 109s. He entered the formation of enemy fighters and began firing at the plentiful targets all around. When he landed back at Kenley unscathed, he said he had got four Messerschmitts. The authorities did not believe him, eventually allowing him two probables and two possibles.[16]

The Germans had a piece of luck that morning when one of their bombs severed the main electricity grid, putting the whole of the Kent radar system off the air. Throughout the rest of the day, the attackers were thrusting into a breach they did not know was there.

Amongst them were Erprobungsgruppe 210, now temporarily led by the Commander of the 1st Staffel, Martin Lutz.[17] Their target was Biggin Hill. At about six o'clock in the evening they came in at about 1,000 feet taking the defences by surprise and dropping sixteen bombs. They destroyed one hangar containing two aircraft, the workshops armoury and stores, the cookhouse and NAAFI, the transport yard, and the Sergeants' mess, barracks and the WAAF quarters. One of the bombs landed on top of an air-raid shelter, killing thirty-nine airmen. The telephone lines, gas, water and electricity mains were all cut off. The station went down and Hornchurch took over control of the Sector until emergency power was established.[18] Biggin Hill had escaped lightly so far. Now its trial was to begin. Erprobungsgruppe 210 slipped unmolested back to Calais-Marck.

At about four in the afternoon a raid was reported to the north of the Thames Estuary. There were about sixty Heinkels of I./KG1 and II./KG53 and, as it was too far for Bf 109s, their escorts were drawn from II./ZG2, II./ZG26 and II./ZG76. It looked as if they were after the airfields again. 11 Group called for support, and 12 Group began scrambling the squadrons at Duxford. In fact they were after two factories. The raid split up, with I./KG1 heading north for the Vauxhall works at Luton and II./KG53 west for the Handley-Page factory at Radlett, which was producing the new Halifax heavy bomber. They did nothing to stop production at Radlett, but did cause casualties at the motor works in Luton. The raiders lost six Heinkels and five Bf 110s, with damage to several others.

One of the squadrons to intercept them was 242 Squadron from 12 Group. This was a largely Canadian unit which had returned rebellious and demoralised from a mauling in France, so on 23 June Leigh-Mallory had appointed Douglas Bader as their new C/O, with the task of turning them around. He had restored their morale to the point that it was now very high, and they wanted to get into action. They had been declared operational on 9 July but had hardly seen a German aircraft since then, although neighbouring squadrons, particularly 19 Squadron, had. Bader himself was boiling with frustration. The 30th was their first action as a squadron.

The controller asked Bader to patrol North Weald at 15,000 feet in response to 11 Group's request. They saw a large German formation to their left stepped up between 12 and 20,000 feet, and dived on the lower group, which were Bf 110s. Bader had the late afternoon sun behind him and was higher – just what he wanted. There were no Bf 109s. When Bader got back his men were elated and Leigh-Mallory congratulated him. They claimed twelve definite kills. With more fighters, Bader told Leigh-Mallory, he could have shot down even more. Leigh-Mallory agreed, and suggested a wing.[19]

242 were probably partly responsible for a couple of the Bf 110s.[20] Bader's men all got home after a very successful first day, even if not quite as successful as they thought. Bader may not have been aware, but the raid was attacked by five 11 Group squadrons as well as his own, and it was they who accounted for the remaining nine German aircraft destroyed. 242 Squadron nevertheless got a message of congratulation for their twelve kills from no less than the Secretary of State for Air and the Chief of the Air Staff that evening.[21]

Other first days were less triumphant. After their troubles in the morning, 253 Squadron lost another two planes and a pilot that afternoon, bringing their losses for the day to five Hurricanes and three pilots. 222 Squadron's first day ended predictably. They lost six Spitfires, four of them in a dogfight over Kent in the early evening in which one of their pilots was killed, and three more damaged.

One more squadron made its debut that day, though it was unscheduled. Squadron Leader Kellett had taken the Poles of 303 Squadron's B-Flight out on a training flight to practise interceptions with some Blenheims. They found the Blenheims over St Albans at 1635, when the raids on Radlett and Luton were in progress. Flying Officer Paszkiewicz spotted some of the raiders under attack nearby, and waggled his wings in front of Kellett to attract his attention. Kellett had seen them too, and decided to turn his practice flight from an interception into an escort mission, with the aim of getting the Blenheims back to safety as quickly as possible. Paszkiewicz wanted none of that, so when his leader ignored him, he dived on the raiders and hit one. When he joined his six colleagues back at Northolt claiming a Do 17, they were cock-a-hoop over it, and Kellett decided to ignore the breach of discipline and ask for the squadron to be declared operational. They were, and it was a decision Dowding never regretted.[22]

The next morning, Saturday, 31 August, the Kent radar was back on the air and picked up four hostile formations at 0800. Kesselring was trying out a trick again, for they were all fighters. As this was realised, the intercepting squadrons were ordered back, but the inexperienced Canadians of 1 Squadron RCAF were too slow and were bounced out of the sun, losing three aircraft.

Even experience did not save 56 Squadron. They engaged a raid of over 200 aircraft over Essex, but were bounced by III./JG26 and III./ZG26 and lost four aircraft, including those of both of their veteran Flight Commanders. Flight Lieutenant Innes Westmacott baled out wounded and was hospitalised, but Flight Lieutenant Percy Weaver was killed. His DFC was announced that evening. 56 Squadron made only one claim. They had been in action since July and were very tired. They moved out to Boscombe Down the next day.

Part of the raid 56 Squadron had engaged headed for North Weald whilst another split off for Debden. 111 Squadron, which was now operating from the Debden satellite of Castle Camps, engaged the force attacking its new Sector Station, which was made up of the Dorniers of II./KG2 and some Bf 110 escorts. Both sets of raiders got through. They dropped about 100 bombs on Debden, damaging the sick quarters, some barracks and four Hurricanes, but leaving its operations unaffected. Despite the size of the raid, North Weald suffered little damage. As it withdrew, the Debden force was attacked by 257 Squadron, led by Flight Lieutenant Beresford, based at the North Weald satellite of Martlesham Heath near the Suffolk coast. They got a Bf 110, but at the cost of two Hurricanes, one of whose pilots was killed and the other wounded. However, one far more experienced 11 Group squadron, 601, which had been moved from Tangmere to Debden on 19 August, managed to bounce V./LG1 on the way back, and shot down two Bf 110s at the cost of one damaged Hurricane.[23]

Further north, a separate raid was making for Duxford, the first time a 12 Group Sector Station had been targeted. At 0810, the Duxford controller, Wing Commander Woodhall, sent 19 Squadron to meet them and asked 11 Group for help, as neither 242 nor 310 Squadrons were up to state and able to take off.[24] 19 Squadron, operating from the Duxford satellite of Fowlmere, tried to intercept with their unreliable cannon-armed Spitfires but lost three of them and one pilot for only two claims. Park sent in 1 Squadron from Northolt, who lost a Hurricane and also made several claims.

It was only 0900, and things were not going well for Fighter Command. Kesselring maintained the pressure, moving it south. A group of escorted Dorniers bombed Eastchurch, doing a bit more damage to buildings, and a fighter sweep strafed Detling with little effect. But these moves were just to get the defences to commit before the real threat emerged: one wave of heavily escorted Dorniers aimed at Biggin Hill, and Erprobungsgruppe 210 heading, this time deliberately, for Croydon. There was no worrying now about the niceties of whether or not Croydon was part of London. Kesselring had decided to let his fighter-bomber specialists finish the job they had accidentally begun.

Peter Townsend's 85 Squadron were just taking off from Croydon when Erprobungsgruppe 210 arrived. Twelve raiders came in low and damaged a hangar. Townsend and his men pursued them, thirsting for revenge. 'I was so blind with fury that I felt things must end badly for me,' he has written. 'But I was too weary and too strung up to care.'[25] They got a Bf 110 which crashed on Wrotham Hill, possibly having been hit by Patrick Woods-Scawen, and damaged two others, but three of their Hurricanes were shot down, including Townsend's. He landed in a small wood near Hawkhurst with a bad pain in his left foot. After a quick patching-up and a pint at the Royal Oak, he was taken to Croydon General Hospital and had a cannon splinter removed from his foot and a toe amputated. He stayed there for two weeks.[26] Now he was out of it – another experienced leader gone. Patrick and Sam Allard now had to lead the squadron.

The Biggin Hill raid was carried out at the conventional height of 12,000 feet. The bombs hit the living quarters again, and made some more craters. Everyone available was put to work filling them in so that the station's squadrons could land. 610 Squadron were just leaving for Acklington that day, to be replaced by 72, who were unlikely to be impressed. The resident 79 Squadron had themselves only arrived on the 25th.

As the raiders left, they were attacked with particular savagery by 253 Squadron. Starr had taken them out that morning to intercept one of the early raids. Starr's Hurricane had been hit and he had baled out, but was found dead with a bullet through the heart. Word got back to Gleave that his old pupil had been murdered while dangling on his parachute. In command of 253 once more, Gleave wanted vengeance, and, as with Townsend, his anger made him careless. As he launched a climbing attack on the bombers, a Bf 109 hit him from below and behind, and his Hurricane burst into flames. Tom Gleave baled out on his second day of combat to become Archibald McIndoe's Chief Guinea Pig at the East Grinstead burns unit, where he was to spend many months.

Hornchurch was next. The raiders had come in over Dungeness in parallel with those attacking Biggin Hill. The controllers got somewhat confused when they carried on past Biggin Hill, and haze prevented the Observer Corps from getting a good view of their heading. When they got to Hornchurch, the long-suffering 54 Squadron were still on the ground. 603 Squadron were 'released', and Richard Hillary was walking across the airfield towards dispersal. Like 85 Squadron at Croydon, 54 took off with the bombs falling, but the rear section was unlucky. A bomb burst amongst them, throwing them back onto the ground. One of them was Alan Deere, who used up his ninth life ploughing a hundred yards along the runway upside down, hanging on his straps with the top of his helmet scraping along the ground. He continued to hang there with the smell of petrol growing ever stronger, until the pilot behind him, who had also crashed, levered him out of the cockpit. None of the three colleagues were badly hurt and all flew again the next day. Their Spitfires were write-offs.[27] Richard saw it all happen as he ran towards a shelter, thinking, 'That's the shortest flight he's ever taken,' as Deere hit the ground. Taking stock of the actual damage caused, he thought it to be 'striking proof of the inefficacy of their attempts to wipe out our advance fighter aerodromes'.[28]

Most of the bombs had burst around the edge of the airfield. The barracks' windows blew in, but operations were unaffected. The raiders had bombed from 15,000 feet, from which height hits on anything vital were mainly a matter of luck.

In the afternoon some snap attacks on coastal radar stations put them off the air for a few hours, in preparation for a second round against Hornchurch and Biggin Hill.

A mixture of Ju 88s and Bf 110s dropped a few bombs on Hornchurch, destroying two Spitfires. This time, 603 Squadron were scrambled and both Richard Hillary and his quiet, thoughtful friend Peter Pease scored hits on Bf 110s. Brian Carbury claimed no less than five, which, coming from most pilots, would have been dismissed as exuberance. However, it was already clear that Carbury was a man to take seriously, and, unlikely though the total might be, all five were confirmed.

Biggin Hill was the object of a low-level attack at about 1800. A Staffel of Dorniers of the low-level specialists III./KG76 put in their first appearance since Kenley two weekends before.[29] They hit two of the three remaining hangars, and cut the telephone lines, which had just been repaired. But this time they also got the Operations Room. At 1835 Kenley advised the Observer Centre at Bromley that all lines to Biggin Hill were down and asked for the call signs of 72 and 79 Squadrons so it could take them over. They diverted 79 Squadron to Croydon, but 72 managed to land at the shambles of their new home.

For the first time since Eagle Day, an important element of the command and control system had been taken out. The other elements of the system closed in round the wound as repairs were started, and power was restored to the Operations Room. By the following morning, 1 September, Biggin Hill was working again.

The afternoon's action had been followed by Winston Churchill from 11 Group Operations Room in Uxbridge. His last visit had been prompted by excitement. This one was prompted by concern. The previous evening, he had been given the week's casualty figures showing more civilian deaths from bombing than ever before. He watched the controllers deciding which raids were the most threatening and how to meet them. It had brought the war home to him, he told Colville afterwards.

That evening Churchill invited Dowding and Portal to dinner at Chequers. Colville was impressed that Dowding stood up to Churchill, refusing to be particularly unpleasant about the Germans but also showing no signs of complacency. There was a long discussion of the ethics of shooting men on parachutes. Dowding told Churchill what he later wrote, to the effect that if a British pilot was coming down on British soil and would be a combatant the next day, the Germans were entitled to shoot at him. Churchill was horrified, comparing escaping pilots to drowning sailors.[30]

Among the pilots at this time, there were more and more stories about such incidents, told by both sides. The very afternoon that Harold Starr was believed to have been shot on his parachute, Hasso von Perthes of I./LG2 arrived in hospital in Sussex after successfully baling out of his Messerschmitt with his legs full of machine-gun bullets. He died a short while later. It had been 303 Squadron's first day. They had seen Warsaw burn and they fought to their own rules. The fighting was becoming hard, merciless and brutal.[31]

Kesselring seems to have understood that only persistence would win the day. The morning of 1 September was warm and sunny, so he made the best of the opportunity.

At about 1030 he sent out two groups of raiders which then split up. One group hit Eastchurch, another bombed Detling, a third raided Tilbury Docks in London and the fourth went for Biggin Hill again. They were Dorniers, operating from medium altitude. They cratered the runway again and blew up one of 610 Squadron's Spitfires which had been about to leave for Acklington. The Station Commander, Group Captain Grice, was in the village attending a funeral service for those killed two days before. They took cover, then finished the service. The station continued to operate.

The early-evening raid, now a regular feature of life at Biggin Hill,came in under cover of fighter sweeps which strafed Detling, Lympne and Hawkinge. The power went down and the Operations Room was hit again. This time, the repairmen focused their attention on the site planned for such an eventuality. They set up an emergency Operations Room, located in a shop in Biggin Hill village, until a more permanent site – the old mansion of Towerfields in the nearby village of Keston – was ready. The engineers worked through the night, and the next morning it was up and running. It was decided to move 72 Squadron to Croydon for the time being. 79 Squadron stayed at Biggin Hill.

Debden was also attacked that Sunday and, after a long respite, Kenley was subject to some attention, but the defence was fierce and most of the bombs fell over Caterham. The most serious damage was done to the defending fighters. This action finished 85 Squadron. Climbing from 5,000 feet below the bombers when the escorts pounced, they lost four Hurricanes, one of them belonging to Patrick Woods-Scawen. Two pilots were wounded, one of whom later died in hospital. Two more were missing, one of them Patrick. His plane was found half buried in the ground of the recreation field at Kenley, but he was not inside it. He must have baled out. When Bunny got the news, she was very worried, and everyone waited for him to turn up.

Churchill had gone back to Uxbridge that afternoon, watched what was going on, and talked to Park. On his return to Chequers, he remarked to Colville: 'The Admiralty is now the weak spot; the air is all right.'[32]

On 2 September, the attacks followed the same pattern as the day before: two groups which split into four simultaneous thrusts, each by a Gruppe of bombers protected by a Geschwader of Bf 109s, directed at Eastchurch, Rochford, North Weald and Biggin Hill. Eastchurch was cratered again and more buildings were destroyed. The Rochford force missed the airfield and bombed the perimeter of Gravesend instead, doing little damage. The North Weald raid did not get through but the Biggin Hill raid did, coming in at low

level. There was not much left to hit. 603 were one of the squadrons to intercept the North Weald raid, and Richard Hillary added two Bf 109s to his
score.

Hornchurch was raided in the afternoon, but most of the bombs dropped
outside the perimeter. Eastchurch was attacked for a second time, exploding a
bomb dump. More dangerous was the attack on Brooklands at Weybridge in
Surrey. Both the Vickers factory making the Wellington bomber, which was hit,
and the Hawker factory assembling Hurricanes, which was not, were attractive
targets.

43 Squadron were part of the force intercepting the Eastchurch raid on its
way back. Tony Woods-Scawen was leading Yellow Section. He had not heard
about Patrick. He had been showing signs of fatigue, and quietly told the medical officer that his eyes were playing up, something he did not usually
complain about. 43 found some Bf 109s, and got into a dogfight. Tony was seen
to follow a 109 down, but as usual he was hit. Over Romney Marsh he baled
out, as usual. Two boys cycling nearby saw him. His plane was very low and his
parachute did not have time to open properly. A parson also saw him come
down and went over to pick him up. He was dead.[33]

On the 3rd, Biggin Hill suffered just two minor raids. The only major raid
of the day was on North Weald. Again, there was a lot of destruction to buildings, including hangars, and there were the usual craters, but again the station's
operations were unimpaired. As the raiders returned, they were attacked by
several squadrons, including 603. Peter Pease got a Bf 109. Richard Hillary got
behind another one. He gave it a two-second burst and saw some hits. He followed it. He wanted a certain kill. He fired a second, longer burst. Then the
control column was knocked out of his hand by a terrific bang, and his Spitfire
burst into flames.

His machine had had a new hood fitted, which did not slide very smoothly
in the runners. It took him a long time to get out. He hit the waters of the
North Sea off Margate and bobbed up and down in great pain. As time passed
he decided to drink sea water in order to hasten his end, but then he thought
of some words of Goethe to the effect that no-one who had not yet realised his
full potential had the right to take his own life. So he stopped. Three hours
later, the Margate lifeboat picked him up, and he was taken to East Grinstead,
where he joined McIndoe's Guinea Pigs.[34]

The Duxford squadrons played their part in the defence of North Weald.
310 Squadron claimed five Bf 110s and a Dornier for the loss of one Hurricane,
but 19 Squadron's guns jammed again and, after vigorous protestations, eight
conventional Spitfires were flown in for them. They were a bit old and battered,
but their guns worked.

In contrast to previous days, most of the German losses were bombers and
Bf 110s. I./ZG2 was badly mauled, losing five aircraft. The Bf 109s were less in
evidence. This was partly because of the range needed to reach North Weald,
but also a sign that the German single-seaters were becoming exhausted.

On the following day, the 4th, the Bf 110s once more bore most of the burden. The attack on Brooklands was repeated, and again the Wellington factory was badly damaged, with production halted for several days, but the Hurricane factory escaped unscathed. The raiders were Bf 110s: Erprobungsgruppe 210 was back in action under their new permanent Commander, Hans von Boltenstern. He led them for the first and last time. He crashed into the Channel trying to manoeuvre to repel what he thought was an imminent attack. He was their only loss. Their Bf 110 escorts from V./LG1, however, lost four aircraft and III./ZG76 lost six, with Pat Hughes and Bob Doe from 234 Squadron prominent amongst their tormentors. As soon as the Bf 109s failed to appear in large numbers, German losses mounted. In all, seventeen of the twenty-eight aircraft the Luftwaffe lost on 4 September were Bf 110s, the same as the total losses suffered by Fighter Command. It was the worst day the Zerstörer force ever experienced.

The only airfield to be raided was Eastchurch, which was attacked in two waves, during which the Bf 109s made their only appearance. They gave a rough handling to 66 Squadron, who were on their first combat sortie, having arrived at Kenley the day before. They lost three Spitfires and suffered three more damaged, with five pilots wounded. 222 Squadron lost another two pilots with their machines.

Given that Biggin Hill had been quiet, Group Captain Grice decided to take things into his own hands. Only one hangar was still standing, and he had realised that the Luftwaffe based their target selection on aerial reconnaissance. Grice went up in a Magister to have a look and, on his return, ordered the hangar to be blown up. It disappeared with a big bang at six o'clock that evening. It was, after all, perfectly useless. He was later censured in a Court of Enquiry, but no action was taken.[35]

Kesselring went back to Biggin Hill just once more, on 5 September, to make sure. About thirty escorted bombers were scattered by 79 Squadron, but managed to make a few fresh craters and cut the telephone again. Kesselring launched a large number of small raids on the other usual airfields, but they were all met and turned back, with Bob Doe and Pat Hughes scoring again over Kenley. The biggest raid, and a new departure, was on the oil storage depot at Thames Haven, on the Essex coast of the Thames Estuary. 19 Squadron met the raid, but lost Squadron Leader Pinkham to the escorts. The oil tanks were hit. For the first time, there were big fires within sight of London.

Churchill addressed the Commons that afternoon. He outlined the plans to compensate those who lost their homes through bombing, and warned that although August had been 'a real fighting month' in the air, neither side had yet applied its full strength, and heavier fighting must be expected in September. The RAF was achieving rates of three to one in machines and five to one in men, and was stronger than in July. The Germans had claimed 1,921 British aircraft in July and August. The reality was 558. He did not know, he said, if

Hitler believed his figures, but he hoped he did: 'One is always content to see an enemy plunged in error and self-deception.'[36]

The Luftwaffe came back to stoke the fires at Thames Haven further on the 6th, and tried to get through to the airfields, once more in small numbers, but they were again thwarted. Erprobungsgruppe 210 also returned to Brooklands, but without much effect. They again lost one Bf 110. After the losses of the Zerstörer over the previous two days, most of the escort missions were flown by Bf 109s, and they in their turn suffered accordingly.

Dowding had been concerned by the raids on the factories, and on the 5th Park had issued an instruction specifying how they were to be protected. He stressed the need to intercept well forward to prevent bombing, and 10 Group were alerted to form a second line of defence against anything that got through 11 Group. Time permitting, squadrons were to be scrambled in pairs, with Spitfires going in high to attack the fighters and Hurricanes going in lower to tackle the bombers. In addition to the Hawker and Vickers factories that had been attacked, he mentioned the Southampton aircraft factories as being 'of vital importance to the RAF'[37] They were where the bulk of Spitfire production was still going on.

Kenley Lane runs from Kenley Common to Kenley Station, just north of the airfield. It is a sunken road, with high banks on either side, and not much travelled. The houses along it are large and secluded. On 6 September 1940, someone went into the garden of a house which had been standing empty. The garden was overgrown, but they found what they had been searching for between the weeds. It was Patrick Woods-Scawen. His parachute had failed to open.

Bunny and Patrick's widowed father had attended his brother's funeral at Folkestone the day before. Now they would have to plan another one. Neither 'Wombat' nor 'Weasel' got their girl. She was numbed for several months. The following year she joined the WAAF. She was nineteen.[38]

23. THE AIRFIELDS

In attacking the airfields, Kesselring was consciously trying to do two things: force the British to come up and fight or face destruction on the ground; and make their bases unusable. He was quite unconsciously doing a third and far more important thing, which was attacking the command and control system, represented by the Operations Rooms of the Sector Stations. Kesselring had no idea these rooms existed.

Although the attacks reached their greatest intensity during the fortnight up to 6 September, which is often identified as a separate phase of the Battle, some damage had already been done in the first week of Eagle. The table on p. 287 summarises the Luftwaffe effort against airfields up to 6 September, including all the raids which either involved substantial forces or were destructive or both.

This table shows Kesselring's first problem: identifying his targets. Taking the number of raids as a rough guide, it can be said that the Luftwaffe wasted a third of its effort on targets other than Fighter Command. Only 40% of the raids were directed against Sector Stations, and the bulk of these did not begin until the end of August. One airfield in each category was singled out for special attention: Manston was raided six times, Eastchurch nine times and Biggin Hill had the honour of being the most bombed airfield in the RAF, both in terms of the number of raids and their concentration. Eleven were delivered in total, all but one in the space of a week, during which it was left alone on only one day. The Battle of Biggin Hill showed the Luftwaffe at its most determined.

The bombing of airfields not belonging to Fighter Command was not due to ignorance. Beppo Schmid had done his job long before, and produced a complete Order of Battle for Fighter Command as of 1 January 1940, detailing where every squadron was located.[2] Initially, part of the reason for the lack of focus was the unclear strategy. The RAF was the target from the outset, but not until the conference of 19 August did everybody finally agree it was really Fighter Command that mattered. In any case, it was clear that fighters could use any airfield, so what in practice dictated target selection were the reports from the daily reconnaissance flights. If they reported aircraft on the ground – and from the heights at which they operated it was not always easy to tell if they were fighters or something else – the airfield would be attacked. The hope was that a lot of parked aircraft would be destroyed.

The northern airfields were a problem because of the Bf 109's range. Several raids were actually turned back, whereas most of the attacks further south got through. The southern bases also lay directly between the Pas-de-Calais and London, and Göring's concept was to systematically clear a path, starting from the coast.

Specific choices were opportunistic. The presence of 266 Squadron at Eastchurch on the 13th misled the Luftwaffe into singling it out. They concentrated on Manston rather than Hawkinge because the land around Manston is flat, whereas Hawkinge is sheltered by low hills. There was no good reason to concentrate on Biggin Hill rather than Kenley. The post-raid reports on the 18th seem to have convinced them that Kenley was done for, so they only came back once after that. Aerial photographs of Kenley after the 18th would have shown every building to be wrecked or destroyed. Group Captain Grice's decision to destroy Biggin Hill's last hangar himself was very rational. It had already effectively become surplus to requirements.

The most obvious effect of the attacks on the airfields was the cratering of runways, but craters were usually filled within hours. Dowding observed that damage to aerodrome surfaces was 'not a major difficulty', particularly in view of the large number of landing grounds available.[3]

All the attacks destroyed buildings, but this produced more discomfort than anything else. Personnel were billeted in the neighbourhood[4], and the lost equipment was replaced. Repairs, maintenance and refuelling were carried on around the perimeter.

The main danger was from unexploded and delayed action bombs. Particularly in low-level attacks, the Luftwaffe often got the timing of the fuses wrong and a lot of bombs failed to explode. In many ways such errors were a bigger problem for the defenders than when they did what they intended. The presence of a large number of unmarked live bombs at Manston was a major factor in the RAF's decision to abandon it. Elsewhere, there was always enough time to make the area safe before the next attack.

Less than twenty fighters were destroyed on the ground.[5] Only four Hurricanes were lost at Kenley, though others were damaged, and a handful were written off at Biggin Hill and Hornchurch. A few squadrons, such as 65 at Manston on the 13th, 615 at Kenley on the 18th or 85 at Croydon on the 31st, were taking off when the raids began and had narrow escapes. The only squadron to lose aircraft in this way was 54 at Hornchurch, but all three pilots had miraculous escapes. The only case of a squadron caught on the ground refuelling was of 266 at Manston on the 18th, and this was due to the unusual initiative of a single officer at I./JG52.

Major Attacks on Airfields			
Date of Attack	Fighter Command Sector Stations	Other Fighter Command Airfields	Airfields not Connected with Fighter Command
12 August		Hawkinge Lympne (twice) Manston	
13 August			Andover Detling Eastchurch
14 August	Middle Wallop	Manston	Sealand
15 August	Middle Wallop	Croydon Hawkinge (twice) Lympne Manston Martlesham Heath West Malling	Driffield Eastchurch
16 August	Tangmere	West Malling	Brize Norton
18 August	Biggin Hill Kenley	Croydon Manston	Ford Gosport Thorney Island
24 August	Hornchurch North Weald	Manston (twice)	
25 August		Warmwell	Driffield
26 August	Debden		St Eval
28 August		Rochford (twice)	Eastchurch
30 August	Biggin Hill (twice)		Detling
31 August	Biggin Hill (twice) Debden Hornchurch (twice) North Weald	Croydon	Detling Eastchurch
1 September	Biggin Hill (twice) Debden Kenley		Detling (twice) Eastchurch
2 September	Biggin Hill Hornchurch	Gravesend Lympne	Detling Eastchurch (twice)
3 September	Biggin Hill (twice) North Weald		
4 September			Eastchurch (twice)
5 September	Biggin Hill Hornchurch		

Given that one of the Luftwaffe's prime goals was to catch aircraft on the ground, the rarity of such cases is a real tribute to the efficiency of the defences and the watchfulness of Park's controllers. In Poland and France, the Luftwaffe had been used to finding lines of aircraft parked on runways. The RAF's policy of dispersing planes round an airfield perimeter, and protecting them with the simple but effective E-shaped blast pens Dowding had ordered in 1938, meant that even if the planes were on the ground, a direct hit was needed to destroy each machine. The Luftwaffe's happy days of gaining air superiority in a few hours were not to come again until June 1941, when the Russians offered them even longer rows of aircraft lined up as if for target practice, and they wiped out thousands of them before they even took off.

People were killed on the ground, though the numbers were surprisingly small. The Kenley raid cost nine dead. The thirty-nine killed at Biggin Hill on the 30th was the worst single incident, and an unlucky one. By and large, the protection afforded to ground staff was effective.

Of course, it was people who kept things going. It took courage. If at Manston the courage of some indeed failed, at Biggin Hill it signally did not. Marking out unexploded bombs with flags was a vital but very hazardous task, which by the time of Churchill's visit had become impossible at Manston. After the first raid on Biggin Hill on the 18th, Sergeant Elisabeth Mortimer continued doing so after one bomb had gone off near her, and she was ordered to stop because it was too dangerous. She was awarded the Military Medal. For their bravery in remaining at the switchboard throughout the raids on 1 September, two WAAFs, Sergeant Helen Turner and Corporal Elspeth Henderson, were also awarded the Military Medal. For her conduct during this and the previous days, Felicity Hanbury, the Assistant Section Officer in charge of the WAAFs at Biggin Hill, was awarded a Military MBE. The Battle of Biggin Hill put an end to the concerns some RAF officers had about whether WAAFs would go to pieces under fire. They helped the station to justify its motto, 'The Strongest Link'.

Park was concerned about the airfields because he wanted his men to get proper food and sleep, and the destruction of the airfield infrastructure would jeopardise both. However, his real worry was damage to the Sector Operations Rooms. In the event, the Luftwaffe only got one, and the example shows just how resilient the system was. Two other Sector Stations took over Biggin Hill's role whilst it was out of action, and this period lasted a few hours. Thanks to Gossage's foresight, an emergency room was already prepared.[6] In accordance with a recommendation in the post-damage report to the Kenley raid,[7] the Kenley Operations Room was pre-emptively moved down into a disused butcher's shop in Caterham village on 3 September. Both of these cases give some measure of the task facing Kesselring. The Operations Rooms could have been anywhere. Even if the Luftwaffe had tried to raze Biggin Hill and Caterham villages to the ground, only a direct hit would have put the rooms out of action. Then they would have been moved somewhere else. Given the inability of Luftwaffe intelligence to find out what a Sector was, let alone a Sector Operations Room, it was hardly likely to have been able to identify Spice & Wallis, Quality Family Butchers of 11 Godstone Road, Caterham as a key strategic target in their struggle for world domination.[8]

Nevertheless, although the system did not go down, it was degraded for some periods of time. The real vulnerability of the Operations Rooms was loss of power, which is what took Kenley off the air for two hours, and this was proving to be the main threat to the radar network as well. When these coincided, things became hairy, as they did on the 30th because of the chance hit on the Kent grid, which helped Erprobungsgruppe 210 to get through to Biggin Hill.

There was in all of this a discernible pattern which, had it been properly recognised, could have gained the Luftwaffe some measure of success: early attacks on radar stations to put them down for a few hours, followed by low-level attacks on the Sectors. The Luftwaffe could not destroy the system but it could disrupt it for short periods and do a lot of damage while it was out of action. But only low-level attacks would work. The casualties suffered by 9./KG76 and by Erprobungsgruppe 210 convinced them they were too costly, but the widespread use of such tactics could have put Park under enormous pressure.[9]

The Luftwaffe probably flew something like 13,500 sorties from Eagle Day to 6 September, and the 20 or so aircraft of Erprobungsgruppe 210 probably accounted for no more than 2–3% of them. Yet the damage they did in putting out the radar system, damaging Biggin Hill, rendering Manston unserviceable and damaging the Vickers works at Weybridge represented a greater threat than almost everything else put together. As far as the rest of the bombing was concerned, there was a great deal of sound and fury, but its military significance was almost nothing.

Park was nonetheless little inclined to lie down and accept the damage that was done. In his report for Evill he stressed the damage, claiming that, 'contrary to general belief and official reports', it was 'extensive', and complaining about the inadequacy of land lines at the emergency Operations Rooms and the Air Ministry's arrangements for repair – just as Churchill had after his visit to Manston – saying he had made the point repeatedly in writing since mid-August. It is not surprising that he took the damage seriously, nor that he took the opportunity to berate the Air Ministry, which frustrated him as much as it frustrated Dowding and which was then gearing itself up for some serious criticisms of his own handling of the battle. He also wanted to make the point that it was important to defend the airfields in the air by intercepting before bombing could take place. This was already a bone of contention with Sholto Douglas, who was at the Air Ministry.[10]

Park continued by specifying the real danger. After the damage inflicted on Biggin Hill, the destruction or cutting-off of the Operations Rooms of neighbouring Sector Stations would have put London's defences into a 'parlous state'. 'There was', he wrote, 'a critical period between 28 August and 5 September when the damage to Sector Stations and our ground organisation was having a serious effect on the fighting efficiency of the fighter squadrons, who could not be given the same good technical and administrative service as previously.' This period, he continued, was 'tided over' as the result of immense hard work, but the effect of the dislocation was 'seriously felt for about a week in the handling of squadrons by day to meet the enemy's massed attacks.'

Park nevertheless concluded by saying that, at the time of writing (12 September), 'confidence is felt in our ability to hold the enemy by day and to prevent his attaining superiority in the air over our territory, unless he greatly increases the scale or intensity of his attacks'.[11]

Dowding commented on these remarks in his covering letter to Park's report. He agreed that the damage was serious, but pointed out that, despite over forty attacks on airfields in the Group, only Manston and Lympne were unfit for flying for more than a few hours, and that the repair organisation had been rapidly strengthened.[12]

Park's remarks have given some credence to the belief that by 6 September the Luftwaffe was achieving its goals and Fighter Command was close to collapse. It is perfectly true that if the Luftwaffe had managed to do to Kenley and Hornchurch what they had done to Biggin Hill and sustain it, squadrons would have had to be moved out of Kent and Surrey. However, this concedes that, in order to do any real damage, they had to tear a big hole in the network. It had taken them three weeks, and some luck, to get as far as they had. Park's exact words are telling. He was concerned about a loss of efficiency, not collapse. In fact, the Luftwaffe was barely able to continue as it had done. It had a very limited precision-bombing capability and was using up its fighter force at an alarming rate. The best it could hope for in continuing to attack the airfields would be a further degrading of the command-and-control system, but this in itself, whilst making life increasingly difficult for Park, would not have destroyed Fighter Command. The clock was ticking: Sealion was supposed to be launched in a week. Kesselring was actually worried that he might succeed and force Park to move the bulk of his forces north of London. They could still defend the capital from there, but would themselves be still harder to attack.

One might indeed wonder why Park did not do so. Some of the pilots who had to land at Manston wondered at the time, and afterwards, why it was not abandoned much earlier. Using it was not a lot of fun. Once the Channel battle ceased, it was not a lot of use, and it seemed to many an expensive luxury, kept going for propaganda reasons.[13] In his despatch, Dowding took a very relaxed view. He says that Manston, Hawkinge and Lympne were only used for topping up fuel when maximum range was required, and were only temporarily abandoned. 'This is not to say,' he adds, 'that they could not have been used if the need had been urgent, but, for interception at or about our own coastline, aerodromes and satellites farther inland were quite effective.'[14]

Park took a very robust view of keeping his airfields in operation, but he had good reasons. He saw his task as the defence of a territory that began at the coastline. He was not going to concede ground without a fight, and to some extent the morale aspect of the situation played a role. He knew full well that any airfield could remain usable as long as the damage were cleared up after every raid, and he regarded it as the duty of each station to do so. He therefore waited until he was certain it was no longer worth the effort. If he had withdrawn to the north, he would have achieved at a stroke of the pen what Kesselring was trying to do with tons of bombs – degrade the efficiency of his system. A Sector operated best when it controlled two to four squadrons. If he had overloaded North Weald, Debden and Northolt, control and servicing would have been impaired. Facing its sternest test, he wanted the system to work at maximum efficiency, and that meant keeping all the sectors operating.[15] It was beginning to get difficult, but all of them were.

On the evening of 6 September the country's air defences were battered but intact, and quite capable of resisting another week or two weeks of the sort of treatment it had been withstanding so far. Whether the Luftwaffe chose to attack airfields or something else made no difference to what took place in the air. On 31 August, Fighter Command suffered its highest ever losses in the air in one day. The question was, as in any battle of attrition: who would give up first.

24. THE PILOTS

These two weeks were the most nerve-wracking for Park and Dowding and the most exhausting for the pilots. Some of them got so tired they fell asleep in their cockpits as soon as they landed. It had become a grim business. Attritional warfare is dreadful for the participants. There is no sense of achievement and little sense of purpose. There is just killing and the attempt every day to avoid being killed. Each side continues until one realises it is getting nowhere and gives up. The body-count matters.

The count of aircraft had changed. The Luftwaffe lost 380 machines to Fighter Command's 286, a ratio of 1.3 to 1. During the first week of Eagle the ratio had been 2.4 to 1. The intensity of the fighting had also increased. The first week had cost Fighter Command 125 aircraft. It was now losing an average of 140 a week. Whereas the first week cost the Luftwaffe nearly 300 aircraft, its loss rate had dropped to more like 200 a week. So although the Luftwaffe was wearing itself out faster than it was wearing down Fighter Command, the balance of losses had shifted in its favour. Perhaps, if it carried on in the same way, regardless of what it attacked, it could win the battle in the air after all.

There were two reasons for this change in pattern.

The first was the change in the mix of aircraft the Luftwaffe was now sending over. The ratio of fighters to bombers was now often four or five to one. The British pilots had no more Stuka parties and it was harder to get through and inflict heavy casualties on the bomber formations. More of the combat was between fighters, and the German fighters were now led by the best aerial tacticians and practitioners they had.

The other reason was the mix of units Fighter Command was now sending into the battle, and the losses that were resulting. Fighter Command's losses were of three quite different kinds.

First, the front-line squadrons were, as before, suffering steady attrition of experienced pilots. It was not noticeably increasing. Ten Hurricane aces were lost between 8 and 19 August and twelve between 20 August and 6 September.[1]

Exhaustion and stress took an inevitable toll. Townsend is a case in point, as were Weaver and Westmacott of 56 Squadron who were shot down the same day, the fateful 31 August. Their luck ran out, as the pilots themselves would have said. Every now and again, one of the old hands bought it.

Secondly, the existing squadrons were also suffering steady attrition of replacements, at five to six times the rate of experienced men. This had also been happening the whole time, and it was just as true on the other side of the Channel.[2] Every squadron had a story about a bright youth who arrived from his training unit with twelve hours on type and disappeared on his first mission. Because of the intensity of the fighting, there was no time for any of the novices to learn. However, those who filled the gaps in units like 111, 501, 609, 32 or 43 Squadrons had experienced old hands to learn from, some of whom were aces, but all of whom knew how to survive. So they had a chance.

The new phenomenon was the loss of whole units that were posted down from the north as replacements. It began to occur at this stage because there were more exhausted units in need of replacement and the air had become extremely dangerous. In a lot of these units, nobody at all knew what they were doing, and each squadron had to learn for itself the hard way. The fatalities were largely caused by the continued use of the official RAF tactics, the Fighting Area Attacks, and the vic formation. The effect on these units was devastating.

The pattern of transfers between Groups made during August and the first week of September is shown on page 295. The squadrons identified in bold are new ones coming into the thick of the fighting for the first time.

Park was the one who first identified what was going on. In a secret memo to Fighter Command HQ written on 26 August, he drew attention to the heavy casualties suffered by reinforcing units sent from the north, but drew a sharp distinction between the performance of those sent from 13 Group and those from 12 Group.

He quoted three cases of 13 Group squadrons. Since arriving in 11 Group, he noted, 41 Squadron had made thirteen claims for one pilot casualty, 152 had claimed four for one and 602 Squadron had claimed twenty six for two, and added that Station Commanders had commented on their 'high standard of flying and fighting efficiency'. He then quoted the sad records of 266 and 616: nine claims for six pilots and eight claims for seven pilots. Both of these units had been sent from 12 Group. Park's meaning is clear: it was Leigh-Mallory again, sending him lambs to the slaughter.

Park concludes by observing that he expected intense fighting to continue for at least a month, and that the environment in 11 Group meant only experienced units could survive intact. He 'urgently recommended' that, following Saul's practice, 'only experienced squadrons be provided when exchanges are necessary during the next rather critical month.'[7]

Dowding supervised the movement of squadrons, but deferred to his Group Commanders in choosing the squadrons to move in. Park was writing to him to draw his attention to what was happening. Leigh-Mallory was indeed selecting relatively inexperienced units and, despite Bader's yearning for action, kept him in 12 Group.[8] He got on well with Leigh-Mallory, and was ideally suited to helping him develop some of his ideas on tactics. He had also already attracted some good publicity. His lone interception of a Do 17 meterological flight on 11 July had been fêted by the press.[9] He stayed where he was.

Little was to change for another week after Park's memo.

Of the thirteen squadrons moved into 11 Group from other Groups up to 3 September, eight had claims-to-loss ratios of less than two; in other words, they claimed to have shot down only twice as many aircraft as they lost themselves. This probably meant they were in reality losing more aircraft than they destroyed. To them should be added the newly formed 1 Squadron RCAF, which had its first day of action on the day Park wrote his memo. These nine squadrons between them suffered almost 40% of Fighter Command's air combat losses over the last week of August and first week of September, but made only 25% of the claims. It is likely that, because of their inexperience, their claims contain an unusually high number of errors, so these submissions probably overstate the real damage they were doing to the Luftwaffe. Their losses were not in doubt. Removing their claims and losses from the overall figures for all fighter squadrons over this period reveals that the experienced squadrons were continuing to shoot down German aircraft at the rate of over 2:1.

The pattern of these units' losses is similar. Most of them suffered a dramatic loss in one action because they were bounced by Bf 109s. 79 Squadron lost four aircraft and their pilots on the 31st, three days after their arrival at Biggin Hill; 603 Squadron lost three aircraft and pilots on its first day; 222 Squadron arrived in Hornchurch on the 29th, took off on the 30th and lost six aircraft and three pilots for just one confirmed claim; 253 lost five aircraft and their pilots on their first two days at Kenley, making only eight claims, including the four erroneously filed by Tom Gleave; 46 Squadron lost one aircraft for one claim on their first day and three aircraft and pilots for two claims on their second; 66 Squadron lost five aircraft and two pilots on their first two days and were granted one confirmed kill in return. On the 31st, 1 Squadron RCAF lost four aircraft and three pilots and made three claims.

The specific reason for these catastrophes was that they still used prescribed RAF formations and tactics. Des Sheen was with 72 Squadron when it arrived at Biggin Hill. He was shot down himself when the weavers failed to spot a bounce coming in and the rear flight was destroyed. His two companions were killed. The squadron lost thirteen aircraft and five pilots in six days, claiming fourteen in return. Sheen himself was high-quality material, a well-trained pre-war pilot who was to become an ace.[10] He and his colleagues were not inexperienced flyers, like the boys who came as replacements to the old squadrons: they were inexperienced fighters. If that had been all, they might have learned quickly enough to survive. Their learning was fatally held up because, as disciplined professionals, they flew as they had been taught and

Squadron Moves Between Groups, 8 August to 7 September[3]

Date	Unit	From	To	Type of Move
8 August	41	11 (Hornchurch)	13 (Catterick)	Exchange
	54	13 (Catterick)	11 (Hornchurch)	Exchange
13/14 August	74	11 (Hornchurch)	12 (Wittering)	Exchange
	266	12 (Wittering)[4]	11 (Hornchurch)	Exchange
	145	11 (Westhampnett)	13 (Drem)	Exchange
	602	13 (Drem)	11 (Westhampnett)	Exchange
	249	12 (Church Fenton)	10 (Boscombe Down)	Reinforcement
19 August	64	11 (Kenley)	12 (Leconfield)	Exchange
	616	12 (Leconfield)	11 (Kenley)	Exchange
21 August	74	11 (Hornchurch)	12 (Wittering)	Withdrawal
	266	11 (Hornchurch)	12 (Wittering)	Withdrawal
27/28 August	32	11 (Biggin Hill)	13 (Acklington)	Exchange
	79	13 (Acklington)	11 (Biggin Hill)	Exchange
	603	13 (Turnhouse)	11 (Hornchurch)	Reinforcement
29 August	264	11 (Hornchurch)[5]	12 (Kirton-in-Lindsey)	Exchange
	222	12 (Kirton-in-Lindsey)	11 (Hornchurch)	Exchange
	615	11 (Kenley)	13 (Prestwick)	Exchange
	253	13 (Prestwick)	11 (Kenley)	Exchange
31 August	610	11 (Biggin Hill)	13 (Acklington)	Exchange
	72	13 (Acklington)	11 (Biggin Hill)	Exchange
1 September	151	11 (Stapleford Tawney)	12 (Digby)	Exchange
	46	12 (Digby)	11 (Stapleford Tawney)	Exchange
	56	11 (North Weald)	10 (Boscombe Down)	Exchange
	249	10 (Boscombe Down)	11 (North Weald)	Exchange
	607	13 (Usworth)	11 (Tangmere)[6]	Reinforcement
3 September	54	11 (Hornchurch)	13 (Catterick)	Exchange
	41	13 (Catterick)	11 (Hornchurch)	Exchange
	616	11 (Kenley)	12 (Coltishall)	Exchange
	66	12 (Coltishall)	11 (Kenley)	Exchange
5 September	257	11 (Debden)	12 (Martlesham)	Withdrawal
	504	13 (Catterick)	11 (Hendon)	Reinforcement
7 September	601	11 (Tangmere)	10 (Exeter)	Exchange
	213	10 (Exeter)	11 (Tangmere)	Exchange
	605	13 (Drem)	11 (Croydon)	Reinforcement

fought according to the handbooks.[11] Over Dunkirk in June, and even over the Channel in July, it had been possible to do that and survive. Over Kent, Surrey and Sussex in August, it was not. There were too many Bf 109s about.

The contrast with the other reinforcements is very revealing.

249 Squadron had a claims-to-loss ratio of almost 4:1, and were never massacred. They in fact suffered their heaviest losses on the 16th, when they lost Nicolson's machine and those of his two companions, one of whom was killed. Their only claim was Nicolson's Bf 110. Their first day had been the 15th, and they claimed five for no loss. This was against the raid on Worthy Down which consisted of Ju 88s and Bf 110s. After the 16th, the squadron saw further action in 10 Group, so by the time they went to 11 Group on 1st September, they had had two weeks in a less intensive environment during which to learn. Six of its pilots went on to become aces.

602 Squadron were moved to Tangmere's satellite, Westhampnett, which is on the border between 10 Group and 11 Group, and therefore also faced fewer Bf 109s. Their claims-to-loss ratio for the period was over 6:1. Though they had not fought at Dunkirk, they had engaged a stream of lone raiders in Scotland, including the first German aircraft shot down over Britain. In the south, they enjoyed a début against Stukas on the 16th, and took part in the final Stuka party on the 18th. They had modest losses, with just three pilots wounded over the two weeks, and claimed steadily. They did not have any celebrities in their ranks, but one star performer, Archie McKellar, had flown with them from the beginning of the war until he was posted to 605 Squadron as a Flight Commander and eventually their leader. They also seem to have been very cohesive and were well led by Sandy Johnstone, who was to become an ace, as were three of his men.

The most telling story is that of 234 Squadron. They were also in 10 Group. In their two first disastrous days they lost six Spitfires and three pilots. However, from 17 August to 6 September, the squadron only lost two more aircraft, and they built up claims fast because they had two hunter-killers in their ranks: Pat Hughes and the young Bob Doe. Between them, these two accounted for half the squadron's claims. Doe's progress is a model of what every novice had to do, and a microcosm of Fighter Command itself. Its survival and effectiveness largely depended on how many like him were in its ranks.

The only newcomers to survive being plunged directly into the maelstrom of the south-east were not newcomers at all, but the most experienced squadron in the RAF: the Poles of 303. The first day they fought as a unit, the 31st, they claimed six for no loss. The next day they claimed three, the next day eight and the next day seven. By 7 September, they had a claims-to-loss ratio of over 8:1. So it went on. By November, they had claimed 126 kills, the highest of any squadron in the Battle of Britain. 602 were next with 102. The Poles did not give a damn about RAF formations and could not read the manuals about Fighting Area Attacks even if they had wanted to.

The Poles were wonderful, but they were not a solution. Dowding realised that moving units south was not working, but he had to find some way of relieving and reinforcing the pilots down there. Finally, and with some reluctance, he decided to create three categories of squadron: 'A' squadrons were those in or adjacent to 11 Group and were to be kept as far as possible at full strength, fed by replacements; 'B' squadrons, outside 11 Group, were also to be kept at full strength and used as a reserve, to be moved in if necessary; pilots for both were to be provided by 'C' squadrons. All but five or six experienced pilots in these units were to be posted to 'A' or 'B' squadrons, and the remainder sent to quiet areas to train new pilots in combat flying and tackle any unescorted bombers they met. Dowding's reluctance to do this was because of its impact on the self-esteem of the 'C' squadrons, which numbered some proud units such as 32, 54, 85, 111 and 610. It was only temporary, but he did not like it.

The Luftwaffe did not have the same problem with inexperienced units. All the fighter Geschwader of Airfleets 2 and 3 had seen action in France and had been at the Channel front since the beginning of August at the latest. They all flew in the brilliantly effective Schwarm created by Mölders in Spain, and fighting tactics formed part of basic training. Nevertheless, one new unit did enter the fray. I./JG77, the unit transferred from North Germany, entered the battle in late August and on the 31st lost seven Bf 109s and another damaged, about a quarter of its strength. Six of the pilots were killed or captured. Their last action had been the invasion of Norway in April. Since then they had been involved in coastal defence against the odd unescorted bomber. They had had an easy war, and the charnel house of southern England chewed them up in the same way it did the British newcomers.

However, the problem with new pilots sent as replacements existed equally in the Luftwaffe. On 20 August, Erhard Milch began a five-day tour of the air force he had created with a view to checking morale, identifying and remedying equipment deficiencies and making recommendations about the new wave of promotions Göring was contemplating. He wrote his report on the 26th. In it he comments on the inadequate experience of the new pilots being rushed to the front from the training schools, whom he found to be of 'very variable' quality. The fighter Geschwader were complaining that they were getting boys who had only done ten landings in a Bf 109, and no firing training with cannon.[12] Milch made a particular point of noting that green pilots were being sent as replacements to Erprobungsgruppe 210, which he thought, in view of the unit's special role, particularly aberrant.

Milch also discovered that, despite the replacements, the units he visited were under-strength in equipment too, a handicap the British did not suffer at all. The differences in industrial output were beginning to make themselves felt at the front. He cited a litany of shortages:

- eleven Bf 110s, one Bf 109 and ten crews at Erprobungsgruppe 210;

- thirty pilots at JG26;
- ten Bf 109s at JG3;
- nine crews and twelve radio operators (who had suffered particularly heavy casualties) at II./KG2, fifteen crews at III./KG2 and seven crews and eight Dorniers at I./KG2, at which five crews were on the sick list; KG2 was short of seventeen aircraft in total;
- ten Heinkels at I./KG53, fifteen at III./KG53 and seven at II./KG53 which had also run out of spare engines.[13]

Milch did another round between 27 August and 4 September. Things had got worse, in particular with equipment. Serviceability rates, which were acceptable at Stuka units, were running at 75% with Bf 109s, 70% with bombers and 65% with Bf 110s, indicating shortages of spare parts. All units were also well below establishment. Out of an establishment of about 35–40 aircraft in a Gruppe, the bomber units averaged 20, Bf 109s averaged 18 and the Bf 110s even fewer. The attrition was beginning to tell, particularly on the fighters. Milch lets it pass without comment.[14]

For Fighter Command the concern was the recent increase in losses. On the eve of Eagle Day, there had been 1,396 operational pilots. After the losses and replacements of the following fortnight there were twenty fewer. The addition of four new squadrons had raised the number to 1,422 a week later, but the week of heavy fighting had brought the number back down again to 1,381 by the end of the first week of September. The overall trend was up: Fighter Command still had more pilots than it had had at the beginning of July.[15] However, Dowding did not know how long it would go on, and had few remaining sources of reinforcements. His goal, as ever, was to build up at least fifty squadrons to establishment strength, and he was worried about the immediate trend.

On 2 September, Evill prepared an analysis of the Command's pilot strength and the trends produced by the latest fighting, which showed pilot losses outstripping replacements. He calculated that the loss-rate was running at about 125 a week and the training units would, under existing arrangements, only provide the squadrons with 150 new pilots by 21 September. As of 31 August, the squadrons were 150 below establishment, based on an establishment target of 16 per squadron. He proposed re-training thirty ex-Battle pilots and finding another forty trained pilots for rapid conversion to Spitfires.[16]

The idea of re-training Battle pilots was not new. Dowding had wanted this done in early August when he was trying to build up his strength before the expected assault. He had run up against Sholto Douglas at the Air Ministry, who found the suggestion 'very unpalatable', as in his opinion the lumbering Battles would be 'extremely useful if and when an invasion occurs, since they are particularly well adapted to deal with troops landing on, and advancing from the beaches.' Perhaps aware that the Battles were less well adapted to dealing with Bf 109s, he added that plans to re-equip their squadrons were in progress. Douglas suggested that some figures about pilot strength be prepared so that all could get a clear picture of what the problem was, admitting at least that there might be one.[17] Some pilots were re-trained. Now Evill was suggesting taking some more.

Frustrated by what appeared to be complacency at the Air Ministry, Dowding called Sholto Douglas to meet Evill, Park and himself at Bentley Priory, so that the three of them together could try to get through to him. Dowding felt he had spent his life fighting for resources. He had come close to seeing his Command whittled away through piecemeal destruction in France, and now, under direct attack and with the possibility of a crisis in the offing, Douglas and others at the Air Ministry were prevaricating while his force wasted away through attrition. He had raised the squadron establishment to twenty-six in order to allow his pilots some rest. Now he was only targeting sixteen. He knew what even that meant for the boys in the front line. They were all doing everything asked of them and, as Park knew from his daily visits to the squadrons, morale continued to be high, but how much could a leader ask of his men? Dowding was angry.

His anger comes through in the minutes of the meeting, held on 7 September, which are unusually detailed, suggesting Dowding wanted a very clear record of exactly what was said. He had a shorthand typist take everything down.

Dowding opened aggressively by stating that the purpose of the meeting was to decide the steps to be taken to 'go down hill' in the most economical fashion, should it be necessary, so as to leave the pathway back up hill as easy as possible as the situation improved. He outlined his proposal for creating 'A', 'B' and 'C' squadrons and the reasons for it. He promised to provide some graphs which would show that, provided the Air Ministry continued their great efforts in removing the bottleneck at the Operational Training Units (OTUs), which were turning new pilots into operational pilots, 'enough men would be provided to meet wastage greater than any incurred so far'. His proposal effectively added more OTU capacity in the form of 'C' squadrons. It also kept up the strength of 11 Group, so that the opposition the Luftwaffe was meeting was unchanged. He then asked for comments.

Douglas queried whether the C-in-C was not being a little bit too pessimistic in talking of 'going down hill'. Dowding strongly disagreed that he was being pessimistic. Douglas said he had understood that, though there may be a shortage of experienced pilots, there was no shortage of pilots as such. Dowding explained what he meant by a trained pilot – one who is operationally trained and capable of fighting effectively. Douglas said that the Ministry was actually making arrangements to get the OTUs up to full establishment, which should provide an extra forty pilots a month. That ought to keep Fighter Command up to strength.

At that point in the meeting, Evill and Park joined in. Evill pointed out that at current rates the OTUs were turning out 280 Hurricane and Spitfire pilots a month, and that losses in the previous four weeks had been 348. Accidents, illness and so on would make things worse. That morning, Park said, nine squadrons had less than fifteen pilots, and the day before some squadrons had been sent up as composite units. 'It must be realised,' said Dowding, 'that we are going down hill.' Park agreed with him, and said it was better to have twenty-one squadrons with twenty-one pilots each than more squadrons with fewer, which was part of the point of the scheme. Morale would suffer, Dowding said, if the pilots were overtired and overworked, and morale was extremely important. The steps he was planning were essential if the Germans maintained their pressure. Some squadrons were flying fifty hours a day, Park added. With their aerodromes being bombed, they were getting less rest and a lower standard of meals. They had 'felt the shock'. 'I want you to take away from this meeting,' Dowding said, looking at Douglas, 'the feeling that the situation is extremely grave.'

It was becoming clear to Douglas that this was not just Dowding being irksome as usual. There was a veiled accusation: Fighter Command was not satisfied that everything was being done to increase output from the OTUs. So he stated that 'there were one or two things which could be done'. One was the introduction of a further OTU. The others were not impressed. It would take too long. Another thing they could do, suggested Douglas, was to call on pilots from other squadrons. Dowding mentioned that some had already been taken from Battle and Lysander squadrons. There was no objection from Douglas this time.

The discussion turned to the fighting. Park doubted that the enemy could keep up its pressure for more than three weeks. Dowding said that it could go on much longer – it depended on politics, Göring's personal ascendancy and other factors. Given recent appraisals of German air strength, one should reckon on a long campaign. It was agreed, after some arguing about the figures, that the supply of aircraft would not be a problem, or a constraint on expansion.

Whereupon the group parted company.

Dowding's plan was put into action the following day, and Evill sent the minutes of the meeting to the participants. Douglas replied a few days later, complaining that it read as if he had been given the part of the 'Mutt' who asks foolish questions in a music hall turn. 'Frankly,' he wrote, 'I consider the minutes were drafted by someone with a distinct bias in favour of everything said by a member of Fighter Command,' and went on to criticise the number of 'C' squadrons. Evill sent an apologetic reply.[18] But Douglas was to get his revenge.

Knowing that their enemy was preparing to 'go down hill' would have been cold comfort to the Luftwaffe. They assumed the enemy had been doing that for some time. In fact they believed he ought to be at his last gasp. General Stapf had reported to Halder on 30 August that the British had lost 800

Hurricanes and Spitfires since 8 August out of a front-line strength of 915.[19] Given Schmid's estimate of their production capacity of 200–300 a month, the British could therefore only have 3–400 left at the outside. After another week of pounding in September, they must indeed be down to their last 200 machines.

In fact, on the evening of 6 September, Fighter Command had over 750 serviceable fighters and 1,381 pilots available to it, about 950 of whom flew Spitfires or Hurricanes. It needed 1,588 pilots to be at full establishment, which is of course what Dowding wanted, so from his point of view he was 200 short.[20] From the Luftwaffe's point of view, he had almost 200 more pilots and 150 more planes than he had had at the beginning of July when they set out to destroy him.

There are many who believe that Fighter Command was on its knees after the attacks on the airfields. It was a strange way of kneeling. Given Evill's calculations, and taking the worst scenario of no increase in output from the training units, if the Luftwaffe had continued its attacks on the airfields and continued to destroy aircraft in the air at the most favourable rate it ever achieved, there would still have been about 725 Hurricanes and Spitfires ready to take to the air in the third week of September.

As he was getting ready for the meeting at Bentley Priory, Park had had a talk with his Chief Controller, Lord Willoughby de Broke. 'I know you and the other controllers must be getting worried about our losses,' Park said. Willoughby de Broke replied that he had indeed been getting concerned. 'Well,' Park said, 'I've been looking at these casualty figures, and I've come to the conclusion that at our present rate of losses we can just afford it. And I'm damned certain that the Boche can't. If we can hang on as we're going, I'm sure we shall win in the end.'[21]

The Germans were getting nowhere. Even worse, they did not know it. They had tried almost everything. Almost, but not quite. They had one more trick up their sleeve.

25. LONDON

In late summer, few parts of the world are as congenial as south-east England. It is usually warm, but, thanks to the maritime air, rarely oppressively hot. Seldom has the impact of man on nature been so benign as in the Weald, where the ancient forest has given way to a scattering of villages whose houses, built of local brick and tiles, seem to have grown out of the earth.

In 1940, the inhabitants went about their business as usual, just occasionally peering into the sky at the vapour trails which appeared almost every day. After work, they drank their warm beer in the multitude of pubs, just now and then disturbed by the distant chatter of machine-gun fire above them or the more ominous sound of a crashing aircraft or explosion. In the village of Elham near Hawkinge, schoolteacher Mary Smith kept up her diary: '*21 August*. Two bursts of AA during morning. Explosions – some AA during the afternoon. Ginger came to tea. *23 August*. Quite normal except for some distant gunfire. Made Sambo a pillow out of my old dressing gown. *31 August*. Not quite so bad. Fierce scrap overhead at 9 a.m. Nazi came down by parachute in Hog Green. Saw him. Only slightly wounded.'[1] People collected souvenirs from the numerous crashes, German ones being especially prized. They were not supposed to approach wrecks, but the authorities were never quite quick enough in posting guards on them. Small boys arrived within minutes. They had never known such fun. Richmond Golf Club issued a set of temporary rules to deal with the changing times, specifying, for example, that 'A player whose stroke is affected by the simultaneous explosion of a bomb may play another ball from the same place. Penalty one stroke.'[2] Kent, Sussex and Surrey were a patchwork of hedgerows full of birds. The farmers, many still using horse-drawn ploughs, were in their fields harvesting early. These were the killing fields.

As the English idyll of the pastoral poets and cheap illustrators, still a reality then, was played out quietly below, the German fighter pilots glanced down at the familiar patchwork with increasing bitterness. As they crossed the

Channel, they glanced down with loathing. Its waters, cold and choppy even at the height of summer, would kill within four hours if ditching did not kill you first. Better to bail out. But still, you should carry a gun to make a clean end of it, as Horst Tietzen had done.[3] Even if they were found, their ruthless enemy would try to shoot them down in their rescue plane.

In many units, morale was beginning to crack. They had been in continuous action since late July, flying several times a day. The sortie rate had increased among the Bf 109 pilots to reach even as much as six or seven on some days. They were not rotated or sent south to rest as Dowding sent his boys north to rest. Attrition had been relentless. Furthermore, despite the number of Tommies shot down, they just kept on coming. It was a sickening round of continual killing which seemed to be having no effect. They were beginning to lack a sense of purpose.

Tensions were mounting with the losses, as the pressure on those remaining grew. 'For the first time,' wrote Hellmuth Ostermann of III./JG54, 'some of the pilots started to talk about being transferred to a quieter front.' In the evening, the conversations got resentful. Why were all the medals going to the prima donnas? It was the Katschmareks that got shot down! One more white stripe on the tail meant one more wingman lost. 'The picture looked grim,' Ulrich Steinhilper has reflected. 'I was thinking we were all fighting to rid the sky of the RAF, and what was really developing was that many individuals were using this battle as a stage upon which they could further their own careers and personal scores'.[4]

But it was the Channel above all that dogged them. 'There were hardly any of us who had not had to ditch with a shot-up machine or an empty tank,' wrote Oberleutnant von Hahn of I./JG3. Nearly all the pilots headed to the latrines after mission briefings. At JG53 they took to holding the briefings there.[5] That was normal, and the men still flew. But '*Kanalkrankheit*' or 'Channel sickness' had reached epidemic proportions.[6] Pilots had stomach cramps, could not eat and grew irritable. Cigarette and alcohol consumption rose. The number of missions aborted because of hot engines, drops in oil pressure and instrument failure steadily went up. It seemed as if the machines themselves were sick. These were all old tricks. A new one was a sudden case of appendicitis. Cases of this were so numerous that German Battle of Britain veterans used to ask after each other's appendectomy scar.[7] Steinhilper reports that when Hauptmann Eschwege, Gruppenkommandeur of I./JG52, returned from Luftflotte 2 HQ with a new Iron Cross First Class and announced with regret that he would have to depart for a spell to have his appendix removed, there was almost mutiny.[8] It was all combat fatigue – in other words, cracking-up.

It did not just happen on the fighters. Not for nothing did Milch find 25% of the crews of I./KG2 in the sick bay. They were not suffering from flu. The bomber crews flew fewer sorties than the fighters, so the strain was less. But when they did fly, it was a harrowing experience. Park's tactics may have frustrated Osterkamp, but knowing you are the target every time leads to worse than frustration. A Ju 88 pilot, Peter Stahl, who had the good luck to fly with KG30 over in Luftflotte 5 and to miss the action on 15 August, wrote in his diary as early as 25 August: 'It is being said that the British are already on their last legs, but when one hears what the operational pilots – and particularly the bomber crews – have to report, we're obviously still a long way from victory. The losses suffered on our bomber units must be terrible.' By the beginning of September, even in his Geschwader, which was on the fringe, two Gruppen had suffered such losses that they were only conditionally operational.[9]

There was growing tension between the fighter and bomber units. It was not just about the cock-ups, but about the principle of how much close escort to give and how much time should be spent on sweeps. It was an emotive subject because it was actually about who was going to die. If the fighters just did sweeps, the British would always get through to the bombers and the bomber crews died; if the fighters flew close escort the bombers had some protection, but the fighter pilots were disadvantaged in the inevitable dogfight and some of them died. Galland describes the ideal in the form of the policy he introduced on taking over JG26: one Gruppe flying close escort, one as loose top cover and one out ahead on a sweep. Not all the Geschwader adopted this arrangement.[10] Not all of them had enough aircraft to do so. Göring explicitly and quite rightly left it up to the Kommodoren, so it was their problem.

Nevertheless, it was to Göring that the bomber leaders complained when he came to the Channel in early September. Having listened to their complaints, he summoned the fighter leaders, hauled them over the coals for their lack of aggression and the bombers' losses and demanded that they devote more resources to close escort. The Bf 109 was designed to bounce from height. Try to dogfight in one, and even a Hurricane could give as good as it got, let alone a Spitfire. Playing the role of escort, you could only dogfight. Adolf Galland is the only witness to have given an account of this heated conversation, but he is also the one who has made it famous. Having finished berating them, Göring, as usual, turned on the charm and asked what he could do for his pilots. Mölders asked for uprated engines for his Bf 109s. Galland asked for a squadron of Spitfires. Apparently, Göring's sense of humour failed him at this point.[11]

The conclusions of the conference on 19 August were quite clear, and offered the only solution to a problem the whole Luftwaffe was facing because of Park's interception policy. Göring could not afford to have his bombers decimated, and he shared with others the suspicion that his top aces were more interested in their own scores than Dorniers crashing into the Channel.[12] It was his way of dealing with it the pilots found intolerable. He was disparaging and offensive, and that served to undermine morale all round. Thus did Park confound his enemies.

Göring thought he might have found an answer to the problem of bombers and escorts: fighter-bombers. After all, the results reported by Erprobungsgruppe 210 were impressive. On 2 September he issued a document

suggesting that the British aircraft industry could be destroyed by a few precision attacks. He wanted targets in the north to be attacked by single bombers.
Their crews should be experienced volunteers. However, targets within range of
the Bf 109 should be attacked by fighter-bombers. A bomb-carrying version
existed (the Bf 109E-4/B) and would be provided in increasing numbers. In the
meantime, fighter pilots were to be given training in bombing.[13]

This was all a bit late. Being asked to fly bombing missions was the last
straw for the fighter pilots, but preparations were begun in some units. In any
case, Kesselring had another agenda.

On 30 August, Hitler had finally lifted his ban on attacking London.
Bombs had already fallen on it, but there had been no deliberate mass attack.
The ban was lifted because of a succession of predictable mistakes by the
bomber forces.

On the night of 24/25 August, a small force of Heinkels from KG1 had
been trying to drop a few bombs on the Thameshaven oil terminal. It was per-
ilously close to London, and trying to hit it at night was a long shot. In the
event, the bombs fell across the East End, damaging the church of St Giles,
Cripplegate. The following morning a telegram from Göring arrived at KG1
HQ demanding to know the identities of the crews responsible, as he wanted
them transferred to the infantry.[14]

In response, the War Cabinet sanctioned the first raid on Berlin. On the
night of 25/26 August, the Hampdens of 49 and 50 Squadrons left for a raid on
Tempelhof airfield, whilst a force of Wellingtons tried to find the huge Siemens
works nearby. North Germany was covered in cloud, but they dropped their
bombs anyway. Six of the Hampdens failed to return, three of them ditching in
the sea when they ran out of fuel. There was a strong headwind on their return
flight and Berlin was at the limit of their range. The bombs they dropped
destroyed a summer house in the garden of a house in the Berlin suburb of
Rosenthal, injuring two people. The rest fell outside the city, mainly on farm-
land, which gave rise to the local joke that now the British were trying to starve
Berlin out.[15]

The following night, Bomber Command raided Leipzig, Leuna, Hannover
and Nordhausen in Germany as well as sending eleven Whitleys to bomb Turin
and Milan. Air-raid warnings sounded in London as a few of Sperrle's night
raiders tried to get at outlying targets like Northolt, North Weald and
Hornchurch. Churchill was at No.10 and came down in his golden dragon
dressing gown to pace the lawn for some time before going to his shelter.
Colville heard Big Ben chime midnight, watched the searchlights and heard the
sound of 'a distant gun'.[16] Churchill decided he was not interested in Leipzig
and sent a minute to the Chief of the Air Staff the next day: 'Now that they have
begun to molest the capital, I want you to hit them hard, and Berlin is the place
to hit them.'[17]

So on the night of 28/29 August, Bomber Command included Berlin in its
plans again, sending some Hampdens of 83 Squadron there, though they sent

about seventy planes to raid five other German towns and some airfields in France as well. This time the Hampdens hit civilian areas around the Görlitzer railway station, killing eight people and wounding twenty-one others. Hitler was at the Berghof, and when he got the news that the Greater Berlin area had been bombed for the first time, he returned to his capital. The next day, he gave the Luftwaffe carte blanche.[18]

Göring met his commanders on 3 September in the Hague. That very day Hitler was going to state that the earliest date for S-Day, the launch of Sealion, was no longer to be 15 September, but the 21st, and its exact date would be finally decided three days in advance.[19] The ostensible reason for this was that, because of the damage the RAF had done to the Dortmund-Ems canal on the night of 12/13 August, during which Learoyd won his VC, preparations for Sealion were behind schedule. However, Göring knew that Hitler did not believe the Luftwaffe were ready anyway. They now had a bit more time. Something had to be done.

The differences between Sperrle and Kesselring were still unreconciled, but Kesselring now had the chance to get what he wanted, and urged an all-out attack on London. He argued that Fighter Command was concentrating its forces in the northern airfields now that Biggin Hill was wrecked. He feared they might withdraw to them completely, which would pose him a real problem because of the Bf 109's range. In fact, he could not really understand why they had not already done so, unless it was just a question of not being seen to abandon territory. From the loss reports he and his staff believed he had more or less established air superiority, and the key thing was to attack something within the Bf 109's range that the British would have to come up and defend. They could abandon airfields – they had lots of them. They could not abandon London.

Sperrle disagreed. He was sceptical about the loss reports. He had seen all that before in Spain. Fighter Command was far from its last gasp, and the attacks on its infrastructure should continue.

Kesselring insisted. There was no point in trying to attack British aircraft on the ground, because they were not there. Hardly any fighters had been caught on the airfields. The only place to get them was in the air, and the only issue the perennial one of how to force them up so that Galland, Mölders, Oesau or Balthasar could then shoot them down. The Luftwaffe was not getting any stronger. It should concentrate the forces it had, argued Kesselring, and launch massed attacks on a single target. London was the only candidate.

Kesselring was now pushing at an open door. Göring's view was political and his concern, as Dowding observed with insight on the 7th, was his personal standing. He had infamously claimed in public that, if enemy bombs were ever to fall on Berlin, people could call him 'Meyer'. The jokes were already doing the rounds. His relationship with Hitler was no joke. He had said Berlin was safe from attack, yet it had no air defences at all. The British could come and go as they pleased. People were shocked. They had believed themselves to

25 & 26. Fighting tactics: (top) four Bf 109s showing the standard 'Schwarm' formation to the cameras, though in practice they would fly further apart; and (below), 85 Squadron demonstrate the standard RAF 'vic' formation. They really did fly into action this close together. The survival of RAF fighter pilots depended to no small extent on how quickly they gave up what the Germans called the 'Idiotenreihe'.

27, 28 & 29. Three potential prey in the aerial hunting ground: (top) the Boulton-Paul Defiant, designed as a bomber-destroyer with a heavy power-operated turret and no forward armament, which, thanks to Dowding's opposition, equipped only two squadrons, both of which were massacred; (centre) a Ju 87B Stuka of the 3rd Staffel of StG/77 with its cheerful crew and ground staff. It was far more accurate but also far slower and more vulnerable than the Luftwaffe's medium bombers and withdrawn from operations after 18 August, when this Staffel alone lost five aircraft; (bottom) the He 59 seaplane used by the Germans for air-sea rescue, and attacked as a matter of policy by the British, despite its Red Cross markings, which outraged many Germans at the time and still rankles with some veterans today.

30 & 31. Two Adolfs who were outstanding air leaders: (left) Adolf Galland being helped into his life jacket by one of his ground-crew; (right) the South African Adolf Malan, who dropped his first name in favour of 'Sailor' when he joined the RAF, pictured in early 1943 on becoming Station Commander at Biggin Hill.

32. A Heinkel He 111 over Docklands at 1848 on 7 September 1940, the first daylight raid on central London.

33. The Operations Room at Fighter Command Headquarters at Bentley Priory in 1940.

34. Pilots of 501 Squadron at Gravesend doing a scramble for the benefit of newsmen on 16 August. Two days later, seven of them were shot down in their most costly day of battle, four of them in a repeated bounce by Gerhard Schoepfel, Gruppenkommandeur of III.JG26. The leading figure, Kenneth Lee, was his final victim, and never saw his assailant. The figure behind Lee far right is Flight Lieutenant George Stoney, killed later in the day when pressing on alone to attack some bombers after the rest of the Squadron were embroiled with their escorts. The man who killed him, Hauptmann Foezoe of JG51, said he was 'a very brave man, the only English fighter in the whole wide area'.

35 & 36. 'Weasel' and 'Wombat'. (Above left) Flight Lieutenant Patrick Woods-Scawen of 85 Squadron - 'little Patrick who smiled with his eyes' - and (above right) his younger brother, Pilot Officer Tony Woods-Scawen of 43 Squadron - 'who looked like a rabbit and was as blind as a bat'.

37. Their widowed father pictured in 1941 outside Buckingham Palace having just collected their DFCs from the King. Next to him is Una Lawrence, the childhood sweetheart the boys called 'Bunny' and with whom they both fell in love, and their cousin George, who was killed in October 1941 while serving with 92 Squadron.

38. Squadron Leader Peter Townsend pictured in May 1940 while still at 43 Squadron having been awarded the DFC for shooting down three lone raiders. He took command of 85 Squadron on 23 May. Here he is demonstrating to his rigger and fitter why his life jacket was known as a 'Mae West'.

39. Last in a dramatic set of pictures taken at 1210 on 15 September 1940, showing the remains of the fuselage section of the Do 17 piloted by Rudolf Zehbe of I./KG76 plunging down to crash next to Victoria Station, having been claimed by nine pilots, the last of whom rammed it. Its bombs landed in the grounds of nearby Buckingham Palace. The Operations Record Book of 11 Group unblushingly recounts that on that day 'one enemy aircraft made a deliberate dive-bombing attack on Buckingham Palace'.

40 & 41. An image of merry pilots turned into an icon by its use in the official Air Ministry pamphlet issued in 1941. The picture was staged for official photographers by 249 Squadron on 21 September shortly after their arrival in North Weald. (Below) Compare the images of the figures fifth from left and second from right with these, taken in November after several weeks of intensive combat. The faces of Pilot Officer Tom Neil (left) and Flying Officer Richard Barclay (right) show the meaning of the term 'exhaustion'. By then, one of the pilots pictured above was dead and two were in hospital. Both Neil and Barclay carried on flying without a rest. Barclay was killed in Africa in 1942, but Tom Neil happily survived the Battle of Malta and the war.

42 & 43. Bob Doe standing by his new Spitfire at Leconfield in early 1940 and (inset) sixty years later.

44 & 45. Flight Lieutenant 'Sandy' Sanders DFC in 1940 and Wing Commander James Sanders in 2000.

be immune, and suddenly they were vulnerable.[20] Furthermore, the Führer did not believe that the Luftwaffe was clearing the skies over England, and said so on the 30th. Göring was in trouble.

Bombing Berlin was a political act requiring a political response. Hitler was going to give that response to the German people, and it needed to be acted upon. For very different reasons, Göring agreed with Kesselring that they had to attack London. There was no alternative.[21]

There was by now a strong groundswell of opinion within the German military hierarchy that this step was overdue. It had been Hitler's sacred cow for too long. Jodl had always been in favour of trying it. At a meeting with Hitler which took place on Eagle Day itself, he had strongly recommended a ruthless air attack on London the day before the invasion. A mass exodus of the population would result in a stream of refugees comparable to that which had clogged the roads of France a few weeks earlier and made movement impossible for the Allied armies.[22]

In any case, it did not really matter too much if the Luftwaffe could not knock out the RAF and Sealion had to be postponed. There was more than one way to defeat England. An attack on London could be the beginning of extended economic warfare and a U-boat siege. Then Gibraltar and Egypt could be taken from her. As the cost of prosecuting the war grew, England would come round. The key thing was to break her will to resist by the Spring of 1941, when it would be Russia's turn. Invasion was not the only, nor even the best, way.[23]

Hitler had reiterated on 22 August that Sealion would only be carried out if the conditions were particularly favourable. In the meantime, Franco was approached about co-operating on Gibraltar.[24] There were plenty of options. So the Luftwaffe might as well have its last try at creating particularly favourable conditions for Sealion.

On 4 September, Hitler chose the opening of the Winter Relief Campaign at the Sportpalast in Berlin for his political response. His audience largely consisted of women nurses and social workers, precisely the people who would be the closest witnesses to the effects of bombing Berlin.

Hitler opened with a joke. The English were full of curiosity, he said, and kept asking, 'When is he coming?' 'Don't worry,' exclaimed Hitler. 'He's coming! He's coming! They should not be so curious.' The audience found this very funny.

He then came to the subject of Mr Churchill's 'new invention', the night attack. The British had to attack at night because they could not fly over Germany in daylight. The Luftwaffe, of course, was darkening the skies over England every day.

He returned to his peace offer of 19 July, and said his patience was at an end. He thought the British would stop this pointless war, but clearly they thought his offer was a sign of weakness. Now the Luftwaffe was answering them night after night. If the British say they will attack German cities, he thundered, we will wipe theirs out. 'The time will come,' he averred, 'when one of us will break, and it will not be National Socialist Germany!'

The crowd leapt to their feet in ecstasy. 'Never! Never!' they shouted.[25]

The bombs on the Görlitzer station had killed eight civilians. The crowd wanted revenge. They got it. Those upon whom they wrought their vengeance then wanted it for themselves. They were to get that as well. By the time it all stopped 60,000 British and 600,000 German civilians had died, and half of Europe was turned to ashes and ruin.[26]

On the morning of 7 September 1940, the Air Ministry issued Invasion Alert No.1 ('Attack Imminent') to its Commands. Park was due to see Dowding, Evill and Douglas at Bentley Priory. He had made his dispositions the night before and Willoughby de Broke could handle things well enough. As long as the air-fields were covered, things would be all right. But before he left, he issued Instruction 12 to his controllers. During the previous week, he wrote, it had become apparent that bombers had on numerous occasions been getting through undisturbed. In the case of one raid during the 6th, only seven out of eighteen squadrons intercepted and, during another, seven out of seventeen. This was because controllers sent the interceptors in too high and the pilots then added a few thousand feet themselves. Bombers got in below 15,000 feet and were only intercepted after they had bombed. The instruction went out, and Park left for Stanmore.

This was a difficult issue. Just as the German fighter pilots wanted to fly high on sweeps in order to bounce, so the British pilots wanted to fly high in order to prevent just that from happening. Escorting bombers had its prob-lems, but so did intercepting them. Both sets of pilots were understandably concerned about self-preservation. Given that height was the least reliable reading provided by the radar system, Park's men preferred not to take a chance.

It was a bright and sunny day. Everyone waited. Things were tense. What was going to happen? Something was up.

Nothing happened. Perhaps the German troops were getting onto their barges.

In fact, Göring was arriving at the Pas-de-Calais in his own train, *Asia*, to take personal command of the day's action, a rather hypothetical idea given that the plans had all been set. He had a new uniform, and was carrying his unique baton, the gold baton of a Reichsmarschall. As his cooks unloaded the cases of wine he had brought along, Kesselring and Loerzer greeted him with the pomp of a state visit. Then he went on an inspection of the fighter unit I./LG2 to have a chat with his boys and show them he was still himself a fighter pilot at heart. He tried and failed to get into the narrow cockpit of a Bf 109, which caused much amusement. When that was over, they picked up a few bot-tles of the better vintages and went for a picnic on the cliff-tops to exercise command and enjoy the show through binoculars.[27] The show was big enough and significant enough for it to be given a name, the name used throughout for London: '*Loge*', the God of fire. The next day would be the 25th anniversary of the first Zeppelin raid on London, when the German air force first introduced the world to bombing cities from the air. It now meant to celebrate in style.

It was at 1554 that a WAAF at Bentley Priory placed the first 'hostile' counter on her board. The raid looked as if it would be a big one. At 1616 the Observer Corps reported that 'many hundreds' of aircraft were approaching the coast. Five Kampfgeschwader had put up their full strength of 348 bombers, and they were accompanied by everything Osterkamp could muster, a total of 617 Bf 109s and Bf 110s. It was a maximum effort. They were stepped up between 14,000 and 23,000 feet in one huge formation.

By 1630, all the 21 squadrons within 70 miles of London were either in the air or at readiness. A few minutes later, the first of them made contact. They had never seen anything like it.

One of the first to arrive was 602 Squadron, scrambled together with 43 Squadron from Tangmere. They climbed through haze to 16,000 feet, and as they broke through the top, they saw them. 'I nearly jumped clean out of my cockpit', their leader, Sandy Johnstone, has recalled. 'Ahead and above a veritable armada of German aircraft . . . Staffel after Staffel as far as the eye could see . . . I have never seen so many aircraft in the air all at one time. It was awe-inspiring.'[28] Another said that the formation looked like the escalator at Piccadilly Circus.

Behind 602 came the Hurricanes of 43 Squadron. They were also amazed. But, as Churchill had said, they were undaunted by odds, and following past practice, three of them climbed in order to hold off the 600 fighters and the other six headed for the 350 bombers. Their new leader, the South African Caesar Hull, did not come back, and neither did the Australian-born Dick Reynell, a Hawker test pilot who had joined up to see some action.

It was new, and not very subtle, but it seemed to be working. The controllers had also been taken by surprise. They had been expecting attacks on airfields. This time the formation did not split up as it had done before, but ploughed straight on like a battering ram towards London. The controllers gave the squadrons the wrong vectors, so the interceptions were scrappy. KG1, KG30 and KG76 all began their bomb runs on Docklands unscathed. Following Park's Instruction on the 5th, squadrons were scrambled in pairs, with Hurricanes detailed for the bombers and Spitfires for the fighters, but the single German formation was too big for any pair to break it up. So when the German pilots did see British fighters, there did not seem to be many of them. Perhaps the intelligence reports were correct and the RAF really was finished.

Nevertheless, the armada was so big it was hard to miss, and, as Kesselring had hoped, a huge fight developed.

Up at Duxford, Leigh-Mallory seized his chance to try out his big idea for the first time and send in a whole wing under Douglas Bader. The wing was scrambled at 1645 and ordered to patrol North Weald/Hornchurch at 10,000 feet. Bader decided that this was too low. They tried to form up and eventually the two Hurricane squadrons, 242 and 310, arrived over North Weald at 15,000 feet with 19 Squadron strung out behind them. They saw a formation of bombers coming from the Thames Estuary and then they were bounced by the high cover escorts. The 109s shot down one aircraft of each of the Hurricane squadrons, killing one pilot and seriously wounding the other, and damaged four others, including Bader's.

The fighting drifted over the Isle of Sheppey, and soon involved over 1,000 aircraft from the two sides.

By 1745, the bombers had delivered their loads and were heading home, their formations battered but largely intact. They left the docks on fire and, as night fell, a second wave returned to keep them burning. Fighter Command had nothing but a few Blenheims and searchlights to oppose them with. From now on in London there would be blitzy nights as well as blitzy days.

The two sides assessed their gains and losses for the day. The sight of so many Germans had clearly got the Poles very excited. They claimed fourteen in exchange for the two they lost.

The Duxford wing claimed twenty-two: five from 19 Squadron (only a few of whom arrived in time to engage), six from 310 and eleven from 242. Given the nature of the fighting, it is impossible to say how many they actually accounted for. A great many of the German planes were hit by several fighters. From a comparison of actual German losses with pilots' combat reports it seems likely that the wing accounted for three Bf 110s and shared in the destruction of two others. They may also have got a couple of Bf 109s.[29]

The two 10 Group squadrons from Middle Wallop, 609 and 234, claimed six and seven respectively, but at the cost of Squadron Leader O'Brien, who had taken over 234 Squadron on 17 August, and Pat Hughes, who collided with a Dornier he was attacking, and crashed at St Mary Cray in Kent.[30] He had got married on 1 August. The pilots of 234 Squadron were waiting outside to meet his young bride, Kay, when she arrived at Middle Wallop that evening. She had said he always reminded her of Errol Flynn. After 38 days of anxious happiness, she learned for the first time, she said, what true grief was. She wept until she could cry no more.[31]

234 Squadron moved out back to St Eval on 11 September. Bob Doe does not remember much about the first week of the month because he was so tired. He does remember that after arriving in Cornwall he slept for most of the time until returning to the Battle on 28 September.[32]

In all, *Loge* cost the Luftwaffe only fourteen bombers, a loss rate of 4%, which was quite moderate compared with the horrors of Black Thursday. The fighters had done their job well, but it had cost them sixteen Bf 109s, with two pilots killed and ten captured, and seven Bf 110s together with their crews. The British could not really get through to the bombers, but they had done well this time when encountering the escorts. With the addition of some reconnaissance machines German combat losses for the day totalled forty-one.

All seven of the Bf 110 escorts lost were from ZG2, which had already suffered heavily. It was withdrawn from the battle and converted into a night-fighter unit. At about the same time, I./ZG76, the unit which had been desperately depleted in the single engagement over the North Sea on 15 August, was re-trained for night-fighting and converted into II./NJG1.[33] Bomber Command's raids on Germany, particularly the recent ones on Berlin, had made the need clear. It had also become clear that the Zerstörer would always take very heavy losses when used as fighters over England in daylight. ZG2 had been flying close escort to KG53, which attacked Newhaven. Nevertheless, the remaining six Zerstörer Gruppen soldiered on.

Fighter Command lost twenty-three aircraft and six pilots in combat, with another seven wounded. Overall fighter losses on both sides were the same. Significantly, although the Germans lost fewer single-engined fighters they lost twice as many of their pilots. It may also not be coincidence that five of the twelve Bf 109s lost were from JG51, which had been in action since early July, longer than any other unit.

When he landed at Duxford, Douglas Bader stomped to the phone in a fury and called the Operations Room, demanding to know why they had been scrambled so late. The Controller told him that he had been sent off as soon as 11 Group had called.[34] 11 Group had called as soon as they had realised the target was London. No-one at 11 Group knew that Bader wanted to form up a wing. Had he not spent time doing so, 19 Squadron, in their faster Spitfires, could have been above him over North Weald, and might have prevented the bounce. As a result of the lack of communication about tactics, one man was dead, and Bader had come as close as he cared to joining him. Instead of Leigh-Mallory's wing theory withering on the vine, attitudes began to harden.

Park got back to Uxbridge just as the raid was ending. After a quick discussion with Willoughby de Broke, Park left for nearby Northolt and took off in OK1 to have a look for himself. The docks had been the target, just as at Portsmouth, Liverpool and elsewhere many times before. But the East End was ablaze. Whatever the military intent, civilian areas had been badly hit. It was dreadful. It was his job to protect these people. But his airfields were now probably safe.

After Park had landed, he got a call from Churchill to tell him that there was an invasion alert. The church bells had been rung across the home counties and the Home Guard were at their posts. Neither he nor Churchill was particularly disturbed. Park had actually received a call from the Air Ministry to prepare to evacuate his southern airfields, but he had ignored it.[35] After a while the fuss died down.

Dowding and Park met the following morning. Both of them believed that the previous day's events signalled a fundamental change and that attacks on London would continue. They were both heartily relieved that the pressure was off the airfields, and they were about to implement a scheme to take the pressure off the pilots as well and reduce losses in the air.

Just as Kesselring thought that Dowding had made a mistake in not withdrawing from the south, so Dowding thought Kesselring had made a mistake in turning on London. Most people have agreed with him ever since. Kesselring did not know how important the Sector Stations were, but Dowding did, so his relief on being free of the danger of losing Operations Rooms is understandable. In fact, it made little difference. Even if he had known what he was doing, Kesselring is unlikely to have succeeded. In any case, Dowding did not know that Kesselring only had another week, and that he now wanted a decisive action. To Dowding, the whole battle was one of attrition, and could go on indefinitely. To Kesselring, that phase was over. If Kesselring's gamble on London paid off, either the invasion could take place or the British government would face such chaos and loss of civilian life that it would come to the negotiating table. If it did not pay off, it would be the beginning of a protracted campaign against the British war economy.

Dowding and Park agreed the next set of moves. Two grand old squadrons, 43 at Tangmere and 111 at Croydon, would move to 13 Group and become category 'C' units. It was sad, but they had the skill and experience to whip some youngsters into shape. At Biggin Hill, 79 Squadron had lost seven Hurricanes in the last ten days, and if attacks were from now on going to be on London, Park wanted fast-climbing Spitfire squadrons at Biggin Hill to get at the escorts early on. So 79 were pulled out, and for the last time Dowding risked a transfer from the north to replace them. It had to be 92 Squadron. They were unusual – they had not seen much action since Dunkirk, but they had something of a reputation. They included some colourful characters and good fighter pilots, men like Don Kingaby, Brian Kingcome, 'Wimpey' Wade and Bob Stanford Tuck. They were worth taking a chance on.

There was a different plan for Tuck, though. 257 Squadron had a miserable record. Since May, it had lost eleven out of its twenty original pilots and was now leaderless. The two Flight Commanders had been shot down and killed the previous afternoon. One of them, Hugh Beresford, had in fact been leading the squadron; their nominal Squadron Leader was a wash-out. He could go to a training unit and Tuck could have a bash at turning them around.

There were only a few raids that day. The poor weather made interception difficult. The Luftwaffe lost more machines in accidents than in combat, though the gunners claimed a few.

At midday, Churchill visited the docks and the East End with his brother Jack, Duncan Sandys and his Chief of Staff, Lord Ismay. Their car moved slowly through the narrow, partially blocked streets. They found a shelter that had taken a direct hit, killing forty people. Churchill broke down in tears. Ismay wrote to Churchill afterwards: 'They stormed you, as you got out of the car with cries of, "It was good of you to come, Winnie. We thought you'd come. We can take it. Give it 'em back . . ." I heard an old woman say, "You see, he really cares, he's crying."'[36]

The Luftwaffe waited for darkness. Then they came with a vengeance. Fires raged, 412 people died and another 747 were seriously injured. *Loge* had come to London, and his reign would last for fifty-seven nights.

On 9 September, OKL explicitly showed that it was backing two horses, decision and siege, by issuing detailed orders for the round-the-clock bombing of the British capital. The weather was poor, but several raids were launched, the biggest in the afternoon. It was directed against the southern suburbs and the airfield at Farnborough. Eight squadrons, including the Duxford wing, attacked them over Croydon. Some of the experienced squadrons entered the fray with some success. 602 Squadron claimed five for the loss of one Spitfire. 41 Squadron, who had been resting at Catterick after their work over the Channel (which included wounding Werner Mölders), and had arrived at Hornchurch on the 3rd, claimed seven for no loss. Bader's three squadrons claimed twenty between them, eleven of them from 242. However, 242 Squadron lost two Hurricanes and 310 lost two more in a collision as they went into action. In each case, one of the pilots died. Two of 19 Squadron's Spitfires were also damaged.[37]

All told, Fighter Command lost seventeen planes and six pilots, five of the aircraft and three of the pilots being from 607 Squadron which had moved to Tangmere on 1 September, but seen no action until the 9th. Their story needs no telling. The Luftwaffe lost twenty-four aircraft in combat, including thirteen Bf 109s and ten of their pilots. At that rate, Kesselring needed a decision soon.

Park was unhappy, however. Only twelve out of twenty squadrons scrambled managed to intercept. This may have been because of the weather but, as far as Park was concerned, it still was not good enough. He wanted to inflict heavy casualties. It was also clear that to stop a single mass attack like this he needed to concentrate his forces first. He sent a signal to controllers the following day asking them to send up pairs of Spitfire squadrons at the escorts and pairs of Hurricane squadrons at the bombers. Clearly concerned about the numbers engaging, he issued Instruction 16 the next day, reiterating this in more detail. As far as possible, squadrons at the same station were to work together; failing that, those in adjacent stations. Controllers should specify the base for rendezvous and the squadron that was to lead, but give all orders to both squadrons so they could operate separately if necessary.[38]

The 10th was washed out by the weather, and the forecast was poor. Hitler therefore postponed the date for his decision on Sealion to the 14th.

The weather did not stop Bomber Command; in fact it probably helped them. It had had a bad night, losing ten aircraft in various operations. But during the day, its planes struck at Eindhoven airfield and destroyed nine Heinkels of II./KG4 on the ground without loss to themselves.

There were also some deliberations about tactics. Bader flew to 12 Group HQ at Hucknall to meet Leigh-Mallory and examine the results of the past few days. They decided that part of the problem they had been having stemmed from the three-squadron wing being too small. More Spitfires were needed to hold off the high-flying escorts. The wing should really be made up of five squadrons. So Leigh-Mallory gave Bader 611 and 74 Squadrons, which had just been re-equipped with the new Spitfire Mark IIs, to add to 242, 310 and 19.[39] 74 replaced 616 at Duxford. Their leader was 'Sailor' Malan, who had his own ideas about air fighting.

The morning of the 11th was cold and windy. It was not until about 1530 that a raid appeared, a force of bombers escorted by about 200 fighters. Nine squadrons attacked them, but could not get through the fighter screen. It turned into a fighter battle, in which the 109s generally had position on their side. The Duxford wing, now a Big Wing, went into action under Brian Lane, the C/O of 19 Squadron. Malan dutifully tagged along with 74 Squadron to join 19, 266 and 611 in the dogfighting over Kent. The Bf 109s, using up fuel in the fighting, had to head for home, and the bombers, from KG26, went on alone under constant attack. More waves of Bf 109s on sweeps came over to protect the raiders as they returned, but the bombers had been alone long enough to be exposed, and lost seven Heinkels.

There was also some activity further west. Erprobungsgruppe 210 had been moved across to Cherbourg after their raid on Brooklands to deal with another, even more worthwhile target that needed their skills – the Spitfire factory at Woolston on Southampton Water. Whilst production of the new Mark II at Castle Bromwich near Birmingham was rising, the bulk of the Mark Is then equipping the squadrons were assembled at Woolston, Itchen and Eastleigh, all in or near Southampton.[40]

Erprobungsgruppe 210 came down in a shallow dive and the first bombs fell at 1613. They did some damage, and escaped unscathed. They had hit the wrong factory, the Cunliffe-Owen works, which assembled Hudsons for Coastal Command and made parts for Stirlings. The Spitfires were safe for the time being, but reconnaissance flights showed Woolston to be undamaged, so Erprobungsgruppe 210 would have to return.

At the end of the day, the Germans had come off best in the fighter battle. They lost eleven bombers and seven Bf 110s, but only three Bf 109s, a total of twenty-one. The RAF lost twenty-seven Spitfires and Hurricanes, and two Blenheims which had been given the dreadful task of escorting a raid on Calais.

Some of the squadrons did well. The old hands of 74 Squadron claimed five for no loss and 303 predictably claimed sixteen, though they lost two themselves. But the newcomers, 46 Squadron, lost four aircraft and two pilots and only claimed one in return.[41] 92 Squadron lost three Spitfires, but they ebulliently claimed nine. 266 and the Canadians lost one and two respectively for scant return. It was the same problem, whether the attacks were on the airfields or London. 11 September was one of the days the Luftwaffe had hoped would be typical, one of the very few in which they inflicted more casualties than they suffered, almost one and a half times as many. The level of delusion was also reversed. The RAF claimed eighty-seven, four times the actual number.

On the evening of what was thought to have been a good day, Churchill broadcast to a population which was now 'taking it' all over the country.

The German effort to secure daylight mastery of the air over England was of course, he said, 'the crux of the whole war.' These efforts had so far failed, and cost them dear. The RAF was stronger now than at the beginning of July. On the other hand, he said, 'there is no doubt that Herr Hitler is using up his fighter force at a very high rate, and that if he goes on for many more weeks he will wear down and ruin this vital part of his Air Force.' Yet if they did not win the air battle, an invasion would be too hazardous for the Germans to contemplate. They were preparing for one, and if it were to come at all, it had to be soon. He then put the situation into the sort of terms he had used in his rallying call of 18 June:

> Therefore, we must regard the next week or so as a very important period in our history. It ranks with the days when the Spanish Armada was approaching the Channel, and Drake was finishing his game of bowls; or when Nelson stood between us and Napoleon's Grand Army at Boulogne. We have read all about this in the history books; but what is happening now is on a far greater scale and of far more consequence to the life and future of the world and its civilisation than these brave old days of the past.

He finished by dealing with the bombing, and Hitler's hope that he might thereby 'terrorise and cow the people ... and make them a burden and anxiety to the Government.' Instead, he said, Hitler had kindled 'a fire in British hearts' which would burn on 'until the last vestiges of Nazi tyranny have been burnt out of Europe', and he called upon everybody to unite until victory was won.[42]

Indeed, 7 September must be the day on which any possibility of a negotiated peace finally evaporated in the fires lit by the Luftwaffe's incendiaries. Hitler had given up on England. Hoping until then to make the people turn on their leadership, he instead united them, just as the fires the RAF was to light in Berlin were to weld the German people to him, and as every act of bombing has united its victims with each other, their cause and their leader, whoever he may be, ever since.

On the next two days, the weather was so bad that there was hardly any flying. Luftwaffe incursions were restricted to reconnaissance flights and lone nuisance raiders making use of the heavy cloud. One of these solved a political problem which had begun to concern the government since the raids on the East End on the 7th – Harold Nicolson, a junior minister, confided to his diary on 12 September that 'everyone is worried about the feeling in the East End where there is much bitterness; it is said that even the King and Queen were booed the other day'. On the 13th, however, the Luftwaffe completed the job of creating solidarity amongst the British population when bombs fell on Buckingham Palace, wrecking the Royal Chapel. It meant, as the Queen said,

316 THE MOST DANGEROUS ENEMY

that the Royal couple could 'now look the East End in the face', which they did,
and their popularity soared.[43]

The press and the authorities seized their chance and made as much capital as they could out of it. Later wartime accounts of the Battle of Britain
hammered home the message:

> For some obscure reason the Nazis wished to kill the King and
> Queen! There is no possible doubt that the attacks on Buckingham
> Palace were deliberate . . . Seduced by the glamour of regicide, or
> acting on orders, the Nazi airmen ignored . . . important military
> objectives in an area which fairly bristles with them . . . Hitler had
> tried to kill the King. After that all Londoners were in the same boat,
> and there was not the ghost of a chance of the misery and suffering of
> the multitude taking a revolutionary turn. Instead of that, a flame of
> hatred of the Nazis . . . illuminated all classes.[44]

The possibility of popular disillusion with the war leading politicians to get rid
of Churchill and negotiate an armistice was Hitler's main hope, so it was
important to deny it could ever have occurred. Nobody explained how an aircrew could have found and then deliberately hit Buckingham Palace through
unbroken cloud cover.

Nevertheless, the story needed completion by finding a pilot who shot
down the wicked Hun perpetrating the deed. 'Ginger' Lacey was on patrol that
day and hit a Heinkel over Maidstone. Return fire from the Heinkel hit his radiator and he baled out at 1345, coming down near Leeds Castle. The bombs had
fallen on the Palace much earlier in the morning, but this was a detail. Even
after the war, Lacey's biography was marketed as being of the pilot who 'shot
down the Heinkel that bombed Buckingham Palace'.[45] The only Heinkel to
come down over Britain on 13 September was one which collided with a balloon cable and crashed in Newport, South Wales, at 3.30 a.m. Two others
crashed on return to France from operational flights over England. It may be
that Lacey's victim was one of these. Whether they had actually been engaged
on a mission that would have been not only politically inept but also, given the
weather conditions and the navigational and bomb-aiming technology of 1940,
a matter of luck, has never been ascertained.

Park used the break in the weather to study the action in more detail by
going through combat reports. On the 13th he sent round a note to his Sector
Station Commanders summarising his observations. Several things stood out:
the effectiveness of head-on attacks, which should be employed as often as possible; the need for squadrons to keep together, for the size of German
formations now encountered made flights and sections totally ineffective; and
the number of pilots wasting their time on lame ducks, most of which went
down anyway. Park reminded his pilots that 'their primary task should be to
engage enemy aircraft which have not previously been attacked.' He knew why

they did it. They should not follow their victims down: 'If you still have ammunition left, help your mates in the main engagement. It is unfortunate not to have the pleasure of seeing your victims crash, but this serves no useful purpose.'[46]

On the afternoon of Friday the 13th, Churchill as usual drove to Chequers for the weekend, and, as was becoming usual, stopped briefly at 11 Group HQ on the way.[47] There was nothing going on. Perhaps his next visit would be more interesting.

On the 14th, the weather let up slightly, and there was some activity, mainly Bf 109s on sweeps. The day followed the pattern of the 11th. Again, the new boys suffered. Galland had been out prowling and JG26 alone made seven claims, though they lost one of the Staff Flight of I./JG26 to a Hurricane of 253 Squadron over Maidstone. 222 Squadron and 66 Squadron lost two each, and 73 Squadron were given a hammering over Kent when they were bounced, losing three Hurricanes with four more damaged. In the confused fighting they were set upon by some Spitfires as well. 73 had flown in from 12 Group, where they had been re-fitted after having been almost destroyed in France. The tally for the day was eleven British to eight German machines. Though the numbers were small, it was another of Fighter Command's worst days.

Yet there was a silver lining to the cloud. Since the 7th, the weather had prevented much fighting, giving the pilots a little time to rest. It made interception difficult, and that, combined with the confusion on the 7th, led the Luftwaffe to believe opposition was weakening. What they found was scrappy. Perhaps the RAF really was down to its last 200 planes. Perhaps there were even fewer. Perhaps one more push would do the job.

Hitler decided to postpone his decision about Sealion once again. The day before he seemed to be inclining towards forgetting about it altogether, but he finally decided to leave it till the 17th. The last day of favourable tides would be the 21st, so this was his last chance to launch Sealion before 1941. He by no means wanted to force the issue, he said – it all depended on having air superiority. The threat of invasion should in any case be continued in order to exercise moral pressure on the British government.[48] He discussed the air situation with Milch and Luftwaffe Chief of Staff Jeschonnek. The raids were to be kept to the dock areas. Hitler did not want an attack on the civilian population yet. It was a pity that the weather had prevented the Luftwaffe from gaining mastery of the air over the last week. Now, at last, the weather forecast was improving.[49]

It looked as if it would be fine in London the next day. Then everyone would find out where things stood.

26. BATTLE OF BRITAIN DAY

On Sunday, 15 September 1940, dawn broke at 6.34 a.m. At 0700 hours GMT, which was 0800 British Summer Time, the Met. Office reported slowly rising pressure, heralding unsettled weather. The UK was sandwiched between an area of low pressure to the north-east of Norway and an area of high pressure to the south-west around the Azores, giving a light westerly breeze that dispersed the layer of strato-cumulus cloud which had been hanging over London. By dawn, most of it had gone, leaving just a few puffs of cumulus and a trace of stratus higher up. Visibility on the ground was four miles, a light mist soon burning off. The temperature was 14° Centigrade, 57° Fahrenheit.[1] It was a beautiful late summer day. Many went to church after the Prime Minster's broadcast on Wednesday evening. It was also perfect weather for tending the garden, strolling to the pub or launching major air attacks.

The day began badly for Keith Park. It was rare indeed for him to be wrong-footed, but this time he was caught napping. Over breakfast, his wife, Dol, casually mentioned that it was her birthday. He had forgotten. History has not recorded his exact response. He had, after all, been rather pre-occupied with the defence of Western civilisation, but whether he used this as an excuse or not we do not know. We do know that he was apologetic – a judicious recovery gambit, given his weak position. This move seems to have been successful, as it put his wife into a conciliatory mood, and she told him that 'a good bag of German aircraft would be an excellent present.'[2]

Having thus avoided potential disaster on the home front, Park left his house through the green wooden door at the back of his garden which led directly to the entrance of the 'bunker' at RAF Uxbridge. Having negotiated the several flights of steps, he entered his Control Room. One squadron at each Sector Station had been brought to readiness at 0700. There were the usual reconnaissance flights, and in 10 Group 87 Squadron shot down one Heinkel over the sea near Exeter at 0830.

However, Park was soon to be confronted with another problem. At about 1030, he received word that the Prime Minister wanted to drop in.

Over breakfast at Chequers, Churchill's mind had been on the offensive operations he wanted to launch in 1941. Having dictated a letter to Admiral of the Fleet Sir Dudley Pound, urging him to ensure that adequate numbers of landing craft were built 'as soon as possible', he took a look at the weather and decided that it was going to be a blitzy day.[3] He therefore resolved to visit Uxbridge again on his way in to London and, together with Mrs Churchill, John Martin and an armed bodyguard, he set off in a car at breakneck speed. 'He liked to drive very fast,' Martin is reported as saying, 'and would urge the driver to go faster. The car was fitted with a police gong so it could ignore traffic lights and hazards like that; there was very little traffic anyway.'[4]

On Churchill's arrival, Park had the tricky job of explaining to him, as he had on every previous visit of this kind, that the air-conditioning system in the underground Operations Room could not deal with cigar smoke. The Prime Minister grunted and observed the unfolding drama with an unlit Havana clenched between his teeth.[5]

Nothing happened. The plotting board was clear, and Park said he did not know whether or not there would be much activity.

The main forces available to Kesselring were close to 500 bombers, 120 Bf 110s and just over 500 Bf 109s. Dowding had 126 Hurricanes and Spitfires in 10 Group, 194 in 12 Group and 310 in 11 Group, with what was effectively a strategic reserve of another 172 in 13 Group, now made up of 'B' and 'C' squadrons. The 500 Bf 109s therefore had to deal with 630 Spitfires and Hurricanes in the front line. The Spitfires and Hurricanes had to defend their airspace against 1,120 German aircraft. The margins on both sides were narrow. No-one could afford to make a mistake.

Kesselring chose III./KG76, the veterans of Kenley and Biggin Hill, commanded by the stalwart Bavarian Alois Lindmayr, to open his attack. However, as they only had nineteen Dorniers left out of an establishment of thirty, they were joined by the even more depleted I. Gruppe, which could now muster only eight machines. They took off at 1010, joined up and headed for Cap Gris Nez to rendezvous with their escorts, but not before having lost ten minutes searching for each other in clouds, during which two planes got lost and returned to base. The escorts took off as ordered at 1100, but had to burn up fuel over Calais while they waited for the Dorniers. The CH radar at Dover picked them up at 1104.

Underground at Uxbridge, Churchill saw a WAAF put down her knitting and move over the table to place a small wooden block marked with the letters 'H06 30+' on it. This denoted 'hostile' raid number 6, of at least 30 aircraft. Park excused himself and walked over to the main gallery to join Willoughby de Broke. Were they just fighters or was it a real raid? Park decided to scramble 92 and 72 Squadrons at Biggin Hill and get them over Canterbury at 25,000 feet. From that height they could take on the high escorts if he chose to engage.

At Biggin Hill, the pilots of 92 Squadron had been up since 4.30 in the morning. They waited in the dispersal hut round a pot-bellied stove which the Duty Ops telephone operator lit every morning. Some dozed fitfully in the iron cots around the walls, some played with flying helmets or oxygen tubes, others studied aircraft identification charts. There was a poster on the wall with black crosses painted on it, and beneath it the words: 'Remember the Hun in the Sun'. Suddenly an engine roared into life on the other side of the airfield. 'God, how I hate this waiting,' someone said. 'Why don't the buggers come?' At that moment, the Ops phone went. Flying Officer Brian Kingcome grabbed it. They called him 'King-Pin Kingcome', and he often led them in the air. There was silence and all eyes were on him. 'OK, chaps, it's scramble Angels twenty, rendezvous with 72 over base.' As they rushed for their Spitfires 72 Squadron were already taking off.[6]

The first marker was swiftly followed by 'H04 30+' and 'H10 40+'. Lindmayr and his escorts had finally made contact. Park decided that it was a serious raid. It was 1115. He called out his orders: 'Northolt, Kenley, Debden'. He watched the board. Nothing else was coming. If this was the real one, he needed to meet it in force. At 1120 he called out, 'Hornchurch, North Weald,' and ordered 10 Group to scramble Middle Wallop. He now had two squadrons high and forward over Canterbury, four over Biggin Hill and Maidstone at 15,000 feet to meet the bombers and a pair over Chelmsford to back them up. The Hornchurch squadron, 603, would head for Dover at 20,000 feet, so it should arrive just after 92 and 72 had made their first attack on the high escorts, by which time the dogfight would have descended somewhat and they could get at the close escorts. The pair from North Weald would head for Maidstone so that, if the bombers got through, they would run into them over London. The squadron from Middle Wallop would cover the flank for Park and guard a vital target by patrolling over Brooklands.

Park paused. The raid would arrive over London at about noon. If Kesselring behaved as he had usually done, most of the force would be fighters. Park's squadrons would have their hands full stripping them away. With a bit of luck, once the bombers were over London, they would be very exposed, and London had to be protected. There was also the nagging question of his northern airfields, though raiders attacking those had always come via the Thames Estuary. It was time to call for support and see what Leigh-Mallory's 'Big Wing' was made of. It was 1125. He issued his next order. 'Call Stanmore. 12 Group to scramble Duxford and patrol Hornchurch at 20,000 feet.' They would be to the west of the bombers and a good 5,000 feet higher. They could take them out of the sun. If Leigh-Mallory could get there in time.

The wing was now a Big Wing. 74 Squadron and their tough, sceptical leader had been posted away from Duxford to Coltishall as a category 'B' Squadron on the 13th and replaced by the second Polish squadron, 302, which had seen little action. So when Woodhall got the message from Fighter Command that Sunday morning, he sent off 19, 310, 302 and 611 Squadrons, led by 242 Squadron under Douglas Bader as Wing leader. These fifty-six aircraft headed for Gravesend.

Alois Lindmayr's escorts had arrived. JG27 and JG52 were on a sweep ahead, JG53 formed top cover and JG3 had drawn the short straw and were flying close escort. Lindmayr was a stickler for tight formation flying, for the bombers' survival might well depend upon it. He did not know how long he would enjoy the company of the 109s. As a result, the bombers were travelling so slowly in their efforts to keep tight that some of the Bf 109s had to fly with their flaps down in order to hold position, which made them sitting ducks.[7] They crossed the coast near Folkestone at 1136.

At about that time, twenty-one Bf 109s of II./LG2 were just taking off. They were part of Göring's new scheme for using the Bf 109 as a fighter-bomber. They were to arrive over London before KG76, drop the bombs they had beneath their fuselages and then play the role of fighters. This was not exactly the low-level precision bombing role that Göring had envisaged. It was supposed to be a nuisance raid to distract the British from the real one. The pilots hoped they would not be too distracted, for with 550lb bombs under them, the Bf 109s would be easy meat. Taking off when they did, they should overhaul the Dorniers quite soon.

At 1142, more markers appeared on the table at Uxbridge. There seemed to be a second wave. Park wanted to engage this one as it came in and also keep up the pressure on the Germans whilst his first squadrons were re-arming and re-fuelling. Half an hour had passed since his first scramble. He now ordered off six more squadrons, keeping the remaining four on the ground at Tangmere and Hornchurch. As the forces closed, something like 120 Bf 109s and 25 Dorniers were facing 254 Hurricanes and Spitfires.

The Dorniers were moving through the air slowly enough, but they were moving even more slowly over the ground. At the height they were flying, 16,000 feet, there was a strong head wind. It would take them all even longer to reach the target, and the escorts would run out of fuel even sooner. It would also speed the British interceptors on their way. Thank God, Lindmayr's men thought, there weren't too many of them left.

As the Biggin Hill squadrons met up and climbed in a left-hand circuit to their operational altitude, the Sector Controller directed them to their interception. 'Hello, Gannic Leader! Gannic Leader! Carfax calling! 200-plus coming in over Red Queen. Vector 120. Angels 25. Watch out for snappers above.'

They arrived over Canterbury at 25,000 feet as instructed, and saw JG53 some 3,000 feet below over Ashford, with KG76 and JG3 another 6,000 feet below them. Anxious eyes scanned the sky above for 'snappers', but there were no specks to be seen. They were above the top cover. In a minute or two they would be south of them and could then curve in and bounce them out of the sun. That was just what they did.

It was at 1150 that the ground controllers heard Flight Lieutenant 'Pancho' Villa of 72 Squadron call out, 'Tennis Squadron, tally-ho'. Seconds later they

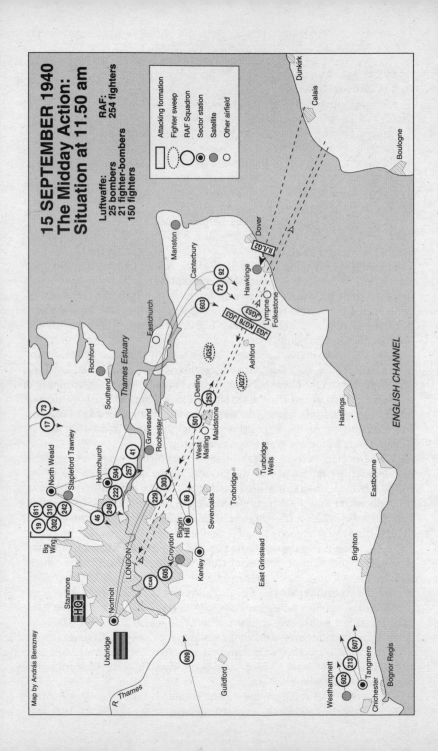

Map by András Bereznay

15 SEPTEMBER 1940
The Midday Action:
Situation at 11.50 am

Luftwaffe:
25 bombers
21 fighter-bombers
150 fighters

RAF:
254 fighters

Attacking formation
Fighter sweep
RAF Squadron
Sector station
Satellite
Other airfield

ENGLISH CHANNEL

Dunkirk
Calais
Boulogne

Dover
Hawkinge
II/LG2
Folkestone
Lympne JG3 KG76 JG63
JG63
JG53

Manston
Canterbury
Eastchurch
Ashford
JG52
JG27
Detling
Maidstone
West Malling
253
501
92
72
603

Hastings
Tunbridge Wells
Tonbridge
Sevenoaks
East Grinstead
Eastbourne
Brighton

Rochford
Southend
Thames Estuary
Gravesend
Rochester
Hornchurch
North Weald
Stapleford Tawney
Big Wing
73
17
41
257
504
222
242
310
611
19
302
249
46
303
229
66
Biggin Hill
Kenley
Croydon
LONDON
1CAN
605
Northolt
HQ
Stanmore
Uxbridge

R. Thames
Guildford
Westhampnett
Chichester
Tangmere
Bognor Regis
602
213
607
609

15 SEPTEMBER 1940
The Afternoon Action:
Situation at 14.20

Luftwaffe:
114 bombers
20 heavy fighters
340 fighters

RAF:
276 fighters

▭	Attacking formation
⬭	Fighter sweep
◯	RAF Squadron
◉	Sector station
●	Satellite
◯	Other airfield

Map by András Bereznay

ENGLISH CHANNEL

Dunkirk

Calais

Boulogne

Manston

Canterbury

Dover

Folkestone

Hawkinge

Lympne

LG22

Eastchurch

603

Southend

Rochford

Thames Estuary

Chatham

Detling

JG26

Maidstone

607

JG77 92

41 222

KG3 KG26

213 KG53

605 KG53

JG3 JG53

501

JG51

West Malling

Sevenoaks

17 257

Hornchurch

73

249

504

Bexley
Gravesend

North Weald

Stapleford Tawney

46

229
DCM

66

72

Tonbridge

Tunbridge
Wells

Hastings

Eastbourne

611
310
242

19 302

Big Wing

West Ham

LONDON
Docks

303

Croydon

Biggin Hill

253

Kenley

East Grinstead

Brighton

Stanmore

HQ

Northolt

Uxbridge

238

Guildford

609

602

R. Thames

Westhampnett

Chichester

Tangmere

Bognor Regis

heard, 'Tally-ho right, Gannic. Here they come, chaps'. It was Kingcome's voice. 'OK, boys, let's go!' The lights on the 'tote' board at Uxbridge under 72 and 92 Squadrons lit up against 'Engaged'.

The pilots of JG53 were also scanning the sky. Suddenly there was a call: *'Achtung, Indianer!'* Almost simultaneously, the aircraft of Feldwebel Alfred Müller, who was temporarily leading the 1st Staffel, belched smoke and went into a shallow dive. Müller called out over the R/T that he had been hit, but then it was every man for himself. In the first pass, the Spitfires hit four or five Bf 109s of I./JG53, and dived through to get at the bombers. Then 603 Squadron arrived to join the dogfight.

Park had peeled away the first layer of the onion. Now for the bombers. It was 1205. The Kenley Squadrons, 253 and 501, should be approaching the front of the formation at the same height.

They were, and they delivered a head-on attack. So disciplined were Lindmayr's men, however, that the formation remained intact, and JG3 waded into the Hurricanes as they re-formed for another pass, shooting down two from 501. The Northolt squadrons, 229 and 303, were now arriving. One of 229's Hurricanes collided with a Messerschmitt of JG52 over Staplehurst. As more British squadrons arrived, the Dorniers ploughed doggedly on. By 1207 they were over Lewisham, still together but for one machine of the I. Gruppe, piloted by Oberleutnant Robert Zehbe, which had engine trouble and was trailing half a mile behind. But the formation was isolated, the escorts embroiled over Kent. Half the British fighters had yet to engage.

The first to run into the bombers were the North Weald pair, 504 and 257 Squadrons. On this occasion, 257 was led by Peter Brothers, a veteran of 32 Squadron helping Tuck, in Debden, to turn the 'shower of deadbeats' he said he'd found on taking them over three days before, into an efficient unit. They had been doing fighting practice since Tuck had turned up, and now put it to good use.[8] The Dorniers were assailed on all sides, with particular attention reserved for the straggling machine piloted by Zehbe. Two planes from each squadron concentrated on him until, with two crewman dead, Zehbe ordered the other two to bale out, set the aircraft on auto-pilot, and followed them. He landed in Kennington near the Oval and, hanging by his parachute from some power cables, was set on by an angry mob, including several women with bread knives and pokers. He was rescued by the army and driven away, but he died of his wounds soon afterwards. Meanwhile, his Dornier flew on into history.

The main formation of Dorniers were just completing their bomb run on the railway lines running between Clapham Junction and Battersea power station when, still beset on all sides, they saw a collection of dots approaching from the north-west. They had seen their escorts bounced by what they thought were the last fifty Spitfires, then watched another last fifty Spitfires join the dogfight, then been attacked by yet another last fifty themselves, and here were the Spitfires back again. It was Bader with his now very Big Wing of five squadrons.

It was 1209. Lindmayr's force, flying over Battersea at 16,000 feet, kept formation and turned for the flight home. There were now so many British planes in the sky that they had to queue up to have a go at the Dorniers. When it was the Big Wing's turn, there were so many of them that they got in each other's way and had to break off to avoid colliding with or shooting at each other. KG76 held on grimly like an encircled wagon train.

Robert Zehbe's damaged Dornier, now empty and flying by itself, was attracting a swarm of fighters. It was attacked by five pilots from three squadrons. Finally, Sergeant Ray Holmes of 504 Squadron saw the lone machine flying on below him and dived to attack. As he pressed his gun-button nothing happened. He was out of ammunition. 'The machine looked so flimsy,' he said, 'I did not think of it as something solid and substantial. I just went right on and hit the Dornier.' The tail came away and the plane see-sawed, imposing enormous forces on the wings, which broke off beyond the engines. It spun viciously, the g-forces ejecting its bombs, which fell on Buckingham Palace. The remains of the fuselage landed at the corner of Wilton Road on the forecourt of Victoria Station. Holmes's Hurricane went into a vertical spin and he baled out, landing on a three-storey block of flats only yards from the railway lines. His parachute caught in some guttering, and he hung with his feet resting on the top of an empty dustbin. Cutting himself free, he kissed two girls who appeared in the next-door garden and, having inspected the nearby wreck of his kill, went to Chelsea Barracks to have a celebratory drink in the mess.

Only fifteen of Lindmayr's Dorniers remained in formation, and most of them were damaged. Six had been shot down and the other four were making back alone. As the main body retired, they were met by a covering force of Bf 109s and landed in France without further molestation, but with stories to tell about how close Fighter Command was to defeat. It is a tribute to their leader that they got back at all.

The fighter-bombers of LG2 had already come and gone. Coming in high, they looked like the usual fighter sweep, and Park had left them alone. Over London, they saw a railway station, went down in a 45° dive, released their bombs and flew back. They only saw one British fighter.

The attacking force had lost six bombers and twelve Bf 109s, eighteen machines in all, which was 12.5% of its strength. The returning British pilots made eighty-one claims, twenty-six of them from the Duxford Wing. Zehbe's Dornier alone was claimed nine times.

Still, it was a victory, if hardly a resounding one. Fighter Command lost thirteen fighters. They had held their own in the fighter battles and taken out a quarter of the bombers. Park would not have been pleased to learn that, after he had stripped a small bomber force of its protection to leave it flying over the middle of London surrounded by about a hundred fighters, three-quarters of it survived. By the end of the day, he began to suspect.

Still, his prescriptions of four days before had worked precisely. Churchill was impressed. As the plots faded away, he went down from the balcony to the floor of the room, cigar between his teeth, and said, 'Well done,' to the girls.

The intention of the midday raid had just been to wear the defenders down. As the British fighters were landing, the forces constituting the real thrust were forming up into five blocks. Their battle order was to be twenty-five Dorniers of III./KG2 followed by the eighteen of II./KG2 on the left, twenty-four Heinkels of I. and II./KG53 in the centre and nineteen Dorniers of II./KG3 followed by twenty-eight Heinkels of I. and II./KG26 on the right. It is significant that by this stage Kesselring was forced to amalgamate Gruppen to put together a proper formation of 114 aircraft.

They were just the bait. The main force consisted of 340 Bf 109s and 20 Bf 110s. Five Gruppen from JG3, JG53, JG77 and LG2 flew top cover while JG51 and the hunting masters JG26 were out on a free sweep ahead. Only one Gruppe, from JG54, flew close escort. For the sake of appearances, I./ZG26 and V./LG1 represented the Zerstörer, flying close escort for KG26.

There were 475 aircraft. It was only half the size of the armada which had first battered its way through to London the weekend before, but instead of there being twice as many fighters as bombers, now there were four times as many. Nor could the German fighter Kommodoren complain about being tied to the bombers: the bulk of them were high and mobile or on a free hunt.

They were picked up at 1345, and Park and the Prime Minister watched the plots build. This time, to get a better fix on the numbers and make-up of the raid, the controller scrambled a 'spotter', Flight Lieutenant Alan Wright of 92 Squadron, who had been sitting all alone at Hawkinge waiting for such an order. By 1405, Wright was at 26,000 feet and reporting back. He could also see six Bf 109s climbing up to get him, so he decided to get them first and dived on them. His speed increased to the point where his controls froze up and he could not manoeuvre for a shot. He went straight through the 109s, reduced pressure on the stick and the Spitfire pulled itself out of the dive, blacking him out. It had been trimmed for straight and level flight. When he came to, Wright made for Biggin Hill as fast as he could.

Park had already ordered the first scrambles, putting two squadrons over Sheerness at 20,000 feet, backed up by two over Chelmsford and another pair at Hornchurch at 15,000 feet. He also got Kenley airborne. Five minutes later, the plotters distinguished the three columns. They seemed to be coming on in the same old way, so he would throw them back in the same old way. He reinforced the squadrons east of London by sending two more to Hornchurch at 20,000 feet, put one more over the docks, and then established a forward line of seven squadrons between Biggin Hill and Kenley. Becoming certain that this was as close to a maximum effort as the Luftwaffe was going to make that day, at 1415 he called on 10 Group for another squadron over Kenley and contacted Stanmore to ask for the Big Wing over Hornchurch. He hoped it would indeed go there.

Certain that their target was London, Park was no longer intercepting as far forward as he used to. He held the bulk of his forces over north Kent and London to draw them in. He would hit them hardest at the point the Germans called '*die grosse Angstkurve über London*' ('the dreaded big turn over London'), when the Bf 109s were beginning to get uncomfortable but the bombers had yet to release their loads. This would also ensure that most of the fighting was over land, to protect his pilots and further imperil his enemy's.

He nevertheless needed all the time he had from when the raiders crossed the coast to strip off the fighter cover, but he wanted to do so economically. He sent the two Spitfire squadrons, 41 and 92, which had rendezvoused over Hornchurch together with 222, forward at 25,000 feet to Romney Marsh. At 1415, just after the raid passed over Dungeness, they heard: 'Mitor and Gannic Squadrons, tally-ho, tally-ho!' Twenty-seven British fighters plunged into the formation of 475, 'undaunted by odds' once again. But Park had given his young braves height and surprise, for there were too few of them to be easily spotted against the sun. As the calls of '*Indianer!*' and '*Achtung, Spitfire!*' crackled across the Bf 109s' R/T sets, the intrepid 'few' were already through them and away, claiming fourteen for the loss of only one Spitfire. Behind these few lurked a few more between Angels 15 and 20 – 250 of them – and behind those a few others were waiting on the ground – 630 in all: enough to do their country loss, and also inflict serious loss on the 114 bombers they were after.

As his forward units engaged, Park ordered up his own reserve, his Praetorian Guard of 602 and 303, to patrol Northolt and Biggin Hill respectively, and asked 10 Group to put the veteran 609 Squadron over Brooklands again.

As the raid moved forward, more and more squadrons engaged. 607 Squadron headed south from Kenley and delivered a frontal charge against the right-hand column, led by KG3's Dorniers. Horst Schulz watched in horror as a Hurricane filled the Plexiglass in front of him, its wings winking as its eight Brownings delivered Sorley's carefully worked-out bomber-killing package right at him. It roared overhead, there was a tremendous crash, bits of metal showered down in front of him, and Schulz saw a Dornier from somewhere above him spiral down, its starboard wing shattered. The Hurricane turned on its back, allowing Pilot Officer Paddy Stephenson to jump clear and land in Cranbrook with a broken ankle. The Dornier entered an accelerating spin, its g-forces pinning the crew to the inside of the cabin. They were still there when it plunged into a wood near Lamberhurst.

The Dorniers tried to hold formation as the escorts attempted to ward off the attackers, but more of them were coming in fast. 605 and 501 curved in from the flank and, as they were doing so, Flying Officer Cooper-Slipper's Hurricane was hit and he knew he would have to bail out. He was overtaking a Dornier from behind, so he stayed long enough to give it a bump. 'My overtaking speed was about 50mph and I was surprised at the small force of the impact,' he said afterwards. Both he and the Dornier crew took to their parachutes.

After delivering this attack, the fighters had broken off in all directions. Sergeant 'Ginger' Lacey of 501 Squadron found himself alone, but then saw some other fighters in the distance and set off to join up with them. He was approaching them head-on, but had been spending most of his time looking behind him, so only when he was close did he realise that they were 109s, and dived beneath them. As they flew straight on, he looped upwards behind them and, still inverted, picked off the rear machine from 150 yards. As there was still no reaction, he opened up on a second one from 250 yards and hit it as well. This time he was noticed and, with the whole of the Messerschmitt formation curving round on him from both sides, he put the nose of his Hurricane down and escaped into clouds.[9]

As the bombers passed over Chatham on their way to the docks, the gunners had a go. As the AA shells burst around them, two bombers fell out of formation, making them easy prey for the fighters.

It was 1435. At Uxbridge, Churchill watched Park as he stood behind Willoughby de Broke, his hands folded behind his back. He looked at the counters on the board below and glanced at the fascinating panels of lights in front of him. Under all the squadrons, the lights glowed red against 'Engaged'. He understood now, after his past visits, something of how it all worked. He knew that Park's forces were committed. He had seen it happen on his first visit a month before, and remembered Ismay's anxiety when, with the eye of a general, he saw that there were no reserves. The forces of 10, 12 and 13 Groups were not shown on the board at Uxbridge. He sensed the tension. Park seemed nervous in a way he had not before. Churchill had remained silent then, but now he posed the question he had hesitated to ask on that previous occasion, the same question he had posed to General Gamelin at that dreadful meeting on 16 May, when Gamelin gave the reply that had left him incredulous and he had realised that France was finished. He spoke to Park. 'What other reserves have we?' he asked. Park turned round to him. 'There are none,' he replied. Churchill said nothing. Park later observed that he 'looked grave'. 'Well I might,' wrote Churchill afterwards. 'What losses might we not suffer if our refuelling planes were caught on the ground by further raids of "40 plus" or "50 plus"! The odds were great; our margins small; the stakes infinite.'[10]

Park was nervous at that time because he did not trust Leigh-Mallory, and if the Big Wing failed to turn up, or turned up somewhere else, he could be in trouble. Otherwise, everything was normal. It is a measure of the strain he had had to bear throughout six long weeks that the Prime Minister, who was not exactly a worrier, should feel so concerned at the weight of the burden Park was carrying. Indeed, if his squadrons were to be caught on the ground in large numbers, he could lose the war in an afternoon. He knew that. It was part of the job. In fact, at that moment he was pretty sure that Kesselring had nothing much left and there was plenty of cloud over his airfields. His first squadrons would soon be getting back to refuel, so he would have some cover. In the meantime, he wanted to deal Kesselring a blow he would not forget and he wanted to deliver it over London. He needed the Big Wing for that.

In the meantime, nineteen fresh squadrons, 185 fighters, had hurled themselves at the three columns in an area of sky stretching from Gravesend to the eastern outskirts of London. Park wanted to break them up before they could bomb. Then he would go for the kill.

Given his earlier dispositions, most of his squadrons came from the north-west, and so it was the right-hand column, already mauled, which took most punishment. The Bf 109s were scattered now. Six squadrons went for the bombers, including 257, the shower of deadbeats. The debonair showman Bob Stanford-Tuck had got back to lead them personally, and they followed him down and then up in a graceful, shallow curve towards the bombers' unprotected bellies.

The centre column was attacked by four squadrons that still used the old tactics, but today they were in luck. Knowing that they were unused to the fighter battles in the south-east, Park had kept them back until now. The situation was one they had trained for: a large formation of (almost) unescorted bombers. With a couple of weavers above, Squadron Leader Rupert Leigh led 66 Squadron in one of the Fighting Area Attacks, moving into line astern from in front and below, each section going in, firing and breaking away. One of the weavers was a rather nervous Bobby Oxspring. He was right to be nervous, for he was terribly exposed. He spotted some Bf 109s above him, and tried to gain some height while not losing speed in the process. They could have bounced him. They stayed where they were, and cruised on high above the mêlée. Perhaps they did not see him. Perhaps, as German bomber commanders had observed before, they were too concerned about their fuel situation to want to fight. Perhaps they had had enough. Oxspring turned back and dived into the bombers.

The left-hand column was the most intact, and JG53 came down to protect it. They became embroiled with the Poles and 253 Squadron while 73 was able to deliver a head-on attack.

Meanwhile, having been called for at 1405[11], the forty-nine pilots of the Big Wing were still climbing. Around 1500, they emerged between Maidstone and Kenley at 16,000 feet, in the vicinity of the left-hand column of KG2. JG26 were above them.

Adolf Galland had not been having a good day. Mölders had got thirty-seven confirmed kills. Another three and he would get Oak Leaves to add to his Knight's Cross. Then there was that young blood Helmut Wick over at JG2 who was scoring very fast. Galland had got number thirty-two the day before, but this afternoon he had been hunting around for a good ten minutes without getting a bag, just dogfighting some Hurricanes, which was no use. He just needed a bit of luck. Then he saw the Big Wing below looking like a huge flock of pheasant. At last! He took his men down to bounce 310 Squadron. He and his wingman both got a Hurricane, and two others each hit a Spitfire of 19 Squadron, one of which came down. It was one pass and away for JG26, and they headed off before the red warning lights came on. They had no wish to try out the services of the Seenotflugkommando's seaplanes. Galland was relieved. That was number thirty-three. Just another four and he would be level with Mölders. Another seven and it would be off to Berlin for the Oak Leaves for *his* Knight's Cross. As KG2 began their bomb run on the Surrey Commercial Docks they were alone over the enemy's capital without any fighter escort.

As KG2 approached the river, however, they found the whole target area obscured by cloud, so they turned back as well. Seeing them turn without dropping their bombs, their assailants felt they had triumphed. It may have been at this time that a lone Hurricane appeared on the scene and made a headlong charge at the Dorniers. Group Captain Stanley Vincent, Northolt's Station Commander, had decided to 'have a go' along with his Poles. He did not hit anything, but he did see the Dorniers he attacked turn away.

Having turned, they scattered their loads over Bexley, Dartford and Crayford in Kent. The other formations found the Royal Victoria Docks also shrouded in cloud, but neighbouring West Ham and the Bromley-by-Bow gas works were visible, so they bombed them instead.

Then began the bombers' most difficult task, a fighting withdrawal. Many were damaged and their escorts were gone or dispersed. There would be no protection until the withdrawal cover arrived nearer the coast. At least there was cloud. Some of them had lost their formations and played a dangerous game of hide-and-seek with marauding fighters.

The rear group of the right-hand column, KG26, was pretty much intact. They had only lost one, a straggler. Leutnant Roderich Cescotti was beginning to feel some relief when he saw something that shook him. He suddenly spotted a lone Spitfire ahead dive steeply through the still-intact escort of Bf 109s and, ignoring them completely, come tearing right at him. As he watched, Cescotti saw a Bf 109 appear behind the Spitfire and open fire, striking its tail. To his astonishment the British plane took no evasive action, but continued straight for him, opening fire. Cescotti shielded his eyes from the shards of Plexiglass flying around the cabin as some of the Spitfire's rounds hit. The fighter pulled up, swept through the formation on its back, and dived down trailing smoke.

Flying Officer Peter Pease of 603 Squadron, son of Sir Richard and Lady Pease of Richmond, crashed into the ground at Kingswood, just south of Leeds Castle in Kent, at 1505.

The withdrawal cover arrived over mid-Kent at about 1515, but the British fighters harried them all the way. 238, 602 and 609 Squadrons now joined in for the first time, and shot down a Heinkel and two Dorniers.

At Uxbridge at 1525 the lights on the tote began to change. Several lit up against 'Ordered to Land', others against 'Landed and Refuelling'. Then, against 213 Squadron at Tangmere: 'At Readiness'. The apparent crisis had lasted fifty minutes. No new plots appeared.

Park turned to Churchill. 'I am very glad, sir, you have seen this,' he said. 'Of course, during the last twenty minutes we were so choked with information that we couldn't handle it. This shows you the limitations of our present resources. They have been strained far beyond their limits today.' Churchill appears to have been a little surprised by this. He asked if there were any results, adding that the attack seemed to have been repelled very satisfactorily. Park was not satisfied at all. Not enough raiders had been intercepted, and the Luftwaffe had got through to London.[12] That was not good enough.

Others thought it was. 257 Squadron had drinks in the mess with their new Squadron Leader that night. They had got three and a 'probable' for no loss. The Biggin Hill pilots crowded out the bar at the White Hart. The owners, Kath and Teddy Preston, had watched the fighting above them that afternoon, and there was an unusual level of excitement in the evening. For once, the rule that nobody talked shop was waived as the pilots compared notes on their victories.[13]

Douglas Bader had mixed feelings. On the one hand, the claims showed they had gained a great victory: the Wing had got twenty-six and eight 'probables' for the loss of three aircraft and two pilots, with two other pilots wounded in damaged aircraft. On the other hand, it had been a bit hairy. All because they were scrambled too late – again.

Churchill left Uxbridge as the raiders began landing, or crash-landing, on their airfields. He returned to Chequers and went for his usual afternoon nap.

The day was not over, however. At 10 Group, a small raid was picked up at 1505. As it grew nearer, it became apparent that it was a large raid directed at Portsmouth, and 152 Squadron were scrambled. They got to them, twenty-seven Heinkels of KG55 with no fighter escort, as they were heading home, managing to shoot down one and damage another. It could have been a massacre.

Things went quiet until 1725, when something else was picked up in the west. This one looked big. 10 Group scrambled three squadrons and 11 Group scrambled four. It was in fact just thirteen aircraft from Erprobungsgruppe 210, speeding low over the water to try their luck for a second time at Woolston. Nobody had any luck. The interceptors went in too high and missed them completely. Erprobungsgruppe 210 mistook the target and missed Woolston completely, which was just as well for Dowding.

A lone raider was shot down at dusk. By 2000 it was dark. That was when Churchill woke up. He was clearly emotionally exhausted, for he had uncharacteristically slept through. His Principal Private Secretary, John Martin, brought him the news, all of which was bad. 'This had gone wrong here,' Churchill subsequently wrote in Their Finest Hour; 'that had been delayed there; an unsatisfactory answer had been received from so-and-so; there had been bad sinkings in the Atlantic.' 'However', Martin said, 'all is redeemed by the air. We have shot down 183 for the loss of under 40.'[14] Churchill had been getting more and more confident about the air. In future he could sleep easily. He had seen it all for himself, and he had watched a master at work.

The sirens started in London. Despite the bombing, the presses at Fleet Street began whirring. Buckingham Palace had been bombed – the Nazis were trying to target the Royal Family again. Despite these dastardly tricks, *The Times* reported that the RAF had shot down 175 planes. Thirty British fighters were lost but ten of the pilots were safe. Several large bomber formations turned tail and fled when they saw our boys approaching. Some of them took fright and turned tail at the sight of a single Hurricane. So the numbers, and the tales, rolled on.

They travelled far and fast. On 16 September, the British flying boat *Clare* landed in New York carrying mail and passengers from Poole in Dorset. The crew were greeted with congratulations for the RAF's record bag of 185, a number the German Embassy tried in vain to correct. They were engulfed by a wave of sympathy for their cause, and a group of pro-British Americans placed a full-page advertisement in the *New York Times*, demanding political union with the 'six British democracies', pointing out that they were no longer dealing with George III but with Hitler.[15]

It took the Germans longer to put their story together. But on 17 September, the *Völkischer Beobachter* announced that reprisal attacks against London had continued, causing widespread damage. In a great air battle the Luftwaffe had shot down seventy-nine British aircraft for the loss of forty-three of their own.

Not all the bombs that fell on the night of the 15th fell on London. In the darkness, Bomber Command went out as usual on one of its cold, dangerous and uncelebrated journeys over occupied Europe. On the night of Battle of Britain Day, Sergeant John Hannah, who was eighteen years old, fought the fires which gripped his Hampden over Antwerp with such determination and disregard for his own safety that he got badly burned and was awarded the Victoria Cross.

Park was livid when he got the claims returns. Claiming nearly 200 on one day was nonsense. Especially that bloody wing of Leigh-Mallory's. More damage should have been done. There were too many inexperienced leaders in the squadrons, interceptions were being missed and the pilots spent too much time on stragglers and lame ducks which were no military threat. Things needed tightening up: that was the lesson of 15 September 1940!

The claims were indeed inflated. The RAF claimed 81 in the morning engagement and 104 in the afternoon, with the Big Wing accounting for one third and one quarter of them respectively. The Luftwaffe lost eighteen aircraft in the morning and thirty-five in the afternoon, which, together with two reconnaissance machines and the single Heinkel from the evening raid on Portsmouth brought their combat losses for the day to a total of fifty-six. British combat losses were twenty-eight, giving a loss ratio of exactly 2:1, which was good, but not their best. The body count, as was to be expected, showed a greater discrepancy. The Luftwaffe lost eighty-one aircrew killed, thirty-one wounded and sixty-three taken prisoner. Fighter Command lost twelve pilots killed, fourteen wounded and one taken prisoner when Sergeant Potter of 19 Squadron was picked up in the Channel by an He 59.[16]

Fighter losses on both sides were about equal in both engagements. In the morning, about half of the twelve Bf 109 losses were incurred by I./JG53 when they were bounced by the Biggin Hill Spitfires. The Germans got in one bounce of their own, getting two of the Canadians. Otherwise, British losses were incurred through dogfighting, return fire from bombers and collisions. In the afternoon, the Germans lost three Bf 110s and eleven Bf 109s and the British fifteen Hurricanes and Spitfires, three of them when Galland bounced Bader's Wing.

The big difference between the two engagements was in the bomber losses. The vast mêlée over London at midday cost KG76 six bombers, but the ferocious head-on charges and savage beam attacks by the pairs of 11 Group squadrons in the afternoon did for twenty-one of them. In each case the fighter protection had been peeled away by the time the bombers were trying to make their bomb runs.

Fighter Command therefore had greater success when it faced the 475-strong phalanxes of the afternoon than it did against the 145 raiders of the morning which it had outnumbered almost 2:1. The ratio of fighters to bombers was only 3:1 in the afternoon versus 5:1 in the morning, and there were more targets. The more bombers Kesselring sent over, the more he lost.

Kesselring was back where he started. Park's handling of the two actions of 15 September was a masterpiece of aggressive defence, yet he was never under the pressure he had experienced on days like 31 August when the air activity was so confusing and fragmented it was hard to control. A big set-piece slugging match played right into his hands.

Some other analysis of the fighting was underway. Two days later, on 17 September, Leigh-Mallory submitted to Dowding a report on Wing Patrols, which Evill forwarded to the Air Ministry a week later. It covered the operations of the Wing on 7, 9, 11 and 15 September. Leigh-Mallory explained that the Wing had three Hurricane squadrons to destroy bombers and two Spitfire squadrons to attack any escorts that tried to interfere. On the morning of the 15th, he wrote, the Wing took off 'before noon', and on finding the Dorniers 'were able to destroy all they could see'. One squadron saw a further smaller formation 'and promptly destroyed the lot'. 'The enemy were outnumbered in the action,' he concluded, 'and appeared in the circumstances to be quite helpless.' In the afternoon, the Wing produced satisfactory results, but could not break up the bomber formation because they had not had enough time to reach patrol height, and so were attacked by Bf 109s while trying to get into position. Leigh-Mallory appended some tables of casualties the Wing had inflicted and sustained. In total, they claimed 105 destroyed, 40 probably destroyed and 18 damaged for the loss of 14 aircraft and 6 pilots.

Evill added in his covering letter to the Ministry that the figures of enemy losses should, in his opinion, 'be regarded only as approximate'.[17] However, there they were. And Douglas had got them. They were just what he had been looking for.

The numbers did not actually matter as much on 15 September as they had before. Both sides had suffered more in the past. The 56 missing German aircraft were 19 short of the 75 that had failed to return on the 15th of the previous month. But in a way those 56 hurt more. They were the heaviest since the 69 lost on 18 August. Having spent the interval trying to destroy Fighter Command, the Germans now seemed to be looking at the bad old days of Eagle again. 15 September was the day when some, though not all, of the people who mattered realised what had been going on, and acted accordingly. This began a slow process of enlightenment. It is for that reason it has become known as Battle of Britain Day.

Enlightenment often begins with pain and fear, and so it was in this case. It began as the crews returned. Most of the bombers had dead and wounded men on board, and many were badly shot up. Twenty-five of them were seriously damaged, two of them beyond repair.

At the worst-hit units, men were quiet. They were too shaken. KG3 had lost six of the nineteen aircraft that had taken off. Only the day after did it become clear that a third of their unit had been wiped out in an hour. 'We came to realise,' Horst Schulz has recorded, 'that if there were any more missions like that, our chances of survival would be nil.' Fink's KG2, the first bomber unit to become active on the Channel front, lost eight aircraft and crews, with further crew casualties amongst the five aircraft which returned damaged, the heaviest losses the unit had ever suffered in one day.[18] It was losses of this order of magnitude to individual units that had led to the withdrawal of the Stukas. If, after all this, the rest of the bomber fleet were just as vulnerable, despite the protection of most of Osterkamp's dwindling fighter force, what did it mean for daylight bombing?

Those who had come off more lightly were still shaken, for different reasons. KG26 only lost one aircraft, but Roderich Cescotti could not get the image of that lone Spitfire out of his mind. The sheer ferocity and determination of the attacks made his blood run cold. Some of them, like that one, had seemed suicidal. There had been four collisions, three of them deliberate. Stories of ramming got about quickly. Most of the incidents were very visible. Nobody knew at the time whether they were deliberate or not, but they looked it. Any pilot making a head-on attack was certainly taking a risk, and most of the Germans saw plenty of those.

Had they been Josef Goebbels, they would have seen this as a sign of desperation, the last throw of a gallant but mortally wounded enemy. But the swarms of fighters that allowed them no respite from the coast to London and back gave this the lie. The appearance of Bader and his Wing over London in the morning had shocked them. Militarily ineffective, the Big Wing was a powerful psychological weapon, and this was its real contribution to the day.

At a stroke, all the experience of the past week of weakening opposition, which had made so much sense after the incessant pounding of the previous fortnight, was confounded. The opposition had always been there, of course, but it had been unable to find them, first because of controllers' errors, and then because of bad weather. The Sunday sunshine had revealed a foe who appeared to be, and was in fact, stronger than ever before.

Fighter Command did not win the Battle of Britain on Battle of Britain Day. It had done that already. It had won it in the last week of August and first week of September by filling in craters, repairing and servicing its machines and manning the Operations Rooms as the bombs fell. It had won it by having enough Bob Does who managed to learn to live and turn themselves from spring chickens into hawks, and enough Al Deeres who overcame their fear and exhaustion and took off again. It had won because it had endured.

Moreover, unless Park had committed crass errors and been caught on the ground, the Luftwaffe could not have won the Battle of Britain on Battle of Britain Day. If it had been as successful on that day as it had ever been in the past, if it had lost twenty-eight aircraft and Fighter Command had lost fifty-six, Dowding would have replaced 11 Group's losses from his 'C' squadrons and carried on. During the day's two engagements, Fighter Command only used half its strength. It would have met the Luftwaffe again, as usual, on the morrow.

There was an uncomfortable conference at Karinhall the following day. It seems to have been conducted in an atmosphere of fantasy curiously presaging the conferences held in Hitler's bunker in 1945.

The British had clearly withdrawn from large areas in order to concentrate everything they had around London, including cannon-armed Hurricanes.[19] The raids in the west in the evening had met no opposition. Another four or five days would be sure to break them. In some places there would be no fighter opposition at all. To stop any more fighters appearing, the aircraft industry had to be a special target, especially the works at Filton near Bristol. Attacks on London were to continue – if the British fighters refused to appear, their capital would be laid in ruins. London was to be subject to round-the-clock bombing. Winter quarters were to be prepared and Sealion should not disturb the Luftwaffe in the pursuit of its goals.

Osterkamp put the problems of the previous day down to the British introducing the new stratagem of attacking them with massed formations, which had surprised the escorts. Göring was delighted. That was what he had always wanted. If they came in masses, they could shoot masses down.

Finally there was a warning that, as the nights grew longer and the weather got worse, drivers should be particularly careful when chauffeuring irreplaceable people like Mölders and Galland. They did not want to lose them in an accident.[20]

It was not until 23 September that General Speidel gave OKW and Hitler a full report on the course of the aerial campaign. Things had been going well during the first phase of operations, during which resistance had been seen to weaken. However, there had been an unfortunate delay in getting permission to attack London and open the second phase. There had only been one day of good weather, so it had not been possible to carry out the attack as planned. By the time it was resumed, the British had used the interval to get every pilot they could out of the training schools and put every machine they could find into the front line, some of them straight from the factory still unpainted. They had sent completely raw units into the fight, some of them so inexperienced that all they could do was to ram bombers. Therefore, it had become necessary to open a third phase, attacking London by night and using fighters during the day. There were in fact only about 300 British fighters left, with some 250 a month being produced. 'Our own forces,' Speidel concluded, 'still feel themselves to have the upper hand over the enemy, and are completely confident that the air war can be prosecuted successfully.'[21]

So it had been the last-minute measures of the desperate defenders and the damned English weather that had led to this tiresome prolongation of operations. Summer's lease had had too short a date.

Hitler was not that bothered. Sealion had always been a huge risk, even with air superiority, and he had been convinced since the end of August that the Luftwaffe would not achieve that. He had burned his boats now anyway. The war with England would have to go on. Let them suffer throughout the winter, and in the spring he would eliminate Russia and their last hope would be gone. Then they would negotiate. He would maintain the pressure by keeping the threat of invasion going. But it would not be this year.

On 17 September, five copies of a lapidary order, 'Nr. 00 761/40 g. Kdos.' went out from Hitler's Supreme Headquarters to the High Commands of the Army, Navy and Luftwaffe. It stated that order 'Nr. 33 255/40 g. Kdos. Chefs.' of 3 September, fixing S-Day, the launching of Sealion, for 21 September, was postponed until further notice.

So it was that, a little later in the war, US Air Force General Hap Arnold could say with some truth: 'On 8 August 1940, the RAF Fighter Command took off to save everything, and between then and the end of September they saved it all.'

27. BLUFFING

Göring had never believed in Sealion, and Hitler had long been sceptical about Eagle. Both now went their separate ways, but that suited them. Hitler wanted someone to keep the pressure up, and Göring wanted to do so.

On 19 September, Hitler ordered the assembly of invasion barges already earmarked for Sealion to continue, but to add no others. However, there was increasing concern about the damage Bomber Command was doing to the inviting targets offered it by the barges, and the job of keeping the army in readiness was becoming a strain. So it was decided that, as it would be sufficient if the invasion force could be reassembled with a three-week warning, the bulk of the troops could be moved east.[1]

In England, the results of the indefinite postponement of an invasion were not readily apparent. In a secret session on the 17th, Churchill warned Parliament that the next few weeks would be 'grave and anxious'. There were 1,700 barges and 200 sea-going ships in the invasion ports, capable of carrying half a million men, and if this were 'all a pretence and stratagem to pin us down here, it has been executed with surprising thoroughness and on a gigantic scale'. He pointed out that the coastline from the Wash to the Isle of Wight was as long as the front in France from the Alps to the sea, and that landings could make use of fog or artificial fog.[2] The coming of winter brought the danger of surprise landings in bad weather. On the 18th, Park issued a secret document to all Station and Squadron Commanders called 'Measures to Counter an Attempted German Invasion, Autumn 1940.' It explained that Germany's economic situation would compel her to make every attempt to defeat Britain before the winter, and that an invasion should therefore be expected. Park impressed upon his men that the first twenty-four or at most seventy-two hours would be critical, and that they should expect to fly six sorties on what was to be their longest day.[3]

Colville commented in his diary on 21 September that it was daily becoming more apparent 'how well prepared the enemy is for invasion'. 'The PM seems rather more apprehensive than I had realised about the possibility of invasion in the immediate future,' he added, 'and he keeps on ringing up the Admiralty and asking about the weather in the Channel.' Dowding and Lord Gort came to dinner that evening and discussed counter-invasion preparations as well as the air fighting. Dowding paid tribute to the Poles, whom he described as 'very dashing but totally undisciplined', and it was generally agreed that they were 'magnificent fighters'. 'When we have abolished Germany', added Churchill, 'we will certainly establish Poland – and make them a permanent thing in Europe.' Dowding had produced a paper on night interception in which he laid out the prospects for using airborne radar in Beaufighters combined with wireless-controlled searchlights and AA guns. Churchill described it to Beaverbrook as 'masterly'. One worry was that the Germans would themselves exploit technology and use the beam they had for guiding aircraft to help invasion forces to land in fog.[4]

That very night, a telegram arrived from Roosevelt warning that the invasion would be launched at 3 a.m. Churchill had gone to bed and nobody woke him because there was a storm in the Channel. When he learned of it, he was sceptical and his wife and daughter Mary treated the whole thing 'as a most entertaining joke.' Over lunch the next day, Churchill promised that if the Germans did land, they would be shown no quarter. The 'reliable source' behind this scare was the American Chargé d'Affaires in Berlin, Alexander C. Kirk, who had correctly predicted the invasion of Belgium and Holland to within the hour, but had got it wrong this time – perhaps a sign that Berlin was full of rumours and that the Germans were as confused as anyone.[5]

Whilst British reconnaissance flights indicated that the size of the invasion fleet was being reduced, vigilance was maintained. Radio traffic intercepted by the Enigma code-breakers during September indicated that preparations were still being made. In Germany, the population was anxious for the invasion to take place, as it would mean the end of the war. An SS report on 24 September noted 'a certain disappointed impatience.'[6]

On 12 October, Hitler issued an order saying that henceforth all preparations for a landing in England were to be conducted purely in order to exercise pressure. Should a landing be considered once again in 1941, fresh orders would be issued. In the meantime, the winding-down of preparations was to be conducted in such a way that the English would continue to expect a landing on a broad front, but also so as to minimise the cost to the German economy.[7] In other words, it was all a bluff.

On 27 October, the Enigma decryptors picked up some radio traffic referring to training for Sealion. If the Germans were still training, an invasion could not be imminent. Only then did these reports, linked with clear signs from aerial photographs of the barges leaving the embarkation ports, finally lead Churchill to conclude that the immediate danger had passed.[8]

Having only reluctantly ordered the preparation of Sealion, Hitler proved equally reluctant to abandon it completely. In Directive 18 of 12 November, he stated that Operation Sealion might be needed in 1941 and that the Wehrmacht should continue to try to create favourable conditions for it.[9] He was also toying with the idea of invading Ireland, an operation appropriately coded '*Fall Grün*' ('Case Green'), and 6th Army carried out exercises for it on 21 November.[10]

However, on 18 December, Hitler issued Directive 21. It stated that the Wehrmacht must be prepared to destroy Russia in a quick campaign even before the war with England had been concluded. The operation was to be called 'Barbarossa'. His following two directives covered his back as far as England was concerned. Directive 22, issued on 11 January 1941, gave orders for the support of the Italians who were fighting the British in the Middle East, and being roundly defeated. Directive 23, issued on 6 February, observed that the most effective means of destroying the British war economy was to sink its merchant fleet. The impact of air attacks on British industry was hard to ascertain and there had been no appreciable adverse effect on the morale of the civilian population. He accordingly ordered the intensification of the U-boat war, and the concentration of air attacks on targets valuable to the merchant fleet.[11] The strategy against England was now unambiguously one of siege, combined with attacks on the periphery of the Empire.

Sealion was never cancelled. On 5 February 1944, the Naval High Command ordered that preparations should be temporarily discontinued, and the German High Command stipulated that the provisions made for it be available for other urgent purposes. Four months later, on 6 June 1944, an Anglo-American army disembarked in Normandy, which did indeed lead to some urgency in various parts of the Wehrmacht, and the resources allocated to Sealion were redeployed.[12]

Bluff or not, the killing went on.

For the week following 15 September, Kesselring sent over fighters. Park ignored them, so Kesselring tried a few bombers. When he sent over a fresh unit of Ju 88s, III./KG77, on the 18th, they were met by fourteen squadrons, including the Duxford Wing, and lost eight of their number, including their Gruppenkommandeur. The Wing claimed twenty-four destroyed, four shared, three probables and one damaged. Once again, 242 Squadron, which had claimed twelve destroyed, received messages of congratulation from Newall and Sinclair.[13] They were being noticed in very high places.

Increasingly, the casualties were suffered by civilians as the night Blitz on London intensified and Bomber Command raided Berlin, sending out 129 bombers on the night of the 23rd. This was the first time that Bomber Command concentrated its main strength on just one German city, targeting seven railway yards, six power stations, two gasworks and two aerospace factories.[14] Appropriately, on the same day, King George VI announced the institution of the George Cross as the equivalent of the Victoria Cross for civilians. Over the Channel, the German Army High Command played a war game to practise Operation Sealion. It was all a great success.[15]

In accordance with Göring's orders of the 16th, the British aircraft industry was the object of some attention. The Luftwaffe was finally beginning to concentrate on important targets. Erprobungsgruppe 210 had already made a couple of attempts on Supermarine in Southampton. There were two factories, the main one at Woolston on the River Itchen off Southampton Water and a second just up-river at Itchen, where Spitfire fuselages were assembled.

At 1300 on the 24th, Erprobungsgruppe 210 tried again. They hit the Itchen works without causing much damage to the factory, but killing forty-one workers and seriously injuring another sixty-three. They lost one Bf 110. The following day, they attacked Portland to divert attention from the main action, which was a raid by the He 111s of KG55 on the aircraft factory at Filton near Bristol. Bf 109s accompanied the Heinkels to the coast, but their main escorts were provided by III./ZG26. Brand thought the raiders were making for the Westland factory at Yeovil, so he concentrated his fighters there. As a result, they only intercepted KG55 after they had bombed, halting production, but they got four of them as well as four of the Bf 110 escorts.

Erprobungsgruppe 210 were under orders to bomb the Supermarine works until they were flattened. On the 26th, they joined forces with KG55 and this time they were successful. Seven bombs hit Woolston and one hit Itchen. They killed thirty-seven people, and production was brought to a standstill.[16] Beaverbrook reacted by ordering production to be dispersed but, although Spitfire deliveries slowed for about three weeks, this did not matter as there were plenty at Maintenance Units.

On the 27th, there was action all along the front.

Groups of Bf 110s and Bf 109s flew over Kent and Surrey to try to exhaust the defences before a serious raid on London was launched. Some bait was provided by about fifteen Ju 88s of I./KG77, but Park peeled away their protective layers by engaging the Bf 109s of JG27 near the coast. By the time they reached north Kent they were alone with some Bf 110s of V./LG1 and ZG76 in defensive circles. Four of the Ju 88s were shot down, and the others never reached London. ZG76 managed to time their break well and got back with the loss of only two.

This left V./LG1 to engage 11 Group's full attentions. Seven of the ten Zerstörer were lost, with eleven crewmen killed, including their Gruppenkommandeur, Horst Liensberger, and the other three taken prisoner. They were cut up when they broke the circle to get back, with Liensberger being pursued by the twenty-one-year-old Percy Burton of 249 Squadron. Liensberger raced low over Sussex with Burton on his tail firing occasional bursts until, just north of Hailsham, he ran out of ammunition. When the Hurricane stopped firing Liensberger probably realised why, so he slowed down and pulled up in front of Burton to make him overshoot and then get away. He misjudged the manoeuvre, and they collided at about 200 feet and went in, killing all on board both aircraft.[17]

To the west, the target was the Parnall aircraft component factory at Yate near Bristol. Erprobungsgruppe 210 paired up with KG55 again, with the Bf 110s of ZG26 once more acting as escorts. Bf 109s of JG2 flew over the Channel with them, but then left them to the mercies of 10 Group. This time, Brand was waiting with five squadrons, including 504, which had moved to Filton after the raid of the 24th. It was 504 that found them first. ZG26 formed a circle and Erprobungsgruppe 210 flew on. 504 Squadron accounted for two machines from ZG26 and two more from Erprobungsgruppe 210, including that of their Commander, Martin Lutz. As more British fighters arrived, there was a wild chase towards the Channel, during which a Spitfire of 609 Squadron collided with another Bf 110. Two more Bf 110s, one each from ZG26 and Erprobungsgruppe 210, crashed on land, and three more, one flown by Wilhelm-Richard Rössiger, the Staffelkapitän of 2nd Staffel of Erprobungsgruppe 210, went down in the Channel. ZG26 had lost six aircraft and Erprobungsgruppe 210 four, with yet another leader gone. They had had to jettison their bombs before reaching the target. KG55's attack was broken up over Yeovil, and they scattered their bombs over Sherbourne before making off. The only British loss in the whole action was caused by the collision.[18]

Further east, the main thrust on London was being prepared. In the early afternoon, the remaining two Gruppen of the luckless KG77 appeared over the south coast with an escort of Bf 109s. Amongst them was Ulrich Steinhilper, who found himself leading I./JG52, now down to thirteen aircraft. Then from nowhere, he saw thirty to forty Hurricanes and Spitfires tearing towards them in what he describes as 'a wall of aircraft'. He ordered his men to turn into them. His own Schwarm followed him, but the others, who did not know him very well, did not, and he lost them. Steinhilper was by now very experienced, and he knew that one of the advantages the Bf 109 had over its British opponents was its climbing ability. He ordered his men to turn and climb with about 60° of bank and as high a nose attitude as possible. They came close to stalling and it felt very dangerous to fly the plane to its limits like that, but it worked, and they all got away. The others did not. They lost seven Bf 109s and the Gruppe was effectively written off.[19] Disaster also overtook the bombers. II. and III./KG77 lost eight Ju 88s, making twelve losses that day for the whole Geschwader. They could not take much more of this.

The whole day had been a shambles. For the loss of nineteen Bf 109s, twenty-one Bf 110s and seventeen bombers, a total of fifty-seven aircraft, the Luftwaffe's fighters had only been able to shoot down twenty-nine of the defenders. None of the targets had been molested, and the German casualties were as heavy as they had been on the 15th. As a result of its losses, V./LG1 was disbanded and the survivors moved to Germany to form the nucleus of a new night fighting unit, I./NJG3. The Bf 110 would be more use against the British bombers flying in increasing numbers over Germany by night than against fighters during the day.

Bader had done one uneventful patrol in the morning, but was scrambled at 1155 with 242, 19, 310 and 616 Squadrons and ordered to patrol London in case the early afternoon raid got through. He knew better, however, and flew south to engage the raiders. They claimed only thirteen this time, and probably got some, but at a cost of four aircraft with two pilots killed and one wounded.[20] He was lucky the raid did not get through.

The following day, the 28th, Kesselring used small groups of Ju 88s to attract British fighters and accompanied them with all the fighters he could. This time, he had remarkable success. The Bf 109s managed to catch a lot of the defenders on the climb and the tally for the day was sixteen British aircraft for only four German. It was the sort of day the Luftwaffe had needed from the first. Now it was too late and made no difference.

The Luftwaffe had its last serious fling on the last day of September. A mixed wave of 200 aircraft was turned back over Maidstone by eight squadrons, and another 100 further west were also repulsed. In the afternoon, two more successive waves of about 200 crossed into Kent, but they too were broken up and the action dissolved into sporadic dogfighting.

One of them involved a classic and costly cock-up caused by reliance on new technology. II./KG30 were to bomb London through cloud, using the Knickebein radio beacon for navigation. The leader followed the beam guiding him towards London but missed the one intersecting it which told him when to release his bombs, and flew on. By the time they turned for home their escorts, with whom they could not communicate because of their different radio frequencies, had used up two-thirds of their fuel. The 109s could not leave the bombers because they were under constant attack. Instead of taking the shortest route back, II./KG30 headed out over the Isle of Wight. When finally the 109s did break for home, it was said that many had to ditch. The Kommandeur of II./KG30 was court-martialled.[21]

The last serious raid was on the Westland factory at Yeovil. It was down to KG55 and ZG26 again. They got through, but Yeovil was obscured by cloud, and most of the bombs fell on the town rather than the factory. ZG26 escaped with the loss of only one plane, and KG55 lost four Heinkels.

One of these Heinkels was shot down by the new Flight Commander of 238 Squadron, Bob Doe. He had been awarded the DFC and transferred from 234 Squadron to 238 on the 28th. As 238 flew Hurricanes, he had to get used to the new aircraft, and the 30th was his first day of action since the 7th.

In the course of the fighting, Fighter Command lost nineteen aircraft. The Luftwaffe lost a total of forty-three: fourteen bombers, one Bf 110 and no less than twenty-eight Bf 109s. These were the heaviest day's losses ever suffered by the German single-seaters, with Fighter Command more than avenging its defeat of two days before. All the Jagdgeschwader took a beating. JG52 and JG53 each lost four, JG2 and JG 26 lost five, JG27 lost seven and the rest were shared amongst the others. Many of the loss records simply indicate 'missing' – probably cases of pilots having to ditch because they ran out of fuel. However, the fighting went badly as well. It was JG26's worst day, and all five of their losses were due to British fighters. Galland's wingman, Hauptmann Kienzle, was shot down by the Poles. Only one of the pilots got back, and he was wounded. They filed three claims in return.

None of the attacks were pressed home in the way they would have been a month before. The heart had gone out of the offensive.

Luftflotte 3 thought it worthwhile announcing in its post-action report that Hauptmann Wick had scored his 35th and 36th aerial victories. He had been made Kommandeur of I./JG2 on 7 September, and was scoring faster than either Mölders or Galland, though it is doubtful whether his headline score represented the actual damage he was causing to Fighter Command. His marketing was good, though, and he was becoming a familiar face to the readers of newspapers in Berlin. With the daylight bombing campaign running out of steam, Goebbels was concentrating more and more on the fighter aces. Ulrich Steinhilper had made friends with Wick when they were cadets together before the war. Wick was left out of a round of promotions after he had applied to marry a divorcée. His officers told him he was too young and turned his application down, but he thought it was nothing to do with age, just that they did not want any whiff of scandal in the Officer Corps. He attributed his lack of promotion to his marriage application. 'When the fighting starts,' he confided to Steinhilper, 'I will show them all up by becoming an ace, and then they won't talk about me like that any more.'[22]

30 September was also the day on which the King named Hugh Caswall Tremenheere Dowding as Knight Grand Commander of the Order of the Bath. Clearly, it was time for him to go.

The Luftwaffe opened the new month of October by sending forty-eight Bf 109s of JG2 and JG53 and the remaining thirty-two Bf 110s of ZG26 on a sweep over Portsmouth. They claimed twelve Hurricanes and Spitfires. In fact, they got two. The only German aircraft shot down was a Bf 110. Bob Doe led down the six Hurricanes of 238 Squadron in a bounce from 5,000 feet above them, and got the Messerschmitt from below as he pulled up from the dive. He reported seeing some four-engined Focke-Wulf 200 bombers – usually used for maritime reconnaissance – in the formation, which the fighters may have joined as they set out for the western approaches.[23]

LG2's Bf 109s took part in some sweeps over Kent, with the usual inconclusive results. The aircraft were Bf 109E-7s, a new version equipped with shackles under the fuselage so that it could carry a long-range fuel tank or a 250kg bomb. These supplemented the E-4/Bs already at the front. LG2 had pioneered the use of the Bf 109 as a fighter-bomber on the 15th and tried it out again on the 20th. Since then the pilots of other fighter units had been doing some perfunctory training in bomb-aiming and, at the end of the month, each Geschwader was ordered to nominate one Staffel in every Gruppe, a third of its aircraft, to act as fighter-bombers.

JG53 had the pleasure of trying out its first fighter-bomber ('*Jagdbomber*' or 'Jabo' in German) mission on 2 October, which was a beautiful day. During training none of the pilots had been very keen, and they took off very worried about the impact the bomb had on their fuel consumption and ability to defend themselves. 8./JG53 was the Jabo Staffel of III. Gruppe and they were escorted by their colleagues of I./JG53. The escorts flew over at 30,000 feet and saw nothing but the glorious blue autumn sky and thin layers of cloud over London. The Jabo Staffel could not fly as high as that and, whilst their colleagues enjoyed the sunshine, they were bounced over the Thames Estuary by 603 Squadron, who were learning. They shot down the four leaders and the rest dropped their bombs and fled.[24]

This set the tone for such operations amongst the 109 pilots. The whole thing was regarded as aberrant. In fact the idea was very good, but its timing and execution made it a farce. It was what had become of Göring's order of 2 September to use Bf 109s in the fighter-bomber role. If the pilots had been properly trained in fast low-level bombing, and been used extensively to attack airfields and radar stations in August, Park would have had his hands full. The avowed rationale for sending over half-trained pilots at high altitude to jettison a few small bombs over London was to paralyse the economy by constantly forcing Londoners down into their air-raid shelters. It was a waste of lives, and the 109 pilots were not fooled. There was an increasing feeling of every man for himself, as witnessed by the behaviour of escorts, which were tending to leave their charges to get on with it.

Even Erprobungsgruppe 210 was losing its touch. If anyone knew how to use fighter-bombers they did, but when they attacked West Malling on 5 October under their new acting leader, Oberleutnant Werner Weymann, the 1st Staffel ran into 303 Squadron who hacked two of them down, including Weymann himself. 501 and 92 Squadrons damaged two more. The Bf 109s of 3rd Staffel managed to bomb West Malling, but they did little damage. The day's fighting cost the Luftwaffe a total of eight Bf 109s, one Ju 88 and a Henschel Hs 126 reconnaissance machine as well as the two Bf 110s – a total of twelve aircraft and crews. The RAF lost eleven aircraft and two pilots. Helmut Wick was responsible for two of these, and probably damaged two others. He claimed five, which got him promotion to Major and Oak Leaves to add to his Knight's Cross. Only he, Galland and Mölders had been awarded that.

On the 6th the weather was bad, but on 7 October, the Bf 109s returned to the south-east. In the course of the clashes during the day, the Luftwaffe lost ten fighters to the RAF's seven. In the afternoon, II./KG51 launched the last major daylight bombing raid of the campaign, covered by ZG26, the whole of JG2 and a Staffel from JG53. The target was Yeovil.

Only one of KG51's Ju 88s was lost. It was once more due to Bob Doe, whose fire hit the oxygen tank stored in the rear fuselage and blew its tail off. However, ZG26 lost seven Bf 110s. Little damage was done to the Westland factory, but one bomb hit a shelter in the town, causing serious casualties. The

RAF lost six fighters to the Bf 109 escorts. After this raid, the fighting was left almost entirely to the German single-seaters.

Since mid-September, there had been some active debate within the Luftwaffe about how to use the Zerstörer force. It was felt that, although their successes in air combat (i.e. their claims) justified their losses, they were too high. One idea was to mix them with Bf 109s, but Osterkamp argued that they should only be used when the distance to the target demanded it, or for night-fighting. He saw them primarily as a defensive weapon. Kesslering agreed, and on 4 October issued his summary of the debate, coming down on the side of Osterkamp.[25] Accordingly, after the raid on Yeovil they were withdrawn from the front-line. Between 7 October and the middle of November, the Zerstörer force lost only fourteen machines, a reflection not of reduced vulnerability, but of reduced operations. Their crews had had the most dangerous job of any participants in the Battle of Britain. They lost a total of 223 machines, a sobering 94% of their initial strength.

Intercepting the Jabos and their escorts which flew in above 30,000 feet was causing Park some problems. Warnings were very short, height readings endemically unreliable, and it was not clear which 109s were carrying bombs and which were harmless. If they went for the Jabos, British pilots found the escorts to be potentially very dangerous. Hurricanes struggled at these heights though Spitfire Mark Is could hold their own, and the more powerful engines of the new Mark IIs gave them an edge. To help gain better information, a Spitfire reconnaissance unit called 421 Flight was used to patrol the coast at high altitude. Park instructed his controllers to hold back pairs of squadrons and let them get above 25,000 feet before sending them to their patrol lines.[26]

High altitudes were to say the least uncomfortable, given 1940s technology. Temperature decreases by about 2° Centigrade with every 1,000 feet of altitude, so at 30,000 feet it was pretty cold, whatever the temperature on the ground. There was no pressurisation or cockpit heating. The Hurricane, which had gaps and draughts everywhere, was the most uncomfortable machine, so its pilots were no doubt grateful that it could not perform very well at high altitude and that Spitfires were usually chosen for this work. Windscreens misted or iced up, which was disconcerting for a pilot to whom vision was life. It was a hazard faced by all, but the Spitfire was sometimes fitted with a small, flat panel on the side of the canopy to give a clear view to the side.

The fighting dragged on, with pilots on both sides finding it increasingly futile. As October wore on, things got into a routine. The Spitfire squadrons used to cruise at about 27,000 feet where they could still perform well, and the Bf 109s cruised past at 30,000 feet. Increasingly, they left each other alone. 'If the Germans wanted to come down and mix it with us, they could jolly well do so,' Sandy Johnstone of 602 Squadron has commented. 'We were not going to go up after them because they were doing no harm up there . . . We cruised around trying to entice them down and a couple of them did come down.

They'd just whiz down and go right up again. They didn't wait to fight it out. That's when we began to think the tide was turning.'[27]

The fighting was of low intensity, but there was a trickle of attrition on both sides. Accidents increased. On 8 October, 303 Squadron's Josef Frantisek crashed at Ewell in Surrey on a routine patrol and was killed. He was the highest-claiming RAF pilot of the Battle with seventeen victories. 303 had flown their last combat mission of the Battle of Britain just one day before, and on 11 October they were withdrawn to Leconfield. Since entering battle on 31 August they had filed 126 claims, more than any other squadron in Fighter Command, for the loss of nine pilots.[28] Their claims-to-loss ratio of 14:1 was among the best in Fighter Command. The most effective German fighter wing was Galland's III./JG26, which at the end of the Battle was also the most highly decorated, all of its Staffelkapitäne and its Gruppenkommandeur being Knight's Cross holders. Within it, the best record was enjoyed by 9th Staffel, which filed 26 claims for the loss of three pilots between 24 July, when it first went into action, and 31 October, giving it a claims-to-loss ratio of 8.7:1, well below that of the Poles. The highest-scoring stars of the Luftwaffe usually flew in the Stabschwarm, and their victories are therefore not counted amongst those of the individual Staffeln. However, even if a third of the twenty-eight victories of the Gruppenstab claimed by the likes of Gerhard Schöpfel and Galland himself are added in, 9th Staffel's claims-to-loss ratio does not rise above 12:1. Even though it was equipped with the Hurricane, the least effective of the three main fighters, 303 Squadron was by most measures the most formidable fighter unit of the Battle of Britain.[29]

On 10 October, Bob Doe was scrambled against a high-flying fighter raid, despite the fact that he was now flying Hurricanes. He got separated from his companions in some cloud and, as he emerged from the top of it, he was suddenly hit very violently from in front and behind, with a knock on his left side and left hand, and an explosion from under his seat. He did what he had always trained himself to do, which was to push the control column forward immediately, and baled out to land in a sewage drainage pit on Brownsea Island. He was taken to Poole Hospital and had a bullet removed from his left hand and a piece of cannon shell dug out of his right foot. More seriously, he had damaged his spine. This was to restrict his mobility long after the end of the war.[30]

For him, the Battle of Britain was over. With fifteen confirmed victories, most of which can be verified from German records, he was one of the highest scoring RAF aces of the Battle, just behind Frantisek, Ginger Lacey, Eric Lock and Brian Carbury, and about level with Archie McKellar, Colin Gray and his own mentor, Pat Hughes.

Just after 9 a.m. on 27 October, Ulrich Steinhilper took off from Coquelles with seven other Messerschmitts, which was all that I./JG52 could muster. His own machine was being serviced, so he had to take an old one that had been standing idle for some time. He had written to his mother a few days before and mentioned that the British were now using new Spitfires that the old 109 'Emils' could hardly keep up with. Still, it was a machine he knew and trusted, for it was the one he used to fly. They were to escort some Bf 109 Jabos, and that meant operating at the limits of their service ceiling.

He knew when the British would get them: just as they turned for home. Trouble started on the way out. He could not get the propeller to move from coarse to fine pitch – like driving a car stuck in second gear. No doubt with the machine standing unused for so long condensation had collected in the grease of the pitch gear and at the high altitude it had frozen. Too bad. He settled for coarse pitch, taking the risk that the engine would over-rev.

Just as they were turning back, somebody saw them. '*Achtung, sie Kommen! Sie kommen!*' '*Aus der Sonne!*' He turned and saw 'a staircase of Spitfires'. It may have been just as well he did not know which ones. It was 74 Squadron, flying Spitfire Mark IIs, with Sailor Malan at their head. He turned, lost his wingman and dived hard, with the rev counter winding up. He glanced at it: 2,800 – 400 over the limit! Suddenly, there was a bang on his left. He did not know if he had been hit, or whether it was his supercharger going, but he was losing oil. He saw some Hurricanes ahead and darted into cloud. The temperature gauge was reading 130° C. He drifted down, with hostile territory below. Then the engine seized. He had to bale out, but as he jettisoned the hood, a blast of air jammed him against the back of the cockpit. He used all his strength and came free, tumbling over and over. He pulled the ripcord and felt a sharp pain in his leg as the parachute lines twisted round it. He freed his leg and came down in the middle of a herd of cows. As he tried to get his parachute there was a shot, and a man with an arm-band shouted, 'Get up!' His war was over.

He had flown on I./JG52's last mission. The Gruppe had lost his wingman and one other pilot as well that day. Of the thirty-six pilots who had been with the unit in July, four now remained. The unit was withdrawn to Antwerp and then sent to Krefeld to rest and re-fit.[31]

For Britain's official historians, the line is drawn under the Battle of Britain on 31 October.

For others, the fighting was not over. The exhausted 109 pilots carried on. On 1 November, the Stukas returned to bid a last farewell. JG26 escorted a wing of them to attack a convoy off the Nore. They managed to get away with the loss of only one.

For some, it offered a new opportunity. There had been repeated discussions between Hitler and Mussolini about military co-operation. Mussolini wanted Hitler's support in the Mediterranean, and he was anxious to help in northern Europe. Despite grave misgivings amongst Luftwaffe commanders, units of the Regia Aeronautica turned up in Belgium in mid-September under the name of Corpo Aereo Italiano, and began training. They were armed with obsolete Fiat CR 42 biplane fighters, and obsolescent BR 20 bombers and G 50 monoplane fighters. They were unused to northern weather conditions and tended to get lost.

However, they were gallant men and their morale was high. At 1330 on 11 November, Essex radar picked up a plot made by about a dozen BR 20s and a dozen CR 42s heading for Harwich. 257 Squadron were scrambled, and, with some help from 17 and 46 Squadrons, shot down nine of them without loss. They described it as 'a turkey shoot'. The birds never returned.[32]

For others, the old opportunity was too bound up with their existence to give up now. In early November Erprobungsgruppe 210 got a new leader, the former Gruppenkommandeur of II./ZG2, Major Karl-Heinz Lessmann. On the 17th, he led them on an attack on the airfield at Wattisham near Ipswich, escorted by JG26. They were intercepted by 17 and 257 Squadrons and lost three Bf 110s. These were their last combat losses in 1940. On 24 April 1941 they were re-designated 'Schnellkampfgeschwader 210', and transferred to the east.

For one or two, the fighting ended for unexpected reasons. On 28 October, Karl Bertram, a Sergeant Pilot with the night-fighter unit III./NJG1, was killed when his Bf 110 crashed in Schleswig-Holstein. On 30 September, his brother, Hans, had been killed over Sussex when flying with I./JG27. There was a third brother, Otto, who was Gruppenkommandeur of III./JG2. When Karl was killed, his family invoked the 'last surviving son' rule: Otto was given the Knight's Cross and withdrawn from combat operations.[33]

For a few it did not seem futile. On 20 October, Otto Bertam's opposite number at I./JG2, Helmut Wick, was made Kommodore of the whole of the 'Richthofen' Geschwader. At twenty-two, he was heir to the greatest ace of all time, the man whose spirit animated the whole of the Luftwaffe. They no longer talked about him as they had done in training school.

Mölders claimed his fiftieth victory on 22 October, Galland his on the 30th. On 29 October, Mölders shot down his fifty-fourth victim. Wick claimed three victories on 5 November and five more the next day. He flew whenever he could, and kept on scoring. Mölders had no luck at all during November.

In the middle of the month, Wick did it. At about the same time as the Richthofen Geschwader celebrated its 200th aerial victory, Wick chalked up his fifty-fourth to draw level with Vati Mölders, the Oswald Boelcke of the new Luftwaffe. It was the last lap. Galland was languishing on fifty-two. Then, on 17 November, Wick got a shock, for Galland had claimed three that one day, taking him to fifty-five.

At 1310 on the afternoon of 28 November 1940, Helmut Wick climbed into the cockpit of his Bf 109 at Querqueville near Cherbourg in Normandy and took off with the Staff Flight on a sweep up to the Isle of Wight. They were accompanied by most of the rest of JG2 and a flight from II./JG77 who were invited to come along to watch the fun. Georg Schirmböck of JG77 was astonished to observe that all these aircraft were under orders not to make kills themselves, but simply to protect their Kommodore as he did so. That morning, the latest edition of the *Berliner Illustrierte* carried a photograph of a smiling Göring visiting his own old unit, the Richthofen Geschwader, with its good-looking new Commander, the direct heir to the position he had once held, laughing next to him. An hour later Wick touched down again, and his ground crew welcomed him in as he taxied up, anxious to hear the news. Yes! Another Spitfire, number fifty-five! He was ahead of Mölders and level with Galland. Then disaster struck. At 1500, JG2 got a telephone call from JG26 Headquarters to say that Galland had just shot down a Hurricane.

There was still plenty of light. The Bf 109s were quickly re-armed and re-fuelled, and at 1530 Wick led the Stabschwarm back out over his favourite hunting ground over the Needles. Just after he had taken off, a signal arrived at the Geschwader Headquarters. Major Wick was grounded with immediate effect. He was too valuable a personality to be risked in combat.

South-west of the Isle of Wight, Wick and his wingman, Erich Leie, together with the two pilots of his second Rotte, Franz Fiby and Rudi Pflanz, spotted some Spitfires climbing to meet them. They were 152 and 609 Squadrons. The Germans dived on them, and Wick hit the Spitfire flown by Paul Baillon who had only just joined 609 Squadron. The plane began to smoke. Wick had to make certain of this one. He fastened on to the crippled Spitfire and gave it another burst. Baillon baled out into the Solent at 1613. Number fifty-six! Helmut Wick was now Germany's greatest ace! It was a sweet moment.

At just that moment, Squadron Leader Michael Robinson of 609 Squadron heard a familiar and exuberant voice over the R/T: 'I've finished a 109, whoopee!' It was John Dundas. 'Good show John!' Robinson replied. That was all he heard.[34]

Hugh Dundas had recovered from the wounds he had received on 22 August. On Friday 29 November he drove to visit his parents. He arrived at tea-time and was shocked to learn that his father had had a telegram saying that his brother John was missing. 'Poor Mummy!' Hugh wrote. 'If John is killed – and I did my best to persuade her otherwise – I believe that even her brave heart will be broken.'[35]

John never turned up. He lies somewhere out to sea off Bournemouth, as does the 109 he finished, and its pilot, Helmut Wick. Rudi Pflanz saw Wick hit and bale out. Just as the attacking Spitfire turned away, Pflanz managed to get it in his sights and send it into the Channel as well. No trace of either pilot or their planes has ever been found.

Siegfried was slain.

PART III:
AFTERMATH

28. FEUDING

At 3.30 p.m. on Thursday 17 October 1940, an extraordinary meeting was convened in the Air Council room at the Air Ministry in London to discuss 'major day tactics in the fighter force'. Present were: Sir Charles Portal, who had been designated to take over as Chief of the Air Staff from Newall a week later and was thus effectively Britain's most senior airman; Sir Philip Joubert de la Ferté, the Assistant Chief of the Air Staff with responsibility for radar, reporting to Douglas; Air Commodores Slessor and Stevenson and Group Captain Crowe from the Air Ministry, who worked for Douglas; Sholto Douglas himself; Dowding; Park and Brand; and Leigh-Mallory, who brought with him a guest, Squadron Leader Douglas Bader.

The meeting had been called by Sholto Douglas. He also chaired it in his role as Deputy Chief of the Air Staff because his boss, Newall, was unable to be present, 'owing to indisposition'.

Douglas opened the meeting by declaring that it had been convened to discuss three propositions: that it was desirable to out-number the enemy when they were met; that intercepting fighters should work with a plan so that escorts were held off while the bombers were tackled; and that, if possible, the interceptors should have the advantage of height.

These propositions were hardly worth holding a meeting about, let alone one so august. All assembled only needed to nod in agreement and break up for tea. They were not what it was really about at all.

Relations between Park and Leigh-Mallory had been deteriorating steadily since 15 September. Park had been enraged at Leigh-Mallory's report on wing operations which had been sent to the Air Ministry. On 22 September, Dowding sent the Air Ministry a copy of Park's own report on operations between 8 August and 12 September. It contained some undiplomatic remarks about the dilatoriness of the Air Ministry's arrangements for repairing airfields. Airing his rancours in such a way was not wise.

Meanwhile, Leigh-Mallory's report had been passed around in London and aroused much interest. The Adjutant of 242 Squadron, Flight Lieutenant Peter Macdonald, also happened to be the Tory MP for the Isle of Wight. In mid-September he had spoken to Sinclair's Deputy, the Under-Secretary of State for Air, Harold Balfour, in the Commons, asking to see Churchill. Balfour told him that he was not going to arrange anything, but as an MP he had the right to seek an interview with the Prime Minister. Macdonald did so, with the result that enquiries issued from the Prime Minister's office.[1]

Dowding too found Leigh-Mallory's report interesting, and treated the matter as if he were unaware of the sour relations between his subordinates. Douglas was supportive of Leigh-Mallory and highly critical of Park, particularly because he did not deal with night-fighting.[2]

This subject had become a bone of contention between Douglas and Dowding. Dowding was working slowly and methodically, as was his way, on developing the radar-based system he had explained in the paper Churchill found so 'masterly'.[3] Douglas wanted immediate results and felt, as he put it after the war, that Dowding had become 'a little blinded' to the 'more simple hit or miss, trial and error, use of single-engined fighters', and that 'the effort had to be made'.[4]

Dowding was making progress, even if it did not yield spectacular results. On 9 September, he began the 'Kenley experiment', in which gun-laying radar sets were mounted at searchlight posts in the Kenley Sector and linked to the Sector Station, which then guided fighters with Air Interception (AI) radar onto the incoming bombers. One of the pilots working on this was Sandy Sanders. One foggy night, he was called up and told that Dowding and Churchill were coming and that he was to go down to the Operations Room in Caterham to answer any questions they might have. He recalls listening to Dowding explain things to Churchill. 'Sir,' he said, 'I envisage a night-fighter taking off on a night such as this using only his instruments. He will be vectored onto the enemy in the middle of cloud, in the middle of the night, he will shoot it down and be brought back and land safely in the fog.' 'The man's a bloody lunatic,' thought Sandy. Churchill looked bewildered. Both thought that doing what Dowding envisaged would take years, if indeed it would ever work at all. 'Yet, do you know', remembers Sandy, 'just a couple of months later, old John Cunningham and Jimmy Rawnsley took off and did just that – that very thing. I never believed it could happen. So Dowding was right, absolutely right'.[5]

At the time there was a powerful lobby convinced he was absolutely wrong. On 14 September, Beaverbrook intervened, writing to Sinclair to inform him that a committee was to be formed to look into night defence under one of his staff, a former CAS, Marshal of the Royal Air Force Sir John Salmond. The Salmond Committee produced its report within days. It contained eighteen points, many of them critical of Dowding and backing up Douglas. Salmond also wrote to Trenchard, who, though retired, still exerted considerable influence with his reputation of being the 'father of the Royal Air

Force'. Salmond told Trenchard that Dowding lacked humanity and imagination and was living on the reputation gained by his pilots in daylight combat. He had attached a private note to the copy of his report to Beaverbrook recommending that 'Dowding should go'. He added that he had said the same thing to Churchill, who practically blew him out of the room, but was coming round. Were Churchill not to come round, Salmond was prepared to go to the King.[6]

Dowding received a copy of Salmond's report and marked it with a blue crayon in his usual way. Of the eighteen points, three got ticks, five got question marks and nine got crosses. He was going to carry on regardless, in his usual way.

The battle over the daylight battle intensified. On 29 September, perhaps because he sensed what was going on, Park fired off an irritable memo called 'Major Tactics in Home Defence' to Dowding, praising Brand and condemning Leigh-Mallory. Leigh-Mallory, he wrote, did not send the requested reinforcements where and when they were needed, as a result of which the airfields north of London had been bombed whilst 11 Group squadrons, believing their bases to be safe, were engaging the enemy further forward. Indeed, Leigh-Mallory sent his Wing down to Canterbury without telling anyone. To the 11 Group controllers, the Wing looked like a German raid, and squadrons needed to intercept the Luftwaffe went up to intercept Bader and his men instead. Park asked Dowding to make 12 Group co-operate with his requests and not to waste time 'forming up into a mass of five squadrons' when he asked for two or three single ones.[7] That Park knew he was on the defensive is shown by the fact that he felt moved to write another memo on the use of wings to his own station commanders a few days later. He pointed out that no more than two squadrons could use the same radio frequency anyway.[8]

Given the number of friendly-fire incidents during the Battle of Britain, it is a mercy that Bader's roving Wing was not attacked by its own side. Squadron Leader Miles Duke-Woolly took over command of 253 Squadron in late September, and has written of one close shave. Having climbed to 31,000 feet over Canterbury, which was unusual for Hurricanes but at just the sort of height at which 109s were then operating, he saw a 'black mass' bearing down on him from the north. He realised in time that it was the Duxford Wing, but they did not recognise him as friendly. When he set off to tag along behind, they thought they were being stalked, and orbited for some minutes until their fuel ran low and they retired. As a result of another similar encounter they 'returned in disorder to their bases'.[9] The Wing was of course very vulnerable to being bounced and it often was for real, which is no doubt why the pilots in it were wary. Had 253 Squadron been a *Staffel* of Messerschmitts, they could have put an end to the Wing's patrol and a few lives with ease.

At Stanmore, Evill, Dowding's SASO, reacted as always with conciliatory reasonableness to Park's testy note, and told Dowding that the two Groups were operating on different principles and that they needed to co-operate. On

8 October, Dowding sent Park's note to Leigh-Mallory, asking for his comments. Leigh-Mallory replied mellifluously the next day, saying that he hoped the C-in-C did not think, as Park had implied, that he was only after 'a good bag'. He suggested that if the Wing were called when the Germans were assembling their massed raids over Calais, it could be over Biggin Hill by the time the Germans arrived. He was, after all, 'only too anxious to co-operate with 11 Group'.[10]

Park did not call the Wing when German aircraft were assembling over Calais because it was not clear where the raiders were going and he did not want anyone to get caught on the ground re-fuelling after having been dispatched towards a feint. Kesselring, after all, was no slouch. Nor did he want to call them before committing his own forces because that was not how the system worked. 12 Group's primary responsibility was for its own area, and the best use of it was in defending the many lucrative targets north of the capital. However, it would have done no good even if he had called them when the potential raiders were still over Calais. Assuming it climbed at its optimal speed, a Spitfire would take about twenty-three minutes to cover the 70 miles from Duxford to Canterbury. It could take off about five minutes after the first radar warning of a build-up over Calais. A bomber travelling at 180 mph would reach Canterbury in fourteen minutes. Even without adding in time for forming up, and even assuming the Wing used Spitfires rather than the slower Hurricanes which would take longer, a German bomber formation would be over Canterbury in half the time it would take a single fighter from Duxford to get there.[11] The whole thing was absurd.

As far as the fighting was concerned, all of this had become academic. When Dowding suggested to Park that he employ the Big Wing in one of his sectors, Park wrote back on 10 October to explain, with the use of track charts from recent raids, why this was impossible, and suggested instead that 12 Group relieve his squadrons from the burden of their many patrols.[12] They had both missed the point.

It was on 14 October that they received their invitations for what was termed 'a small conference' to be held in London that Thursday. The attached agenda was clear enough. It listed ten items in the form of questions. The first read: 'Is it agreed that the minimum fighter unit to meet large enemy formations should be a wing of three squadrons?' and continued in similar vein, challenging all Park's beliefs and his past practice.[13] All at the Air Ministry were clearly agreed.

Park wrote to Stevenson at the Ministry on 15 October asking him to circulate to the conference participants two of his instructions on the use of two or three squadrons at a time within 11 Group and the results of his five months' experience in trying to engage 'BEFORE THE BOMBER RAIDS HAVE REACHED VITAL OBJECTIVES' (upper case in the original), adding that 'conditions of time and space do not permit squadrons in 12 Group engaging incoming raids'.[14] He also prepared a list of ten points for the conference, which reiterated the main principles of his interception policy. But this was one of Park's few attempts at interception which came too late.

As he entered the Air Council room on 17 October, Dowding was astonished to see Bader, and, Bader's biographer reports, he 'looked at him severely'. No pilot from 10 or 11 Groups was there to put an alternative case, and no-one had suggested that bringing one or two along would be appropriate. Park realised that Bader was there 'to make room for Leigh-Mallory', and that he had been stitched up.[15]

The minutes of the conference show Park defending himself against overwhelming odds and Dowding appearing to be mildly unconcerned and talking generally about the problems of interception. Leigh-Mallory was only too willing to help 11 Group, but all agreed with Squadron Leader Bader that time was a problem. This seems to have been Bader's only contribution to the discussion.[16] The items on the prepared agenda were all agreed, with some riders about conditions needing to be suitable. Portal seems to have been the only sceptic with regard to wings, asking Leigh-Mallory how he could defend his local area if all his strength were so concentrated. Leigh-Mallory assured him that 'satisfactory plans were prepared'. Douglas summarised the results as agreement that: 'The employment of a large mass of fighters had great advantages, though it was not necessarily the complete solution to the problem of interception. In 11 Group, where the enemy was very close at hand, both the methods described by AOC 11 Group and those of AOC 12 Group could, on occasion, be used, with forces from the two Groups co-operating.' So all were agreed, and everyone was right. Towards the end of the conference, the subject turned to night defence. Douglas suggested forming a wing of two Defiant and two Hurricane squadrons for night-fighting. Dowding stated that diverting Hurricanes to night defence was 'dangerous and unsound', but reluctantly agreed to experiment with a 'fighter night' over London, though it was not a course he would recommend.[17] With that, the meeting was adjourned, and so they went their own ways.

When the minutes were circulated, Dowding, Brand and Leigh-Mallory each sent back a short note with some suggested corrections. Park wrote back with a set of detailed amendments and a two-page statement. In a minute sheet, Stevenson noted that the DCAS (Douglas) had decided to leave the minutes as they stood and omit the statement in view of its length and the fact that he did not think all of the remarks were appropriate.[18]

'Mutt' had got his revenge.

On 26 October, Sinclair visited Duxford, and talked to both Bader and the Sector Controller, Woodhall. A week later, Balfour turned up and wrote a report on his visit. He confirmed Sinclair's fears that there was a conflict between Park and Leigh-Mallory, and said that it had become a personal issue between the pilots, with 12 Group feeling resentful against Park and his Group as well as against the Air Ministry. There had been no improvements as a result of the conference and the Wing was still being called too late. 11 Group resented 'poaching' on its territory and its pilots were 'unnecessarily shaken in their morale' because they were constantly out-numbered. The memo was copied to Sinclair, Portal and Douglas, and Douglas forwarded it to Dowding, asking him to act decisively, and get Park to make better use of the Wing. He added that he had been asked by Balfour to ensure that Bader did not get into trouble.

Dowding replied, rebutting every point, but saying that he would now assume direct control of combined operations between the groups. As for Bader, he said, he had been responsible for a good deal of the ill-feeling and, whatever his other merits, suffered from 'an over-development of the critical faculties'. It might be better to move 'young Bader to another station where he could be kept in better control'. His 'amazing gallantry' would probably protect him from disciplinary action.[19]

Nobody actually asked any 11 Group pilots about their morale. Some have since been outraged to hear the suggestion that it was poor. Park, on the other hand, was worried about 12 Group's morale. He was of the opinion that the 12 Group squadrons transferred to him had been taught that it was not safe to fly about in anything but a wing of four to five squadrons, and that he had to un-teach them quickly when they arrived in the south-east.[20] Many pilots got to hear about what was going on between their Group AOCs and whilst some took sides, others saw it as a 'peevish tiff'. One of them was Tom Neil, then a Pilot Officer in 249 Squadron which fought with 10 Group until 1 September when it moved to North Weald in 11 Group:

> I . . . began to feel that the group commanders . . . were demeaning themselves. To us, as might be expected, Park was the hero and Leigh-Mallory the villain, though never once did we approach the point of being openly critical of either.
>
> Squadron Leader Douglas Bader . . . was generally regarded as being the main advocate of the Balbo . . . Acknowledged everywhere as being a tremendously gutsy character, flying as he did with artificial legs, he also had the less enviable reputation of being somewhat over-devoted to his own interests, a characteristic which did not endear him to everyone, particularly those of us who suffered as the result of his personal enthusiasms. All too frequently, when returning to North Weald in a semi-exhausted condition, all we saw of 12 Group's contribution to the engagement, was a vast formation of Hurricanes in neat vics of three, steaming comfortably over our heads in pursuit of an enemy who had long since disappeared in the direction of France. Our reactions on such occasions, though mostly of resigned amusement at first, grew to be more harshly critical later on.[21]

Not all the pilots in 12 Group approved of wings either. Flight Lieutenant Douglas Blackwood led 310 Squadron and has observed that it was often chaos at the back of the formation with people being left behind, though of course Bader was always at the front and never saw this. Bernard Jennings was a Sergeant Pilot in 19 Squadron and remembers the Wing being very cumbersome even when led by his own C/O Brian Lane, who was 'a wonderful pilot'. More outspoken is his colleague on 19 Squadron, Flying Officer Frank Brinsden, who thought the Wing 'a disaster' which achieved nothing because in any case 'the Wing disintegrated almost immediately battle was joined.'[22]

Dowding, Leigh-Mallory and Park tried in the following days to work out some form of modus vivendi which would satisfy the needs of the fighting and Leigh-Mallory's desire to use wings. On 7 November, Park sent Dowding his report on operations between 11 September and 31 October, in which he devoted some space to the use of wings. He claimed that the Duxford Wing had been used 'on every possible occasion during the last half of October'. He attached a table showing its record. In ten sorties, it had managed to intercept once and had shot down one German aircraft.[23]

Dowding passed the report on to the Air Ministry on 15 November. No-one was interested. The previous night, the Luftwaffe had used its Knickebein beams to raid Coventry in strength. Over 500 civilians had died, over 1,000 had been injured and the town had been devastated. That was the price of Stuffy's stubbornness over night defence. He could not control his subordinates, would not work with the Air Ministry and had out-of-date ideas. He had become an isolated and increasingly eccentric old man, who had been supposed to retire long ago anyway. On the other hand, as some at the Ministry had pointed out, he could do some very good work in America.[24]

29. THE SPOILS OF WAR

On 25 November, Dowding was retired from his post as C-in-C Fighter Command.[1] Churchill said it 'nearly broke his heart'.[2] Before he left, Dowding went round to every office in Bentley Priory and said 'I think you know that I am going. Thank you very much'. At all the operational units of Fighter Command, a final signal arrived from the Commander-in-Chief:

> My dear Fighter Boys,
> In sending you this my last message, I wish I could say all that is in my heart. I cannot hope to surpass the simple eloquence of the Prime Minister's words, 'Never before has so much been owed by so many to so few.' The debt remains and will increase.
> In saying good bye to you I want you to know how continually you have been in my thoughts, and that, though our direct communication may be severed, I may yet be able to help you in your gallant fight.
> Good bye to you and God bless you all.

He went to America to work on the delicate issue of obtaining aircraft and supplies from the US. Dowding was not a great diplomat, and the mission was not a great success. He returned in May 1941. Nobody knew what to do with him, so the Air Council asked him to write a despatch about the Battle. He finished it in August and his retirement from the RAF was gazetted on 1 October.

Churchill had always had the highest regard for Dowding, and reacted with his customary vigour when he read the news, firing off memos which quickly developed from the enquiring to the indignant. He said that he should have been consulted, and demanded that further employment be found for Dowding. So it was that the mess over fixing his retirement date continued beyond it. His retirement was cancelled, and he was given the job of improving manpower efficiency in the RAF. This time, Dowding took control of his own fate, turned down the job and asked to be placed back on the retired list. Sinclair agreed, but Churchill did not, and asked to see him. In a very frank interview, Dowding told Churchill that he neither liked nor trusted Sinclair, which shocked Churchill, for Sinclair was an old friend. Churchill prevailed and Dowding carried out his task, finally retiring at his own request in July 1942. When the retirement submission came before the King for signature, he asked whether Dowding should not be made Marshal of the Royal Air Force, the equivalent of Field Marshal, in view of his 'really wonderful service to this country'. Sinclair consulted Portal and wrote a painful reply about how it might provoke comment, as Dowding had already retired once, and how the Battle of Britain finished two years before and it should have been done then or not at all. He might, however, be considered for a reward at the end of the war.

He was not. Churchill, though, proposed him for a Barony in 1943. Dowding accepted, and chose the title 'The Lord Dowding of Bentley Priory'.[3]

In retirement he devoted much of his energies to cultivating an interest in spiritualism. In October 1942 he was guest of honour at a dinner given for Battle of Britain pilots at the Savoy. During his speech he told them that he was in regular communication with their dead comrades and that they were all in good shape and quite happy.[4] His surviving fighter boys thought he had lost his marbles.

It was probably not fortuitous that his post was taken over by Sholto Douglas. His offensive spirit was more suited to the needs of Fighter Command now that the defensive battle had been won; he was much younger than Dowding, articulate and able, and he was well-placed to influence Sinclair, who leaned on him heavily. He was also an old friend of Balfour's. After all, the support of politicians is important if senior service officers are to be effective.[5]

On 4 December, Park was received by the King and made a companion of the Most Honourable Order of the Bath (CB). On 18 December, in view of his tiredness and the heavy load he had been bearing, he was removed to Training Command and replaced as AOC 11 Group by Leigh-Mallory. Several members of his staff wrote to him congratulating him on the CB and expressing regret at his departure. To one he replied that he felt quite fit and had been looking forward to the spring offensive. The C/O of Hornchurch, Group Captain Cecil Bouchier, wrote that he had not only ensured but inspired ultimate victory, and felt that with his departure 'so much heart was going out of the group'. Park also wrote one letter of congratulation, to Richard Saul, who replaced Leigh-Mallory at 12 Group, and whom Park felt should have replaced him. On the day of Park's departure, Leigh-Mallory did not show up, so Park handed over to his SASO.[6]

The new brooms introduced wings into the Fighter Command organisation. One of the first was the Tangmere Wing which was led by Douglas Bader until he was shot down by one of Adolf Galland's men on 9 August 1941. One of those who learned about air fighting from him was Hugh 'Cocky' Dundas, who shared the feelings of all his pilots that Bader was the most inspiring leader he ever served under. He helped Bader to work on squadron formations, which resulted in 1941 in the invention of the 'finger four', a re-discovery of Mölders' 'Schwarm', and a variant of the 'fours in line astern' introduced in 74 Squadron by 'Sailor' Malan in 1940. Working out the 'finger four' formation, together with the direct impact he had on the men he led, was Bader's most important contribution to the war in the air. Dundas ended the war at the age of twenty-four as the youngest Group Captain in the RAF.

After he returned from captivity in 1945, Bader led the Battle of Britain flypast over London, and became the country's most celebrated fighter pilot, the only one to have his biography, *Reach for the Sky*, turned into a film. It became one of the most popular in the history of British cinema.

On 29 January 1941, Leigh-Mallory ran an exercise reproducing the airfield raids Fighter Command experienced in early September. His airfields were bombed while the planes were still on the ground. He remarked that he would do better next time.[7] He and Sholto Douglas were busy with other things. Wanting to take the battle to the enemy, they adopted a policy they called 'leaning towards France'. In leaning in this direction during the summer of 1941, Fighter Command lost 194 pilots. The Luftwaffe lost 128 aircraft, and recovered most of their pilots. The Germans wanted to get on with the real war in Russia, so left only about 160–200 fighters from JG2 and JG26 in France, which proceeded to do to Leigh-Mallory what Park had done to them. They did not overly care if France was bombed, so they were particularly choosy about when and how they engaged, and ambushed the huge wings in Staffel or Schwarm strength. The confused mêlées in the air led to the sort of overclaiming characteristic of the Big Wing in 1940, so Leigh-Mallory thought he was doing rather well, and carried on. In the second half of the year, Fighter Command claimed 731 German aircraft for the loss of 411. The actual German losses were 154, only 92 of which were incurred in opposing Leigh-Mallory's 'circuses' and 'rhubarbs' over France. The Luftwaffe's kill-ratio of over 4:1 was about what they would have needed to have won the Battle of Britain. Fighter Command was fortunate that the whole campaign was of little strategic significance, conducted mainly to show Stalin that Britain was trying to do something in Europe.[8]

The only occasion on which fighting reached the sort of intensity it had in 1940 was in the operation to cover the disastrous Dieppe raid on 19 August 1942. Leigh-Mallory overruled objections from his deputy SASO, Group Captain Harry Broadhurst, and used multiple wing formations. The RAF lost ninety-seven aircraft in action, but claimed ninety-six confirmed, thirty-nine probables and a hundred and thirty-five damaged in return, so declared victory. The Luftwaffe lost forty-eight. Fighter Command lost forty-seven pilots and another seventeen were made POWs. The Luftwaffe lost thirteen fighter pilots. Broadhurst flew over Dieppe three times during the day to see what was happening, and saw small groups of Fw 190s bounce the unwieldy wings time and again. He lobbied to get single squadrons and flights sent over to counter them, and had some success. At least the air umbrella was successful in protecting the shipping and troops from most of the Luftwaffe's attempts to bomb them.[9]

In late 1942, Douglas moved on to the Middle East and Leigh-Mallory replaced him as C-in-C Fighter Command. As such, Leigh-Mallory was heavily involved in the planning for Overlord, and became the C-in-C of the Allied air forces in Normandy. He was posted to take over in South East Asia, but was killed in an air crash on his way out there on 14 November 1944. Douglas ended the war as C-in-C of Coastal Command.

When Keith Park arrived at 23 Group, Flying Training Command in December 1940, he found that it was working at two-thirds capacity and following peace-time routines, which put his shortage of pilots in a new light. He shook it up before being moved to Egypt in January 1942 to take over responsibility for the air defence of the Nile Delta.

On 14 July 1942 he took over command of the air defences of Malta from Air Vice-Marshal Hugh Lloyd. He faced Kesselring again, and gave him another beating. Lloyd had led the defences against truly daunting odds with the supply of aircraft several times threatening to run out. By July that crisis was over, but Malta was still the most bombed place on earth. Park took the offensive, using pairs of squadrons to intercept the raiders well forward. Within a fortnight, the bombing had been stopped, and the number of aircraft destroyed on the ground reduced from thirty-four to four. On 20 November, the first convoy to reach Malta unmolested sailed into Grand Harbour, and the siege was over. From then on Park concentrated on further offensive operations to support the Allied landings in Sicily, where the Allied air forces managed to establish and maintain air superiority.

Park served in Egypt for one further spell, but when Leigh-Mallory was killed in 1944, he was appointed as Air C-in-C of South East Asia Command in his stead. He supplied 14th Army from the air during Slim's re-conquest of Burma, and was present when Mountbatten accepted the formal Japanese surrender on 21 September 1945. In 1946 he received a letter from Lord Tedder, the CAS, telling him that the RAF had no suitable positions available for him and that he would be retired at the end of the year. He went home to New Zealand, where he embarked on a new career in civil aviation.

Tedder made amends, however. In February 1947, at the annual dinner of the New Zealand Society in London, Tedder made a speech about Park in which he observed: 'If ever any one man won the Battle of Britain, he did. I don't believe it is realised how much that one man, with his leadership, his calm judgement and his skill, did to save not only this country, but the world'.

Park's main opponent, Albert Kesselring, continued to prosecute the air war against England during the winter of 1940–41, in what the British call 'the Blitz' but was increasingly involved in the planning of Barbarossa, the assault on Russia. In June 1941, he moved to the east with the rest of Luftflotte 2, which was the largest of the three Airfleets taking part in the campaign, with the task of supporting Army Group Centre, whose target was Moscow. The air war in the west was now left to Sperrle and Airfleet 3, and Sperrle stayed in France up to and beyond the Allied invasion in 1944.

The role of the Luftwaffe in Russia was explicitly to support the army, and Kesselring worked closely with his Army Group Command. In November 1941, with the German army grinding to a halt in front of Moscow, Kesselring was moved to Italy as theatre C-in-C and took Luftflotte 2 with him. The British had become active in the Mediterranean and were sinking a lot of ships, and the Afrika Korps needed help. There then began an air war over the supply routes in the Mediterranean, the centrepiece of which was Operation Hercules, the plan to invade Malta, which became an attempt to subdue the island from the air. Kesselring may have had a sense of déjà vu about this as the invasion plans vacillated and reports that the British were at their last gasp kept on coming in. That sense must have been further strengthened in July when Park turned up again. Facing this opponent for a second time was a hard fate, and the result was the same as it had been the first time round.

As the German military crisis in North Africa deepened, Kesselring took overall control of the theatre and exercised direct operational command of the German army in Italy. The years 1943–45 were Kesselring's finest hour as he conducted a stubborn and brilliant defence until the war's end, tying down an Allied army substantially larger than his own. Controversially indicted at Nuremberg, he was imprisoned until 1952 and died in 1960, still trying to clear his name.

Adolf Galland went on to run the German fighter force on the Channel coast, which he did very well against heavy odds, giving Leigh-Mallory a drubbing over the Channel dash of the *Scharnhorst* and *Gneisenau* in February 1942. As Inspector General of Fighters, he was responsible for the defences during The Battle of Germany fought against the US 8th Air Force from 1943 onwards. However, this was one battle he was bound to lose. After the war he became Germany's best-known pilot and became a good friend of his former prisoner, Douglas Bader. He also made friends with Bob Stanford Tuck, who was shot down by flak in 1942 on one of Leigh-Mallory's 'rhubarbs' and joined Bader in prison. After the war they discovered that shooting with each other was more fun than shooting at each other.

Galland's old enemy Ulrich Steinhilper was sent to a prisoner of war camp in Sheffield and then evacuated to Canada. One of his fellow prisoners was Franz von Werra, the Adjutant of II./JG3, who had been shot down over Marden in Kent on 5 September. Everybody talked about escape, and when von Werra actually succeeded, Ulrich decided to emulate him. He made five unsuccessful attempts, and was finally released on 6 December 1946. His early interest in technology enabled him to embark on a successful career as an executive at IBM, where he was one of those responsible for inventing the word-processor.[10]

Fate had not finished with Al Deere, but his guardian angel did not desert him. Technically, he had used up all his nine lives by the time he was finally withdrawn from the Battle on 3 September, but only six of them had been used up actually flying. Fate clearly took the more generous view and decided he had three to go. After 54 Squadron had moved north, Deere collided with a young Sergeant Pilot when training him, baled out with his parachute partially torn from his back, and landed in a cesspool. On 5 June 1941, he crash-landed on a cliff-top at Ayr when his engine seized on another training flight. Finally, his Spitfire was hit in a dogfight in August and he force-landed at his favourite airfield – Manston. After a tour of the USA and some staff duties, he became Wing Leader at Biggin Hill in 1943, commanded another wing over Normandy, and became Biggin Hill Station Commander just after the war ended. In his account of the Battle of Britain, the German writer Cajus Bekker paid tribute to Deere, citing him as an example of the toughness and tenacity of the defenders.[11] None, it must be said, went through quite as much trauma as he did. The RAF recognised his extraordinary courage and resilience with a DFC and a DSO, which seems a little mean.

Peter Townsend recovered from the wounds he suffered on 31 August, and re-joined 85 Squadron as they were converting into a night-fighter unit in line with Douglas' scheme. He scored their first night victory on 25 February 1941, but Dowding had been right, and it was only when they re-equipped with Defiants and American-built Havocs that they began to have consistent success. In April 1942, Townsend became Station Commander at Drem, and had a series of staff appointments until becoming Equerry to King George VI in 1944. He ended the war a Group Captain, and achieved notoriety in the 1950s when he fell in love with Princess Margaret, and she with him, which was understandable.

He left the RAF in 1956, went on a journey round the world and retired to France where he married a beautiful French girl, Marie-Luce, in 1959. He became a writer and died at his home in France in 1995, a much loved and respected man.

When Richard Hillary was recovered from the water on 3 September he was very badly burned. He did not leave hospital until the end of 1941. Whilst enduring multiple operations he got to know the girlfriend of Peter Pease who flew to his death on 15 September. Inspired in part by his memory, and in part by feelings of guilt at having survived whilst so many of his friends had died, he wrote a self-questioning memoir, *The Last Enemy*, which has become a classic since its publication in June 1942. With his hands turned into twisted claws despite all that surgery could do, he was hardly fit to fly, but he persisted and was posted to a training unit to convert to night fighters. On the night of 18 January 1943, whilst he was circling a beacon in very bad weather, his aircraft, an old Blenheim, spun in and he was killed. He became a symbol of the doomed youth of Fighter Command, his story being most recently explored by Sebastian Faulks in *The Fatal Englishman*.

James Sanders stayed in the battle zone in a variety of flying roles until the Battle of Britain petered out and turned into the Blitz. After his attachment to 253 Squadron he was briefly posted to 66 Squadron on 2 October 1940, was attached to the Fighter Interception Unit and then, on 14 October, formed 422 Flight (which in December became 96 Squadron) to develop night-interception techniques. He was posted to 255 Squadron, flying Defiant night-fighters, on 4 March 1941 and was credited with three kills at night. From then on he had various training appointments, and was Station Commander at three airfields. He ended the war at SHAEF (Supreme Headquarters, Allied Expeditionary Force) in Brussels, and left the RAF in 1947 as Wing Commander flying at Mingladon in Burma.

In 1943, he had a brush with the authorities that paralleled 'Sailor' Malan's in 1937, but in this case he was not the escorting officer, he was the accused. Sandy had recently married the girl for whose sake he had stayed at Kenley. She had been attached to his friend Bill Fowler in the role of his 'Command Reserve'. Bill had another lady friend as his 'Initial Equipment', so his 'Command Reserve' had pursued Sandy and was eventually successful. In 1943 Sandy was posted to Shropshire and she was billeted with him. One day he visited 41 Squadron nearby, where his old friend Douglas Hone was acting Squadron Leader, and borrowed a Spitfire so that he could 'beat up' his wife in time-honoured manner, just as 'Sailor' Malan had done to his girlfriend, by doing a slow roll over her lodgings. Unfortunately, he frightened the local Chief of Police who observed what he took to be a Spitfire flying close to his home supposedly 'inverted' about '10 feet off the ground'. The Chief of Police made a note of Sandy's code letters, which were EB-M, and sent the details on to the Air Ministry together with the observation that the culprit was a disgrace to the Air Force and should be severely punished. This time it was a real court martial. However, Sandy had a spot of luck. He looked in the authorisation book and saw to his relief that EB-W had been in the air at the same time. He wrote out the code letters on a piece of card, took it to the hearing and when asked what he had to say for himself, he showed the court the card, turned it upside down and explained that his accuser must have been mistaken – he had seen EB-W flying the right way up. It was in any case impossible to fly upside down at 10 feet, he argued. The President of the court martial was Darley Pyne, known as 'Barley Wine', who knew Sandy from the days when he had been Station Adjutant at Northolt. The case was washed out, but it had been a close call.

Robert Francis Doe left hospital in the winter of 1940, and flew again for the first time on Boxing Day 1940. He took over command of 238 Squadron, but crashed and was seriously injured in a night landing accident at Warmwell in January 1941. His face was smashed, with one eye dislocated, his jaw broken and his nose pushed up onto his forehead. He spent some months in hospital and had twenty-two operations. He recovered to join 66 Squadron on 16 May 1941, where he flew convoy patrols and sweeps over France, before having several postings as an instructor. In late 1943 he was sent to Burma and ended the war as Squadron Leader of 10 Squadron, Indian Air Force, which he both formed and commanded. He retired from the RAF in 1966 as a Wing Commander. Having left school at fourteen, he had no qualifications, so he sat down, not for the first time in his life, and thought about what to do.

In 1941, Mr. Philip Woods-Scawen, accompanied by Bunny Lawrence, went to Buckingham Palace to receive the DFCs awarded to his sons Patrick and Tony. Bunny married four years later, and had six children and fourteen grandchildren. She has said that she has such memories of the boys as will never die.

30. APPRAISAL

Attempting to gain daylight air superiority over south-east England cost the Luftwaffe 1,887 aircraft. Stopping them cost Fighter Command 1023. Whilst the battle for air superiority was going on, Bomber Command lost 376 aircraft in helping to stop an invasion, and Coastal Command, which supported both efforts, lost 148.[1] Total aircraft losses to the RAF were therefore 1,547. In comparing the cost to the air forces of each side, the Luftwaffe lost only 20% more aircraft than the RAF.

In the air fighting, however, the Luftwaffe as a whole was directly confronted by Fighter Command. It destroyed all but a handful of the 1,887 aircraft the Germans lost, achieving an overall kill-ratio of 1.8:1. The margin of victory was not narrow. The Luftwaffe never came close.

Fighter Command's victory was decisive. Not only had it survived, it ended the battle stronger than it had ever been. On 6 July its operational strength stood at 1,259 pilots. On 2 November, the figure was 1,796, an increase of over 40%.[2] It had also seriously mauled its assailant. In a lecture held in Berlin on 2 February 1944, the Intelligence Officer of KG2, Hauptmann Otto Bechtle, showed that from August to December 1940 German fighter strength declined by 30% and bomber strength by 25%.[3]

Many believe that the Luftwaffe did come close in the last week of August and the first week of September. In fact, all their fury achieved very little. The only Sector Station to go down at all was Biggin Hill, and it was non-operational for just a few hours. 11 Group's efficiency was impaired, and Park was vociferous about that, in part because he wanted to make the point that it did indeed matter whether interceptions took place before or after bombing, and in part because of his rage with 12 Group for not protecting his airfields when he asked them to.

Dowding was more objective, commenting in his letter accompanying Park's report on the period of 8 August to 10 September:

I agree with the Air Officer Commanding 11 Group that the damage done by air attack to aerodromes has been serious, and that it was beginning at one time to affect materially the efficiency of our fighter operations. Nevertheless, I must point out . . .

(i)   That 13 aerodromes in the Group underwent a total of over forty attacks in three weeks, but Manston and Lympne were the only two that were unfit for day flying for more than a few hours.

(ii) That although the scale of attack certainly exceeded the capacity of the works organisation existing at the outset, this was rapidly strengthened, and I do not wish to express any dissatisfaction with the measures taken to effect this improvement.'[4]

Park could not afford to be complacent, but Dowding states the facts.

It remains very difficult to make an airfield unusable. In the Falklands War of 1982, the British raided Port Stanley airfield repeatedly with Harriers and twice with a Vulcan, but the Argentineans continued to land supplies there until it was captured by ground troops.[5] Forty-five years after the Battle of Britain, the RAF took delivery of the first weapon designed to destroy airfields, the JP 233 'runway denial' bomb. Even with the immense advance in bombing and navigation technology over the intervening years ground defence technology kept pace, and the Tornados which delivered them in the Gulf War of 1991 suffered loss rates of three times the Allied average.[6] They were the heirs of Erprobungsgruppe 210. The difficulty of the task facing the Luftwaffe in 1940 had barely diminished in the intervening years.

The Luftwaffe's turn on London was a relief, but it was not critical. Even if the Luftwaffe had continued to pound the airfields, the counter-measures put in place and the robustness of the system would still have ensured its survival. Whether they attacked London or Biggin Hill or any other target made no difference whatever to the loss-rate in the air. Some of the Luftwaffe's most successful days of air fighting, 11, 14 and 28 September, came after they had turned on the capital.

They did so primarily for military reasons, not because Hitler wanted to avenge the bombing of Berlin. That event simply persuaded him to relax his stricture *not* to attack London. Many German commanders had suggested it from the outset. The actions over London on 15 September were not militarily, but psychologically, decisive. No single day decided the outcome. Hitler had to make a decision on the 17th. If the Luftwaffe had had a good day and Hitler had decided to launch the invasion, the end result could have been even worse. Sealion was set up to be the greatest military disaster in German history. It was just as well for them they never tried it.

The balance of losses in the air, although always against them, shifted in the Luftwaffe's favour because of their profligate use of Bf 109s and the moving of inexperienced British units into the area of intense fighting. Novice pilots were no more of a problem for Fighter Command than they were for the Luftwaffe, but novice squadrons were. Fighter Command's greatest point of vulnerability was its traditional devotion to neat formation flying and its very un-British contempt for the experience of the past.

Despite this, the Luftwaffe was soundly beaten in the air-fighting. The defences never weakened in their ability to meet any raid in whatever strength was necessary, whilst the German fighter arm was wearing itself out. Some idea of the attrition rates they suffered can be got from an analysis of the monthly Luftwaffe personnel records for fighter units:[7]

	Bf 109 pilots Available	Bf 109 pilots Operational	% Operational	Losses as % of Available
July	1126	906	80%	11%
August	1118	869	78%	15%
September	990	735	74%	23%

The number of pilots available includes all those at operational training units. From July to September this figure declines, but the number of pilots operational at front-line units declines even faster, showing how the Luftwaffe training organisation failed to make good losses and how the average experience level amongst Bf 109 pilots, though starting at a higher level, declined in the same way that it did in Fighter Command. The number of pilots available declined by 136, but the number of those actually operational declined by 171.

The losses are calculated as a percentage of those available at the beginning of each month. The percentage loss-rate rose both because absolute losses increased and because the number of pilots available declined. The strain on them rose as their numbers dwindled. They all stayed constantly in the front line – there was no system of rotation as there was for their British counterparts.

The fundamental dilemma facing the German fighter pilots had been recognised by Osterkamp right from the start. They needed a very high kill ratio, which meant selecting only favourable opportunities, but they also needed a high absolute level of kills, which meant using every opportunity for fighting. In practice, this was a contradiction: they could either have good results or big battles, but not both. The only days on which they inflicted more losses than they suffered themselves were, with one exception, days on which there was not a great deal of air activity and the overall level of losses in air combat was not high:[8]

Date	RAF Losses	Luftwaffe Losses	Luftwaffe Kill Ratio
19 July	10	4	2.5:1
7 August	4	3	1.3:1
11 September	27	21	1.3:1
14 September	11	8	1.4:1
28 September	16	4	4:1

11 September was a day of confused fighting in which the Bf 109s managed to bounce several squadrons new to the fighting. Taken together, on these, its most successful days of air-fighting, the Luftwaffe only managed to account for sixty-eight British fighters, less than 7% of Fighter Command's total aircraft losses.

In contrast, on every day of intensive combat the results of the fighting in the air were either in balance or in favour of Fighter Command:

Date	RAF Losses	Luftwaffe Losses	RAF Kill Ratio
11 August	17	20	1.2:1
12 August	20	27	1.4:1
13 August	13	47	3.6:1
15 August	32	75	2.3:1
18 August	34	69	2:1
30 August	23	23	1:1
31 August	37	33	1:1
7 September	23	41	1.8:1
15 September	28	56	2:1
27 September	29	57	2:1

The total combat losses for these ten days account for 25% of Fighter Command's losses during the Battle, and 24% of the Luftwaffe's. The outcome of the whole campaign was determined by days like these. On those days on which it launched its greatest efforts, the best the Luftwaffe managed to do was to shoot down as many aircraft as it lost itself. The last two days in August saw several RAF squadrons getting bounced and on 30 August, British losses were affected by the loss of the radar system during the morning. It is perhaps a fitting irony that 13 August, Eagle Day itself, was the day on which the RAF achieved its best loss ratio of all.

Within these overall figures, the Bf 109 pilots did well, probably as well as they could have reasonably expected. Against total British fighter losses of 1,023, the Germans lost 873 fighters of both types. This is only to be expected, as the only targets the Germans had were fighters, and the British were con-centrating on their bombers. Of these 873 German fighters lost, 223 were Bf 110s and 650 were Bf 109s. Assuming, in broad terms, that some 75% of British fighter losses were caused by the Bf 109s – and it is impossible to establish unique causes in every case – it appears that the German fighter pilots shot down about 770 Hurricanes and Spitfires, giving them a favourable kill ratio of 1.2:1. They were therefore less successful than the British, who achieved an overall kill ratio of 1.8:1, but still meted out more punishment than they took. The trouble was that it was not nearly good enough. The 5:1 target Osterkamp set his men in July was never remotely within reach.

These figures demonstrate the Luftwaffe's real problem. The Bf 109's margin of superiority over the Hurricane was too small to allow the sort of aerial massacres it needed, and the Spitfire became an obsessive worry to them. They started with the advantage of greater experience and better fighting tac-tics, but as an increasing number of RAF squadrons gave up Fighting Area Attacks and vics, the advantage eroded.

They did perform better against Hurricanes than against Spitfires, but not by much. Of the 2,741 claims made by Fighter Command between 10 July and 31 October, 1,552, or 55%, were made by the 34 squadrons flying Hurricanes, and 1,189, or 43%, by the 19 squadrons flying Spitfires.[9] Included in the Hurricane claims were plenty of Bf 109s. Taking the claims as an indi-cator – they are all too high by an average factor of 1.5 – the Spitfire squadrons achieved a better claims-to-loss ratio. In round terms, the average Hurricane squadron claimed 45 German aircraft for a loss of 8 pilots; the average Spitfire squadron claimed 63 victories for a loss of 8.4 pilots.[10] This means that the Hurricane squadrons claimed 5.7 German aircraft for every pilot they lost themselves, but the Spitfire squadrons claimed 7.4, which is 30% better, suffi-ciently large a difference to be significant.

How much Britain relied on this pair of fighters can be seen by what made up the balance: Blenheims, which were mainly night-fighters, and the Defiants, which should have been. The two Defiant squadrons, 141 and 264, claimed twenty-two German aircraft between them, but lost twenty-eight air-crew. Of course these included gunners as well as pilots, but the price they paid for their victories is clearly out of all proportion to the other two types. Dowding showed prescience in many ways during the 1930s, but marginalising the Defiant against the wishes of the Air Ministry was not the least important of his achievements.

A Swiss historian of the Battle sums up its position in the history of air warfare by saying: 'Fighter defence achieved here a qualitative peak of striking power and efficiency which is unique in the history of air warfare and will probably remain so.'[11]

In the summer of 1940, the RAF dealt the Luftwaffe a body-blow from which, as Osterkamp ruefully observed, it never recovered, and it heralded a feckless decline.[12] Despite its impressive victories in Russia in 1941, it was never again to be as strong, relative to its enemies, as it was in July 1940, and by 1943 it was in desperate straits. In the first half of 1944, the Mustang defeated it decisively in its own skies. The German crews lost in 1940 were all highly trained, and standards steadily declined. Despite appalling attrition rates, almost half the 107 German fighter pilots to claim 100 or more kills (mainly in the east) were veterans of the Battle. Only eight of them joined their units after mid-1942.[13]

The human cost of the air battle was strongly imbalanced, as many of the German aircraft were multi-crewed bombers. The Luftwaffe lost 2,698 airmen, Fighter Command 544. It is difficult to understand what these numbers mean in terms of attrition. For example, Fighter Command's pilot losses were about 40% of their initial strength in July, but only 18% of all those who fought in the Battle. The steady flow of replacements, who were themselves more likely to be casualties than those already there, means that it is wrong to say that 40% of those who were there at the beginning became casualties. Equally the casualty figures cannot be compared with the number of all those who flew during the Battle, as some flew for four months and some for four days.

To gain insight into the experience of the pilots themselves it is necessary to look at an individual unit, and see the grim rhythm of losses and replacements over the period of the Battle. 501 was the only squadron in Fighter Command to fight in 11 Group throughout the Battle, apart from a period in 10 Group (at Middle Wallop) from 5–25 July. It also, as one might expect, suffered the heaviest casualties of any squadron. The Squadron served in France, so most of the pilots who were with the unit in July had some combat experience.

501 Squadron had eighteen operational pilots on state on 10 July and thirty-one operational pilots on 31 October, an increase of 72%. Over the same period, Fighter Command also grew stronger as a whole, but only by 50%. 501 were a Category 'A' Squadron, so they got more replacements than the average. A total of sixty-four pilots served with them at some time.

Of the original eighteen, eight survived and were flying with the Squadron at the end, two more survived and were posted to other units, four were killed and four were wounded badly enough to be incapacitated. The mortality rate was therefore 22%. However, of the forty-five who joined the Squadron during the Battle, fifteen were killed, a rate of 33%. Lacking the experience of the original members of the Squadron, they suffered more severely. The value of experience in increasing the chances of survival is further shown by the fact that of the original eighteen, the four killed all died during the first month. Having got through that period, the remainder of this group got through the whole Battle with only another three being wounded. One of the newcomers, P/O Rose-Price, the brother of the actor Dennis Price, arrived from 10 Flying Training School on the morning of 2 September, took off on one uneventful patrol, took off on a second patrol in the afternoon, and never returned. He was twenty-one. Four were killed within a week of joining, and four more within a

No less than sixteen pilots baled out or force-landed, four of them twice. Sergeant James Lacey, their highest scorer, did so three times. It is reasonable to assume that had they been fighting over enemy territory, a good number of them would have been captured and lost. This would have brought the Squadron's losses from 47% (nineteen killed and eleven wounded) to 72%, which would have been unsustainable. This gives some measure of the advantage the RAF had in fighting over its own territory, and of the wisdom of Park's strictures about not flying over the Channel.

501 Squadron filed claims for 100 German aircraft. Of these, twenty were down to one man: Ginger Lacey. The top 5% of scorers (Lacey, Gibson and Glowacki) accounted for 36% of the claims, which is almost exactly in line with the general rule. The top 10% of pilots (the top six) made 55% of the claims. Thirty-five of the pilots, over half, made no claims at all, some no doubt because they joined late in the fighting and had no opportunity.

The survivors did not discuss the fate of their comrades. Some were close friends, some were barely familiar faces. Some were posted, some were in hospital, some were dead. They did not dwell on it or they would not be able to keep going. Death was an absence, like a posting. Of those who survived the Battle, just over half – thirty-four – survived the war. The survival-rate for Fighter Command as a whole was rather better than that. After the war, the RAF identified 2,917 airmen who had flown at least one operational sortie with a squadron which was deemed to have participated in the air-fighting between 10 July and 31 October. Of these men, 544 (i.e. 19%), lost their lives in the course of the Battle. Of the 2,373 who got through it alive, 1,578 (i.e. 66%), survived the war.

Even during the Battle of Britain, when operations had not reached the intensity they were to do in later years, Bomber Command lost 801 pilots and aircrew – almost 50% more than Fighter Command – and another 200 were taken prisoner. A further 103 were wounded. The cause of about half of their losses is unknown: they were simply posted 'missing'. Another third of them were killed in accidents, whether in training flights or returning from operations low on fuel, getting lost or crash-landing in the dark. They are the forgotten 'few'. When Coastal Command's losses are taken into account, RAF aircrew losses add up to only about a thousand less than the Luftwaffe's. Making some further allowance for those killed on the ground, the Battle of Britain probably cost the lives of about 5,000 military personnel on both sides. Compared with any other major campaign of World War II, it is still a very small number. Never has so crucial a battle been won at so low a cost in life.

It has commonly been argued that the Luftwaffe failed because it was not properly equipped for its task. It was a tactical air force trying to carry out a strategic role without two vital pieces of equipment: a heavy bomber and an effective long-range fighter. Neither argument stands up to examination.

The short range of the Bf 109 is high on Galland's catalogue of woes, along with poor radio communications and Hermann Göring. It certainly

THE COUNTRY GIRL, THE LADY AND THE VAMP: VITAL STATISTICS

Data for the Hurricane is taken from Francis K. Mason, *The Hawker Hurricane*, Aston Publications, 1987. Data for the Spitfire is from the A & AEE assessment of N3 171 of March 1940, slightly adjusted to reflect a typical service machine of mid-1940 as suggested by Alfred Price in *The Spitfire Story*. Data on the Bf 109 is from R. Cross & G. Scarborough, *Messerschmitt Bf 109, versions 8–E*, Classic Aircraft No. 2, Patrick Stephens 1972. Turning circles are as calculated by John Ackroyd of the Manchester School of Engineering.

restricted their operations severely, and it also tested the nerves of the pilots. Any mistake in navigation or dwelling too long over the combat zone could be fatal. However, it was not the key factor in their defeat.

Suppose the Bf 109 had in fact had the range of a Mustang. What would the Luftwaffe have done with it? The Mustangs needed the range in order to get from East Anglia to Berlin and back. Similar endurance in the 109 would have allowed the Luftwaffe to send escorted bombers to John O'Groats. Why would they have wanted to do that? Given the goal of establishing local air superiority, there was no point whatever in attacking any target north of London, indeed precious little point in attacking London. A bit more endurance would have helped in raiding Hornchurch, North Weald and Debden, but unless the British could be caught on the ground, attacking airfields was not in itself going to win the Battle. The key aircraft factories were at Kingston-upon-Thames and Southampton, which were within range. The range of fighter escorts was only critical if the plan was to conduct economic warfare as part of a long-term siege. It was not critical to gaining air superiority over the invasion beaches.

Had they had an extra margin of fifteen to twenty minutes, the Bf 109 pilots would probably have been able to do a bit more damage and somewhat reduced their own losses. They would certainly have been far more relaxed. However, their cannon only had seven seconds' worth of ammunition and, although they had sixty seconds' worth of machine-gun rounds, their two machine guns alone would have greatly reduced their effectiveness. So if their fuel had not been used up, their bullets would have. Any pilot who spent more than five minutes in a dogfight would have been exhausted anyway. When the Mustangs went to Berlin they spent most of their time getting there and getting back, not dogfighting. When Fighter Command took the offensive in 1941, the pilots carrying out sweeps over northern France in order to draw up the Luftwaffe complained about many things, but not about the range of the Spitfire. It was only when the target was further away that range became critical.

Another reason often advanced for the German failure is that they lacked a strategic bomber of the kind Wever wanted to develop. The cancellation of the Do 19 and Ju 89 in 1936, it is argued, robbed them of victory in 1940.[14]

Germany could never conceivably have produced sufficient long-range heavy bombers to have had an impact. German industry was incapable of producing the 400 originally planned and then cancelled, but even if it had, it would not have been enough to wage a successful strategic campaign. It took Britain until 1942, with its industry going flat out, to produce enough bombers of all types to mount a raid of a thousand aircraft. However, that raid had little military impact. From 1943 onwards, Germany was attacked by two air forces round the clock for two-and-a-half years, each one of them launching frequent 'maximum efforts' with resources way beyond Germany's capacity. Those attacks did not end the war or force Germany to capitulate.

Had the Luftwaffe launched heavy bombers against southern England in daylight instead of the medium bombers it in fact launched, they would merely have presented Fighter Command with bigger targets. Even the B-17, which was designed to fly unescorted, suffered crippling losses in daylight over Germany. Heavy bombers would have delivered heavier loads, but no more accurately, and it was accuracy, not the volume of bombs, which counted.

The Luftwaffe did not fail because it was wrongly equipped. It failed because it did not use its equipment properly. The failure came from the top, from a leadership which asked its men to do the wrong things in the wrong way. The plan they produced meant that they entered the Battle with the odds of success stacked heavily against them. However, nothing in history is inevitable. Alternative plans could have been produced which could have shifted the odds significantly in their favour.

The first and most obvious thing the Luftwaffe had to do was to concentrate on its target: Fighter Command. In order to defeat it, the Luftwaffe had to destroy its early-warning system, its command and control system and then its aircraft and pilots, in that order, and to maintain its own fighter force more or less intact. The ground targets were the radar stations, airfields and aircraft factories, all of which were small.

It had all and precisely the weapons it needed at its disposal. What mattered in attacking the ground targets was bombing accuracy. Stukas could deliver the accuracy, but were too vulnerable and were needed later to attack the Royal Navy when the invasion commenced. The key weapon was the Bf 110. Had *all* the Zerstörer crews been retrained to deliver fast, low-level pinpoint attacks in the way that Erprobungsgruppe 210 were, Göring would have had a war-winning weapon in his hands.

The radar stations were difficult to destroy, but they were all on the coast, which made them vulnerable to two tactics: air attack by squadrons of Bf 110s, and commando raids.

The British later showed how the commando raids could have been carried out. In 1942, the newly formed Parachute Regiment carried out a raid on a Würzburg radar station on the heavily defended French coast at Bruneval. Led by the same Major John Frost who was to gain fame at Arnhem, the raid was brilliantly successful.

The Germans could have done the same thing on a larger scale in 1940. The men to do it were actually part of the Luftwaffe, and were noted for daring *coup-de-main* exploits. A few paratroopers could easily have been put ashore at night, for although Admiral Raeder did not have any battleships, he did have E-boats. Several simultaneous raids could actually have achieved what was so hard to do from the air: destroy the masts themselves. The British could only have countered this by providing the stations with heavy ground defences, but these would have been vulnerable from the air. In early May the Germans had taken out Fort Eben Emael in Belgium by landing three gliders of paratroops on top of it and blowing it up. Coastal raids would have involved less precision and co-ordination.

In any case, the system only had to be put down for a week or two. After the commando raids, the sites could have been attacked two or three times a day from the air to prevent repairs and, with luck, to cut off power supplies – a flight of aircraft would have sufficed each time. It would then have been possible to mount low-level saturation attacks on the Sector Stations, with the chance of surprise, albeit the Observer Corps would have made it hard to achieve with consistency. With the radar down, conventional bombers could also have been used, but strafing runs by fighters alone would have been effective. Each airfield would have to have been attacked about three times a day, in order to produce the effect achieved at Manston. It would have been costly, but Göring could have afforded to expend his whole Bf 110 force on this task.

His Bf 109s, on the other hand, had to be preserved to protect the invasion forces. They could have been largely used for sweeps, some going in low over airfields and others flying high, aiming to catch British fighters on the climb after they had been flushed up by an airfield attack, using radio intercepts as I./JG52 did on their snap raid on Manston. If applied with consistency and determination for about ten days, these tactics might have had a reasonable chance of forcing the abandonment of 11 Group's area. The Bf 109's range limitations would not have mattered. They only had to dominate the skies above and behind the beaches.

Attacking the aircraft industry would have been more difficult, but all the Luftwaffe really had to do was to disrupt it for a couple of weeks in order to stop the flow of replacement aircraft. The most obvious target was the Spitfire plant at Woolston, which they astonishingly left alone until 11 September. Castle Bromwich was out of range of the 109 but was only just gearing up production. It could still have been attacked by Bf 110s, or, using the Knickebein navigation system which enabled the Luftwaffe to raid Coventry in November, attacked at night. Hurricanes were produced by Gloster in Gloucestershire, and a few were shipped in from Canada, but most were built by Hawkers at Kingston-upon-Thames and Langley in Buckinghamshire. Both were at the limit of Bf 109 range, but were also vulnerable to the Bf 110. In the case of the Kingston factory, they once again waited too long before trying.

In practice, it was too little too late. Erprobungsgruppe 210 attempted to take on the job the whole of the Luftwaffe should have attempted to do from the beginning. The final raid on Woolston was successful. It may be that his note on using fighter-bombers on 2 September was a sign that Göring was realising what was needed, but when it was put into practice, it was a travesty. Kesselring had the fixed idea that the RAF had to be defeated in air combat, and his fighter pilots were trained to fly high and look for bounce opportunities. They had an aversion to low-level operations because it made them feel vulnerable. Manston is the only airfield to be repeatedly strafed by Bf 109s. It worked there, but there are very few examples of Bf 109s being used in this way anywhere else.

This was the strategy Park feared most, and there was not a lot he could have done once the radar was down. His worst moments during the Battle were when he was blinded for a time, as on 30 August. Ground defences could have been strengthened, especially with light AA guns and machine guns, and the Sector Operations Rooms could all have been relocated. However, if the attacks had been frequent enough, he would not have had enough time to reorganise his defences. The effectiveness of such attacks depended on intensity, and the weather could therefore have prevented them from being kept up. However, Knickebein would have enabled raiders to find target areas in dirty weather, and poor visibility was good for them: it was easier to get surprise and escape. Erprobungsgruppe 210 showed the Luftwaffe the way.

So it is that just as they had defeated the great French Army through the onrush of a few thousand armoured vehicles, the Germans might have conquered Britain by the prowess of a few thousand airmen.

Churchill's mythologisation of 'the Few' has led to a general belief that they were a superior breed to their German counterparts. They were not. The key *difference* in military performance between the antagonists was not in the pilots. The distinction which really made the difference was in the leadership. The Germans were out-generaled.

The most fundamental reason for the German defeat was a failure of strategy. Most of the decisions which determined the outcome of the Battle had been made before it began. Given the defence system, the aircraft, the training and the plans, all put in place by the decisions of a few people in leadership positions on each side, the odds were stacked heavily against the Luftwaffe from the first.

However, even with all the advantages the British had, their commanders could still have lost. History is full of cases where advantage is frittered away or not exploited. But whereas the Germans had to come up with something extraordinary, the British just had to avoid gross errors.

The defence was actually conducted by quite a large number of people. There were the Observer Corps and the radar operators, the ground controllers and the WAAFs on the stations, the gunners and searchlight operators, the riggers and fitters, the repair and maintenance engineers and the ferry pilots, all of whom were subjected to attack, and there were the crews of Bomber and Coastal Commands who raided the invasion ports. On 1 October 1940, the Royal Air Force had a strength of 437,473 people, including over 17,000 women, and most of them played some part in the Battle of Britain.[15]

Beyond the actual combatants were the many more non-combatants who suffered, particularly the factory workers and the civilian population of London and the South-East. Had factories like Woolston, Itchen and Kingston, such obvious targets, been abandoned early on, the flow of fighters would have stopped. Had Londoners panicked, as many on both sides thought they might, Churchill could have been forced to resign. To this extent, the Battle was fought by the nation as a whole. The pilots had by far the most dangerous job, and they did what was asked of them like everybody else. Their courage and endurance were highly visible, and at the point of contact with the enemy all was indeed in their hands. So it was that all seemed to depend on them. But they in their turn depended on everybody else, and everybody engaged in the fighting depended on the work done by others in the years before.

If the Battle of Britain was fought by a broad section of British society, then it must equally be said that some individuals within that collective made unique contributions. They were only effective as part of teams, but they took decisions others could have made differently or had insights which others would not have had. There are ten men – one general, two scientists, three engineers, one politician and three airmen – who in this sense could not have been substituted for. They were the few without any one of whom the outcome could have been different.

The first was Major-General E. B. Ashmore, who was in charge of London's air defences in World War I. In 1940, aged sixty-eight, he commanded a battalion of the Home Guard. In 1917 he had been the architect who laid down the principles of Dowding's system, the creator of the Observer Corps, the plotting and reporting system, gridded maps and counters, the telephone network and the gun lines. The biggest difference between 1918 and 1940 was the replacement of sound locators with radar. When he took over Fighter Command in 1936, Dowding resurrected Ashmore's system and developed it. Without Ashmore's work, Dowding would not have been ready in 1940.

The second and third were Henry Tizard and Robert Watson-Watt. Tizard led the team of scientists responsible for putting the RAF at the forefront of applied technology. He sorted out crackpot ideas from important innovations at a time when the difference between them was hard to discern. Watson-Watt at the National Physical Laboratory turned the crackpot idea of a death-ray into Radio Direction Finding, and pursued it until it worked well enough to be used in war.

The fourth, fifth and sixth were Sydney Camm, Reginald Mitchell and Ernest Hives. They led and inspired the teams that produced the crucial weapons. Camm's Hurricane was cheap to make, easy to repair and robust, and gave Fighter Command the numbers it needed in the air in 1940. Without it, the thin blue line of defenders would have been too thin to hold. Mitchell's Spitfire matched the Bf 109. Without it, losses would have been far heavier. Neither aircraft would have performed without the Merlin engine. Its development was driven by Hives, who not only led the team which developed the 'R' series in the 1920s and 30s, turning it into a totally reliable service engine, but as Works General Manager introduced to Rolls-Royce the production reforms needed to build it in numbers. He was so successful that by January 1939 deliveries of the Merlin were running ahead of the Air Ministry's programme.[16]

The seventh was Ralph Sorley. He was given a job to do, like the others, but he took up the armament issue like a personal crusade. He combined experience with theory and pursued the radical consequences of his thinking until he had seen what must have seemed impossible in 1933 become reality. As a result, the RAF in 1940 was the only air force in the world with eight-gun fighters, and although the need for still heavier armament was becoming clear, if it had not been for him, the Hurricane and Spitfire would have gone into battle with four machine guns, and many of their opponents would have survived to fight another day.

The eighth was Hugh Dowding. He built on and supported all the these efforts, drew them together and created a weapons system which was not only unique in its ability to create clarity out of a mass of constantly changing data without using computers, but was also extremely robust – perhaps its most important characteristic. During the Battle, he devoted all his energies to keeping the system supplied and resourced, developing a new night-fighting capability and managing the overall deployment of his forces without ever deviating from his main strategic goal. He made resistance possible and laid the foundations of victory.

The ninth was Winston Churchill. He decided to use Dowding's weapon. He got the Battle fought, and conducted the nearest-run campaign of the summer against the peace lobby. He convinced the nation that his battle was inevitable, inspired all, and intervened decisively on critical issues. No other person alive at the time had the willpower, personality and the set of talents needed to achieve what he did.

The tenth was Keith Park. He wielded the weapon that Dowding created and Churchill decided to use. Had he failed, as he could have done, the efforts of all the others would have come to nought. Throughout the long months of strain, Park hardly put a foot wrong, making all the major tactical decisions, attending to relevant details, visiting pilots and airfields himself, and fighting an internal political battle. Tedder was right: if ever any one man won the Battle of Britain, he did.

Park's performance was extraordinary. In the way in which he anticipated and countered every move of his opponent, it has many parallels with Wellington's at Waterloo; but whereas Wellington sustained his concentration and bore the strain for some five hours, Park ran the Battle for five months. He consistently showed complete mastery of his weapon, of events and of his opponent. Even today, with hours of leisure to ponder decisions he took in minutes, and with full knowledge of hindsight and what was happening on the other side, it is difficult to find ways of improving on his conduct of operations.[17]

Only as post-war research has pieced together the evidence about what actually occurred has the correctness of his tactical principles and their application become clear. The wing theory was at best an irrelevance. Park often brought superior numbers of fighters into play against individual raids, but he did not waste time getting them into a single formation first. Quite rightly, he was deeply suspicious of the claims filed by the Big Wing while most others believed them. Only now do we know that they were unusually inflated and would have been even without Bader's exuberance, for analysis of air combat has shown that mistaken and duplicate claims rise with the number of aircraft involved. Nobody knew that in 1940. It is symptomatic of Park's profound insight into the new art of aerial warfare that he suspected it.

His intellectual grip of his task, both in terms of broad principles and fine detail, was matched by Dowding. As a leader, however, Park surpassed his chief. He was the only one among his peers to regularly visit his men, talk to them, hear their views and keep them informed. The Public Record Office is full of documents he produced during the Battle: instructions to controllers, memos on tactics to unit commanders, full reports on German tactics and methods, summary lessons from combat reports and messages of congratulation to units or stations which performed well. The volume of communications from him easily surpasses that of all the other Group Commanders put together. This had a real impact on the experience of the pilots.

Bob Doe's most enduring complaint is that nobody ever told him anything, and that nobody else seemed to know what was going on or why. He never saw any senior officer, and felt completely isolated from start to finish. He fought the whole of the Battle in 10 Group. Had he served under Park, he would have felt differently. Tom Neil started in 10 Group and then moved to 11 Group under Park, and writes in his autobiography of the striking difference between Middle Wallop, which was Bob Doe's Station, and North Weald. At North Weald, they were 'invariably kept informed before the event and controlled with understanding and helpful information throughout the interception. At Middle Wallop, we were frequently given just the scramble instruction, after which – silence!'[18]

Neil served under Leigh-Mallory in 1941 and points the contrast between him and Park. 'Park I felt I knew', he writes, and tells how he landed at North Weald shortly after Neil's squadron had arrived there and stopped his Hurricane outside the pilots' dispersal hut. Neil ran outside, not knowing who he was, and peremptorily ordered him to move. Park did so and apologised to this young Pilot Officer for his thoughtlessness. When Neil learned whom he had just ticked off, he was embarrassed. 'Somehow', he reflects, 'I couldn't see Leigh-Mallory doing that.'[19] Frank Brinsden flew with 19 Squadron in 12 Group, and has commented: 'I do not believe that any of us in 12 Group at squadron pilot level realised that we were engaged in a full-scale battle, nor how important the outcome would be if we lost. Intelligence and general briefing was sadly lacking.'[20] Sandy Sanders, who served under Park the whole time, has no doubts: 'Keith Park was wonderful. He understood Dowding and he did exactly what Dowding asked him to do and he was a great, great man. He was modest, he was sincere, he didn't brag – no, he was a great man.'

Those he fought also formed their views. In early 1944, Air Ministry Intelligence obtained some German appraisals of some of their main opponents. They considered Leigh-Mallory to be 'a pedantic worker with a preference for administrative questions, who gives his subordinates little room for personal decisions. He is therefore known as "The Flying Sergeant"'. Park was regarded as efficient with staff work, but a courageous man of action. He, they said, had earned the title 'Defender of London'.[21]

What Park achieved in the Battle of Britain is in itself enough to place him amongst the great commanders of history. But his performance in 1940 was not a one-off. In 1942 in Malta, Park took the offensive and turned Kesselring's defeat into a rout. After that, he directed the air operations that enabled Slim to expel the Japanese from Burma. He was as adept at offence as he was at defence, and, like Wellington, he never lost a battle. His record makes him today, without rival, the greatest fighter commander in the short history of air warfare.

One has to have some sympathy with Kesselring. He was a very fine soldier, and under the circumstances he did well in 1940, but he lacked the depth of understanding of air operations which might have enabled him to pull something out of the hat, which is what he needed to do. He was unlucky to be up against Park, and doubly so to face him again in the Mediterranean. He is the only one of the senior Luftwaffe commanders to give an account of the Battle, and it is typical of his outlook that he pays generous tribute to his opponents, as one professional to another:

> I gladly agree with Churchill's words of praise when he says that the RAF 'far from being destroyed, was triumphant'. The British airmen unquestionably deserved praise for their pluck and skill, as did the whole defence for its exemplary reaction to new technical methods.[22]

However, he worms his way out of the admission of defeat that is the logical obverse of the RAF being 'triumphant'. He believes the early battles were quite successful, and that the raids on factories and ports had 'remarkable psychological results' (the nature of which he does not specify) and did indeed disrupt the British economy (which they did not). He goes so far as to claim that air superiority had in fact been achieved within a restricted area in early September, but could not be sustained.[23] He then follows the ploy of claiming that there was just a change in tactics on 7 September – how odd that Kesselring should change his tactics just when he claims he was winning – which saw the initiation of full-scale economic warfare. The rest of the daylight battle and the Blitz were therefore just a second way of achieving his goal, whatever that was. His overall conclusion is sporting and thoroughly British:

> I cannot accept that the first attempt ended with a decisive defeat for the Luftwaffe in the months of July, August and September. To break

off a battle that is going well is not by any means the same thing as
being decisively defeated . . . In a word, in this struggle two worthy
enemies were matched who surpassed each other in the performance
of their highest duty.[24]

So it was a draw. The Germans were scoring well, but decided to declare just as
bad light stopped play. It is understandable that Kesselring should seek to justify his record, but we do not have to accept this sort of thing as a cogent
reading of history.

Sperrle did not disgrace himself. He had a better understanding of what
was going on than his colleague and argued against turning on London, for he
knew that Fighter Command was far from being at its last gasp. But the
Luftwaffe needed more than competence to overcome an opponent like Park.
In 1940 they lacked the insight into air operations and knowledge of their
adversary which might have led them to concentrate on low-level pin-point
attacks on the key targets. They did not have access to the staff paper Park had
written in 1922 which might have pointed them in the right direction.

Göring's performance reflected the ideology he espoused: arrogant,
incompetent, egotistical and divisive. For all that, post-war German accounts
have tended to saddle him with too much blame. He did not issue orders
shackling the Bf 109s to the bombers, he rightly left it up to the fighter leaders
how best to protect them. Some of them had to fly close escort if the bomber
losses were to be limited. It was a cruel choice, but Park manoeuvred them into
making it. Göring's most serious error was to allow the radar stations to be
ignored. He gave his own version of events briefly after the war. He told one of
his interrogators at Nuremberg that the Luftwaffe was enormously successful
in 1940 and that its losses were not serious. The invasion did not take place
because there was not enough shipping. If there had been, his fighters would
have kept the bridgehead clear of British planes and the invasion would have
succeeded.[25]

Hitler showed little interest in the air campaign and, like the army generals, awaited events without intervening. Had he played a more active role,
he could certainly have added energy and purpose. On the other hand, given
the leadership style he demonstrated when things started to go wrong later in
the war, he could have done more harm than good. Had he started directing
individual raids in the way in which he directed individual battalions in
Russia in 1944, the German defeat could have been even more costly than it
was.

On the other hand, no-one could have injected greater energy or purpose
into the defence than Churchill. His contribution was not restricted to inspiring rhetoric. He visited the 'front', both by inspecting bomb damage and seeing
for himself how Park handled the Battle. His account of his visit to Uxbridge on
15 September shows very clearly that he made no attempt to interfere with the
purely military aspects of the fighting.

When he did intervene he did so in a manner fully consonant with his role as Prime Minister and Minister of Defence and was very effective. The way in which he picked up Sinclair's statement about a growing pilot shortage in the Cabinet meeting of 3 June and harried the Air Ministry with memos to ensure that action was taken is typical of the way in which, with a few deft lines on small pieces of notepaper, he turned a spotlight on critical issues and focussed the efforts of those with the power and knowledge to deal with them. He shared with Hitler an ability to deal with detail as well as the overall picture. Unlike Hitler, he was able to select the details that mattered and to concentrate on them. Churchill's running of the machinery of government is an object lesson in how to apply leverage to the efforts of others and to goad and focus the efforts of large, complex and inherently sluggish organisations faced with crisis.

One of the lessons graphically illustrated by the events of 1940 is that the performance of an organisation deteriorates if the human relations between its leaders are poor and improves if they are good.

The Nazis undermined honest and respectful dealings between men wherever their polluting doctrine spread and the Luftwaffe was a prime example of that. Few of its top leaders got on to the extent of even being able to work as a team, and most hated each other. Both Udet and Jeschonnek were to commit suicide.

In the RAF, Park and Brand offered a seamless defence line along the south coast and both worked in complete harmony with Dowding. Weaknesses in the British defences only appeared when Park and Leigh-Mallory had to work together: bombers got through to their targets unmolested, valuable resources were wasted, energy was expended on pseudo-issues and frustration was felt by all, including the pilots. The argument about the Big Wing was an irrelevance. The issue was squadron tactics. The whole affair was sad and unnecessary, rooted more in a personality clash than in substance, and Dowding should have put a stop to it.

This is the main point of criticism which one can level against 'Stuffy' Dowding, one which, to his credit, he accepted after the war. He regretted not having exercised stronger control over Leigh-Mallory, commenting that he 'should have known better'. He also admitted that the Air Staff 'got in first' and that 'perhaps because of that there is something in the criticism that is made of me'.[26] Dowding did in fact know about the Big Wing dispute as soon as it blew up.[27] What he failed to do was to realise how much personal rancour was involved and the deleterious effect this could have. He did not like interfering and tried to remain 'hands-off' for too long:

> I did not want to have to say you mustn't do this and you mustn't do that. I expected more of my Group Commanders than that. And that was why, by mid-October, I had come to realise I would have to do something about what was going on and get rid of Leigh-Mallory.[28]

Given that a lot of air fighting was still going on, he still hesitated to be decisive, a decisiveness which could have stopped well short of dismissing Leigh-Mallory. By then it was too late. Dowding was unable to perceive the bitterness between his subordinates. In the light of after-events, he admits to feeling sorry 'that at the time I did not take that firmer action.'[29]

This defect was part and parcel of Dowding's virtues – his own integrity and task-orientation. His services were not rewarded as they might have been during and immediately after the war, but some amends have been made since, and his statue now stands outside the RAF church of St Clement Danes in the Strand.

Keith Park has no memorial in Britain, though his control room in Uxbridge can still be visited by appointment and contains a small museum. He should have found a place in the Battle's mythology, for he was in fact the lone hero who seized the magic weapon which the old wizard Dowding had forged, and slew the dragon. There is a fitting irony in the fact that he came from the other side of the earth to win a battle whose name declares it to be for a country not his own. The name is in many ways unfortunate, for although it defines the territory fought over, it was not in fact a battle for Britain, but for Europe, indeed, for the world.

In 1945, after the defeat of Germany, the Russians asked the Wehrmacht's most senior operational commander, Field-Marshal Gerd von Rundstedt, which battle of the war he regarded as most decisive. They were expecting him to say 'Stalingrad'. What he said was: 'The Battle of Britain'. They put away their note-books and left.[30]

At first sight, this is a strange judgement. Victory in the air achieved a modest strategic goal, for it did not bring Britain any closer to victory in the war, but merely avoided her defeat. Indeed, it has been argued that it did not even do that. The invasion never took place because Hitler never meant it to. He was too scared of the Royal Navy.[31]

Hitler seems to have been little concerned about the choice between siege and invasion, and the Luftwaffe's failure to eliminate Fighter Command decided the matter. Gambler that he was, he thought that attacking their population might bring the British to the negotiating table, so by postponing the invasion indefinitely on 17 September, he kept that possibility open and allowed the siege to begin. It was the result of the air battle which tipped the scales against invasion and in favour of this course, one which was to lead nowhere.

A political result had always been the most likely outcome. If Dowding had been forced to withdraw 11 Group, leaving the south-east to be patrolled unchallenged by the Luftwaffe, the pressure on the War Cabinet would have become immense. Under such circumstances, the Germans would only have had to offer generous terms, such as a non-aggression pact and the return of a few colonies, to give Halifax new impetus. Nobody at the time knew whether or not 'London could take it'. Other cities appeared not to have been able to. 'Taking it' would certainly involve great destruction and loss of life, and when added to the threat then posed by the Wehrmacht could have led to a reconsideration of the virtues of continued belligerence. The issue would have been decided within the government and Parliament, and not a few would have felt their view of Churchill as a dangerous, unrealistic adventurer to be confirmed. His heroic gestures and lack of judgement had cost the country dear in the past. Would they have allowed him to sacrifice the whole nation, when its security and that of the Empire could have been had at the price of a little flexibility and the recognition of what after all was the reality of the situation?

Of course, it never came to that. But the scenario is not fanciful. On 8 August, the former War Minister, Hore-Belisha, is reported to have said that:

> the Tory party in the House were not very interested in the war, were afraid for their possessions and of the rise of Labour . . . they might one day bring peace terms upon us and DM *(David Margesson, the Tory Chief Whip)* would get his legions into the lobby in favour of it even if the country was dead against it. It might be a *fait accompli* and Hitler would stiffen his terms the next day and insist on a government of his own like Pétain's.[32]

In July 1942, with both the USSR and the United States fully engaged in the conflict, Churchill faced a vote of no confidence in the House. He won, but twenty-five MPs voted against him and another forty abstained. Britain had changed Prime Ministers in May 1940. MPs might have concluded in September that the new one had had his chance, tried bravely, but failed, and that the interests of the nation came first. If the government had changed, what would the people have done? In September 1939 some of them had marched through the streets demanding peace. What if, which is very hard to imagine, others had marched through the streets a year later demanding war? It was their right to protest, but protests do not bring down governments. It was Fighter Command which ensured this question did not arise.

As German strategy against Britain slid into a siege, it pointed to a long, hard road ahead for both sides. One more critical battle had to be fought in order to ensure Britain's survival as a belligerent power, the Battle of the Atlantic. Churchill has put it on record that the U-boat peril was the only thing which ever really frightened him during the war, adding that he was even more anxious about it than he was about the Battle of Britain.[33] Both were campaigns which Britain had to win. The outcome of the Battle of the Atlantic was more uncertain, even after America joined in, because the means of defeating the U-boat had to be created during the course of the campaign itself, whereas the RAF already had the means of defeating the Luftwaffe when the Battle was joined.

However, if the Battle of Britain had not been won, the Battle of the

Atlantic could not have been fought. To that extent, the Battle of Britain was a necessary pre-condition of all the later successes, and by the same token a necessary if not sufficient condition of the victory ultimately won by the Western Allies. Winning it did not make victory inevitable, but it did make it possible. Britain was never closer to defeat than in the summer of 1940. By the following spring, she was far stronger both in the air and on the ground. From the summer, she had the Soviet Union as an ally, the country which was to carry out the war's most formidable and important task, that of breaking the German Army.

Having won the two defensive battles in the air and on the sea, Britain could fulfil its prime strategic role, which was to act as a base for an Allied army to invade continental Europe and defeat the German army in the West. Without the continued British participation in the war made possible by the Battle of Britain, there could have been no Battle of Normandy, and indeed, it is doubtful whether America would have entered the European war. Had Britain left the fight, even if Hitler had declared war on America after Pearl Harbor, America would have had no means of attacking Germany.

Their failure over Britain hampered the Germans considerably. The Luftwaffe had been weakened. Aircraft losses were made good, but the force which attacked Russia in June 1941 was soon to need every machine and every pilot it could get. A clear victory in 1940 would have given Hitler a free hand in the east in the early spring of 1941, which is when he wanted it. The delay was to cost him dear, and as his troops engaged ever more deeply with the Red Army, he was to find that he had to devote increasing resources to defending Germany against air attack from Britain.

Hitler made the most crucial decisions of his life in 1940 and in that summer OKW lost its grip on German grand strategy and made fateful mistakes. They were to win many more battles, but they set themselves off in a direction which made them likely to lose the war. They made choices that could have been otherwise. Hitler's impatience to attack Russia and his failure to develop a proper strategy for defeating Britain were to prove a fatal combination. The best approach to the problem of England would probably have been the one OKW briefly discussed but never seriously pursued, which was to concentrate on her overseas interests. This would have meant attacking the periphery, which is why it never really appealed, though it worked when applied on Germany in reverse.[34]

Britain's success convinced many, particularly in America, that their cause was not hopeless and it also aroused widespread admiration. In the occupied countries, too, it was vital to the incipient resistance movements which Britain was to succour in the coming years. It was Germany's first defeat. Her second, in front of Moscow, was to be a long time in coming. Until then, the Battle of Britain was the only ray of light in a darkened world, a symbol of hope that defiance was not futile, but would in the end lead towards the sunlit uplands Churchill had promised.

31. MEANINGS

In the summer of 1947, a new Noël Coward play opened in the West End. It was called *Peace in our Time* and was based on the fiction that Britain was successfully invaded in November 1940 following defeat in the air. It tells of the British resistance up to the time of the country's liberation in May 1945. At one point, two characters discuss whether it would have been better if the Battle of Britain had been won:

ALMA:	It might have been better for America and the rest of the world, but it would not have been better for us.
FRED:	Why not?
ALMA:	Because we should have got lazy again, and blown out with our own glory. We should have been bombed and blitzed and we should have stood up under it – an example to the whole civilised world – and that would have finished us.'[1]

It nearly did.

World War II made the USSR and the USA world powers and hastened the end of the British Empire. In and of itself, this was probably no bad thing, both for the countries which formed part of the Empire and for Britain itself, for even by the 1920s the Empire had become an intolerable economic burden. In the 1950s it became an insupportable political one as well. But choices made in the conduct of the war weakened Britain itself far more than appeared to be the case when it ended in triumph.

In August 1940, the War Cabinet made the deliberate decision to build an army of fifty-five divisions and expand aircraft production to nearly 3,000 a month. The purchases of equipment from the United States that this entailed cost £3,200 million in the first twelve months at a time when Britain's reserves amounted to some £490 million. In March 1941, Britain technically became bankrupt, and was kept going by the loan of gold from the Belgian government in exile and the passing of the Lend-Lease Act by the US Congress. By 1945, Britain was in debt to America to the tune of £27 billion.[2]

So it was that in the summer of 1940, whilst the German High Command made decisions that made Germany likely to lose the war, the British Cabinet made decisions that made Britain likely to lose the peace. When Churchill said, 'We shall defend our island, whatever the cost may be', he meant it, and went further. He intended to prosecute an aggressive war, whatever the cost might be.

He did not have to. He could have done what was necessary to survive and waited for the Americans to come in, an option which appears never to have been contemplated. Before the twentieth century, it would have been regarded as aberrant to engage in wars the country could not afford. In 1940, it seemed to be the natural course to take. Little thought was given as to whether or not this was prudent or in the country's long-term interests. Britain was alone, confronting the forces of evil, fighting a world cause. She had to do so with all the powers at her disposal, regardless of the consequences. It was just bad luck that for a time the whole burden fell upon her, so she got on with it. In choosing to exert such an effort, she went beyond the limits of national self-interest and beyond the call of duty. She was to get little reward. It was an act of self-sacrifice.

Despite the wastage of assets entailed by the decision to prosecute total war, a decision which undoubtedly enabled the Allies to achieve total victory by 1945, the subsequent peace-time decline was not inevitable. It was the result of many other decisions rooted in the 'dreams and illusions'[3] of Britain's post-war leaders and shared by much of her population. The events of 1940 and the perceptions of them at the time were instrumental in perpetuating these illusions, and helped to create some of them. As the characters in Coward's play observe, the Battle of Britain was a dangerous victory for the British people, for it did them psychological damage. The mythology around it led them to misunderstand themselves as well as the world about them, whilst its real lessons remained hidden.

The first illusion was that victory depended on acts of collective and individual heroism of which only the British were capable because of some innate national qualities they alone possess.

This belief was fostered by some facts. Every other country faced with aggression had gone under, and in war the virtue on most prominent display is courage. It was therefore easy to assume that victory was the result of superior courage and to ignore the many other virtues, such as hard work, co-operativeness and careful thinking, which are also necessary. The decision to go on fighting was driven through by Churchill with the support of most, but not all, of Parliament. Most of the population had little choice but to endure the resulting suffering, just as the Germans had little choice but to endure the far worse bombing inflicted upon them in the later years of the war.

The Russian population endured far worse than either. No nation has a monopoly of courage or determination, for what comes into play under these circumstances is basic human psychology, which is much the same regardless of nationality.

The second was that it was a victory against all the odds, with the common suggestion that it was miraculous.

'The miracle of Dunkirk' is still a standard phrase in the mythology of 1940, derived from Churchill calling the evacuation a 'miracle of deliverance' in his speech of 4 June. The only miraculous thing about Dunkirk, perhaps better called 'good luck', was that the sea remained so calm. The rest was down to excellent organisation by the navy, skill on the part of the RAF, generally good discipline in the BEF, and a lot of human effort. Hitler had many reasons, good and bad, for holding back his Panzers, but divine mercy was not one of them. The Battle of Britain seemed to be a fight against impossible odds because people believed pre-war German propaganda about the strength of the Luftwaffe and did not understand either the power of the defence system or the difficulty of the task the Luftwaffe set itself. The pilots were usually outnumbered in the air at any given point in time because by attacking successively in squadron strength they could get at the raiders earlier and cause more casualties than by attacking as a single formation. Operating Dowding's system in the way Park did put heavy demands on the pilots' courage and their confidence in him, but they showed that they had plenty of both. Given the preparations made on both sides, when Eagle was launched on 13 August, a German victory was very unlikely.

The third was that the British were terribly unprepared and just muddled through, showing their national genius for improvisation.

With regard to the Battle of Britain, this is complete nonsense. It is true that the British army was poorly prepared for war in 1939, but the navy was not, and began as it finished, sinking German ships everywhere from the North Sea to the South Atlantic and annihilating the Italian navy in truly Nelsonian fashion within a few months of Mussolini's declaration of war.[4] Within the RAF, Bomber Command was unprepared for the war it wanted to fight, but Fighter Command was the best prepared fighter force in the world, by a considerable margin. In 1940 it was given the opportunity of fighting almost precisely the battle it had planned for since its inception in 1936, the only difference being the proximity of its enemy along the whole Channel coast. It did not need to improvise, there was very little muddle, and it all worked out much as expected. Both its pilots and commanders felt supremely confident.

The British economy also got onto a war footing at tremendous speed, and made use of innovative measures to disperse production and make use of shadow factories. By July 1940 it was far better prepared than Germany's to keep turning out planes and guns in large quantities for as long as it needed to. The British are capable of planning and organising quite brilliantly when they have a mind to do so.

National unity is another theme of the myth.

It arose because Churchill asserted that the nation was united, and because many ordinary people remember the spirit of co-operation and friendliness they met with from complete strangers. Most, though not all, of the population seem to have been united, but the Cabinet was not. A minority of people opposed the war throughout its course, and the peace lobby came close to getting their way in 1940. It would have been quite remarkable given the deep and widespread pacifism of the 1930s if all had suddenly become ardent sons of Mars and rallied without question behind Churchill. In a democracy it would also have been unhealthy.

These elements of the myth have had a nefarious influence on the way the British have understood themselves. They suggest that we came through by the skin of our teeth, because of innate superiority and divine providence (usually called 'good luck'). These things saw us through then, so it must be all right to rely on them in the future. By the same token, if everything starts to go wrong, there is not much we can do about it. Either we are in fact worthless after all, or the gods have deserted us. So we either run ourselves down or blame circumstances outside our control. Both of these reactions are counsels of despair and both are based on complete fantasies. The way in which the Battle was actually won offers us far more worthwhile lessons, both for the present and the future.

The nature of that achievement has become clearer as the years have gone by.

It has often been said that 1940 was a critical year in British history, a turning point to be placed alongside 1588 and 1805 when would-be conquerors were thwarted. It was in fact not a turning point at all, for it ensured that things continued much as before. This was in many ways unfortunate, for by 1945 the world had become a very different place. The real long-term significance of the Battle of Britain was not to be felt in Britain at all, but far beyond its shores.

In 1940, the issues were qualitatively different from what they had been in 1588 and 1805. Had the Armada succeeded in 1588, Britain would have become Catholic. Had the French succeeded in 1805, Britain would have adopted the Code Napoleon. Otherwise, life would have gone on. Failure in 1940 would, by contrast, have led to prolonged human suffering on a scale dwarfing anything that had gone before. King Phillip's Spain and Napoleon's France were civilised powers. Nazi rule would, as Churchill said, have brought civilised life to an end.[5] In that sense, what was at stake made the Battle of Britain far more important in its human consequences than either of those previous threats to her sovereignty.

It was not only crucial that the Nazis be defeated, but also of vital importance who did it. The fact that Britain remained belligerent kept a Western presence in Europe, a presence which had immense implications for the world which would emerge out of the war.

If Britain had given up in 1940, the war could have had one of two possible outcomes: Nazi or Soviet domination of Europe. Hitler would have invaded the Soviet Union as he did anyway, only under rather more favourable circumstances. There the main war would have been fought out as it in fact was, a war of annihilation with one side being the victor.

If Hitler had won, all Europe from the Atlantic to the Urals would have come under Nazi rule, the consequences of which, in terms of human suffering, hardly bear thinking about. The death camps could have carried out their work unhindered on many more millions than they actually managed to round up. Resistance, though it would have seemed utterly hopeless, would no doubt have continued, with corresponding reprisals spread across all the occupied countries. America could have done little even if she had wanted to. She might have invented the atom bomb before Germany (though she was a long way behind in developing a missile-based delivery system) and intervened with that, if she had found a base near enough to launch it from. Without the stimulus of actual hostilities, however, she would probably never have pursued the project. However that may be, this scenario is one of the most awful one can contemplate. Europe was spared all that.

On the other hand, as is probably more likely, things may still have ended in a Soviet victory. The Red Army would have taken longer to defeat the Wehrmacht, but when it had eventually succeeded, it would not have had to stop its march westwards at the Oder-Neisse line, but would have continued to the Atlantic and down into Italy. The whole of Europe, lacking any Western presence on the battlefield, would have been occupied by the Soviets. There would probably have been less killing than under the Nazi alternative, but what Soviet rule would have meant only became fully apparent in 1990. Assuming that Communism would have collapsed anyway – and it might have lasted a good deal longer than it did – the whole of Europe would have been on its knees, with only the United States to pick up the burden of reconstruction. There would in particular have been no Federal Republic of Germany to fund the recovery of its smaller sister state. The tensions which have arisen in the former Soviet Union and the wars which have broken out there, and more bitterly still in Yugoslavia, could have been far more widespread. The world would have been not only much poorer, but much more dangerous than it is today.

Had the Battle of Britain not been fought, or had it been fought and lost, one of these two things must have been the consequence. Britain could not win the war in the West, only America could do that, and even after America entered, she could have failed to win. The Battle of the Atlantic could have been lost to the U-boats, the invasion of Normandy could have been defeated. There are many possibilities. But the British participation in the war secured in 1940 was a condition *sine qua non* of a Western presence in Europe in 1945.

Had the Red Army fought and defeated the Wehrmacht alone, the country to have suffered most would have been Germany. As it is, the bulk of the

German population has been allowed to live in a state with remarkable democratic institutions, which offer some of the best protection of the rights of the individual of any state apparatus in the world. They have enjoyed unprecedented levels of prosperity, earned largely by their own efforts, but made possible by Britain's original maintenance of a Western presence on the continent. The Federal Republic is, if measured by its ability to foster the greatest good of the greatest number, by far the most successful state in German history. Never has so much been owed by the vanquished to its victors. The Germans have much reason to be grateful that Britain declared war on them in 1939, for in the end that saved them both from the Russians and from themselves.

The contrast between the Battle of Britain and the war in the east could not be starker. More Russian soldiers alone died on every *day* of that conflict than were killed on both sides during the whole of the Battle of Britain. Barbarossa opened the most brutal and destructive war in history, costing the lives of 4–5 million Germans and perhaps 25 million Soviet citizens, two thirds of them civilians. The contrast is not just one of extent. For all the ruthless demands that they made on their pilots, both Dowding and Park cared passionately about both the lives and the welfare of their men. In the east, both the Soviets and the Germans fought without the slightest regard for the lives of their own people, let alone the other side's. The Russians in particular treated their own soldiery with brutality, and were directly responsible for the deaths of many of them. Many Russians captured by the Germans were imprisoned or executed for treason by the Soviets after their re-capture. Battles like Stalingrad give us a chilling glimpse into the heart of darkness. The war in Russia was purely destructive of life and of the soul. In 1940, the West took the first step towards preserving itself from being totally dominated by whichever régime emerged the victor of this savage butchery.[6]

Totalitarianism reached its high-water mark in 1940. It is thanks to Britain that this proved to be a breaking wave. Since then, gradually at first, and then more recently in a sudden flood, ever more states have adopted liberal democracy. In his analysis of the progress of democratic forms of government, Francis Fukuyama shows that though in 1919 there were twenty-five democracies in the world, in 1940 there were only thirteen. By 1990 he could count sixty-one.[7]

In the east, the less malevolent of the two régimes prevailed, but Stalinism was still devoid of respect for human life or dignity. The story of the Soviet-German war is one of negation. Out of the Battle of Britain, on the other hand, there emerge some values worthy of affirmation.

The Battle of Britain first showed the bankruptcy of the warrior-hero, who seemed to have vindicated himself and the new order he believed he would establish in the Battles of Poland, Norway and France. There the élan, military professionalism, drive, daring and fighting prowess of the warrior-hero had overcome the outmoded and decadent states of the West.

Trusting again to superior fighting prowess, the Luftwaffe hurled itself against Britain and failed. The Germans began by feeling superior, and with good reason. The RAF, whilst showing a level of self-confidence which bemused outside observers, was under no illusions about how tough things would get. Humility led to extraordinary effort, and victory. The big egos of Germany's score-chasing hunter-killers were beaten by the team-players.

It is ironic that the British and the Germans swapped the characteristics they commonly attribute to each other:

- the British were run by hard-bitten air force professionals who had devoted years to mastering the task they were to face; the Luftwaffe High Command was headed by an amateur, a swashbuckling adventurer politician. His key commander, Kesselring, whom he himself named alongside von Richthofen as the best in the Luftwaffe,[8] was trained as an artilleryman and had spent less that one third of the time his main opponent had as an airman;
- the British had a carefully prepared system which fully applied all the resources of modern technology, and was flexible enough to cover the eventualities which arose without on-the-spot improvisation; the Germans improvised their attack and neither exploited the potential of the technology available to them, nor understood the use their opponents were making of it;
- the British fought with a high level of discipline and control which still left room for initiative in the air; with their unclear strategy, the Germans looked to their airmen to come up with a heroic *tour de force*, and Göring berated them when they unsurprisingly failed to do so;
- the British worked as disciplined teams and played down the role of individuals both in the air and on the ground; the Germans worked as individuals, who lived in an eccentric old-world culture of the aristocratic hunting fraternity;
- the British commanders were determined and ruthless, and most of the foreign, and some of the British, pilots felt hatred for their enemies. They knew they were not playing cricket and did not play the nastier game they were playing for the game's sake, but in order to win, which probably contributed to their doing so; the Germans thought of themselves as knights of the air, jousting against noble opponents of whom they spoke with generosity and towards whom they generally behaved with some chivalry.[9]

In their 'finest hour' the British behaved quite differently from the way in which they usually seek to portray themselves. They exhibited a talent for planning and organisation which, in its Teutonic thoroughness, far outstripped that of the Germans. They left little to chance, planned for the worst case and did not rely on luck. Given all this, it is hardly surprising that they won. It is, on the other hand, quite extraordinary that they should imagine they could have won by doing the opposite.

If the British behaved like Germans at their best, these qualities were tempered and refined by a value system which was distinctly theirs. It was not articulated, but informed the way in which people saw themselves, their roles and their working relationships with others.

The most effective individuals viewed themselves as taking part in a collective effort and had a realistic view of the value of their own effort's contribution to it, which led them to espouse modesty as a virtue. They had an entirely unheroic view of what they did, regarding it as a job, and recognised that in order to achieve anything they had to put in a lot of hard work, much of which was unglamorous. They put the achievement of their task above their own glory, and were stimulated to great efforts by a desire not to let down their fellows. Where mutual respect governed their interactions, all went well. When it did not, things broke down.

They also displayed courage. During the fighting, physical courage was necessary. Moral courage – the willingness to represent unpopular views, to keep on trying in spite of failures and set-backs and to have the integrity to say what one thinks – was displayed in the years of peace as well as during the war. The greatest efforts were from people who contributed to the collective, but were not buried by it.

These values were exemplified in all the important steps that led to the ultimate victory. Mitchell's design team is one good example. Mitchell has often been called a genius. If so, he was a very hard-working one. He put his team first, and encouraged internal criticism and debate. When Britain won the Schneider Trophy outright in 1931, the names of everybody involved, down to the met officer, were broadcast in the press, with one exception: that of Mitchell himself. He put the development of the Spitfire before his own health, and after producing a complete failure in his first response to F7/30, the Type 224, started all over again and produced one of the greatest aircraft designs there has ever been.

Dowding and Park displayed it in the way Fighter Command was built up and run. Dowding was utterly selfless in his dedication to building Britain's air defences, and showed determination to the point of pig-headedness in getting things to happen once he was convinced they were necessary. He was generous in his praise of Park, who showed respect and loyalty in return. Park got no less from those who worked directly with him. He was irked by the direct and implied criticisms of his tactics, but he continued to do what he believed was right, all at a time when he was under immense strain.

The pilots displayed it in the Battle. It is perhaps most clearly embodied in the way in which Fighter Command's most outstanding air leader of the period, 'Sailor' Malan, ran 74 Squadron. There was no score-chasing, least of all from Malan himself; there was constant practice and debate on tactics; there was emphasis on mutual support and teamwork. This all worked as well in the air as it did on the ground.

These values did not just make the strains on individuals less of a burden, they were effective. They are not martial virtues, but they can make a peaceful nation a formidable opponent in war. They make for high levels of achievement in any sphere, and they make life a good deal more pleasant than it would otherwise be.

Perhaps the most telling symptom of the value system espoused by the British protagonists, and the feature commented on more than any other, particularly amongst the pilots, was the humour. It was pervasive, usually ironic and often self-deprecating. It was not in order on the other side of the Channel, where Osterkamp records being taken to task by his Corps Commander, Bruno Loerzer, for sending a message out of keeping with the seriousness of the war situation.[10] The Luftwaffe took itself very seriously, the first step towards hubris.

Fighter Command was an international force, and had created an ethos which those who joined it from other countries willingly espoused, and they in their turn were integrated very quickly to a degree which surprised many observers. Not many of the pilots were classic military types. They lived a student lifestyle and in many cases captivated and charmed those who knew them in a way that fighting men have seldom done. Soldiers throughout the ages have been feared by civilians as brutal, amoral and potentially dangerous. With the recruitment of civilian armies, this began to change. With the pilots of 1940, the centuries-old view of the military professional became inverted, for they seemed to many to be the finest embodiment of the civilised values for which they were fighting. They were able to fight hard but preserve their humanity. Their passing was bitterly mourned, as is recorded in particular by some of the women who served with them:

> Off they pelted, day after day, those glorious, radiant boys. We were with them in sound and spirit . . . But that feeling of lead in the stomach when they failed to return was all too familiar . . . There were so many. I remember when Caesar Hull was killed – we all admired him. The gay and gallant American Billy Fiske; the two Wood-Scawens, inseparable brothers, devout Catholics, charmers both – and all of them so young and so well-endowed, and such a wicked, wicked waste. I mourned them then, now and for ever.
>
> The fighter boys were a breed apart, sadly lost, in those days for ever; and I and all who knew them were very privileged.[11]

In the end, one has to come back to the cause for which they were fighting, for in the end, it makes a difference.[12] At its most fundamental, the different values were embodied in the two national leaders.

A glance through any part of *Mein Kampf* is enough to show that Hitler's

dominant emotion was hatred and that his basic attitude to others was contempt. He did not love Germany. He thought that the laws of nature had
marked the Germans out as a master race, but this was something they had to
prove by winning the struggle he pushed them into. When they failed to do so,
he interpreted the result as a judgement upon them, and accepted that they
should go under as they had shown themselves to be less strong than he had
thought. He concluded that they deserved their fate.

Churchill did not hate the Germans, he simply opposed them. In January
1941 he remarked to Colville that he 'hated nobody and didn't feel he had any
enemies – except the Huns and that was professional!' Few men, Colville added,
were as 'good natured' as Churchill.[13] There was, on the other hand, a great deal
that he loved. He loved France, and was devastated by her defeat. He felt great
affection for America, his mother's country. And he loved Britain and her
people, and decided to fight in order to preserve what mankind had achieved
in creating modern civilisation and what Britain stood for within that. He was
not ashamed to show what he felt in public. Tough old bird that he was, there
are not a few occasions on which he was observed to be in tears.

The British fought to preserve the ethos of a post-heroic age against the
last destructive manifestation in Europe of the master-hero ethic. They fought
for the right of people to decide on their destiny by themselves and the right to
say and think what they like. They fought for the right to be wrong, the right
to be vague, the right to be fed up. They fought for ordinariness, being nice to
people and minding your own business. They fought for a sort of Englishness
as it then was.

A few fought because they were brave. Some fought because they agreed
with Churchill that Hitler was a threat to Western civilisation. But most people
did not know much about Western civilisation. A lot of them fought because
they thought Hitler was a bully and needed taking down a peg or two. He
shouted and showed off and that annoyed them. Probably most people fought
because Churchill told them they had to, so they just got on with it. The Battle
of Britain was won on the whole by people just getting on with it. Whether out
of courage or bloody-mindedness, obedience to their leader or lack of imagination, they were led unconsciously to perform an act of self-sacrifice which is
unprecedented. That sacrifice saved civilisation. As Churchill observed after it
was all over:

> Not every government called into being by democracy or despot-
> ism, and not every nation, while quite alone, and as it seemed
> abandoned, would have courted the horrors of invasion and dis-
> dained a fair chance of peace for which many other plausible excuses
> could be presented.[14]

But this is precisely what his government and the nation did. They did so successfully, but they paid the price in full. It was presented as self-defence, and just

as well, for there are not many instances of nations consciously sacrificing themselves for others laid low by their own folly. But sacrifice it certainly was, and it was quite clear, as Churchill repeatedly affirmed, that the fate of Europe, and not just of Britain depended upon it.[15] However it was conceived and understood at the time, it was not the meanest of acts among nations.

If we must have heroes, we could do a lot worse than look back to 1940.[16] Compared with any other period in its history, Europe is living today on broad, sunlit uplands. We are apt to despair because of the clouds that continue to pass, and forget that it is not long ago that Europe stared into an abyss. By comparison, all we have to deal with are shadows. The non-martial, non-heroic values that won the Battle of Britain have lost none of their potency in peace.

Few events in history, and almost none in the history of warfare, are so uplifting and life-enhancing as the story of the Battle of Britain. No battle has benefited so many at the cost of so few. Few battles have ultimately proved to have such positive consequences for the defeated. Looking back over the century whose course it so decisively determined, hideous epoch though that century may have been, one can feel justified in saying that the Battle of Britain was one of humanity's finest hours.

Epilogue

When he left the RAF, Bob Doe talked to some people he knew to see if they had any opportunities, and he joined a family-run garage in Kent with a self-drive car business. In the end, he bought out the owners, sold off the cars and ran the garage, where he served the petrol himself. He managed to buy a lovely house with a large garden over the border in Sussex. None of his customers knew who he was. He did not talk much about the past and did not go to reunions. He did not like to display his sores in public, he said.

That changed in 1985, when he appeared in a Channel 4 documentary called 'Churchill's Few', which also featured Ulrich Steinhilper. The morning after the broadcast, a roadsweeper walked in, shook his hand, said 'Thanks', and walked away. An old lady came up to him and kissed him and his customers started calling him 'Sir'. He was in tears. In 1991 he finally published a slim volume of his recollections.

We met at his home on a lovely summer afternoon, sipped some beer and 'had a natter', as he put it. He does not work at the garage any more, leaving it to his wife, Betty. His old wounds are playing up, he has had a double hip replacement and moving about is not as easy as it was. He has time to reflect, and wants to set the record straight. 'Everyone talks about the wrong people,' he said in his deep, rich voice, 'the self-publicists. Now who has ever heard of Pat Hughes? He saved our squadron, and he shot down a lot more than others I could name. But he died you see. That was a blow. They sent us away to Cornwall after that.' He wonders why nobody ever told them anything. 'I never saw Dowding. Nobody did. I think he was very, very good in what he did until the battle started, but he fell down as a leader after that. The man who won the battle was Keith Park. He was marvellous.'

Bob Doe is a quiet, gentle man. He understates, and he is still self-deprecating. Wasn't he taking a terrible risk that day he attacked a whole gaggle of Messerschmitts? 'Not really. I was alone and up-sun, so they couldn't see me. I had position, and that was everything. I was a bit concerned when the engine stopped, mind you, but I just got into some cloud and then it started again. The key to air fighting was shooting. You had to fly the aeroplane through the gun-sight, and treat yourself and the plane as a flying gun.'

He dismisses the glamorous image of the Knights of the Air. 'It wasn't very romantic, you know. We had a job to do, so we got on with it. We had to stop them – we were the only ones who could. I was defending my home.' However, he remembers one chivalrous act of his own. 'I only actually saw the enemy once. I had a snap shot at a 109 which then dived for the sea. I followed it for some time, caught it up and got it again. Its engine stopped and the pilot got rid of his canopy. I flew up alongside and looked at him. He was a big, blond man in a blue flying suit. We looked at each other. I was getting low on fuel, so I turned round, and looking back I saw him splash into the sea. I suppose he could have got back and shot me down later on, but I couldn't have shot him in cold blood. After the war, a German pilot, quite a famous one, heard of this story and wrote to me, saying it was him.'

We walked around in the garden and inspected the roses. Bob has returned to his origins. His main job now is in the greenhouse where he has special responsibility for the nursery. Once the seedlings are big enough, his wife takes over and plants them out.

Underneath the gentleness, one can nevertheless perceive a steely core built around moral values. He has a strong sense of duty and a very clear idea about right and wrong. He is very proud of his son, a policeman who got a commendation for 'courage and professionalism' in tackling a man with a knife. And he can be very definite about some things. He once had a row with another pilot whom he thought left him in the lurch. He felt very strongly about it at the time.

As I left, I thanked him. 'For someone of my generation,' I said, 'meeting you is almost like meeting one of Nelson's men who was at Trafalgar'. He laughed. 'Don't forget to tell them about Park,' he said. 'People ought to know about what he did.'

Every year, 615 Squadron hold a reunion at Kenley on the weekend closest to 18th August, the day of the big raid. The first to arrive was a gentleman with an aquiline nose and a shock of white hair. He had piercing eyes and did not wear glasses. He looked like a bird of prey. Pointing at a photograph on the wall with his stick he said 'There, that's me. That was in France. I'm the only one left out of that lot.' The picture showed a group of pilots sitting outside a hut, and he pointed at one standing at the back lighting a cigarette. I looked. It was indeed the man next to me. This was Wing Commander James Sanders.

'I left the RAF in 1947,' he said, 'and never had anything more to do with the Air Force, out of deference to my second wife, whom I married after the war. She had been married twice during the war, both times to an RAF officer, and they were both killed flying. She was engaged to a third one and he was killed too. I was the fourth, and she meant to hang on to me, so she made me give up flying and have nothing to do with it. I hardly ever went to reunions and did not talk to historians. But she died a few years ago. She was lovely. We were very happy. We can talk if you like.'

So we met at his house in a quiet London suburb. As we chatted over tea, it began to feel not just like meeting one of Nelson's men, but someone who had been on the upper deck of the *Victory* at Trafalgar. He had been there at the centre of things from the beginning. He was the third man to fly the first monoplane fighter ever delivered to the RAF, Hurricane L1547; he had worked with the units developing tactics before the war and argued in vain against tight formations; he had been sent to France in Gladiator biplanes in 1939; he had fought in France, Dunkirk and throughout the Battle of Britain; he had been one of only a handful of pilots to intercept German bombers at night in a single-engined fighter; he had watched Dowding at work convincing Churchill of his night-fighting strategy; and he had probably saved Churchill from an untimely end at the innocent but over-curious hands of his own wife in 1939!

After the war he became an executive at an insurance company, and since retirement has concentrated on enjoying his own large family and cultivating his love of music. Several operations, including hip replacements, do not stop him from getting about and he generously invited me to one of the Proms, which he attends regularly. Whilst he quite enjoyed the Bruckner symphony it was the première of contemporary composer James MacMillan's 'Quickening' which aroused his real enthusiasm. Perhaps it was something of the same enthusiasm for the new that found him in the cockpit of a Hurricane in 1937.

We talked a lot about prima donnas and why he fought them. There was more to it than standing up for himself against his four sisters at home. James was brought up in Italy at a time when Fascism was gaining its grip. He went to school in Genoa and remembers an occasion when he was nine years old when he and his classmates had to sing the slave song from Verdi's *Nabucco* for Mussolini's arrival at Staglieno sports arena. He deeply resented it and felt the dictator looked silly with his melodramatic poses. It was in Italy that he first got into trouble with the authorities. When he was in his late teens he faced a judicial hearing. The toilet paper in his school consisted of sheets of newspaper and at the time Mussolini was on almost every page. James was overheard to remark that he wiped his bottom with Mussolini. That was enough to get arrested. They let him off because he argued that if he was given newspaper for the purpose he had no choice but to use the Duce's image in that way. There was no answer to that. He left Italy because he was convinced there would be a war and he wanted to join up. Challenging authority had become natural to him. So, ultimately, did fighting dictatorships. By 1940, the whole country had joined in.

He had a lot of respect for the enemy. 'The 109 was unstable,' he said, 'especially at low speed near the ground. But flown by a good pilot it was deadly. It was slightly smaller than our two fighters, stayed completely under control when inverted, and had two very nasty cannons. I once met a pilot who flew it. It was after the war in Italy. He was an Italian aristocrat actually and he said he was at the Pas de Calais during the Battle of Britain. He said the 109s were too dangerous and he pulled all the strings he could to get out of flying them. He was a prince, so he succeeded. He transferred to miniature submarines and was one of the ones who put a limpet mines under the *Valiant* and *Queen Elisabeth* in Alexandria Harbour. He was obviously brave, but perhaps he was the wrong type for fighters. You had to have the right temperament.'

'I had a pilot once, a Yorkshireman called Dick Pexton, who was not a fighter type. He was a farmer, and when we went up, he'd get on the R/T and say "Sandy" – I used to be called "Sandy" – "look down there, that's a bloody good barley-field." "Never mind the barley-field," I said, "look up here or the 109s will get you." Well they did, of course. He joined up with a whole formation of them. He just formated on them. He didn't have a clue. They riddled him with bullets, but he baled out and got away with a bullet in the leg. When he got back from hospital, I said "Dick, you're no good as a fighter pilot. You should go to bombers. You've got the right attitude. All you have to do is to stick right in the centre of the formation, and the only things you have to worry about are flak or if someone above drops an incendiary on you." So he did. In no time at all, he was a Squadron Leader. He collected all the gongs. I saw him a few years later, and he said, "Sandy, that was the best piece of advice I've ever had".'

Sandy flew Defiants at night, and once, when the guns had jammed after damaging a Heinkel, he remonstrated with his gunner to bale out so that he could saw the bomber's tail off with his propeller. 'He didn't like that idea. As we argued about it, the German disappeared. I heard he came down actually, on the coast somewhere south of Grimsby.' 'Didn't you think it was a bit dangerous, ramming a bomber?' I asked. 'Dangerous? No, not really. Didn't think about it. The Defiant's got a nice big open cockpit. You can bale out easily. You're a birdman, you see. I was so frustrated, I just wanted to get the thing, make sure of him.'

He thought for a bit. 'We had an easy war in a way, you know, we fighter pilots.' He looked at me. 'Oh, I know you're thinking "You were confronting the enemy every day" and all that. But we were very lucky. We had marvellous food in the mess, we had a bed to go back to, we had an aircraft with an armoured windscreen, armour plate behind us, a parachute underneath and a nice big engine in front to take any bullets, and eight machine guns. What a wonderful way to fight a war. We didn't deserve any medals. It was the bomber pilots, especially the ones on the early Blenheims, that deserved them, all of them. I saw them going down. They used to catch fire easily and it was a ghastly sight. I know people make a lot of fuss about heroes, but it's all nonsense. Take Bader. Pilots in 11 Group actually had very little time for Bader and his Wing. There was no way the Big Wing could be operated. He was a gentleman, though, and he was a marvellous inspiration to the disabled. I remember after the war, I went to a do with my wife Josephine at the Green Room and Bader was Guest of Honour. He gave up his seat to her, you know, with his spindles and all that. "Good for you", I thought, "at least you are a gent."'

He feels deep respect for his leaders. 'Dowding and Park won the Battle of Britain, there's no doubt about that. Above all Dowding. Maybe Churchill won the war, but Dowding saved the country. Park was a great man. I think I'd take my hat off to him. He understood exactly what Dowding wanted and he knew how to do it. But it was really Dowding who was behind it all. You cannot imagine all the things he was doing, well before the war. He was working on so much. I saw it.'

Like Bob Doe, James Sanders' behaviour in 1940 was driven by a strong set of core values. He showed extraordinary resilience, carrying on in action without a break despite two hair-raising escapes from France. He expected to die, as did most of his comrades, but he had developed a lot of skill, and it enabled him to cheat death often enough to come through alive. He was not a callow youth with twelve hours on Hurricanes, but a young man of twenty-five with 1,000 hours. That probably saved him.

He is modest about his own achievements. By the end of the Battle of Britain he was 615 Squadron's leading ace, being accredited with sixteen destroyed and five damaged, but he paid little attention to the business of scores at the time. He lost his log-book in France, and some of his claims from that time went unrecorded, but he is unconcerned. He was willing to sacrifice the goodwill of his superiors in order to speak out for what he believed to be right. 'There were a lot of prima donnas in the Air Force, you know. They just had to sit in an aeroplane and the press would be there and they'd get a gong.' His promotion probably suffered because he did not care about currying favour with his superiors. For him, stating the truth and standing up for it is what matters. He has a strong sense of right and wrong, and a very clear sense of the difference between exuberant behaviour and doing harm. Like Bob Doe, he is proud of his family's achievements. His son Patrick went to Cranwell and became the official RAF aerobatic pilot on Jaguars.

James often mentioned the names of the men he flew with then who died when cruelly young. There was 'dear old Conny', Mike Ferriss and Michael Robinson at 111 Squadron, there was Bill Fowler at 615, who escaped from Colditz but killed himself in a Typhoon at Boscombe Down – 'you'd have really loved him, he was such tremendous fun' – and many others. All in all he had a wonderful time in the Air Force, enjoying the company of some delightful people who were witty and outrageous, talented and amusing, adventurous and brave. There is a sense of the irretrievable loss of some of the best of a generation, still remembered with great fondness. The waste and brutality of war have left an indelible impression.

The stupidity of war is summed up for James in the story of Margot, the elderly French woman with whom he was billeted at Vitry-en-Artois during the winter of 1939–40. A widow of World War I, she still wore black. Each night when he came back from his mess at the Hôtel de Bretagne she would be waiting for him with 'des briques chaudes pour le lit' – a tray of heated up house bricks under a cloth to warm his bed during the bitter winter. Every morning at dawn she would be standing by the corner of the front door counting her rosary with hot coffee for him. 'C'est pas nécessaire, Margot' he would plead every day, but every day she carried on just the same. She used to worry about the Boche coming. 'C'est pas possible,' he would reassure her, as the British would never allow them to. He went to find her after the war, to apologise for getting this wrong. When he asked after her in the Hôtel de Bretagne he got some dark looks, and was told that she was 'une collaboratrice'. This could not be his Margot. When he found her still at the old house, she was overwhelmed to see him. He asked her about being a collaborator. She told him that after he had gone the Germans did come after all, and billeted a pilot with her. 'Margot,' he said, 'did you get him warm bricks for his bed and bring him coffee?' 'Of course,' she said. 'And he told me the English would never come back. But you did. I told him so.' 'When?' asked James. 'A few weeks ago when he came over to apologise for telling me the British would never come back.'

'Margot was no collaborator,' he reflected, 'she was a mother. She just saw two young men away from home who needed looking after. We were the same to her. She was protecting the sons she never had because her husband was killed. How ridiculous and cruel to condemn her.'

In a lifetime of rich experience, James Sanders' memories of the summer of 1940 are still more vivid than any others. 'Looking back,' he reflected, 'you never stop talking about it, but I was lucky to get away with it. I did France, Dunkirk and the Battle of Britain, the whole thing. I was with 11 Group right from the beginning to the end. I was lucky. I think I possibly am the only person around now who did the whole lot like that, you know, the only one left.'

James 'Sandy' Sanders died peacefully at home on 12 August 2002, aged 88.

Postscript

I now live at Oxted in Surrey, near the Kent border. With both Biggin Hill and Kenley just four miles away, the Battle of Britain seems closer than it was in my childhood. On 15 September 1990, I took the train to London. As we passed Whyteleafe at the end of the Caterham Valley, I saw a glider turning gently above us. It was from just over the hill in Kenley. The airfield is used by 615 Squadron Gliding School, the heirs of 615 'County of Surrey' Squadron, whose Honorary Air Commodore was Winston Churchill. Mostly people just walk their dogs there and boys daub graffiti on the overgrown bunkers. There was no memorial then, but one was put up in 2000, unveiled just sixty years after the big raid in 1940.

I got out at Victoria and walked along the back streets towards Buckingham Palace. The crowds thickened until I reached the south side of the Palace and had to stop. A service was in progress to commemorate the 50th Anniversary of the Battle of Britain. There was some movement in the crowd, then we heard the sound of jet engines and an RAF fly-past began. Aircraft of every sort flew overhead in perfect formation. Their noise died away, and there was a brief pause. Then I picked up another sound. It was lower and easier on the ear than the whining cacophony of the jets, something between a buzzing and a growl. As it grew more distinct a boy sitting on his father's shoulders in front of me suddenly pointed up over the Mall and cried out: 'Look, Dad! A Spitfire!'

Just over the gate they flew, very low in line abreast, like a pair of ageing ballroom dancers holding hands. On the right was the humped outline of a Hurricane, stubby and purposeful. Next to it was The Lady Herself, skimming the trees of the Mall. She looked as she always does, dainty and deadly, beautiful and brave.

Suddenly as they reached the Victoria Memorial they broke, the Hurricane to the right and The Lady to the left, where we were standing. And there, for a brief second, a piece of obsolete mechanical engineering with a silly name flew over our heads, showing off That Wing. She still flirts with anyone and everyone. The crowd burst into applause. The little boy shouted and waved. In a moment she was gone, and the growling faded away. For a while, we stood around wondering what to do, but nothing could follow that, so we slowly dispersed.

Just ten minutes' walk away, inside the entrance to Westminster Abbey, visitors can pass by a stone set in the floor which bears the words: 'Remember Winston Churchill'. In the main, they should probably get on with their lives and concentrate on the future. But every now and again, perhaps, they should do as it says.

Perhaps you too, especially if you are not British, should not completely forget about the Battle of Britain. For this, if anything of ours, is worth your memory.

LUFTWAFFE ORDER OF BATTLE, 13 AUGUST 1940[1]

LUFTFLOTTE 2, Brussels, Generalfeldmarschall Albert Kesselring

Wettererkundungsstaffel 26, Reg. Rat Krug: weather reconnaissaince

—	Brussels-Grimberghen	Do17/He 111/ Bf 110	8

I Fliegerkorps, Beauvais, Generaloberst Grauert

Kampfgeschwader 1, Oberstleutnant Exss: bombers

Stabschwarm	Amiens-Glisy	He 111	4
I. Gruppe	Montdidier	He 111	23
II. Gruppe	Amiens-Glisy	He 111	29
III. Gruppe	Rosières-en-Santerre	He 111	15

Kampfgeschwader 76, Oberstleutnant Frölich: bombers

Stabschwarm	Cormeilles-en-Vexin	Do 17	5
I. Gruppe	Beauvais-Tilles	Do 17	29
II. Gruppe	Creil	Ju 88	28
III. Gruppe	Cormeilles-en-Vexin	Do 17	19

Aufklärungsgruppe 122, Hauptmann Bohm, long-range reconnaissance

5. Staffel	Haute-Fontaine	Ju 88, He 111, Do 17P	5

II Fliegerkorps, Ghent, General Lörzer

Kampfgeschwader 2, Oberst Fink: bombers

Stabschwarm	St. Léger	Do 17	4
I. Gruppe	Épinoy	Do 17	27
II. Gruppe	St. Léger	Do 17	31
III. Gruppe	Cambrai-Sud	Do 17	32

Kampfgeschwader 3, Oberst von Chamier-Glisczinski: bombers

Stabschwarm	Antwerp-Deurne	Do 17	3
I. Gruppe	Le Culot	Do 17	28
II. Gruppe	Antwerp-Deurne	Do 17	32
III. Gruppe	St. Trond	Do 17	25

Kampfgeschwader 53, Oberst Stahl: bombers

Stabschwarm	Lille-Nord	He 111	1
I. Gruppe	Lille-Nord	He 111	27
II. Gruppe	Lille-Nord	He 111	15
III. Gruppe	Lille-Nord	He 111	24

Stukageschwader 1, Hauptmann Keil: dive bombers

| II. Gruppe | Pas-de-Calais | Ju 87 | 30 |

Lehrgeschwader 1, Hauptmann von Brauchitsch: dive bombers

| IV. Gruppe | Tramecourt | Ju 87 | 28 |

Lehrgeschwader 2, Hauptmann Weiss: fighter-bombers

| II. Gruppe | St Omer[2] | Bf 109 | 31 |

Erprobungsgruppe 210, Hauptmann Rubensdörffer: fighter-bombers[3]

Stabschwarm	Denain/Calais-Marck	Bf 110	3
1. Staffel	Denain/Calais-Marck	Bf 110	9
2. Staffel	Denain/Calais-Marck	Bf 110	9
3. Staffel	Denain/Calais-Marck	Bf 109	9

IX Fliegerdivision, Soesterberg, Holland, Generalmajor Coeler

Kampfgeschwader 4, Oberstleutnant Rath: bombers

Stabschwarm	Soesterberg	He 111	5
I. Gruppe	Soesterberg	He 111	12
II. Gruppe	Eindhoven	He 111	25
III. Gruppe	Amsterdam-Schiphol	Ju 88	23

Kampfgruppe 100, Hauptmann Aschenbrenner: pathfinder bombers[4]

–	Vannes	He 111	19

Küstengruppe 126, minelaying

–	Various	He 111	8

Aufklärungsgruppe 122, Oberstleutnant Koehler: long-range reconnaissance

3. Staffel	Eindhoven	Ju 88, He 111	9

Jagdfliegerführer 2, Wissant, Generalmajor Osterkamp: fighters

Jagdgeschwader 3, Oberstleutnant Vieck/Lützow[5]: fighters

Stabschwarm	Samer	Bf 109	3
I. Gruppe	Colembert	Bf 109	32
II. Gruppe	Wierre au Bois	Bf 109	22
III. Gruppe	Desvres	Bf 109	29

Jagdgeschwader 26, Major Handrick/Galland: fighters

Stabschwarm	Audembert	Bf 109	4
I. Gruppe	Audembert	Bf 109	34
II. Gruppe	Marquise	Bf 109	35
III. Gruppe	Caffiers	Bf 109	38

Jagdgeschwader 51, Major Mölders: fighters

Stabschwarm	Wissant	Bf 109	4
I. Gruppe	Pihen	Bf 109	32
II. Gruppe	Marquise	Bf 109	33
III. Gruppe	St Omer	Bf 109	30

Jagdgeschwader 52[6], Major von Merhert/Trübenbach: fighters

Stabschwarm	Coquelles	Bf 109	1
I. Gruppe	Coquelles	Bf 109	33
II. Gruppe	Peuplingues	Bf 109	32

Jagdgeschwader 54, Major Mettig/Trautloft: fighters

Stabschwarm	Campagne-les-Guines	Bf 109	2
I. Gruppe	Guines	Bf 109	24
II. Gruppe	Hermelinghen	Bf 109	32
III. Gruppe	Guines	Bf 109	40

Lehrgeschwader 2, Major Trübenbach/Ihlefeld: fighters

I. Gruppe	Calais-Marck	Bf 109	36

Zerstörergeschwader 26,[7] Oberstleutnant Huth/Schalk: heavy fighters

Stabschwarm	Lille	Bf 110	3
I. Gruppe	Yvrench	Bf 110	33
II. Gruppe	Crécy	Bf 110	32
III. Gruppe	Barly	Bf 110	24

Zerstörergeschwader 76, Major Groth: heavy fighters

II. Gruppe	Abbeville	Bf 110	6

LUFTFLOTTE 3,[8] Paris, Generalfeldmarschall Hugo Sperrle

Wettererkundungsstaffel 51, Reg. Rat Dr. Felber: weather reconnaissaince

—	Versailles-Buc	Do17/He 111	3

IV Fliegerkorps, Dinard, General Pfugbeil

Lehrgeschwader 1, Oberst Bülowius: bombers

Stabschwarm	Orléans-Bricy	Ju 88	1
I. Gruppe	Orléans-Bricy	Ju 88	23
II. Gruppe	Orléans-Bricy	Ju 88	24
III. Gruppe	Châteaudun	Ju 88	23

Kampfgeschwader 27, Oberst Behrendt: bombers

Stabschwarm	Tours	He 111	1
I. Gruppe	Tours	He 111	22
II. Gruppe	Bourges/Dinard	He 111	21
III. Gruppe	Rennes	He 111	23

Kampfgeschwader 40, Oberstleutnant Geisse: long-range reconnaissance

| Stabschwarm | Brest-Guipavas | Ju 88 | 1 |
| I. Gruppe | Brest-Guipavas | Fw 200 | 3 |

Kampfgruppe 806, Hauptmann Linke: maritime bombers

| – | Nantes and Caen | Ju 88 | 22 |

Stukageschwader 3, Oberst Angerstein: dive bombers

| Stabschwarm | Caen | Do 17, Ju 87 | 5 |

Aufklärungsgruppe 31, Hauptmann Sieckemus: long-range reconnaissance

| 3. Staffel | Rennes | Bf 110, Do 17, Ju 88 | 6 |

Aufklärungsgruppe 121, Hauptmann Kerber: long-range reconnaissance

| 3. Staffel | North-West France | Ju 88 | 6 |

V Fliegerkorps, Villacoublay, Generalleutnant Ritter von Greim

Kampfgeschwader 51, Major Schulz-Heyn[9]: bombers

Stabschwarm	Paris-Orly	Ju 88	1
I. Gruppe	Melun-Villaroche	Ju 88	21
II. Gruppe	Étampes-Montdésir	Ju 88	24
III. Gruppe	Étampes-Montdésir	Ju 88	25

Kampfgeschwader 54, Evreux, Oberstleutnant Höhne: bombers

Stabschwarm	Evreux	Ju 88	0
I. Gruppe	Evreux	Ju 88	29
II. Gruppe	André-de-l'Eure	Ju 88	23

Kampfgeschwader 55, Villacoublay, Oberst Stöckl: bombers

Stabschwarm	Villacoublay	He 111	1
I. Gruppe	Dreux	He 111	35
II. Gruppe	Chartres	He 111	28
III. Gruppe	Villacoublay	He 111	33

Aufklärungsgruppe 14, Hauptmann von Dewitz: long-range reconnaissance

4. Staffel	Cherbourg	Bf 110, Do 17	9

Aufklärungsgruppe 121, Hauptmann Kerber: long-range reconnaissance

4. Staffel	Villacoublay	Ju 88, Do 17	7

VIII Fliegerkorps, Deauville, Generalmajor Freiherr von Richthofen

Stukageschwader 1, Major Hagen: dive bombers

Stabschwarm	Angers	Do 17, Ju 87	3
I. Gruppe	Angers	Ju 87	27
III. Gruppe	Angers	Ju 87	26

Stukageschwader 2, Major Dinort: dive bombers

Stabschwarm	St Malo	Do 17, Ju 87	7
I. Gruppe	St Malo	Ju 87	29
II. Gruppe	Lannion	Ju 87	33

Stukageschwader 3, Hauptmann Sigel: dive bombers

I. Gruppe	Caen	Ju 87	24

Stukageschwader 77,[10] Major Graf von Schönborn: dive bombers

Stabschwarm	Caen	Do 17, Ju 87	4
I. Gruppe	Caen	Ju 87	33
II. Gruppe	Caen	Ju 87	25
III. Gruppe	Caen	Ju 87	37

Lehrgeschwader 1,[11] Hauptmann Liensberger: heavy fighters

V. Gruppe	Caen	Bf 110	29

Lehrgeschwader 2, long-range reconnaissance

7. Staffel	Böblingen	Do 17	9

Aufklärungsgruppe 11, long-range reconnaissance

2. Staffel	Bernay	Do 17, Bf 110	6

Aufklärungsgruppe 123, long-range reconnaissance

2. Staffel	Paris	Do 17	4

Jagdfliegerführer 3, Deauville, Oberst Junck: fighters

Jagdgeschwader 2,[12] Major von Bülow/Schellmann/Wick: fighters

Stabschwarm	Evreux/Beaumont-le-Roger	Bf 109	3
I. Gruppe	Beaumont-le-Roger	Bf 109	32
II. Gruppe	Beaumont-le-Roger	Bf 109	28
III. Gruppe	Le Havre	Bf 109	28

Jagdgeschwader 27, [13] Oberstleutnant Ibel: fighters

Stabschwarm	Cherbourg-West	Bf 109	4
I. Gruppe	Plumetot	Bf 109	32
II. Gruppe	Crépon	Bf 109	32
III. Gruppe	Carquebut	Bf 109	32

Jagdgeschwader 53, [14] Major von Cramon-Taubadel: fighters

Stabschwarm	Cherbourg	Bf 109	6
I. Gruppe	Rennes/Guernsey	Bf 109	37
II. Gruppe	Dinan/Guernsey	Bf 109	34
III. Gruppe	Brest	Bf 109	35

Zerstörergeschwader 2,[15] Oberstleutnant Vollbracht: heavy fighters

Stabschwarm	Toussus-le-Noble	Bf 110	3
I. Gruppe	Caen-Carpiquet	Bf 110	35
II. Gruppe	Guyancourt	Bf 110	34

Zerstörergeschwader 76, Laval, Major Grabmann: heavy fighters

| Stabschwarm | Laval | Bf 110 | 0 |
| III. Gruppe | Laval[16] | Bf 110 | 11 |

LUFTFLOTTE 5, Stavanger, Norway, Generaloberst Hans-Jürgen Stumpff

X Fliegerkorps, Stavanger, Generalleutnant Geisler

Kampfgeschwader 26, [17] Oberstleutnant Fuchs: bombers

Stabschwarm	Stavanger	He 111	6
I. Gruppe	Stavanger	He 111	29
III. Gruppe	Stavanger	He 111	26

Kampfgeschwader 30, [18] Denmark, Oberstleutnant Loebel: bombers

Stabschwarm	Aalborg	Ju 88	1
I. Gruppe	Aalborg	Ju 88	34
III. Gruppe	Aalborg	Ju 88	27

Jagdgeschwader 77, [19] Hauptmann Hentschel: fighters

| II. Gruppe | Stavanger, Trondheim | Bf 109 | 37 |

Zerstörergeschwader 76, [20] Hauptmann Restemeyer

| I. Gruppe | Stavanger | Bf 110 | 32 |

Küstenfliegergruppe 506, Major Eisenbeck: maritime patrol

1. Staffel	Stavanger	He 115	6
2. Staffel	Trondheim, Tromsö	He 115	5
3. Staffel	List	He 115	6

Aufklärungsgruppe 22, Oberstleutnant Thomas: long-range reconnaissance

| 2. Staffel | Stavanger | Do 17 | 5 |
| 3. Staffel | Stavanger | Do 17 | 4 |

Aufklärungsgruppe 120, Major Schub: long-range reconnaissance

| 1. Staffel | Stavanger | He 111, Ju 88 | 3 |

Aufklärungsgruppe 121, Hauptmann Klinkicht: long-range reconnaissance

| 1. Staffel | Stavanger | He 111, Ju 88 | 6 |

Aufklärungsgruppe Ob. d. L.: long-range reconnaissance

| 3. Staffel | Stavanger | Do 215, He 111, Bf 110 | 7 |

Wettererkundungskette X Fl. Korps, Reg. Rat Dr Müller: weather reconnaissaince

| | Stavanger | He 111 | 2 |

OBERBEFEHLSHABER DER LUFTWAFFE, Berlin, Reichsmarschall
Hermann Göring

Aufklärungsgruppe Ob. d. L., Oberstleutnant Rowehl: long-range
reconnaissance

1. Staffel	Various	Ju 86P, Ju 88, He 111, Bf 110, B&V 142, Do 215, Do 217	20
2. Staffel	Various	Do 215, He 111	5

Wettererkundungsstaffeln Ob. d. L.: weather reconnaissaince

1. Staffel	Oldenburg	Do17/He 111	5
2. Staffel	Brest	He 111	2

SEEFLIEGERVERBÄNDE, Berlin, Generalmajor Ritter

Küstenfliegergruppe 406, Major Stockmann: maritime patrol

3./406	Hörnum	Do 18	10
2./106	Rantum	Do 18	6
2./906	Hörnum	Do 18	8

Küstenfliegergruppe 706, Oberstleutnant Lessing: maritime patrol

1./406	Stavanger	Do 18	8
2./406	Stavanger	Do 18	7

Küstenfliegergruppe 606, Major Hahn: maritime patrol

1./606	Brest	Do 17	11
2./606	Brest	Do 17	11
3./606	Brest	Do 17	10

Küstenfliegergruppe 106, Major Emonds: maritime patrol

1./106	Nordeney	He 115	12

TOTALS				
	Airfleet 2	Airfleet 3	Airfleet 5	OKL	Total
Bombers	485	380	123	0	988
Dive-bombers	58	253	0	0	311
Reconnaissance	26	46	27	32	131
Coastal	8	0	17	83	108
Fighters	568	303	37	0	908
Heavy fighters	130	101	32	0	263
Total	1275	1083	236	115	2709

FIGHTER COMMAND ORDER OF BATTLE, 1 JULY 1940[1]

11 Group, Uxbridge, Middlesex: Air Vice-Marshal Keith Park

	Squadron		Serviceable Aircraft	Pilots	
Sector A – Tangmere					
Tangmere	43	Hurricanes	13	18	S/L Lott[2]
Tangmere	145	Hurricanes	11	17	S/L Peel
Tangmere	601	Hurricanes	15	19	S/L Aitken[3]
Tangmere	F.I.U.	Blenheims	4	10	W/C Chamberlain
Sector B – Kenley					
Kenley	64	Spitfires	10	19	S/L Odbert[4]
Kenley	615	Hurricanes	12	21	S/L Kayll
Croydon	111	Hurricanes	12	17	S/L Thompson
Croydon	501	Hurricanes	10	18	S/L Hogan
Sector C – Biggin Hill					
Biggin Hill	32	Hurricanes	12	16	S/L Worrall[5]
Biggin Hill	79	Hurricanes	12	14	S/L Joslin[6]
Hawkinge	245[7]	Hurricanes	15	16	S/L Whitley
Gravesend	610	Spitfires	14	20	S/L A. T. Smith[8]
Manston	600	Blenheims	8	22	S/L de B. Clarke

Sector D – Hornchurch

Hornchurch	65	Spitfires	11	16	S/L Cooke[9]
Hornchurch	74	Spitfires	10	20	S/L White[10]
Rochford	54	Spitfires	12	18	S/L Leathart

Sector E – North Weald

North Weald	56	Hurricanes	16	20	S/L Manton[11]
North Weald	151	Hurricanes	14	20	S/L Donaldson[12]
Martlesham	85	Hurricanes	15	21	S/L Townsend[13]
Martlesham	25	Blenheims	6	22	S/L McEwan

Sector F – Debden

Debden	17	Hurricanes	14	19	S/L MacDougall[14]

Sector W – Filton[15]

Pembrey	92	Spitfires	11	19	S/L Sanders
Exeter	213	Hurricanes	14	20	S/L McGregor
St. Eval	234	Spitfires	9	21	S/L Barnett[16]

Sector Y – Middle Wallop[17]

Middle Wallop	238	Hurricanes	10	17	S/L Baines[18]
Middle Wallop	236	Blenheims	11	19	S/L Drew[19]

Sector Z – Northolt

Northolt	1	Hurricanes	10	18	S/L Pemberton
Northolt	609	Spitfires	15	18	S/L Darley
Northolt	604	Blenheims	10	21	S/L Anderson
Hendon	257	Hurricanes	13	17	S/L Bayne[20]

12 Group, Watnall, Nottingham: Air Vice-Marshal Trafford Leigh-Mallory

Sector G – Duxford

Fowlmere	19	Spitfires	9	25	S/L Pinkham

Sector J – Coltishall

Coltishall	242	Hurricanes	11	25	S/L Bader
Coltishall	66	Spitfires	12	26	S/L Leigh

Sector K – Wittering

Wittering	229	Hurricanes	14	20	S/L Maguire
Wittering	266	Spitfires	8	21	S/L Hunnard[21]
Colly Weston	23	Blenheims	10	20	S/L Bicknell[22]

Sector L – Digby

Digby	46	Hurricanes	15	17	S/L MacLachlan
Digby	611	Spitfires	3	21	S/L McComb
Digby	29	Blenheims	10	15	F/Lt Adams[23]

Sector M – Kirton-in-Lindsay

Kirton-in-Lindsay	222	Spitfires	14	16	S/L Hill
Kirton-in-Lindsay	264	Defiants	12	21	S/L Hunter[24]

Church Fenton

Church Fenton	73	Hurricanes	8	22	S/L More[25]
Church Fenton	87	Hurricanes	14	23	S/L Dewar[26]
Church Fenton	616	Spitfires	11	19	S/L Marcus Robinson
Leconfield	249	Hurricanes	10	23	S/L Grandy

13 Group, Newcastle, Northumberland: Air Vice-Marshal Richard Saul

Catterick

Catterick	41	Spitfires	11	21	S/L Hood
Catterick	219	Blenheims	10	19	F/Lt Little

Usworth

Usworth	607	Hurricanes	10	17	S/L Vick
Acklington	72	Spitfires	12	19	S/L Lees[27]
Acklington	152	Spitfires	8	25	S/L Devitt

Turnhouse

Turnhouse	253	Hurricanes	13	19	S/L Gleave[28]
Turnhouse	603	Spitfires	10	19	S/L Denholm
Turnhouse	141	Defiants	14	20	S/L Richardson
Drem	605	Hurricanes	8	17	S/L Churchill
Drem	602	Spitfires	10	23	S/L Johnstone

Dyce

Grangemouth	263	Hurricanes[29]	3	7	S/L Eeles

Wick

Church Fenton	3	Hurricanes	12	18	S/L Godden
Church Fenton	504	Hurricanes	12	15	S/L Sample

Total			640	1103

Appendix III

FIGHTER COMMAND ORDER OF BATTLE, 1 SEPTEMBER 1940

10 Group, Box, Wiltshire: Air Vice-Marshal Sir Quintin Brand[1]

	Squadron		Serviceable Aircraft	Pilots	
Sector W – Exeter					
Exeter	213	Hurricanes	8	19	F/Lt Macdonald
Exeter	87	Hurricanes	9	18	S/L Mills
Sector Y – Middle Wallop					
Middle Wallop	234	Spitfires	12	19	S/L O'Brien[2]
Middle Wallop	609	Spitfires	11	20	S/L Darley[3]
Middle Wallop	604	Blenheims	11	20	S/L Anderson
Warmwell	152	Spitfires	12	19	S/L Devitt[4]
Boscombe Down	56	Hurricanes	9	18	S/L Pinfold
Pembrey					
Pembrey	92	Spitfires	12	19	S/L Sanders[5]
St Eval					
St. Eval	238	Hurricanes	11	20	S/L Fenton[6]
St. Eval	236	Blenheims	12	22	S/L Montague

11 Group, Uxbridge, Middlesex: Air Vice-Marshal Keith Park

Sector A – Tangmere

Tangmere	17	Hurricanes	12	19	S/L Miller
Tangmere	43	Hurricanes	10	19	F/Lt Hull[7]
Tangmere	607	Hurricanes	16	22	S/L Vick[8]
Westhampnett	602	Spitfires	12	19	S/L Johnstone

Sector B – Kenley

Kenley	253	Hurricanes	10	17	F/Lt Cambridge[9]
Kenley	616	Spitfires	12	20	S/L Robinson[10]
Croydon	85	Hurricanes	13	17	S/L Townsend[11]

Sector C – Biggin Hill

Biggin Hill	72	Spitfires	15	20	S/L Collins[12]
Biggin Hill	79	Hurricanes	10	17	S/L Heyworth
Gravesend	501	Hurricanes	12	22	S/L Hogan

Sector D – Hornchurch

Hornchurch	54	Spitfires	11	14	S/L Leathart[13]
Hornchurch	222	Spitfires	12	18	S/L Hill
Hornchurch	603	Spitfires	13	18	S/L Denholm
Hornchurch	600	Blenheims	9	23	S/L de B. Clarke

Sector E – North Weald

North Weald	249	Hurricanes	15	18	S/L Grandy[14]
North Weald	25	Blenheims	14	24	S/L Loxton[15]
Stapleford	46	Hurricanes	15	20	S/L MacLachlan[16]

Sector F – Debden

Debden	111	Hurricanes	11	19	S/L Thompson[17]
Debden	257	Hurricanes	12	20	S/L Harkness[18]
Debden	601	Hurricanes	12	22	S/L Sir A. Hope

Sector Z – Northolt

Northolt	1	Hurricanes	10	14	S/L Pemberton
Northolt	1 (Can)	Hurricanes	13	24	S/L McNab
Northolt	303 (Pol)	Hurricanes	13	24	S/L Kellett

12 Group, Watnall, Nottingham: Air Vice-Marshal Trafford Leigh-Mallory

Sector G – Duxford

Duxford	310 (Czech)	Hurricanes	10	24	S/L Blackwood
Fowlmere	19	Spitfires	9	25	S/L Pinkham[19]

Sector J – Coltishall

Coltishall	242	Hurricanes	11	21	S/L Bader
Coltishall	66	Spitfires	10	19	S/L Leigh[20]

Sector K – Wittering

Wittering	74	Spitfires	11	20	S/L Malan
Wittering	266	Spitfires	8	17	S/L Spencer[21]
Wittering	23	Blenheims	11	26	S/L Heycock
Bircham Newton	229	Hurricanes	12	18	S/L Maguire[22]

Sector L – Digby

Digby	151	Hurricanes	9	17	S/L West[23]
Digby	611	Spitfires	12	23	S/L McComb[24]
Wellingore	29	Blenheims	10	23	S/L Widdows

Sector M – Kirton-in-Lindsay

Kirton-in-Lindsay	264	Defiants	8	18	S/L Garvin

Church Fenton

Church Fenton	73	Hurricanes	11	19	S/L Robinson[25]
Leconfield	302 (Pol)	Hurricanes	14	23	S/L Satchell
Leconfield	64	Spitfires	12	22	S/L MacDonell

13 Group, Newcastle, Northumberland: Air Vice-Marshal Richard Saul

Catterick

Catterick	41	Spitfires	14	20	S/L Hood[26]
Acklington	32	Hurricanes	8	15	S/L Crossley
Acklington	610	Spitfires	9	18	S/L Ellis
Leeming	219	Blenheims	10	19	F/Lt Little

Turnhouse

Turnhouse	141	Defiants	9	22	S/L Richardson[27]
Drem	605	Hurricanes	12	19	S/L Churchill[28]

Dyce

Dyce	145	Hurricanes	9	18	S/L Peel
Grangemouth	263	Hurricanes[29]	5	10	S/L Eeles

Wick

Wick	3	Hurricanes	15	22	S/L Godden[30]
Castletown	504	Hurricanes	14	21	S/L Sample
Total			648	1142	

Sources

The first scholarly work devoted to chronicling the events of the Battle of Britain as a whole which based its conclusions on the losses each side admitted to have suffered was *The Narrow Margin* by Derek Wood and Derek Dempster, first published in 1961. Actual daily losses were made available by the RAF, and German losses were taken from the returns prepared by the Luftwaffe Quartermaster General which had been captured after the war. These returns were not universally accepted at the time because of the enormous discrepancy between them and RAF claims. However, the purpose of the returns was to make up losses with replacement aircraft and crews, so it was in the interests of all involved to make them as accurate as possible. They played no role in propaganda. They showed the margin of victory in the air to have been far smaller than had previously been supposed. Hence the title of the book.

Further research into the events of the Battle of Britain could only begin with the release of RAF records kept secret until 1970 under the thirty-year rule. One excellent general account of 1940, *The Breaking Wave,* by the US Army Intelligence Officer Brigadier General Telford Taylor, based on captured German documents, appeared in 1967. The public's understanding of the Battle of Britain was largely based on biographies, autobiographies and personal reminiscences, and the accounts of events written by some who lived through it, like Alexander McKee or Americans like Drew Middleton and Herbert Agar who worked as journalists in London in 1940 and admired Britain's lone stand.

It was not until the appearance of Francis K. Mason's *Battle over Britain* in 1969 that accounts of the fighting were able to go into more detail than the summarised daily chronicle provided by Wood and Dempster, who in any case devoted about half of their book to an account of the pre-war background and the build-up. The bulk of Mason's text is a day-by-day account of the fighting followed by the details of each aircraft and crew casualty suffered by each side. Mason was given access to RAF records before their release to the Public Record Office and used a copy of the Luftwaffe records.

Mason's book remains invaluable, but it inevitably contains numerous inaccuracies. Though both attempted to be accurate, neither the German nor the British loss records are completely reliable, and some of Mason's inaccuracies of detail stem from his sources. Beyond this, however, he allows himself what he calls in his introduction 'a fair degree of extrapolated opinion' (p. 5), some of which has since been shown to be erroneous. For all that, *Battle over Britain* remains an important source for any serious student of these events and a remarkable achievement for its time.

Whilst valuable biographical accounts and irritating pot-boilers continued to appear throughout the 1970s, our understanding of the events was taken to a new level by two key publications. One was Alfred Price's *The Hardest Day*, published in 1979. This was the first full-length book to be devoted to the events of one twenty-four-hour period, Sunday 18 August. It contains carefully researched statistical data on the losses and is based not only on original records but also on extensive interviews with eye-witness survivors on both sides. The result is a new level of insight. Price followed up this success in 1990 with a sequel, *Battle of Britain Day*, which corrects many popular tales about the fabled 15 September.

The second key publication appeared just after *The Hardest Day* and set new standards of accuracy and detail as far as losses were concerned. This was *The Battle of Britain Then and Now*, edited by Winston Ramsey for After the Battle Publications. In After the Battle's customary style, it contains histories of the airfields with comparative photographs of the sites as they were in the late 1970s, and documents the discoveries of the then-burgeoning and sometimes controversial aviation archaeology movement. This consists of groups of amateur enthusiasts, most of whom are very knowledgeable, dedicated and serious, who locate and excavate the sites of crashes to recover remains for display in museums (for example, the one at the Kent Battle of Britain Museum at Hawkinge). It was when human remains were discovered in some of the wrecks that the MOD began to take an interest and these activities are now more strictly regulated than they were in the 1970s.

It also contains a full list of British aircrew casualties. Just after the war, an official Roll of Honour was compiled to commemorate the RAF casualties, but it was soon discovered to be incomplete. John Holloway, an RAF officer who retired in 1958, set out to put this to rights. He identified 2,946 pilots and aircrew and collected as many signatures from them as he could. *The Battle of Britain Then and Now* contains a list from Holloway's research of the 537 who died during the Battle.

However, the greatest value of *The Battle of Britain Then and Now* is in the 400 or so pages detailing all the aircraft and aircrew losses of both Fighter Command and the Luftwaffe compiled over many years by Peter Cornwell, who also supplied the data used by Price in *The Hardest Day* and *Battle of Britain Day*.

Cornwell began his work in the 1960s with the same basic sources as Mason, but spent years checking them through, often working with the aviation archaeology fraternity to verify individual cases. For example, he corrected

British errors by checking through airframe histories and corroborating casualty records from parish archives, and corrected German ones from other archive sources and interviews with survivors. *The Battle of Britain Then and Now* was first published in 1980, but has since appeared in five subsequent versions, each adding a bit more. Peter Cornwell kindly made available to me a list of corrections and additions he has compiled over the intervening twenty years, though these are relatively minor, a tribute to the thoroughness of his original efforts.

Peter Cornwell's tables are the main source of Fighter Command and Luftwaffe losses used in this book, but they have been supplemented by John Foreman's *Battle of Britain – The Forgotten Months* (Air Research, 1988) and *Fighter Command War Diaries*, Vols I and II, published in 1996 and 1998 respectively. These are arranged differently, and usefully give details of the claims made by each squadron. There is no full list of German claims, but claims made by Luftflotte 3 can be found in their operational records, of which I have obtained a complete set from the Bundesarchiv in Freiburg.

Neither Cornwell nor Foreman covers Bomber Command, and details of its losses have been drawn from W. R. Chorley's *RAF Bomber Command Losses of the Second World War, 1939–40* which appeared in 1992.

In more recent years other important work has been done illuminating particular aspects of the Battle. Of special note is the book by another amateur researcher, John Vasco, called *Bombsights over England*, published by Vasco's own press, JAC Publications, in 1990. This is the only available history of Erprobungsgruppe 210, which played a crucial role in the Battle. Based on extensive study of archives and interviews with veterans, it has been researched in painstaking detail, surpassing in accuracy anything written before about the subject. It was followed in 1995 by a history of the whole Bf 110 force in 1940 called *Zerstörer*, for which Vasco collaborated with Peter Cornwell. There have been other high-quality histories of particular units such as Chris Goss's *Brothers in Arms* (1994), which covers JG53 and 609 Squadron, and specialised series such as Osprey's *Aircraft of the Aces* provide further sources of accurate information based on modern research. Dilip Sarkar is another enthusiast who has shed light on specific issues. As well as numerous interviews with eye-witnesses, his books contain transcripts of original documents, which makes them particularly useful for those wanting to go deeper into the subject without making the trip to Kew themselves.

One further aspect of events that has been the object of careful and revealing study in the 1990s is the role played by Dowding, his relations with the Air Ministry and the various moves to get rid of him. The two most insightful works are *The Battle of Britain – New Perspectives*, published by a retired schoolmaster, John Ray, in 1994, and *Dowding and Headquarters Fighter Command* by Peter Flint, published in 1996. They come to similar conclusions.

Another recent book which offers new insights is *Spitfire on my Tail* by Peter Osborne and Ulrich Steinhilper (1990). Steinhilper, who flew with JG52 in 1940, is the only German fighter pilot apart from Adolf Galland and Theo Osterkamp to produce a full-length work covering his experiences of the Battle, and will now probably remain so.

For the rest, I have tried where possible to base my case on original archive material from the Public Record Office at Kew, the Imperial War Museum, the RAF Museum at Hendon and the Bundesarchiv-Militärarchiv at one of my old University towns, Freiburg.

Acknowledgements

I have not been assiduous in interviewing veterans, as so many have already made their views public in (auto)biographies, television interviews or interviews with historians which can be found among the literature. However, I would like to express my particular thanks to the ever-modest, ever-charming Bob Doe and the ever-iconoclastic, ever-indefatigable James Sanders, both of whom have provided me with delightful hours and marvellous stories, and both of whom read early versions of this text and saved me from some gross errors. I also benefitted from conversations with the late Wing Commander 'Laddie' Lucas, and Sebastian Cox of the RAF Air Historical Branch.

Cliff Kenyon has shed some light on the workings of a Sector Operations Room, and Chris Wren gave me an instructive private tour of Keith Park's 'bunker' at Uxbridge. Sally Hine of the BBC Sound Archive and Chris Mobbs of the National Sound Archive helped me to sort out the vexing case of Winston Churchill and Larry the Lamb, and Dr John Ackroyd of the Aerospace Engineering Division of the Manchester School of Engineering was extraordinarily indulgent of my nagging doubts about the turning circles of the Spitfire, Hurricane and Bf 109, finally laying them firmly to rest with a scholarly paper full of algebra from which I hope his students may continue to benefit in the years to come. My old friend and colleague Anthony Miles also rescued me from the brink of printing a falsehood with a neat piece of analysis about the performance of pre-war fighters and bombers.

Invaluable help on the factual content of the manuscript has been provided by John Vasco and Peter Cornwell, both of whom read an interim version, and further information about the Bf 109 was generously provided by Michael Payne. My thanks to Geoff Nutkins, who runs the delightful little Battle of Britain Museum at Shoreham in Kent, for putting us in touch and providing the details of some local events.

I would also like to express my gratitude to Atalanta Beaumont for arranging my flight in Spitfire ML407. I had to wait three years, but it was the ride of a lifetime.

Numerous friends and colleagues have also lent a hand in various ways, mostly by taking on the unenviable task of reading and commenting on early drafts of the text. They include Jill Black, David Brownell, Les Colquhoun, Alastair Dick, Patrick Forth, Anthony Miles, Neil Monnery, Perry Keenan, Ian Smith, Peter Truell, Neville Walton and Peter Williamson. Heather Farmbrough applied her journalistic skills to editing the unwieldy monster which originally formed Part I. Paul Beaver has been consistently encouraging and offered valuable advice, and John Deere gave me access to his father Alan's memorabilia. I would like to thank my agent David Grossman for his faith in this early monster and the persistence he showed which finally took us to Aurum Press. My editor, Graham Coster, has immeasurably improved what he got saddled with. Given all the help, the failings of the end product are all my fault.

Bibliography

This bibliography lists only works that have been cited at least once in a footnote. I have not listed original documents, but have included their sources, in the case of the PRO listing the main categories used.

A. PUBLISHED BOOKS AND ARTICLES

1. Military and Political Background

Atkinson, Max, *Our Masters' Voices*, Methuen 1984

Barnett, Corelli, *The Audit of War*, Papermac 1987

Barnett, Corelli, *The Lost Victory*, Macmillan 1995

Beevor, Anthony, *Stalingrad*, Viking 1998

Calder, Angus, *The Myth of the Blitz*, Pimlico 1992

Cannadine, David (ed.), *Blood, Toil, Tears and Sweat – Winston Churchill's Famous Speeches*, Cassell 1989

Cecil, Robert, *Hitler's Decision to Invade Russia 1941*, Davis-Poynter 1975

Churchill, Winston S., *The Second World War*, Vol. I, *The Gathering Storm*, Chartwell Edition, The Educational Book Company Ltd. 1949

Churchill, Winston S., *The Second World War*, Vol. II, *Their Finest Hour*, Chartwell Edition, The Educational Book Company Ltd. 1949

Churchill, Winston S., *Into Battle* (Speeches 1938–1940), compiled by Randoph Churchill, Cassell 1941

Churchill, Winston S., *The Unrelenting Struggle* (Speeches 1940–1941), compiled by Charles Eade, Cassell 1942

Collier, Basil, *The Defence of the United Kingdom*, Imperial War Museum 1957

Costello, John, *Ten Days That Saved the West*, Bantam Press 1991

Cox, Richard (ed.), *Operation Sealion*, Thornton Cox 1975

Dixon, Norman, *On the Psychology of Military Incompetence*, Jonathan Cape 1976

Eade, Charles, (ed.), *Secret Session Speeches by the Right Hon Winston S. Churchill*, Cassell 1946

Ellis, John, *The Sharp End*, Windrow & Green 1990

Fleming, Peter, *Operation Sealion*, Simon & Schuster 1957
Fukuyama, Francis, *The End of History and The Last Man*, Penguin 1992
Gelb, Norman, *Dunkirk – The Incredible Escape*, Michael Joseph 1990
Gilbert, Adrian, *Britain Invaded*, Random Century 1990
Handel, Michael I. (ed.), *Intelligence and Military Operations*, Frank Cass 1990
Hastings, Max, *Overlord*, Pan 1985
Hitler, Adolf, *Mein Kampf*, translated by Ralph Manheim, Pimlico 1992
Hubatsch, Walther (ed.), *Hitlers Weisungen für die Kriegführung 1939–1945*,
    Bernard & Graefe 1983
Irving, David, *Churchill's War*, Avon Books 1987
Keegan, John, *The Battle for History*, Hutchinson 1995
Kieser, Egbert, *Hitler on the Doorstep*, Arms & Armour Press 1997
Kissinger, Henry, *Diplomacy*, Simon & Schuster 1994
Knightley, Phillip, *The First Casualty*, Pan Books 1989
Lamb, Richard, *Churchill as War Leader*, Bloomsbury 1991
Liddell Hart, Basil, *History of the Second World War*, Cassell 1970
Liddell Hart, Basil, *The Other Side of the Hill*, Pan Books 1983
Livesey, Anthony (ed.), *Are We At War? – Letters to The Times 1939–45*, Times
    Books 1989
Lukacs, John, *The Duel*, Bodley Head 1990
Lukacs, John, *Five Days in London*, Yale Press 1999
Macksey, Kenneth, *The German Invasion of England, July 1940*, Greenhill Books
    1980
Overy, Richard, *Why the Allies Won*, Pimlico 1996
Overy, Richard, *Russia's War*, Penguin 1998
Pocock, Tom, *Nelson*, Pimlico 1994
Ponting, Clive, *1940 – Myth and Reality*, Hamish Hamilton 1990
Quarrie, Bruce, *Hitler – The Victory that Nearly Was*, David & Charles 1988
Roberts, Andrew, *Eminent Churchillians*, Phoenix 1995
Shirer, William L., *The Rise and Fall of the Third Reich*, Secker & Warburg
    1971
Shirer, William L., *The Nightmare Years*, Bantam Books 1985
Schom, Alan, *Trafalgar*, Penguin 1992
Taylor, A.J.P., *The War Lords*, Penguin 1978
Taylor, Telford, *The Breaking Wave*, Weidenfeld & Nicolson 1967
Thompson, Laurence, *1940 – Year of Legend, Year of History*, Collins 1966
Thompson, R.W., *Generalissimo Churchill*, Hodder & Stoughton 1973
Wells, H.G., *War in the Air*, Odhams 1908

2. Technical and Aviation Background

Aeroplane Monthly, IPC Magazines Ltd, August & September 1995
Balke, Ulf, *Der Luftkrieg in Europa – Die Operativen Einsätze des Kampf-
    geschwaders 2 im Zweiten Weltkrieg*, Teil 1, Bernard Graefe 1989

Bekker, Cajus, *Angriffshöhe 4000 – Kriegstagebuch der deutschen Luftwaffe*, Gerhard Stalling Verlag 1964

Bowyer, Chaz, *Spitfire*, Bison Books 1980

Bowyer, Chaz and van Ishoven, Armand, *Hurricane and Messerschmitt*, Ian Allan 1993

Brooks, Robin J., *Kent Airfields in the Second World War*, Countryside Books 1998

Burns, Michael G., *Bader – The Man and his Men*, Arms & Armour Press 1990

Caidin, Martin, *Me 109*, Purnell 1969

Caldwell, Donald, *JG26 – Top Guns of the Luftwaffe*, Airlife Publishing 1991

Caldwell, Donald, *The JG26 War Diary*, Grub Street 1996

Chorley, W. R., *Bomber Command Losses 1939–40*, Midland Counties Publications 1992

Corum, James S., *The Luftwaffe – Creating the Operational Air War 1918–1940*, University of Kansas Press 1997

Cossey, Bob, *Tigers – The Story of No. 74 Squadron RAF*, Arms & Armour Press 1992

Crossland, John, 'Britain's Air Defences and the Munich Crisis' in *History Today*, Vol. 38 (September 1988)

East, R. A. and Cheeseman, I. C., Mitchell Memorial Symposium, *Forty Years of the Spitfire*, Royal Aeronautical Society 1976

Faber, Harold (ed.), *Luftwaffe – An Analysis by Former Generals*, Sidgwick & Jackson 1979

Flint, Peter, *RAF Kenley*, Terence Dalton 1985

Foreman, John, *Fighter Command War Diaries*, Vol. I, September 1939 to September 1940, Airlife 1996

Foreman, John, *Fighter Command War Diaries*, Vol. II, September 1940 to December 1941, Airlife 1998

Franks, Norman, *The Greatest Air Battle*, Grub Street 1992

Garnett, David, *War in the Air*, Chatto & Windus 1941

Gretzyngier, Robert and Matusiak, Wojtek, *Polish Aces of World War II*, Osprey 1998

Hastings, Max, *Bomber Command*, Pan Macmillan 1993

Holmes, Tony, *Hurricane Aces 1939–41*, Osprey 1988

Hooton, E.R., *Phoenix Triumphant – The Rise and Rise of the Luftwaffe*, Arms & Armour Press 1994

James, John, *The Paladins*, Macdonald 1990

Johnson, Air Vice-Marshal J. E. 'Johnnie', *The Story of Air Fighting*, Arrow Books 1987

Jones, Ira 'Taffy', *Tiger Squadron*, W. H. Allen 1954

Kaiser Verlag, *Die Großen Luftschlachten des Zweiten Weltkriegs*

Kaplan, Philip, *Fighter Pilot – A History and a Celebration*, Aurum 1999

Killen, John, *The Luftwaffe*, Sphere Books 1967

Latham, Colin and Stobbs, Anne, *Radar – A Wartime Miracle*, Sutton Publishing 1996

Mason, Francis K., *The Hawker Hurricane I*, Profile Publications
Middlebrook, Martin and Everitt, Chris, *The Bomber Command War Diaries*, Midland Publishing 1985
Mitchell, Gordon, *R.J.Mitchell – Schooldays to Spitfire*, Clifford Frost 1997
Mondey, David, *British Aircraft of World War II*, Hamlyn 1994
Murray, Williamson, *Luftwaffe*, Allen & Unwin 1985
Neil, Wing Commander Tom, *From the Cockpit – Spitfire*, Ian Allan 1990
Ogley, Bob, *Biggin on the Bump*, Froglets Publications 1990
Onderwater, Hans, *Gentlemen in Blue – 600 Squadron*, Leo Cooper 1997
Overy, Richard, *The Air War 1939–45*, Papermac 1987
Peters, Thomas and Waterman, Robert, *In Search of Excellence*, Harper & Row 1982
Price, Alfred, *Heinkel He 177*, Profile Publications
Price, Alfred, and Ethell, Jeffrey L., *Target Berlin*, Arms & Armour Press 1981
Price, Alfred, *The Spitfire Story*, Arms & Armour Press 1982
Price, Alfred, and Ethell, Jeffrey L., *Air War South Atlantic*, Sidgwick & Jackson 1983
Price, Alfred, *Spitfire – A Complete Fighting History*, Ian Allen 1991
Price, Alfred, *Sky Battles!*, Arms & Armour Press 1993
Price, Alfred, *Spitfire Aces 1939–41*, Osprey 1996
Quill, Jeffrey, *Spitfire*, Arrow Books 1983
Ray, John, *The Night Blitz 1940–41*, Arms & Armour Press 1996
Rendell, Ivan, *Reaching for the Skies*, Orion Books 1988
Ritchie, Sebastian, *Industry and Air Power*, Frank Cass 1997
Russell, C. R., *Spitfire Postscript*, 1994
Scutts, Jerry, *Fighter Operations*, Patrick Stephens 1992
Sims, Edward H., *The Fighter Pilots*, Cassell 1967
Smith, J. Richard, *The Dornier Do 17 & 215*, Profile Publications
Smith, J. Richard, *The Junkers Ju 87A & B*, Profile Publications
Spick, Mike, *The Ace Factor*, Airlife 1988
Spick, Mike, *Luftwaffe Fighter Aces*, Greenhill Books 1996
Stockman, Rocky, *The History of RAF Manston*, RAF Manston 1986
Stuart, Major Oliver, *The Strategy and Tactics of Air Fighting*, Longmans 1925
Terraine, John, *The Right of the Line*, Hodder & Stoughton 1985
Völker, Karl-Heinz, *Dokumente und Dokumentarphotos zur Geschichte der deutschen Luftwaffe*, Stuttgart 1968
Wallace, Graham, *RAF Biggin Hill*, Putnam 1969
Wallace, G. F., *The Guns of the RAF 1939–45*, William Kimber 1972
Weal, John, *Bf 109D/E Aces 1939–45*, Osprey 1996
Weal, John, *Junkers Ju 87 – Stukageschwader 1937–41*, Osprey 1997
Weal, John, *Messerschmitt Bf 110 Zerstörer Aces of World War Two*, Osprey 1999
Wells, Mark K., *Courage and Air Warfare*, Frank Cass 1995
Windrow, Martin C., *The Heinkel He 111H*, Profile Publications
Windrow, Martin C., *The Junkers Ju 88A*, Profile Publications

Windrow, Martin C., *The Messerschmitt Bf 110*, Profile Publications
Zamoyski, Adam, *The Forgotten Few*, John Murray 1995

3. The Battle of Britain

Allen, Wing Commander H. R. 'Dizzy', *Who Won the Battle of Britain?*, Weidenfeld & Nicolson 1974
Barker, Ralph, *That Eternal Summer – Unknown Stories from the Battle of Britain*, Collins 1990
Blandford, Edmund, *Target England*, Airlife 1997
Bowyer, Michael J. F., *The Battle of Britain – 50 Years On*, Patrick Stephens 1990
Collier, Richard, *Eagle Day*, Dent 1966
Deighton, Len, *Fighter*, Grafton 1987
Flint, Peter, *Dowding and Headquarters Fighter Command*, Airlife 1996
Foreman, John, *Battle of Britain – The Forgotten Months*, Air Research 1988
Garnett, Graham (ed.), *Against All Odds*, RAFA./Rococco Group 1990
Gelb, Norman, *Scramble*, Pan 1986
Goss, Chris, *Brothers in Arms*, Crécy 1994
Haining, Peter, *Spitfire Summer*, W. H. Allen 1990
Hough, Richard and Richards, Denis, *The Battle of Britain – The Jubilee History*, Hodder & Stoughton 1990
Johnson, David Alan, *The Battle of Britain*, Combined Publishing 1998
Johnson, Air Vice-Marshal J. E. 'Johnnie', and Lucas, Wing Commander P. B. 'Laddie', *Glorious Summer*, Stanley Paul 1990
Jullian, Marcel, *The Battle of Britain*, Jonathan Cape 1967
Kaplan, Philip and Collier, Richard, *The Few*, Cassell 1989
Knight, Dennis, *Harvest of Messerschmitts – The Chronicle of a Village at War – 1940*, Wingham Press 1990
Mason, Francis K., *Battle over Britain*, Aston Publications 1990
McKee, Alexander, *Strike from the Sky*, Grafton Books 1990
Middleton, Drew, *The Sky Suspended*, Secker & Warburg 1960
Munson, Kenneth and Taylor, John W.R., *The Battle of Britain*, New English Library 1976
Price, Alfred, *The Hardest Day*, Arms & Armour Press 1988
Price, Alfred, *Battle of Britain Day*, Sidgwick & Jackson 1990
Probert, Henry and Cox, Sebastian (eds.), *The Battle Re-Thought*, Airlife 1991
Ramsey, Winston (ed.), *The Battle of Britain Then and Now*, Mk IV, After the Battle Publications 1987
Ray, John, *The Battle of Britain – New Perspectives*, Arms & Armour Press 1994
Robinson, Anthony, *RAF Fighter Squadrons in the Battle of Britain*, Arms & Armour Press 1987
Sarkar, Dilip, *Angriff Westland*, Ramrod Publications 1994
Sarkar, Dilip, *Bader's Duxford Fighters*, Ramrod Publications 1997

Townsend, Peter, *Duel of Eagles*, Weidenfeld & Nicolson 1970
Townshend Bickers, Richard, *The Battle of Britain*, Salamander Books 1990
Van Ishoven, Armand, *The Luftwaffe in the Battle of Britain*, Ian Allan 1980
Vasco, John, *Bombsights over England*, JAC Publications 1990
Vasco, John and Cornwell, Peter, *Zerstörer*, JAC Publications 1995
Von Eimannsberger, Ludwig, *Zerstörergruppe*, Schiffer 1998
Weber, Dr Theo, *Die Luftschlacht um England*, Flugwelt Verlag 1956
Willis, John, *Churchill's Few*, Michael Joseph 1985
Wood, Derek, with Dempster, Derek, *The Narrow Margin*, Tri-Service Press 1990
Wright, Robert, *Dowding and the Battle of Britain*, Macdonald 1979
Wynn, Kenneth G., *Men of the Battle of Britain*, 2nd edition, CCB Associates 1999
Young, Neil, *The Role of Bomber Command in the Battle of Britain*, Imperial War Museum Magazine

4. Biographies and Autobiographies

Bartley, Tony, *Smoke Trails in the Sky*, Crécy Publishing Ltd 1997
Brickhill, Paul, *Reach for the Sky*, Collins 1954
Bryant, Arthur, *The Turn of the Tide 1939–1943* (A Study Based on the Diaries and Autobiographical Notes of Field Marshal The Viscount Alanbrooke), Collins 1957
Charmley, John, *Churchill – The End of Glory*, Hodder & Stoughton 1993
Collier, Basil, *Leader of the Few*, Jarrolds 1957
Colville, John, *The Fringes of Power*, Vol. I, Hodder & Stoughton 1985
Deere, Air Commodore A.C., *Nine Lives*, Wingham Press 1991
Doe, Wing Commander Bob, *Bob Doe – Fighter Pilot*, Spellmount 1991
Douglas of Kirtleside, Lord and Wright, Robert, *Years of Command*, Collins 1966
Dundas, Hugh, *Flying Start*, Stanley Paul 1988
Forrester, Larry, *Fly For Your Life*, Muller 1956
Franks, Norman, *Sky Tiger*, Crécy Books 1994
Galland, Adolf, *The First and the Last*, Bantam 1978
Gilbert, Martin, *Finest Hour*, Minerva 1989
Hillary, Richard, *The Last Enemy*, Pan 1956
Irving, David, *The Rise and Fall of the Luftwaffe: The Life of Luftwaffe Marshal Erhard Milch*, Weidenfeld & Nicolson 1973
Irving, David, *Göring – A Biography*, Macmillan 1989
Johnson, Air Vice-Marshal J. E. 'Johnnie', *Wing Leader*, Chatto & Windus 1956
Johnstone, Air Vice-Marshal Sandy, *Spitfire into War*, Grafton Books 1988
Kent, Group Captain J. A., *One of the Few*, William Kimber 1971
Kesselring, Albert, *The Memoirs of Field Marshal Kesselring*, introduced by Kenneth Macksey, Greenhill Books 1988

Lewis, Cecil, *Sagittarius Rising*, Penguin 1977
Londonderry, Marquess of, *Wings of Destiny*, London 1943
Macksey, Kenneth, *Kesselring – The Making of the Luftwaffe*, B. T. Batsford 1978
Mason, Peter D., *Nicolson VC*, Geerings of Ashford 1991
Neil, Wing Commander Tom, *Gun Button to Fire*, William Kimber 1987
Newton Dunn, Bill, *Big Wing – The Biography of Air Chief Marshal Sir Trafford Leigh-Mallory*, Airlife 1992
Orange, Vincent, *Sir Keith Park*, Methuen 1984
Osterkamp, Theo, *Durch Höhen und Tiefen jagt ein Herz*, Vohwinkel 1952
Page, Geoffrey, *Tale of a Guinea Pig*, Wingham Press 1981
Pile, General Sir Frederick, *Ack-Ack*, Harrap 1949
Pimlott, Ben (ed.), *The Second World War Diary of Hugh Dalton, 1940–45*, Cape 1986
Preston, Kath, *Inn of the Few*, Spellmount 1993
Stahl, Peter, *The Diving Eagle – A Ju 88 Pilot's War Diary*, William Kimber 1984
Steinhilper, Ulrich and Osborne, Peter, *Spitfire On My Tail*, Independent Books 1990
Tedder, Lord, *With Prejudice*, Cassell 1966
Toliver, Colonel Raymond, and Constable, Trevor J., *Fighter General – The Life of Adolf Galland*, AmPress 1990
Townsend, Peter, *Time and Chance*, Methuen 1978
Townshend Bickers, Richard, *Ginger Lacey – Fighter Pilot*, Blandford Press 1988

B. NEWSPAPERS

Battle of Britain, Daily Telegraph Editorial Supplement, June 1990
Guardian Weekly, 26th August 1990

C. UNPUBLISHED SOURCES

Bundesarchiv-Militärarchiv, RL/2, RL/7
Imperial War Museum Department of Documents:
    Greiner, Helmuth, OKW Tagebuch, EDS AL 1054/1
    Greiner, Helmuth, 'Das Unternehmen Seelöwe', EDS AL 1048/1
    Halder, Generalleutnant Fritz, Tagebuch, Bd IV/ii (EDS Series)
    Milch Papers
    OKW M.1.14 (various)
Manchester School of Engineering, Manchester University, Aerospace Division, Aerospace Internal Report No. 9701, 'A Comparison of Turning Radii for Four Battle of Britain Fighter Aircraft' by J. A. D. Ackroyd and P. J. Lamont
Public Record Office, Kew:
    AIR 2 – Correspondence
    AIR 6 – Air Council

AIR 8 – Chief of the Air Staff Papers
AIR 16 – Fighter Command
AIR 19 – Private Office Papers
AIR 20 – Unregistered Papers
AIR 24 – Operations Record Books, Commands
AIR 25 – Operations Record Books, Groups
AIR 27 – Operations Record Books, Squadrons
AIR 28 – Operations Record Books, Stations
AIR 41 – Air Historical Branch: Narratives and Monographs
RAF Museum, Hendon:
Dowding Papers
Evill Papers
RAF Air Historical Branch Narrative
Saundby Papers
Sorley Papers

D. TV AND VIDEO PRODUCTIONS

Campbell-Jones, Suzanne, *Battle for Britain*, TVS Productions for ITV, 1990
Charlton, Lindsay, *Divided We Stand*, Laurel Productions for Thames Television 1990
Creation Company Films Ltd, *Pilot's Eye – The Spitfire*, 1993
Gilbert, Martin, *Churchill*, BBC-TV Productions 1992
Isaacs, Jeremy, *The World at War*, Vol. II, Thames Television 1980
Johnson, Brian, *Spitfire*, Thorn EMI Video Ltd., 1983
Johnson, Brian, *Spitfire*, Uden Associates production for Channel 4's *Equinox* 1990
Willis, John, *Churchill's Few*, Yorkshire Television 1985

Notes

INTRODUCTION

1. Mythological accounts continue to appear, such as *The Battle of Britain* by John Frayn Turner, Airlife 1998, which turns one archetypal hero, Douglas Bader, into its central character.

2. This fixed epithet, which literary scholars call a '*topos*' can be found in the most serious and scholarly works on the Battle some fifty years on. See, for example, Francis K. Mason, *Battle over Britain*, Aston Publications 1990, p. 222 or Richard Hough and Denis Richards, *The Battle of Britain – The Jubilee History*, Hodder & Stoughton 1990, p. 136.

1. THE REASON WHY

1. Amery Diary II, 8 May 1940, p. 611, quoted in Charmley, *Churchill – The End of Glory*, Hodder & Stoughton 1993, p. 393.

2. Charmley, pp. 394–5.

3. John Colville, *The Fringes of Power*, Vol. I, Hodder & Stoughton 1985, p. 141.

4. Churchill, *The Second World War*, Vol. I, pp. 522–3.

5. Costello, op. cit., p. 51.

6. Fire warden Les Linggard, quoted in Norman Gelb, *Scramble*, Pan Books 1986, p. 68.

7. *The Second World War Diary of Hugh Dalton, 1940–45*, ed. Ben Pimlott 1986, 28 May 1940, p. 26.

8. Colville, op. cit., p. 142.

9. Angus Calder, *The Myth of the Blitz*, Pimlico 1992, p. 77. Calder gives an account of the mixture of arguments, honest soul-searching and specious rationalisations to which the left subjected itself after September 1939 (pp. 77–89). It should be remembered that they had not only to face up to the Nazi-Soviet pact, but the Soviet Union's sharing in the spoils of the German conquest of Poland. The Katyn massacre was only one of many unpleasant truths unknown at the time.

10. As reported in *Divided We Stand* by Lindsay Charlton, Laurel Productions for Thames Television, 1990. For a full account of the Right Club's origins, activities and what is currently known about its membership see Costello. op. cit., pp. 113 ff., 157–162 and Appendix 2.

11. Russell changed his mind in June, and was followed by other pacifists. See Laurence Thompson, *1940 – Year of Legend, Year of History*, Collins 1966, p. 133.

12. Charmley, p. 399.

13. See Basil Collier, *The Defence of the United Kingdom*, Imperial War Museum 1957, p. 123. The renaming of the LDV was done at Churchill's instigation on 27 June, as he found the administrative tone behind LDV uninspiring and had hankered after the name 'Home Guard' since October 1939 (see Churchill, *History of the Second World War*, Vol. II, pp. 129–30). It is typical of his attention to details, particularly those which could have an impact on morale.

14. See Arthur Bryant's account of the war from the diaries of Lord Alanbrooke, *The Turn of the Tide, 1939–43*, Collins 1957, p. 188.

15. Charmley, p. 403.

16. ibid., pp. 403–4.

17. ibid., p. 404.

18. ibid.

19. Norman Gelb, *Dunkirk*, Michael Joseph 1990 p.116.

20. This account is based on Charmley, pp. 405–6, which is in turn based heavily on Dalton's diary and book *The Fateful Years*. Charmley describes this meeting as 'perhaps the most crucial of 1940'.

21. ibid. p. 406.

22. Charmley, p. 405.

23. *Divided We Stand*, Thames Television 1990.

24. Thompson, op. cit., p. 143.

25. Costello, op. cit., pp. 397–8.

26. ibid. p. 419.

27. For an account of the tradition in English thought of looking towards the United States as an English-speaking ally rather than a rival see Calder *The Myth of the Blitz*, p. 52–3.

28. Its actual progress has been charted by Francis Fukuyama in *The End of History and The Last Man*, Penguin 1992, passim, but esp. pp. 39–51.

29. See Henry Kissinger, *Diplomacy*, Simon & Schuster 1994, pp. 17–28.

30. Address to the House of Commons, 13 May 1940.

31. Charmley, p. 407.

32. Thompson, op. cit., p. 172.

33. A view very similar to this one is expounded by R.W. Thompson in his book *Generalissimo Churchill*, Hodder & Stoughton, 1973. Thompson is himself a romantic English writer of the old school, but despite some inaccuracies, his account of Churchill's disastrous interference with his Generals' conduct of the war is borne out by many eye-witness accounts of those involved. He concentrates on the period up to 1942, and in particular the North African campaign.

34. John Keegan, for example, expounds the political case for involvement in Greece in his work *The Battle for History*, Hutchinson, 1995, pp. 18–21.

35. The psychologist Anthony Storr has remarked that Churchill was able simply to give reign to his romantic fantasy life so that people became heroes (*Churchill* (Part 2), BBC-TV 1992).

36. Churchill, speech to the House of Commons, 13 May 1940 in *Blood, Toil, Tears and Sweat – Winston Churchill's Famous Speeches*, ed. David Cannadine, Cassell 1989, p. 149. The phrase is a conscious echo of Garibaldi's words to the Italian patriots of the Risorgimento: 'I offer you hunger, thirst, forced marches, battle and death. Anyone who loves his country, follow me.'

37. ibid.

38. Cannadine, ibid. For such a Romantic as Churchill, this is an unexpected echo of the Enlightenment.

39. Max Atkinson identifies the 'list of three' along with 'unfavourable references to them and favourable references to us' and the use of 'contrastive pairs' as the three most commonly used devices used by politicians to gain audience approval. See *Our Masters' Voices*, Methuen, 1984, esp. pp. 57–73.

40. Cannadine, ibid.

41. Cannadine, p. 147.

42. Colville, p. 158.

43. Cannadine, p. 152.

44. Cannadine, ibid. p. 154. The passage is a shortened version of I Maccabees, Chapter 3, verses 58–60.

45. Gelb, *Dunkirk*, p. 171.

46. ibid., p. 218.

47. Cannadine ed., p. 157.

48. ibid., p. 160. Churchill here repeats the words used by the Liberal leader, Sir Archibald Sinclair, an old friend of Churchill's whom he made Secretary of State for Air. In the Norway debate of 7 May, Sinclair had said: 'The right hon. Gentleman *(Chamberlain)* today told us that south of Trondheim and north of Trondheim we had succeeded, by a masterly policy, in evacuation with no losses. Wars are

not won on masterly evacuations.' (Gilbert, *Finest Hour*, p. 291).

49. Cannadine, p. 160.

50. On 8 July, Air Vice-Marshal Keith Park, the Commander of 11 Group, Fighter Command, who ran the air fighting over Dunkirk, submitted a report on the air fighting in France in which he stated that 603 German aircraft had been shot down for the loss of 120 pilots, giving a 'highly satisfactory' ratio of five to one (PRO, AIR 2/7281, 'No. 11 Group Report – Operations over France, May-June 1940', p. 5). In fact British aircraft losses over Dunkirk were 177, and German losses 240. Pilot losses on one side cannot be compared with aircraft losses on the other.

51. Cannadine, p. 161.

52. ibid., pp. 160–1. Churchill's examples can be found in Park's report (AIR 2/7281, p. 6) which was a serious document prepared for the Air Ministry, and contains a critical examination of the lessons of the Dunkirk fighting on the part of a man who had a very real interest in ascertaining the truth.

53. ibid., p. 161.

54. The idea was first articulated by H.G.Wells, whose work Churchill read avidly. In *The War in the Air*, which was written in 1907, Wells describes the enforced passivity of the civilians subjected to aerial bombardment and comments: 'The balance of military efficiency was shifting back from the many to the few, from the common to the specialised' (Chapter VI, §2).

55. ibid., p. 162.

56. ibid., pp. 164–5.

57. ibid., p. 165. Thematically, this passage bears a strong resemblance to what Churchill had said to the French Prime Minister, Reynaud, General Weygand and Admiral Darlan in France on 31 May, and to what he later told them on 11 June. See Gilbert, *Finest Hour*, pp. 444 & 509. He was subsequently asked by Lord Lothian, the British Ambassador in Washington, exactly what he had

meant by his reference to the New World. He replied that the words had been addressed primarily to Germany and Italy. He continued by explaining that if Britain were to break, a pro-German government would get easier terms by surrendering the fleet, 'thus making Germany and Japan masters of the New World'. By remaining on the side-lines, the US ran 'the terrible risk that their sea-power will be completely over-matched' (ibid., p. 486).

58. Cannadine ed., p. 155.

59. ibid.

60. Charmley, p. 411.

61. The idea has gained currency that the speech was broadcast by the actor Norman Shelley, who played Larry the Lamb, Dennis the Dachshund, Winnie the Pooh and others on the BBC's Children's Hour during the 1930s. (See Clive Ponting, *1940: Myth and Reality*, Hamish Hamilton 1990, p.158, Charmley, op. cit., p. 411 and David Irving, *Churchill's War*, Avon Books 1987, p. 313.) This issue generated some heat in the letters pages of the *Guardian* in 1991. In fact the speech was not broadcast that evening at all. In a Radio 2 interview on 4 October 1978, shortly before he died, Shelley told the story that the British Council had approached Churchill, asking him to record the speech for a broadcast in the US. Churchill pointed out that he had rather a lot on his plate at the time, but if they could find an actor to do it, that was fine, subject to his approval of the results. The British Council found Shelley, Churchill heard the recording and was much amused, and so it – presumably – passed across the Atlantic. There is no record of what happened to it, though it is possible, but unproven, that it is still in currency. Churchill recorded several of his most famous speeches for Decca in Chartwell after the war, and these are currently available on the Argo label. My thanks are due to Sally Hine of the BBC Sound Archive and Chris

Mobbs of the National Sound Archive for their help in sorting this out.

62. Charmley, pp. 411–2.
63. ibid., p. 412.
64. Charmley, p. 417.
65. Hansard.
66. Cannadine, p. 177.
67. ibid., pp. 177–8.
68. The phrase 'broad sunlit uplands' is another echo of a phrase from H.G. Wells – 'the uplands of the future'. It occurs in *The Discovery of the Future*. See Calder, *The Myth of the Blitz*, p. 181.
69. In a minute about air raids of 26 June, Churchill suggested that they should be treated 'as if they were no more than thunderstorms' (Gilbert, *Finest Hour*, p. 603). In a letter to Chamberlain on 24 September, he wrote: 'Let us go on together through the storm' (ibid., p. 812).
70. At 1125 on the morning of 21 October 1805, as his fleet was closing with the enemy, Nelson hoisted the signal 'England expects that every man will do his duty'. Given the formal and standardised nature of the navy's relatively new signalling procedures, it was very complicated, though simpler than the signal Nelson had originally wanted to send (see Alan Schom, *Trafalgar*, Penguin 1992, p. 320). The bulk of his sailors set up a great cheer, but Nelson's second in command, Collingwood, irritably wondered what all the fuss was about. 'What is Nelson signalling about?' he is reported as saying. 'We all know what we have to do.' (see Tom Pocock, *Nelson*, Pimlico 1994, p. 325.) There were some who echoed those sentiments in reaction to Churchill in 1940.
71. Colville, op. cit., p. 192.
72. John Lukacs, *The Duel*, Bodley Head 1990, p. 150.
73. Charmley, pp. 418–9.
74. Lukacs, *The Duel*, p. 147.
75. Colville, op. cit., p. 193. Churchill did indeed imbibe prodigious qualities of alcohol, a common theme of Nazi propaganda. However, there are few if any reports of his ever being drunk. It seems that, as he once remarked, he got more out of drink than it took out of him.
76. Lukacs, *The Duel*, p. 184.
77. Ibid., p. 148.
78. Charmley, op. cit., p. 418.
79. Richard Lamb, *Churchill as War Leader*, Bloomsbury 1991, p. 74 and Laurence Thompson, op. cit., p. 140.

2. THE THREAT

1. The author's own original suggestion was: 'A Four and a Half Year Struggle Against Lies, Stupidity and Cowardice: A Reckoning with the Destroyers of the Nazi Party Movement', which, whilst giving a better flavour of the contents of the book, shows a limited flair for marketing.
2. Churchill, *The Second World War*, Vol. I, 'The Gathering Storm', Chartwell Edition 1954, p. 9.
3. Hitler, *Mein Kampf*, Verlag Franz Eher Nachfolger GmbH, München 1933, p. 21.
4. Ibid., p. 82.
5. Ibid., p. 159, author's translation.
6. Ibid., p. 158, author's translation.
7. Ibid., p. 700, author's translation. On the preceding see pp. 691–700.
8. Ibid., pp. 712–6.
9. Ibid., pp. 720–5 & 755–8.
10. Ibid., pp. 742 & 749–752.
11. Popular anti-Semitism was endemic in the western Soviet Union and Krushchev described Stalin as 'a dyed-in-the-wool anti-Semite'. See Richard Overy, *Russia's War*, Penguin 1998, pp. 135ff.
12. Even such an ardent admirer as Milch confessed to having managed to get through only the first twenty pages (Irving, *The Rise and Fall of the Luftwaffe*, Weidenfeld & Nicolson 1973, p. 39). He was not alone. See William L Shirer, *The Rise and Fall of the Third Reich*, Secker and Warburg 1971, pp. 80–81. Most of the OKW generals such as Brauchitsch, Halder or Blumentritt who heard Hitler discourse about England were quite taken aback by his admiring tones,

but his words on these occasions echo quite precisely just what he had written in *Mein Kampf*. (See, for example the passages quoted by Liddell Hart, *History of the Second World War*, Cassell 1970, p. 83, or Telford Taylor, *The Breaking Wave*, Weidenfeld & Nicolson 1967, pp. 64–5.) Their ignorance of their Leader's thinking and intentions is striking. One wonders whether the generals' plotting to remove Hitler might not have reached maturity earlier if some of them had bothered to read his book.

13. *Mein Kampf*, pp. 167–8, author's translation.
14. See David Irving, *Göring – A Biography*, Macmillan 1989, pp. 155, 175, 184, 193, 217–8, 258–68 & 275–8.
15. Churchill, 'The Gathering Storm', pp. 172–3.
16. See William Shirer, *The Rise and Fall of the Third Reich*, Secker & Warburg 1959, pp. 545–622, especially p. 618.
17. Liddell Hart, *History of the Second World War*, Cassell 1970, pp. 72–84. For further details and discussion of this see Costello, op. cit., pp. 173–183, and on further peace moves pp. 183–196.
18. In his account of an army conference with von Brauchitsch on 11 July, Halder mentions an intelligence report about 'dissonances' between Churchill and Halifax, concluding that Churchill had succeeded in maintaining a policy of 'war to the end' (Halder Tagebuch, Bd. IV/ii, IWM Dept. of Documents, EDS Series, Blatt 101).
19. William L. Shirer, *The Rise and Fall of the Third Reich*, Secker & Warburg 1971, p. 759.
20. Ibid., pp. 760–1.
21. Karl-Heinz Völker, *Dokumente und Dokumentarfotos zur Geschichte der deutschen Luftwaffe*, Stuttgart 1968, pp. 460–466.
22. Alfred Price, 'Could Sealion have Succeeded?' in *The Battle of Britain*, ed. Munson & Taylor, New English Library 1976, p. 100.

23. Wood & Dempster, *The Narrow Margin*, Tri-Service Press 1990, p. 156.
24. Kesselring *Memoirs*, Greenhill Books 1988, pp. 66–7 and Macksey *Kesselring*, B T Batsford 1978, p. 74.
25. Kesselring, op. cit., p. 62.
26. See Costello, op. cit., pp.183–196, 344–8 and 375–8, and Shirer, op. cit., pp. 785–792.
27. John Lukacs, *The Duel*, Bodley Head 1990 pp. 187–8.
28. It became known as the 'Niegelungenlied', i.e. the 'never succeeded song', a pun on 'Nibelungenlied'.

3. THE ASSAILANT

1. Quoted in Caidin, *Me 109*, Purnell 1969, p. 9.
2. Ibid., pp. 56–61.
3. See John Killen, *The Luftwaffe*, Sphere Books, 1967, pp. 72–3 and Irving, *The Rise and Fall of the Luftwaffe*, p. 46.
4. Quoted by Costello, op. cit., p. 214.
5. Ibid., p. 379.
6. Ibid., pp. 203–4.
7. On all of the following see Mason, pp. 42 ff. and Williamson Murray, *Luftwaffe*, Allen & Unwin 1985, pp. 15ff.
8. See David Irving, *The Rise and Fall of the Luftwaffe*, Weidenfeld & Nicolson 1973, pp. 16–22.
9. Ibid., pp. 4–10 & 23–5.
10. David Irving, *Göring, A Biography*, Macmillan 1989, p. 83.
11. Ibid., pp. 42–3.
12. See Murray, op. cit., p. 32.
13. Ibid., p. 24.
14. See R.J. Overy, *The Air War 1939–45*, Papermac 1987, pp. 129–30 & 159.
15. Irving, *The Rise and Fall of the Luftwaffe*, p. 55.
16. Cf. *Luftwaffe – An Analysis by Former Generals*, edited by Harold Faber, Sidgwick & Jackson 1979, p. 9.
17. For figures on Germany see Murray, op. cit., p. 26 and for Britain see Corelli Barnett, *Audit of War*, Papermac 1987, p. 145.
18. In particular the lack of good engines. See James S. Corum, *The Luftwaffe*, University Press of Kansas 1997, pp. 170–3.

19. Murray, op. cit., pp. 38–9.
20. Ibid., p. 39.
21. See Wood & Dempster, pp. 19–25.
22. See Faber (ed.), pp. 170–177.
23. Steinhilper reports how his unit was always constrained through lack of aircraft even before the war broke out. See *Spitfire On My Tail*, Independent Books 1990, pp. 102 & 115.
24. Overy, op. cit., pp. 141–2.
25. Ibid., p. 143.
26. Ibid., pp. 186–7.
27. Caldwell, *JG 26*, Airlife Publishing 1991, p. 44.
28. See Steinhilper, op.cit., pp. 126–9.
29. Ibid., pp. 197–8.
30. See John Weal, *Junkers Ju 87*, Osprey 1997, p. 18.
31. Steinhilper, op. cit., p. 225.
32. E. R. Hooton, *Phoenix Triumphant*, Arms & Armour Press 1994, pp. 110–111.
33. Ibid., pp. 157–8, and Steinhilper, op. cit., p. 101.
34. Ibid., p. 151.
35. See Peter Stahl, *The Diving Eagle*, William Kimber 1984, pp. 38–9 for a description of such a crash and some reflections on the causes of the high accident rate.
36. Hooton, p. 159.
37. Steinhilper, op. cit., pp. 88–9.
38. Ibid., pp. 127, 130 & 197.
39. Hooton, op. cit., p. 166.
40. Overy, op. cit., p. 10.
41. Wood & Dempster, p. 21.
42. Murray, op. cit., p. 34.
43. Irving, *The Rise and Fall of the Luftwaffe*, pp. 38–9.
44. See Overy, op. cit., pp. 179–80.
45. J. Richard Smith, *The Dornier Do 17 & 215*, Profile publications, pp. 3–4.
46. Ibid., p.6.
47. Martin C. Windrow, *The Heinkel He 111H*, Profile Publications, pp. 3–5 & 12.
48. Faber (ed.), p. 149.
49. The first Junkers prototype was ironically powered by a Rolls-Royce Kestrel engine. It crashed due to tail flutter and a new square tail was fitted to the second prototype which had a Junkers Jumo engine. This was the machine which won. See J. Richard Smith, *The Junkers Ju 87A & B*, Profile Publications, p. 3.
50. Martin C. Windrow, *The Junkers Ju 88A*, Profile Publications, p. 3. One of the machine's two designers was an American, Al Gassner, who was spending some time working in Europe.
51. Faber (ed.), p. 152. In the report issued by RAE on a captured Ju 88, they noted that the normal dive angle was 50°, with provision to adjust it between 30° and 70° (van Ishoven, *The Luftwaffe in the Battle of Britain*, Ian Allen 1980, p. 30).
52. Windrow, op. cit., p. 5.
53. See Irving, *The Rise and Fall of the Luftwaffe*, pp. 75–6 & 107–8. Udet's obsession reached the apogee of farce with the five-year attempt to make the huge four-engined He 177 into a dive-bomber. See Faber (ed.), pp. 153–5 and Price, *Heinkel He 177*, Profile Publications.
54. See van Ishoven, op. cit., pp. 27–30 and Peter Stahl, *The Diving Eagle*, Kimber 1984, pp. 24–27 and 40–45.
55. See Bowyer and van Ishoven, *Hurricane and Messerschmitt*, Ian Allen, 1993, pp. 167–169 and 176–7.
56. Ibid., pp. 177–180.
57. Caidin, *Me 109*, p. 17.
58. van Ishoven, op. cit., p. 187.
59. Caidin, op. cit., p. 17.
60. Ibid., pp. 28 & 47.
61. The interim solution was to move from the original two-bladed wooden Schwarz propellers to metal Hamilton-Standards, imported from the United States. See Caidin, op. cit., p. 38.
62. Ibid., pp. 196–201.
63. I am grateful to Michael Payne for clarifying this point. There is some confusion in the literature. The first Bf 109 to actually be fitted with a cannon which fired through the spinner was the Emil's successor, the Bf 109F, which did not enter service until 1941, after the Battle of Britain.
64. See, for example, Theo Osterkamp, *Durch Höhen und Tiefen jagt ein Herz*, Vohwinkel, 1952, pp. 336ff.

65. Martin C. Windrow, *The Messerschmitt Bf 110*, Profile Publications, p. 3, Weal, *Messerschmitt Bf 110 Zerstörer Aces of World War 2*, Osprey 1999, pp. 6–8 and John Vasco and Peter Cornwell, *Zerstörer*, JAC Publications 1995, pp. 9–10. Though they might have been Göring's favourites, the Zerstörer units were not part of an élite. There were no élite formations in the Luftwaffe at all in 1940, any more than in the RAF.
66. Irving, *The Rise and Fall of the Luftwaffe*, pp. 52–3.
67. Ibid., p. 58.
68. *The German Organisation for Air Operations*, pp. 25–6, Evill Papers, RAF Museum, Hendon, AC 74/8/34.
69. Irving, op.cit, p. 63.
70. Ibid., pp. 73–4.

4. AIR DEFENCE
1. Francis K. Mason, *Battle over Britain*, 1969, pp. 16–17.
2. Sebastian Cox, 'Radar' in *Against All Odds*, ed. Graham Garnett, RAFA./Rococo Group 1990, p. 68
3. Mason, p. 13.
4. Lord Northcliffe was a press baron who owned, amongst other things, *The Times* and the *Daily Mail*. He began a campaign to make Britain 'air-minded' in 1906 and coined this phrase even before Blériot crossed the Channel. See Mason, pp. 28 & 32.
5. Mason, p. 17.
6. Quoted by Max Hastings in *Bomber Command*, Pan Macmillan 1993, p.48, as reported in H.A. Jones, *The War in the Air*, Oxford 1937.
7. Wood and Dempster, *The Narrow Margin*, Tri-Service Press 1990, p.40.
8. See Mason, p. 60. They were grossly exaggerated, but had their effect.
9. Wood and Dempster, p. 44.
10. Caswall was his grandmother's maiden name and Tremenheere his mother's.
11. Robert Wright, *Dowding and the Battle of Britain*, Macdonald 1979, pp. 58–9.
12. John Ray, *The Battle of Britain – New Perspectives*, Arms & Armour Press 1994. p.16.
13. Basil Collier, *Leader of the Few*, Jarrolds 1957, pp. 108–9.
14. Pile, *Ack-Ack*, Harrap 1949, p. 109.
15. Stanley Baldwin, Speech to the House of Commons, November 1932.
16. See John Crossland, 'Britain's Air Defences and the Munich Crisis', *History Today* Vol. 38 (Sep. 1988), p. 44.
17. Quoted by John Terraine, 'The Dowding System' in *Battle of Britain*, (Part 1), *The Daily Telegraph*, Editorial Supplement, 16 June 1990, p. XI.
18. Terraine, 'The Dowding System', p. X.
19. See Mason pp. 67–70.
20. Conversation with Cliff Kenyon, 3 October 1999. Cliff worked at Kenley Operations Room from 26 July 1940.
21. Mason, p.70.
22. Ibid.
23. Ashmore also invented the gridded map, counter and reporting system Dowding used. His role in creating the air defence system is generally passed over, but in many ways he, rather than Dowding, should be regarded as its architect and Dowding the builder. See Derek Wood, 'The Dowding System' in *The Battle Re-Thought*, ed. Air Commodore Henry Probert & Sebastian Cox, Airlife Publishing, 1991, pp. 3–4 and the discussion pp. 56–7.
24. The Luftwaffe did carry out some low-level attacks, but because of their difficulty they could in practice be performed by only a few units, notably Erprobungsgruppe 210 and III./KG 76, both of which were specially trained for the purpose. The rationale for these tactics was not stealth, however – though it was always hoped that might be a useful by-product – but bombing accuracy. Erprobungsgruppe 210 also suffered very heavily throughout its intensive Battle of Britain career largely because it was so heavily used. Against an average operating strength of twenty to twenty-five machines, the unit lost thirty-five aircraft and fifty-four crewmen killed or captured (including three commanding

officers and one acting commanding officer) between its formation on 1 July and the end of October (see John Vasco, *Bombsights over England*, JAC publications, 1990).

25. The delegation of tactical control to the groups was resisted by some staff officers, but Dowding was rightly insistent on decentralisation. Had Bentley Priory attempted to run the air battles which took place in August and September 1940 the system would have quickly imploded. See Vincent Orange, *Sir Keith Park*, Methuen 1984, p. 69.

26. Cliff Kenyon, conversation with the author, 3 October 1999

27. Wood, 'The Dowding System', op.cit., p. 7.

28. It might be characterised as 'simultaneously loose-tight'. See Peters and Waterman, *In Search of Excellence*, Harper & Row, 1982, Chapter 12.

29. Wood, 'The Dowding System', op.cit., p. 6.

30. He was to be criticised for this both during and after the battle. See Ray above.

31. H.C.T. Dowding, *Battle of Britain Despatch*, §147 in PRO AIR 8/863.

32. See *The Battle Re-Thought*, p.58.

33. A point also made by Wood, op.cit., p. 8.

34. It is the main subject of Ray's book, op.cit. above. Ray suggests that the system *was* flawed, in that it was unclear how the role of group commanders was to be interpreted: 'Park surmised that 12 Group aircraft were to provide a source of reinforcement for him, when he requested; Leigh-Mallory believed that his squadrons should be allowed to operate in their own right over 11 Group's area (p. 76). This is not really a system fault. Many bureaucracies attempt to spell out responsibilities and procedures in minute detail and the result is usually a manual nobody ever reads. The principles behind the system and above all the intention were clear, and as group commanders were big boys it was reasonable to expect them to work out how to co-operate effectively. Park and Brand did, Park and Leigh-Mallory did not. It was a personnel problem, not an organisational one.

35. See Wood & Dempster, *The Narrow Margin*, p. 90.

36. Wood & Dempster, p. 93.

37. Ibid., p. 88.

38. The Luftwaffe had a less finely-tuned three-stage system. Stage 1 was ready for take-off within one minute, the pilots being strapped-in or sitting next to the aircraft in deckchairs. Stage 2 was ready for take-off in one hour and Stage 3 was released until a specified time (see Ulrich Steinhilper and Peter Osborne, *Spitfire on my Tail*, Independent Books 1990, p.227). This clearly shows that the Luftwaffe was thinking offensively and not about how to utilise its pilots as fully as possible in a resource- and time-constrained defensive situation.

39. The working up and improvement of the system, and the equally important assessment of its technical limitations is described by Vincent Orange in *Sir Keith Park*, pp. 73–8.

40. Price, *The Hardest Day*, Arms and Armour Press 1988, p. 39.

41. A.C. Deere, *Nine Lives*, Wingham Press 1991, p. 39. For details of the 'Battle of Barking Creek' see Tony Holmes, *Hurricane Aces 1939–40*, Osprey 1998, pp. 9–11.

42. The incident, in which one pilot died, is now well documented. See, for example, Hough & Richards, p. 67.

43. Price, *The Hardest Day*, p. 157.

44. Even more paradoxically, for a land power which could reasonably have expected to fight most of its wars well away from water, the Germans had an imperfect but serviceable one.

45. Price, *The Hardest Day*, p. 30.

46. Pilot Officer W.D.David, as quoted by Hough & Richards, p. 340.

47. Wood & Dempster, op. cit. pp. 152–3 & 222–3.

48. As related by Johannes Steinhoff in the ITV documentary *Battle for Britain*, TVS Productions for ITV, written by Suzanne Campbell-Jones, 1990.

49. Quoted by Wood in *The Battle Re-Thought*, p. 10.
50. Galland may be being disingenuous. He tends in most of his post-war commentaries to stress the impossibility of the task facing the Luftwaffe in 1940. He knew very well that Germany developed a radar-based control system for the defence of Germany. He commanded it.
51. The German pilots listened in to the RAF's frequencies and speculated about what was going on. Steinhilper thought that the squadron call-signs were 'a system of cover names and special phrases, supposedly to confuse us' (op. cit., p. 275). In fact these call signs – the two he mentions, 'Weapon' and 'Dogrose' were for 601 and 610 Squadrons respectively – had been introduced in order to make communication simple, rapid and clear. The high frequency radios used in the late 30s were of poor quality and experiments had shown that short two-syllable words were the easiest to understand unambiguously over the interference-prone airwaves. Fighter Command was far more interested in being able to talk to itself than in confusing the Luftwaffe.

5. THE FIGHTERS

1. The Fox was never used in large numbers by the RAF. Of the 177 built, some went to Peru and 94 served with the Belgian air force. These were still in the front-line when war broke out, and when Belgium was invaded in 1940 they were in continuous action for the eighteen days of Belgium's courageous but hopeless resistance (David Mondey, *British Aircraft of World War II*, Hamlyn, 1994, p. 86). On the subject of the relative performance of pre-war fighters and bombers I am indebted to Anthony Miles.
2. Mason, p. 39.
3. Sorley Papers, *Origins of the Hurricane and Spitfire*, 1957, RAF Museum Hendon, AC 75/27/18. An edited version of this essay was published in *The Times* on 14 September 1957.
4. Ibid., p. 3.
5. Ibid.
6. Ibid., pp. 5–6. As a back-up, a specification was also issued to Gloster Aircraft Co., for an eight-gun fighter with a Bristol air-cooled engine as opposed to the liquid-cooled Merlin.
7. The specifications are reproduced in Alfred Price, *The Spitfire Story*, Arms & Armour Press 1982, pp. 27–35.
8. Mason, p. 61.
9. See Deighton, *Fighter*, p. 75.
10. Wood & Dempster, p. 53.
11. Letter from Sir Sydney Camm to Air Marshal Sir Robert Saundby, 14 May 1965, in Saundby Papers, RAF Museum Hendon, Box 8.
12. Sorley Papers, *Factors Involved in the Conception of the 8 Gun Fighter*, 1945, p. 8.
13. See Wood and Dempster, p. 53.
14. See Alfred Price, *The Spitfire Story*, p.11. There was no tailwind.
15. Deighton, op. cit., p. 95 and K.G. Mitchell, 'Some Personal Observations' in *Forty Years of the Spitfire*, Proceedings of the Mitchell Memorial Symposium, 6 March 1976, Royal Aeronautical Society 1976, p. 131.
16. Vickers had bought a controlling interest in Supermarine in 1928.
17. *The Spitfire Story*, pp. 17–18.
18. Ibid., p. 19.
19. A skilled team of four armourers could nevertheless change the ammunition boxes, feed the belts through, swab out and cock the guns of a Spitfire in under ten minutes.
20. *The Spitfire Story*, p. 20.
21. Ibid.
22. See Jeffrey Quill, *Spitfire*, Arrow Books 1983 pp. 177 ff.
23. The precise date is a matter of some doubt because the Chief Test-Pilot, Mutt Summers, noted it in his diary as 5 March, but Jeffrey Quill thought it was the 6 March. In 1982, Alfred Price came down in favour of the 6 March (see Price, *The Spitfire Story*,

p.37). Subsequently, Price has found a Vickers document detailing the cost of developing the prototype (a princely £14,637) on which the company secretary wrote 'Flew on 5 Mar 36' (Price, *Spitfire – A Complete Fighting History,* Ian Allan 1991). Such is the current balance of evidence. It hardly matters.

24. Price, *The Spitfire Story,* p. 40.

25. Gordon Mitchell, *R.J.Mitchell – Schooldays to Spitfire,* Clifford Frost 1997, p. 130.

26. Leslie Howard's propaganda film made in 1942 portrayed Mitchell as 'The First of the Few'. By suggesting that Mitchell had worked himself to death in order to finish work on the Spitfire in time, Howard added to the mythology surrounding the man and the machine. See Calder, p. 206.

27. An interesting comparison from the point of view of a modern aircraft restorer is given by Tony Bianchi in the Uden Associates production *Spitfire* written by Brian Johnson for Channel 4's *Equinox* series in 1990.

28. The failings of UK industry throughout the war are candidly if tendentiously exposed by Corelli Barnett in *Audit of War,* especially Chapters 3 to 9.

29. See Hastings, *Overlord,* Pan Books 1985 pp. 220–231.

30. For an appropriately unbiased view from a German source see *Die Großen Luftschlachten des Zweiten Weltkriegs,* Kaiser Verlag, pp. 54–61. This ability to keep pace with performance needs without going to a fundamentally new design enabled Britain to keep its fighter forces equipped without major disruption to production and with relatively little time loss, which was important in winning the war of numbers. Whilst the original Mk I took 330,000 man-hours to design, all fifteen subsequent marks of Spitfire were developed in only 620,000 man-hours. Likewise, tooling-up for the Mark I took 800,000 hours as against an average of 69,000 hours for each of the subsequent marks

(Overy, *The Air War 1939–45,* p.178).

31. Price, *The Spitfire Story,* p. 211. Mitchell did not *quite* take piston engined fighter design as far as it had to go. There was one more technological generation to come. The North American P51 Mustang used the only wing design which could be considered superior to the elliptical wing and this gave it a performance to match. Even so, later marks of Spitfire were fully comparable to the P51, except in range.

32. Likewise, Quill was the first to call the machine 'a real lady'.

33. See for example the reaction provoked by an article by former test-pilot Roland Beamont in *Aeroplane Monthly* in February 1994, in which he compared aspects of the Spitfire unfavourably with the Hurricane. Rod Smith, an ex-RCAF Spitfire pilot, leapt indignantly to his old girlfriend's defence in the August 1995 issue, followed up by no less than Alex Henshaw (the Spitfire's production test-pilot) and Jeffrey Quill in September. Beamont had not meant to insult a lady, and wrote a letter in reply in the October issue in which it became clear that he had been motivated by a desire to give the Hurricane its due rather than denigrate the Spitfire. There was clearly more at stake than mechanical engineering.

34. This was a propaganda exercise in good Beaverbrook style. There was no shortage of scrap aluminium to begin with and pots and pans were not suitable for aircraft production. (See C.R. Russell, *Spitfire Postscript,* 1994, pp. 125–6.) Useless as the piles of cooking utensils may have been, as Beaverbrook's son, the pilot Max Aitken has remarked, it was 'all good stuff' (*The World at War,* Thames Television).

35. Quill, *Spitfire,* Arrow Books 1985, p. 77.

36. Foreword to *Spitfire* by Alfred Price, Ian Allan 1991, p.9.

37. *Forty Years of the Spitfire*, R.A.S. 1976, p. 90.
38. Quoted in *Spitfire* by Chaz Bowyer, Bison Books 1980, p.13.
39. Bob Doe, *Fighter Pilot*, Spellmount Ltd., 1991.
40. Hugh Dundas, *Flying Start*, Stanley Paul 1988, p.19. In a study published on 27 January 1945, Dr Douglas D. Bond of the USAF pointed out that many pilots showed a great love of their aircraft, a phenomenon he called 'libidinisation'. He believed that this channelling of their most powerful feelings helped them to resist the stresses of combat. See Mark K. Wells, *Courage and Air Warfare*, Frank Cass 1995, p.95.
41. Conversation with the author, 23 July 1996.
42. Though they came very late, as a result of a pilot's call to de Havilland in June 1940. The effect on service ceiling was so clear that the Air Ministry approved and 1,050 had been retrofitted in the field by mid-August. See Deighton, p. 104.
43. Wood & Dempster, p. 60.
44. The Air Staff were well aware of this. Sir Wilfred Freeman, the Air Member for Research and Development, said in 1938 that the Hurricane and Spitfire would continue to have genuine value in 1940, but not much beyond that. The Air Council was already looking for a replacement and favoured the Westland Whirlwind (see Crossland, op. cit., pp. 43–4). The Hurricane was indeed taken out of front-line service as a day fighter in Europe, but was used in other theatres throughout the war. Three RAF and eight Indian air force squadrons were flying them in the Far East on VJ Day 1945 (Bowyer & Ishoven, op. cit., p. 133). Joseph Smith and Rolls-Royce between them saw to it that all expectations about the Spitfire were to be confounded. Jeffrey Quill tells how in July 1942 he was invited to Farnborough to take part in comparative evaluations between the Spitfire, a captured FW 190 and the new Hawker Typhoon. The objective was to see by how much each of the new fighters beat the Spitfire. Quill flew down in a new Mk. XII, powered by a Griffon engine. The order of finishing was Spitfire, Typhoon, FW 190, which caused a considerable sensation. (Quill, *Spitfire*, pp. 217–8).
45. Quoted by Williamson Murray, *Luftwaffe*, Grafton Books, 1988, p. 431.
46. See David Mondey, *British Aircraft of World War Two*, Hamlyn 1982, pp. 40–42.
47. See John Crossland, 'Britain's Air Defences and the Munich Crisis' in *History Today*, Vol. 38, September 1988, pp. 44–5, and Vincent Orange, *Sir Keith Park*, pp. 69–70.
48. On Dowding's opposition to the Defiant, see Peter Flint, *Dowding and Headquarters Fighter Command*, Airlife 1996, p. 98.
49. See Dundas, op. cit., pp. 4–6.
50. How those few who were commissioned were selected is obscure. Tom Neil recalls being one of five out of a course of forty-two and having no idea why he was chosen (*Gun Button to Fire*, William Kimber 1987, p. 29).
51. See Mark K. Wells, *Courage and Air Warfare*, Frank Cass 1995, pp. 122–4.
52. See Gelb, op. cit., p. 43.
53. Quoted in Wells, op. cit., p. 12.
54. Gelb, op. cit., pp. 40–41.
55. A resumé of the activities of this committee and the state of these experiments as at 27 May 1940 can be found in AIR 6/59.
56. See Hooton, op. cit., p. 160.
57. Ibid., p. 133, n. 21.
58. The various perils are examined by Wells, op. cit., pp. 28–32.

6. THE BOMBERS

1. The absolute number understates the peril. The loss-rate, i.e. the chance of getting killed each time a man went out on an operation, made flying with Bomber Command the most dangerous occupation of the war except for sailing with a German U-boat. The army lost a total of 126,734

killed in all theatres (John Ellis, *The Sharp End*, Windrow & Greene, 1990, p. 156). Losses in rifle companies, however, if treated in isolation could also approach 90%.

2. Britain, France and Germany had all agreed to President Roosevelt's proposals, sent to them on the outbreak of war, to exercise restraint in selecting targets, and Bomber Command was not allowed to attack private property, let alone civilians.

3. W.R. Chorley, *Bomber Command Losses 1939–1940*, Midland Counties Publications 1992, pp. 11–12.

4. Ibid., p. 13. Max Hastings gives a detailed account of the raid on the 18th in *Bomber Command*, Macmillan 1993, pp. 15–35.

5. Hastings, *Bomber Command*, p. 34. For a full account of the psychology behind this sort of thing see *On the Psychology of Military Incompetence* by Norman Dixon, Jonathan Cape 1976. The psychology it describes is by no means restricted to the military.

6. Neil Young, 'The Role of Bomber Command in the Battle of Britain', *Imperial War Museum Review*, No. 6, 1991, p. 77.

7. Ibid., pp. 78–9.

8. Ibid., p. 79.

9. See ibid., p. 85.

10. Details from the RAF Air Historical Branch Narrative, 'The RAF in Maritime War' Vol II, 1947, pp. 123–373, RAF Museum Hendon.

7. STRENGTH FOR BATTLE

1. Overy, op. cit., pp. 28 and 150.

2. See Kenneth Macksey, *Kesselring – The Making of the Luftwaffe*, Batsford, 1978, p.59.

3. See David Irving, *Göring – A Biography*, Macmillan 1989, pp. 227–8 and 276.

4. Overy, op. cit., pp.152–3.

5. See Corelli Barnett, *The Audit of War*, Macmillan 1986, p. 139.

6. Incompetence on the part of Vickers-Supermarine and its sub-contractors also played a role. For example, sub-contractors found that the component drawings they had been given were inaccurate (John Crossland, 'Britain's Air Defences and the Munich Crisis', *History Today*, Vol. 38, (Sept. 1988), p. 44). See Barnett, op. cit., p.140, and for a general account of the weaknesses of the country's aeronautical production capabilities pp. 125–158. Less recriminatory accounts of the initial production problems with the Spitfire are given by Quill, op.cit., pp. 114–20 and Price, *The Spitfire Story*, pp. 61–69, and overall by Overy (see above).

7. Price, *The Spitfire Story*, pp. 67 and 107–8, and C.R. Russell, *A Spitfire Postscript*, 1994, pp. 116–125.

8. Russell, op. cit., pp. 60–63.

9. Churchill was one of the believers who added to the Beaverbrook mythology. See, for example, *Their Finest Hour*, pp. 249–50. According to Lord Tedder, who worked at the MAP at the time, it took Beaverbrook only six months to create such chaos as to be a threat to the safety of the country, and he wrote to Sinclair in November 1940 to tell him so. See Tedder, *With Prejudice*, Cassell 1966, p. 14 and John Terraine, *The Right of the Line*, Hodder and Stoughton 1985, pp. 191–2. On the overall role of the MAP see Ritchie, op. cit., pp. 228–40.

10. Ibid.

11. See Overy, ibid., pp. 155 and 159–166.

12. The Marquess of Londonderry, *Wings of Destiny*, London 1943, p. 29.

13. Ibid., pp. 115 and 136.

14. See Flint, op. cit., pp. 7–11, 17, 47–8, 73, 84–5 and 89, Ray, op. cit., pp. 22–4 and 52 and Orange, op. cit., p. 70. As a rule of thumb, most calculations were based on a fighter strength of 30% of an opponent's total air strength. Dowding was shocked after the war when Churchill wrote in *Their Finest Hour* that Dowding had told him he needed 25 squadrons. Well he might have been. Given the plethora of numbers to choose from, it is odd that Churchill picked one which was never

mentioned. Unless somebody got the 52 the wrong way round ...

15. Flint, op. cit., pp. 47–8.
16. Political correctness had not been invented in 1939, and this story is told as I heard it.
17. Conversation with the author, 20 August 1999. The incident was witnessed and confirmed by two other pilots there at the time, Bryan Young and Dick Pexton.
18. Wright, op. cit., pp. 111–2. The original document now hangs in the Royal Air Force College at Cranwell.
19. Flint, op. cit., pp. 79–80.
20. Ibid., pp. 334–5, 337–41, 346, 350–4, 366 and 370. Cf. Flint pp. 48, 51–3, 73–80 and 82–4 and Ray, pp. 24–30.
21. Flint, op. cit., p. 85.
22. Ibid., p. 79.
23. Ibid., pp. 53–4.
24. Ray, op. cit., pp. 26–7.
25. Gilbert, *Finest Hour*, pp. 416, 434–5, 441, 450–1, 456–8, 460–1, 470–1, 479–85, 492, 506 and 517–8.
26. Wright, op. cit., p. 129. Dowding had more reason than most to harbour these sentiments, but he was not the only one to do so. King George VI wrote to his Mother: "Personally I feel happier now that we have no allies to be polite to and pamper." (Gelb, op. cit., p. 32).
27. AIR 19/162.
28. AIR 19/162.
29. Gilbert, *Finest Hour*, p. 760.
30. Osterkamp, op. cit., p. 236.
31. Overy, op. cit., p. 23.
32. Ibid., p. 28. Hooton, op. cit., gives the same figures specifying aircrew casualties of 413 dead and missing and 126 wounded (p. 188).
33. Hooton, op. cit., p. 236. The British total includes the Fleet Air Arm and 43 aircraft lost on board HMS *Glorious*.
34. See Hooton, op. cit., p. 207.
35. Ibid., pp. 204–8.
36. Overy, op. cit., p. 29.
37. Hooton, op. cit., pp. 267–8 and Murray, op. cit., p. 77.
38. Figures for the Luftwaffe are taken from Murray, op. cit., p. 93, which are those given in the AHB translation

VII/83 of the numbers prepared by the Luftwaffe Quartermaster General's 6th Abteilung for 29th June. The RAF fighter strength is from Mason, op. cit., p. 98, giving the order of battle at 0900 hours on 1 July. The figure for Bomber Command is from Churchill, *Their Finest Hour*, Appendix C, p. 553, and is for 11 July. The figure for Coastal Command is given as approximate by John Terraine in *The Right of the Line*, Sceptre 1985, p. 234.
39. The RAF used both bombers and fighters for reconnaissance purposes, and did not break them out separately.
40. The Luftwaffe also had 408 transport aircraft not included here.
41. Wood and Dempster, op. cit., Appendix 20C, p. 355.
42. Ibid.

8. SEALION

1. Compare the States of Readiness for July and September shown by Churchill in *Their Finest Hour*, pp. 209–210.
2. The German Airborne Forces Commander, General Student, told Liddell Hart after the war that he had advocated such a move, despite its dangers. See Liddell Hart, *The Other Side of the Hill*, Pan Books 1983, pp. 220–1.
3. Kenneth Macksey, *The German Invasion of England*, July 1940, Greenhill Books 1980.
4. David Shears, 'The German Invasion Plans', in *Operation Sealion*, edited by Richard Cox, Thornton Cox 1975, p. 158.
5. Halder, op. cit., Blatt 86.
6. Taylor, op. cit., pp. 209–10 and Halder, op. cit., Blatt 87.
7. Taylor, op. cit., pp. 208–9, and IWM Dept. of Docs., M.1.14/92.
8. Halder, op. cit., Blatt 91.
9. Ibid., Blatt 101. Cf. Gilbert, *Finest Hour*, p. 599.
10. Taylor, p. 66. This phrase was used by the army in its first meeting to discuss Sealion on 3rd July (Halder, op. cit., Blatt 89).

11. Taylor, pp. 64–5 and 216–8.
12. IWM Dept of Docs., M.1.14/94.
13. Taylor, pp. 66–7 and 219–220.
14. Hitler had got Lloyd George's mood right. On the 24th, Chips Channon noted in his diary that Lloyd George's 'affection for Churchill has noticeably cooled of late' and that he was predicting that the country, though currently 'hysterically infatuated' with him, would turn on him after his first great blunder (Gilbert, *Finest Hour*, p. 676).
15. Ibid., pp. 67–8, 72–3 and 220–1 and Halder, Blatt 114.
16. Shears, ibid.
17. Taylor, op. cit., pp. 69 and 221–2, Halder, op. cit., Blatt 120.
18. Halder, op. cit., Blatt 122.
19. Ibid., Blatt 123, 124, 125.
20. Taylor, pp. 70–5 and 222–3 and Halder, op. cit., Blatt 126–9. Russia was not England's last hope. Churchill wrote to Stalin on 25 June in an attempt to establish better relations, but was under no illusions about his chances. He received no answer and had not expected one. See 'Their Finest Hour', pp. 103–7. Involving the United States was, of course, the corner-stone of his long-term political strategy. For a careful examination of the full context of the momentous decisions taken by Hitler and his Staff in the summer of 1940 and the relationship between Sealion and Barbarossa, see Robert Cecil, *Hitler's Decision to Invade Russia 1941*, Davis-Poynter 1975, esp. pp. 68–84.
21. IWM Dept. of Docs., M.1.14/106.
22. Liddell Hart, *The Other Side of the Hill*, pp. 219–220.
23. Taylor, op. cit., p. 22.
24. Basil Collier, *The Defence of the United Kingdom*, IWM 1957, p. 440.
25. Shears, ibid., p. 165.

9. EAGLE

1. '*The Memoirs of Field Marshal Kesselring*', introduced by Kenneth Macksey, Greenhill Books 1988, p. 67.
2. See Murray, *Luftwaffe*, pp. 372 ff.
3. Kesselring, ibid., p. 68.
4. He was, amongst other things, Speaker of the German Parliament, head of Stormtroopers, Prime Minister of Prussia, Special Commissioner for the four-year-plan and President of the Reich Defence Council. Most of these titles were empty, but some of the other jobs he had taken on, such as setting up the Gestapo and the first concentration camps, were more onerous.
5. John Weal, *Bf 109D/E Aces 1939–41*, Osprey 1996, p. 72.
6. Chris Goss, *Brothers in Arms*, Crécy Books 1994, p.179.
7. Osterkamp, op. cit., p. 125 (author's translation).
8. On Kesselring's qualities and his development up to 1940 see Kenneth Macksey, *Kesselring – The Making of the Luftwaffe*, pp. 15–65.
9. Irving, *The Rise and Fall of the Luftwaffe*, p. 67.
10. See Deighton, op. cit., pp. 150–1. He characteristically set up his HQ at the luxurious Palais de Luxembourg in Paris, one-time residence of the Medicis.
11. See Murray, op. cit., pp. 246 & 374 and Killen, op. cit., pp. 81–3, 102, 107, 165, 254 & 280–1.
12. RL/2/II 27. See Taylor, op. cit., p. 120, Peter Townsend, *Duel of Eagles*, Presidio Press 1970, pp. 254–5 and Wood & Dempster, op. cit., p. 158.
13. Ibid., pp. 127–130.
14. Karl-Heinz Völker, *Dokumente und Dokumentarfotos zur Geschichte der deutschen Luftwaffe*, Stuttgart 1968, pp. 454–460.
15. Wood & Dempster, op. cit., p. 162.
16. They actually had about 675.
17. Osterkamp, op. cit., pp. 324–7. Osterkamp tellingly entitles his account of the conference 'Utopien'.
18. Taylor, op. cit., pp. 132–3.
19. Kesselring, op. cit., p. 70.
20. Osterkamp, op. cit., pp. 314–5.
21. Ibid., pp. 318–9.
22. Edmund Blandford, *Target England*, Airlife 1997, pp. 86–9.

10. THE DEFENDERS

1. See Ray, *The Battle of Britain – New Perspectives*, pp. 13–14 & 16–17, and Collier, *Leader of the Few*, op. cit., pp. 168–70. For Dowding's feelings about the manner in which the issue was handled see Wright, op. cit., pp. 60–65, 69, 72–76, 85–6, 95–7, 136–143, 156–8 & 242–3. His dismissal has been viewed by some as a scandal in itself. Dowding himself accepted retirement and resisted later attempts by Churchill to give him further duties. What he objected to was the style rather than the substance. 'I want it to be quite clear that I had no grievance on that score,' he is quoted as commenting. 'It was the way it was done that hurt, when I was sent away as if I had been rather an indifferent sort of commander' (Wright, p. 242).
2. See Ray, op. cit., pp. 30–32.
3. Vincent Orange, *Sir Keith Park*, Methuen, 1984, p. 28.
4. Ibid., p. 37.
5. Ibid., pp. 70–83.
6. Ibid., p. 76.
7. Ibid., p. 165. For views on Park's character see ibid., pp. 34, 119, 129, 144, 149, 165, 177–8 & 265.
8. Ibid., p. 40.
9. Ibid., p. 89.
10. For these and other examples of his communication style see ibid., pp. 40, 89, 150, 165, 170 & 173.
11. Ibid., pp. 112–3, 116–7, 150 & 162.
12. Ibid., pp. 47, 53 & 83.
13. AIR 16/122. Park argued, on purely military and operational grounds, for keeping Tangmere within 11 Group rather than moving it to 10 Group but for leaving Duxford in 12 Group, and Dowding agreed. As things turned out, he would have been better advised to have suggested the opposite.
14. On Leigh-Mallory's early career see Bill Newton Dunn, *Big Wing*, Airlife 1992, pp. 1–66.
15. Orange, op. cit., p. 78.
16. Ibid., p. 80.
17. Ibid., p. 120 and Wright, op. cit., p. 94.
18. See the comments of Wing Commander Hancock in Probert and Cox (eds.), *The Battle Re-Thought*, p. 71.
19. See the comments of Sir Kenneth Porter, who served under both Leigh-Mallory and Park, ibid., pp. 71–2.
20. AIR 2/3034.
21. AIR 16/367. Sholto Douglas sought to have these principles recognised and applied operationally after he took over from Dowding as C-in-C Fighter Command in November 1940. See Peter Flint, *Dowding and Headquarters Fighter Command*, pp. 179–182.
22. The best size of tactical formation had been a matter of some debate before the war. The air exercises conducted in 1939 suggested that the squadron was the largest formation which could be effectively controlled in the air. Large raids could simply be met by several squadrons acting in concert, but without wasting time forming up together into a single large formation. See Dilip Sarkar, *Bader's Duxford Fighters*, Ramrod Publications 1997, pp. 14ff.
23. See Mason, op. cit., p. 98.
24. One of Dowding's former pilots, 'Dizzy' Allen, has described these dispositions as being 'calculated to lose an aerial battle over south-east England', and the number of units placed in the North to show 'no military logic of any kind'. In his view, all the best fighters, the Spitfires, should have been packed into 11 Group, Hurricane pilots should have been re-trained to fight on Spitfires, and the Blenheims and Defiants should have been removed. See H. R. Allen, *Who Won the Battle of Britain?*, pp. 108–9 & 112–3.
25. Flint, op. cit., pp. 92–4.
26. On attitudes to the Germans in Europe and beyond see John Lukacs, *The Duel*, Bodley Head 1990 pp. 205–210.

11. THE ENEMY AT THE GATE

1. A transcription of large parts of the broadcast can be found in *Spitfire Summer* by Peter Haining, W.H. Allen

1990, pp. 13–21. The broadcast itself can be heard at the National Sound Archive.

2. Gardner's efforts at live recording were topped by his German opposite numbers, some of whom flew with the Luftwaffe and actually broadcast from bombers flying over London. These men were attached not to newspapers but to Goebbels' 'Propaganda Kompanien', which were part of the army. They were trained as soldiers, expected to fight if necessary, and given a military mission, that of influencing the outcome of the war by psychological means. There was no nonsense about objectivity. See Phillip Knightley, *The First Casualty*, Pan Books 1989, pp. 220–1 and 233.

3. *Are We At War? – Letters to The Times 1939–45*, ed. Anthony Livesey, Times Books 1989, p.75.

4. Ibid.

5. Ibid. pp. 75–6.

6. Ibid., pp. 76–7.

7. Ibid., p. 77.

8. 615 Squadron, Form 540, PRO AIR 27/2123.

9. 'A War of the Unknown Warriors', 14 July 1940, *Into Battle*, pp. 247–251.

10. Gilbert, *Finest Hour*, p. 665.

12. THE CHANNEL: JULY

1. 'Allgemeine Weisung für den Kampf der Luftwaffe gegen England', 30.6.40, RL/2/II 27.

2. At the beginning of July it consisted of two Stuka Gruppen, II./StG1 and IV.(St)/LG1, and the Dorniers of KG2. (See Ulf Balke, *Der Luftwaffe in Europa, Teil 1*, Bernard und Graefe 1989, p. 128). Erprobungsgruppe 210 became operational on 17 July. The fighters, under Osterkamp, originally consisted of his own JG51 and ZG26.

3. Marcel Jullian, *The Battle of Britain*, Jonathan Cape 1967, p. 38. 'Kanal' means 'sewer' as well as 'channel'. 'Kanakafü' has echoes of 'Kacke', a baby word for faeces.

4. See Ivan Rendell, *Reaching for the Skies*, Orion Books 1988, pp. 61–4. The statue is still there.

5. Fink as quoted in Blandford, *Target England*, Airlife 1997, p. 83. See also Wood and Dempster, p. 170.

6. Wood and Dempster, p. 170.

7. See Weal, *Bf 109D/E Aces 1939–41*, pp. 44–5.

8. 'Allgemeine Weisung für den Kampf der Luftwaffe gegen England', 30.6.40., RL/2/II 27, § 1 'Zielsetzung' (author's translation).

9. Osterkamp, op. cit., pp. 318–23 and 328–9.

10. Michael J. Bowyer gives a list of the targets bombed up to 12 August in *The Battle of Britain 50 Years On*, Patrick Stephens 1990, pp. 85–87, from which can be gauged how widespread they were.

11. The daily operational reports for Airfleets 2 and 5 have been lost, but those for Airfleet 3 covering the period of the Battle are largely extant in the Bundesarchiv in Freiburg under RL/7/88-92.

12. See Gilbert, *Finest Hour*, pp. 82–98.

13. This was an He 111 of Wettererkundungsstaffel 1, shot down by two Hurricanes of 3 Squadron at 8.30 a.m. on 25 July. Four crewmen were killed and a fifth picked up by a RN destroyer.

14. *The Battle of Britain Then and Now*, Mk IV, After the Battle Publications 1987, p. 538.

15. See Mason, p.121.

16. As suggested in *The Battle of Britain* by Richard Townshend Bickers, Salamander Books 1990, p. 114.

17. See Mason, op. cit., pp. 120–1, Townshend Bickers op. cit., pp. 110–3 and Hough and Richards, op. cit., pp. 123–8.

18. Ira ('Taffy') Jones, *Tiger Squadron*, W.H. Allen 1954, p. 225.

19. W. R. Chorley, *Bomber Command Losses*, pp. 87 and 90.

20. Halder op. cit., Blatt 101.

21. See John Vasco and Peter Cornwell, *Zerstörer*, pp. 83–88.

22. *The Battle of Britain Then and Now*, p. 538. According to Mason, the He 59 had to ditch with engine trouble when out looking for downed aircrew. It was assisted by another,

but spotted by the Cornish coastguard, and the Royal Navy put out two destroyers with an escort of three Blenheims of 236 Squadron to capture them both. A Ju 88 of I./KG51 attacked the destroyers but was shot down by the Blenheims. A Heinkel He 111 was also chased off, but the destroyers never found the seaplane, which was probably scuttled (op. cit., p. 124). Mason gives his source as a private diary and the ORB of 236 Squadron, but he may be indulging his admitted penchant for 'extrapolated opinion'. Cornwell is usually more reliable.

23. *The Memoirs of Field Marshal Kesselring*, ed. Macksey, p. 70.
24. Ulrich Steinhilper and Peter Osborne, *Spitfire on my Tail*, pp. 277–8.
25. Dowding *Despatch*, § 156, AIR 8/863.
26. Alan Deere, *Nine Lives*. His account of the collision and the He 59 incident, with his and others reactions to it, can be found on pp. 89–96. Deere mistakenly gives the date as 11 July.
27. Fighter Command pilots had indeed filed claims for fifty 'confirmed' and thirty-one 'probable' kills over those days, for the loss of thirteen aircraft. Churchill had no doubt heard the figure of fifty and related it to about ten for the RAF. They had in fact destroyed twenty-four, a rate of two to one. At this time, the British did not understand claims inflation any more than the Germans did.
28. Colville, op. cit., p. 228, and Wright, op. cit. pp. 142–3.
29. For an account of the speech and the British and German reactions see Shirer, *The Nightmare Years*, pp. 551–4.
30. Colville, op. cit., p. 234.
31. See Mason, op. cit., p. 138 and Osterkamp, op. cit., pp. 336–340.
32. This incident is told by Dowding's personal assistant, Robert Wright (op. cit., pp. 144–5). Though there is no reason for Wright to make it up, there is no other record of Churchill visiting Bentley Priory on or around the 19th.

33. Gelb, op. cit., pp.126–7.
34. AIR 16/217.
35. 'Besprechung Reichsmarschall am 21.7.40' in RL/2/II 30.
36. Osterkamp op. cit., pp. 360–3.
37. John Weal, *Bf 109D/E Aces 1939–41*, p. 68.
38. Compare the traditionalists Mason, op. cit., p. 154 and Franks, *Sky Tiger*, pp. 57–8; with the revisionists Anthony Robinson in the *Daily Telegraph* Editorial Supplement 'Battle of Britain', 16 June 1990, p. XXI, and *RAF Fighter Squadrons in the Battle of Britain*, Arms and Armour Press 1987 pp. 70–71 and 141–2 and, most forcefully, John Foreman, who asserts in *Fighter Command War Diaries Volume 1*, Airlife 1996, p. 128, that Malan was definitely not involved as he had left the scene after a dogfight with III./JG26. The first person to challenge the traditional view was Peter Cornwell, who published the revised version of events in a Postscript to the Mark II version of *The Battle of Britain Then and Now* (pp. 718–9) in 1982. Mölders' own account, in which he is unsurprisingly greatly outnumbered and hit by a lucky shot, is reproduced in van Ishoven, *The Luftwaffe in the Battle of Britain*, Ian Allan 1980, pp. 25–6.
39. Bill Felstead, quoted in Bob Cossey, *Tigers – The Story of No. 74 Squadron RAF*, Arms and Armour Press 1992, p.72.
40. Cossey, op. cit., p.87.

13. THE MEN

1. Quoted in Alfred Price, *The Hardest Day*, p. 14.
2. See Spick, *Luftwaffe Fighter Aces*, p. 45.
3. From 1943 this was refined, and an elaborate system of points was instituted, based on how valuable certain kills were and how difficult it was to get them. They ranged from half a point for bringing down a twin-engined aircraft which had already been damaged to three points

for the full destruction of a multi-engined bomber. In the West, a Ritterkreuz was earned with 40–50 points, whereas in the East it took 75, because getting victories against the Red Air Force was so much easier. See Spick, pp. 13–14.

4. Steinhilper, op. cit., p. 302. Steinhilper gives expression to his personal sense of bitterness about this in a footnote.

5. See Steinhilper, op. cit., pp. 181–2 for a revealing story about the importance of decorations to Galland.

6. Caldwell, op. cit., pp. 40 and 49.

7. Ibid., p. 63 and After the Battle, p. 666.

8. Caidin, op. cit., p. 141.

9. See Caldwell, op. cit., p. 32 and pp. 69–71 for a comparison of Geschwader performance. It is worth noting that the average claims-to-loss ratio for the whole of Fighter Command was 5.5:1.

10. Milch, 'Besichtigungs-Bemerkungen bei Verbänden der Luftflotte 2 vom 20. – 25.8.40' in Milch Papers, IWM Dept of Documents, Vol. 51/54.

11. Steinhilper, op. cit., p. 263.

12. See for example the interviews with Galland, Lange and Steinhoff in the *Guardian Weekly*, 26.8.90, pp. 26–7. Their attitude was shared by Göring. See David Irving, *Göring – A Biography*, p. 272.

13. Ibid.

14. Gelb, op. cit., p. 120. Johnnie Cock, an Australian, survived the battle and the war. Dewar, a Wing Commander, was killed on 12 September on a routine flight from Exeter to Tangmere, and was the only RAF casualty on that day and the highest-ranking British casualty of the battle.

15. Dowding Despatch §§ 158–60.

16. Quoted in Gelb, op. cit., p. 64.

17. Wells, op. cit., p. 146.

18. On Lacey's and other pilots' different reactions to combat stress and fear see Richard Townshend Bickers, *Ginger Lacey – Fighter Pilot*, Blandford Press 1988, pp. 97–100. The Flying Personnel Research Committee investigated the problem of flying stress and concluded that more stress was caused by being on stand-by than by flying. The Committee, which consisted of academic scientists, wisely counselled that in order to lessen the problem, it was 'of the utmost importance that personnel, when standing-by, should be engaged in some interesting and profitable occupation, such as studying languages' (AIR 6/59). No doubt Paddy Barthropp and his colleagues could have made some alternative suggestions.

19. Pilot Officer Roland Beamont, in Gelb, op. cit., p. 146.

20. Ibid., pp. 146–7. Squadron Leader 'Shovel' Gregg crash-landed near Abbotsbury at about 6 p.m. on 15 August and was thrown clear of his cockpit. His clothing was on fire and he had bullet wounds in his arms and legs. He was already dead.

21. P/O Peter Brown, 611 and 41 Squadrons, in Gelb, op. cit., p. 189.

22. Gelb, op. cit., pp. 26–7.

23. See Deere, op. cit., pp. 101–8, and Larry Forrester, *Fly For Your Life*, Muller 1956, Panther edition pp. 110–2.

24. The stories of early leadership failures in 234 and 57 Squadrons are recounted in *Churchill's Few* by John Willis, Michael Joseph 1985.

25. Dowding Despatch, § 219.

26. Peter Townsend, *Time and Chance*, Methuen 1978.

27. Richard Hillary, *The Last Enemy*, Pan 1956, p. 87.

28. Max Aitken in *The World at War*, produced by Jeremy Isaacs, Thames Television 1980, Vol. II.

29. Brian Kingcome, ibid.

30. Pilot Officer Bob Kings, Gelb, op. cit., p.62.

31. Douglas Bader as quoted by Burns, *Bader – The Man and his Men*, Arms and Armour Press 1990, p. 60.

32. *Sagittarius Rising*, Penguin 1977, p. 31.

33. *Against All Odds*, ed. Garnett, p. 174.

34. Some of them were actually Americans. See David Alan Johnson, *The Battle of Britain*, Combined Publishing 1998.

35. Ibid., pp. 177–181. Canada also made a major contribution to the Allied war effort by acting as a training ground for aircrew. It produced the bulk of the 200,000 aircrew trained during the war under the Empire Air Training Scheme, but the first of these men were only just beginning to arrive in Britain as the battle ended.

36. Adam Zamoyski, *The Forgotten Few*, John Murray 1995, pp. 81–5. See also Robert Gretzyngier and Wojtek Matusiak, *Polish Aces of World War II*, Osprey 1998.

37. Zamoyski, pp. 58–70.

38. Ibid., pp. 75–7.

39. Ibid., p. 75.

40. Ibid., p. 97.

41. Kent, *One of the Few*, William Kimber 1971, p. 100.

42. Ibid., pp. 126–7.

43. Zamoyski, op. cit., p. 83.

44. An account of the circumstances of his death is given by Kent in *One of the Few*, pp. 125–6.

45. Zamoyski, op. cit., p. 72.

46. See ibid., pp. 5 and 23.

47. Personal statement recorded in *Battle for Britain*, TVS Productions, Suzanne Campbell-Jones 1990.

48. Gelb, op. cit., p. 41.

49. Bob Ogley, *Biggin on the Bump*, Froglets Publications 1990, pp. 124 and 128.

50. Wynn, *Men of the Battle of Britain*.

51. See Johnson, op. cit.

52. *Against All Odds*, p. 169.

53. The effects of burns and the long, hard road to recovery embarked upon by those who suffered them were described in one of the most famous pieces of writing to come from the war, Richard Hillary's *The Last Enemy*. Hillary was killed in a flying accident in January 1943. One who has lived with his injuries into old age is Geoffrey Page, nephew of Frederick Handley Page, and a Pilot Officer who flew with 56 Squadron until shot down and severely burned on 12 August. He had seventeen operations during the war, returned to end the war as a Wing Commander, and has had another twenty or so operations since. His biography is appropriately called *Tale of a Guinea Pig*, and was published in 1981 by Wingham Press.

54. Geoffrey Page has admitted to this on *Churchill's Few*, Yorkshire Television 1985. This was not to be recommended, particularly as his were made of nylon. Fortunately for him, this was not the day he was shot down in flames.

55. Sergeant Jack Perkin in Gelb, op. cit., p. 172.

56. Tom Neil, *From the Cockpit – Spitfire*, Ian Allan 1990, p. 56.

57. Ibid., p. 46.

58. This may have been what did for Hans-Joachim Marseille, the 'Star of Africa', who had claimed 158 victories when he baled out of a 109 over the desert on 30 September 1942. He had not even been in action – his machine developed engine trouble. He might also have hit the tail. Nobody knows. He made no attempt to open his parachute.

59. This is precisely what happened to Steinhilper (op. cit., p. 17).

60. This method was successfully employed by Geoffrey Page (op. cit., p. 95) and in slightly varied form by Peter Townsend (op. cit., p. 267). Both books convey a good impression of what it was like to bale out and parachute into the sea, in the one case unwounded and in the other severely burned.

14. THE CHANNEL: AUGUST

1. Colville, op. cit., p. 250.

2. The destroyers were based at Dover in order to give early warning against an invasion. Portsmouth had always been seen as a suitable alternative on the south coast. See 'Invasion – General Naval Appreciation', 29.5.40., p. 4 in ADM 205/7. The use of destroyers for early warning had become redundant by July and the policy was strongly criticised by the C-in-C Home Fleet, Admiral Forbes. See Peter Fleming, *Operation Sea Lion*, Simon and Schuster 1957, pp. 161–3.

3. AIR 16/341. See also Orange, *Sir Keith Park*, pp. 98–9. The offensive spirit behind this is typical of Sholto Douglas, who was to succeed Dowding at Fighter Command and embark on a policy of 'leaning towards France' which was to cost his men dear in the years that followed.
4. See for example RL/2/II, 21.7.40.
5. RL/2/II 30.
6. See Mason, p. 172–3.
7. Ralph Barker, *That Eternal Summer*, Collins 1990, pp. 121–3.
8. RL/7/90, Einzelmeldung 9, Abschuß-Erfolge. The Bf 109s of JG2, JG27 and JG53 claimed 38 between them, the bombers claimed 2 and the Bf 110s of ZG2 claimed a fanciful 17.
9. Colville, op. cit., p. 257.

15. THE NUMBERS GAME

1. For example, on 11th November 1937, the German Embassy in London wrote a letter to the Foreign Office in Berlin about the construction of what they called 'Reservefabriken' being planned for the production of aero-engines and aircraft parts, attaching a report of a press conference on the subject given by the Air Ministry. These were the shadow factories and dispersals organisations, the location of which was an important piece of information on which little action seems to have been taken. See BA-MA, RL/2/II 101.
2. Boog, op. cit., pp. 350–3.
3. Ibid., pp. 353–5.
4. Only the Appendices now survive.
5. Boog, op.cit., pp. 355–6.
6. Wood and Dempster, op. cit., p. 65, and RL/2/II 411.
7. Boog, op. cit., p. 362.
8. In his report on his visit to the Luftwaffe in January 1937, Evill commented: 'They have a great respect for the possibilities of AA fire, and appear to think that it will be necessary to bomb at high altitudes and high speeds.' (*The German Organisation for Air Operations*, p. 12, Evill Papers, RAF Museum, AC 74/8/34).
9. RL/2/II 935. For a translation of Schmid's report and some pertinent comments see Wood and Dempster, pp. 66–8.
10. RL/2/II 727.
11. Ibid., pp. 27–8.
12. See *Radar – A Wartime Miracle*, by Colin Latham and Anne Stobbs, Sutton Publishing 1996, pp. 1–8.
13. Sebastian Cox, 'A Comparative Analysis of RAF and Luftwaffe Intelligence in the Battle of Britain, 1940' in Handel (ed.), op. cit., p. 437.
14. 'Bemerkungen zum Einsatz der Luftwaffe Nr. 6', Ob.d.L. Ia Nr.1670/40 geh. (III), 1st May 1940, §29, in BA-MA RL 2/II/58.
15. See the report made by Luftflotte 5, Nielsen, Stab Luftflotte V to Ob. d. L. Ia, 22 February 1941, in BA-MA RL 2/II/359.
16. Price, *Battle of Britain Day*, Sidgwick and Jackson 1990, pp. 49, 53–8, 63–4 and 117. See also *After the Battle*, ed. Ramsey, pp. 644–5, which includes photographs of the Dornier's spectacular end and the crash sites.
17. Cf. Caldwell, *JG 26*, pp. 68–9.
18. Cox, op. cit., pp. 430–1.
19. John Vasco and Peter Cornwell, *Zerstörer*, JAC Publications 1995, pp. 87, 146–7 and 196.
20. Cox, op. cit., p. 432.
21. Despatch, § 115.
22. See Air Historical Branch report, Appendix 36, AIR 41/16.
23. The data on Fighter Command and Luftwaffe aircraft and pilot losses on which all the analysis in this book is based have been compiled since the 1960's by Peter Cornwell and published by After the Battle Magazine in *The Battle of Britain Then and Now*, edited by Winston Ramsey. I am grateful to Peter Cornwell for providing me with a list of amendments compiled since the publication of the original material in 1982. It is a tribute to the thoroughness of the original work that the revisions are minor and have had little impact on the overall shape of the story which emerges. Bomber Command losses are drawn from

W.R. Chorley's *Bomber Command Losses of the Second World War*, Vol. 1, Midland Counties 1992.

24. By John Vasco, op. cit., pp. 97ff.

25. Osterkamp, op. cit., pp. 329–336.

26. 'Notes of a Meeting held at Air Ministry Headquarters, Whitehall, on Wednesday, 3 April 1940, to Consider the Prevention of Avoidable Accidents', AIR 6/59.

27. Ibid.

28. Mondey, *British Aircraft of World War II*, pp. 61–2.

29. Once the day threat had receded, several Hurricane squadrons were converted to night operations. For accounts of the near futility of this, written by those involved, see Bowyer and van Ishoven, *Hurricane and Messerschmitt*, Ian Allan 1974, pp. 120–9 and Peter Townsend, *Time and Chance*, Methuen 1978, pp. 112–5. The hapless Defiant, once withdrawn from daylight operations, found a more useful role as a night fighter.

30. See Hastings, *Bomber Command*, p. 234.

31. Neil, *Spitfire*, Ian Allan 1990, p. 51.

32. See his letter accompanying Park's report of 22 September, AIR 19/60.

33. Tom Neil, *Gun Button to Fire*, William Kimber 1987, p. 92.

34. Halder, Blatt 121.

35. See Vasco, op. cit., pp. 24–5.

36. Ralph Barker, *That Eternal Summer*, pp. 1–17.

37. Despatch, § 228.

16. EAGLE DAY

1. This unit had an unusual history which made it particularly suitable for use as part of Erprobungsgruppe 210. It had originally been equipped with Stukas and, together with two Staffeln of Bf 109s, formed a naval unit, Trägergruppe (Carrier Wing) 186, intended for use on the German Navy's only aircraft carrier, the *Graf Zeppelin*. The ship was never finished, and after the campaign in Poland, 4./TrGr186 re-equipped with the Bf 109 and was re-stationed in North Germany for coastal defence. The pilots thus had experience of dive-bombers and fighters (see Weal, *Bf 109D/E Aces 1939/41*, pp.12 and 21). Experience on type proved to be more important than experience in dive-bombing technique. In his report on his inspection of the unit on 26 August, Milch stated that the second Staffel, which had been a Stuka unit, had suffered heavier losses and had poorer morale than the other two, which he attributes to their relative lack of familiarity with the Bf 110 (Milch Papers Vol. 51, IWM).

2. See Vasco, op. cit., pp.10–11 and 28–9 and Mason, op. cit., pp. 182–3.

3. Jeffrey Quill, *Spitfire*, pp. 167–9.

4. Vasco, p. 31. Probably because of the misidentification of the aircraft at the time, Mason (p. 183) reports that Hawkinge was attacked by Ju 88s of II./KG76.

5. Claims according to Wood and Dempster, op. cit., p. 200.

6. Despatch, § 134.

7. See Bowyer, op. cit., pp. 126–7 and Chorley, op. cit., pp. 87–8.

8. Richard Collier tells the story that the only radio operator in KG2 to pick up the long-range signal from Kesselring was suffering from flu, and through his bunged up ears mistook the message as confirmation that the attack was to go ahead. See *Eagle Day*, Dent 1966, p. 51.

9. RL/2/II, 360, Merkblatt, 'Über den Einsatz von Jagd- und Zerstörerverbänden zum Begleitschutz und zur Aufnahme von Kampfverbänden und Aufklärern', I 5.

10. Cf. Vasco, *Bombsights over England*, pp. 33–4.

11. Macksey, *Kesselring – The Making of the Luftwaffe*, p.79. Kesselring would have been the one holding the tirade if Fink had in fact disobeyed his order of 4 August and been without any escort.

12. Mason ascribes this action to later in the day as part of the main raid on Portland (op. cit., pp. 188–192). Luftflotte 3's operational records give the take-off time as 1210, which was 1110 BST, and state clearly that it was

a 'freie Jagd', not an escort mission (RL/7/90). An account of the fight itself from a German point of view can be found in Bekker, *Angriffshöhe 4000*, Stalling Verlag 1964, pp. 188–90.

13. None of the published accounts of the morning's activities in the west can be fully reconciled with the operational records of Airfleet 3, which have been followed here, with additions from Vasco and Cornwell's *Zerstörer* and von Eimannsberger's *Zerstörergruppe*. Different raids are mixed up and the Luftwaffe's intentions misinterpreted. For example, commentators usually say that Andover was bombed by mistake, the real target being Middle Wallop. This would have made sense, but the records clearly show Andover to have been the intended target.

14. In its report to OKW, the Luftwaffe said it destroyed 90 British fighters and 8 barrage balloons against losses of 28 (Greiner, OKW Tagebuch, IWM Dept of Documents EDS AL 1054/1, p. 36). It at least knew its own losses for sure, so this could have been a deliberate attempt to impress Hitler. On the other hand, it may have been based on an early and incomplete assessment.

15. Colville, op. cit., p. 261.

16. Hastings, op. cit., pp. 70–73.

17. Operations Record Book of 600 Squadron as quoted by Vasco, op. cit., p.37.

18. He kept an eye on both of them. On the 19th he moved 111 to Debden in 12 Group and 601 from Tangmere to Exeter.

17. THE GREATEST DAY

1. The identity of the raiders on the 15th is unclear. Mason (op. cit. p. 199) identifies the raiders as II./ZG76, but if so, this would be the only occasion on which they carried bombs. Robin Brooks (*Kent Airfields of the Second World War*, Countryside Books 1998, p. 165), says it was Erprobungsgruppe 210, whilst

mistakenly attributing the two aircraft they lost to the ground defences on the 14th to this raid. Vasco (*Bombsights over England*, p. 38) cites evidence that the unit flew five missions on the 15th, amongst which only the Martlesham Heath and Croydon raids have been positively identified. This could have been one of the others.

Deighton, meanwhile, describes with some relish a complete disintegration of morale at Manston (*Fighter*, pp. 207–9 and 240–3). This has caused some offence to those who were there. He does not name any sources, and the veracity of some has been questioned. One story, about Squadron Leader Leathart having to restrain another officer from threatening cowering ground staff with a gun, which has been denied elsewhere by Leathart himself (Hough and Richards, op. cit., p. 226), appears to have originated in Al Deere's account (op. cit., p. 127). There was an air-raid warning in force and the men were told to go to the shelters and stay there. Morale was poor at Manston, but there is no evidence of a mutiny. See Rocky Stockman, *The History of RAF Manston*, RAF Manston 1986, pp. 39–40 and 43–4, and Hans Onderwater, *Gentlemen in Blue – 600 Squadron*, Leo Cooper 1997, pp. 129 and Appendix XVI, pp. 447–453, which gives a line-by-line refutation of Deighton's claims.

2. He is thought to have been flying a Bf 110D-0 with a built-in long-range tank. The aerodynamic penalties this tank imposed led to its being abandoned in the more numerous D-1 version which had jettisonable fuel tanks. Most of the unit were probably flying this version. It does not seem to have helped them much. One of those who did get back was Gordon Gollob, who became the first German fighter ace to score 150 victories and took over from Galland as Inspector of Fighters in January 1945.

3. Mason, along with most others, claims Rubensdörffer was pursued and finally shot down by S/L John Thompson, whose cine-gun film from the 15th shows Rubensdörffer's aircraft, coded S9+AB, under attack (p. 206). Vasco disputes this and claims he was probably finally shot down by P/O Duckenfield of 501 Squadron, whose log describes shooting down a Do 215 at the right place and the right time to fit with Rubensdörffer's machine, which could easily be mistaken for a Do 215 (pp. 41–52). It may well be that Thompson hit and damaged him and somebody else delivered the coup de grace. We will probably never know.

4. RL/2/II, 360, Besprechung am 15.8.40, and RL/2/II 30, Besprechung Reichsmarschall.

5. Deere, op. cit., pp. 112–9.

6. Roberts, *Eminent Churchillians*, pp. 175–7.

7. Colville, op. cit., p. 263.

8. *Their Finest Hour*, p. 249.

18. THE HARDEST DAY

1. See Mason, op. cit., p.212, Caldwell, *JG26*, pp. 44–5 and Hough and Richards, op. cit. pp. 193 and 231.

2. See Hough and Richards, op. cit., p.196. This account states that Greenshields body was washed up on the beach, but the evidence about his fate given in *The Battle of Britain Then and Now*, pp. 362–3 is persuasive.

3. See in particular David Alan Johnson, *The Battle of Britain*, Combined Publishing 1998, pp. 119–22. Johnson focuses on the American perspective of the battle. Other Americans, claiming to be Canadian, may have been earlier casualties.

4. See above. The award seems to have been something of a burden to Nicolson, who was plagued by the belief that he had not earned it, a view shared by many pilots who knew of similar cases and did not like one of their number being singled out and made a fuss of. Nicolson was posted to India in 1942, and killed in 1945 when the Liberator he was travelling in crashed into the sea south of Calcutta.

5. Barker, op. cit., p. 125.

6. See Gilbert, *Finest Hour*, p.736. The thought probably originated with H.G. Wells and the phrase with Shakespeare. See Chapter 1.

7. Ibid., p.110, Doe, op. cit., pp. 22–3 and conversation with the author, 23.7.96.

8. Middlebrook and Everitt, *The Bomber Command War Diaries*, Midland Publishing 1985, p. 74.

9. See Price, *The Hardest Day*, pp. 192–3.

10. Thanks largely to Alfred Price, op. cit.

11. This eye-witness account can be found in the Shoreham Aircraft Museum in Shoreham village north of Sevenoaks, which is run by aviation artist Geoff Nutkins. The witness was Private Manchip and the account was written by Leonard Smith on 10 June 1990. It fits Lamberty's own account, in which he was clear about being under attack from Hurricanes until just before he crashed (see Alexander McKee, *Strike from the Sky*, Grafton Books 1990, pp. 184–5), and the combat reports filed by F/Lt Brown and Sgts Craig and Dymond of 111. The other twin-engined machine seen by Private Manchip could have been either of those piloted by Raab or Maasen, the other planes in the 1st Kette. Lamberty's aircraft was also shot at by a separate detachment of the Addington Home Guard, who claimed it themselves. This was the best version of all as far as morale was concerned, so the *Daily Mirror* duly reported on 19 August that the Home Guard had 'bagged a plane at 50 feet' (see Haining, *Spitfire Summer*, pp. 124–5). It is very unlikely that they hit it at all.

12. Mason (p. 179) gives an account of this episode which shows how much confusion can arise in war. Two Blenheims of 604 Squadron with an escort of three Spitfires from 152 Squadron were ordered out by the

Station Commander of Middle Wallop to look for ditched aircrew, as a number were missing. They found an He 59 on the water with an escort of 109s above, so they attacked the seaplane while the Spitfires held off the escorts. One Spitfire and Blenheim were lost. A second He 59 put out to the area, but was shot down by 610 Squadron, who themselves then tangled with some 109s and lost two pilots.

13. On the following see Price, *The Hardest Day*, p. 60, Caldwell, op. cit., pp. 45–6 and Spick, *Luftwaffe Fighter Aces*, p. 74

14. Price, op.cit., p.173

15. The most remarkable case of this technique being used was when Hans-Joachim Marseille, regarded by many as the most gifted of all Germany's aces, attacked the Tomahawks of 5 Squadron SAAF near Bir Hakeim in Libya on 6 June 1942. The Tomahawks, inferior to the Bf 109F flown by Marseille, saw him and went into a defensive circle, but by repeatedly diving on them, Marseilles shot down five and damaged a sixth. (See Edward H. Sims, *The Fighter Pilots*, Cassell 1967.) The method was widely used, being a particular favourite with Galland, who was clearly an influence on Schoepfel. See Spick, *Luftwaffe Fighter Aces*, pp. 68–70.

16. RL7/90.

17. Barker, op. cit., pp. 126–7.

18. A full and painstaking account of the day's fighting, from which this summary is largely derived, is given by Alfred Price in the work which gave this day its name. First published in 1979, it remains one of the best books yet written about the Battle of Britain.

19. THINKING AGAIN

1. Toliver and Constable, *Fighter General*, Ampress 1990, pp. 102–5.

2. The results of this meeting were documented in a summary of Göring's comments distributed down to the level of Gruppenkommandeur

on the 22nd, and a separate set of remarks sent to the Airfleet Commanders. Both are found in RL/2/II 360.

3. See Steinhilper, op. cit., pp. 283–4.

4. Wing Commander John Dewar was killed in unknown circumstances on a lone flight from Exeter to Tangmere on 12 September. He commanded 87 Squadron at Exeter and was also the Station Commander there. When his body was discovered attached to a parachute harness and riddled with bullets, it gave rise to more nasty speculation about the shooting of pilots who had baled out.

5. As defined by Park himself on p. 2 of his report on the fighting in this period prepared for the Air Ministry on 12 September. See AIR 19/60.

6. Speech to the House of Commons, 20 November 1950.

7. Churchill, *Into Battle*, Cassell 1941, pp. 252–62.

8. Colville, op. cit., p. 267.

9. Deere, op. cit., p. 126 and Gelb, p. 265.

10. Gelb, op. cit., p. 265. The last may have been Squadron Leader Michael Crossley, the C/O of 32 Squadron, who happened to be awarded a DSO to add to his DFC on the 20th. The quip may have multiple originators.

11. Gilbert, *Finest Hour*, p. 742.

12. P/O Dennis David in Gelb, op. cit., p. 165.

20. HUNTERS AND HUNTED

1. Mike Spick, *The Ace Factor*, Airlife 1988, Introduction.

2. See M.J.F. Bowyer, *The Battle of Britain 50 Years On*, Appendix 2, pp. 226–9.

3. Such errors naturally occurred on both sides. On 8 September Ulrich Steinhilper saw a 109 from a different unit shoot down one of his comrades (Steinhilper & Osborne. *Spitfire on my Tail*, p. 293). Galland's illustrious career was nearly terminated after Dunkirk by the distinguished *Experte* Wilhelm Balthasar, who was demonstrating to his admiring men how to shoot down a Hurricane

which was just stooging along unconcerned by his presence. Galland was listening to Balthasar's commentary over the r/t when lines of tracer streaming past his cockpit made him realise that he was the dopey Hurricane (Johnnie Johnson, *The Story of Air Fighting*, Arrow 1987, p. 107 and Spick, *Luftwaffe Fighter Aces*, pp. 46–7).

4. For this and the following see Mike Spick, *The Ace Factor*, pp. 1–31.

5. Experienced Luftwaffe pilots defending Germany against the heavily armed B-17s of the US 8th Air Force later in the war used to attack from head-on, as the bombers could put up a formidable amount of fire from the rear. See, for example, Jeffrey L. Ethel and Alfred Price, *Target Berlin*, Arms & Armour Press, 1981, p. 24 and diagram, p. 50.

6. The shot also dropped as it lost energy and curved downwards at an ever increasing angle. At a range of 400 yards the bullets would drop 5 feet by the time they reached the target (*Spitfire*, written by Brian Johnson, Thorn EMI Video 1983). Bob Doe has pointed out that guns were harmonised to allow for this.

7. Donald L. Caldwell, *JG 26*, p. 50.

8. Ibid. The Germans did not have as much of an issue with the Bf 109, as the guns were mounted more closely together.

9. See for example, Doe, *Fighter Pilot*, p. 30.

10. See *Battle of Britain*, *Daily Telegraph* Editorial Supplement, Part 1, 16 June 1990, p.XX.

11. Larry Forrester, *Fly for your Life*, Panther 1959, p. 37. This need for intimacy with the aircraft, acquired only after plenty of flying, may in part explain the reluctance many aces had to change mounts, even when a superior aircraft was available. Galland stuck to his Bf 109E even when the 109F was available, and when the clearly superior FW 190 was first introduced many German pilots still preferred to fly their old 109s.

12. P/O Peter Brown in Gelb, op. cit., p.153.

13. For pilots' own assessment of this ability see Gelb, op. cit., pp. 163–4.

14. See Wells, op. cit., pp. 36–9.

15. Norman Franks, *Sky Tiger*, p.12.

16. He took up big game hunting after the war with his friend Adolf Galland, and practiced skeet shooting whenever he could during the war.

17. Forrester, op. cit., p.23. Tuck's most famous feat of marksmanship was accomplished, ironically, when he was shot down by AA fire on a low-level 'Rhubarb' over France on 28 January 1942. Bringing his damaged Spitfire in to crash-land whilst still being fired at from the ground, he saw an AA gun shooting at him from the end of the field he was planning to belly-land in and fired at it. He not only shot up the crew but also put a shell down the barrel of the gun, to the amusement and admiration of his captors (Forrester, op. cit., p. 183). It was luck, of course, but 'Tuck's luck' was part of what made him successful. In his own comments on the importance of marksmanship he stresses the need for precision flying, particularly the avoidance of skidding, for getting in close and then delivering a two-second burst. If more than that were needed, the shot had not been properly prepared. See *Forty Years of the Spitfire*, Mitchell Memorial Symposium, Royal Aeronautical Society 1976, p. 98.

18. Toliver, *Fighter General*, pp. 18–19.

19. Steinhilper, op. cit., p. 211.

20. Osterkamp, p. 320.

21. Bob Doe has remarked that they always had the numerical odds against them, but they never disengaged because of it.

22. See Mike Spick, *Luftwaffe Fighter Aces*, pp. 12–13.

23. See the account given in *The Battle of Britain Then and Now*, Mark IV Edition, pp. 306–313, and the authorised biography *Nicolson VC* by Peter D. Mason, Geerings of Ashford,

1991, passim. No Bf 110 was in fact lost in circumstances corresponding to Nicolson's combat report. He himself wrote that he had no reason to believe the Messerschmitt was out of control and was not even sure his gun-button was on 'fire' (*Nicolson VC*, p. 37).

24. One of them died.

25. The Secretary of State for Air had written that he wanted to honour the recent exploits of the RAF by finding a suitable candidate for the VC. Dowding passed this on to his Group Commanders and when Nicolson's Station Commander at North Weald, Victor Beamish, recommended him for the DFC on the advice of his Squadron Leader, John Grandy, Park changed it to the VC 'for this outstanding act of gallantry and magnificent display of fighting spirit'. Dowding concurred, and after some discussion the RAF's Personnel Services agreed to pass the recommendation to the RAF Awards Committee (see Mason, *Nicolson VC*, pp.51–3).

26. *Sagittarius Rising*, Penguin edition 1985, p. 46.

27. That prisoners were killed on both sides during World War II is well documented. See, for example, Hastings, *Overlord*, pp. 249–51.

28. As observed, for example, by F/O Wright of 92 Squadron, in *Battle of Britain, Daily Telegraph* Editorial Supplement, Part 1, 16 June 1990, p. XXI. Park became so concerned about the frequency of such reports that on 13 September he wrote to his station commanders ordering pilots to leave cripples alone (AIR 16/735).

29. Hugh Dundas, op. cit., pp. 1–3.

21. TACTICS

1. John James, *The Paladins*, 1990, p. 222.

2. For a visual display of the Fighter Area Attacks see the superb diagrams in *The Battle of Britain* by Richard Townshend Bickers, Salamander Books 1990, pp. 97–102. They are accompanied by a suitably ironic commentary from Air Vice-Marshal Johnnie Johnson.

3. *The Battle of Britain* by Richard Townshend Bickers, p. 99. See also Gelb, op. cit., pp. 88–90.

4. Vincent Orange, *Sir Keith Park*, Methuen 1984, p. 71.

5. Norman Franks, *Fighter Command 1936–1968*, Patrick Stephens 1992, p.38.

6. On the following see Dilip Sarkar, *Angriff Westland*, Ramrod Publications 1994, pp. 61–63.

7. See Vincent Orange, *Sir Keith Park*, pp. 96–7. Whilst head-on attacks were later used by the Luftwaffe against B-17s, the preferred tactic was to invert and dive away before meeting the formation rather than fly through it, but in practice a lot of German pilots did fly straight through, exposing themselves to dangerously concentrated cross-fire from the defensive 'box' formation the Americans used.

8. *The Battle of Britain Then and Now*, pp. 361 and 578.

9. Gerry Edge and Paddy Barthropp as quoted in Norman Gelb, *Scramble*, pp. 114–5.

10. Stanford-Tuck, quoted in *Glorious Summer*, ed. Johnson & Lucas, Stanley Paul 1990, p. 94.

11. See Burns, p. 80 and Sorley Papers, RAF Museum, Hendon, AC 75/27/18.

12. Keith Park had argued for the use of heavier-calibre 0.5 inch machine-guns instead of standard rifle-calibre 0.303s in 1938 (Vincent Orange, *Sir Keith Park*, pp. 70–71). This was to be the standard weapon adopted by the USAF, which agreed with him. 'Dizzy' Allen flays the decision to use the 0.303 rather than the 0.5 as yet another example of RAF incompetence (op. cit., pp. 63–70). The arguments governing the choices at the time were complex and always controversial. See G.F. Wallace, *The Guns of the RAF 1939–45*, William Kimber 1972.

13. *The Battle of Britain Then and Now*, p. 500.

14. For Townsend's graphic and charmingly self-deprecating account of this engagement see his own book about the Battle of Britain, *Duel of Eagles*, pp. 263–8.

15. This epithet, which is clearly an epic *topos*, is so stubbornly attached to the Stuka that it appears in books published fifty years after the events (e.g. Toliver, *Fighter General*, 1990, p.94) and in the work of the most serious and erudite of historians (e.g. Mason, p. 222).

16. It served usefully in secondary theatres as long as the Luftwaffe had air superiority, and was a very effective tank-buster in Russia, where the Luftwaffe's supremacy was not seriously challenged until 1943.

17. On the following see Price, *The Hardest Day*, pp. 117–8.

18. Galland can be heard complaining about this, as he complains about almost everything else which happened to him in the summer of 1940, in the TVS television documentary production *Battle for Britain*, ITV 1990.

19. Unteroffizier Heinz Sellhorn, quoted by Price, *The Hardest Day*, p.126.

20. As in the case of the Stuka, neither time nor erudition can erode the strength of the glue between this epithet and the maligned Bf 110. See, for example, Hough and Richards, 1990, p. 136.

21. See Spick, *Luftwaffe Fighter Aces*, pp. 54–6.

22. It took part in some of the early massacres of Wellingtons and Blenheims, notably that on 18 December 1939.

23. Osterkamp, op. cit., p. 329.

24. Vasco and Cornwell, *Zerstörer*, p. 49.

25. Ibid., pp. 55–6.

26. See Mason, p. 121.

27. See Spick, *Luftwaffe Fighter Aces*, pp. 59–60.

28. See Vasco, op. cit., pp. 71–2.

29. Even before Mölders worked out his flying tactics, Luftwaffe training manuals put a lot of emphasis on fighting techniques, as witnessed by the 'Jagdflieger Anleitung' from the 1930s in BA-Ma RL/2/II 283.

30. *Hurricane and Messerschmitt* by Chaz Bowyer and Armand Ishoven, Ian Allan 1993, pp.207–9.

31. Probably the clearest and best-illustrated account of Luftwaffe fighter tactics in English is Johnnie Johnson's previously cited essay in *The Battle of Britain* by Richard Townshend Bickers, pp. 94ff. On the development of the Schwarm in Spain see Spick, *Luftwaffe Fighter Aces*, pp. 23–5.

32. The tactical gambits opened up by the use of the Schwarm formation are explained by Spick in *Luftwaffe Fighter Aces*, pp. 17–27.

33. See Johnnie Johnson, *Wing Leader*, Chatto and Windus 1956, pp. 29–30 and *The Story of Air Fighting*, pp. 112–3.

34. Stuart, *The Strategy and Tactics of Air Fighting*, Longman 1925, p. 10.

35. Ibid., passim, especially pp. 32–6, 44–7 and 65–76.

36. Ibid., p. 193.

37. AIR 16/735.

38. Sergeant Jack Perkin, who flew with 600, 615 and 73 Squadrons during the battle, in Gelb, op. cit., p. 89.

39. Dowding Despatch, § 220.

40. Wing Commander Roland Beamont in *Hurricane and Messerschmitt* by Bowyer and Ishoven, pp. 32–3.

41. See Spick, op.cit., p. 13.

42. Air Commodore Henry Cozens, in Price, *Spitfire*, p. 19.

43. A revealing pilot's-eye view of the Spitfire and the 109 is given by Squadron Leader Paul Day in the Yorkshire TV production on the Spitfire in the series *Equinox*, written by Brian Johnson, Uden Associates, Channel Four 1990.

44. Ergonomics is now a science but was in its infancy in 1940. The Flying Personnel Research Committee reported on this too, making a few suggestions about the positioning and lighting of instruments in future designs, but these were just based on a few conferences, rather than empirical investigation. See AIR 6/59.

45. Ulrich Steinhilper describes how, on 27 September, he used this characteristic to save his life and get away from an aggressive crowd of Spitfires and Hurricanes (op. cit., pp. 309–11).
46. I am grateful to Michael Payne for pointing this out.
47. See the A & AEE report on flying a captured 109 written in May 1940 reproduced in Bowyer and van Ishoven, op. cit., pp. 298–304.
48. Rod Smith, 'In Defence of the Spitfire', Aeroplane Monthly, August 1995, p. 31.
49. As claimed by the RAE in Bowyer and Ishoven, op.cit., p. 302.
50. It is also said that 5% of all Bf 109s were written off in landing accidents. As 30,000 were built and 1,500 is 5% of 30,000, it may be that these two statements have been confused.
51. See the remarks by Tony Bianchi on the Spitfire's old-fashioned skinning (Yorkshire Television Equinox).
52. Bowyer and Ishoven, op.cit., p. 302.
53. Ibid., p. 218.
54. I am grateful to Dr John Ackroyd, of the Dept of Aerospace Engineering at the Manchester School of Engineering, for indulging my curiosity and producing a paper, together with P.J. Lamont, which checks the results given by Deighton (in Fighter, Grafton 1977, p. 106) and also Mason in his Profile No. 111 on the Hurricane (1967), from which source Deighton seems to have got his data. Both assume vertically banked turns that are not possible, and the data and calculations are wrong. The critical values are the respective wing loadings and lift coefficients. The turning radii for the three aircraft under achievable combat limits are: Bf 109 854 ft, Spitfire 684 ft and Hurricane 663 ft (Ackroyd and Lamont, Aerospace Internal Report No. 9701).
55. Rod Smith, op.cit., p. 30.
56. See Graham Leggett in Bowyer and Ishoven, op. cit., p.52.
57. Whilst (according to the trials carried out with Mk I N 3171 in March 1940) the Spitfire took 7 minutes 42 seconds to reach 20,000 feet, the Hurricane took 8 minutes 30 seconds. (Figure quoted for a late Mark I in Francis K. Mason, The Hawker Hurricane I, Profile Publication 111, p. 20).

22. SUMMER'S LEASE

1. In October, when escorting fighter-bombers, this rose to as much as seven. Steinhilper, op.cit., p.234.
2. The minutes of the meeting of 21 July, when the fighting was still close to the fighter bases, already contains a note at the end to ensure tight flight discipline, adding: 'Materialverbrauch Bf 109!!' ('Bf 109 fuel consumption!!') (RL/2/II).
3. Gelb, op. cit., p. 180.
4. See Vasco, op. cit., p. 56. Since the raid on Croydon, the unit had been involved in a couple of small attacks on convoys, losing one machine.
5. Stockman, op. cit., p. 41.
6. Deere, op. cit., pp. 128–9.
7. Dundas, op. cit., pp. 40–3.
8. Doe, op. cit., pp. 31–2. His victim may well have been one of the four 109s lost by JG 53 which was on a 'freie Jagd' in Geschwader strength over the Channel during the operation against Portsmouth between 1550 and 1710. Three of them are reported to have come down near Cherbourg. Claims were filed by pilots of 43 and 610 Squadrons as well as 234.
9. AIR 41/16.
10. AIR 16/330.
11. Flight Lieutenant Ash, the most senior ranking Defiant gunner who flew with S/L Garvin, managed to bale out, which was very lucky for a gunner in the cramped, electrically operated turret. However, he was found dead. He may have been hit by bullets, or he may have hit the tailplane, a very real danger. See Caldwell, op. cit., p. 51.
12. Deere, op. cit., pp. 135–6.
13. See Steinhilper, op. cit., p. 288.
14. Gilbert, Finest Hour, p. 761.
15. Hillary, op. cit., pp. 102–3.

16. Mason believes (op. cit., pp. 256–7), that he did get not four but five, a claim repeated by Wood and Dempster (op. cit., p. 240), and quotes extensively from Gleave's own account. The German losses recorded by Peter Cornwell do not bear this out (op. cit., p. 607). On 30 August, JG27 lost four Bf 109s due to combat. Three were from I. Gruppe. Two of these force-landed near Ashford, which was about where Gleave was, and the pilots were taken prisoner, but they were lost much later in the day, probably to 603 Squadron. The third was lost over Dungeness and went into the sea. A fourth, from III. Gruppe, was shot down over the Thames Estuary at 1830. A further machine of Stab III./JG27 crashed on landing at Guines after a combat sortie and was damaged, and one more from III./JG27 was damaged when it belly-landed following mechanical failure after an operational sortie.

17. Vasco, op. cit., pp. 56–7. Most accounts attribute this raid to some unidentified Ju 88s, which is what those on the ground thought they were. The log books of pilots from Erprobungsgruppe 210 make it clear that they were responsible. A new leader, Hauptmann von Boltenstern, was posted in on the 26th, but it is not clear that he led the raid.

18. Mason op. cit., p. 257 and Bob Ogley, *Biggin on the Bump*, Froglets Publications 1990, p. 64.

19. Sarkar, *Bader's Duxford Fighters*, pp. 78–83. Burns, *Bader and his Men*, Arms and Armour Press 1990, pp. 59–63 gives a more traditional account, which has Bader ignoring the controller, flying higher and further west in order to bounce from out of the sun. The 242 Squadron records quoted by Sarkar contradict this. The account of the conversation with Leigh-Mallory comes from Bader himself. Bader did not mention a wing.

20. As usual, a lot of German losses were caused by more than one attacker. In

this case, there are reasons to believe that one or both of these two claims (by Christie and McKnight), which were indeed actual losses, were shared by 1 Squadron. See Sarkar, op. cit., pp. 77–80.

21. Ibid., p. 80. It was quite unusual for messages like this to arrive from such august quarters.

22. See Robinson, op. cit., pp. 250–1 and Kent, *One of the Few*, p. 105. Another Hurricane, probably flown by P/O Wicks of 56 Squadron, attacked the same machine, and Wicks also claimed it as a Bf 110. As Paskiewicz claimed it as a Do 17, Fighter Command probably counted it twice. Wicks was right: it was in fact a Bf 110 of 4./ZG76 (Vasco and Cornwell, op. cit., pp. 152 & 187), part of KG53's escort.

23. Later on, however, 601 Squadron lost four Hurricanes, with one pilot missing and another wounded, in a clash with some Bf 109s over the Thames Estuary at about 1330.

24. Mason, p. 260. 242 Squadron took off from Coltishall at 0825 and 310 Squadron went up from Duxford at the same time. Both landed an hour later without having seen action (Sarkar, op. cit., p.86).

25. Townsend, *Time and Chance*, Methuen 1978, pp. 111–2.

26. See Townsend, *Duel of Eagles*, pp. 373–5.

27. Deere, op. cit., pp. 142–7. Despite their exhaustion, they still managed to joke. When Deere got into his Spitfire the next morning, he was given an envelope from George Gribble containing an open train ticket to Hornchurch with the message that he thought he might need it.

28. Hillary, op. cit., pp. 106–8.

29. Mason attributes these late raids on the radar stations, Hornchurch and Biggin hill to Erprobungsgruppe 210 (p. 262), as do Hough and Richards (p. 238). They could not physically have done them all. In fact log books show that they returned to Denain in the afternoon. Bekker (op. cit., p.209)

more plausibly names the raiders as III./KG76. All agree it was a low-level attack.

30. Gilbert, op. cit., pp. 764–6 and Colville, op. cit., pp. 276–8.
31. See Knight, *A Harvest of Messerschmitts*, p. 116. Their attitude was shared by the Czechs. Squadron leader Hess of 310 Squadron told his controller that he had made two passes at the crew of a Dornier he had forced down, intending to machine-gun them on the ground. However, he reported, 'I do not shoot . . . I think it is no use, I am become too bloody British!' He had recently heard that his wife and daughter had been killed by the Nazis. See Sarkar, op.cit., p. 86.
32. Colville, op. cit., pp. 279–80.
33. Barker, op. cit., pp. 134–5.
34. Hillary, op. cit., pp. 5–10.
35. See Mason, p. 260, Ogley, op. cit., p. 71 and Graham Wallace, *RAF Biggin Hill*, Putnam 1969, pp. 186–7. On the night of the enquiry, Grice and some pilots went down to their favourite haunt, the White Hart at Brasted, to celebrate. They started putting their names on the black-out screen in front of the bar door. It became famous and can be found today behind the door at the Shoreham Aircraft Museum only a few miles from Brasted. See Kath Preston, *Inn of the Few*, Spellmount 1993, p. 33.
36. *Into Battle*, pp. 263–271. Whilst the text of this speech gives the loss statistics, Gilbert plausibly states that they were not divulged to the Commons, but only to the Chiefs of Staff Committee. No doubt Churchill could have trusted Parliament, but the delusion of the German High Command about what was actually going on was strategically so important that he may well have reserved this information for the inner circle.
37. Instruction No. 10, AIR 41/16.
38. Barker, op. cit., pp. 135–7.

23. THE AIRFIELDS

1. Based on Appendix 8 of the account written by the RAF Air Historical Branch, AIR 41/16. This list contains some serious omissions which have been filled in from various other sources.
2. RL/2/II, 471.
3. Despatch §145.
4. Not everybody co-operated. After the first raids on Biggin Hill, the senior WAAF officer, Felicity Hanbury, toured the village to find accommodation for her girls. Most of those they asked were very willing to help, but some house owners told them what they thought of the RAF for building an airfield next door which put their lives in danger and slammed the door. See Wallace, op. cit., p.180 and compare Ogley, op. cit., p. 71.
5. Price, *Sky Battles!*, Arms and Armour 1993, p.43.
6. After moving to Towerfields, in late September it was moved on once again to a place called the Rookery in 1941 because Towerfields was too small. See *The Battle of Britain Then and Now*, Mark IV, pp. 738–9.
7. AIR 41/16, Air Historical Branch Appendix 8.
8. See Peter Flint, *RAF Kenley*, Terence Dalton 1985, pp. 88–91.
9. They were not in fact as costly as all that. We do not know for sure, but Erprobungsgruppe 210 probably flew 300–350 combat sorties between 12 August and 6 September and suffered casualties of thirteen aircraft destroyed and nine damaged. Their resulting ratio of total losses per sortie of 3.5–4.5% is about the same as the long-term average suffered by the US 8th Air Force in its daylight campaign against Germany later in the war. The American Commanders regarded this as acceptable. The bulk of the losses were incurred over Croydon when Erprobungsgruppe 210 lost their escort, and 9./KG76 suffered heavily because of the mix-up over the timing of the Kenley

raid. Other units suffered similarly for similar reasons in carrying out conventional raids. Low-level attacks were not inherently as perilous as the Luftwaffe seemed to believe.

10. Dowding has also commented that the amount of damage 'has been generally underestimated' (Despatch §144).

11. Park report of 12 September, pp. 6–7, AIR 19/60.

12. AIR 19/60, letter of 22 September, p. 2.

13. See for example, Deere, *Nine Lives*, pp. 128–9.

14. Dowding Despatch §135, AIR 8/863.

15. See Orange, op. cit., p.96.

24. THE PILOTS

1. Tony Holmes, *Hurricane Aces 1939–40*, Osprey 1998, pp. 82 & 87–8.

2. See Weal, *Bf 109 D/E Aces 1939–41*, p. 68.

3. Source is the data given by Bowyer, op. cit., pp. 133–4, usually corroborated by at least one further source. Moves within Groups have been excluded except in cases where they effectively meant moving a tired unit to a quiet sector.

4. They arrived in Tangmere from Wittering on the 9th and operated from there and Eastchurch before moving to Hornchurch on the 14th. They saw no action in the air until the 16th.

5. They moved from Hornchurch to its satellite, Rochford, on the 27th, and began leaving for Kirton-in-Lindsey on the 28th.

6. Saw no action until 9th September.

7. AIR 16/330.

8. See Sarkar's analysis, *Bader's Duxford Fighters*, pp. 69–70.

9. Ibid., pp. 48–9.

10. Several of the massacred squadrons contained outstanding individuals such as Denys Gillam who was with 616, or Brian Carbury of 603, both to become well-known aces. Both were in fact involved in the massacre of I./JG77 on the 31st. See Knight, op. cit., p. 115.

11. See the account by Tony Holmes in Price, *Spitfire Aces 1939–41*, Osprey 1996, pp. 83–6.

12. Steinhilper gives an example of such a youth sent to JG52. He was unable to use his oxygen or radio equipment and his navigation skills were such that he headed straight for England when he was ordered to return home, and had to be led back (op. cit., pp. 303–4). Steinhilper's Gruppe were also short of aircraft.

13. Milch Report of 26/8/40, Milch Papers Vol. 51/54, p. 9, IWM Dept. of Documents.

14. Ibid., Report of 9/9/40, p. 3.

15. Figures from Wood & Dempster, op. cit., p. 348.

16. AIR 16/903.

17. AIR 20/2759.

18. AIR 16/330.

19. Halder, op. cit., Blatt 157.

20. Figures on pilot and aircraft availability from Wood & Dempster, op. cit., pp. 344 & 348.

21. Conversation with Willoughby de Broke as reported by Wright, op. cit., p. 192. It is not the only time during the period under which he was under the greatest pressure that Park expressed confidence. When Churchill returned to Uxbridge on 1 September after his visit on 31 August, the day of Fighter Command's heaviest losses in air combat during the whole battle, Park 'confirmed the PM's view that the Germans must already have developed their maximum attack and could not stand the strain much longer' (Colville, op.cit., p. 279). This view was right on both counts.

25. LONDON

1. Dennis Knight, *Harvest of Messerschmitts*, Wingham Press 1990.

2. Collier, *Eagle Day*, p. 155.

3. Tietzen's body was washed up on the French coast with a single bullet wound to the head. His case was not isolated, and side-arms were banned in September. See Steinhilper, op. cit., p.335.

4. Steinhilper, op. cit., p. 284.
5. Goss, op. cit., p. 151.
6. See Steinhilper, p. 286ff & 302, Bekker, op. cit., p.210, Collier, op. cit., p. 172ff, Hough & Richards, pp. 236–7.
7. Johannes Steinhoff as quoted in *Guardian Weekly*, 26.8.90, p. 27.
8. Steinhilper, p. 287.
9. Peter Stahl, *The Diving Eagle*, Kimber 1984, pp. 58–9.
10. Donald Caldwell, *The JG26 War Diary*, Grub Street 1996, p. 61, and *JG26*, p. 49.
11. Galland, *The First and the Last*, Bantam 1978, p.31 and Toliver, op. cit., pp. 111–2. Osterkamp must have been at this meeting, but he makes no mention of it. However, it has been confirmed by Osterkamp's Chief-of-Staff Viek, as well as Fink and Weitkus of KG2, all of whom were interviewed by Alexander McKee (McKee, op. cit., p. 165). It has given rise to the misleading impression that Göring was responsible for shackling the Bf 109s to the bombers. Galland's own practice at JG26 was in fact what he was after.
12. Galland notes Göring's observation that the bombers were more important than record bag figures (ibid.). If directed at him personally, score-chaser that he was, it should be said that Galland was also a responsible leader and JG26's record in bomber protection was second to none.
13. RL/2/II 360.
14. Bekker, op. cit., pp. 214–5.
15. Middlebrook and Everitt, *The Bomber Command War Diaries*, p. 77.
16. Colville, op. cit., p.271.
17. Gilbert, op. cit., p. 757.
18. Greiner, *Kriegstagebuch*, p.77.
19. IWM MI 14/101.
20. For an account of the political and psychological impact of bombs falling on Berlin, see Shirer, *The Nightmare Years*, pp. 589–591.
21. There is no surviving direct documentation of this meeting. An account of it was given by Beppo Schmid after the war. See Taylor, op. cit., pp. 156–8, Wood & Dempster p.

256, Mason p. 294, Bekker, op. cit., pp. 214–5.
22. Greiner, op. cit., p. 41.
23. Ibid., p. 47.
24. Ibid., pp. 64 & 67.
25. Shirer, op. cit., pp. 592–3.
26. On the motivation for the attack on London compare John Ray, *The Night Blitz* 1940–41, Arms & Armour Press 1996, pp. 97–103.
27. Hough and Richards, p. 254–5.
28. Sandy Johnstone, *Spitfire into War*, Grafton 1988, pp. 172–3.
29. See Vasco and Cornwell, op. cit., pp. 194–6 and Sarkar, op. cit., pp. 98–104.
30. The wreck of the Dornier has been excavated and a British bullet case found in its wing. It has also been suggested from the examination of the wreck of Hughes' Spitfire that he was hit by friendly fire. With so many aeroplanes in the sky, it is unlikely to have been the only case. See Foreman, *The Fighter Command War Diaries, Vol II*, Air Research Publications 1998, p. 16.
31. Willis, op. cit., pp. 86 & 135.
32. Doe, op. cit., p. 35.
33. Vasco and Cornwell, op. cit., p. 117.
34. Burns, op. cit., pp. 79–80.
35. Orange, op. cit., pp. 107–8.
36. Gilbert, op. cit., p. 775.
37. Sarkar, op. cit., p. 109–10. Sarkar points out the curious fact that 242 Squadron not only made a lot of claims, but that all of them were 'definites', unlike most other squadrons which had numbers of 'probables' and 'damaged' in most of their claims.
38. AIR 16/217.
39. Burns, op. cit., pp. 85–6. There is no documentary record of this meeting. The original source of what happened there is probably Bader himself. Burns gives no specific source.
40. Castle Bromwich produced 37 Spitfires in August and 56 in September.
41. The Squadron had fought heroically in Norway and been wiped out when they were coming back in June on the aircraft carrier *Glorious* and it was

sunk by the *Scharnhorst*. The
Squadron was re-built around the
two survivors. They were having to
learn from scratch.

42. *Into Battle*, pp. 272–5.
43. Roberts, op. cit., pp. 49–50.
44. David Garnett, *War in the Air*,
Chatto and Windus 1941, pp. 131–2.
Garnett was an Intelligence Officer
at the Air Ministry. The dust-jacket
describes the book as being written
for 'those who want to understand
the facts.'
45. See Richard Townshend Bickers,
Ginger Lacey – Fighter Pilot, pp.
111–4 for his account of the action.
46. AIR 16/735.
47. Gilbert, op. cit., p. 781.
48. Greinert, op. cit., pp. 113–4.
49. IWM, MI4/14/118.

26. BATTLE OF BRITAIN DAY

1. Price, *Battle of Britain Day*, p. 22. The
following account of the action draws
on multiple sources, but Price is the
most detailed and reliable and has
generally been followed when
secondary sources conflict,
particularly on losses.
2. Orange, *Sir Keith Park*, p. 109.
3. Gilbert, *Finest Hour*, p. 783 and
Churchill, *Their Finest Hour*, p. 255.
4. Price, op. cit., pp. 27–8.
5. Orange, ibid.
6. The experiences of one 92 Squadron
pilot are described by Tony Bartley in
Smoke Trails in the Sky, Crécy 1997,
pp. 30–35. Memory may be playing
tricks with regard to some matters –
the day is referred to as 13 September,
when there was almost no flying, but
clearly describes the 15th, even if not
in every detail.
7. Chris Goss, *Brothers in Arms*, Crécy
1994, p. 146.
8. On Tuck's efforts at 257 Squadron see
Willis, op. cit., pp. 141–2, 144–6,
165–7 and 178–9 and Forrester, op.
cit., pp. 96–116.
9. See Price, *Battle of Britain Day*, p. 62,
for a factual account of the incident
and Richard Townshend Bickers,
Ginger Lacey – Fighter Pilot,
Blandford Press 1988, pp. 114–5 for a

heroic one, which alludes to Lacey's
opponents as 'the vaunted Abbeville
wing'. JG26 became known as 'the
Abbeville boys' during 1941 because
they were based there. They were not
based there in 1940 and suffered no
losses on 15 September. The German
unit actually involved has not been
clearly identified. The propaganda
value of Lacey's combat report did
not go unnoticed. The incident was
chosen by the Air Ministry to show
the Germans' inability to profit from
their superiority in numbers in its
official pamphlet on the Battle of
Britain published by HMSO in 1941
and reprinted in 1989 (see p. 28). The
fanciful illustration accompanying
the text shows the Messerschmitts
improbably arranged in RAF-style
'*Idiotenreihen*', as the Luftwaffe called
them.
10. Churchill, *Their Finest Hour*, pp.
257–8.
11. Time given by Sarkar, op. cit., p. 123.
Price gives 1415 (p. 77).
12. Churchill, ibid., p. 258.
13. Kath Preston, *Inn of the Few*, p. 30.
14. Churchill, *Their Finest Hour*, p. 258.
15. Egbert Kieser, *Hitler on the Doorstep*,
Arms & Armour Press 1997, p. 272.
16. All three crew of a Beaufighter night
fighter from 25 Squadron were killed
when it crashed near Biggin Hill at
1820. It had nothing to do with the
day's engagements, so has been
omitted from the statistics. It was
probably shot down by Fw Neuhoff
of JG53 who claimed a Blenheim at
about this time.
17. AIR 2/7281.
18. Balke, op.cit., p. 173.
19. This curious observation seems to
have caused great excitement: '*Es gibt
daher nur ein Motto – Alles muss sich
auf die Kanonen-Hurricane stürzen*.'
There was indeed such an aircraft. It
was first flown in action by F/L
Roddick Smith of 151 Squadron on
14 July and he claimed a Dornier
with it on 13 August. That was that.
151 Squadron left for Digby on 1
September and never took to the air
on the 15th.

20. This extraordinary document can be found under RL/2/II 30.
21. Greiner, op. cit., pp. 127–9.

27. BLUFFING
1. Greiner, op. cit., p. 150.
2. Churchill, *Secret Session Speeches*, ed. Charles Eade, Cassell 1946, pp. 22–3.
3. AIR 16/212.
4. Colville, op. cit., pp. 289–90.
5. See Colville, op. cit., pp. 290–2, Gilbert, op. cit., p. 802, and Egbert Kieser, *Hitler on the Doorstep*, Arms & Armour Press 1997, pp. 254–5.
6. Kieser, op. cit., p. 255.
7. IWM, Md. 14/86.
8. Gilbert, op. cit., pp. 878–9.
9. Walther Hubatsch, *Hitlers Weisungen für die Kriegführung 1939–1945*, Bernard & Graefe 1983, p. 71.
10. Kieser, op. cit., pp. 259–60.
11. *Hitlers Weisungen für die Kriegführung*, pp. 84–103.
12. Kieser, op. cit., p. 262.
13. Sarkar, *Bader's Duxford Fighters*, p. 134.
14. Middlebrook and Everitt, op. cit., p. 85.
15. RL 7/44.
16. See Russell, op. cit., pp. 47–58.
17. See *Battle of Britain Then and Now*, pp. 741–4 and Ludwig von Eimannsberger, *Zerstörergruppe*, Schiffer 1998, pp. 137–158. Some take the view that Burton rammed Liensberger. In 1992, an Austrian air-force accident investigator visited the crash site and concluded that a collision was more likely.
18. See Mason, pp. 336–7 and Vasco, op. cit., pp. 65–70.
19. Steinhilper, op. cit., pp. 309–311.
20. Sarkar, op. cit., pp. 140–5.
21. Steinhilper, op. cit., pp. 315–7. During the whole of the Battle of Britain only two Bf 109s can be positively identified as lost through running out of fuel, and a further eight were damaged in the same way. Lack of fuel may have been the cause of some losses simply reported as missing.
22. Steinhilper, op. cit., pp. 107–9.
23. This aircraft, called the Condor, was flown by KG40, which was attached to Airfleet 3 at this time. German records contain no mention of any mission flown by the unit on 1 October, but they were used for nuisance raids on distant targets as well as reconnaissance, usually in small numbers. One of them carried out a nuisance raid on Liverpool during the night.
24. Goss, op. cit., pp. 152–3 and Mason, pp. 347–8.
25. RL 2 II, 361.
26. Park, Instruction 24, AIR 16/217.
27. Gelb, op. cit., p. 260.
28. Robinson, op. cit., p. 273.
29. Data on JG26 derived from Caldwell, *The JG26 War Diary*.
30. Doe, op. cit., pp. 46–8.
31. Steinhilper, op, cit., pp. 9–19 and 232–8.
32. See Mason, pp. 384–5. Though this was the Italians' only daylight sortie they did take part in six night raids before the end of 1940 (Peter Cornwell).
33. Weal, *Bf 109D/E Aces*, 1939–41, Osprey 1996, p. 82.
34. See Michael Payne, 'The Helmut Wick Story', *Aviation News* 9–22 November 1990, pp. 584–8.
35. Dundas, op. cit., p. 54.

28. FEUDING
1. See Ray, *The Battle of Britain – New Perspectives*, pp. 159–60.
2. Ibid., pp. 102–11.
3. Significantly, perhaps, Churchill's scientific adviser, the eccentric Professor Lindemann, who was involved with the Night Defence Committee, muttered that the paper contained Dowding's first admission of a number of facts which had been impressed on him for ages (Colville, op. cit., p. 291).
4. Lord Douglas of Kirtleside and Robert Wright, *Years of Command*, Collins 1966, p. 103.
5. Wing Commander James Sanders, conversation with the author, 20.8.99.
6. Ray, op. cit., pp. 135–140.
7. AIR 16/330.
8. AIR 2/7281.
9. Quoted in Sarkar, op. cit., p. 138.

10. AIR 16/330.
11. Calculations from Sarkar, op. cit., p. 160, who makes the same point.
12. AIR 16/330.
13. AIR 2/7281.
14. Ibid.
15. Sarkar, op. cit., pp. 162–3.
16. Bader's biographer, Paul Brickhill, has him do most of the talking. See *Reach for the Sky*, Collins 1954, pp. 237–9.
17. AIR 2/7281.
18. Ibid.
19. Ray, op. cit., pp. 161–2.
20. See point 7 of his 'Points for Air Ministry Conference', AIR 16/735 34397 and his letter to Evill of 27 October, AIR 16/330 32533.
21. Neil, *Gun Button to Fire*, p.120.
22. Sarkar, op. cit., pp. 153 and 192–3.
23. AIR 2/5246.
24. On the full background to this see Ray, op. cit., *passim* and Flint, op. cit., *passim*.

29. THE SPOILS OF WAR

1. Robert Wright unleashed some controversy over the manner of his going by claiming, on the basis of Dowding's recollections, that he was summarily dismissed in a phone call from Sinclair (op. cit., pp. 241–4). Dowding was very pained by the way in which it was done, but his memory appears to be at fault, for there is documentary evidence of a proper interview. For a full account of what really happened see Ray, op. cit., pp. 164–7.
2. Ray, op. cit., p. 140.
3. See Flint, *Dowding and Headquarters Fighter Command*, pp. 187–93.
4. Dundas, op. cit., p. 99.
5. For an innocent account of these reasons see Ray, op. cit., pp. 167–9.
6. Orange, op. cit., pp. 137–8.
7. Orange, op. cit., p.138.
8. See John Terraine, *The Right of the Line*, Hodder and Stoughton 1985, pp. 282–8.
9. See Norman Franks, *The Greatest Air Battle*, Grub Street 1992, especially pp. 63, 80. The whole operation was an appalling waste of life and the pilots were not fooled. See p. 182.

10. Willis, op. cit., pp. 220–32. Von Werra's story was turned into a film, *The One That Got Away*.
11. Bekker, op. cit., pp. 208–9.

30. APPRAISAL

1. Coastal Command losses are derived from the RAF Air Historical Branch account, *The RAF in Maritime War*, Vol. II, Appendix XIV, p. 411, RAF Museum Hendon.
2. Wood and Dempster, op. cit., p. 348.
3. Air Historical Branch translation, A.I.12/USAFE/TE 53.
4. AIR 19/60.
5. See Jeffrey Ethell and Alfred Price, *Air War South Atlantic*, Sidgwick and Jackson 1983, pp. 52–9, 72–3, 77–8, 135–7, 144 and 201–3.
6. See Jerry Scutts, *Fighter Operations*, Patrick Stephens Ltd, 1992, pp. 152–73.
7. Figures from Murray, op. cit., pp. 88 and 89.
8. These are just the losses incurred in air combat. The total aircraft losses on both sides were higher due to the usual accidents.
9. Claims totals are taken from Kaplan and Collier, *The Few*, Cassell, 1989, p. 221 and the pilot losses from Ramsey, op. cit., p. 255. Losses are pilots killed. Included in the totals are a few Hurricane squadrons which gained official qualification but saw little action. Two of them (245 and 263) made no claims. 263 was re-equipping with the Whirlwind. These depress the averages for Hurricanes.
10. 269 Hurricane pilots and 160 Spitfire pilots lost their lives.
11. Dr Theo Weber, *Die Luftschlacht um England*, Flugwelt Verlag, 1956, pp. 204–5 (author's translation).
12. Osterkamp, op. cit., p. 385.
13. Cf. Murray, op. cit., pp. 412–3. Figures derived from Appendix 2 in Spick, *Luftwaffe Fighter Aces*, pp. 225–37.
14. E.g. Mason, op. cit., p. 50.
15. John Terraine, *The Right of the Line*, p. 701.
16. On Hives' role in this regard see Ritchie, *Industry and Air Power*, pp. 115–121.

17. As Johnnie Johnson has also observed in *The Story of Air Fighting*, p. 149. Ironically, both he and Wellington were in fact criticised for the way they won their victories.
18. Neil, op. cit., p. 80.
19. Ibid., p. 221.
20. Sarkar, op. cit., p. 150.
21. Orange, op. cit., p. 143.
22. Kesselring Memoirs, op. cit., p. 84.
23. Ibid., p. 71.
24. Ibid., p. 84.
25. Interrogation of Göring, 1 June 1946, BA-MA RL/2/VI 165. The interrogation notes add that von Brauchitsch had already said that the Luftwaffe's losses had been so high it had been forced to give up.
26. Wright, op. cit., pp. 197, 199 and 209.
27. This is documented by a telex from 11 Group to HQ Fighter Command on 9 September, which references a discussion with Dowding on the 7th about the strength and timing of 12 Group support (AIR 16/330).
28. Wright, op. cit., p. 217.
29. Ibid., pp. 228 7 250.
30. Drew Middleton, *The Sky Suspended*, Secker and Warburg 1960, p.230.
31. A view taken, amongst others, by the indefatigably vituperative 'Dizzy' Allen, who argues that he and his colleagues in Fighter Command had lost the battle by the beginning of September, due largely to incompetent leadership, but that England was saved by the Kriegsmarine getting the attacks switched to London in order to sabotage Sealion. The Battle of Britain was a 'silent victory' for the Royal Navy, which would have smashed the invasion had it been launched (op. cit., pp. 178–9 and 182). Allen flew with 66 Squadron, one of the inexperienced units transferred south in early September. It lost five Spitfires in its first two days. From his point of view, the Luftwaffe did have air superiority (see p. 163).
32. Quoted by Roberts, op. cit., p. 175.
33. *Their Finest Hour*, p. 455.
34. For an account of how a strategy conducted along these lines could have won Hitler the war, see Bruce Quarrie's *Hitler – The Victory that Nearly Was*, David and Charles 1988.

31. MEANINGS

1.   Quoted in Calder, *The Myth of the Blitz*, p. 251.
2.   See Corelli Barnett, *The Audit of War*, p. 144.
3.   Corelli Barnett, *The Lost Victory*, Macmillan 1995, p. xiv.
4.   At Taranto in November 1940 and Cape Matapan in March 1941.
5.   In a broadcast on 24 August 1941, he made this very point in comparing Hitler to Napoleon, adding that Hitler had at his disposal far more effective means of oppression, which were the 'sadly perverted product of modern science', echoing the phrase 'lights of perverted science' which he used in his 'finest hour' speech on 18 June 1940. See *The Unrelenting Struggle*, Cassell 1942, p. 234.
6.   It is only since the opening of Soviet archives after the fall of Communism that it has become clear what depths of inhumanity were plumbed by both sides. They are graphically exemplified in Anthony Beevor's *Stalingrad*, Viking 1998, and laid out in full in Richard Overy's *Russia's War*, Allen Lane 1998.
7.   *The End of History and the Last Man*, Penguin 1992, pp. 49–50.
8.   Interrogation of Göring, 29 June 1946, BA-MA RL/2/VI 164.
9.   Theo Osterkamp, who was something of a romantic himself, as evidenced by the title of his autobiography, commented at the time on the contrast between the 'strongly romantically coloured German leadership' and the sober British method of conducting war 'with a slide rule, as was always the English way'. *Durch Höhen and Tiefen Jagt ein Herz*, p.281.
10. Osterkamp, op. cit., p. 361.
11. ACW Anne Turley-George and plotter Edith Kup, quoted in Hough and Richards, op. cit., pp. 336 & 353.
12. As is argued by Richard Overy in *Why the Allies Won*, Pimlico 1996, pp. 282–313.

13. Colville, op. cit., p. 414.
14. *Their Finest Hour*, p. 175.
15. A point affirmed by John Lukacs in *Five Days in London – May 1940*, Yale University Press 1999, pp. 213 ff.
16. As was recommended by the coroner at the inquest of a Battle of Britain pilot, Denis Noble, whose remains were finally found and buried in 1996. He contrasted the dead pilot with 'highly paid footballers' whom he characterised as 'one type of what today are called heroes'. See *The Times*, 19 December 1996, p. 5.

APPENDIX 1

1. The main source is Balke, *Der Luftkrieg in Europa*, Anlage 4, but has been modified where other sources seemed more reliable, including the records of Airfleet 3 (RL7/89 and 90). Units moved about and anomalies probably remain. Figures are for aircraft serviceable on Eagle Day, for which I have generally followed Balke. The list excludes:
   - the night-fighter division under Oberst Kammhuber which consisted of the three Gruppen of NJG1 and was based in Germany. On 7 September, II./NJG1 was reorganised to form I./NJG2 and subsequently further units operating the Bf 110 joined the expanding night-fighter force;
   - KG77 which was forming at Laon with Ju88s as part of Fliegerkorps I in Airfleet 2. It was not operational at this time, having its baptism of fire on 17 September;
   - 39 He 59s of the air-sea rescue service which were organised into five Seenotflugkommandos, based at Brest, Cherbourg, Boulogne, Wilhelmshaven and Stavanger;
   - various short-range reconnaissance Staffeln equipped with the Hs 126 which were not used on operations against England.
2. Transfered from Böblingen in Germany in mid-August.
3. Figures for each Staffel are not known, but they are recorded to have had seventeen Bf 110D-0, four Bf

110C-6s and nine Bf 109E-4Bs serviceable on 13 August. Based at Denain, they used Calais-Marck as a forward base.
4. Transferred to IV Fliegerkorps in Airfleet 3 on 17 August.
5. The second name is that of the replacement chosen in late August after Göring's re-shuffle.
6. The III. Gruppe was also based at Coquelles from 24 July, but promptly lost its Gruppenkommandeur, Hauptmann Wolf-Dietrich von Houwald, and two Staffelkapitäne the same day. It was withdrawn to Zerbst in East Germany within the week.
7. I. and II. Gruppen also used St Omer, and III. Gruppe used Arques, which is just to the east of St Omer. ZG26 transferred to Luftflotte 3 on 25 September.
8. Not included is KGr. 606 which first flew on operations on 28 August with 29 Do 17s based at Cherbourg and Brest.
9. The original commanding officer, Oberst Dr. Fisser, was killed leading the raid on Portsmouth Dockyard on 12 August.
10. The unit was quartered around Caen in Flers, la Ferté and Maltot, and also used Cherbourg as a forward base.
11. Quartered at Rocquancourt just outside Caen, V. (Z)/LG1 regularly used Cherbourg as a forward base.
12. JG2 also used the forward airfield of Querqueville, just to the west of Cherbourg.
13. JG27 was transferred to Luftflotte 2 on 28 August.
14. Transferred to Luftflotte 2 in late August. III. Gruppe was based at Le Touquet. I.Gruppe was based at Montreuil-Neuville, later moving to Etaples, and II. Gruppe at Sempy, all near Le Touquet. While in Luftflotte 3, they used the forward airfield of Cherbourg-East.
15. After heavy losses, ZG2 was withdrawn to Germany on 7 September to re-form as a night-fighter unit.
16. They regularly used the forward airfields of Dinard and Lannion on the northern coast of Brittany.

17. Transferred to Luftflotte 2 in late August. Stab and II. Gruppe were based at Gilze-Rijen, and I. Gruppe at Moerbeke and Courtrai.
18. Transferred to Luftflotte 2 in late August/early September. Stab and I. Gruppe were based at Brussels, and II. Gruppe at Gilze-Rijen.
19. I./JG77 was moved from North Germany to Marquise on 25 August. III./JG77 stayed in Germany till late November.
20. Redeployed to Germany as night-fighter unit in early September.

APPENDIX 2

1. Main source is Mason, p. 98, with biographical details from Wynn.
2. Wounded on 9 July, one day before the official beginning of the Battle, Lott handed over to S/L Badger. He did not qualify for the Battle of Britain clasp, but was awarded the DSO on 30 August 1940. Badger was shot down on 30 August and died of his wounds on 30 June 1941. He was replaced by F/Lt Caesar Hull.
3. Posted on 20 July, Aitken's place was taken by S/L Hobson, who was replaced by the senior Flight Commander, Sir Archibald Hope, on 19 August.
4. Aged thirty-one in 1940, Odbert was posted to Northern Ireland on 19 July and replaced by S/L MacDonell.
5. Though aged twenty-nine, Worrall led the Squadron until late August when he became Senior Controller at Biggin Hill and handed over command to F/Lt Mike Crossley.
6. Replaced by S/L John Heyworth on 12 July.
7. The squadron flew over Dunkirk, was moved to Turnhouse in July and then Aldergrove in Northern Ireland (13 Group), where it stayed throughout.
8. Killed on 25 July attempting to land at Hawkinge after an action with Bf 109s, and replaced by F/Lt Ellis.
9. Replaced by S/L Sawyer on 8 July. Sawyer crashed on take-off on a night patrol on 2 August and was killed. On 14 August he was replaced by S/L Holland.

10. White was posted to HQ Fighter Command on 8 August and replaced by F/Lt 'Sailor' Malan.
11. On 31 August, Manton was promoted to Wing Commander and posted to Manston as Station Commander. He was replaced by S/L Pinfold.
12. Posted to 5 FTS on 5 August, and replaced by S/L Gordon. Gordon was shot down and hospitalised on 18 August. He was replaced by S/L E.B. King, who had been flying as a supernumerary with 249 Squadron, on 21 August. King was shot down and killed on 30 August. The Squadron was taken over by S/L West on 8 September.
13. Townsend was wounded and hospitalised on 31 August, but returned to the Squadron on 21 September. It had moved north to Church Fenton on 5 September and become a Category 'C' squadron.
14. Posted away on 18 July, and replaced by S/L Cedric Williams. Williams was killed on 25 August and his place was taken by S/L Miller on 29 August.
15. Formed part of 10 Group when it was formed on 8 July.
16. Relinquished command on 13 August and replaced by S/L O'Brien on 17 August.
17. Formed part of 10 Group when it was formed on 8 July.
18. Baines was 31 and posted away on 15 July. He was replaced by S/L Fenton, who was wounded on 8 August, but returned to the Squadron, without relinquishing command, on 13 September. From 16 August the Squadron was led by F/Lt Blake.
19. Drew was shot down and killed on 1 August when escorting bombers attacking Querqueville aerodrome. He was replaced on 15 August by S/L George Montagu. Originally a night-fighter unit, 236 was transferred to Coastal Command in July and used for maritime patrols and escort duty.
20. Bayne, who had a wooden leg, was posted to HQ Fighter Command on 22 July and his place was taken by S/L Harkness.

21. On 6 July, the squadron was taken over by S/L Wilkinson, who was killed on 16 August. He was replaced by S/L Spencer, though the squadron was generally led by the senior Flight Commander, F/Lt Dennis Armitage.

22. On 9 August, Bicknell was replaced by S/L Heycock.

23. S/L Widdows took over command from 16 July.

24. Hunter failed to return from combat on 24 August. S/L Garvin, who had joined the squadron on 8 August, assumed command.

25. On 8 August, More was promoted to Acting Wing Commander, and was posted to 9 Group on 4 September. On his promotion, S/L Maurice Robinson assumed command of the squadron.

26. On 12 July, Dewar was promoted to Wing Commander and made Station Commander of the new station of Exeter. He was shot down and killed while on a lone flight to Tangmere on 12 September. Dewar was replaced by S/L Lovell-Gregg, who was shot down and killed in his first action on 15 August. After this, Dewar or F/Lt Gleed usually led the squadron in the air. On 24 August, S/L Mills was posted in to take over command.

27. On 26 July, Lees was posted away from the squadron, though he returned on attachment on 31 August, only to be shot down on 2 September. S/L Collins assumed command from 18 July.

28. Aged thirty-two, Gleave handed over command to S/L Starr on 9 August, but stayed with the squadron, taking over command again briefly after Starr's death on 31 August, before being shot down himself at 1300.

29. The squadron took first deliveries of the new secret fighter, the Westland Whirlwind, in July and began operational trials.

APPENDIX 3

1. 10 Group took over adminstrative reponsibility for the south-west from 11 Group on 8 July 1940.

2. O'Brien was shot down and killed on 7 September. He was replaced by Acting S/L Blake on 22 September.

3. On 4 October, Darley was posted to Exeter as Station Commander, and replaced by F/Lt Michael Robinson.

4. Posted to 9 Group at the end of October, Devitt was replaced by his senior Flight Commander, F/Lt Boitel-Gill.

5. On 20 September, Sanders landed his damaged machine at Biggin Hill. He lit a cigarette, but his clothing was soaked in petrol and he suffered serious burns. He was replaced by S/L Lister who was shot down and wounded on the 24th. He was replaced by S/L MacLachlan on the 26th, though the squadron was effectively led in the air by F/Lt Brian Kingcome. On 25 October, MacLachlan was replaced by F/Lt Johnny Kent, posted in from 303 Squadron.

6. Fenton was absent, having been wounded. Until his return on 13 September, the squadron was led by F/Lt Blake.

7. Hull was shot down and killed on 7 September. His place was taken on 16 September by the remaining Flight Commander, F/Lt Morgan.

8. Posted to HQ 14 Group on 12 October.

9. After the loss of Starr and Gleave on 31 August, the senior Flight Commander, F/Lt Cambridge, took over the squadron. On 6 September, his aircraft gave trouble on a routine patrol, and he baled out but was killed. After the short attachment of S/L Bitmead, Acting S/L Duke-Woolley took over temporary command on 27 September.

10. Marcus Robinson was posted away as an instructor on 3 September and replaced by Acting S/L Burton.

11. Hospitalised until 21 September.

12. Collins was posted to 46 Squadron on 5 October and replaced by F/Lt Graham.

13. Leathart was posted to the Air Ministry on 18 October and replaced by F/Lt Dunworth.

14. Grandy was wounded on 6 September, and returned to the squadron on 19 September, but did no further flying. He was posted to HQ Fighter Command in December. The squadron was led in the air by the Flight Commanders, F/Lt Barton and F/Lt Lofts.

15. Replaced by S/L Mitchell on 25 September.

16. Posted on 6 October, replaced by S/L Collins, and from December by F/Lt Rabagliati.

17. Posted to 11 Group on 5 October, and replaced by S/L Biggar.

18. Posted to Boscombe Down on 12 September and replaced by F/Lt Stanford Tuck.

19. Pinkham was shot down and killed on 5 September. His post was filled by F/Lt Brian Lane.

20. Posted to HQ 13 Group on 18 October, he was replaced by F/Lt Atholl Forbes.

21. Spencer was posted on 10 September. S/L Mermagen took his place until 17 September, when F/Lt Pat Jameson took over command.

22. Maguire was posted to 6 OTU on 6 September. He was replaced by S/L Banham, who had been a Flight Commander on 264 Squadron, and had been shot down in his Defiant on 26 August. On 15 October, Banham was shot down once more, badly burned, and sent to the burns unit at East Grinstead. On 19 October, 229 was taken over by the senior Flight Commander, F/Lt Freddie Rosier.

23. From 8 September.

24. Posted on 19 October and replaced by S/L Bitmead.

25. Posted away on 26 September and replaced by S/L Murray.

26. Hood was killed on 5 September when he collided with F/O Webster, who also died. His place was filled by S/L Don Finlay.

27. Posted away and replaced on 13 September by S/L Wolfe, who converted the squadron to night-fighting.

28. Posted on 29 September to form 71 (Eagle) Squadron from American pilots. He was replaced by F/Lt Mckellar who had been leading the Squadron since 11 September because of Churchill's eye trouble. On 1 November, McKellar was killed.

29. The squadron was engaged on working up the new secret fighter, the Westland Whirlwind, although only eight had been delivered by the end of 1940.

30. Godden was posted to HQ 9 Group on 6 September, leaving in charge S/L Tyson, who had joined the squadron as a supernumerary in August, until being replaced by S/L Chater on 22 September.

Index

THE MAIN BATTL

Legend:
- **HQ** Fighter Command H.Q.
- Group H.Q.
- ⊙ Sector Station
- ● Satellite Airfield
- ○ Other airfield
- Chain Home RDF Station
- Chain Home Low RDF Station
- Mobile Freya radar

Coventry

12 Group
10 Group

Oxford

Brize Norton

Yate

Cardiff

⊙ Filton

Colerne
○

Bristol

Box

Upavon ○

Andover

Middle Wallop
○ ⊙

Boscombe Down ●

10 Group
11 Group

Yeovil

Sherborne

Salisbury

○ Worthy Down

Southampton

Exeter
⊙

Bournemouth

Portsmouth

The Solent

Warmwell
●

Worth
Matravers

Brownsea
Island

The
Needles

Isle of Wight

Weymouth

Ventn

Isle of Portland

ENGL

West Prawle

Map by András Bereznay

Map by András Bereznay

AIRFLEET 2,
Brussels

Amsterdam

Schiphol
III./KG4

Soesterberg
I/KG4

Den Haag

Rotterdam

Eindhoven
II./KG4

II./KG3
Deurne

Ostend

Antwerp

Le Culot
I./KG3

Brussels

Calais

Dunkirk

St Trond
III./KG3

Liège

Boulogne

inset

KG53

IV./LG1
Tramecourt

Lille

I./KG2

Erp.Gr.210

Epinoy

Denain

II./ZG26

Barly

Crécy

III./ZG26

Cambrai

Yvrench

III./KG2

I./ZG26

St Léger

Abbeville

II./KG2

II./ZG76

Amiens
II./KG1

Rosières-en-Santerre
III./KG1

Dieppe

Montdidier
I./KG1

Beauvais
I/KG76

Cormeilles-en-Vexin
III./KG76

Creil
II./KG76

Roger

Evreux
I./KG54

III./KG55

André-de-l'Eure
II./KG54

Villacoublay

PARIS

Guyancourt
II./ZG2

Melun
I./KG51

Dreux
I./KG55

Étampes
II&III./KG51

Chartres
II./KG55

Châteaudun
III./LG1

Orléans
I&II./LG1

I./KG27
Tours

BASES OF LUFTWAFFE COMBAT UNITS,
13 AUGUST 1940